Nature, Woman, and the Art of Politics

Nature, Woman, and the Art of Politics

Edited with an Introduction by

Eduardo A. Velásquez

ROWMAN & LITTLEFIELD PUBLISHERS, INC.
Lanham • Boulder • New York • Oxford

ROWMAN & LITTLEFIELD PUBLISHERS, INC.

Published in the United States of America
by Rowman & Littlefield Publishers, Inc.
4720 Boston Way, Lanham, Maryland 20706
http://www.rowmanlittlefield.com

12 Hid's Copse Road, Cumnor Hill, Oxford OX2 9JJ, England

Copyright © 2000 by Rowman & Littlefield Publishers, Inc.

All rights reserved. No part of this publication may be reproduced, stored in a retrieval system, or transmitted in any form or by any means, electronic, mechanical, photocopying, recording, or otherwise, without the prior permission of the publisher.

British Library Cataloguing in Publication Information Available

Library of Congress Cataloging-in-Publication Data

Nature, woman, and the art of politics / edited by Eduardo A. Velásquez.
    p. cm.
  Includes bibliographical references and index.
  ISBN 0-8476-9246-9 (cloth : alk. paper) — ISBN 0-8476-9247-7 (paper : alk. paper)
    1. Women in literature. 2. Politics and literature. 3. Feminism and literature. 4. Sex role in literature. 5. Women in politics. I. Velásquez, Eduardo A., 1961–

PN56.5.W64 N37 2000
809'.933352042—dc21

                                                99-048708

Printed in the United States of America

♾™ The paper used in this publication meets the minimum requirements of American National Standard for Information Sciences—Permanence of Paper for Printed Library Materials, ANSI/NISO Z39.48-1992.

Forever Andrea

Contents

Acknowledgments   ix

Introduction
    An Apology   xi
    Eduardo A. Velásquez

1. **Male and Female Created He Them: Some Platonic Reflections on Genesis 1-3**   1
   Ronna Burger

2. **The Tragic Heroine: Medea and the Problem of Exile**   19
   Domnica Radulescu

3. **The "Woman Drama" of *Republic* Book V**   53
   Steven Berg

4. **Women and Slaves in Arisotle's *Politics* I**   73
   Evanthia Speliotis

5. **Livy, Lucretia, and Rome's Republican Founding: A Reading of Female Rape and Masculine *Virtù***   95
   Melissa Matthes

6. **Plutarch on Philosophic *Eros* and Married Life**   115
   Matthew B. Crawford

7. **Women and/as Princes in Machiavelli's Comedies**   137
   Arlene W. Saxonhouse

8. **The Natural Rights Family: Locke on Women, Nature, and the Problem of Patriarchy**   149
   Lee Ward

9. **Convention and Constraint in the Education of Rousseau's "Natural Woman"**   181
   Deborah L. Winkle

10. **Honor, Civility, and Civilization: David Hume on the Refinement of Sexual, Moral, and Civic Relations** 209
    Eduardo A. Velásquez

11. **When Vanity Leads to Virtue: Self-Regard in Jane Austen and Adam Smith** 245
    Inger Sigrun Brodey

12. **Virtue and Friendship in *Persuasion*: Jane Austen's "Aristotelian" Understanding of Happiness** 265
    Germaine Paulo Walsh

13. **Evolving Conceptions of Women in Modern Liberal Culture: From Hegel to Mill** 295
    Nicholas Capaldi

14. **Nietzsche's Woman as Friend: The Paradox of Distance and Proximity** 313
    Denise Schaeffer

15. **What Death Will Buy: Escaping Gender in Emily Dickinson** 329
    Lesley Wheeler

16. **Wild Women and Graceful Girls: Toni Morrison's Winter's Tale** 341
    Marc Conner

Index 371

About the Authors 383

Acknowledgments

Much of the impetus for this book comes from a symposium held during April and May 1998 at Washington and Lee University. To the participants in the symposium (Ronna Burger, Arlene Saxonhouse, Denise Schaeffer, Germaine Paulo Walsh, and Stuart Warner) I owe many debts. Their engagement with faculty and undergraduates at our small college vividly demonstrated for us how serious and sustained reflection on texts that seem increasingly to have less and less of a hold on our imagination can indeed provide necessary illumination to the question of how we should live. I thank the students enrolled in the spring term seminar that accompanied the symposium for their diligence and enthusiasm. Without the generosity and trust of Larry Peppers, dean of the Williams School of Commerce, and Bob Strong, chair of the Department of Politics, neither the symposium nor subsequent collection of essays would have seen the light of day. Their support in these and in so many endeavors while I have been a faculty member at Washington and Lee University has made the marriage of teaching and scholarship both possible and enjoyable. From them I also gained access to the William Lyne Wilson II Endowment Fund, without which even the best-laid plans would have come to naught. Jennifer Ashworth performed painstaking and incomparable service on behalf of this collection. Her astonishing gifts, on display while editing and formatting the various essays, made this collection far better than it would have been by my meager editing efforts alone. Alexander Sedgwick's contribution to the seminar that planted the seed for this book, and his assistance during the final stages of book production also elevated and corrected my labors in ways I cannot properly repay. Nicholas Ryan-Lang's help with the last copy editing details also proved invaluable. Any errors which remain are of course my own.

I sincerely hope the work of so many is not diminished by my conclusion that the greatest debt I owe is to Andrea, my wife. Aside from putting up with the repeated absences needed to get this book together, she nonetheless understood the necessary dereliction of my duty to her and my son Diego that accompanies the life of junior faculty members. More importantly, it is from her example that I learned much about my place in the world, how one goes about living in such a way that prevents our speculative flights from sapping our native attachments of their essential vitality. Such wisdom is found in no book. I trust I might be forgiven for supposing that dedicating this one to her offers a modest recompense.

Introduction

An Apology

Eduardo A. Velásquez

A book bearing a title in which the words "nature" and "woman" appear in close proximity to each other requires at least an explanation, but perhaps more appropriately a full-fledged apology. If the word "nature" is intended to stand for "essence," and if the title thus suggests that the contents of this book are focused on the "essence" of woman, how could anyone responsibly advance such an argument in light of our current understanding of masculinity and femininity as social constructions? To suggest that one can readily collapse male into man, and female into woman, is to ignore the overwhelming evidence (psychological, social, political, cultural, and multicultural, to cite only a few sources) that demonstrates how much the constitution of masculinity and femininity owes to society's conventions. Or if the word "nature" is intended to stand for the rational or Providential "whole," as if to insinuate that we are about to immerse ourselves in studies that indicate the "proper place" of woman in the whole, one ignores the very visible accomplishments of women that call into question any supposed moral and intellectual superiority on the part of man. Or if in the most basic sense "nature" were to refer to female reproductive functions, would not the innovations of modern science convincingly undermine arguments that try to assign a place for woman in society on the basis of biological necessity? These questions do not capture much less exhaust the problems created by the proximity of "nature" to "woman." But they do indicate that the need for an apology depends on what we (authors and readers) understand by both "nature" and "woman." It is here that matters get significantly more complicated.

This collection of essays does *not* purport to give an answer to the question of what are "nature" and "woman," at least not in an immediate, definitive sense. Rather, the comprehensive aim here is to reopen *questions* as to the "nature of nature," the "nature of woman" (if you pardon the expressions), with consideration given to the consequences of pairing some understanding of "nature" with that of "woman." The practical pairing of "nature" and "woman" is a task for what I have here called the art of politics, a discussion of which we get to in an instant. Incumbent upon us first is to consider why such fundamental questions tend to be obscured. In so doing, we must explain why the attempt to shed new light upon these questions is necessarily good. The necessity and goodness of this return to questions must contend against the charge that the various ills that plague our current political practices require concrete programs for action. For such critics, the questions are no doubt important. But in the final analysis *answers* are what we most need, and the merit of endeavors such as these rests on our capacity to deliver good ones.

As for the questions, let us begin by taking a step back. Starting roughly in the seventeenth century and finding steam in the eighteenth, several influential thinkers took it upon themselves to reinterpret the terms by which we understand and participate in the activity we call politics. Among the most powerful and revolutionary terms they bequeathed to us is "rights." In speaking about politics in terms of rights, the founders of our liberal modernity sought to assert the primacy of freedom, chiefly against the claims of altar and throne, but also in its own right. The quest to live by the dictates of our own consciences, to pursue happiness on our own terms, to reap the fruits of our own undisturbed labors, to bind ourselves to laws *only* of our own making, was seen as *the* most basic and powerful human aspiration. Initially, early moderns such as Thomas Hobbes and John Locke understood these rights as *natural* rights, that is, as freedoms whose intelligibility was accessible only by the light shed upon them by what they called "nature."

The juxtaposition of the prescriptions of nature, on the one hand, and freedom, on the other, is problematic, however. How do we understand the relation between the bounds set by nature and the boundlessness of freedom? When we consider that the early moderns, and particularly the founders of *this* (American) republic, understood "nature" in terms of the "*law(s)* of nature and nature's *god*," the tension if not the outright opposition between nature and freedom becomes even more pronounced. To make a long story short, it took the imagination of Rousseau and Kant to help persuade us of the opposition between freedom and nature. Henceforth, no enlightened person would refer to rights as *natural* rights. Instead, we are at ease speaking only of *human* rights. To be fully human is to be fully free.

This admittedly incomplete account nonetheless helps us to appreciate how the dissociation of nature from freedom (implied in the term "human rights") opens up uncharted possibilities for human emancipation. Human beings are free to make of themselves what they "will." We are, to use a familiar word, free to "construct." By the same token we are free to "deconstruct." One can only deconstruct what is constructed. The possibility for construction and deconstruction is fueled by new hopes for individual autonomy no longer bound to the "law(s) of nature and nature's god." If freedom asserts its primacy over nature, and if indeed we can go farther to assert that there is no nature (*phusis*) to speak of, then there is no good reason to entertain metaphysical questions. "Liberalism without foundations," to evoke a popular term, captures the spirit of our moral and political regime. Not truth, but appearance. Not reality, but perspective. Not permanence, but flux. Not nature, but culture or "History." And for our present purposes, not sex, but gender.

But in fairness to the advocates of freedom and autonomy, some of whom have much to recommend them, could we not just as readily turn this history or genealogy on its head? For example, were one to survey the various accounts of "nature" as articulated in the great works of political philosophy, one is likely to find as many conceptions of "nature" as there are authors. Aristotle or Hobbes? Plato or Locke? Thomas or Machiavelli? We would discover that those eager to jettison the word "nature" find themselves falling back on some other building block—say, the "will to power," "custom," "divine will," "tradition," to name only a few—upon which their respective philosophical and political edifices are erected. However antithetical to older conceptions of "nature" such appeals undoubtedly are, they are nonetheless supposed to hold the same authority for us as do the apparently unbending standards of "nature." Even when there is supposedly no "nature" to speak of, there remain appeals to a quality or feature that is said to define us as humans. One need not turn to the highfalutin utterances of now obscure political thinkers to encounter the difficulty I am alluding to here. Attention to everyday speech reveals the extent to which many of us hold different views of justice. These views are almost always buttressed by what each of us takes to be most fitting, appropriate, or dare I say "natural" for human beings. Various conceptions of the "natural" find their way back into our thinking, although we are not entirely conscious of them. When the original force of "nature" is in question, we are nonetheless inclined to speak in terms of a so-called second nature.

The foregoing is not an argument for relativism, nor is it an admonition that we should all dogmatically hold to our own idiosyncratic conceptions of the "nature" of things. The point I make here is that under the current dispensation—according to which freedom is the moral imperative, and freedom is understood largely as the absence of restraints—there is a tendency to banish the question of whether there is some moral order that accords with justice or the human good (save for the justice of freedom idiosyncratically understood). At the same time, the authority of "nature," used as it is for a variety of political purposes, also potentially stands in the way of inquiry. For part of what makes "nature" authoritative is that it is beyond question. "Nature" is what is. Not a few political philosophers and divines claim to have seen into the "nature of nature," and thus derive from that insight a set of dicta, conformity to which is necessary for human happiness and perfection. To speak in this way is not to disparage our various commitments to what we think is true, good, or just. Life makes immediate and compelling demands on each of us. It requires hard choices that cannot be made by simply suspending judgment. Judgments we must make, and these are always with some view to what we think is good. To say that these judgments always take place after thorough deliberation and only on the basis of a full understanding of "nature" may be nothing short of self-delusion. However controversial the term "nature" may ultimately appear under scrutiny, its authority is necessarily with us. Dogma on behalf of freedom and nature does not provide fertile ground for philosophy.

Charting a course between our desire for freedom, on the one hand, and the necessity to abide by laws, customs, and dare I say *obligations* that enrich us as individuals and members of communities, on the other, strikes me as the sovereign and pressing question of the day. It may very well be the perennially sovereign and pressing question. The choice for human beings is not between some open-ended and abstract concept of freedom, against which any restraint is understood as falling nothing short of a most perfect tyranny. Human beings find much latitude for thought and action. Our creative and inventive powers transcend established bounds, especially at those moments when we think we have exhausted our capacity to think and live in novel ways. Cultural variability continues to be pronounced within and among nations, at times not in spite of the homogenizing effects of the market, but on account of the market's liberating potential. Yet for all of the awesome differences that astound, honor, and horrify human nature, we remain creatures that persistently feel the pinch of physical and moral necessity. Granted, the latter proves contentious on account of the disparity between moral opinions. But differences between us do not eclipse but rather affirm our status as moral creatures. Our moral differences often call for adjudication, and therefore standards by which we must determine the relative merit of our competing goods. The problem of adjudication takes on added gravity when thinking of ourselves in relation to others as we must, that is, as members of distinct and often overlapping communities; as professionals engaged in life's labors; as parents, children, and members of a family; and as spiritual beings who think about a common purpose and destiny. At stake here is what we expect from ourselves *and* others. No one wants his or her freedom violated or transgressed with impunity by others. Even those who quickly disparage restraints on their own behavior nonetheless expect some restraint from others.

If upon reflection we discover that we cannot escape questions about how and to what end we must govern ourselves—questions that inevitably implicate the meaning, regulation, bounds, and end(s) of freedom—then we are also compelled to think about the goodness, propriety, or justice of the limits we place on human freedom. There is, of course, an immediate answer on behalf of "utility" that has hovered in the background of our discussion thus far. We are restrained only because we want others to be likewise restrained. This is barebones liberalism. But such a simple answer begs deeper questions. For as human beings we are not only concerned about our preservation and security, though no one doubts the importance of these goods. We think about how we might live well, nobly, and justly. We seek beauty and order. We think about what might be appropriate to us given the kind of creature we are. In a word, we think about *happiness*, for ourselves *and* for others. These reflections always bring us back to questions about our constitution, or, in a word, our "nature." Do we have moral needs just as we have physical needs? Are those needs the demands of a "nature"? But to repeat, let us not allow the terms of our inquiry to ossify. Our inquiry into our moral constitution should be entertained in full view of just how plastic human beings seem to be. We have to recognize different aptitudes, callings, and chiefly the capacity to educate our native endowment and to acquire skills and desires that once seemed entirely foreign to us. Even so considered, we are not speaking of boundless freedom or creativity. We are speaking about *how* we marry the limits that seem to impress themselves upon us by virtue of our human constitution and setting, and our capacity to push whatever the natural endowment might be in a variety of different directions. The necessary marriage between our limits and possibilities is a human contrivance that calls for a peculiar kind of *art*. It is not self-evident *how* the various natural and conventional parts can and should go together. Since this marriage takes place in the context of what is appropriate to ourselves and in relation to others, it may be rightly called a *political* art.

The discussion thus far is framed in terms of the "human being" as such. Between the limits placed on us by virtue of our communal existence and our freedom falls an activity or art we call politics by which we determine the right admixture of competing claims. But as the attentive reader may already suspect, such abstraction ignores, among other things, the fact that there is no "human being as such." There is male and female. If the questions before us were not sufficiently complicated, any consideration of whether there is a "nature," of which "human nature" is a part, cannot proceed without taking into account the distinction between male and female. Granted, there are obvious physical and anatomical differences that distinguish females from males. But do those physical differences extend to make *moral* claims upon the two sexes? Anatomy, for example, has an effect on preparations for and the performance of the sexual act. Couple these distinctions with the superior strength of males, and immediately we are compelled to contemplate questions about the proper use and government of sexual desire. Do the traditional virtues ascribing to man the "leading role," and to the woman her place as "helper" or "surrogate," to some degree follow from biological facts? How do we account for the prevalence of attaching one set of virtues to male and another to female? In the case of modesty and chastity, two of the premier examples of so-called feminine virtues, do these virtues emerge from the fact that the female carries the child? From the uncertainty of the male in regard to his seed? But then what of freedom? Returning to the creative process we have here called the "art of politics," just which of the sexual and moral differences do we take into account when contriving our common political existence? Or do we rather under the demands of equality ignore those differences altogether? In other words, justice is not difference, but rather sameness. But if we try to banish from consideration the distinction between male and female, and thus exercise our political existence as if our nakedness did not matter, then just what (if anything) stands for the "human nature" under which we are all supposedly subsumed? If there is such a thing as "human nature," how is sovereignty of the "human nature" supposed to stand over and above our "sexual nature"?

While the authors take into account the moral bearing of physical distinctions between male and female, we explore a less obvious relationship between "nature" and "woman." This book opens with an essay on what is arguably the defining story about woman. We, of course, know Genesis 1-3 as the account of the human "Fall." But it is also the story of the woman's search or desire for wisdom. It is Eve, not Adam, who is first tempted by the fruit of the

Tree of Knowledge, and it is Eve who eats first. This is not the place to recount Ronna Burger's remarkable reading of the first transgression (chapter 1). Burger's essay, like all the others in this volume, speaks for itself. Let us note only that the book opens with a story that identifies "woman" as the first philosopher, and then explores the reasons that her search for wisdom is punished. The numerous suggestions and complications this first essay invites us to consider live in each of the subsequent essays of this book. They live in recurring questions. How do we understand woman's quest for wisdom? Is there a kind of wisdom peculiar to woman, acquired either by her initial encounter with the serpent or her subsequent subordination to man? In thinking about the wisdom peculiar to woman, we are compelled to think about wisdom itself. Is there a relationship between wisdom and the feminine? If there is a feminine side to wisdom, what does this mean for man and his search for wisdom? Is there some part of wisdom that woman imparts to man? If so, what is it, and how is it imparted? These questions are hardly exhaustive. Bringing together "nature" and "woman" is by no means as condescending as it first appears and should not be understood in terms of some easy-going biological reductionism. At stake here are pressing questions about the nature of wisdom itself and the relationship between sex and wisdom.

I trust that we can now better appreciate why the reopening of questions proposed by this book is necessary and important. Before we can answer the questions, we need to know what they are. We need to learn *how* to question. We need to shake our prejudices. The essays in this collection aim to recover the questions and the important and delicate art of questioning. Easy and immediate answers are eschewed in the service of making readers participants in the questioning process. The texts and interpreters are united in their desire that we interlocutors recover our sense of wonder. But even if we succeed on these levels, difficulties remain. A glance at the table of contents will reveal a collection of diverse texts across a vast expanse of time. While authors and interpreters are united by their probity, the works under scrutiny are not united by the answers they give to similar questions. What could be said on behalf of Nietzsche (and post-Nietzscheans who, for example, recognize the incommensurability of "perspectives," or the malleability of "nature,") cannot be said of the likes of Aristotle, who, as one representative among many, is *supposedly* the advocate of natural slavery, natural hierarchy, and other potentially pernicious, misogynist, and rigid teachings about "nature." It is, therefore, not so much the questions that matter, but rather the answers. The answers demonstrate the inherent superiority of the old over the new, and a greater awareness on the part of late-twentieth-century thinkers of the possibilities available to women for advancement and self-fulfillment. The assertion of the superiority of our contemporary and near contemporary answers is based on a repudiation of antiquated biological and metaphysical views that simply no longer hold up under scrutiny. This is a tempting criticism.

The charge against the possibility and utility of recovering perennial questions requires us to attend to the character of and relationship between history and philosophy. Now, it is within neither my power nor my scope here to fully explicate what is meant by "history" and "philosophy." However, there are some immediate issues related to the general thrust of this introduction that can be illumined. Bringing together texts and authors covering such a vast expanse of time is intended to demonstrate that the questions are indeed recurring. And the persistence of questions across time is itself by no means an insignificant matter. The persistence of questions points to the persistence of problems, and thus to the insufficiency of answers. This is not to say that all answers are created equal. But the persistence of problems and questions speaks to something about our condition as human beings. It is not easy to define just what that "something" is. For some authors the human situation is understood in terms of the opposition between our animal and spiritual "natures"; for others, the opposition between necessity and freedom, nature and convention, the human and the divine. In each of these essays, the reader will discover the concentrated attempt to come to terms with the peculiarities of the human situation, as it speaks to us as humans, and especially as it speaks to the character and social standing of woman. Understanding the questions and problems provides a door to reflection on this situation in a way that answers do not. While the questions open us to wonder, answers always aim at closure.

None of this is to say that Plato saw every question, or that Plato's answers should be ours. The Greek *polis* is not Hume's Scotland, much less is it Morrison's America. Yet the participation in similar questions directed at persistent problems suggests that the old can illumine the new, and the new the old. This collection challenges the view that the so-called canon of Western civilization is inherently misogynist. This book as a whole captures a dialogue across time, demonstrating that Plato may be as keenly aware as Morrison of the key issues of gender. By looking backward we can appreciate where we came from. By seeing where we came from we might better understand where we are. Perhaps we might be able to anticipate where we are going, whether forward or backward. What is thus proposed by the sum of these essays is a delicate blend of both history and philosophy. Just as the choice for human beings is rarely between unencumbered freedom and tyranny, neither is the choice between unadulterated nature and convention. No human being stands wholly outside of convention. This means that whatever we claim on behalf of our nature must be seen in light of the conventions that shape our natural endowment. We are all historical beings, members of different political regimes, the product of customs, laws, and particular socialization processes. Any meaningful discussion of the large questions anticipated by this introduction demands careful attention to the particularities of place, time, and circumstance. We have not ignored history, nor the possibilities that shape the kinds of answers humans can indeed give within time and place.

We leave, as we must, the task of judging the merits of this explanation and defense to our able readers. We lay before them a book that takes aim at dogmas of various kinds, and that attempts to revive questions that live, but sometimes dimly. Between the instability of unbounded freedom and the ossification of various claims on behalf of "nature," we propose a middle ground that takes into account both our capacity to create freely and the demand that we live in accordance with what is fitting for us, individually and collectively. The relationship between freedom and nature so understood is explored in the context of woman—of what various philosophers, religious divines, and literary geniuses have said about the peculiar powers, insights, and circumstances of woman. The constraints and possibilities of time and place are not ignored. Perennial questions receive different answers in response to new possibilities or changing circumstances. But every answer has its price. A comprehensive gaze at the historical and philosophical landscape can help us to appreciate our advances and retreats, where we are, and where we might need to go.

Chapter 1

Male and Female Created He Them: Some Platonic Reflections on Genesis 1-3

Ronna Burger

> And God said: Let us make Adam in our image, after our likeness . . . and God created Adam in his own image, in the image of God created he him; male and female created he them.
> —Genesis 1:26-27

The Bible's first reference to the human being is a riddling one: What is this Adam who is at once "him," or perhaps "it," but also "them," male and female? Our perplexity is extended when the following chapter starts all over again. The human being of Genesis 1, defined by its likeness to God, emerges as the last step in the establishment of the cosmic order, within the structure of light and dark, day and night, heaven, earth, and sea, among living creatures of distinct kinds, with dominion over all. With the new beginning of chapter two, the cosmic whole recedes; this account starts out with the creation of the human being and directs all its concern to the characteristic experiences of human life—birth and death, pain and work, fear and shame, desire and the need for companionship.

It is this new beginning that first gives us woman and man as two separate beings, neither identical with the original human from which they are derived. We will be told of how they might overcome their partial status by together "becoming one flesh"; but it is not clear that such a union would reproduce the whole human created originally after the likeness of God. Its insufficiency is suggested by the story, in Genesis 3, of the first human deed, which adopts a very different means toward the end of becoming like God. This deed is initiated by the woman. While she apparently obtains the sought-for end—at least in some potential form—that achievement results in a transformation of her relationship to man: what was at first the pairing and partnership of two partial beings becomes a hierarchical relation of ruler and ruled. These developments belong to an account of the fundamental features of human existence that unfolds, in the first eleven chapters of the Book of Genesis, as a story about the coming into being of life as we know it out of an original condition different in kind. This account is framed by two poles: its culmination, in a tale of the political division of diverse peoples, produced by the fragmentation of a unified humanity, looks back to its starting point, in the natural division of man and woman, produced by the fragmentation of the whole human being.

The conception of the primordial Adam as an androgynous being who must undergo division is an ancient one: it appears in Rabbinic commentary on the opening chapters of Genesis and seems to be familiar to the New Testament writers.[1] In this notion of the androgynous Adam, however the interpreters of Genesis may have come to it,[2] one hears the remarkable resonance of a Platonic conception: according to the speech on eros that Plato puts into the voice of the comic poet Aristophanes, every human being is a fragmented half longing for re-unification with the other who could restore it to the whole it once was.[3] A reading of the first chapters of Genesis with Plato's Aristophanic speech in mind opens up several questions:[4] What is the meaning of the original whole human being created in the image of God? What is God's intention in splitting this whole? What does it mean for each of us to be a man or a woman if that is understood as the product of such a division? Is the original condition set forth as a reality that once was and could be restored, or that once was but is now forever lost? Or is it meant to show by negation what human life is not and can never be? Or could the starting point stand for some end toward which we might aspire, but only on an indirect path in the course of which its meaning would necessarily be transformed?[5]

Eros as the Desire for the Whole Self:
The Speech of Aristophanes in Plato's *Symposium*

Aristophanes sets out to explain the power of Eros, who should be worshiped as the god most friendly to human beings, since he is the physician concerned with those ills of the human condition that, if they could be healed, would lead to the greatest happiness. Whatever Eros the healing god may be able to accomplish, eros as it emerges in the course of Aristophanes' speech proves to be the disease itself from which we are suffering, and it looks incurable. This disease is the product of a fall, through which we have experienced the loss of our "ancient nature." In our primordial form (*eidos*), each of us was a spherical body with four arms and four legs, two faces on a cylindrical neck, and two sets of genitals; when we began running fast, we looked like spinning circles turning cartwheels. We were, as this shape attests, offspring and images of the cosmic gods, and thus belonged originally to three sorts: those descending from the sun, who were composed of two male halves; those from the earth, combining two females; and the offspring of the moon, who were androgynous—half man, half woman. Our kinship with the cosmic gods should have led, one might surmise, to a characterization of humans as essentially rational, subjects whose greatest fulfillment should lie in contemplation and emulation of the cosmos as an ordered whole. Aristophanes does acknowledge the self-sufficiency we experienced in our primordial form and the tendency to "thinking big" that it induced; but what he means by "great thoughts" is the ambition to conspire against the gods. When the spherical beings displayed their will to power by scheming to mount to the heights of heaven, Zeus and the other Olympians—gods of the city, not the cosmos—were threatened by the assault, but at a loss about what to do.[6] If they eliminated humans, as they already had the rebellious giants,[7] there would be no one left to pay them honors. Zeus at last hits upon a strategy: if he were to split the whole humans in two, they would be at the same time weaker and more plentiful, hence more useful as worshipers. And if human pride makes it necessary, Zeus warns, he can fragment once again the half-beings, so that each of us would have to go hopping about on one leg. Apparently this threat is not sufficient in itself: once Zeus has sliced the spherical beings in half, he orders Apollo to turn their faces toward the cut side, in order to induce moderation by the sight of their punishment. Our human shape, in all its comic contingency—including the wrinkles Apollo left around the belly button—is to be a constant reminder of the fall from our ancient nature and the possibility, always looming on the horizon, of a further diremption of our already fractional selves.

Eros, as Aristophanes presents it, is a derivative product of the gods' punishment for the more primordial impulse of human ambition: once we have been split, eros arises as the longing we experience to discover our other half and grow together with it into one again. The force of this desire at first proved to be so powerful that no practical needs could compete with it, so that the fragmented beings began to perish of hunger and indolence. Zeus, this time in pity, came up with another device: he moved the genitals on each half-being to the front. From now on, if a man were to unite with a woman, there could be generation by the male in the female, preserving the genus; and if a man came together with a man (Aristophanes is silent about a woman with a woman), there would be some satisfaction so they could get on with their lives. Sexual pleasure is at best a momentary relief that makes possible survival and, as a by-product, reproduction of the species. But it cannot fulfill the end eros seeks, in its effort to heal the essential wound of human nature by permanently reconstituting an original one out of its fragments.

Each of us is only a "tally," one notched stick missing its matching other. Aristophanes captures quite powerfully our ideal of the exclusivity of eros, the uniqueness of the beloved, the sense that we can only be completed by union with the one other who is destined for us. Of course, he had mentioned in passing—this was the sight that aroused Zeus's pity—how, upon the death of one half, the other goes seeking and embracing any half of the whole woman, or any half of the whole man (191b): what can be made intelligible, Aristophanes indicates, is not our attraction to a unique individual, but only an orientation reflecting a crude typology of three classes. These three, in Aristophanes' eyes, are hardly on a par. The original androgynous whole is the source of men who are women-lovers and women who are men-lovers, the former largely adulterers, the latter adulteresses. Eros, he seems to suggest, must remain beyond the constraints of the law, and it can be present in heterosexual relations, therefore, only outside of marriage. Aristophanes has nothing at all to say about the female pairs. He turns his attention, rather, to the male pairs, whose manly nature leads them, in maturity, to become men active in the city: the political life is the closest fallen humans come to the original assault on the heavens that expressed the pride and strength of the spherical beings. The male lovers, who lead the political life, rank highest among human types; they have no competition from any pair seeking to recover, by their relation to each other, some kind of imitation of the order of the cosmological whole from which they are descended.

Behind the class division he has proposed, Aristophanes identifies a universal feature that characterizes all the fragmented beings alike: every lover is mystified by the experience of eros. The thrill of one fragmentary being meeting up with his kindred leaves each inarticulate; none is able to say what he really wants from the other. They know they are seeking something more than the pleasures of sex; but the end for which each reaches out is something the soul only darkly divines. Aristophanes recalls Homer's story of the adulterous lovers, Ares and Aphrodite, caught in the net of Hephaestus. If, he imagines, the forger god came to any two lovers and asked them, What do you want?, they would be, to begin with, utterly perplexed; but if asked once again, Do you want to live a single life and die a single death, fused eternally in Hades?, none, Aristophanes surmises, would refuse. The erotic experience is, finally, some kind of practice of dying.[8] Eros, Aristophanes concludes from his tale, is the desire for and pursuit of the whole (193a): whatever his definition might imply, the whole he has in mind is nothing but the self each longs for and feels he has a right to restore because it is what he once was. Of course, permanent reunification with our missing half would be possible, Aristophanes has acknowledged, in death alone—or more precisely, in one death shared by the two lovers followed by their continued existence as one in Hades. If this is the best thing, the next best possibility open to us is to find a favorite to our liking, which is the work of the god Eros (193c). But the longing by which he has defined the human condition, Aristophanes has shown, is a wound that either cannot be healed—at least not after the first generation of fallen humans—or could be healed, only in a state that would obliterate us as we are and destroy the individuality we thought eros would restore.[9]

In what ways, we can now ask, does Aristophanes' comic portrait with its tragic core resonate in the opening chapters of Genesis? Certain discrepancies are immediately striking. However much it may share the formal structure of eros as Aristophanes describes it, the biblical account seems to be concerned only with the relation between man and woman. In Genesis, moreover, God's splitting of the original whole human into two is not the punishment for a deed of human ambition; if there is such a deed at all, the subject who performs it is the already fragmented being, whose motivation may reflect that status. Or is it possible that the biblical God is just more prescient than Plato's Zeus, and he foresees the need for a preemptive strike, necessary to prevent the human being from becoming, as God eventually puts it, "one of us" (Gen. 3:22)?

The Splitting of Adam into Man and Woman: Genesis 1 and 2

> God created humankind in his image,
> in the image of God did he create it,
> male and female did he create them.
> —Genesis 1:27, Everett Fox translation

The Adam originally created by God is a being that either abstracts from the difference between male and female or somehow comprehends both.[10] The Hebrew words (*zachar unekava*) are not the terms for man and woman, which will be discussed shortly; they apply to all animals alike—the pairs, for example, that Noah is to take with him on the ark (6:19).[11] Now that which God might conceive of in his own image, which is both male and female or neither, would understandably be "humankind," but how could it be the species itself that God brings into being? While he might conceive of the class, what he brings into being would seem to have to be, rather, a paradigmatic member of the class. The "it," then, which is at the same time a potential "them" could only mean, so the rabbis reason, one being with two aspects, or a whole of two fundamental parts.[12]

The duality in one which makes up the primordial human looks as if it is being traced back to God himself: Let *us* make Adam in *our* image and after *our* likeness, God exhorts, before acting as *he* (Gen. 1:26). This happens to be the very first biblical quotation Maimonides cites in his *Guide of the Perplexed*, and it poses a fundamental problem that is to be confronted in the course of the work as a whole. The citation from Genesis introduces an analysis of the terms "image" and "likeness," which, Maimonides is at pains to establish, do not refer to physical looks or shape: the term "image," he argues, is applied to the natural form—"the notion in virtue of which a thing is constituted as a substance and becomes what it is"—and "likeness" is to be understood in reference to some conceptual respect. What makes the human in the image and after the likeness of God is what distinguishes human from beast, and that is the faculty of intellect. It is mind, Maimonides indicates, that the perfect whole of Genesis 1 represents. None of us, as a man or a woman, is simply that; yet it indicates what it would mean for the human to become what it is.[13]

God and his human creature together look very different once the stark abstraction of the first account of creation is replaced by the concrete imagery of the second. God not only acquires a new name—the universal Elohim becomes the individual Elohim YHWH—but he is now a potter molding man (Adam) from the dust of the earth (*adamah*), then breathing life into his nostrils; the human being of Genesis 1—the being that could plausibly be identified with mind—has thus been replaced by a compound of dust and breath, that is, body and soul. God's plan, it appears, is for this creature to dwell in a garden that supplies all his needs, filled with every tree pleasant to sight and good for food (2:9), under only one restriction: he is forbidden to eat from the fruit of the tree of knowledge of good and evil. The restriction, in the form of a prohibition, looks like God's imposition of his authoritative will, which almost inevitably invites violation; if the genetic account were reconstructed into an articulation of the nature of things, it would express the necessary character of Adam's life of ease and innocence, which precludes knowledge of good and evil.[14]

As soon as he issues his prohibition, God expresses an insight that must be based on his own knowledge of good and evil. While he had pronounced the product of each day of cosmic creation good (with one exception), and the whole very good,[15] he now acknowledges for the first time something that is not good—for Adam to be alone. Assuming that there is nothing bad about God's solitude, this would be a sign of the fundamental gap between divine and human—unless, of course, what God sees in his human creature is a mirror of his own condition, and in understanding what it means for Adam to be alone he recognizes at the same time his own motive for the creation of Adam. God's solution is to produce for Adam an other, over against him; for what makes solitude not good for the human being is presumably his incompleteness and need of an other. Or could it be, on the contrary, that this is still the whole Adam of Genesis 1 and what God finds not good is precisely his completeness? The requisite other, in any case, is now brought into being not by an addition to but by a separation from Adam. While God first forms every beast of the field and fowl of the air out of the ground (*adamah*)—Adam's own element—none of these creatures is an other that is ultimately his own; in being brought before Adam to be named, they bear only the mark of his dominion over them. Adam must be put into a deep sleep—a kind of death—from which he will awaken with a permanent alteration of his very being: out of his rib—that is, one side of his body[16]—God will have formed woman as the sought-for counterpart that can complete himself. Adam immediately recognizes her as his own—flesh of my flesh and bone of my bones.[17] And this recognition leads him to new self-understanding, which he puts into speech: she shall be called "woman" (*esha*), because she came from "man" (*esh*). Adam's pun reflects the derivative being of woman; but his own designation, as "man," appears now too for the first time. Woman only makes explicit what must be true of her partner as well: each half is as partial as the other, neither identical with the whole that is their common source.

God's splitting of Adam into man and woman is a unique event, but the narrative is interrupted at this moment to draw from it a universal principle:[18] Therefore a man leaves his father and mother and clings to his wife and they become one flesh (2:24). It is this passage that the New Testament writers seem to have in mind as *the* grounds for the prohibition against divorce: "What therefore God hath joined together, let not man put asunder" (Matt. 19:6, Mark 10:9). When Mark and Matthew quote Genesis in support, they follow the Septuagint, where the line is altered to read "and they twain shall be one flesh."[19] It is "twain" who become one because it is not only divorce that is being rejected, but also polygamy: if marriage is the re-creation of the original androgynous Adam, nothing but the permanent union of one man and woman could live up to that norm.[20] For the rabbinic tradition, in which neither divorce nor polygamy is against the law, the passage from Genesis 2 is called upon to defend some determination of forbidden relations, though not necessarily to exclude everything but the permanent monogamous union of man and woman. Most fundamental, perhaps, is the appeal to the passage as support for a prohibition against intercourse with beasts; the aspiration in "becoming one flesh," such a reading understands, is an attempt to reconstitute the lost wholeness of the human as such.[21]

Whatever degrees or kinds of restriction it may have been used to defend, however, the primary concern of the biblical passage is clearly with the union of man and woman. In this it stands in striking contrast with Aristophanes' speech, in which the male-female pair is only one of three, and demoted to a merely instrumental role, serving the utilitarian good of preserving the species. Whether the biblical union of man and woman, however, promises the satisfaction Aristophanes denies to his pairs of lovers remains in question. In Genesis, too, the primordial whole being would be, for every man and woman after the first, only a fictional standard, and a man's "cleaving" to his wife suggests an ever-receding goal. What they can achieve, momentarily, is to become one flesh; but that seems to be more a compensation for than a re-creation of the human being of Genesis 1, a corporeal displacement at best of the meaning of the whole being created in the image of God.

By the end of the second chapter of Genesis, man and woman stand over against each other as fragments of a whole, but they do not understand themselves this way: they are naked and not ashamed (2:25). The self-awareness they lack, which belongs with awareness of the other, comes only as the result of disobedience of God, and it is the woman who is responsible for this ambiguous accomplishment.

Woman and the Desire for Wisdom: Genesis 3:1-10

The story of this deed of disobedience, which is told in the third chapter of Genesis, begins with a question, the first in the Bible,[22] raised by a talking serpent, the first mythological creature in the Bible. We are told only that this creature is the most subtle or clever (*arum*) of all beasts in the field. The prior chapter just ended with the observation that the man and woman were "naked" (*arumem*, in the plural) but not ashamed: a surprising pun connects the simplicity of man and woman with the cunning of the serpent. To understand it, we must know what it means to be clothed; for it is that condition which indicates, by its joint absence, the common ground between the diabolical intelligence of the serpent and the innocence of the humans.

The talking serpent, who addresses himself specifically to the woman, appears out of nowhere; as soon as he finishes speaking, he vanishes and the woman sees for herself the tempting features of the forbidden fruit. It is as if a thought or impulse in the mind of the woman, which is in conflict with some other, had to be projected as something independent and given, through personification, a will of its own; once this thought has become fully conscious, that externalized voice disappears. The dialogue of the woman with the manifestly fictional serpent looks, then, like an externalized representation of her own activity of thinking, an image of the inner dialogue she is carrying on with herself.[23] Woman, as a result of this dialogue, emerges as the being who experiences doubt or conflict; but precisely because of this internal doubleness she has a certain transparency, whereas man, who is simple, remains altogether opaque.

The woman's vulnerability to the line of the serpent might be explained in part by her lack of clarity about the command. She was not, after all, the direct recipient of God's decree, but through Adam, presumably, has had the law passed down to her.[24] Woman, then, is the representative of all of us who are not direct recipients of divine revelation, but stand in a tradition subject to distortion over time.[25] The serpent taunts the woman with an overly harsh version of God's prohibition—Were you not forbidden to eat from any tree in the garden?—intending, it would seem, to arouse her resentment. She corrects him, but only while displaying the lack of understanding behind her obedience to a command she has exaggerated in her own way: they are not to eat or even touch the forbidden fruit, though it is not, she protests, every tree that has been prohibited, but only that which stands in the middle of the garden. Either she is unaware there are two that fit that description—the tree of life and the tree of knowledge of good and evil (2:9)—or she thinks of the two as one. This apparently false assumption will prove to be in some way true: eating from the tree expressly forbidden requires expulsion from the garden in order to preclude eating from the other; for it is only the two together—knowledge of good and evil and immortality—that constitute the divine as something other than the human, and expulsion from the garden is meant to preserve that otherness.

God had supplemented his prohibition with an announcement of the consequence of violating it: on the day you eat of it, he warned Adam, you shall surely die (2:17). What sounds like a threat of capital punishment would have to be understood differently if the genetic account were reconstructed into an account of the nature of things: it would express the character of the condition of mortality that makes it coeval with human knowledge of good and evil. The serpent refuses to admit this connection. He assures the woman that God was only concealing the reward for humans eating the forbidden fruit: their eyes will be opened and they will become like gods. Knowledge of good and evil, he implies, is sufficient for divinity, and it is a jealous God whose will alone prevents humans from sharing in it. There is no real effort required for human beings to achieve this state and no price to be paid for it; becoming like God should be their right, for it would be a restoration of the original human state. And yet, it is a criminal path to which the serpent tempts the woman: the way back to the human defined by likeness to God can be followed only in defiance of divine authority.

Looking upon the tree after the serpent speaks, what the woman sees is fruit good for food, a delight to the eyes, and desired to make one wise (3:6). Maimonides, working out his account of Genesis 2 in the second chapter of his *Guide*, refers to the fruit perceived as good to taste and a delight to the eyes: these were the two characteristics, though stated in the opposite order, originally attributed to all the trees in the garden (2:9). Maimonides leaves out, then, precisely what the woman adds on her own—recognition of the fruit as desired to make one wise. Thanks to this careful omission, he can assign the blame for the deed on sensual desire and the pleasures of imagination— fruit good to eat and delightful to the eye. But the reader who notices, as Maimonides must hope, the discrepancy between his quotation and its biblical source must draw a different conclusion: as a challenge to God's rule, sensual pleasure and imagination are nothing in comparison with the desire for wisdom.[26] And it looks as if, once humans have tasted the forbidden fruit, that desire cannot be simply suppressed.

We see the woman's deed only after hearing her dialogue with the serpent and being told of her perception of the fruit. If, as that perception implies, it is indeed the desire for wisdom that moves her, the Bible's first woman, in this first human deed, would exhibit something other than the *Symposium*'s model of the Aristophanic half longing for its whole self; she would point to the response Socrates offers through a fictional character of his own invention— the prophetess, Diotima—who teaches him that the paradigm for eros as an awareness of neediness is the love of wisdom.[27] Yet it hardly seems to be philosophic eros that is projected in the image of the serpent, who instigates the woman's doubts. Should we not rather hear, in the serpent's promise of becoming like God, the voice of spiritedness, which makes the woman chafe against the bit of the supreme authority and its prohibition?[28] Are spiritedness and the desire for wisdom, then, so inextricably intertwined that neither can be excluded from the woman's motivation in all its complexity? That motivation has become a question for us, in any case, precisely because of the signs of an inner life that are explicit, however ambiguous. She must, for just that reason, be understood to act deliberately;[29] only man can be said to "drift" into disobedience.[30]

Immediately upon eating the fruit, the eyes of the man and woman, as the serpent predicted, are opened. Realizing now for the first time that they are naked—or what it means to be naked—they cover themselves with fig leaves: shame is *the* mark of their newly acquired knowledge of good and evil, just as its absence was of their prior ignorance.[31] What they have come to see is their difference as a sign of defectiveness, measured against the whole being from which they originated: to be man or woman is to fall short of the standard of the human as such. Of course, the human as such was itself defined as that which is in the image and after the likeness of God.[32] The measure of human defectiveness is the divine. When they now hear the voice of God, who is walking in the garden in the cool of day, they conceal themselves, and when God asks, "Where are you?" Adam answers, "I heard your voice in the garden and I was afraid because I was naked, and I hid myself" (3:8-10). The new experience man and woman have of shame before each other brings with it fear before God.[33]

Ruler and Ruled (Genesis 3:11-24, 11)

Who told you that you were naked? God asks Adam, recognizing at once *the* sign of his having obtained the forbidden fruit of knowledge. Man, quite reasonably, throws the blame on the woman; in fact, he pushes it back a step and tells God, the fault lies with the woman whom *you* gave to me. The woman, in turn, passes the blame on to the serpent, and God seems to concur. He turns to that creature and curses him from among all cattle and beasts of the field: the serpent is a degenerate beast of the field, and the cleverness that set him above the others now acquires an image of its true character in his distinctive motion—slithering on his belly, eating dust all his life. From this moment and forever there is to be enmity between him and the woman, between his seed and hers: not just in their founding crime, but for all time there is, apparently, an indissoluble bond that locks the serpent to woman in particular and seems to confirm his status as a projection of some feature in her complex nature from which she cannot ever be entirely freed.

In serving as the recipient of God's malediction, the serpent takes on for the woman the burden of being cursed herself. Her deed has necessitated God's replacement of his original plan—for a potentially immortal pair to dwell in the ease of the garden—by a new one—preservation of the human species through sexual reproduction; and the function woman is now assigned, in childbirth, is simply the means for the implementation of this plan. And yet, although the woman is not cursed, it does look as if she is being punished; at least the pain and labor attached to childbirth seem to be explained here by no purpose other than to serve as a reminder of the criminal deed that brought an end to the original human condition.

God spells out one further consequence for woman: your desire, he tells her, will be unto your husband, and he shall rule over you (3:16). Adam was at the outset assigned dominion over the other living things (1:28); but at this moment human beings themselves have become divided, on the most primary level, into classes of ruler and ruled.[34] Once the original Adam was divided, man was naturally inclined to cleave to woman, as the missing part that could make him a whole. What attracted her, on the other hand, was the possibility of becoming like God by obtaining knowledge of good and evil.[35] It must be either the spiritedness of that aspiration on which God now finds it necessary to impose constraints, or the love of wisdom it embodied, or both. The means for control, in any case, is the rechanneling of woman's desire: that desire has now been given an impulse of its own, directed toward man.[36] The result is woman's subordination to man's rule, which seems to be in turn an imitation of divine authority.

By God's intervention, man and woman, who began as partners, have come to stand in a hierarchical class structure. What is being explained by this genetic account is the conventional role of the husband as head of the household, with no obvious signs whether it is being endorsed or criticized.[37] That it is, in any case, recognized as a convention is clear from the stories of the patriarchal families that follow in Genesis, which show us that the hierarchy of husband and wife decreed by custom does not always coincide with the relation warranted by their individual natures. The plot of these stories ties the problematic convention of the husband's authority over his wife to another problematic convention—the right of the first-born son, which does not necessarily coincide with natural fitness for authority. As the story of Rebecca and her relation to Isaac makes especially vivid, the failure of custom to bring about the proper order poses a challenge for a wife of superior insight and strength of will.[38] While one might not wish for the convention that calls for her subordination, one has to admire the excellence displayed under those conditions.[39]

After assigning woman her position as ruled, God turns finally to the man, but not to confirm his position as ruler. Instead, he issues a curse, not indeed on Adam, but for his sake on the ground (*adamah*). Laboring over the unyielding earth is to be a constant reminder that man is dust and will return to dust: work too is a sign of the reality of mortality. Adam makes no response to this announcement of his fate. He reverts, instead, to his role as authoritative namegiver and now bestows on woman a proper name—Eve (Hava), because she is "mother of all the living" (3:20). Woman, as he now sees her, is in her essence not philosopher but giver of life. The woman had sought to achieve likeness to God through the acquisition of knowledge of good and evil; Adam accepts, in its place, a completeness to be achieved by sexual union as the cause of perpetuation of the species.[40]

The creation of man and woman from Adam and their experiences in the Garden of Eden make up a "myth": an understanding of the way things are, that is to say, is presented in an imaginative genetic account of how they came to be. The relation between husband and wife as simply equals, according to this genetic account, belongs in a picture of life with no division of labor, no work necessary for self-preservation, no reproduction of the species. This picture shows us, by negation, certain necessities of human life and the consequences that follow from them, including hierarchically ordered relationships, beginning with the primary level of human association. If the genetic account is indeed a mythological presentation of the way things are, its intention could not be to induce nostalgia for life before the "fall." Is it, then, meant to disclose how, without birth and death, labor and pain, knowledge of good and evil, fear, shame, and desire, relations of ruler and ruled, we would be less than human, or other than human—either godlike or beastlike?[41] Perhaps, though, the postulated original condition of the Bible's genetic myth is not meant simply to disclose what human life is not; it appears, rather, to reveal a deep ambiguity in what it means to be human. For being human was characterized, to begin with, by a completeness that comprehends or transcends the division between man and woman; to be human was to be a whole defined by likeness to God. That starting point disappears from the surface of the account, but only, it seems, to lurk on the horizon as a standard—first, for the reunification of man and woman, then for the woman's deed of disobedience. It may not be the pursuit of this standard, then, that is being rejected, but only the direct and unmediated way of seeking to attain it. The possibility would remain, in that case, of an indirect path to the same end.

Such a possibility is suggested by the puzzling gesture with which God concludes his encounter with Adam and his wife, when he clothes them in garments of animal skins he has made for them (3:21). Now the man and woman have already covered themselves with the readily available leaves of a tree; but God, it seems, wants to be responsible for artfully covering over human nakedness. What, then, is the "clothing" that can conceal the defective condition of human beings in their natural state? In light of everything that unfolds in the Hebrew Bible from this beginning, that "clothing" would seem to have to be the law. The law is a necessity for beings who experience sex, birth, labor, desire, and death; although it does not belong to our nature as they do, we would not be distinctively human without it. It replaces the lost state of innocence prior to the experience of shame and fear by covering over the nakedness that elicits that experience.

Of course, God's "clothing" of the man and woman is only an image; the actual giving of the law requires a further development in the human situation. That development turns out to be one more reverberation of Aristophanes' tale of the whole human beings, impelled by their "great thoughts" to assault the heavens. All humanity made up a kind of whole, Genesis 11 tells us, with a shared language. Out of the strength of this unity they undertook to build a city and tower reaching into heaven. If this is what they begin to do, God worries, there is no limit to what they will attempt. "Let us go down," he exhorts, and confuse their language, so that they will be scattered over the face of the earth. God speaks to himself in the plural once again, as he did when he formulated his plan to create the human being in his image. The whole human being of God's original creation had to undergo what seems to be the primary natural division, between man and woman; the unified humanity building the Tower of Babel has to undergo a political division, into a plurality of peoples with diverse languages. This fragmentation is intended to prevent human beings from their ultimate imperial project of attempting by art to reach the heavens: it is to guarantee, as God indicates, that human beings recognize some limit. This seems to be the fundamental principle of the law. The law, which will be given to a particular people, does not return human beings to the original condition of Genesis 1; in fact, it might appear to constitute the ultimate barrier to that return. Yet it looks as if it must allow for more than slavish obedience: if it is the offering God provides for beings who have acquired, in some potential form, knowledge of good and evil, it would seem to have to be the source for the actualization of that knowledge.

God's preventive measure, in destroying the Tower of Babel, is foreshadowed by the expulsion of Adam and Eve from the garden, with which Genesis 3 concludes: Adam, God announces, is become like one of us, knowing good and evil and now, lest he put forth his hand and take also from the tree of life and eat and live forever ... (3:22). The impossible consequence remains unstated. Knowledge of good and evil is a trait humans share with God; if they acquired immortality as well, eating from the tree of life, they would be gods. If this preventive measure served, retrospectively, as the model for God's original splitting of the primordial Adam, that too must have been meant to prevent, before the fact, some kind of "imitation of God" that would deny the distance between divine and human. Splitting the human as such into man and woman, however, proved insufficient. For woman—either out of an illusion of her completeness or some awareness of her incompleteness or a paradoxical combination of both—violated obedience to divine command in favor of striving to imitate God. The price she paid for this deed—having to stand in relation to man as ruled to ruler—looks like the means for God to complete what his division of man and woman began. And yet what God acknowledges in expelling man and woman from the garden is the success of the deed by which, precisely through striving to imitate God, the woman initiated the path along which the human being can become fully human.

Notes

I would like to thank Eduardo Velásquez, who, with his students and colleagues at Washington and Lee University, made my visit there the occasion for stimulating discussion of the ideas presented in this paper.

1. The notion of the androgynous Adam is invoked in the Midrashic commentary, *Genesis Rabbah* VIII, see note 12 below. David Daube analyzes the role this notion plays for Mark (10:2-12) and Matthew (19:3-10) in supporting the rejection of divorce (see *The New Testament and Rabbinic Judaism* [Salem, NH: Ayer Co. Publishers, 1984] 71-79 and note 20 below).

2. A plausible candidate for the transmission would seem to be Philo (c. 20 B.C.E.-50 C.E.), as is suggested by the allusions to Plato's *Symposium* in his commentary on Genesis (see notes 10 and 17 below).

3. See *Symposium* 189c-193d. The intriguing idea of a correspondence between Aristophanes' speech and the opening chapters of Genesis was first suggested to me by Seth Benardete. There is a tradition, as noted above, aware of the common structural pattern—the splitting of the whole human into incomplete halves. Benardete goes further when he observes, "Since the division in the self [in Aristophanes' speech] is presented corporeally, it is not possible to translate it entirely into psychic terms; but Aristophanes seems to assign the soul two layers, an original pride and a subsequent shame, that cannot but remind us of the Biblical Fall" (Seth Benardete, "On Plato's *Symposium*," Munich: Carl Friedrich von Siemens Stiftung, 1994, 53). Cf. note 32 below.

4. "Platonic reflections" in the title of this paper is meant to indicate a reading guided not just by the appeal to Aristophanes' speech as a model, but more generally by certain themes and structures of thinking represented in and by the Platonic dialogues. Leo Strauss implies such an intention, it seems, by including his reflections on the Bible, in "Jerusalem and Athens," as one chapter of a volume to which he gave the title *Studies in Platonic Political Philosophy* (Chicago: University of Chicago Press, 1983). Strauss's "Platonic" way of proceeding can be characterized, minimally, by contrast with the historical-critical study of the Bible's layers of composition; although it does not deny such claims, its concern is with trying to discover the biblical teaching by starting from "the uppermost layer—from what is first for us, even if it may not be the first simply"

(151). Cf. Kenneth Hart Green's remarks in the "Editor's Preface" to the volume in which he reprints Strauss's studies of the Hebrew Bible (*Jewish Philosophy and the Crisis of Modernity: Essays and Lectures in Modern Jewish Thought* [Albany: State University of New York Press, 1997], xiv n.4).

5. The Hebrew title of Genesis, taken from the first word of the book, "*Bereshith*," would, in that case, refer to the beginning or "first things" not simply as the origin, but as the principle out of which the human evolves precisely by the attempted return to it. *Bereshith*, that is, would mean what the earliest Greek philosophers meant by "*arche*," that out of which things come to be and into which they return, the origin that is also the ruling principle (Aristotle, *Metaphysics* A 983b6-8).

A group of heretics challenge Rabbi Simlai to explain the verse, *And God said, Let us make man*. . .; he responds by calling their attention to the singular in the next verse "*And God created*." But after the heretics leave, his disciples ask him whether he has a more satisfying answer for them. "In the past," he explains, "Adam was created from dust and Eve was created from Adam; but henceforth it shall *be In our image, after our likeness*; neither man without woman nor woman without man, and neither of them without the Divine Spirit." (*Genesis Rabbah* VIII.9).

6. With his story of the tyrant god Zeus, threatened by the assault of the powerful spherical beings, Aristophanes reinterprets the earlier speech of Pausanius, which referred to the two lovers, Harmodius and Aristogeiton, legendary heroes of the Athenian democracy, whose union gave them the strength and determination to overthrow the reigning tyrant (*Symposium* 182c-d).

7. Aristophanes takes as his model Homer's story of the giants, Otis and Ephialtes, who threatened to mount to heaven and assault the gods (*Odyssey* XI. 305).

8. Aristophanes' speech thus puts into question what might have seemed a simple opposition between the *Symposium*, which identifies philosophy with eros (203e-204b), and the *Phaedo*, which identifies philosophy with the practice of dying (64a).

9. Aristotle provides a profound comment on Socrates' "best city in speech" when he compares the communism of women and children in *Republic* V to Aristophanes' ideal of the erotic relationship (*Politics* II, 1252b4-16).

10. Genesis 1, according to Philo, speaks of the creation of the ideal human or the species; and while man and woman have not yet received their essential forms—that belongs to the account of material creation in the following chapter—male and female are contained in the original human the way species are contained in a genus, for those with eyes sharp enough to see (*de opificio mundi* 76).

11. Yet in Genesis 1, as Leo Strauss observes, this division is applied only to the human being created in the image of God, at the same time that a plurality is ascribed to God himself ("Jerusalem and Athens," 153).

12. According to Rabbi Jeremiah ben Eleazar, "When the Holy One, blessed be He, created Adam, He created him an hermaphrodite, for it is said, *Male and female created He them and called their name Adam* (Genesis 5:2)." Rabbi Samuel ben Nahman explains: "When the Lord created Adam, he created him double-faced, then He split him and made him of two backs, one back on this side and one back on the other side." When the objection was raised, that God is said to have taken one his ribs, he explained that this term means "one of his sides," referring to Exodus 26, where "the rib of the Tabernacle" means the side (*Genesis Rabbah* VIII.1; cf. *Babylonian Talmud*, Erubin 18a). We are told (*Genesis Rabbah* VIII.11) that in the Septuagint (the Greek translation of the Hebrew Bible), Genesis 1:27 was altered, with King Ptolemy in mind, to read, "a

male with his female parts" (in order to imply that it could not be two separate beings God would create in his own image?). I am grateful to Rabbi Geoffrey Spector for helping me locate these passages.

13. See *The Guide of the Perplexed* I.1, trans. Shlomo Pines (Chicago: University of Chicago Press, 1963) vol. I, 22.

14. Compare the description of life in the Age of Cronus in the myth told by the Eleatic Stranger in Plato's *Statesman*, in particular the question of whether philosophy would be possible under such conditions (271c-272d). There is a connection, Leo Strauss suggests, between the prohibition against eating from the tree of knowledge of good and evil and the central theme of the original account of creation, which is the demotion of heaven, that is, of cosmological speculation ("Jerusalem and Athens," 155). While Strauss finds in the first chapter of Genesis an "articulation of the permanently given whole," which is "not fundamentally different from a philosophic account," the integration of this biblical cosmology into an account of creation uncovers a "deep opposition" between the Bible and cosmology ("On the Interpretation of Genesis," reprinted in *Jewish Philosophy and the Crisis of Modernity*, 361, 369). And the connection to the prohibition of knowledge of good and evil indicates, as Strauss puts it in the lecture "Progress or Return?," a "perfect agreement, as to the decisive biblical message, between the first account of creation and the second account of creation, the account which culminates in the story of the Fall" (*Jewish Philosophy and the Crisis of Modernity*, 115).

15. The one day of creation on which God fails to pronounce his work good is the second—the day he makes the dome or firmament to separate the waters above from the waters below: the chaos it was meant to isolate will eventually flood into the ordered world below. At the end of the sixth day, God pronounces the whole "very good"; but he did not pause before that assessment to call his creation of Adam in particular good. For the being who is not simply created good, knowledge of good and evil looks like a necessity.

16. Maimonides explains how the Sages understood the passage: "The expression, *one of his ribs*, means according to them one of his sides. They quote as proof the expression, *a rib of the tabernacle*, which [the Aramaic translation] translates: a side of the tabernacle. In accordance with this, they say that ["one of his ribs"] means: of his sides. Understand in what way it has been explained that they were two in a certain respect and that they were also one; as it says: bone of my bones, and flesh of my flesh" (*Guide of the Perplexed* II.30; cf. note 12 above).

17. This is the moment, Philo observes, when love supervenes and brings together into one the divided halves, as it were, of one being (*de opificio mundi* 152).

18. On the difference between law appealing to an example (God's creation and subsequent splitting of the original Adam) and law based on a general precept (Therefore a man shall cleave unto his wife . .), see Daube, *New Testament and Rabbinic Judaism*, 67-89.

19. Paul cites the line in this form in 1 Corinthians (6:17) and Ephesians (5:32), where the two that are to become one body—a "mystery with many implications"—is said to refer to the relation between Christ and the Church.

20. This explains, Daube argues, what Mark assumes (10:11-12) when he has Jesus declare that it is adulterous for a man or woman to remarry after divorce: this "esoteric" teaching, which Mark has Jesus explain in private to his disciples, assumes the androgynous Adam as the basis for marriage being indissoluble and monogamous,

otherwise a man's remarriage would not count as adulterous (*The New Testament and Rabbinic Judaism*, 71-79). Matthew, unlike Mark, does not present Jesus' response to the question of divorce as a private teaching; and in quoting Genesis 2, he includes the phrase, "Therefore a man shall cleave to his wife," because, Daube reasons, he no longer connects the verse with the notion of marriage as a re-creation of the androgynous Adam, and therefore requires the precept to justify the rejection of divorce (83).

21. That a man should "leave his father and his mother" supported, in rabbinic interpretation, the prohibition of certain incestuous relations; that he should "cleave to his wife" was appealed to as grounds for rejecting homosexuality and adultery; that "they shall be one flesh," as Rabbi Akiba (second century C.E.) explained, is possible only in a union between human beings (see the reference in Daube, *New Testament and Rabbinic Judaism*, 81-82).

22. See Robert Sacks, *A Commentary on the Book of Genesis* (Lewiston, NY: Edwin Mellen Press, 1990), 28. In the next chapter, Sacks observes, God acts "in imitation of the serpent as it were," when he calls out, *where are you?*, to the man and woman who are hiding in the garden.

23. On thinking as inner dialogue, see Plato, *Theaetetus* 189e-190a and *Sophist* 263e. There is a "duologue," as Umberto Cassuto sees it, taking place in the woman "between her wiliness and her innocence, clothed in the garb of a parable" (*A Commentary on the Book of Genesis*, Part I [Jerusalem: Magnes Press], 142). Cf. note 28 below.

24. Of course, man too has been derived from the original Adam, but the two ways of coming to be are not exactly symmetrical: while woman comes from the original Adam by the separation of a part, man is the being that remains of the original once that separation has been performed.

25. See Strauss, "Jerusalem and Athens," 156.

26. If biblical wisdom is, ultimately, something other than wisdom as the Greek philosophers understand it—for wisdom that begins with fear of the Lord is not the same as that which begins in wonder (Strauss, "Jerusalem and Athens," 149)—what the Bible represents in the striving of the woman is the alternative to what it will identify as true wisdom.

27. See *Symposium* 203e-204c; cf. Seth Benardete, On Plato's *Symposium*, 73-79.

28. The figure of the serpent would confirm, then, the psychological account Socrates offers in *Republic* IV, where *thumos* is shown at work handling internal dissension by treating the conflicting force as if it were an external subject, standing over against the unified self (see 439e-440a, 440e-441c).

29. In "Eve and Adam: Genesis 2-3 Reread," (reprinted in *Eve and Adam*, ed. Kristen E. Kvam, Linda S. Schearing, and Valarie H. Ziegler [Bloomington: Indiana University Press, 1999]: 431-38), Phyllis Trible takes up the story of the "fall" in an effort to save it from the charge of legitimating male supremacy. Addressing the question of why the serpent speaks to the woman and not to the man, she criticizes those who suggest that the woman is weaker or more cunning or more sexual than the man: "Both have the same Creator... both are equal in birth... there is complete rapport, physical, psychological, sociological, and theological, between them... they are equal in responsibility and in judgment, in shame and in guilt, in redemption and in grace. What the narrative says about the nature of woman it also says about the nature of man" (435). But she raises the question again and goes on to speculate: "Throughout the myth, she is the more intelligent one, the more aggressive one, and the one with greater sensibilities"

(435). It is true that the first characterization seems to follow from the account of the creation of woman in Genesis 2, the second from her action in Genesis 3: but how are they to be put together? The apparent contradiction needs at least to be acknowledged. If there were no significant difference in the coming to be of woman and man (but see note 24 above), why is woman singled out for the role she goes on to play? If she is indeed superior, why is she the cause of a development that is, as Trible sees it, simply a "fall" from a desirable state to a disastrous one? And if she is superior, would restoration of a relation between equals be, as Trible maintains, a fitting ideal?

30. "The Bible," Strauss asserts, "says nothing to the effect that our first parents fell because they were prompted by the desire to be like God; they did not rebel high-handedly against God; they rather forgot to obey God; they drifted into disobedience" ("Jerusalem and Athens," 156). It is not obvious why Strauss goes beyond his earlier statement about the man alone, who "drifts into disobedience by following the woman." In doing so, he seems to echo Nietzsche, who contrasts the "Aryan" Prometheus myth, with its "sublime view of active sin" and its "masculine" understanding of the dignity of sacrilege, and the "Semitic" myth of the fall, with its account of the passive and pre-eminently feminine origin of evil (*Birth of Tragedy*, section 9).

31. This might appear to support the surface teaching in chapter 2 of Maimonides' *Guide*: the fall of man is from pure intellection—cognition of reality only in terms of true and false, which is, presumably, what it means to be in the image and likeness of God—to reliance on "knowledge of fine and bad," which is mere convention. Yet Maimonides introduces this account by first defining *elohim* as rulers; and rulers would need knowledge of the human things, which is more than convention, albeit not intellectual intuition of pure truth and falsehood. Rulers can neither be outside the cave simply nor prisoners within; their understanding requires interpretation of life in the cave, where shame may be ineradicable.

Cf. Steven Berg's discussion, in chapter 3 of this volume, of the central and complex role of shame in the argument of *Republic* V.

32. Benardete contrasts the shame experienced in the biblical account by man and woman, who realize that neither is in the image of God, with the shame Aristophanes' human being experiences in being subject to gods in whose image he has been reconstructed ("On Plato's *Symposium*," 55-57).

33. In Plato's *Euthyphro*, the relation between fear and shame becomes thematic once Socrates gives up on seeking with Euthyphro an "idea" of the holy (12a-d); at the same time, Socrates' appeal to Euthyphro's own passions of fear and shame has been guiding the action of the dialogue, as we discover at the end (15d-e).

34. The only prior mention of "ruling" is that of sun and moon over day and night (1:16)—not, as Strauss observes, over the earth, let alone man ("Jerusalem and Athens," 153).

35. If, as Maimonides argues, in the phrase "becoming like God," the term *elohim* should be translated "rulers" (see *Guide* 1.2 and note 31 above), it is in response to her striving for knowledge befitting rulers that the woman is consigned to the class of the ruled.

36. The line about woman's desire and her husband's rule has a striking repetition in the following chapter. When Cain's countenance falls, after God rejects his offering in favor of his brother's, God asks why he is angry: "If you do well, shall it not be lifted up? And if you do not, sin couches at the door, and its desire is unto you, but you can rule over it." (4:5-7). Sin, in this personification (cf. note 28 above), stands in relation to

Cain, as woman does to man—with the qualification that in Cain's case domination is not a description of the way things will be, but only a possibility.

37. That the eventual fate of woman is to be ruled by her husband is, Phyllis Trible argues, a pattern being condemned, not condoned, in Genesis 3. "Whereas in creation man and woman know harmony and equality, in sin they know alienation and discord. Grace makes possible a new beginning" ("Eve and Adam: Genesis 2-3 Reread," 80). This view presupposes: that the original condition was once a reality, and could therefore be restored; that the departure from it is unambiguously a decline (the serpent, who is the impetus for it, is assumed to be "the tempter"); that the relation of ruler and ruled, at least between husband and wife, is not a necessity; that the "solution" is "grace," which in this case means a return to the supposedly perfect harmony and equality postulated as our original condition.

38. Isaac's eyes are dim, and not just his eyes, as he prepares to bestow the blessing of the firstborn on Esau; when he sends him out first to hunt for venison, he provides Rebecca with an opportunity for the wise deception that will establish her younger son, Jacob, in the position for which he is naturally right (see Gen. 27). Rebecca's stature is suggested by her monogamous relation to Isaac. But one might compare Sarah, persuading Abraham to cast out Hagar and her son Ishmael so as to prevent him, the eldest son, from sharing the inheritance with Isaac (21:8-11), or Rachel bargaining with Leah, in her effort to bear Jacob a son (30:14-24)—the son, Joseph, whose path to his position of leadership will be a long and complicated one.

39. This is not to deny that the Genesis stories reveal problems concerning the status of women, some of which might be improved by law. Calum Carmichael sheds light on some of the otherwise obscure legislation of Deuteronomy by seeing in it the legislator's response to such problems and his search for legal solutions that would uphold the honor and dignity of women. See *Women, Law, and the Genesis Traditions* (Edinburgh: University Press, 1979).

40. Use of the language of knowledge to express the sexual relationship begins with the first line of the next chapter: "And Adam knew his wife . . ." (4:1).

41. Cf. Aristotle, *Politics* I, 1253a25-29.

Chapter 2

The Tragic Heroine: Medea and the Problem of Exile

Domnica Radulescu

> Out of the ash
> I rise with my red hair
> And I eat men like air.
> —Sylvia Plath, "Lady Lazarus"

Medea, that terrifying name that conjures up in our minds all sorts of grisly scenes of blood, sorcery, and human devastation—Medea, the female figure who has haunted the Western imagination from at least as far back as the seventh century B.C.E. and has made her way through Greek and Roman antiquity into our own century—might have a lesson or two to teach us. Her name alone, that eerie combination of open vowels framed by the round labial [m] and the metallic dental [d], is enough to send many of us into various tirades on the destructive aspects of jealousy, or on the horrors of evil parenting, or on the devastation brought about by uncontrolled human anger, and as we would go about our heated arguments we would probably be pretty sure we are the ones to teach her a lesson or two. Fair enough. This essay, however, does not attempt to do that. It does not attempt to support or justify Medea, or search to castigate her, but to dispel some of the Halloweenesque haze surrounding this character and reveal her as a complex symbol of human nature and more particularly of female nature and the plight of women.

This chapter explores the Medea figure as a tragic heroine whose tragedy is primordially one of exile and fragmentation. Medea is certainly not a model heroine in whose image we should raise our daughters, and her story does not make for very nice bedtime reading, but neither is she entirely the monster that popular belief has led us to think she is. The fascination of writers and artists for this figure may equal only characters such as Ulysses or Penelope. From archaic myths to the plays of Euripides and Seneca, the paintings on ancient sarcophagi or amphoras, Pierre Corneille's play, Cherubini's opera and Maria Callas's interpretation of it, Jean Anouilh's play, or Diane Wakoski's poetry, the Medea myth has continued to thrive, be created and recreated, considered and reconsidered under many lights and in many artistic forms. One reason may be that she teaches us both what to be and what not to be; she tells us about what to fear and what to face courageously; she is, by various degrees, present in each of us as she looms threateningly above us.

Furthermore, Medea is a mythological figure often associated in ancient Greece with the goddess Hera herself, belonging to various heroine cults before she ever became a literary character, a motif on a painted sarcophagus, or a character in an opera. Taking that mythopoetic background into account as well as the fact that she is a literary character from a literary era, such as Attic tragedy, when most heroes and heroines had the value of archetypes and generalizing symbols, I will try as much as possible to avoid looking at Medea from an immediate or realistic point of view. I will interpret her as a complex character-symbol built on contrasting forces, a symbol based on dualities and ambivalences such as the basic duality of good and evil, or love and hatred.

The association of "gore" with Medea comes primarily from her murder of her own children. But that is not the entire story of the myth or of the literary works based on it. It is only one out of about ten different episodes, and, as with any literary character, it would be fallacious to judge her only on one episode of her life. It would be, in fact equally fallacious to judge an actual human being on one action or instance in her life, even when that one action might exceed all others in horror or nobleness. Furthermore, Medea significantly defies realistic representation, more so than most characters who have entered Attic or Latin tragedy. She is helped by her grandfather Helios, the Sun God, and by the goddess Hera, famous like herself for her scorching jealousy. She concocts rejuvenating potions, puts to sleep fiery dragons, flies on winged serpents or on chariots of fire. She demands to be interpreted as a symbol, with all the dualities, bipolarities, and ambivalences that that involves. For that reason also, Medea, particularly as recreated by Euripides, concentrates some of the most puzzling paradoxes of both the "female nature" and of "human nature" in general. Euripides, whom Nietzsche considered the "destroyer" of Greek tragedy in the Sophoclean and Aeschylean tradition, is, I believe, a progressive thinker who urges us, through his character, to take a closer look at ourselves and to face some of the most disturbing questions about love, relationships between the sexes, power, and politics. He also urges us to face our own inner monsters of hypocrisy, fear, or selfrighteousness.

As I will try to show in the following sections, Medea both fits and defies stereotypical representations of what we have grown accustomed to calling the "female nature." Her character points at once to the inadequacy of these representations in rendering the full complexity of woman as a human being and to the harmful influence that the preconceived ideas about a "female nature" have had in women's lives and their place in society. I would go so far as to say that Medea challenges the essentializing concept of a "female nature." Her character and many of her words and gestures suggest that this concept has served as an ideological tool in the hands of men for the oppression of women, as they are generally perceived either as "cunning," "frail," or "cowardly," or as monstrous and "manly" when too independent and powerful. But she also opens up the concept of "female nature" and allows it to include virtues traditionally associated with men, such as courage, prowess, loyalty to friends, independence, and a need for artistic expression. Furthermore she embraces the concept of a "female nature" in an ironic way, in the sense that she lucidly uses its stereotypes in conjunction with those of "male nature," as a way of accomplishing her revenge and punishing those who have caused her misery.

If we can bear to take a clear look at Medea past her monstrous side, we discover that, in her distorted and frightful way, she opens a path toward some form of liberation from the stifling molds of gender stereotypes. And she does so both on the one hand by suggesting the necessity of transcending the very concepts of a female or male "nature" toward the liberating concept of a "human nature," and on the other hand by enriching the concept of a "human nature" with the specificities of each gender. Medea urges us to go beyond the dangerous habit of forming moral judgments that limit certain virtues to one gender while attributing certain faults to another. In this context, the concept of exile, which will constitute the core of my argument, is crucial in putting together what I call "the Medea puzzle." As we shall see, Medea is both creator and victim of her exile. By a set of unfortunate circumstances, her status of exile becomes, so to say, a second nature, or rather, a mutated nature. She incarnates the status of woman as exile from the world of men, but also as the rebel against this status. Her rebellion attracts the wrath of men who continue to exile her, then transforms her new exile into the no-man's-land of crime, thus exiling herself irrevocably not only from the world of men and structured society, but from herself as well. But in doing so she denounces the many traps set for human beings by their own constructs of gender.

Attic theater was financed and sponsored by the Athenian state and exclusively acted by men wearing masks in front of an audience almost entirely composed of men. Medea seems to be taking this game of masks and cross-dressing to its extreme where the two are either indistinguishable or combined in "mon-strous" ways. It is relevant to point out, I believe, that one of the most radical and influential British feminist theaters of the past several decades was named "Monstrous Regiment," and one of its most provocative and influential plays, *Medea*, is a feminist play written and interpreted by women and inspired by this myth. A relatively recent drama by a South African writer, Guy Butler, entitled *Demea*, makes use of the Medea myth to criticize apartheid practices and racism in general. Finally, British and American feminists at the beginning of this century often opened their rallies with speeches taken from Euripides' *Medea*.

Again, I caution the reader that this is not in any way to say that Medea's "monstrosity" is something to be celebrated, but to question the very concept of her so-called monstrosity, and to suggest that Medea herself, particularly in the Euripides version, calls for a transcendence of this "monstrosity" and for a more complex understanding of it.

Her criminal and supernatural characteristics aside, Medea is a powerful voice for women's liberation. She is a progressive female character with a strongly political dimension who is punished for all of that. She represents at once a leader and a subject, a rebel and a victim; she tries to lead but is castigated by a world and social order structured entirely on patriarchal rules and values. I argue that the deterioration of her character into an image of evil has two principal motivations. First, as the creation of the male imagination, Medea is rendered monstrous to a significant extent by the fear and repulsion of men toward powerful, independent, and intelligent women; second, the "mutation" of her character is motivated psychologically by the successive abuses, exiles, and fragmentations imposed on her by various patriarchal structures or by events dictated by fate or the gods. The figure of Medea poses a challenge to all man-created social and political structures as well as to traditional gender roles by forcing us to reconsider various moral or political concepts such as "power," "courage," "cunning," "exile," "foreign," "leadership," in a new light free of gender biases.

Finally, from an ontological point of view, the Medea story also contains the basic human fear of expulsion and exile from structured society, and, narrowing the ontological sphere to the female gender, it portrays the alienated status of woman in society. Although Medea has stereotypically and in popular consciousness become primarily a symbol of female jealousy and its destructive effects, the two tragedies that have fixed her forever in Western culture and thinking present her— at least during the first part of each drama—equally as victimized by repeated "expulsions" and enraged as a result of the repeated symbolic morcellating caused by exile.

Literary Connections Involving Medea and Exile

The waters of what the Greeks once called the "Pontos Euxinos," today's Black Sea, are often frightfully tumultuous, roaring and writhing, greenish-black—a sailor's nightmare. Every once in a while the sea quiets down to a velvety blue that shimmers in the sun and gives the eye a spectacle so lovely and serene it is hard to imagine the rage of the previous night. On its shores lies a town whose old name is Tomis, from the Greek τέμνω (*temnu*) meaning "to cut," "wound," "maim," "sever," or τομή (*tomé*) meaning "a cutting," "the place from which a thing has been cut: the end left after cutting."[1]

On these shores and in this town the Roman poet of the first century B.C.E, Publius Ovidius Naso, spent the last nine years of his life in exile ordered on him by the emperor Augustus. In his last work, the *Tristia*, in which he laments his bitter fate on these "barbaric" shores, amid the "barbaric" people called Dacians, he also mentions the famous, mythical Medea and explains the etymology of the town name, Tomis. The reference is to her slaying and cutting to pieces of her brother Apsyrtus so that she could distract her father from chasing her as she fled with Jason.[2] Ovid had written about Medea, her love of Jason, and her witchcraft in his *Metamorphoses* and had also written a tragedy called *Medea* (nonextant today).

Grief-stricken, dejected, and lonely, having lost everything he had ever loved— his country, his family, his glory—the great Ovid thinks of Medea, her rage and her murders, as he watches the savage sea and its savage shores. He had never thought, at the time he had written the *Metamorphoses* or *Medea*, that he was going to be so close to this tortured and frightful figure—irony of ironies—in the very town named after Medea's crime. "Swift and fickle is fortune and, swooping down, has torn me from royalty and given me o'er exile" laments Seneca's *Medea*.[3] Ovid, whom "fickle" fortune has struck in a similar way, seems to have a profound understanding of the young maid's psychology and anguish, despite the "many things unspeakable [she] was to dare."[4] Interestingly, the directions of their exiles are almost in perfect opposition: she comes from "barbaric" shores, close to those very "barbaric" shores where Ovid pines in exile, while he comes from civilized and glorious Rome, the equivalent of civilized Greek Corinth, where she goes into exile to follow Jason, and from where she is herself exiled by Jason.

Interestingly, Dante Alighieri mentions Jason as one of the sinners in the circle where seducers are being scourged by horned demons, and describes him as a vile seducer, Medea being one of his victims: "and for Medea, too, revenge is taken."[5] She does not appear in any of the circles of the *Inferno*, but her husband Jason who unjustly sends her into exile, does. Dante too was an exile, bitterly suffering and pining for his beloved Florence. As Ovid was one of Dante's most respected masters of poetry, he most certainly had knowledge of the Medea story from the *Metamorphoses,* which provide a significant amount of the mythological information of the *Inferno*.[6]

Taking the ironic chain of exile even further, the twentieth-century exiled writer of Romanian origin Vintila Horia mentions several times the Roman poet thinking of Medea and hearing her name carried by the winds of these same "barbaric" shores. In his novel entitled *Dieu est né en exile*, Horia tries to reconstruct a possible diary of Ovid during his exile on the shores of the Pontus Euxinus. And there seems to be, in this modern recreated version of the *Tristia,* even more of a compassionate touch in Ovid's attitude toward his character and imaginary companion in exile, Medea of Colchis.[7] This chain of references to the myth of Medea seems to suggest something like a solidarity of exiles across the centuries. Indeed, those whom fortune (or maybe fortune disguised as political action) has torn apart from their homes have no other space that is truly theirs except a suspended, imaginary space that transcends physical boundaries and time, and in which all find each other symbolically related. Exiles are other exiles' symbolic family.

Medea, however, unlike her brothers in exile who have thought of her across the centuries, is doubly exiled. She first willingly exiles herself, following Jason, who becomes her home and her family. Jason, however, decides to marry another woman, daughter of a king, and to send Medea into exile, forcing her thus to separate from her new home and from her own children as well. The symbolism of fragmentation and cutting, as contained in the etymology of the name Tomis, is entirely appropriate for Medea and blends into her story with a poignancy that has, however, escaped criticism. Medea suffers multiple exiles: she has left family and country out of love of Jason, has tried to recreate with him a sense of home and is again chased away—out of her new home and out of Jason's heart. What is left for her as woman, as both woman and "barbarian," as female "barbarian" and exile? Ovid still has his creativity and ability to write intact, and so does Dante, as he transforms his exile into art. Ovid, precisely with the power of his mind, proudly defies the political powers that have sent him into exile: "Behold me, deprived of native land, of you and my home, reft of all that could be taken from me; my mind is nevertheless my comrade and my joy; over this Caesar could have no right" (III. vii. 45-48).[8] As we shall see in the subsequent pages, Medea's exile is much more complete and multidimensional, as it becomes the defining feature of her destiny and takes over her inner life as well.

From the moment of Jason's betrayal of Medea, the point at which both Euripides' and Seneca's tragedies begin, she is symbolically and psychologically cut into pieces, torn, fragmented. Metamorphosed into a monster by this psychological maiming, she, in turn, becomes the author of literal maiming and cutting to pieces: Jason's new bride and her father, the king, are literally torn to pieces by the poisoned dress she has concocted with her witchcraft; and, horrifyingly, she kills her own children, symbolically cutting herself into pieces as she tears her own motherhood apart.

The Medea Myth

The Medea myth is part of the larger "Argonautic" story first mentioned in the seventh century B.C.E. by Eumelus, the "Corinthian poet whose name is associated with the earliest known Argonautic epic."[9] The myth is then recounted in epic poetry by the Greek writer Apollonius of Rhodes in his *Argonautica* of the third century B.C.E., and two centuries later by the Roman writer Ovid Nasso, in his *Metamorphoses*. The Argonautica is also fleetingly mentioned in Homer's *Odyssey*: "That way the only seagoing ship to get through was Argo, / Who is in all men's minds, on her way home from Aietes; / and even she would have been driven on the great rocks that time, but Hera saw her through, out of her great love for Jason."[10] The myth was explored and set in verse by Pindar, the Greek poet of the fifth century B.C.E., in his famous *Pythia* 4. It was first incorporated and developed in the form of drama by the fifth century Attic tragedian Euripides and then five centuries later by the Roman writer Seneca.

The various versions of the myth contain some or all of the following important moments: (1) Jason and his men, called the Argonauts (from the name of their exceptional ship the Argo), start in search of the Golden Fleece of Colchis. (2) In Colchis they are asked by King Aetes to perform various impossible tasks. (3) The king's daughter, Medea, is struck by one of Eros's flashes and desperately falls in love with Jason. (4) She then helps him to obtain the Golden Fleece and to successfully perform three impossible tasks (yolking fire-spitting bulls, killing the giants that arose from the field of Ares, and putting to sleep with the help of a magic potion the dragon guarding the fleece). She then flees with him on the Argo. (5) Her father embarks on the sea with the intention of bringing her back. (6) Medea kills her brother Apsyrtus, cuts him to pieces, and throws the pieces into the sea in order to delay her father, who is forced to stop and perform the funeral rites for his son.[11] (7) Medea and Jason find refuge in Corinth and live in happy marriage for many years. (8) Jason decides to remarry and send Medea into exile. (9) She revenges herself by killing the bride and her father, King Creon. (10) Medea kills her children in order to complete the revenge against Jason. It is largely believed that it is Euripides who added to the myth the episode of the infanticide, although this assumption is still the subject of controversy among scholars.[12] It is also believed that, originally, in the myth, it was the Corinthians who committed the infanticide to punish Medea for the killing of Creusa and her father, King Creon.[13] (11) Medea flees in a magical flaming chariot, drawn by winged serpents and untouched by any punishment![14]

In his study "Medea, the Enchantress from Afar,"[15] Fritz Graf proposes a "horizontal" reading of the Medea story. He looks at the crucial moments in terms of their connection to a specific place or country and thus crosses from myth to literature. According to where a specific event took place, we would thus have the "Colchian story" (Medea's aid to Jason in order to obtain the Golden Fleece); the "Iolcan story" (Medea helps Jason take revenge on King Pelias who had stopped Jason from taking the throne of Iolcos, kills Pelias, and flees with Jason); the "Corinthian story" (Medea's revenge on Jason, which takes place in Corinth, the city where she had settled with Jason); the "Athenian story" (Medea marries Aegeus, king of Athens, and tries to kill his son Theseus, after which she must flee again); and finally, the "Medean story" (Medea finally settles in the Iranian highlands, whose people have been called "Medes" ever since). This division brings out with particular clarity Medea's involvement with the politics of the time, on the one hand, and her status as a perpetual fugitive and exile, on the other hand. As daughter of a king, wife of a hero, and subsequently wife of another king, Medea's role is oblique, either as disobeying the patriarchal order and thus causing political chaos and disorder, or as destroying the patriarchal order altogether. She runs away from the king her father, forcing him to leave his throne and country for the period; she contributes to the death of King Pelias; she kills King Creon, Jason's future father-in-law; she tries to kill King Aegeus's son, Theseus. She continually places herself between powerful men and their power, subverting or destroying it. As Alain Moreau points out, she has made a habit of killing or trying to kill kings and men in general, accumulating thus, like Oedipus, some of the basic crimes: fratricide, regicide, and, finally, infanticide. Her crimes are both the cause of and motivated by her constant fugitive status.[16] She tries to obtain power and/or happiness, is denied one or both; she acts or reacts to the denial/rejection and is forced into exile. In its turn, each new exile functions as both denial and affirmation: denial of her present identity and home and affirmation of her power to both destroy and reestablish homes and herself.

Medea is also giver of power. She is the very reason for Jason's actual glory as the hero who obtained the Golden Fleece. When in love and loved by Jason she has the capacity to be creator of glory and of happiness; with her witchcraft she can create helpful potions and produce helpful magic. Although her creativity is defined mostly in terms of magic, a practice traditionally associated with women, she does have the power to create and transform, power traditionally associated with men. Scholars have pointed out that Medea displays traits that were associated with both maleness and femaleness in ancient Greek society.[17] Alain Moreau, in particular, analyzes with subtlety the specific traits and facts that make of Medea both a feared character and a scapegoat or "*bouc émissaire*," among them the combination of womanhood with intelligence, wisdom, and knowledge of both beneficent and maleficent magic. Mimoso-Ruiz suggests that "this superiority of Medea, affirmed in a sphere of activity reserved to men (the field of Ares, royal power) sends us to the mythical image of Hera who also tends to mark her sovereignty over Zeus himself."[18]

The myth itself, with its many episodes, versions, and spatial plurality, seems to partake of the very fragmentation of its main protagonist, who, wandering from place to place, ultimately exists in a nonspace. It appears that of all the fragments of the myth, each connected to a particular country or shore, it is only the conquest of the Golden Fleece and the Corinthian infanticide that underwent significant development throughout literature.[19] Between power and defeat, happiness and misery, Medea's myth seems to have molded its own aesthetic structure and destiny onto the destiny of its heroine, with its sharp tensions and dichotomies between positive and negative and, most significantly, with its fragmentary and itinerant nature, trying to define itself with each new spatial structure while denying or running away from each previous territory.[20]

Medea exemplifies the famous line that "hell hath no fury like a woman scorned." Her creativity can turn to destructiveness in a swift second. For indeed, "scorned" she is: starting with the moment she flees her father the king, throughout the myth and the literary works based on the myth, she is perpetually exiled, chased, and torn to pieces. In the myth, she finds rest and relative peace only when she has acquired the political power she could have, or would have had, if she had not lived in an entirely male-dominated world: in the end, as the one after whom an entire people is named, she acquires a symbolic queenship among the "Medes." As a woman, she could not have had political power, except vicariously as either daughter or wife of a king. The few powerful queens of the ancient world that are often given as examples of women who acquired political power, the likes of Sheba, Cleopatra, or Dido, are exceptions that support the rule. Moreover, no Greek female political figures or leaders are known. Once her father the king starts chasing her, she loses that vicarious experience as well. She then reestablishes a home and vicarious "hero" status or "queenship" through Jason. But, alas, that too is taken away. The myth is centered around Medea's fugitive or exile status, which she reacquires every time she has a chance at being both politically powerful and personally happy.

Defining the "Tragic" and Medea's "Tragic" Status

From Aristotle to Pascal to Nietzsche to Camus[21] to the vast amount of twentieth-century scholarship, the concept of "tragedy" and the "tragic" has been analyzed, defined in many different ways, argued about. As Geoffrey Brereton points out, in his *Principles of Tragedy*,[22] this century has seen the publication of a lot more books about tragedy and the tragic than it has seen actual tragedies written. Definitions vary and are subject to controversy, particularly between Aristotelian and non-Aristotelian scholars. I rely specifically on two definitions of the tragic and of the tragic hero , that of Brereton and that of Jean-Pierre Vernant, although I refer to other opinions on the subject. I also draw attention to that which is particularly tragic for the female protagonist. Brereton's definition of a "tragic happening" is neo-Aristotelian: "A tragedy is a final and impressive disaster due to an unforeseen or unrealized failure involving people who command respect and sympathy. It often entails an ironical change of fortune and usually conveys a strong impression of waste. It is always accompanied by misery and emotional distress." This definition is somewhat akin to Thomas Gould's discussion of the notion of "pathos" and "pathe."[23] While Plato uses the term "pathos" (Gr. *pathe*) "for affection, punishment and disease," points out Gould, "In the *Poetics*, Aristotle can use pathos as a strong emotion, even though he normally uses *pathéma* in that sense. The adjective *pathétikos* can mean passive, capable of experiencing emotion, characterized by strong emotions, susceptible to devastating passions, dependent on dramatic *pathe* in the technical sense, destined to become the victim of pathos, or able to elicit great pity in other people or in an audience" (64). Jean-Pierre Vernant's definition contains echoes of Aristotle as well: he considers the tragic hero as: "sometimes 'aítios,' responsible for his actions in so far as they express his human character; sometimes a simple plaything in the hands of the gods, victim of a destiny which can haunt him like a *daímon*."[24] All three definitions apply to Medea's tragedy as a human being, but they do not fully describe the qualities of her tragedy as a female protagonist.

In the first part of the story, Medea corresponds to the helper-maiden type[25] and is a positive character, fitting the Aristotelian and neo-Aristotelian definitions of the tragic hero-heroine. She is of noble origins and noble stature. The Greek historian of the first century B.C., Diodorus of Sicily, in fact presents Medea as morally superior to her father. According to him, Medea was a prisoner of her own father, for she refused to sacrifice strangers and use her supernatural powers in maleficent ways.[26] Though the killing of her brother is problematic in terms of her being judged as "noble," and though it anticipates the gory deeds she is to perform later, her action is justified as a means of defending herself and Jason and as an action dictated mostly by despair and love. Furthermore, this love was dictated to her by Eros in the first place, and not of her own choice. In Apollonius's *Argonautica,* we see Medea become entirely the victim of the overpowering force of Eros:

> Meanwhile Eros came unseen through the bright air, . . . He quickly reached the foot
> of the door-post in the vestibule; he strung his bow, and selected from his quiver a new
> arrow destined to bring much grief. . . . He crouched down low at Jason's feet, fitted the
> arrow-notch to the bowstring, and stretching the bow wide in his two hands shot straight
> at Medea. Her spirit was seized by speechless stupor. . . . As when a woman heaps up
> twigs around a burning brand—a poor woman who must live from working wool—so
> that she might have light in her dwelling at night as she sits very close to the fire, and a
> fierce flame spurts up from the small brand and consumes all the twigs, just so was the
> destructive love which crouched unobserved and burnt in Medea's heart.[27]

Her "tragic" dimension as "a mere toy in the hands of the Gods, victim of a destiny which can haunt him like a *daímon*" is traced from the very beginning of her story. It is not without significance that, in Apollonius's version, of all his arrows, Eros chose the "new" kind which were "destined to bring much grief."

Hers is the tragic fate by definition, as it is crossed by unusual grief and cruel irony.

The moment when Jason takes the new bride (the point at which both the Greek and Latin tragedies begin) corresponds to the Aristotelian "peripeteia," reversal of fortune or "an ironical change of fortune." At this point, Medea, who is heard and then seen at the beginning of both Euripides' and Seneca's plays as lamenting and raging against her cruel and painful fate, is someone who "commands sympathy," or "eleos," and terror or "phobos" in Aristotle's definition. She is also "*pathetikos,*" that is, "subjected to devastating passions," as in Gould's interpretation of Aristotle. In Euripides, the chorus supports the idea of her revenge and also laments on her behalf and in heartfelt tones this ironic reversal of fortune: "O hapless thou! / Woe's me for thy misery, woe for the trouble and anguish that meet thee!" (556-58) She is therefore, up to this point, both Vernant's "aitios" (in Greek: at fault, guilty, culpable, accused) and the plaything of the gods—both responsible for her fate and its victim. She has made choices of her own, manifesting her free will, but she is also the victim of Eros, of her father's rage, of Jason's unexpected change of plans, and of Creon's fear of her. The word most used in Euripides' play to express Medea's love for Jason is ἔρως (éros), which means "love: desire for a thing," as well as "the god of love, Eros, Amor," used in ancient Greece to refer to sexual or carnal love, sent on to mortals by either Aphrodite or her son. She is, by all traditional standards, a tragic heroine, poised on the thin line between free will and the will of divine forces and torn between clashing external and internal forces.

But she is also a modern tragic heroine in the sense of the psychological inner tearing resulting from opposing forces that collide within herself; and she is tragic *because* a *heroine,* that is a woman. Even the purity and wholeness of her maidenhood are marked by exile and fragmentation, as she has to leave her home surreptitiously in order to follow Jason. Apollonius gives a gripping account of the way in which Medea is, by Hera herself, deterred from her intention to end her life and influenced to follow Jason. He gives a heartrending account of the moment when Medea flees her home:

> She kissed her bed and both sides of the double door to her chamber, and ran her hand
> over the walls; she cut off a long lock of her hair, and left it in her room for her mother as
> a memorial of her virginity. In a voice of grief she lamented: "As I go I leave you this
> flowing lock, mother, to take my place. Farewell—this is my wish as I depart on a very
> distant journey; farewell, Chalkiope and all my home! Stranger, would that the sea had
> torn you in pieces before you reached the Colchian land!" (IV. 1-38)

As she tears herself away from her old self, she performs a symbolic self-mutilation as she cuts the lock of her hair, symbol of her virginity and prewoman wholeness. And uncannily, as if predicting the many fragmentations, griefs, and crimes that are to fill her grim future, she throws a retroactive curse in which she wishes Jason had been "torn" to "pieces." Medea enters into womanhood, wifehood, and motherhood already an alien and a fragmented being—not on the path of joy and fulfillment, but on that of grief and crime.

Medea tries to resist, question, scorn, and subvert male political power every time it is used unjustly on her, and playwrights were keen to develop this aspect of Medea's character when reworking the myth into their plays. In both Euripides' and Seneca's plays, King Creon, during his encounter with Medea, clearly expresses fear of her unusual powers. It is this very fear that is the cause of her exile. Seneca's Creon calls her "contriver of wickedness, who combinest woman's wanton recklessness and man's strength."[28] Euripides's Creon admits: "I fear thee."[29] In both plays Medea revolts against the arbitrary rule of "these marriage-makers" (Euripides, 367-70). She captures in acrid words the tyrannical nature of the king "who with unbridled sway dissolves marriages, tears mothers from their children, and breaks pledges bound by straightest oath,"[30] and courageously points out the fragility of tyrannical rule: "Unjust rule never abides continually."[31]

The famous speech in which Medea deplores in fiery words the miserable condition of women and their lives projects Medea against the bloody canvas of ancient tragedy as both a female victim and rebel. Through her words Euripides gives the modern reader glimpses of the sociocultural context of the time and of the tragic condition of women; tragic because of the "emotional distress," of the "pathe" and the "victim" status implicit in their very existence and identity within the social order. Heroes "become" tragic as the confrontation between free will and destiny starts to operate. Heroines are already tragic figures due to their difficult status even before this basic confrontation is at work:

> Surely, of creatures that have life and wit,
> We women are of all unhappiest,
> Who, first must buy, as buys the highest bidder,
> A husband—nay, we do but win for our lives
> A master! Deeper depth of wrong is this.
> Here too is dire risk—will the lord we gain
> Be evil or good? Divorce? tis infamy
> To us: we may not even reject a suitor!"
>
> Then, coming to new customs, habits new,
> One need be a seer, to know the thing unlearnt
> At home, what manner of man her mate shall be.
> And *if* we learn our lesson, if our lord
> Dwell with us, plunging not against the yoke,
> Happy our lot is; else—no help but death.
> For the man, when the home-yoke galls his neck,
> Goes forth, to ease a weary sickened heart
> By turning to some friend, some kindred soul:
> We to one heart alone can look for comfort. (230-47)

Whatever the interpretation of this passage might be it is clear that Medea incites women of all backgrounds, ethnic groups, and epochs to rebel, act against male oppression, and subvert the existing patriarchal order. It is hard to believe that, even today, any woman who at any level or degree has experienced the crushing power of male dominance would not identify with and be moved by her words. In terms of this discussion, the pivotal points of her speech are her references to and implications of exile and fragmentation.

In terms of the etymology of the word "exile," of its Greek equivalents further discussed in the subsequent sections, and of the observations on the etymology of the name Tomis, women are presented as "cut off" from the life of the city—aliens, expulsed and tossed around, with no real ties to the community or the family that they are expected to make their one and only universe. The rhythm and structure of Medea's speech point precisely to the shifting and insecure nature of woman's destiny and condition, with the abrupt and often unwanted transitions from maidenhood to marriage to, possibly, the shame of divorce, or better yet to untimely death. And throughout it all: an exile, alone and marginal to life itself! Seneca's Medea vividly describes her predicament in terms of confusion and being "tossed" around: "Perplexed, witless, with mind scarce sane, I am tossed to every side."[32] A different translation renders in fact the very idea of inner tearing and fragmentation: "My mind is ravaged by insanity, / I'm torn to pieces, scattered everywhere."[33] There is no solid ground on which women can ever rest, dependent as they are entirely on male power and will. And Medea, once, twice, three times an exile is also once, twice, three times a tragic figure: she is tragic for all the reasons she herself enumerates in terms of the female condition; she is tragic because she has exiled herself from home, country, and family; she is tragic because she suffers a dramatic "reversal of fortune" and is exiled again by Jason and his future father-in-law, King Creon.[34] At an ontological level, Medea is thus strongly connected to the sea in the myth as well as in the literary works inspired by it. The waves of the sea are the opposite of the solid ground on which she would like to rest. Her actual drama starts on the tumultuous waves of the Pontos Euxinos and she remains forever, symbolically or in actual fact, prey to the whims of the water and not connected to any solid ground.[35] It is no wonder that, in his deep loneliness away from his native Rome, watching the turbulent movements of the Black Sea, the poet Ovid thought of Medea, sister in exile of sorts.

There is also great irony in Medea's tragic status: on the one hand, her "superiority" is "affirmed in a sphere of activity reserved to men (the field of Ares, royal power)," on the other hand she is represented as possessing the powers traditionally associated with women in a negative way: cunning and the fury of the woman scorned. The deeper, ontological meaning of the line "I am tossed to every side" or "I'm torn to pieces" in the context of this tragic irony is that Medea is "tossed" and "torn" in the conflict between various gender stereotypes, conflict that ultimately exiles her from the territory of both genders.

However, in discussing Medea's tragic status, one has to keep in mind that, in both the Greek and Roman versions, the Aristotelian movement of the tragic character from fortune to adversity, or the "reversal of fortune" (peripeteia) is, at least on the surface level, reversed. Medea starts out as a heroine "tossed" by the arbitrary wills of fate and men, exiled and fragmented, and ends as a victorious semigoddess who has completed her revenge against her persecutors. Furthermore, in the Euripides version, the scene between Medea and King Aegeus of Athens suggests that she will find refuge in his kingdom and bed, after the end of the Corinthian episode. The "reversal of fortune" is reversed, and the tragic heroine undoes her tragic status. Or does she? At the first level of the dynamics of tragedy, she does undo her tragic status. She is punished at the beginning at the play without any logical reasons or explanations other than the whims of her husband and the fears of King Creon, and is not punished at the end, when some sort of punishment would be in place. But at a metaphysical level, she is punished at the end as well, for she has done more harm to herself than anybody else has or could have done: she has killed the fruit of her womb and love. She has fragmented herself more than anybody else has or could have done, for by killing her children she has effectuated a triple fragmentation and exile: she has killed the mother in her, and she has transformed herself simultaneously into a murderous and mourning mother, into criminal and victim of her crime. It is no wonder that after this event takes place, the spectator is confronted with an entirely new Medea, a totally new character from the one she was at the beginning of the play. Euripides' much-criticized ending of the deus ex machina technique has much more profound human implications than has been generally believed. At the human level, Medea is obliterated. If she is to survive, she can only survive as a nonhuman being. And this brings us logically to her divine status. As already pointed out, the figure of Medea was part of heroine cults devoted to the goddess Hera. Furthermore, in Greek mythology, the gods and goddesses alone are capable of such shocking duality or multiplicity of faces. Of "inhuman" harshness as well. It is not only Hera, but also Athena and Diana who are known as cruel at times. It is, for instance, the goddess Athena who defends Orestes for the unspeakable crime of matricide, at the end of Aeschylus's trilogy, the *Oresteia*. And it is Apollo and Artemis who, upon request from their mother, Leto, strike all of Niobe's children dead, just to punish her for her pride. In exceeding the limits of what humans can bear to look at, to suffer, or to accept as human, Medea has passed into the realm of the nonhuman. Only this passage is performed by the human mind as well, by the mythmaker, or the playwright. The passage from the human to the nonhuman, to the monstrous or the divine, is ultimately a stylized manner of endowing extreme human fears and/or aspirations with a recognizable face.

There is great irony in Euripides and, implicitly, in Seneca's reversal of the Aristotelian peripeteia, while still keeping the tragic status of their heroines in place. This reversal both cancels and reinforces the tragic status of the heroine. At the human level, Medea's game with gender masks has obliterated her. But it has also enhanced her status above the human and frozen her into a divine figure, a staggering symbol for humans to behold in utter bewilderment, as they both recognize themselves in it and are horrified by it.

The Suffering of Exile

Historical, legal, and anthropological studies have also shown us[36] that women in Greek society were, to begin with, marginal to social life and therefore "exiled" from most of the life of the community outside the home. Young girls were, as a practice, "given" in marriage to older men, with a dowry meant to pay for their upkeep, administered by the husband. A child's citizenship depended on the father's citizenship. While polygamy was widely accepted for a man, women who were considered "adulterous," even if the so-called adultery was the result of rape, could easily be subject to ill treatment and even death if they showed themselves in public or at the temple. These are just a few examples of the marginality of women and the injustices they had to bear as part of the Greek "democratic" social and political system.

If you happened to be, like Medea, a "barbarian," you might as well have remained in your "barbaric" country and given up all hope for justice or happiness. "Medea—as both Pindar and Euripides show—was *the* outsider *par excellence*, a foreign woman who (in Euripides) brutally exposes the risks of all such 'imports,' and in Pindar also represents geographical remoteness and racial and cultural 'difference.' All women were outsiders, but none more conspicuously than Medea."[37] This fact offers to a great extent the "tragic" core of Medea's character. As she starts her famous speech, she laments her initial self-exile, which she chose in order to follow Jason: "O father, O city, whom erst I forsook, for undoing, undoing, / And for shame, when the blood of my brother I spilt on the path of my flight!" (Euripides, 166-67). And Seneca's Medea wonders in her despair: "Had Jason the heart to do this; having robbed me of my father, native land, and kingdom, could he be so cruel as to leave me alone in a foreign land?" (118-20). The Greek word used by Euripides for "forsake" is *apenásten*, the past of the verb *aponáu*, which means "to remove one to another place," "to send away," and which has the same root as *aponémo,* which means "to portion out," "to part off," or "separate." Seneca's Medea uses the verb *eripio, eripere* (stole, robbed) and the expression *exteris deserere* meaning "left outside, deserted," to express that Jason is responsible for her double exile. Later on, in her impassioned speech, Euripides' Medea also blames Jason for her multiple fragmentations, as she mourns her own grim fate as fugitive and exile: "But I, lone, cityless, and outraged thus / Of him who kidnapped me from foreign shores, / Mother nor brother have I, kinsman none, /For port of refuge from calamity." This time the Greek word is *apolis*, from the Greek a, meaning "without" and *pólis* meaning city—literally translated as "cityless"—a word that is used numerous times throughout the play when referring to Medea's exile. It is bad enough that, as she had put it earlier, "of creatures that have life and wit, / We women are of all unhappiest" (Euripides 230-31). Within this miserable lot, Medea, twice foreigner, twice fugitive, and exiled, having destroyed forever her relations with her own kin, having to now tear herself away from her newly established kin, that is, husband and children, is at this point nothing more than an amalgam of broken pieces, suspended in a nonspace. The chorus laments her fugitive state: "Whitherward wilt thou turn thee?—what welcoming hand mid the strangers shall greet thee? / What home or what land to receive thee, deliverance from evils to give thee" (Euripides, 357-60), anticipating Medea's own lament of her lonely and miserable status: "what city will receive me, / What host vouchsafe a land of refuge, home / Secure, and from the avenger shield my life" (387-89).[38] And Seneca's Medea deplores her actual state with magnificent dignity by comparing it to her past situation as beloved daughter of King Aetes, when beautiful and extensive territories belonged to her, reminding us of Francesca da Rimini's famous "there is no greater sorrow than thinking back upon a happy time in misery."[39] The only space where she could have reestablished her home, Jason's heart, has now expelled her.

The abundance of words containing the ideas of separation, banishment, ejection, fragmentation throughout this and the rest of Medea's speeches in the two plays points at once to the vacuousness of the space into which she is thrown and to her own progressively altered wholeness. For instance, in just two lines, Seneca's Medea uses the verbs *eripere* (to rob) and *deserere* (to desert), the adjective *solam* (alone) and the adjective *exteris* (external, foreign). And Euripides' Medea uses four different words that point to the same kind of injury and suffering: ερημος (to desert, to roam forsaken), ἄπολις (without city), υβρίζομαι (to injure, to abuse, also connected to "hubris," which can mean violence and rape), and λελησμενη (forgotten, obscure, from *lanthāno* which means to be unknown, to remain obscure). As if suggestive of the four cardinal points, these clusters of words contain Medea's multidimensional exile from life in general. She is threatened by darkness and nothingness from all directions.

"Perplexed, witless, with mind scarce sane, I am tossed to every side." Medea's suffering, rage, and confusion contain a deeply ontological dimension: they point to the basic human fear of being thrown out of the social order and losing all human bonds, of being condemned to the chaos of perpetual running. After all Adam and Eve are perpetual exiles from happiness. Cain was punished with perpetual exile for the murder of his brother. Leto was punished by Hera out of jealousy, to roam forever and have no place to rest and give birth to the twins Diana and Apollo. Restricting the sphere of human experience by gender, women were already once outcasts. Medea, woman, "barbarian," rejected by her own husband and forced to leave her home and children, is the subject of so many ejections and fragmentations, operated on her by fate, other men, and, to some extent, herself, that her own human and female nature have become the place of exile or rather, the place of no-place.

Often mythology presents us with monstrous female types who initially were beautiful maids like Medea and who, as a result of profound injury, became monsters. Medusa, her name uncannily reminiscent of that of Medea herself, is such an example. She was initially a beautiful virgin who fell in love with Poseidon (god of the seas). She gave herself to him in Athena's temple and Athena turned her into the monster whose gaze turns men to stone and whose hair is made of serpents. Though the mortal one and the weaker of the two, she is punished also for her lover, Poseidon, who had taken her virginity. Although not etymologically connected to it, both names start with the syllable "me" (μή), reminiscent of the Greek word meaning "not." Negation, like an inescapable circle of nothingness, is ironically contained in both their names. Once annihilated in their deepest humanity by male perpetrators, they become in turn annihilators of males. Furthermore, it is rather suggestive that *mēdos* (μήδος) used only in the plural (μήδεα) means "plans, schemes: cunning, craft," but also male "genitals" (like Latin *virilia*). Medea's very name suggests the gender masks and the war between them.

Of course, since most representations of women in the ancient world were the result of male thinking and imagination, as critics have so often pointed out, we have strong grounds to be suspicious of these very "monstrous" portraits and interpret them as symbols of men's fear of women and of more or less conscious attempts to "barbarize" them, to reinvent them as latent or unleashed monsters. Injustice would thus be frozen into law, rationalized and justified. Edith Hall, for example, argues that Greek Hellenic culture of the fifth century is largely responsible for the creation of the very notion of the "barbarian" and that in particular tragedy has played a fundamental role in the elaboration of the theory of the "barbarian." The "barbarians" were also, for the most part in the "democratic" Greek society, slaves taken from wars: "the economic basis of the Athenian empire was slavery, and most of the large number of slaves in fifth-century Athens were not Greek."[40] And going even further down on the social ladder, significant numbers of the slaves were women. In fact, in the Greek legal system, resident aliens, slaves, and women were placed in the same category and subject to similar laws.[41]

There is something fundamentally human and true about the dialectics of transformation, or of psychological and even physical mutations of the human being as a result of excessive abuses and injuries. Euripides plays on the intuition of this truth particularly by portraying Medea as a "tragic" character who elicits "pity" in the first part of the play and by allowing her to give full expression to her outrage, her suffering, and her rebellion in such an eloquent and gripping manner that both audience and chorus sympathize with her up to a point. Thus her mutation and metamorphosis into the frightful figure who does the unspeakable, killing her own children, is to some extent psychologically motivated at least, if not justified. Even if, as Shirley Barlow poignantly argues, in the end Euripides returns to a traditional view of womanhood, with, possibly, the warning that men should beware of women in love, "Glimmers of unease may remain. . . . Euripides made sure that Medea's speech to the women of Corinth universalized her plight, when she made common cause with the Greek Chorus. . . . Not only a *barbarian*, but *any* woman could have gone through and done what Medea went through and did"[42] (45). If the view of the author supported rather than questioned the misogyny of his time, why then would he have wanted to draw the sympathy of the audience toward his character in the first part of the play? Together with Sarah Pomeroy, we can say that "Euripides is questioning rather than dogmatic" and that "he uses the extreme vantage point of misogyny as a means of examining popular beliefs about women."[43]

Medea's suffering as a result of her banishment from Corinth is first mentioned and described in the words of the Nurse (1-48), then directly expressed in progressively vehement language by Medea herself (160-172), then echoed by the chorus in the Antistrophe, then resumed by Medea in her famous speech on the condition of women. It is then repeated in sharp retorts throughout the encounter with King Creon where we see Medea move from the lamenting woman abandoned by her husband ("Ah me! undone am I in utter ruin! / My foes crowd sail pursuing;

landing place / Is none from surges of calamity," 277-79) to the rebellious yet lucid woman who questions popular beliefs and cunningly points to her overly liminal status in society. She then points to her dual condition of powerful heroine and scapegoat (298-305) and finally to the apparently composed woman who pretends to resign herself to her predicament only to gain time and cover up her vengeful plans (307-15). The increasingly agitated rhythm of the expression of her sorrow mixed with rage, followed by the apparent calm (which only hides future turmoil), suggests the rhythm of Medea's own turbulent destiny and seems to find symbolic reverberations in the image of the savage waves of the Pontos Euxinos in stormy weather, followed by a serenity that is invariably outdone by new storms.

The psychological and ontological mutation of Medea takes place under our very eyes as we watch her channel her pain into vengeance and put together the pieces of her fragmented self into a new and monstrous self. This mutation is carved out on the background of the dichotomy between πόλις and ἄπολις, (*pólis* versus *ápolis*), to which Medea keeps returning as if to the very core of her misery. While everybody has a "polis" to find refuge, shelter, home ("Thine is this city, thine father's home, / Thine bliss of life and fellowship of friends"), she is *apolis* ("cityless, and outraged thus." 253-55). Semantically akin with *polis* and *apolis*, the words home (*domon, dómous*), country (*pátris*), land, earth (*ktona*), uttered in this part of the play either by the chorus (360) or by Medea herself (386-87) and preceded by interjections of woe (*u pátris*—"oh my country," 328) or by interrogative particles used rhetorically with the expectation of a negative answer (*é dómon, é ktona; tís pólis, tís dómous*,—"what home," "what land," "what city") suggest the progressive expansion of Medea's exile, the gaping nothingness that encroaches upon her from all sides. The word used by Creon as he pronounces his sentence of banishment is "flight" (*phugas*, 273); Medea also uses the same verb as she refers to her exile again: "I shall go exiled to another land" ("égo d' es állen gáian eími de *phúgas*," 1024). And this same verb, in turn, forms the etymological basis for the Latin verb used numerous times by Seneca's Medea: "to flee" (*fugere*). As the tragedy develops, as the myth is being narrated, recreated, reinterpreted, "flight" becomes the very essence of Medea's destiny. Progressively, as destiny forces itself on her, flight becomes the essence of her very nature and its multiple mutations, just as negation is part of her name. A perpetual itinerant, Medea also continuously flees from herself, denies and tries to recreate herself. With each new re-creation, she advances deeper into crime, thus, on the one hand, restoring herself into evil, sister of Hecate, sister of the Night, and, on the other hand, shredding herself even more as she ends up killing the very fruit of her womb. Not only is there no landing place for Medea, but there is no refuge inside herself either.

Inspired by Euripides, but also incorporating the philosophy and ethics of the Stoics in his art, Seneca presents Medea's great suffering and rage with maybe even more intensity[44] as he projects them on the background of the Stoic belief that that kind of emotional distress is mainly derived from excessive attachment to an exterior object or being.[45] Therefore, the stronger the attachment or the love, the more fierce the pain at the loss of the object of love.

Seneca's Medea is, even more than her Greek double, magnificently and frightfully ablaze in her fury and suffering, at once mother in mourning and murderess mother, at once fragmented by multiple injuries and repeated exiles and striving toward a complete unity of her being through vengeful action. In Seneca, this aspiration is also expressed by her wish to have many children: "Medea is, or wants to be, the mother who concentrates on herself, unfolds and aspires to a large number of children only to better be able to bring herself to unity. A cherished, triumphant unity sufficient unto itself."[46]

Her suffering and wrath take cosmic dimensions, as does the drama of her exile. During her first encounter and dialogue with Jason, she expresses twice the tragic irony of her exile, within a dual linguistic structure that combines negation and affirmation:[47] "All the ways which I have opened for thee I have closed upon myself" (458); "Seeking a kingdom for another, I have given up my own" (477).[48] Medea is not just banished or exiled, she is practically thrown off the earth. There is no longer any place for her that she can call home or where she can rest; like Cain, like Leto, she is condemned to perpetual fleeing. In her answer to Creon she repeats the word "flee" (*fugere*) in breathless rush: "Dost force me to flee? Give back then to the fugitive her ship, yea, give back her comrade. Why dost thou bid me flee alone?" (272-73).[49] When speaking to Jason, she repeats the verb *fugere* at different aspects five times in the first four lines of her speech: "We are *fleeing*, Jason, *fleeing*. Tis no new thing to change our abode; but the cause of *flight* is new—twas *for* thee I was wont to *flee*. I withdraw, I go away, whom thou art forcing to *flee* forth from thy home" (447-49).[50] With stark irony she enumerates to him all the places which are forever closed up to her: "but whither dost thou send me back? Shall I seek Phasis and the Colchians, my father's kingdom, the fields drenched with my brother's blood? What lands dost thou bid me seek? What waters dost show me? The jaws of the Pontic sea through which I brought back the noble band of princes, following thee, thou wanton, through the Clashing Rocks? Is it little Iolcos or Thessalian Tempe I shall seek?" (451-57).

Thus aesthetically and psychologically motivated by the hopelessness of her exile, Medea's wrath and vengefulness rise with superhuman force to encompass all earth, all universe, all that has been denied her: "No whirling river, no storm-tossed sea, no Pontus, raging beneath the north-west wind, no violence of fire, fanned by the gale, could imitate the onrush of my wrath. I shall lay prostrate and destroy all things.... This day shall do, shall do that whereof no day shall e'er be dumb. I will storm the gods, and shake the universe" (409-25). Seneca's Medea is even more hopelessly exiled .than Euripides'. For the Greek play contains a significant episode of the myth which the Latin one lacks: the encounter with King Aegeus, who lends a compassionate ear to Medea's laments and offers her refuge, if she was to ever need it, in his very kingdom. All roads are closed for the Latin heroine. To pun on an old Latin proverb, for Medea, "no roads lead to Rome." As she is even more strikingly a sorceress in Seneca's play than in the Greek one, it may be that the challenge to her powers and the causes of her revenge have to be multiplied, in order to fit her semidivine status better. Or, it may be also that, her condition being more desperate, beyond the limits of human endurance, so does the range of her revenge have to be beyond the limits of human abilities.

But also, on the line initiated by Moreau in his analysis of the Greek Medea as a "scapegoat" (*bouc émissaire*), it can be she is even more of a scapegoat in the Latin play. Patriarchy and male domination were even more conspicuous in Roman society than in the Greek one, which still had significant forms of mother/female/heroine worship and cults. The *Odyssey* is replete with images of strong and complex females from Penelope to Helen to Calypso; Ulysses defines himself in a significant manner through the way in which he relates to and dialogues with women. Even his descent into the Underworld is marked by the moving encounter and dialogue with his mother, Antikleia. The *Aeneid*, on the other hand, the Latin epic of the origins of the Roman empire, traces the avatars and great deeds of Aeneus and, other than sorrowful Dido, and Apollo's Sybil, women are practically nonexistent as characters. Aeneus's trip underground is marked almost entirely by his encounter and discussion with his father, who predicts to him the foundation of the Roman empire and the long line of warriors and patriarchs that were to build it.

A nation of conquerors and empire builders born of the one survivor of Troy, Aeneas, son of Aphrodite and Anchises, builders of an empire whose boundaries stretched as far as the ill-fated Tomis where Medea supposedly killed her brother and where Ovid was sent into exile, the Romans had even less pity on "barbarics" and women, let alone women who were "barbarics" as well. However, as Judith P. Hallet argues, the tension between women's bondage and servitude to men and incipient forms of female liberation in Roman society is a complex matter for scholars to grasp. Roman elegy of the first century B.C., written by Roman poets such as Catullus and Propertius, offers surprising notes of "counter-cultural feminism."[51] Seneca came relatively soon after these poets, in the first part of the first century C.E.; therefore it is quite possible that these very tensions are to some extent expressed throughout his *Medea* as well, his heroine being at once a rebel and a great "matrona."

The gender inversions pointed out by Garrelli-François between Medea and Jason, in which Medea displays male features and Jason displays female traits are similar to the gender inversions discussed by Hallet in the analysis of Roman elegy. To come back to the previous point about the difference in the gravity and expanse of their exiles (between the Greek and the Latin Medea) and, implicitly, the force of their furor, we can see in the latter and in the cosmic range of her revenge, not only an example of what should rightfully befall a "wanton" and treacherous man like Jason but also, as in Euripides, to some extent, a warning against powerful women like Medea and against falling in love with the likes of her. Cynthia, the lover of Propertius present in his elegies, is a Medea type of woman whose jealous rage is depicted with gripping vividness and endured humbly by the male lover who repeatedly acknowledges his fault. Could it be that Seneca's play is also crossed by echoes of condemnation of male "wantonness"? And then again, there is the shadow of that Medea in Dante's *Inferno*, rightfully avenged through Jason's severe punishment in the circle of the "seducers." Dante, with his heritage of classical literature behind him and also a modern man and an exile, guilty of the sin of unfaithfulness himself, condemns wantons and seducers and partially absolves passionate lovers such as Francesca or Dido by placing them in the higher and less painful circles of the inferno. Medea too is the ultimate passionate lover, dangerous as she may be. Her words to that effect ring with great poignancy: "True love can fear no man" (Seneca, 416). To some extent, and in tune with Stoic beliefs, the greater Medea's love, the deeper her suffering. But also, the deeper her suffering, the more vile Jason appears and the more deeply is her rage motivated. Thus the gender inversions may be seen as a way of criticizing gender stereotypes: for if Jason appears as more "feminine" and yet less admirable, and Medea appears as more "masculine" and yet partly justified in her wrath, what the poet is telling us is that it is "human nature" that is at stake here. For men too can be vile, and women too can be justified in their anger at men's lack of virtue. Of course, the reverse can be true as well, namely that the author uses what has traditionally been perceived as typically female flaws in order to justify the vileness of men and, vice versa, what have traditionally been perceived as typically male virtues in order to explain the courage of women. However, whether misogyny and the critique of misogyny coexist, or whether one prevails over the other, some invariable facts remain: both Medeas are, at least in the first half of each play, tragic heroines in the sense already discussed in the previous section; within the respective cultural context of their writers, both are representative of "female" tragedy and suffering in particular; both are torn and fragmented as a result of multiple exiles; and both act on the basis of a fundamental mutation of their nature resulted at least partly from these banishments. Finally, both are represented in terms of certain gender inversions by which the tyrannical nature of gender stereotypes is being relativized and put into question.

Revenge and the Fight against Exile and Fragmentation

Certainly, jealousy is the driving force behind Medea's revenge. It is source of devastating psychological pain, of "pathos" and "emotional distress." But it is not the only source of suffering. Nor is it the only driving force behind her revenge. In the context of Medea's situation, jealousy is incorporated within the psychological fragmentation she is subjected to and is part of the larger suffering of exile. Jealousy is a form of erotic exile, as the lover is being banished from the heart and/or bed of the beloved. Jealousy becomes the spark for her vengeful instincts to emerge to the surface. Her lamentation about the plight of women, then more specifically about her own plight as an exiled woman is restricted in the end to the specific act of adultery. It is ultimately the thought of adultery and of the new bride that helps her shift from the confusion caused by her emotional distress to the single-mindedness of revenge, from lamentation to action, from the stereotypical fearful, passive woman to the "masculine," rebellious woman who fights: "If any path be found me, or device, / Whereby to avenge these wrongs upon mine husband, / On her who weds, on him who gives the bride, / Keep silence. Woman quails at every peril, / Faint-hearted to face the fray and look on steel; / But when in wedlock-rights she suffers wrong, / No spirit more bloodthirsty shall be found" (Euripides, 263).

She is headed, of course, toward destructive action. And this kind of vengefulness, as mentioned earlier, shifts her into another female stereotype, that of the "scorned" woman. However, as has been pointed out by scholars, she is one of the Euripidean tragic heroines who most conspicuously displays traits generally associated with men.[52] This fact derives primarily from the image she gives of herself as she deplores the fate of women: "Thrice would I under shield / Stand, rather than bear childbirth-peril once" (Euripides, 250) and from the other references to battle and fighting throughout both plays. For instance, in Euripides, she describes herself in terms of virtues and traits generally associated with the male warrior type in the line of Homeric heroes such as Achilles or Agamemnon: "Let none account me impotent, nor weak, / Nor spiritless! O nay, in other sort, / Grim to my foes, and kindly to my friends. / Most glorious is the life of such as I" (807-10). She incorporates, or she sees herself as incorporating, the ancient Greek value of *arete*, a mixture of prowess, strength, and loyalty to friends. And as she performs her magical incantations and invokes the darkest powers of the universe to her service, Seneca's Medea cuts herself with the sword in order to harden herself: "Let my blood flow upon the altars; accustom thyself, my hand, to draw the sword and endure the sight of beloved blood" (807-10). (Uncannily, this image of the hardened, warrior Medea appears at the same lines in Euripides and Seneca [807-10].)

I believe that, ultimately, Medea breaks through gender stereotypes altogether. In Euripides, she mocks the little meek passive image of femininity, the woman who "quails at every peril." Then, motivated by her suffering and rage, she moves into another stereotype, that of the female as "bloodthirsty" when "in wed-lock rights she suffers wrong." But in doing this, she symbolically does what men were expected to do and did, what she proclaims to be her occupation of choice, namely warfare, much preferred to motherhood: "Thrice would I under shield / Stand, rather than bear childbirth-peril once." But then, as her resolve to seek violent revenge is taken, she speaks ironically of the very stereotype that men have imprisoned women with, while also claiming she is now going to fit that very stereotype. "I prove me woman indeed! Men say we are most helpless for all good, / But of dark deeds most cunning fashioners." (407-09) And right before sending the lethal gifts to the new bride, she cunningly uses with Jason one of the most common stereotypes of womanhood, that of the tearful feeble creature: "But woman is but woman—born of tears." (227) Seneca's Medea also rises well above stereotypes of the woman as a fragile, tearful being and overturns the stereotype of the woman scorned by the lucid manner in which she chooses revenge, by the irreverence with which she responds to both Creon and Jason while presenting the audience and reader with the image of a fully mature woman fighter who has learned from her sorrows and hardships: "Now I am Medea; my wit has grown through suffering" she confesses.[53] Frederick Ahl gives a more realistic yet shocking translation: "My genius has grown with all these evils I have done." Sister of the Greek heroine, this Medea too resorts to male weapons such as the sword and associates herself and her actions with the traditionally male occupation of war.[54] She does play here as well on the stereotype of the tearful mother, while her intentions are harsh and her tears dry. "Dost refuse a poor mother just a little time for tears?" she asks Creon.⁵⁵ In her conversation with the nurse she reveals the real Medea, unfearing, determined, indomitable in her rage: "great ills lie not in hiding. 'Tis pleasing to face the foe" (156). "Fortune fears the brave, the cowardly overwhelms" (159).⁵⁶ And going even farther than her Greek counterpart, as noted earlier, the Roman Medea breaks through traditional views of both men and women, encompasses both male and female traits and rises to the dimension of goddess as she proclaims: "Medea is left—in her thou beholdest sea and land, / and sword and fire and gods and thunderbolts" (166-67).⁵⁷ And as the play aptly and overwhelmingly proves it, these are not just idle threats.

She consciously tries to beat men at their own game, by choosing warfare, on the one hand, and feeding the stereotype of the woman as either intrinsically "evil" or frail, on the other hand. She consciously shifts from one stereotype to another and uses them to her own advantage. The fact that she makes her choices with clarity of mind and irony raises her above the very stereotypes she is believed to fit.⁵⁸ Ultimately, her deepest drive is to subvert, undermine, and destroy the sociopolitical male order that is responsible precisely for the imprisoning stereotypes cast upon women. The songs of Euripides' chorus illuminate this drive with even more power than her own words lead us to believe, and suggest the possibility of establishing a new order, meant to empower women socially, politically, creatively. They illuminate in a few poignant verses precisely what feminist critics and scholars have been stressing for a long time: namely, that most history, art, and mythology, being the work of man, presents woman in a distorted manner and to her great disadvantage.⁵⁹ It is thus high time for a new order, a new art:

> Upward and back to their fountains the sacred rivers are stealing;
> Justice is turned to injustice, the order of old to confusion:
> The thoughts of the hearts of men are treachery wholly, and, reeling
> From its ancient foundations, the faith of the Gods is become a delusion
> Everywhere change!—even me men's voices henceforth shall honour: My life shall be sunlit with glory; for woman the old-time story
> Is ended, the slanders hoary no more shall as chains
>
> And the strains of the singers of old generations for shame shall falter,
> Which sang evermore of the treason of woman, her faithlessness ever.
> Alas that our lips are not touched with the fire of song from the altar
> Of Phoebus, the Harper-king, of the inspiration-giver! Else had I lifted my voice in challenge of song high-ringing
> Unto men: for the roll of the ages shall find for the poet-sages
> Proud woman-themes for their pages, heroines worthy their singing (410-30).⁶⁰

At one level, these lines subvert the text of the play itself, as they question the value and validity of female portraits created by male artists, such as Medea's own portrait by Euripides. Of course Medea is as she is, the chorus seems to say, because she is the ultimate creation of male imagination: her powers and her inhuman traits are the projection of men's fear of intelligent, willful, and sexually demanding women; her suffering a projection of men's desire to punish and annihilate such women; her crimes a projection of men's panicked warning to all *man*-kind with regard to the dangers posed by either loving, leaving or punishing the likes of Medea. You've created Medea, the chorus seems to tell men, now deal with her! Had we the power to sing our own songs, make our own poetry, choose our own destinies, we would deal with virtuous, strong, exemplary heroines.

Of course, as one attempts to make such statements one feels immediately on guard, particularly in a field like classical studies, where scholars, for the most part male scholars have been warning us for decades, and they keep warning, us against trying to apply our own twentieth-century concepts and views of things to Greek society of the fifth century B.C. or to Roman society of the first century B.C. An eloquent article by Sallie Goetsch[61] brings interesting revelations about the distorting and antifeminist comments and translations by male translators and scholars of classical texts, such as Richmond Lattimore or Robert Fagles, who deliberately choose to neutralize sexually charged lines in their translations, or to reinforce patriarchal attitudes in their commentaries of the texts. Prefacing a production in Greek of Euripides' *Medea* by a New York group of actors, William Arrowsmith, after acknowledging that Euripides criticizes Attic society of his time and that he endows Medea with the famous virtue of the *areté*, traditionally an almost exclusively male value, takes with one hand what he has given with the other and makes it a point to warn his audience against considering Euripides a feminist. The words of Medea's chorus ring true millennia after they have been written, and the attempts of male scholars to hush the voices that try to speak in favor of Euripides' progressive thinking with regard to women continue to allow us to identify with these words as well as with Medea's impassioned speech about the tragic condition of women and their fundamental itinerant and fragmented status in society. I will bring to my support the words of Sarah Pomeroy and ally myself to her as she says, "I can scarcely believe that so subtle a dramatist as Euripides, who called into question traditional Athenian beliefs and prejudices surrounding foreigners, war, and the Olympian gods, would have intended his audience simply to accept the misogynistic maxims."[62]

What would be the value of a work of art and its appeal to each century if we couldn't, to some extent, do just that: apply our own views and interpret works of art of previous periods in ways that make them live for us, today? The fact that one cannot have a full understanding of classical ancient literature without knowledge of the sociohistoric, political, and cultural context in which they were written, is indisputable and needs not be argued. But at the deep human level, at the level of catharsis, of feelings, of immediate reactions to the characters we see on stage or read about, the ultimate test of the power of a play like *Medea* is that it touches, troubles, shakes us even if we do not know much about the mores during the time of Euripides or Seneca. And as one of the more progressive women classicists astutely puts it, "If the wisdom of the past has anything to teach the present (certainly a belief cherished by all self-aware classicists), then the insights of contemporary man should bear on previous human experience as well."[63]

Medea, the great negator, annihilator, murderess, and above all the ultimate exile, is at the same time creator of a new order. Out of the many fragmentations she has been subjected to, her human and female nature mutated and turned to a monster capable of most odious crimes, Medea is nevertheless capable of restoring her wholeness. As both Euripides' and Seneca's texts aptly and movingly display it and as critics have noted,[64] Medea's expression of grief at the thought of the death of her children is considerable and render her up to the last moment a problematic and complex character torn between diametrically opposed forces. No need to say that that is little consolation for the killing of two children. I have deliberately chosen not to treat the infanticide at great length here, and in no way does this study attempt to justify Medea's crimes. Probably no criticism should attempt to either condemn or justify literary characters and their actions as if they were people living among us. If a work is aesthetically and humanly compelling, the receptive reader will assimilate or question its moral lessons and will acquire a deeper understanding of human nature on the basis of which to judge real human beings and life in general. Rather, this study has attempted to explore, understand and illuminate the mechanism of her character and the motivations of her actions in terms of the many dramatic, symbolic and historical factors that account for the creation of her character.

The fact that both in the myth and in the two plays analyzed here Medea rises triumphant at the end of her troubled, grief, and crime-ridden destiny is not without significance. She goes on without punishment in the myth, as pointed out earlier, according to some versions ending up as a symbolic queen of a people whose name derives from her own. In both Euripides' and Seneca's plays, she flies away on a winged chariot, bitterly triumphant and divine in stature. Could it be that the creator of the myth and the creators of the plays felt that ultimately there is some justice in the triumph of a murderess mother, gruesome as that may be, since she has been the victim of many an unjust blow? Could it be that this myth exemplifies the triumph of evil over good and moreover the triumph of the evil female? But then where or who *is* the good in this myth and in these plays? Could it be Jason, whose very hero status has been granted him by his wife, Medea? Jason the "seducer" and the deceitful (the Argonautica myth presents him as a vile seducer even before the Medea episode, in the episode of the seduction of the women of Lemnos and of Hypsipyle), Jason the opportunist who quivers under the authority of the fearful tyrant Creon and gushes in gratitude because he has offered him his daughter as bride? Or could it be that, in its many episodes and versions, the Medea story is at once symbolic of the human experience itself in its most tragic, contradictory, and puzzling dialectics between good and evil, happiness and suffering, triumph and defeat, and, to narrow it down to gender, symbolic of the female experience itself, with its intrinsically tragic core, with the duality of love and hate, eroticism and crime, maternity and jealousy, all on the troubling background of the itinerant status and fragmented identity of the heroine? Mimoso-Ruiz touches precisely on this complicated symbolism of the Medea myth and on its fundamental association with the concept of flight, exile, and strangeness:

> every time that Medea runs away, every passage of the sorceress from one country to another, by sea (on the Argo), or in the air, with the carriage of the Sun, every time that she moves from one status to another—from princess, she becomes a "foreigner" or an exile—Medea performs a symbolic murder. This notion of "passage" would indicate not only that we find ourselves in the presence of a soteriological myth, but also that we are confronted with Medea's privileged

relationship with the world of fugitives. Medea is a figure coming to us from a disquieting "elsewhere."[65]

But then why *is* she in the minds of her male-creators the symbol of this "elsewhere," why are her power, courage, and intelligence connected to sorcery, and why does she always end up as "a stranger or an exile"? Moreau's argument that Medea is a scapegoat comes to mind again, as she is treated as a feminine "pharmakos." As he aptly argues, sorcery is much more commonly associated with women than with men, and myth, literature, film all tend to show us significantly more sorceresses than sorcerers being banished, punished, burned at the stake.[66] The first simple answer that comes to mind is that heroines who rebel and question the existing order, heroines who are more powerful or more intelligent than their male counterparts have to be justified in terms of superhuman or magical powers, in terms of that disquieting "elsewhere" (ailleurs). Haven't woman and devil been also partners in evil for several millennia, in the Judeo-Christian tradition? Woman is the alien, the "barbaric," the exile par excellence, and because an exile, a "source of evil," a convenient scapegoat.

But things are more complicated than that. At the risk of being redundant, I find it necessary to remind the reader again that not only does Medea remain unpunished at the end of both plays, but she soars away as a triumphant goddess. She is not burned at the stake, nor punished in any other way. Euripides's Medea flies away on a chariot of fire, dazzling and all-powerful, her unity restored, a very different heroine from the lamenting fugitive at the beginning of the play. Moreover, given the episode with King Aegeus, the audience can easily guess that she also has a shelter, and not just any shelter but the house of the king of Athens himself. Seneca's Medea is even more awe-inspiring at the end as she regains the pre-Jason, pre-Argonautica, premythical unity of her self: "Now, now have I regained my regal state, my brother, my sire; and the Colchians have once more the spoil of the golden fleece; restored is my kingdom, my ravished virginity is restored. Oh, divinities, at last propitious, of, festal day, oh nuptial day!" (982-86) All the broken fragments of her "barbaric" self are miraculously put back together. It seems that the myth itself is overturned and in some sense annihilated, myth being drama and involving conflict and sacrifice. Medea has annihilated her own annihilation and has come out of it whole. Or has she?

The Medea Puzzle

Triumphant as she may be at the end, I am, as audience and reader, still haunted by the echoes of her laments in the first part of the play, by her irreverent answers to Creon and Jason, still haunted by the words of grief that gush out of her as she contemplates the death of her children, as I am still haunted and horrified by the shrieks of her children as they are about to be smitten dead. As woman, as female human being she remains a tragic heroine, while also a monster. For what has she left at the end? Is she truly triumphant in front of the dead bodies of her own children? Has she a home now? Has she the love of the man she has punished? And her words "I am wretched, wretched" (Euripides, 1250) still ring in my ears. But as goddess, as superhuman being, as symbol? Why the need of the mythical poet and of the playwrights to bring her out of her human condition and project her, triumphant, into the sphere of the divine? The projection into the divine removes her from her tragic status in the Aristotelian sense, for she is not the plaything of the gods anymore, being one herself. Her culpability, her victim status are dissolved. Or are they? Doesn't Oedipus also, at the end of the Sophoclean trilogy, acquire divine stature and exchange his "scapegoat status" with that of "savior"? And then again, if a goddess, why does her itinerant status continue in the myth even after her bitter triumph at the end of the Corinthian episode? She is the ultimate exile, a tragic heroine even by traditional concepts; yet she defies the tragic itself and turns her victim status into power; and then again, she retains, even as an all-powerful female-sorceress-goddess, the sad status of fugitive.

But the two tragic poets, Euripides and Seneca, have chosen to leave the audience with the image of the all-powerful triumphant Medea, the former on a chariot of fire, and the latter on a chariot drawn by two flying serpents, although the audience might well know the subsequent episodes of the myth as well. Another king is dead, Jason is practically annihilated even if not dead, and Medea victoriously proclaims that "now have I regained my regal state." It sounds as though she has regained the political power she has always been deprived of and has always craved. But at what price? What can we make of this intricate and mind-boggling character today, and how are we to interpret the multifaceted symbolism of this female-exile-leader-monster-goddess-mourning mother-scapegoat-queen that is Medea? What I propose is that we look at her as one looks at a kaleidoscope image, mindful of all the colors and nuances and of the way they are interwoven. Medea is arguably more widely and profoundly representative of the female condition, struggle, and tragedy than most mythical and classical heroines. Moreover, she is more connected to politics and more of a political woman than most classical heroines. At the same time she is only vicariously political. She is representative of both our human and socio-political status, or the lack thereof. And her itinerant status continues, to a large extent, to be our own. She is everything at once: what we still are and wish we weren't, what we wish to be and aren't, and also what we dread and hope never to become.

The puzzle is still far from being solved, however. On the often gruesomely colored canvas of Greek mythology, epic poetry, and drama, Medea is far from holding the monopoly on murder and deceit. The valiant Agamemnon sacrifices his own daughter Iphigenia so that the Greek ships will receive the help of the gods; the justice seeker Orestes kills his own mother in cold blood; Atreus kills the children of his brother Thyestes and serves them to him for dinner; and the hero of all heroes, the cunning Ulysses, the protagonist of the epic that is one of the main pillars of Western thought, is also "sacker of cities" (including distribution of captives for rape and possession) whose idea of the Trojan horse ended in the decimation of almost the entire population of Troy, among whom, of course, hundreds of women and children. And what does the Messenger in Seneca's play answer the chorus when they ask by what means Medea has destroyed the king and his daughter? "By the common snare of kings—by gifts," he says.[67] It is by a gift as well that Troy was sacked. Is Medea also, on top of everything else we have found her to be, a female Ulysses? Many similarities could be found between the two, of which their seafaring, fugitive status, their cunning, their ability to survive at all costs, and their jealousy regarding a spouse are not of least importance.

But Medea, at least as she is portrayed in the two classical plays and as we have tried to point out, consciously assumes her "virility," as she consciously assumes her "womanly" guiles. And what does she show us as she becomes "virile," as she incorporates the warrior status? That she can kill in cold blood? That she can be cruel and heartless? History has tired us indeed with this bitter lesson. Maybe by assuming these gender masks, Medea also shows us how aberrant it is to consider the ability to kill virtuous when the killing is done by men and vile when done by women. And how hypocritical to consider "guile" as an intrinsically female attribute. But then, returning for a second to Medea's symbolic kinship to Ulysses, one has to keep in mind that in Euripides' work, Ulysses is far from appearing a hero. On the contrary, in *The Trojan Women* he is portrayed as a reprehensible villain. Yes, it could well be that, marginalized as he was himself as a tragedian, Euripides is also a feminist who has his heroine play with male and female masks, with masks of male and female virtues and flaws, or simply with masks of human virtues and flaws. And Seneca, whom the French theater theorist and poet Antonin Artaud saw as "the greatest of all tragic authors of history, who, initiated into mysteries, was even more capable than Aeschylus to turn them into words,"[68] has Medea continue even further on the line of at once representing and deconstructing the masks of the genders, by pushing both her "female" and "male" traits to the extreme and melting them together in an all-encompassing supernatural force. The last words of Seneca's Medea continue to shock both audiences and critics in their unbridled furor: "If in my womb there still lurk any pledge of thee, I'll search my very vitals with the sword and hale it forth."[69] With this scream suggestive of a potential and violent abortion, Medea denies and revolts against her biological female nature, symbolically rebelling against the very idea of a "female nature" according to which the category of maternity would be indispensable to or implicit in the category of femininity. This final revolt is synchronous with her regaining her "regal state."[70] Her message on politics is not a very cheerful one either, for she seems to tell us that, given the existing male-created political structures, order, and laws, the only way to be politically powerful is by violence and cruelty and by acting against human nature itself, or against that which is humane. Moreover, according to that same order, women and politics can't mix, for if they do, women will either be sorely punished or they will become monsters like Medea. And this is not very far from us today, either. Aren't we still told by males who pine for the "feminine," delicate woman busy at needlepoint that a businesswoman in a suit or a political woman running for office is something of a repulsive image?

Ultimately, in her fluctuating nature and destiny, Medea defies all labels and molds, and she defies not only stereotypes, but also the stereotypical ways we have acquired of criticizing stereotypes. From far away in time and space, her voice mixed with the roar of the many waters she has crossed, Medea seems to urge us to move beyond Medea and perhaps to strive toward that new woman sung by the Corinthian chorus, toward a new discourse filled with "proud woman-themes" and "heroines worthy" of singing. Hopefully, the Creons and Jasons of the world can hear her voice as well.

Notes

1. Liddell, Henry George and Robert Scott, *Greek-English Lexicon* (Oxford: Oxford University Press, 1963).
2. Ovid Nasso, *Tristia. Ex Ponto.*, trans. Arthur Leslie Wheeler (Cambridge, MA: Harvard University Press, 1996). In *Tristia*, III.ix.3-34, Ovid explains the etymology of the name while recounting this particular episode from the Medea story. He starts this part of his discourse with the following words: "sed vetus huic nomen, positaque antiquius urbe, / constat ab Absyrti caede fuisse loco" ("But the ancient name, more ancient than the founding of the city, was given to this place, 'tis certain, from the murder of Absyrtus"). And he ends the letter, in a circular manner, by returning to the etymology of the name Tomis in a more explicit way: "inde Tomis dictus locus hic, quia fertur in illo / membra soror fratris consecuisse sui" ("So was this place called Tomis because here, they say, the sister cut to pieces her brother's body").
3. "rapida fortuna ac levis / praecepsque regno eripuit, exilio dedit." Lucius Seneca, *Tragedies*, trans. Frank Justus Miller (Cambridge, MA: Harvard University Press; London: W. Heinemann, 1917), 219-20. Unless specified, all translations from Seneca's *Medea* will be from this edition, as will be the quotes in the original Latin. Note that the numbers for the Euripides, Seneca, and Apollonius texts refer to the line numbers and not to page numbers.
4. *Tristia*, III. ix. 15-18. Ovid seizes with subtlety the inner battle that is taking place in the young maid's heart, between the "dismay" she feels at the action she herself is about to commit and her "great boldness" and determination to save herself and Jason from her pursuers.
5. "e anche di Medea si fa vendetta." Dante Alighieri, *Inferno*, trans. Allen Mandelbaum (New York: Bantam Books, 1980), canto XVIII, line 96.
6. Dante refers to Jason's stay on the island of Lemnos, and his seduction of the Lemnian Hypsipyle, in Canto XVIII of his *Inferno*. This particular episode does not appear in Ovid's *Metamorphoses*, but many other episodes from the Medea myth, including the Corinthian episode, are retold by the Latin poet.
7. Vintila Horia, *Dieu est né en exil* (Paris: Librairie Arthème Fayard: 1960). The symbolic closeness between Ovid and Medea reaches its climax at the end of the novel, when Ovid actually identifies with Medea and her fratricide and, with moving intensity, relives the moment responsible for the name of the town where he is exiled, Tomis: "Les mouettes criaient: 'Médéeaaa, Médéeaaa!' Elle allait leur répondre d'un moment à l'autre. Elle allait apparaître sur la falaise pour tuer son frère, mon frère. Je tremblais de tout mon corps" ("The gulls were shouting: Medeaaa, Medeaaa! She was going to answer them any moment now. She was going to appear on the shore to kill her brother, my brother. I was trembling all over"), (309).
8. "en ego, cum caream patria vobisque domoque, / raptaque sint, adimi quae potuere mihi, / ingenio tamen ipse meo comitorque fuorque: / Caesar in hoc potuit iuris habere nihil."
9. Edith Hall, *Inventing the Barbarian* (Oxford: Clarendon Press, 1989), 35.
10. Homer, *The Odyssey*, trans. Richmond Lattimore (New York: Harper & Row,

1967), 12:69-72.

11. As Alain Moreau points out in *Le Mythe de Jason et Médée. Le Va-nu-pied et la sorcière* (Paris: Les Belles Lettres, 1994), the actual itinerary of the Argonautica and the geographical data pertaining to its voyage are vague. Connected to both symbolic and actual places on the map, this itinerary is still a subject of controversy among scholars. At some point, says Moreau, the expedition is connected, in the myth, to the colonial expansion of the Greeks. But at what point exactly is still subject to debate (see his chapter "Transformations du mythe. Le Rôle des cités," 157-72).

12. For a very careful analysis of the various sources of the episode of the murder of the children in the Medea story and of Euripides' anteriority with regard to this episode, see Emily A. McDermott, *Euripides's Medea. The Incarnation of Disorder* (Philadelphia: Pennsylvania State University Press, 1989).

13. Analyzing the connection between the Corinthian cults of Hera Akraia and Medea, in her article "Corinthian Medea and the Cult of Hera Akraia," Sarah Iles Johnston argues eloquently and convincingly that "fifth-century authors inherited an infanticidal Medea from myth" and that "the Medea whom we meet in Euripides' play developed out of a folkloric paradigm that was widespread both in ancient Greece and in other Mediterranean countries—the paradigm of the reproductive demon—and that this paradigm is likely to have been associated with the Corinthian cult of Hera Akraia" In *Medea: Essays on Medea in Myth, Literature, Philosophy and Art*, ed. James J. Clauss and Sarah Iles Johnston (Princeton: Princeton University Press, 1997), 45.

14. Moreau quotes Eliade's analysis of the connections between Medea's chariot and Helios, or the Sun, and its implicit kinship with the world of Hades as well, for "l'entrée de l'Hadès s'appelait la 'porte du soleil'" ("for the entry to Hades was called 'the gate of the Sun'"). *Le Mythe de Jason*, 95.

15. Fritz Graf, "The Enchantress from Afar. Remarks on a Well-Known Myth," in Clauss & Johnston, *Medea* 21-43.

16. Alain Moreau, "Médée bouc émissaire?" ("Medea as Scape-Goat?") *Pallas* 45 (1996): 99-110. Alain Moreau astutely analyzes Medea's dual status of criminal and scape-goat, which brings her closer to Oedipus, the ultimate tragic character. Partly relying on René Girard's theories on sacrifice, violence, and the sacred, Alain Moreau demonstrates that Medea enters the category of the "pharmakoi" (107), that is, of the paria, chosen to be sacrificed in order to cleanse the community of violence and misfortunes. See also René Girard, *La violence et le sacré* (Paris: Grasset, 1972) and *Le bouc émissaire* (Paris: Grasset, 1978).

17. See Shirley A. Barlow, "Euripides' *Medea*: A Subversive Play," in *Stage Directions: Essays in Ancient Drama in Honour of E.W. Handley* (London: Institute of Classical Studies, 1995), 36-46. Barlow aptly demonstrates how Euripides has his character both incorporate and question stereotypically female traits, while also endowing her with features and attitudes that were associated with men, such as the prowess of the warrior.

18. "Cette supériorité de Médée, affirmée dans une sphère d'activité reservée à l'homme (le champ d'Ares, le pouvoir royal) renvoie à l'image mythique d'Héra qui, elle aussi, est tentée de marquer sa souveraineté sur Zeus lui-même." Duarte Mimoso-Ruiz, *Médée antique et moderne* (Paris: Edition Ophrys, 1982), 22. For further analyses of the connection between Medea and Hera as well as of the incorporation of Medea in heroine cults dedicated to Hera, see Jennifer Larson, *Greek Heroine Cults* (Madison: University of

Wisconsin Press, 1995) and Sarah Iles Johnston, "Corinthian Medea and the Cult of Hera Akraia," in Clauss & Johnston, *Medea*, 44-70.

19. Mimoso-Ruiz, 16.

20. Mimoso-Ruiz discusses the bipolarity of the Medea myth in tandem with the plurality of the versions of the myth. He points out that this myth contains dichotomic series such as man versus woman, barbarian versus civilized, native vs. nonnative—dichotomies that ultimately can only be reconciled in death. At the same time, Medea's character refuses to let itself be reduced to any one unique label, continuously creating and re-creating itself throughout the many versions and episodes of the myth (23).

21. Aristotles's *Poetics* is the first and probably most influential theoretical work to lay out the principles of "tragedy" and the "tragic hero," in contrast to epic poetry and to comedy. Pascal's *Pensées* explore the tragic dimension of the human condition from the Christian perspective, more precisely the seventeenth-century French Christian movement called Jansenism. In his essay *The Birth of Tragedy*, Friedrich Nietzsche develops a new theory of the tragic based on the exploration of two fundamental tendencies of the human being and of art, which he calls the "Apollinian" and the "Dionysian." Albert Camus's philosophical essay *The Myth of Sisyphus* analyzes the concept of the tragic from the perspective of existentialism and of the notion of the "absurd," using the story of the mythical hero Sisyphus as an all-encompassing symbol for the human condition.

22. Geoffrey Brereton, *Principles of Tragedy* (London: Routledge & Kegan Paul, 1968).

23. Thomas Gould, *The Ancient Quarrel between Poetry and Philosophy* (Princeton: Princeton University Press, 1990), 22-29, 36-49.

24. Jean-Pierre Vernant & Pierre Vidal-Naquet, *Mythe et tragédie en grèce ancienne* (Paris: Maspero, 1973). "tantôt 'aitios', cause responsable de ses actes en tant qu'ils expriment son caractère d'homme; tantôt simple jouet entre les mains des dieux, victime d'un destin qui peut s'attacher à lui comme un *daimon*" (72).

25. In the Introduction to *Medea: Essays on Medea in Myth, Literature, Philosophy and Art,* Sarah Iles Johnston points out, "Narratively, Medea first appears as a lovely and lovelorn princess who enables Jason to steal the Golden Fleece. In this role she fits the paradigm of the 'helper-maiden,' which is found in the fairy tales or myths of virtually all cultures" (5).

26. Vassiliki Gaggadis-Robin, *Jason et Médée sur les sarcophages d'époque impériale* (Roma: Ecole française de Rome, 1994), 66.

27. Apollonius of Rhodes, *The Argonautica*, trans. Richard Hunter (Oxford: Clarendon Press; New York: Oxford University Press, 1993), III:250-338.

28. "tu, tu malorum machinatrix facinorum, / feminea cui nequitia ad audenda omnia / robur virile est." (267-68).

29. "δέδοικα σε." Euripides, IV, trans. Arthur S. Way (Cambridge, MA: Harvard University Press, 1971), 282. Unless otherwise specified, all translations from Euripides' *Medea* are from this edition.

30. "Colpa est Creontis tota, qui sceptro impotens / coniugia solvit quique genetricem abstrahit / natis et arto pignore astrictam fidem / dirimit" (Seneca, 143-6).

31. "Iniqua numquam regna perpetuo manent" (Seneca, 196). See Michael Fartzoff's discussion of power in *Medea*, in his article entitled "Le pouvoir dans Médée," *Pallas* (45, 1996): 153-68. Fartzoff analyzes in depth the apparent power structures versus the underlying power structures in the *Medea;* the struggle for power among Medea, Creon, and

Jason, and the constant shifting of power between the male characters and Medea and particularly between the tyrant (τυραννοs) Creon and Medea. See also Marianne McDonald, "Medea as Politician and Diva," in Clauss & Johnston, *Medea*, 297-323. This article is an excellent resource that points to the many works of art inspired by the Medea myth and Euripides' play, and aptly argues that Medea can be seen as a revolutionary figure. Her role as such is analyzed in modern works of poetry and opera.

32. "incerta vaecors mente vaesana feror / partes in omnes" (123-4).

33. Seneca, *Three Tragedies*, trans. Frederick Ahl (Ithaca: Cornell University Press, 1986).

34. See Vittorio Citti, "Médée et le problème du tragique," *Pallas* 45 (1996): 47-55. Citti discusses the "tragic" of Euripides' *Medea* against the background of Aeschylus and Sophocles' classical drama and places him at a different level, as precursor of the modern conception of tragedy as defined by Goethe: "toute tragicité se fonde sur une opposition inconciliable: si une conciliation se produit ou devient possible, il n'y a plus de tragique" ("the tragic is based on an irreconcilable opposition: if a reconciliation occurs or becomes possible, there is no more tragic") (47). Citti points out that the Sophoclean and Aeschylean type of tragedy, despite the conflict between destiny and individual will, ultimately offers the reconciliation of the two in the sublime, as for instance in the case of Oedipus, who at the end of the trilogy is appeased by the gods and raised to semidivine stature. With Euripides, argues Citti, the old system of values begun with Homer's *Odyssey* and continued through the first part of classical tragedy no longer functions as a measure for the characters' actions and often, as in the case of *Medea*, there is no possible reconciliation between the opposing forces that are at play.

35. See Marie-Hélène Garelli-François, "Médée et les mères en deuil: échos, renvois, symétries dans le théâtre de Sénèque" ("Medea and Mothers in Mourning: echoes, returns, symmetries in the theater of Seneca") *Pallas* 45 (1996): 191-204. Garelli-François mentions the connection between Medea's destiny as exile and the sea with its shores, and its suggestion of solitude and exclusion from the community.

36. For extensive presentations and analyses of the condition of women in ancient Greece or in the ancient world, see the following studies: Edith Hall, *Inventing the Barbarian*; *Women in the Ancient World*, ed. John Peradotto and J. P. Sullivan (Albany: State University of New York Press, 1984); Raphael Sealey, *Women and Law in Classical Greece* (Chapel Hill and London: University of North Carolina Press, 1990).

37. Dolores M. O'Higgins, "Medea as Muse," in Clauss & Johnston, *Medea*, 104.

38. "τίs με δέξεται πόλιs; / τίs γῆν ἄσυλον καὶ δόμουs ἐχεγγύουs / ξένοs παρασχὼν ῥύσεται τοὐμόν δέμαs."

39. Dante, *Inferno*, V.121-22: "Nessun maggior dolor che ricordarsi del tempo felici nella miseria." Francesca Da Rimini, a noble Italian woman guilty of a passionate and adulterous love affair with her brother-in-law, Paolo Malatesta, has become a haunting symbol of the inconsolable nostalgia and sadness experienced in times of misery, at the thought of past happiness.

40. Hall, *Inventing the Barbarian*, 2.

41. See Raphael Sealey's *Women and Law in Classical Greece*.

42. See Shirley A. Barlow, "Euripides' *Medea*: A Subversive Play," in *Stage Directions. Essays in ancient Drama in Honour of E.W. Handley* (London: Institute of Classical Studies, 1995), 45.

43. Sarah B. Pomeroy, *Goddesses, Whores, Wives and Slaves* (New York: Schocken Books, 1995), 107.

44. See Jean-Marie Thomasseau, *Drame et Tragédie* (Paris: Hachette, 1995). In the chapter entitled "Les délices de la fureur," Thomasseau argues that Seneca's theater, "plongé dans la trempe de la philosophie stoïcienne" ("imbued with the philosophy of the Stoics"), goes much farther than its Greek model, in the direction of an unleashed ferociousness and the unbridled poetic expression of this ferociousness and of a certain unprecedented and shocking sensuous vitality. The exacerbation, in Seneca's *Medea*, of her magical powers is in tune with this interpretation, for it creates the artistic medium for the character to express her rage and fury with superhuman intensity and at cosmic levels that, although suggested, are not fully developed in the Greek play.

45. See Martha C. Nussbaum, "Serpents in the Soul. A Reading of Seneca's Medea," in Clauss & Johnston, *Media*, (219-49). Nussbaum presents a profound analysis of Seneca's *Medea* from the point of view of the philosophy of the Stoics and by contrast with Aristotle's theory of the emotions and particularly of love. Thus, by contrast with Aristotle, Seneca's Stoic position on the problem of love would be that love, as all passions, is always prone to lead to violence and murder, hence the "mingling of justification and horror" that is "essential to Seneca's plot" (224).

46. "Médée est, ou veut être, la mère qui se concentre sur elle-même, se replie et n'aspire au grand nombre d'enfants que pour pouvoir se mieux réduire à l'unité. Une unité clamée, unité triomphale qui se suffit à elle même." Marie-Hélène Garrelli-François, "Médée et les mères en deuil," 197. Significantly, this statement is part of her comparative analysis of Medea and Hecuba from the point of view of their motherhood.

47. "Quascumque aperui tibi vias, clausi mihi."

48. "aliena quaerens regna deserui mea."

49. "Profugere cogis? redde fugienti ratem / vel reddem comitem. fugere cur solam iubes?"

50. "Fugimus, Iason, fugimus. hoc non est novum, / mutare sedes; causa fugiendi nova est / pro te solebam fugere. discendo exeo, / penatibus profugere quam cogis tuis."

51. See Judith P. Hallett, "The Role of Women in Roman Elegy: Counter Cultural Feminism," in Peradotto & Sullivan, *Women in the Ancient World*, 241-63.

52. See Barlow, Garelli-François, Moreau.

53. "Medea nunc sum; crevit ingenium malis" (910).

54. See Nicole Loraux, *Tragic Ways of Killing a Woman*, trans. Anthony Forster (Cambridge, MA: Harvard University Press, 1987), 27. Medea aspires to and, to a significant extent, illustrates the Greek value of *arete* which, to quote Nicole Loraux, "belongs to men," for even in funeral epitaphs feminine "worth" is mentioned "in a tentative, not to say reticent, manner." At the same time, she deviates from the model of the tragic heroine proposed by Loraux, namely of the woman who chooses her own death which she performs within the domestic space, thus acquiring the only glory available to women, the equivalent to the glory of men dead on the battlefield. In her speech, Medea chooses precisely the kind of death that endowed a man with eternal glory, the death by sword on the battlefield, and, though tempted at the beginning of the play by the idea of suicide, she moves away from it and turns her vindictive urge unto Jason.

55. Again, Frederick Ahl's translation universalizes less and is more abrupt: "A little time for tears. Can you deny / this much to me in all my suffering?" And the original: "Parumne miserae temporis lacrimis negas?" 293

56. "Fortuna fortes metuit, ignavos premit."
57. "Medea superest—hic mare et terras vides / ferrumque et ignes et deos et fulmina."
58. In "Médée et le problème du tragique," Citti stresses that the heroine's intelligence is triumphant over the male characters but also turns against herself, as she destroys everything that is dear to her (54). He also points out that her desire for vengeance is stronger than her reason and she is ultimately led, not by her rational self but by irrational passion, as she herself states in the famous lines 1078-80, where she actually uses the word *aitios* to describe her predicament: "Now, now, I learn what horrors I intend: / But passion over-mastereth sober thought; / And this is cause of direst ills to men." Rex Warner translates: "I know indeed what evil I intend to do, / But stronger than all my afterthoughts is my fury, / Fury that brings upon mortals the greatest evils" [David Grene and Richmond Lattimore (Chicago: University of Chicago Press, 1955)]. It is true that the element of the irrational plays a significant role in Medea's actions, but to judge her as entirely led by passion and irrationality is to fall again into the fallacy of gender stereotypes which she is trying to defy. For she very clearly states that she is aware of what she is going to do, as she is aware that she is being led by her fury. The Greek word she uses is μάνθα νω which means "to learn by inquiry, to ascertain, to know," as well as "to perceive, understand, comprehend." Even if led to a significant extent by her irrational self, she is nevertheless aware that she is being irrational; she is aware of her tragic status and of the fact that she is both *aitios*, responsible for her actions, and, at the same time, that the *aitios*, the cause of her actions is the *daimon*, the cursed destiny which keeps haunting her.
59. See the quotation given by Barlow, of Bernard Knox's commentary on the words of the chorus: "All the songs, the stories, the whole literary and artistic tradition of Greece, which had created the lurid figures of the great sinners . . . is dismissed; it was all written by men. The chorus has suddenly realized the truth contained in the Aesopian story of the man and the lion who argued about which species was superior. Shown as proof of man's dominance a gravestone on which was carved a picture of a man downing a lion, the lion replied: 'If lions could carve sculptures, you would see the lion downing the man'" (Barlow, *Euripides' Medea*, 40). See also Bernard Knox, *Word and Action: Essays on the Ancient Theater* (Baltimore: Johns Hopkins University Press, 1979).
60. The translation by Rex Warner in the Greene-Lattimore series is surprisingly tamer in its feminist drive: "Cease now, you muses of the ancient singers, / To tell the tale of my unfaithfulness; for not on us did Pheobus, lord of music, / Bestow the lyre's divine / Power, for otherwise I should have sung an answer / To the other sex. Long time has much to tell of us, and much of them." *Euripides IV* (Chicago: University of Chicago Press, 1955). Interestingly, the phrase "arsenun ghena," meaning "valiant" or "manly" women is conveniently avoided and in fact deleted altogether from this translation. As is the translation of the word "moiran" which comes from the Greek "moira" which can mean "that which is meet and right," therefore literally meaning that women should have their fare share in artistic representation of both sexes. Instead, we have here the nondescript and diluted "long time has much to tell of us, and much of them." Indeed, "traduttore, traditore" (Lat. "translator, traitor").
61. Sallie Goetsch, "*Les Atrides* and the History of Reading Aeschylus," *Tulane Drama Review* 38, no. 3 (1994): 75-95. In discussing primarily Ariane Mnouchkine's production of Aeschylus's *Eumenides* at the Théâtre du Soleil, Goetsch touches upon the problem of sexually biased translations such as, for instance the one by Lattimore, which "ignores the

sexual connotations" of certain Greek words, as well as upon that of sexist critical commentaries that betray "a patriarchal attitude worthy of Apollo himself" (90).

62. Sarah B. Pomeroy, *Goddesses, Whores, Wives and Slaves* (New York: Schocken Books, 1995), 107.

63. Hallet, "The Role of Women in Roman Elegy" 246.

64. In the article mentioned earlier, Barlow also analyzes how Euripides is "subverting his own subversion" as he shows Medea overcome by grief and "by the physical bond to her children" ("Euripides' *Medea*," 43). Garelli-François goes further and analyzes the complex coexistence, within the character of Seneca's Medea, of the suffering mother and the infanticidal mother and compares Medea to the tearful mothers of the *Trojan Women* and to Seneca's Hecuba, another ambiguous figure of suffering maternity ("Medea and Mothers," 201- 03).

65. "Chaque fois que Médée s'enfuit, chaque passage de la magicienne d'un pays à un autre, par mer (avec la nef Argo), ou dans les airs, avec le char du Soleil, chaque fois qu'elle passe d'un statut à un autre—de princesse, elle devient une 'étrangère' ou une exilée— Médée accomplit un meurtre symbolique. Cette notion de 'passage' indiquerait bien on seulement que nous nous trouverions en présence d'un mythe sotériologique mais aussi face à un rapport privilégié de Médée avec le monde de l'errance. Médée est une figure venue d'un 'ailleurs' inquiétant" (23).

66. "Medea as Scapegoat," 105-08.

67. "Qua solent reges capi–donis," 881-83.

68. "Le plus grand des auteurs tragiques de l'histoire, un initié aux secrets qui, mieux qu'Eschyle, a su les faire passer dans les mots." Quoted in Thomasseau, *Drame et tragedie*, 37.

69. "in matre si quod pignus etiamnunc latet, / scrutabor ense viscera et ferro extraham" (1012-13).

70. *Renaissance Tragedy and the Senecan Tradition* (New Haven: Yale University Press, 1985). Gordon Braden examines Seneca's apocalyptic vision expressed in tragedies such as *Medea* and *Hercules furens*. He argues that "the Senecan apocalypse is the moment of complete power and vacancy in which rhetoric becomes totally real" (56). Thus, Medea's "reborn virginity" is also "a power, in a sense, over the past itself," while her murder of the children is also "brooding some ultimate revenge upon the future as the last thing that threatens to escape the self's control" (57). The potential abortion she mentions can obviously be seen in the same light of complete annihilation of the future. Her regaining of power coincides with the destruction of the world.

Chapter 3

The "Woman Drama" of *Republic* Book V

Steven Berg

Women and philosophers enter the *Republic* through a digression.[1] By the end of Book IV, Socrates appears to have completed his best city in speech and distinguished within the class structure of its regime the virtues of wisdom, courage, moderation, and justice. Having articulated a similar regime structure within the soul and thereby brought to light the corresponding psychological versions of these same virtues, he is sailing full tilt into the analysis of the defective regimes that he ultimately completes in Books VIII and IX. It is the intervention of Adeimantus at the provocation of Polemarchus, therefore, that lengthens the conversation far beyond what Socrates apparently thought appropriate to the occasion by insisting that he detail the arrangements concerning women and children within the city in speech (450b). Socrates seems to have originally considered it fitting to leave hidden all that is uncovered in Books V through VII. Thus by one measure everything discussed there might be thought to be useless in regard to the chief purpose of the speeches that evening, which seems to involve persuading Plato's brothers, and especially Glaucon, that justice as they understand it—namely, as a moral or political virtue—is worthy of being chosen over injustice because it is "the greatest good" for the human soul (366e). Indeed, from this same perspective, the lengthy speeches of Books V through VII might appear to be worse than useless, since at the peak of this discussion Socrates makes clear that not only justice but all the moral or demotic virtues are unprofitable in the absence of the "greatest study" whose subject matter transcends moral or political virtue altogether—the idea of the good (505a). From a certain perspective then the discussions regarding women and philosophy appear to be, on the one hand, unnecessary and excessive and, on the other, potentially corrupting of the young men who are Socrates' chief interlocutors. It is no coincidence then that at the beginning of V Socrates is put on trial and seems to have doubts about his own innocence, and that at the beginning of VI Adeimantus accuses Socrates of painting philosophy in false colors, since, if we look away from Socrates' speeches to the men themselves, it is clear that philosophers are either useless or bad (487d).

Nevertheless, at the peak of the digression that constitutes Books V through VII, Socrates reminds us that the discussion of the virtues and the soul that was offered in Book IV was "too short" and "deficient in precision" and that a "longer road" was required if the question of the virtue of the soul was to be adequately addressed (504b). By this measure Socrates' "digression" in some way makes up for an earlier discussion that was radically incomplete, since any discussion of soul and its virtue in abstraction from the question of that which "every soul pursues and for the sake of which it does everything" (505d-e) is essentially deficient, and any speech conducted in abstraction from the question of the good itself is partial. Given the broad discrepancy between the two measures according to which Socrates apparently tailors his speeches, the question arises as to how both can simultaneously regulate the movement of his discourse. That which compels Socrates to speak publicly about the public nakedness of women and the presence of philosophy within the best city seems to be in tension with the necessity to "truly persuade" (357a-b) Glaucon and Adeimantus of the attractions of justice by veiling its real character behind the unreality of what they understand to be the "greatest good"—undiluted pleasure (357b, 358b, 363e-364a, 366e, 509a, 587d-e). Doing justice to himself and doing justice to Plato's brothers at first sight appear to be incompatible. For whereas the latter requires that Socrates transpose the class structure of the city and the virtues accompanying it onto the soul, the former, as we will see, requires, on the contrary, that he reshape the city in speech using a transpolitical understanding of the soul and its good as his model. In Books V through VII, therefore, Socrates appears to reverse the procedure he had employed in II through IV (368e-369a). He has prepared us for this reversal from the outset, however, by insisting that the regime established in the city and the justice found within it are to serve primarily as a means by which to understand the "regime" within the soul and the justice that is appropriate to the individual. Both "regime" and the justice of the regime, as expressed in the phrase "minding one's own business," are ambiguous insofar as they can signify either the proper structure and function of the classes within the city, or the autarchy of the individual and the proper function of the soul.[2]

At the opening of Book V, Socrates declares that the arguments they are about to pursue constitute a new beginning and that the motion of these speeches will proceed from a novel source (450a). The character of this novel source is indicated in the first few pages of V, where we are presented with a mock-up of Socrates' trial and defense: the relation between the city and the philosopher is put on stage.[3] Though Adeimantus, Polemarchus, Glaucon, and Thrasymachus (the whole "assembly") have, according to Socrates, "arrested" him (450a), it is Socrates himself who appears to bring forward the most serious charge against him.[4] What looks like Socrates' self-accusation takes the following form. He claims that to speak with knowledge among prudent and friendly men about "what is greatest and a friend" is both safe and bold. But to do so when one is in doubt and inquiring is fearful and slippery, since in stumbling one may drag one's friends down with one and commit a crime of greater magnitude than that of involuntary homicide: one may inadvertently deceive about "the beautiful, the good and the just in laws" (450d-451a). If Socrates' two statements about the safe and the fearful were perfectly symmetrical, then to inquire while doubting about what is greatest and a friend would be fearful perhaps only among men who were neither prudent nor friendly, and to do so among men who were both might therefore be equally safe and even more bold than to speak with knowledge. That Socrates is not among prudent men or friends in the strict sense is made clear by Plato's painting Socrates' interlocutors in the colors of the Athenian assembly before whom his Socrates appears exclusively as a criminal on trial. The present company must be made up then of what Socrates calls his "so-called friends" (382c). Accordingly, Socrates' suggestion that he may drag his friends down with him through such an inquiry in such a context must refer primarily not to Glaucon and Adeimantus, but to that which is Socrates' friend in the strictest sense—that which is "greatest and a friend" (450d-e), namely, philosophy—and to those who are friends of this friend.[5] Thus what at first sight appears as Socrates' self-accusation before the fact—that "it is a lesser fault to prove to be an unwilling homicide than a deceiver about the beautiful, good and just things in laws" (451a)—upon closer inspection reveals itself to be a condemnation of the threat to inquiry from the law and its specious wisdom concerning these greatest things. Socrates is afraid not so much of corrupting Glaucon and Adeimantus through the inquiry they demand he undertake as for the safety of philosophy in the face of the hostility of the law. In fine, it is the inquiry into the true relations among the beautiful, the good, and the just within the context of the law's opposition to such inquiry that Socrates anticipates with fear. He exhibited no such trepidation regarding the inquiry into the just alone that Glaucon and Adeimantus imposed upon him in Book II (368b-c). It is only when the beautiful, the good, and the just are considered in relation to one another that Socrates is forced to reveal what the law always works to conceal: the radical disjunction between the good and the just (505d).

Still, if in Book V the law first comes to light under the aspect of its hostile relation to philosophy, it is nonetheless also the law and the questionable character of its wisdom that first brings the beautiful, the good, and the just together into a relation within the argument of the *Republic*. Thus the law both stands in opposition to and provides a starting point for the inquiry into the greatest things.[6] The inquiry, however, begins not with a discussion of the beautiful, the good, and the just, but with the topic that Adeimantus and company are so eager to have fleshed out: the community of women and children in the best city or, as Socrates calls it, the "woman drama" (451c). Socrates knows in advance that a discussion of women in the best city will necessarily entail a reassessment of the just in the light of the beautiful and the good. Within the plotting of Socrates' "woman drama" the question of the beautiful, the good, and the just first arises in connection with that of the goodness of the public nakedness of women and the possibility of a law that would command it.

The constitution of the best city, Socrates claims, requires that the "females" of the "guardian dogs" both guard and hunt in common with the males (451d). There are at least three oddities in what Socrates says that are worthy of note. First, Socrates has once again effaced the human character of the members of the guardian class by describing them as a species of animal. Second, this is the first time Socrates has said anything about the guardians hunting.[7] It is not, however, the first time he has spoken of hunting: in the midst of Book IV, after having discovered the virtues of wisdom, courage, and moderation, Socrates claimed that he and Glaucon had to proceed "like hunters" if they were to track down justice in the city in speech (432b). Hunting is Socrates' metaphor to describe philosophical inquiry. Finally, although in Book IV Socrates had insisted that the term "guardian" be reserved for the rulers of the city and "auxiliary" henceforth be applied to the warrior class, he now reverts to calling the warriors guardians, that is, he seems to have collapsed the two classes back into one. Be that as it may, if the tasks of guarding and hunting are to be shared by male and female guardians alike, then so must the education in music and gymnastics. For the female guardians to participate in gymnastic training, however, would require, Socrates insists, that they strip and practice naked together with the males. This might, Socrates says, appear laughable in the light of what is customary—particularly when the old and wrinkled among the females doff their clothes and go to the mat. It would thus provide occasion for "the wits" to lend encouragement to such laughter by "making a comedy of it" (452c-d). But Socrates claims that what at one time appears shameful or ugly (*aischros*) and laughable may later appear "better." Just as, though once Greek men were themselves ashamed of public nakedness, later it became evident that "to uncover all such things is better than to veil them and the laughter of the eyes disappeared before that which is best as disclosed by speeches" (452d).

If the shameful is that which must remain publicly concealed or whose open display is impossible according to custom and law, the comic poet seems to ply his trade by shamelessly representing the legally impossible as possible or by putting on stage what, according to law, should never be seen or heard. Nevertheless, he retains the perspective of the law to at least this extent: he portrays this possibility as ugly (*aischros*), if ugly in a harmless way, that is, laughable.[8] The comic poet seems to adopt the perspective of the customary and lawful while simultaneously transcending it. He both reveals and conceals what is hidden by law.[9] Socrates then uses his appeal to comic poetry as a bridge from conventional shame to the shamelessness of disclosure through speeches or philosophy. Having used it, however, he appears to burn his bridge behind him. He demands that the comic poet cease "minding his own business" and adopt a new standard according to which the laughable is the bad and the sole standard of beauty is the good. If he does so he will then understand, Socrates claims, that the nakedness he proposes is not even harmlessly ugly and so laughable, but is in fact beautiful because good. "Minding one's own business" was, of course, the phrase that Socrates employed in Book IV to describe the justice they hunted down and brought to light in the city in speech. This justice was the principle of the vertical articulation of the city in the hierarchy of its class structure. Thus Socrates in effect demands that the poet abandon the just as they have come to understand it in order to embrace the good as a standard of such power that it can make what is present right before one's own eyes—a laughable ugliness—vanish before the brilliance of what speech reveals to be "beautiful" insofar as it is good.[10]

Put simply, Socrates has jettisoned the just as the foundational principle of the city and replaced it with the good. At the same time he has deprived the beautiful of any independent status. While speaking of the stripping of women then, Socrates has himself discarded the veils of the speeches concerning the beautiful and the just that work to conceal the truth about the good. That is to say, he appears to have dispensed with the claims of the city that its class structure provides for what is properly one's own (433a-b), and that the exercise of the plurality of moral virtues provides for the proper function of the human soul (402b-d, 444d-e). Both have been supplanted by a good, that remains as yet undefined. In displacing the just and the beautiful by the good, Socrates appears to have cut the Gordian knot of a fundamental tension within the best regime. For in the case of the city, justice in articulating the class structure of the regime made it necessary that the great majority of individuals within the city—all those who are not members of the ruling class—lack the full complement of virtues or that they remain afflicted with "ugliness" of soul. By contrast, in the case of the individual, justice as the principle of the regime within the soul appeared to allow for the presence of all of the virtues within it. In this latter case then, the just seemed to be merely a means to the realization of the beautiful (444d-e). But when the city claims, on the one hand, that membership within a class provides for what is properly one's own and, on the other, that the proper function of the human soul is the practice of complete moral virtue, then the city and its law display their incoherence insofar as they at one and the same time affirm the naturalness and justice of the regime's class structure and pretend to instill complete virtue in the souls of all its citizens. Be that as it may, it seems to have been Socrates' anticipation of this supplanting of the just and the beautiful by the good that provoked him to effect the reduction of the human to the animal within the guardian class: the elimination of the just and the beautiful seems to leave no room for the specifically human. If this were indeed the case, then a good entirely severed from a relationship to the beautiful and the just could not be a possible good for human beings. But the good must be possible, since an unreal good is simply not a good.[11]

Accordingly, taking the good as his sole standard seems to force Socrates for the first time to speak of the question of possibility in regard to the arrangements of the city in speech. Socrates treats the question of whether the equality of women is possible as if it were interchangeable with the question of whether it is by nature. Since it is determined to be impossible according to custom and ancestral law, it can be shown to be possible only if it is shown to be in accordance with what is thought to be before or in contrast to the law—nature.[12] Thus the participation of women as in some sense the equals of men within the guardian class can be shown to be possible if it can be demonstrated that the nature of the female is such as to be able to act in common with the male in all things or some and especially in war (453a).

At this point, however, Socrates suggests that they grant a fair hearing to those who might dispute that such equality is according to nature by representing them himself (453a). If, as he indicated earlier, first among these disputants is the comic poet and first among the comic poets is Aristophanes then Socrates here allows Aristophanes an opportunity to object to his proceedings. This allowance seems only just in light of Aristophanes' having been silenced in the *Symposium* (212c) when attempting to respond to Socrates' speech, which included an explicit refutation of his own earlier discourse (205e-

206a). There the dispute between Socrates and Aristophanes had revolved around whether eros was primarily of one's own, as Aristophanes had maintained, or of the good and the beautiful, as Socrates' Diotima seemed to insist. If Aristophanes had been allowed to voice his objection on that occasion, he might have pointed first to the manifest contradiction that Socrates' speech seemed to embody—at the opening of his discourse he affirmed that eros was of the good and nothing but the good, while by its end he seemed to have come round to the position that eros was of the beautiful. Aristophanes might further have observed that, whatever the case may be in regard to the beautiful, if the good is to be enjoyed it must be appropriated or made one's own and that, in fact, Socrates was forced to concede this point within his speech even while pretending to prove that love is never of one's own, but always of the good alone (206a). Here Socrates' disputant points to the apparent contradiction between what was said to be the starting point of the city in speech, that "each one must mind his own business according to nature," and what is now being asserted, that men and women must mind the same business in common (253c). In doing so he becomes the defender of the ostensibly natural justice that originally stood at the foundation of that city. The disputant insists that men and women have their own distinctive natures and that they ought to undertake different work that is in accordance with what is their own. Presumably what he has in mind is the fact that women have been assigned by nature the task of bearing and rearing children and that to allow them to enter the guardian class would then violate the founding principle of the city: one man, one job (370b). Thus even if the equality of men and women might appear to be good from some perspective, political or otherwise, it is not in accord with either justice or nature and so impossible, and a good that is not possible cannot be made one's own and, consequently, is no good at all. Aristophanes then attempts to stave off Socrates' displacement of the just by the good by showing that the just preserves what is by nature one's own and that without it therefore the good cannot be appropriated.

It is in the face of this disputant that Socrates confesses that he is overboard at sea and that only some miraculous rescue could preserve him.[13] In lieu of a miracle Socrates begins by accusing the disputant of being a practitioner of the "contradictory art" (*antilogikes*) or of being a sophist,[14] if an unwilling one. One falls unwillingly into sophistry, it seems, when one lacks the capacity to consider speeches by separating out what is said into its *eide* or when one is deficient in dialectics. Still, it is not the case that the *antilogikos* makes no attempt to divide by kinds. Rather his divisions are specious and operate only according to the otherness and sameness of names and not of *eide*. Socrates thus assimilates the poet to the sophist on the basis of the fact that both are practitioners of an art of making false *eide* or images (*eidola*) in speech.[15] In the light of Socrates' example regarding the bald and the hairy, it seems that the false or sophistical character of the poets' images is rooted in the fact that they portray a difference in body as if it were a difference in nature or *eidos*, that is, in soul (454d-c). The poet fabricates false images insofar as he speaks of the soul in terms of the body.[16]

Socrates' argument then is that men and women, despite their obvious bodily differences—as Socrates puts it, "the female bears and the male mounts" (454d)—have a common nature or *eidos* insofar as their souls are distinct from their bodies and as such sexually neutral and therefore that they are capable of minding the same business in common. Whether or not it is legitimate to identify nature and *eidos* and to identify both with soul, it seems safe to say that the sexual difference, whatever its character, is irrelevant to the practice of most arts. Women can build cabinets or bake bread with as much success as men. Socrates' argument, however, goes further in making use of the peculiar assertion that he employed to found the original or "true city" of Book II, namely, that the real natural cut is not between men and women, but between, for example, plumber and bricklayer (370a-b). It is on the basis of the allegedly natural link between soul-type and art that Socrates goes on to argue that, since the variety of soul-types present in men are equally present in women, there are women who are by nature suited to practice medicine, others music, others gymnastics and war, and still others who are by nature philosophical (455e-456a). We recall, however, that in Book II, even while proffering the improbable argument that one is born with a certain soul-type that is by nature fit to practice one and only one art, Socrates had detailed the real ground for the division of labor in the arts, namely, that the perfection and refinement of the arts themselves demand a training in and devotion to one and only one art (370b-c). That such perfection and refinement and therefore the division of labor upon which it is based are potentially infinite gives the lie, if any such proof were needed, to the supposition that the plurality of soul-types lies behind the division of labor. It indicates, furthermore, the endlessly innovative character of the arts. Thus while Socrates pretends to appeal behind convention to nature in order to establish the equality of the sexes and subvert the sexual division of labor sanctioned by the ancestral law as establishing the division between the household and the city (or, as we would say, the private and the public realms), his true appeal is to the innovative character of the arts. He is therefore articulating not so much a division between political convention and what is according to nature, as one between two equally essential aspects of the city that are in fundamental tension with each other. Accordingly, Socrates appears to have replaced justice with dialectic as the power that articulates the fundamental structure of the city. In replacing justice as articulating the structure of the city and in overturning the ancestral law as the source of the division of the human into distinct kinds, his dialectics attacks the root of the sophistry of the poet: the sophistry of the city.[17] Like the poet, the city and its law appear to put forward as natural eidetic cuts, that is, genuine distinctions of soul, what are merely divisions according to bodily looks. The sexual division of labor seems to be a paradigmatic example of this practice and the sex-neutral character of the arts the proof of its sophistical character.

Yet there is an "art" in the practice of which the distinction between the sexes does not appear to be irrelevant. It is the only art, if indeed it is an art, for which something like a particular natural soul-type does seem to be required and it is that one "art" in regard to which Socrates is particularly concerned to demonstrate women's capacity—the "art of war." We recall that the warrior in the strict sense must possess spiritedness in the highest degree. The art of war therefore is the one art that forces us to admit that the bodily difference between men and women corresponds to a significant psychological difference: women's spiritedness, according to Socrates, is even at its strongest "weaker" than that of men (456a). We are surprised then that Socrates, when arguing for the admission of women into the guardian class, hardly touches upon the issue of spiritedness. Rather, certain women are said to be suitable participants within the class on the basis of attributes neither of body nor of soul but of mind: learning, discovery, and thought. The question then slips from that of guarding to that of "hunting," and the philosopher in philosopher-dog becomes preeminent. Thus under the cover of the question of naked women guardians Socrates has smuggled philosophy into the city in speech. Naked women guardians can serve as an image of philosophy insofar as, like the philosopher, the warrior in the strict sense possesses a genuinely distinct nature—as the latter is the spirited, the former is the erotic nature par excellence (485a-b, 490a-b)—and insofar as women cannot be integrated unproblematically into the political order, as the difficulties consequent to their public nakedness demonstrate. Thus Socrates has provided an image in bodily terms—an image compounded of incompatible elements—of the distinctive nature of the philosopher, and under the guise of effacing the division between the sexes in the name of the speciously natural division of labor in the arts, he has pointed to the fundamental natural division within the human, that between the philosophical and the nonphilosophical, a division of "soul-type" that the city and its law cannot possibly recognize. Socrates' dialectics has played off against one another certain divisions within the city in order to reveal the nonpolitical division within the human.[18]

Accordingly, the difficulties resulting from the attempt to incorporate women into the guardian class must ultimately serve to indicate the problematic relationship between the philosopher and the city. Those difficulties are the immediate consequence of the public nakedness of women. Socrates now admits that women practicing gymnastics together with men will provide an occasion for something more than mirth and that whatever virtue these disrobed ladies may clothe themselves in it will certainly not be that of chastity (457a). In turning to the question of sexual arousal as a consequence of coeducational stripping, Socrates shifts his account of precisely what it is that the veils of shame conceal. Whereas previously it seemed that it was the ugly to the eyes but beautiful (because good) in speech, it now appears that it is rather the shameful or ugly (*aischros*) according to custom and law but beautiful in itself that is to be publicly revealed. Having dismissed the comic poet's objections, his conceits are dispensed with as well.[19] Yet the public nakedness of the beautiful, just as the exclusive preeminence of the good, leads to the elimination of the specifically human insofar as man is a political animal and "indiscriminate sexual mixing" is not "holy" (*hosion*) and cannot be allowed in a happy city (258d-e). However, what at first seems to be Socrates' belated concession to the ancestral—that conventional shame supported by the holy allows for the humanizing of sexual eros and the relations between men and women—proves to be another step in its eradication. He appeals to the "sacred" (*hieros*) not in order to reconstitute the human, but to further efface it: "marriage" is put under the auspices of a novel piety antithetical to the ancestral law in order to facilitate breeding the guardians like beasts in the interests of what is beneficial (258c). Once the holy and sacred in the ordinary sense are dispensed with, the household or the private realm, and with it the distinction between private and public, is dissolved: the public nakedness of women leads through the elimination of the holy to communism in regard to the goods of bodily eros.

Socrates initially claims that there can be no dispute that the community of women and children, if it were to prove possible, would be "the greatest good." The only question then is that of its possibility. When Glaucon objects, however, and insists that there might be dispute about both its goodness and its possibility, Socrates proposes that they abstract from the question of possibility and simply assume the existence of the community of women and children and immediately go on to "order the rest" and determine whether such an order would be the most advantageous. Whereas previously the preeminence of the good seemed to nec-essitate the consideration of possibility, now the question of the advantageous is decoupled from that of its possibility. Socrates tacitly admits therefore that the "good" proposed here is impossible. Putting the community of women and children in order turns out to mean instituting a eugenics program to supervise the sexual reproduction of the guardian class. The natural erotic attraction between the sexes aroused in the course of young women practicing naked gymnastics together with men is therefore to be subordinated to a science of eugenics. It is this science that will determine who will have intercourse with whom. With the deferral of the question of possibility, nature is expelled as a standard and admitted or assumed to be defective. The expulsion of the holy brings in its train the artful mastery of errant nature as manifested in the mismatchings of unsupervised eros (cf. 341e).

With the admission that, if individuals strictly suitable to membership in the guardian class are to be consistently produced, nature is insufficient and art must be employed, Socrates concedes that there is no real ground in the nature of the human soul for the division of the arts, and that art is in fundamental tension with nature insofar as it is an attempt to master and correct its defects and deficiencies. This final breakdown of the ostensibly natural link between human nature and the division of labor in the arts was heralded by the objection of "Aristophanes" to the overturning of the principle of this link—one man, one art—with the admission of women into the guardian class and the consequent necessity that they perform two "jobs": guarding and breeding. Thus at the moment in the argument that art or science seems to extend its rule to all aspects of human life, to the very coming to be of human beings, it is admitted that the practice of even the greatest art cannot be a candidate for the activity that constitutes the proper function of the human soul. As both class function (justice) and sex role have been overturned as possible candidates for what is properly one's own, so both the practice of the virtues of the citizen (the beautiful) and the practice of the arts have been eliminated as possible candidates for that activity which is proper to the human soul.

If the eugenics program in the guardian class is ultimately designed to effect the unity of that class by producing a uniform character among its members, its immediate result is grossly to exaggerate a division that has existed within it, we now learn, from the beginning. The principle of this division is not that which was said to distinguish one class from another, namely, justice, since all the guardians mind the same business and the class structure of the city has dissolved. Rather, guardian is distinct from guardian insofar as his native capacity allows him to mind his business well or poorly. There is an aristocracy within the aristocracy of the guardian class based upon distinctions of nature. Art, however, is to master nature through making sure that breeding takes place only through intercourse between the best of the best. The possible opposition between a patrician and plebeian element would lead to faction within the guardian class before the less than perfect can be bred out of the strain, unless, as Socrates suggests, a second art, over and above that of eugenics, is employed to heal the rift that the practice of eugenics itself has opened up. A doctor's art on the political level must be called upon in order to administer certain "drugs" to the guardian class to heal the disease of faction within it. The city as Socrates now describes it will be "purified" then, not in the sense of being cured and restored to health (cf. 399e), but only through constant medical attention. The political "doctor" will therefore practice an art like that of Herodicus rather than the "statesman-like" Asclepius (406c). For the constant sexual conjunction of best with best and worse with worse must be continuously papered over with lies and deceptions, and what is the product of art must be made to appear as the dispensations of chance. The mastery of human nature on the level of the body then requires its complement on the level of the soul: rhetoric. Socrates says that "eminent rulers" will be required to serve as the practitioners of this rhetorical art of soul doctoring. Since the original rulers of the guardian class were themselves chosen on the basis of their inability to distinguish between truth and lie (412d, 420d-e) and they have, in any case, been pushed back down into the warrior class, Socrates can only be looking ahead to the rule of philosophy. It seems then that he has joined the issue of the concealments necessary to bring best together with best in the guardian class to that of the rhetorical tropes employed by philosophy in dealing with its enemies and so-called friends (383c). Be that as it may, the shameless uncovering of the beautiful makes necessary a cover-up of impossible proportions: art's mastery of nature is to be made to appear as the operations of chance, which in their turn are to be called sacred and thereby associated with divine providence.

If one must conceal the split within the guardian class between best and worst, no such concealment is possible or necessary when it comes to a division within the city that is based upon a distinction as natural as that between those of greater and lesser capacity: the old and the young. The law's sexual segregation of these two in certain cases can be perfectly public. The difficulty here is that what is required for the breeding of best with best, and what is required for the breeding of the young with the young, would mesh only if the peak of the body and the peak of the soul or prudence coincided (461a). But Socrates later admits that they do not (460e, 540a; cf. *Symposium* 219a). In any case, it is hard to see why a Socrates or an Alcibiades ought not to continue breeding for as long as humanly possible and why, if we are to allow "sisters" and "brothers" to breed we ought not to allow the best of the best to breed with their like even if they happen to carry the name of "father," "mother," "daughter," or "son." That this will indeed be the case Socrates indicates when he says that the children born in the tenth and the seventh month from the day a man becomes a bridegroom will call him father, while failing to mention those born in the eighth and the ninth months (461d). His double-talk in regard to this issue therefore not only obscures the truth from Glaucon, but seems to suggest that in the city in speech the law's apparent prohibition in regard to intercourse between parents and offspring is simply one of the prescriptions of the soul doctor in the service of the rule of the science of eugenics: law becomes a "drug" employed to obscure from the guardians the truth that breeding best with best sanctions the mixing of young and old in such a way as to make ordinary pederasty look respectable by comparison. It permits the violation of the holiest of ancestral prohibitions. In the interest of the intercourse of the best with the best, the unholy mixing of the old and the young is smuggled into the city under the name of the sacred.

If we recall that the difficulties surrounding the incorporation of women into the guardian class are to serve to indicate the difficulties surrounding the presence of philosophy within the city, then the soul doctor and his rhetorical prescriptions seem to resemble Socrates and his attempt to defend himself before the city against the charges of corrupting the youth and impiety by, on the one hand, arguing that any "ill effects" he may have upon the young through his intercourse with them are perfectly unintended and therefore accidental (*Apology* 26a, 33a-b) and, on the other, by appealing to a superior form of piety: the imitation of the divine (*Apology* 28e-29a, 29d-30a; *Crito* 47c-d, 53b-54e; *Republic* 500c-d). That Socrates' appeal to this "philosophical piety" may not be entirely successful as a means of papering over the radical difference between a philosophical and a nonphilosophical understanding of the divine, however, is suggested by the fact that when philosophical piety is transposed onto the political plane the result seems to be a "legitimation" of the crimes of Oedipus. The philosopher's imitation of the divine is misappropriated as doing what the gods of the poets do.[20] In the present context this politicization of philosophical piety is represented by the "Oedipalization" of the city in speech.

As Socrates immediately makes clear, this Oedipalization is the direct result of taking "the greatest good" as the sole standard of political life (462a). Socrates describes this greatest good in the organization of the city—that which the legislator must take as his end in laying down laws—as that which binds the city together and makes it one (462a-b). The city, he argues, is to be unified by the dissolution of the household and family or what is ordinarily understood to be one's own and the reapplication of the relations within the family to the city or guardian class: thanks to the community of women and children, all the guardians will consider their fellow guardians to be kin or "their own" (463c-464a) However, the apparent extension of "one's own," which Socrates pretends to see as the means to binding together and unifying the city, is accomplished in name alone. Each will, according to the commands of the law, say "my own" in regard to all, but no one will have anything except the body that is indeed his own (464d). Moreover, the unity ostensibly established by the possession in common of women and children is a hallucination produced by the narcotic effect of the drugs of the rhetorical art: women are not held in common, but the best of them mingle only with the best men and the worst with the worst, and since only the offspring of the latter are to be reared, the "common" children of the guardian class are actually the fruit of the loins of the best and the brightest. True kinship and unity will be established among the guardians, if at all, not primarily through the community of women and children, but only through the gradual extinction of the inferior members of the class that the eugenics program is designed to effect. However, even if such a unity were established, it would be only within the class alone, and the guardians would therefore form a breed apart standing over and against their inferiors. Either the city must be reduced to the guardian class or it is in no way unified and subject to the worst versions of political faction.

That even in the case of the guardian class alone such unity will remain a fiction is demonstrated when the consequences of the transgression and dissolution of the boundaries between old and young that the eugenics program requires are considered. Just as, despite laying down nominal prohibitions against incest, Socrates' argument in fact supports the mingling of the young and the old, so his assertion that no violent conflicts will arise between the old and the young men within the guardian class is actually a demonstration of their inevitability: a young man's reverence will be significantly weaker for those who are his father in name alone, and the presence of the sexual transgressions will be complemented by the patricidal violence of Oedipus (464e-465b). Moreover, even in the most benign cases of the tension between fathers and sons, their failure to see eye to eye will, as Socrates himself argues in Book VIII, provide a natural engine for change within the political regime which the most sophisticated science of eugenics will be powerless to control. One need not therefore appeal to ignorance of the nuptial number in order to account for the origin of faction within the best regime (546c-7a). The "generation gap" will prove to be a sufficient condition for the coming to be of the faction that provides the impetus for the decline of the best regime through a series of stages into the worst, namely, tyranny.[21] The attempt, therefore, to artfully eliminate the distinction between best and worst within the guardian class, and by these means effect the unity of the political regime, necessarily results in the transformation of the regime through faction and the reappearance of this distinction on the broadest political level. Art can never gain real mastery over nature on the level of becoming, and therefore the unity that Socrates attributes to the city can exist in speech alone and only in false speech. This good therefore cannot be a good for the city. In what sense then and in relation to what is such unity the "greatest good"?

In appealing to unity as the greatest good, Socrates refers us back to the discussion of the virtues of the soul at the end of Book IV. In accordance with his argument there, that the soul is articulated in a hierarchical structure that mirrors that of the class structure of the city, he had originally identified justice of the soul as strictly parallel to that of the city. As justice was said to be present in the city when each of its three classes minds its own business in terms of ruling and being ruled, so the soul was said to be just in which calculation (*logismos*) in alliance with an apparently subordinate spiritedness (*thumos*) rules over desire, which was said to be "by nature fit to be a slave" (444b).

On the other hand, injustice in the soul was said to be a "certain faction among these three" in which the properly subordinate or enslaved rebelled against the whole in an effort to establish itself as illegitimately ruling. This understanding of justice and injustice in the soul as parallel to justice and injustice in the city, however, was not free of paradox. The first and most obvious difficulty was that when the warrior class first arose and the equality of the arts was displaced by a hierarchical class structure as the dominant mode of articulation within the city, the problem posed was that of preventing the enslavement of the artisan class by the warrior class (375b, 416a-b). That is to say, what Socrates appears to call justice in the soul—the enslavement of the ruled by the ruling element—was, in the parallel case in the city, understood to be a form of pernicious faction, the prevention of which required the education of the warriors in music and gymnastics, the establishment of a ruling class, the promulgation of the well-born lie, and the institution of communism among the auxiliaries. One is forced to conclude, therefore, that what Socrates appears to call justice of soul—that is, the political version of justice of soul—is in reality faction and therefore injustice or "lack of learning," "vice," "sickness, ugliness and weakness" (444b,e).[22] This conclusion is supported by the fact that Socrates' transposition of the structure of the city onto the soul was effected by an appeal to two "poetic" accounts, both of which characterize the soul as "at war" or in "faction" with itself (449e-464e, 441b-c, cf. Homer, *Odyssey*, XX 1-24).

We are hardly surprised, therefore, that Socrates' argument implies a second account of justice of soul that is directly contrary to that of one discrete part of soul ruling over another as master over slave. This second account has no direct parallel in the justice of the city, but is linked to it only through the phrase "minding one's own business," a phrase that must, however, be radically reinterpreted in its transposition from the political to the psychological realm. Whereas in the city justice as minding one's own business served to separate out and prevent the intermingling of the three classes that constitute the parts of the political whole (434b-c) and moderation, at least according to one description, worked to produce a kind of unanimity or accord (432a), when Socrates describes justice as minding one's own business with regard to the soul it has curiously fused with moderation such that it is said to consist in the practice of some activity "with respect to what truly concerns him and his own" through which one "becomes one's own friend." What this seems to mean is that the "parts" of the soul must be "harmonized" in such a way as to "bind them together" in order that they "become entirely one from many, moderate and harmonized" (443c-e). Since wisdom and knowledge "preside over" this unifying "action" and lack of learning and opinion over its opposite (443e-444a), it can only be philosophy that is justice of soul or the proper "business" of the soul or that which truly concerns a human being as such and is truly his own. Accordingly, it is thinking or inquiry and its animating source, namely, philosophical eros, that bind the "parts" of the soul, reason and desire, together into one.[23] Genuine justice of soul therefore would be identical to moderation and coextensive with human virtue simply. That is to say, philosophy, as the source of the unity of the soul, would be the human good in the proper sense (353d-e).[24]

It has become commonplace to take Socrates' description of the community of women and children among the guardians as an explanation of what would be required if the good of the individual (understood in prepolitical terms, that is, the family) were to be entirely subordinated to the city and its ends. However, in taking unity and the binding together of its parts as the good of the city, or in displacing political justice with the justice of the soul as its end, Socrates has in fact taken the transpolitical good of the individual or the human good properly speaking and applied it to the city. As he has forced women to go naked among men, he has forced philosophy into the political realm. It is in this way that he has reversed the procedure upon which the whole of the earlier portion of the dialogue beginning in Book II and culminating in IV seemed to be based: rather than applying the structure of the city and the political good (justice) to the soul, he has applied the unity and harmony of soul or the transpolitical good of the individual (philosophy) to the city.

In the attempt to establish the unity that is the hallmark of the human good on the political plane of the city, Socrates has brought to light certain fundamental divisions present within political life—the tension between the just and the beautiful, the arts and ancestral law, and the best and the worst, on the one hand, and the old and the young, on the other. Having done so he has then proceeded to attempt to resolve these tensions and overcome these divisions through the dissolution of one or both poles of these opposing pairs. At the same time he has collapsed the class structure of the city by reducing the city itself to the guardian class. Through these means he claims to have brought the unity of the "healthy soul" into being within the city in speech. As Aristotle points out in the *Politics*, however, the city that enjoys this sort of unity is no longer a city (1263b 32-4), but, like the lovers of Plato's Aristophanes who in "growing together" "both or one of them disappear" (1262b 11-15), the becoming one of the city dissolves the elements of which the city is compounded and so destroys the city itself. The application of the good of the individual to political life therefore must lead either to the annihilation of political life or to the debasement of the good into the political good (the just) and a specious version of what is one's own or both.[25] This means that, on the one hand, the human good or philosophy cannot be made real on the political plane and is therefore incapable of being politicized and remaining good—that is, what it is—and, on the other hand, that the city can never be relieved of its divisions and fundamental fault lines, that is, to appeal to Aristotle once again, "the city is not naturally one" (*Politics*, 1261b 5). It is necessarily divided against itself or incoherent in its structure.[26]

In pretending to overcome these divisions within political life, therefore, Socrates has in fact uncovered them and demonstrated their necessity. This uncovering has proceeded along the lines of an archaeological excavation. He has stripped away the apparently derivative in order to reveal the primitive that lies beneath it. Thus we move from the properly political: the beautiful and the just, through the prepolitical in the form of the family and the arts, to the inexpugnable elements of nature within the city—the division between, on the one hand, the old and the young and, on the other, the best and the worst. This uncovering of the true divisions within the city is the effect of the failed attempt to bridge the chasm between philosophy and the city or to overcome the fundamental division within human life. However, if we remember that the attempt to politicize philosophy was represented by the entrance of women into the guardian class, it is evident that Socrates' archaeology of the city may be reinterpreted in the following way. If behind naked women guardians stands philosophy, then behind the displacement of the sexual division of labor and the division of labor of the arts by the entrance of women into the guardian class stands the displacement of the class structure of the just and the beautiful as the plurality of virtues by the application of the unity of the good to the city. Moreover, the just and the beautiful reappear behind the split between the old and the young and the best and the worst as well. For not only the tension between the innovative character of the arts and the conservative character of ancestral law, but also that between the reverence for the old as such and the natural preeminence of the best whether old or young, mirror the tension between the city and its law as requiring and articulating a class structure and as claiming to instill virtue in all of its citizens. Thus even as Socrates seems to move within the city from the political via the prepolitical to the natural, at each stage of this apparent descent the issue of the just and the beautiful and their relation to the good is visible beneath the prima facie topics of discussion. This seems to indicate that, though from the point of view of this political "archaeology" the most derivative or latest, and so in one sense of "nature" the least "natural" and most artificial, elements within the city, in another sense the just and the beautiful are those aspects of the city that most immediately lead to an understanding of the nature of the human things. That is to say, the examination of the just and the beautiful point directly, in a way that the issues of the arts, the ancestral law, and the relations between old and young perhaps do not, to the question of the human good: the law's claim to wisdom concerning what is truly one's own (the just) and what is the proper activity of the soul (the beautiful) and the incoherence of that claim points most directly to philosophy.[27] Thus the incoherence that lies behind the apparent coherence of the law, though seemingly furthest removed from the reality of the good, is in fact the real within the city that links it to the reality of that which lies beyond it. And thus the presence of the good in the nature of things seems to display itself in part in what at first sight might appear to be an evil—the irrefragable fragmentation of the political—insofar as it is capable of becoming a condition for the activity of philosophy. This appears to be the meaning of Socrates' assertion that the cave is always open to the light of the sun (514a). What Socrates has shown therefore is that the attempt to publicize the good, or to make it the principle of political life, results in blocking the path through which it can be most directly appropriated. This paradox is represented most clearly in

Socrates' argument by the fact that the extension of one's own to the political level of class membership results in the effective elimination of one's own.

If we remember that the proximate cause of the overturning of the distinction of the public and private realms in the institution of the community of women and children, and therefore of the elimination of the possibility of appropriating the goods of bodily eros (a spouse and children of one's own), was the public nakedness of women within the guardian class, and if we further recall that the legitimation of this public nakedness required the overturning of all shame in regard to these matters, we are forced to conclude that shame, though as Aristotle points out hardly a virtue (*Nicomachean Ethics* 1108a 32), nonetheless serves its purpose. The hiddenness that shame dictates or the legal and conventional impossibility of women's public uncovering appears to make possible the appropriation of certain natural goods that are the objects of bodily eros; shame is therefore a condition of the actual existence of those natural goods. Socrates then, even while pretending to have refuted "Aris-tophanes," has actually expanded and deepened his argument throughout the "woman's song (*nomos*)" (457b). According to this argument, though the division of labor between the sexes is, strictly speaking, neither just nor natural, it is nevertheless the case that the appropriation of certain natural goods requires the more or less strict division between the private and the public realms.[28] That is to say, if these goods are to be made one's own what is required is that certain apparently specious conventional divisions within the human realm and the shame that preserves them be maintained.

If naked women guardians are emblematic of the philosopher in the city, then there would be a parallel to this phenomenon on the level of soul or a philosophical equivalent to conventional shame. That is to say, Socrates' arguments imply that the appropriation of the good, which is the true object of the soul's erotic desire, requires that this good be covered over or clothed. The beautiful and the just seem to be those veils behind which philosophical eros must seek itself and hide itself.[29] The ground for the requirement that philosophy, if it is to be appropriated, must be wrested from hiddenness or discovered through that which it is not seems to be the fact that the good can be grasped in its wholeness only from out of the fragmentation into partial aspects that is the effect of the splitting up of the good into the beautiful and the just. The specious versions of what is one's own and what is the work of the soul are the indispensable means to making the genuine work of the soul one's own.[30] Thus, on the one hand, the threat of the nemesis of the law imposes upon philosophy a necessity of concealment that philosophy itself would otherwise have to invent.[31] But, on the other hand, the specious wisdom of the law provides philosophy not only with the material from which to weave a cloak to cover its nakedness, but with a starting point for inquiry, since it is only through stripping away the false seemings of the law—its incoherent eidetic divisions and specious claims to coherence—that an ascent to the truth can be made.[32] In the argument of Book V, philosophy first seems to come to light in the shamelessness of the naked women guardians and the community of women and children; for the one appears to reflect the shamelessness of philosophy's uncovering of the truth and the other the possibility of sharing that truth perfectly in common. But if philosophy first appears as the enemy of hiddenness and privacy, as the argument unfolds philosophy reappears on precisely the opposite side of this polarity, slipping out of the light into concealment and withdrawal.[33] That, unlike the beautiful and the just, the good need not appear to be good in order to be good (505d) is the ground for the possibility of such withdrawal.

In the light of the preceding, Socrates' ability to do justice in his speeches to both himself and Plato's brothers becomes intelligible. Laying bare the good in stripping away the veils of the beautiful and the just is compatible with simultaneously hiding it behind them because, as we have seen, the "deconstruction" that Socrates performs upon the political is founded upon a prior construction, namely, the attempted fusion of philosophy and the city. This fact is revealed in the "third wave" of Book V when Socrates announces that the "possibility" of the impossible arrangements of the city in speech is dependent upon philosophy being combined with political rule (472c-d). But in persuading Glaucon that the coming to be of the city in speech is indeed possible if philosophers become kings, he demonstrates that the laying bare of philosophy as the human good and as distinct from the political through the failed attempt to make philosophy the principle of the city in speech is at one and the same time the covering over of philosophy as the human good and its veiling behind the just and the beautiful. For this failure is in no way apparent to Glaucon. If it were he would understand that, whatever the philosopher-king represents, it is not as such a practical proposal. Thus Socrates' prudence in weaving together while simultaneously separating his own interest and perspective and those of his interlocutors within his discourse seems to be inseparable from, if not identical to, his dialectical capacity to separate and combine the *eide*.

Notes

1. Cf. Ronna Burger, *The Phaedo: A Platonic Labyrinth* (New Haven: Yale University Press, 1984), 5. A bare citation cannot begin to account for my indebtedness to Ronna Burger. Her guidance in the reading of Plato has been indispensable to me.

2. He reminds us of this fact toward the end of Book V (472b-d).

3. This is not to suggest that the relation between philosophy and the city is not the subtext of Books I through IV. The confrontation between Socrates and Thrasymachus in Book I [cf. Leo Strauss, *The City and Man* (Chicago: University of Chicago Press, 1964), 77-8] and the description of the guardians in Book II as at once savage and spirited and gentle or philosophic makes clear that it is (375c-376c). It is only in V through VII, however, that the relation between the two becomes the explicit theme.

4. Adeimantus charges him only with theft: Socrates, he says, is stealing a whole *eidos* of the argument from them (449c).

5. Seth Benardete, "On Plato's *Lysis*," unpublished paper, 16-17.

6. In order to let himself off the hook, Socrates suggests that the law's leniency in regard to involuntary murder should be applied to his own case as well. Implicit in this suggestion, however, is the much more radical defense that since he is under compulsion to make the inquiry he is about to begin, and since this compulsion is exercised by the community of interlocutors in the role of the democratic city, he has, as it were, been commanded by the law to make this inquiry, and therefore no matter how antinomian its

outcome, he cannot be held responsible for the consequences. The possibility, explicitly entertained only in Book VII, of a city and a law that would command the practice of philosophy, is here already lurking in the background of Socrates' seemingly modest self-justification. Cf. Averroes, "The Decisive Treatise," in *Medieval Political Philosophy*, ed. R. Lerner and M. Mahdi (New York: Free Press, 1963), 165-66.

7. It is worth noting, however, that Socrates' initial description of the character of the "noble puppies" that are to be the members of the guardian class was ambiguous: courage was said to be among their necessary attributes only after Socrates insisted that they must have "sharp senses, speed to catch what they perceive and, finally, strength if they have to fight it out with what they have caught" (375a). This ambiguity was retained in Socrates' characterization of the guardians as both savage and spirited, and gentle and philosophic (375b-376c).

8. Cf. Aristotle, *Poetics* 1449a 35-7. The tragic poet, on the other hand, displays the impossible according to law—e.g., the crimes of Oedipus—as impossible because not simply ugly but destructive and self-destructive. Nonetheless, the tragic poet, like the comic poet, publicly displays what according to the law should be neither seen nor heard. Herodotus' story of Gyges, to which Glaucon alludes in Book II, seems go further than either tragedy or comedy in displaying what the law would leave hidden. Gyges' spying upon the queen in her nakedness is not simply a laughing matter since the queen is young and beautiful and his act of regicide and usurpation of the throne is politically successful (Herodotus, *History* I.8-14).

9. Thus if Aristophanes were to dramatize Socrates' proposal concerning the public nakedness of women in a comedy in which the women in question were old and ugly, he would, as it were, represent the principle of his own comic art on stage. Aristophanes' *Clouds* dramatizes in this way not naked women but philosophy going public.

10. Of course, speech need only perform this office if the naked bodies in question are those of old women. In that of women who are beautiful and young, things may stand in a rather different way.

11. Cf. Seth Benardete, *Socrates' Second Sailing: On Plato's "Republic"* (Chicago: University of Chicago Press, 1984), 153-54.

12. The assumption Socrates appeals to is that there is indeed some human nature to which immediate access is granted apart from the determinations of convention. That such an understanding of nature may be itself but the shadow of the law is suggested by Glaucon's appeal in Book II to injustice as both prior to justice and according to nature: the negatively determined opposite of conventional justice is identified with the genuine core of human nature on the basis of its alleged conformity to a conventional understanding of priority—cf. Strauss, *Natural Right and History* (Chicago: University of Chicago Press, 1950), 91-92; cf. 121-24. This suggestion appears to be confirmed by the fact that, though their possibility is to be established by an appeal to nature, equality and naked gymnastics for women will be institutionalized according to the commands of a novel law.

13. Socrates portrays his situation in terms of the story of Arion from Herodotus's *History* I.23-4—Allan Bloom, *The Republic of Plato* (New York: Basic Books, 1968), 458. Socrates casts himself in the role of Arion. The assembly of his interlocutors is the equivalent of the Corinthian crew and their turning upon him at the opening of V to the Corinthians forcing Arion to walk the plank. The dolphin who miraculously preserves Arion's life against all expectation can only be Plato, who, through his writing, preserves Socrates' life in speech despite the Athenian assembly's having condemned him to death.

14. *Sophist*, 232b.

15. *Sophist*, 234c.

16. Plato's Aristophanes appears to do precisely this when in the *Symposium* he portrays erotic longing exclusively in bodily terms.

17. According to Socrates' arguments of Book VI, the city is the "biggest sophist" (492a).

18. The division and tension between the human in the proper sense and man as a political animal is obliquely indicated by Socrates when he claims that the law that commands that "the guardian women must strip" (457a) not only commands what is possible, but also what is best. He argues that the education provided to the guardians produces "the best citizens," that therefore those women afforded the opportunity to be educated in this fashion will be "the best women," and that, since there is nothing better for the city than that the best possible men and women come to be within it, this law commands what is best (456d-457a). However, Socrates is equivocating in his use of the word "best." What is best for the city is that its members embody virtue as the city understands it or that they be perfectly suited to participation within and fully devoted to the city and its ends, that is, that they be "best citizens." The best citizen is therefore best insofar as he is perfectly instrumental to a political end outside himself. The best men and women simply cannot be instrumental in this way or they would not be best simply, but rather relative to something superior to themselves and their own activity. The best men and women simply must embody not the instrumental virtue of the citizen, but the genuine self-sufficiency of philosophy.

19. Behind this shift seems to lie the difference between Aristophanes' and Plato's portrayals of philosophy in the person of Socrates. Whereas Aristophanes presents Socrates as ugly and ridiculous, Plato offers us a portrait of a Socrates "made beautiful and young" (*Second Letter*, 314c).

20. Cf. *Euthyphro*, 5d-6a; also Ronna Burger, "Making New Gods: On Plato's Eurypheo," in *Plato and Platonism*, ed. Jan Ophuijsen (Washington, DC: Catholic University Press of America, 1999).

21. But since the tyrant is later described by Socrates in terms of the Oedipus of tragic drama (568d-569c, 571a-575e), tyranny seems to be nascent in the best regime from the beginning .

22. "When [Plato] had investigated [the justice generally accepted and applied in cities] . . . it became evident to him that it is complete injustice and extreme evil." Alfarabi, *The Philosophy of Plato*, Sec. 31 (20: 2-3).

23. Insofar as reason and desire are in accord within the soul, that is, insofar as they tend to the same end, the self-mastery and corresponding self-enslavement, of which *thumos* is the agent, find no venue through which to operate. Faction is the element in which *thumos* is alive.

24. Cf. Ronna Burger, "Health of Soul and Psychic Medicine: On the Psychology of Aristotle's *Ethics*," lecture delivered at St. John's College, April 11, 1997, p. 16.

25. It comes as no surprise then that Socrates links the issue of how to prevent the city from destroying philosophy to that of how to prevent philosophy from destroying the city when he considers the problems of the presence of the philosopher and his status within the political community (496c-497d).

26. Having demonstrated the impossibility of employing the good of the soul as a standard by which to order political life, Socrates illustrates the principle of this impossibility by describing the unity of the city first in terms of that of body and soul (462c-d) and finally simply that of the body as a whole of parts (464b): the city willy-nilly understands soul in terms of body. Accordingly, what the city calls virtues of soul are, accordingly to Socrates, merely habits of the body (518d-e).

27. Socrates indicates this privileged status of the just and the beautiful by portraying them in an essentially ambiguous light: the just as minding one's own

business applies both to the city and the individual, and the beautiful is described not only as the plurality of virtues, but also as the object of both eros and knowledge (402b-d).

28. Whether or not this requires assigning the public and private realms to men and women respectively is a separate if related question.

29. Though the good of the body and the good of the soul appear to be similar then insofar as both require a certain hiddenness or privacy if they are to be appropriated, nonetheless if philosophy as the good of the soul is eros in the proper sense then the two are, on a more essential level, fundamentally distinct. The good of the body is the satisfaction of need. Philosophical eros, however, cannot be satisfied in this way and remain what it is—it would be transformed into wisdom. Philosophical eros then is the awareness of need or knowledge of ignorance. The chief sophism of the city therefore is to portray the good of the soul on the model of the good of the body, that is, to understand this good to be not philosophy or knowledge of ignorance but wisdom or knowledge. Plato's Aristophanes seems to fall prey to this sophistry in the *Symposium* where he portrays the erotic longing of the soul in bodily terms and concludes that because this longing can never be satisfied human life is tragic in character.

30. The problem seems to be that the possibility of the good as the unity of the soul in thinking or inquiry is premised upon the essentially problematic character of being that implies the essential limitlessness of thinking or inquiry. But if the activity of inquiry is itself to be understood or thought, and so made one's own in this act of self-understanding, it must be given a limit or definition. This limitation, it would seem, can only be provided by the partially specious eidetic cuts of the beautiful and the just. Thus the "theoretical" pursuit of the truth through the examination of the false divisions of the law and the "practical" task of healing the division in the soul instilled by the law through the unity of desire and reason in inquiry are inseparable in Socratic political philosophy.

31. Cf. Leo Strauss, *Persecution and the Art of Writing* (Chicago: University of Chicago Press, 1952), 21.

32. But if Socrates carries out his inquiries through the examination of the false appearances of the realm of opinion, the realm in which Socratic philosophy persists cannot, as Socrates appears to argue at the end of Book V, be that of being and the epistemic cognition of being. It must rather be the "in between" realm that opinion itself occupies, "somewhere between not-being and being purely and simply" (479b). Philosophy is "neither ignorance nor knowledge" (478c), but knowledge of ignorance and as such may be described as "the wanderer between seized by the power between," finding its way within the realm of the being of non-being. In portraying the philosopher as the knower of pure being, therefore, Socrates portrays philosophy from the perspective of opinion and does so as the first step in his attempt to soothe the anger of those who would attack him and philosophy for having suggested that only the rule of philosopher could ever effect the elimination of evil from the cities of men.

33. Cf. Strauss, *The City and Man*, 115. Ultimately, the nature of philosophy cannot be captured by the political divisions of the public and the private.

Chapter 4

Women and Slaves in Aristotle's *Politics* I

Evanthia Speliotis

Aristotle begins the *Politics* Book I claiming, "those who think statesman and king and household manager and slave master are the same do not speak well. For they believe each of these to differ in greatness and smallness, but not in species [*eidos*] ..." (1252a7 ff.).[1] Presumably Aristotle is going to show, beginning with Book I, how the four differ in kind and what is the species distinction of each. Aristotle pursues his investigation into each kind of rule on the supposition that each is a distinct kind of science. Particular sciences are about, and therefore are determined by, distinct kinds. In order to show that each of the four rulers has a different science and therefore differs in kind, Aristotle needs to identify the distinct object of each science of rule.

The *Politics* is principally concerned with *koinonia* and therefore with the relationships *among* human beings and human actions within those relationships, unlike the *Nicomachean Ethics*, which largely addresses the actions of individual human beings vis-à-vis the individual himself. Distinct kinds of beings by nature engage in distinct kinds of relationships. Diverging radically from the *Nicomachean Ethics*, Aristotle proceeds in the *Politics* as if there were not one universal definition or kind of "human being," but several. He identifies man, woman, master, slave, father, and child as distinct kinds of "human beings," coupled into three distinct kinds of relationships (*koinoniai*) and governed by three distinct kinds of knowledgeable rule.

Man/woman	political	*politike*
Master/slave	mastery	*despotike*
Father/child	kingly	*basilike*[2]

Aristotle underscores the suggestion that there are fundamentally different kinds of human beings when he explicitly states his agreement with Gorgias and his disagreement with Socrates regarding human virtue. "In general, those who say that virtue is to have the soul in a good state or to act rightly or some such thing deceive themselves. For those who enumerate the virtues, like Gorgias, speak far more correctly than those who define them thus" (1260a25-28). On the other hand—and more in keeping with the *Ethics* and with Socrates—Aristotle speaks of the political community (*he koinonia he politike*) as the highest human community, representing the highest goal (*telos*) of human action, as if there were one universal definition of human being, and therefore one universal goal of human action (1252a5-7; 1252b30-32). In order to determine whether *politike, basilike, oikonomike*, and *despotike* are one science or many, therefore, Aristotle must address the question of whether "human being" has one universal definition or whether, by nature, "human beings" are essentially different in kind.

Of the six kinds of human being mentioned in Book I, Aristotle identifies four—man, woman, master, and slave—as the fundamental and essential distinctions.[3] From these fundamentally different kinds of human beings come the two original or foundational human communities: male/female and master/slave.[4] These two communities together constitute the household; a multitude of households together constitute the city.[5] Since the foundational relationships culminate and achieve their perfection in the political community, the city is their end (1252b31). As one moves from nature to household to city, the question is, what is the connection between the different kinds of human beings, "human being," and citizen?

Male and female constitute a community for the sake of procreation (*genesis*), master and slave for the sake of preservation (*soteria*) (1252a26-34). The male/female relationship provides the matter for the city (namely, human beings); the master/slave relationship provides the structure or form. Each of these communities is distinct, according to Aristotle, and both together are necessary.

Both communities are necessary because the city needs material (human beings) out of which to be constituted, and because it needs a hierarchical structure if it is to be a whole or a one.[6] Human beings—the constituent elements of any city—are natural. The composite of body and soul that is a human being is achieved naturally and requires no foresight or mind. For all of Aristotle's claims about the naturalness of the city, however, the city must be constructed by human beings. Unlike a human being or an animal, which is automatically hierarchically arranged into an organic whole from birth, a city must be shaped into a whole.[7] Whereas the material for the city comes from nature, the arrangement of the city seems to be due to art (see 1253a31-32). From the start, therefore, the meaning of the claim that the city is natural is in question, as is the relationship between nature and art or, in this case, the relationship between the naturally given elements—human beings—and the communities into which they can be structured or formed.

The two foundational communities are distinct because each has a different end and because the natures of their constituent members—and the relations between them—are distinct. As Aristotle puts it, "by nature . . . the female and the slave are distinguished, for nature does nothing . . . in a niggardly way" (1252a34-b2).[8] Since "nature is an end, for, that which each thing is when its coming-into-being is completed, that is what we say is the nature of each thing" (1252b32-33), the end of something is its nature. Supposedly, the natures of males and females qua male and female are completed by joining in community with each other and procreating, and the natures of rulers and ruled qua natural ruler and naturally ruled are completed by joining in community with each other and achieving preservation.⁹

"Male" (*arren*) and "female" (*thelu*) are generic terms that apply to plants and animals as well as to human beings. Why then does Aristotle begin with the generic distinction "male/female" and not with the distinctly human distinction "man/woman" (*aner/gune*)? Is the relationship between male and female for the sake of *genesis* (procreation) no different for humans than it is for any other animal? Is Aristotle perhaps suggesting that human beings are not really that far removed from animals, that nonhuman animals and human beings have the same ends, and that even human creations like the city are fundamentally rooted in man's animal nature? Or is there a politically significant analog to the natural relationship between males and females? Is there an aspect to *human genesis* that makes it essentially distinct from mere *animal* procreation (*genesis*), and therefore worthy of being identified as a foundational human relationship (*koinonia*) in the city? Is there a difference between the generic "male" and the more specific "man"? Further, since a man may be a husband (*posis*) and a woman a wife (*alochos*), what is the significance of the fact that it is actually the relationship between husband and wife (not just male and female) that constitutes a foundational community of the city?¹⁰ Finally, is there any connection between Aristotle's claim that the community of male and female exists for the sake of *genesis* (procreation) and his claim that the relation between man and woman is political (1259b1)?

By introducing women first as females, Aristotle seems to be attempting to ground the relationship between men and women as firmly as possible in nature.¹¹ He even goes out of his way to point out that the pursuit of the goal of procreation does not require thought; that is what it means to say this is an end not only for human males and females but also for all nonhuman males and females (1252a28-30). This natural relationship then stands in marked contrast to the seemingly purely conventional relationship of master/slave. Indeed, this very difference between the male/female relationship and the master/slave relationship, which is highlighted from the beginning of Aristotle's argument, may account for why Aristotle has so much to discuss about the naturalness or unnaturalness of "master" and "slave," and why he has virtually nothing to say about the naturalness of "man" and "woman." The suggestion seems to be that, insofar as the relationship of man/woman is simply an extension of the relationship of male/female, it can be taken for granted that it is natural. It seems to be more of a question of whether and how the relationship of master/slave is simply an extension of the relationship of natural ruler/naturally ruled. This question is further underscored because there are at least some who claim that "master" and "slave" are completely conventional distinctions, not at all rooted in nature (see 1253b18-22). Aristotle, therefore, feels compelled to proffer a justification of natural slavery in response to critics of the naturalness of slavery. Since there are no such critics with regard to the distinctions "man" and "woman," he seems to feel no need to provide a similar justification of them.

And yet the relationship of master/slave is itself not without difficulties. Aristotle identifies the master/slave relationship as a particular instance of the natural hierarchy of natural ruler/naturally ruled. The most natural model for natural ruler/naturally ruled would seem to be not the relationship of master/slave but an organic whole, like an animal. Indeed, Aristotle cites the composite of thought (*dianoia*) and body as the primary model for understanding the community of master and slave (1252a31-34).[12] The big difference, of course, between a slave and body and between a master and thought is that both slave and master are themselves organic wholes, hence composites of thinking and body. What does it mean, therefore, that Aristotle offers this particular analogy for understanding the master/slave relationship, and what differences must be accounted for when translating the model to the realm of human beings and human interactions?

As he begins his argument, Aristotle proceeds from two assumptions. First, the kind of rule appropriate for each kind of thing is determined by the nature of that thing, and, second, the appropriate rule is what is necessary in order for each thing to fulfill or complete its nature. To the extent that the male/female and master/slave relationships are the foundational elements of the city, the city's nature is supposedly constituted by—and therefore understood in terms of—these elements. Conversely, insofar as the city is the community of communities, or the community that encompasses all other communities and in which all other communities find their ultimate end, the city is the completion of the male/female and master/slave relationships. As we embark with Aristotle on the analysis of these two relationships and their constituent members, how each is natural, what the nature of each is, how each helps explain the nature of the city, and how each is fulfilled through the city are the central questions of Aristotle's inquiry.

Natural Slave

While Aristotle offers various analogies for the master/slave relationship throughout Book I, the first one he offers seems to dominate the discussion: master is to slave as thought (*dianoia*) is to body (1252a31-34). The master is the one capable of foresight, with intellect, whereas the slave is the one capable of making/acting with the body: the slave is the one who does what the master commands. If a natural slave is going to be useful—and that seems to mean productive—he needs a natural master to tell him what to do and to direct his actions.

Aristotle adds that, since the slave is merely a body capable of acting, he does not belong to himself but to his master (1253b23 ff.). In himself, he is merely a part, of which the master is a whole. Here, the slave is still identified with the body; the master, however, seems to be identified more with the whole individual human being than just with the soul. Body and soul are both parts of a living being and neither one of them alone is the living being—unless of course the soul may be identified with the essence of a living being, which the body may not.[13] And yet, as Aristotle says, unlike the body of a living being, the slave is separable from the master or the whole (1254a17; 1255b11-12).[14] One is led to wonder, therefore, what kind of a whole the master and slave together are. For example, since the slave is separable, does he, as a part, nonetheless enjoy a certain autonomy that makes him more than a part?

In any case, if the body/soul analogy is taken literally, the slave seems very much like an inanimate tool. Indeed, Aristotle explicitly calls the natural slave a tool (1253b23 ff.). And yet Aristotle is clear that a slave must be capable of action. It is a tool but an animate one. The closest analog to what Aristotle seems to mean by a slave under the body/soul analogy is a machine—an artificially animated tool. As machine, it lacks soul—even appetite. Unlike other inanimate tools, however, it is capable of acting as long as it is properly directed (programmed, driven, etc.).

As merely an analog to body, the natural slave has no intrinsic potentiality of its own. It is literally merely the tool the master needs to achieve *his* own ends. As with other tools, it is really the master's or artisan's ends that are thwarted if the tool is not put to use; the tool itself has an end only by analogy. This piece of wood did not need to be made into a shuttle, to be used for weaving. It could have been made into a flute, or it could even have been left alone in nature. It is only made into a shuttle because that is what someone needed at a particular time, and this piece of wood was available. Its being a shuttle is completely accidental, and whatever ends being a shuttle imposes are completely artificial, imposed on the piece of wood from without. As mere body, a mere tool, the slave is valuable, hence useful, only for his strength, his dexterity, or some other such bodily characteristic, and he is useful only insofar as there is someone who has a use for him. Having no intrinsic end, he has no intrinsic worth. He exists only for the master's direction and pleasure. Nothing the master does to him, therefore, is in itself bad or unjust.

Perhaps the chief difficulty with adhering to the soul/body analogy for the master/slave relationship is that slaves are actually animate beings, not artificially moved machines. A far better analogy for master/slave than soul/body, therefore, would seem to be human being/beast, an analogy Aristotle also suggests.[15] Both slaves and beasts are living, hence ensouled, beings. Both slaves and beasts lack thought and foresight. As such neither is capable of intentionally ordering itself or its own actions. They may be ruled by passions and instinct, or they may be ruled by another. A difficulty for Aristotle's discussion, however, is that, having soul, natural slaves and beasts would also seem to have some intrinsic end. Certainly both can participate in mating and procreation without a need for intellect or direction from another. Without direction from another, however, Aristotle says, neither will survive (for long), nor will either be productive in its activity (1254b10-13).

Despite the fact that Aristotle himself suggests the analogy of slave to beast, and despite all the factors slaves and beasts have in common, Aristotle insists that natural slaves are not beasts. This raises two related questions. What do natural slaves have that beasts lack, which qualifies natural slaves as human beings and not as beasts? And what do natural slaves lack that natural masters have, which qualifies natural slaves as slaves and not even potential masters?

The second question is easier to answer than the first. Aristotle says that natural slaves lack the capacity for deliberation (*to bouleutikon*; 1260a13). Referring back to Aristotle's account of the soul from the *Nicomachean Ethics*, the soul has two parts: the rational and the irrational. The irrational part has two parts: the nutritive and the appetitive; the rational part has two parts: the practical and the theoretical. Finally, the four parts[16] may be hierarchically ordered from lowest to highest: nutritive, appetitive, practical reason, theoretical reason. Plants, animals, and humans all have a nutritive soul; animals and humans also have an appetitive soul; but only humans have a rational soul.[17] The difficulty with natural slaves, however, is that they are said to lack *to bouleutikon* which, in the *Ethics*, Aristotle identifies with practical reason. This suggests that natural slaves lack a rational soul. But this, in turn, would seem to preclude them from being human.[18] And if they are not human, then they are not natural slaves but beasts, and there is no moral difficulty in employing them as tools.[19] If natural slaves differ from natural masters because they lack the most fundamental rational capacity, they do not then seem to differ essentially from beasts. But if they do not differ essentially from beasts, then they are not human beings, and—except for some animal rights advocates, which Aristotle is not— how they are treated by human beings is not a question of justice, and the relationship or community between natural masters and so-called natural slaves is not one between human beings.

To deny slaves a share in deliberation, however, is not to deny them *all* reason. Aristotle also says that natural slaves are able to *perceive* reason, while beasts are not and obey their passions (1254b22). He also says that *to nouthetikon* should especially be used with slaves (1260b6-7; "*noutheteteon gar mallon tous doulous e tous paidas*"). While *to nouthetikon* is generally translated as "admonition" and seems to mean spanking, or some other form of corporal punishment, its intention is indicated by the literal meaning of the word: to put mind in. One admonishes in order to instill understanding when the other person lacks the capacity, for whatever reason, to listen to an argument. But admonition will work only if there is some capacity for mind. The suggestion seems to be that human beings are spanked, for example, in order to instill understanding; beasts are beaten because they are only capable of responding behavioristically to pleasure and pain. Natural slaves, therefore, can understand the meaning of the words spoken to them even if they cannot articulate that meaning for themselves; beasts can only be conditioned to seek their master's approval and avoid his disapproval.[20]

This description of the natural slave's capacity sounds very much like Aristotle's description of the appetitive part of the soul in *Ethics* I.13. Both natural slaves and the appetitive part of the soul are said to be capable of listening to reason. In the *Ethics*, Aristotle extends this description one step further, saying that this is like a child who is capable of listening to his father (1103a2). This would suggest that natural slaves were perpetual children and that the proper analogy for understanding the master/slave relationship is mind/appetite. One major difficulty with this model, however, is that mind/appetite is the analogy Aristotle offers for *politike* and *basilike*, not *despotike*. To recapitulate, even if a slave is reduced to having only an appetitive soul, he nonetheless has a soul, and the proper rule over him should be like mind (*nous*) over appetite (1254b4-6), or parent to child (1259b1, b10-17), which Aristotle calls kingly, not despotic, rule.[21]

Of course, one might raise the question of whether it makes a difference that a natural slave is a special kind of child—namely, a perpetual child. Unlike a nonslave child, a natural slave has no potentiality to outgrow his inferiority, dependence, and slavishness. He will always be a slave-child.[22] Perhaps *basilike* or kingly rule only properly applies to helping someone grow into his potentiality as a free, self-ruling individual, and therefore only properly applies to "free" children, not slaves. This would still leave *despotike* to apply to one who, while being able to listen to and obey like a child, must do so in perpetuity.

This may very well be the case, but if it is, an important shift has occurred in the argument. The master as originally described ruled the slave for the master's own ends, hence, the master's own good. This was justified under the soul/body analogy for the master/slave relationship because the slave had no natural ends of his own. If the slave, however, is like a child, albeit a perpetual child, he now has natural ends of his own. They may be no more lofty than comfort and preservation, but they are now *the slave's* comfort and *the slave's* preservation, not the master's. And, in turn, this makes the master in some sense a servant of the slave, commanding for the slave's comfort and well-being, however limited those may be. Rather than the slave being a tool for the master, the master, in a sense, has become a tool for the slave.[23]

But this cannot be correct, for slaves are supposed to be useful. A perpetual child might be a source of joy and delight, but he will also be the cause of toil and hardship. The whole point of the natural slave discussion, however, was to justify masters' subordinating slaves for the masters' ends. Children meet none of the criteria desirable in a slave. They lack the developed bodies necessary for hard manual labor, as well as the mind necessary for developing any real sort of expertise. They are more needy than useful and require too much caretaking to be of real benefit to anyone. And whereas slaves might have the developed bodies necessary for manual labor, if they lack the psychic excellence necessary to perform their function well, they too will require too much caretaking to be of any real benefit to anyone. But a slave who is not beneficial to his master is useless. The last phase of Aristotle's discussion about the natural slave, therefore, turns to the question of virtue.

Certainly a slave, to become excellent at his work, needs training. But he can only fulfill his function once he is trained. This training must include not only the bodily expertise that he will be called on to exercise, it must also include sufficient psychic excellence so that his appetites do not interfere with the discharging of his duties.[24] At the very least, the slave must have and exercise a certain degree of moderation (*sophrosune*, sometimes aptly translated as "self-control"). One can easily imagine that he would also need courage for certain kinds of tasks, and certainly some justice.[25] The difficulty this raises is whether someone who is capable of the degree of virtue sufficient to perform his slavish duties well would still qualify as a natural slave. Aristotle suggests that the natural slave needs only a little share in virtue, just as much as is necessary for him to perform his tasks well. But the way the account has unfolded, certainly if his soul is predominantly—or even exclusively—appetitive, the slave would seem to need a tremendous amount of virtue to get past his appetites and be useful. And if he needs and is capable of any significant degree of virtue, then he would also seem to qualify to be a master, at least over himself.[26]

Aristotle's discussion about the natural slave began from a completely external account of the master/slave relationship and has ended up with a completely internal account. In the beginning, the natural slave is a defective human being, separable from his master, who is nonetheless capable of doing extraordinary deeds that the master can conceive of and dictate but cannot himself do. By the end of the discussion, however, it has been shown that if the slave is to be a distinct human being and if he is going to have the virtue necessary to be a useful agent, then he needs a degree of virtue that disqualifies him as a natural slave.[27] Furthermore, the real slave to be mastered is not the body but the appetites, and the real battleground for *despotike* is not the city but the individual soul. The biggest threat of slavery resides within the individual, in one's appetite, which, when reason is not paramount, drags reason around like a slave. Anything short of this conclusion reduces the so-called natural slave either to a mere body, in which case it is difficult to see how he can be said to be animate, or to a beast, in which case it is difficult to see how he can have any rationality or virtue. In neither case is there a question of injustice. Injustice arises when one treats a *human being* like either a mere body or a beast. In the end, the possibility of a natural slave who is a part of his master, yet animate and separable—hence, the possibility of a science of mastery (*despotike*)—is questionable.

Women

Unlike natural slaves, who are said to be in community with natural masters and to be ruled with *despotike*, women are said to be in community with men and to be ruled with *politike*. The primary difference Aristotle cites to distinguish women from slaves is that women qua women (hence, potential wives) are free, whereas slaves are not nor ever will be (e.g., 1253b4-8; 1259a37-40).

A community of free persons, however, is not sufficient to identify the sphere of *politike*, for such is also true of *basilike*. Whereas Aristotle associates the community of men and women with *politike*, it is the community of father and child that corresponds with *basilike*. As an adult, a woman has already in some sense actualized her potentiality: she is what she is. A child, however, is still in potentiality. That is why Aristotle says the virtue proper to a child is incomplete (1260a14). Presumably, when the child has grown to be a man like his father, he will have actualized the potentiality he had as a child (see 1260b19-20; see also 1259b3-4, 1260a13-14).[28] As a child, however, he is only potentially the equal of his father, not actually so. *Basilike*, therefore, exhibits a hierarchical structure just as *despotike* did. *Politike* alone is the rule of free and equals. Yet the ruler/ruled relationship is hierarchical. Aristotle's purported solution, therefore, is to characterize *politike* as ruling and being ruled in turn.[29]

The difficulty is that Aristotle says that men always rule and women are always ruled. The reason he gives is that men are *kreitton*—stronger—than women (see 1254b13-16; cf. 1259b1-3). Their perpetual rule is justified as the rule of the stronger. This is true both for males and for men, though perhaps not in the same way. Male animals are *in general* bigger and stronger than female animals of the same species.[30] This general rule of the animal world holds true also for the human world: men *in general* are bigger and stronger than women; correspondingly, therefore, husbands *in general* are bigger and stronger than their wives.

This justification for why men perpetually rule and women are perpetually ruled is reminiscent—in two distinct ways—of the master/slave account. There, Aristotle suggested that if nature always fulfilled its purposes, slaves would have big, strong bodies and tiny brains, while masters would have powerful brains and useless bodies, since the slave is the one whose usefulness lies in his body, whereas the master supplies mind (see 1254b16-1255a3). And if indeed nature were always successful in its purposes, everyone would know at a glance who should be master and who slave. Now, the same argument is implied, but in reverse. It is obvious at a glance who is male and who female. Furthermore, the male/female relationship is present throughout nature. In nature, within a given species, the rule exemplified is the rule of the stronger—just what Aristotle claims is the case between men and women. And yet this hierarchy that obviously exists at least among the various animal species in nature does not seem to be the same kind of hierarchy exemplified by the master/slave relationship. The master was said to rule in virtue of mind, whereas the lion is "lord" in virtue of body (size, strength, speed, ferocity). The perpetual rule of men over women, if it is based on physical size and strength, would seem to be nothing else than the perpetual rule of force. *Politike* so described seems to have drawn very close to *despotike*. Either *politike* cannot be read back into the household, or the example of *politike* in the household undermines the pretensions of *politike* in the city.

Kreitton, however, may also be translated as "better" or "superior." Indeed, Aristotle lifts *politike* out of the animal kingdom and places it solely within the community of human beings when he justifies the perpetual rule of man over woman by suggesting that the man is superior to the woman not in body, but in soul (see 1260a2 ff.; cf. 1254b37-1255a1). The difficulty is that this move undercuts his claim that the relationship between men and women is political, for *politike* requires freedom and equality. If women deserve to be perpetually ruled because they have an inferior soul in comparison to men, then women seem to be more like slaves to masters than equals among equals in their community with men.

Women are superior to slaves in that women have *to bouleutikon*, whereas slaves lack it altogether. Women are inferior to men, however, in that, in women, *to bouleutikon* is *akuron* (1260a13-14). Literally, to be *akuron* means to "lack authority." If *to bouleutikon* in women lacks authority over and against the superior strength of their appetites, then women are *the* appetitive creatures, and men the rational, and women *should* be perpetually ruled by men.[31] But if women are merely appetitive creatures, then it is not clear that they truly differ from natural slaves, for, as merely appetitive, women would be permanently inferior to men, as slaves are permanently inferior to their masters. There is, however, a more direct link suggested between women and slaves. Besides saying that natural slaves lacked *to bouleutikon* altogether, Aristotle also said that slaves, unlike animals, were able to perceive reason but not to have it (1254b22). One way of understanding what this might mean is that "having" implies actively using.[32] While slaves may hear the rational command from another, and women may be able to articulate it for themselves, neither slaves nor women *have* reason in the specified sense of *actively using* reason. Both slaves and women need reason to be supplied by another—that is, a master or a man.

There is, however, another possibility. One might be fully authoritative in oneself, i.e., have full authority over oneself, and yet be powerless politically. In such a case, women are only *akuron* because the existing hierarchy refuses to recognize or acknowledge their authority.[33] This possibility seems to be suggested by Aristotle's example of Amasis's foot pan (1259b7-10). Men assumed power to begin with and arbitrarily differentiated themselves from women. Having institutionalized and ossified those differences, men have perpetuated the status quo, which they now try to justify—anachronistically—as rooted in their essentially superior nature. If this is the way in which men are "superior" to women, then women have been enslaved by convention and treated little better than slaves, while deserving to be treated as men's equals. Women, in this case, would be *the* example of a conventional slave.

One might argue in response to this that Aristotle is not denying women *all* authority, merely authority in the city, and that, within the confines of the household, women can be perfectly masterful. The difficulty this raises is by what right are women disenfranchised politically? One possibility is that, as the biological childbearers and natural nurturers (nurses), women are naturally attuned to the needs of their children. And since the proper place for the children is at home, the woman's domain is the home. Women, therefore, rule in the home, while men rule in the city.[34] Two difficulties, however, attend this explanation. First, whenever Aristotle refers in Book I to the nurturing and rearing of children, he mentions only the father as caretaker, never the mother. Second, this argument defines the *political* role of women in terms of the *natural* (biological or animal) function of females. Why then should not men's roles also be determined on the basis of their biological or animal function? But once one embarks on this road, it is not clear how one can avoid returning to the argument that might makes right and women are subordinate politically because, as females, they are weaker.[35]

In the end, the only legitimate justification for why women are always subordinate to men politically is that women are essentially different from men, much as the naturally ruled (slaves) are said to be essentially different from the natural rulers (masters). This might then justify the claim that the proper venue for women to actualize their nature is the household and not the city, and that it is perfectly appropriate for women to rule in the household but not rule at all in the city. Indeed, Aristotle himself seems to be espousing this when he says that Gorgias was correct on this question and Socrates was wrong (1260a20-28).[36]

If women and men have essentially different natures, then there is no one, universal human nature. Once again, the argument points in two directions. Considered biologically, that is, in light of the end of procreation, women and men (qua males and females) certainly have different functions and therefore, presumably, different natures. And, indeed, it was with this biological function that Aristotle began his account. But biological function seems to be closer to the body than the soul. If one turns to consider the soul, one moves away from considering men and women as biological beings, toward considering them as political beings.[37] Further, if one turns to consider the soul, one moves away from considerations of reproductive function and bodily strength, toward considerations of virtue. In order to argue for Gorgias's position and against Socrates', one must argue that, with regard to virtue, there is no one, universal definition of human virtue. And while Aristotle *asserts* this, he does not argue for it. Indeed, Book I as a whole is one long protracted argument against Gorgias' view of human nature and human virtue, and for Socrates' more universal account. But, the *Politics* does not stand alone among Aristotle's works in arguing this; the groundwork is already laid in the *Nicomachean Ethics*, which, from the start, is a discussion about *human* nature and *human* virtue, and which Aristotle explicitly links to the *Politics*.[38]

Human Nature and Human Virtue

Both the arguments about natural slaves and those about women founder when pressed, and for similar reasons. If natural slaves are simply animated bodies, at worst they are machines, at best they are beasts, but it is not at all clear that they are human beings. And if women are simply appetitive creatures, biologically suited for bearing and nursing children, at best they are permanent servants, at worst no better than bodies needing to be kept under control.

And yet the labor slaves perform would seem to require both a certain degree of self-mastery and a certain expertise. After all, the slave is supposed to be able to execute in practice what the master has conceived in theory. The more brilliant the master, the more expert must be the slave in action, lest the master's thinking be for naught. If slaves are essentially body to the master's soul, it is unclear how they could possibly be of much use to the master. In the case of women, on the other hand, the biological functions women as females are able to perform don't necessarily require any great degree of self-mastery nor any great expertise. After all, as Aristotle points out, procreation requires no mind. If women, however, are essentially only biological creatures, it is unclear how their relationship with men can be "political." In the end, the differences between men and women and masters and slaves on which Aristotle insists to justify the perpetual rule of men and masters render it problematic how both men and women and both masters and slaves can be called "human."

Aristotle recognizes these difficulties and turns to address them at the end of Book I (1259b18 ff.). "First then, one might wonder whether there is some virtue of the slave besides his virtues as a tool and a servant, more honorable than these, for example, moderation and courage and justice and the other such characteristics, or whether he has no virtue besides his bodily service? For there is a perplexity in both cases. For if there is some such virtue, then in what way will slaves differ from free men? And if there is not some such virtue, then it is strange since they are human beings and participate [*koinonounton*] in reason. Pretty much the same question arises concerning a woman and a child. . . ." The question is, are slaves merely tools or are they also human beings? Likewise for women. If slaves' only virtue is whatever is necessary to render them well functioning as tools, then they are essentially simply tools. If they share in human virtue, however, then what justifies categorizing them as slaves and not free? And if women are indeed free, as Aristotle repeatedly says, then how can they not share in human virtue, and why should they not share in political rule?

Since Aristotle insists that slaves and women are human beings, as are masters and men, they must at least have the potential for virtue that masters and men have. Perhaps, then, one might argue that men and masters represent perfected or ideal human beings, while women and slaves are examples of different kinds of human imperfections.[39] This would seem to suggest that both women and slaves are, in a sense, like children. If they were simply children, then their virtue would be incomplete, and the ruler's job would be to help them complete it, as the father does for his child.[40] The relationship then would be one of *basilike*, and not of *politike* or *despotike*. Furthermore, as children, they would be contributing nothing to the ends of the ruler. Instead, he would be aiding and nurturing them. If women and slaves are perpetual children, they will not be nurtured toward some perfection, but they will need perpetual caretaking, which would seem to be incompatible with their participation in and contribution to their respective relationships (*koinoniai*).

Aristotle, however, identifies only children as having incomplete virtue (see 1259b3-4; 1260a9-14). Women and slaves have complete virtue, albeit only with regard to their respective jobs. Rulers have complete virtue both with regard to their function as rulers and with regard to what it is to be a human being. But herein lies a difference. One may define virtue in terms of what is needed for a particular job (*ergon*), or one may define virtue in terms of what it is to be a complete or perfect human being. From the standpoint of the tasks necessary for the proper functioning of the city, there are different kinds of jobs, each job has its own distinct virtue, and each individual has one job; consequently, each individual has the virtue appropriate to his or her job. From this standpoint, Aristotle can say, à la Gorgias, that there is a different virtue for men, women, masters, slaves, fathers, and children. From the standpoint of what it is to be a human being, however, there is one universal definition of human being, and therefore one single definition of human virtue.[41] From this standpoint, there aren't essentially different *kinds* of human beings; there are perfect and defective human beings. The women and slaves of Aristotle's argument are examples of essentially defective human beings.

The real question at the heart of *Politics* Book I, which is revealed through an investigation of the discussion about women and slaves, is whether human beings are essentially tools or whether they are essentially free. Are they merely parts of a greater whole, capable only of the completion that is possible through contributing to the work of the whole, or are they in some sense wholes in themselves, working toward the completion and perfection of themselves as human beings? This question requires a reexamination of the relation between the household and the city.

From the start, Aristotle identifies the household as the community (*koinonia*) that provides for life's necessities (see 1252a26 ff.; 1252b12-16). Each constituent relation, or part, of the household addresses a distinct need. And, as we have seen, Aristotle suggests that human beings are naturally fit to do different kinds of jobs. The relationship of man/woman provides a constant crop of human beings to ensure the continued population of the city; the relationship of master/slave provides for the daily needs of that population; and the relationship of father/child ensures that future citizens will be virtuous. Understood thus, human beings essentially differ in kind; each kind is defined in terms of a necessary function; and all human beings are essentially tools.[42] Since Aristotle goes on to identify households as the constituent parts of cities, the protection and preservation of the structures of the household would seem to be essential to the very existence of the city.

If the household were the paradigm for, or even identical to, the city, the city would be indistinguishable from the Cyclopean family. Human beings would be categorized in terms of what job each could best perform. They would be tools contributing to the "good of the whole," but having no intrinsic good of their own. Cannibalism and incest would abound.[43] Furthermore, as most human beings would be perpetually ruled, with only one member of each household serving as perpetual master or king, most human beings would be treated essentially as slaves or—at best—children.

But while the city is constituted for the sake of living (*to zen*), Aristotle says it exists for the sake of living well (*to eu zen*). The goal of the city is not the necessities of procreation and preservation, but the good life, or happiness. And insofar as the political association is the highest goal for human beings and represents their natural end, the good life or happiness suggests individual human flourishing, not just the flourishing of some abstract "whole." Furthermore, unlike the household, with its multitude of useful relationships, the city qua city is constituted by one relationship—*politike*.

Aristotle defines *politike* in various but related ways. It is the community of free equals; it is the community whose members rule and are ruled in turn. It is also the community of rational animals—beings with *logos*. Human being is the being with *logos*. If one qualifies to be called a human being, then one is by nature a political animal and therefore qualified to participate in *politike*. Under *politike* everyone would be recognized as free and equal, and would rule and be ruled in turn. No human being would be delegated to a permanent underclass, and no human being would be denied citizenship altogether. The only nonparticipating members of the city would be children, who would be getting the education necessary, through *basilike*, in order to actualize their potential and come to be full members in the city.

If all that existed were the city, all human beings would enjoy the fundamental equality and freedom proper for a community of human beings. There would be no slaves, and all men and women would coexist as partners, ruling and being ruled in turn. But what about the necessary tasks that master/slave, man/woman, and father/child perform? Either they would not be done at all—in which case the city would be in the untenable position of providing for living well without providing for living—or the city would supervise and enforce their execution. The first alternative is not a genuine possibility. What about the second?

The city might require everyone to perform some necessary task. It might do so either by asking for volunteers (would you like to bear children or sweep the streets?) or by assigning individuals to one task or another. If the city assigns individuals to different tasks, it either must do so arbitrarily or it must do so on the grounds that different individuals have different natures and hence are suited to different tasks. The first possibility looks like the arbitrary imposition of force; the second possibility looks like a return to understanding human beings as being essentially different in kind. Both possibilities fundamentally violate the first principle of *politike*: that all human beings are free and equal. In acknowledgment of everyone's fundamental freedom, the city might offer to pay individuals for performing these necessary tasks.[44] Of course, while the individuals were engaged in the necessary tasks, they would not be participating in the political life. This would mean they would be substituting a wage (the price of the loss or suspension of their freedom) for the good life, an equivalence Aristotle argues most explicitly against in the *Nicomachean Ethics*. In short, if the city gives itself the job of seeing to the necessary tasks, it must treat everyone as if they were merely means, not ends in themselves, which would violate the principles of freedom and equality that lie at its foundation, and it seems to give up (or require individuals to give up) the good life, which is its end.

If the city is to preserve itself as the domain of *politike* (*he koinonia he politike*), it seems that it must distinguish between the nonpolitical and the political, between the necessary and the good, and make room for the household as a separate sphere. This means it must condone the essentially unfree distinctions of male/female (superior/inferior) and master/slave (ruler/ruled) within the household, while recognizing everyone as being in certain essential respects the same, hence, citizens or potential citizens, within the city. Of course, to do this, the city must tacitly acknowledge the fundamental injustice of the household's distinctions. One could, however, argue on behalf of the city that, at least as long as the city carves out a separate sphere for itself, where all human beings are acknowledged as ends in themselves and where they may pursue the good life, it saves everyone from being simply a drudge and sinking into the subjugation of perpetual despotism.

The "solution" of separate spheres for the necessary and the good, however, is not without its own difficulties. The political assumption is that everyone who looks like a human being and who is born of human beings is a human being. And what qualifies one as a human being in the first place is that one is an animal with *logos*. But what does it mean to have *logos*? Does one qualify if one simply possesses the capacity for *logos*, or must one actively use it? At first glance, one would want to say that only those who actively use *logos* qualify as genuine human beings, hence participants in the political community (i.e., citizens). To use *logos* actively, according to Aristotle, is to engage in speeches about the advantageous and the just (1253a14-15) and to have virtue and *phronesis* (1253a34-35). It is not sufficient for one simply to have moral virtue, e.g., self-control with regard to sex and food. One must have virtue *with phronesis*.[45] It is not sufficient, therefore, for one to engage with others in speeches about the advantageous and the just simply to the extent of sharing a common opinion or prejudice about the advantageous and the just. One must either be in community with other knowers of the advantageous and the just or—if one is not wise (*sophos*)—with others who are seeking to discover what is advantageous and just.

The only real citizens of the political community, therefore, would be the philosophers—those who engage in speeches every day about virtue and other such things.[46] For only they, through questioning and investigating opinions and claims about the just and the advantageous, can be sure that they do not blindly accept as just what is in truth unjust. Only philosophers or potential philosophers are working toward true virtue and prudence.

Two difficulties, however, attend the identification of the political community with the philosophical community. First, such a community, while focusing on living well, ignores the necessities of living.[47] Second, such a definition of the political community is too narrow, as it excludes virtually everyone from being a member. It may not be quite as extreme as the *pambasileus* at the end of Book III, but it comes quite close to that. The city where only one person (*pambasileus*) or a mere handful of persons (philosophers) may be citizens once again reduces almost everyone at best to the status of a (perpetual) child, which brings *politike* very close to *basilike*, if not *despotike*.

It seems, therefore, that citizenship should be granted to those who possess the *capacity* for *logos*. They should certainly be capable of perceiving reason when they hear it, and this should allow them at least to be morally virtuous.[48] The difficulty with this definition of human being and citizen, however, is that it sounds very much like the description of the natural slave who was said to perceive reason but not to have it (1254b22-23). Certainly the "natural slave" shows that, if this is the extent of one's share in reason, one hardly qualifies as free. Furthermore, with such a minimal criterion for citizenship, the city will recognize as citizens those who differ as much as children from their fathers. For while some citizens will possess only the capacity for *logos*, others may have a more developed capacity to use *logos*. The city in this case would suffer from the opposite problem of that found in the household. There, equals (namely, human beings) were treated as unequals (master, slave, etc.). Here, unequals (actually virtuous and potentially virtuous individuals) are treated as equals (citizens).[49] It seems just as problematic, therefore, for the city to be all-inclusive and grant citizenship to everyone as it was for the city to be exclusive and grant citizenship only to the virtuous and prudent.

In the end, however, it is far more just to be inclusive rather than exclusive, for a couple of reasons. First, as has been pointed out, to be exclusive with regard to citizenship is to relegate most human beings to the status of perpetual children, which, for adults, looks more like *despotike* than *basilike* as it denies them any autonomy. Second, the only way to determine whether a particular individual is prudent is to engage that individual in dialogue.[50] But to do this is already to involve the individual in the highest community possible for human beings—the community in speeches about virtue.

Aristotle's discussion in Book I points to three distinct ways of understanding "human being," hence, three distinct levels of human activity. On the lowest level is the human being in the household, contributing to what is necessary for life. On the highest level is the human being in the philosophic community, pursuing the discussions and investigations necessary for virtue and the good life. But one also needs an in-between level that recognizes not only actually fulfilled human beings, but also those who have the potential for virtue even if it is as yet unrealized, i.e., those who possess the *capacity* for *logos*. This in-between level corresponds to the actual city.[51]

As Book I has shown through the arguments about slaves and women, the household is essentially the place of what is bestial (slaves) or animal (women) in human beings. The philosophic community, on the other hand, is the place of what is divine (*logos, archon*). But Aristotle states explicitly that human beings are neither beasts nor gods. Human life exclusively within the household descends into savagery (*despotike*). Human life spent exclusively in philosophic discussion is ephemeral (*basilike*). The truly human—that which is neither beast nor god—seems to be most closely identified with the actual city. Although bound to natural necessity (body), human beings have the choice and the capacity to transcend natural necessity by recognizing and cultivating their share in the divine (mind). The actual city that preserves a place for both households and philosophers, while going about its own business of war and peace, serves as the bridge between the merely natural and the genuinely teleological.

Politike, in the end, emerges as the science of human nature and human ends. As such, it may be manifest in different spheres of the city in different ways. Its purest actualization appears to be in the philosophic community, among human beings who are virtuous, hence, genuinely free and equal. Less pure is its actualization in the actual city—which, in preserving a place for the household, acknowledges its origins, and by preserving a place for philosophy acknowledges and preserves its true *telos*. In the end, because this actual (albeit ideal) city does not forget or ignore necessity, it proves to be the real political community, and in it is to be found the most genuine instantiation of *politike*. As for *politike* between man and woman in the household, unless husband and wife can be genuine friends, this does not seem to be a genuine possibility.

Finally, what about the four kinds of rule with which Aristotle began Book I and which he says are mistakenly identified as one science? Certainly there can be an expertise in the direction and use of slaves (*despotike*) and an expertise in the direction and use of the various members of the household (*oikonomike*). But insofar as a particular science is knowledge of an essentially distinct being, neither expertise qualifies as a science. The common object in household and city is human being, and Aristotle's argument seems to suggest that there is one *science* of human being. But which is it, *politike* or *basilike*?

If the *telos* of a human being qua human is to be virtuous and to participate in the political community, the highest form of rule would be *politike*, with *basilike* serving the propaedeutic role necessary for such rule to be possible. Furthermore, to preserve the humanity of human beings and not treat them like perpetual children, *basilike* should be confined to the household, whereas *politike* should be the rule in the city. As kinds of rule, *basilike* and *politike* therefore clearly are different. Are they also two different sciences? The answer to this seems to be yes and no. No, they are not different sciences insofar as the object of both is the complete (*teleios*) human being. And yet to the extent that there is a difference in knowledge between telling someone else what virtue is and actually being virtuous and acting virtuously,[52] they are indeed different sciences. In the end, Plato both did and did not speak correctly.[53]

Notes

I would like to thank Ronna Burger and Peter Vedder for their helpful comments and insightful questions.

1. This is a reference to the beginning of Plato's *Statesman* 258e8-259c4. The one making the claim is the Eleatic Stranger. It is not at all evident that the Stranger maintains this claim all the way through to the end of the *Statesman*.

2. 1259a37-1259b1. Cf. 1253b3-11. Since, in the end, Aristotle identifies households as the constituent parts of the city, and the relations or communities of master/slave, husband/wife, and father/child as the constituent parts of the household, between the household and its parts he accounts for all four kinds of rule he wishes to distinguish from the very beginning.

3. Since a child is potentially like his father, and since every father is either a citizen, master, or slave, "father" and "child" would seem to be less essential distinctions.

4. Actually, Aristotle introduces master and slave as an example of the natural hierarchy of natural ruler and naturally ruled. Whether master/slave is as natural as the natural hierarchy of which it is an example is the focus of Aristotle's discussion in Book I, chaps. 4-7, and is addressed below in the section "Natural Slaves." As for the connection between male/female and man/woman, see the discussion below.

5. Literally, Aristotle says, "The first community arising from several households, for the sake of non-daily needs is the village" (1252b15), and "The community arising from several villages that is complete [*teleios*] is the city" (1252b28).

6. See 1254a28-31: "For whatever is constituted out of a multitude of things and becomes one common thing . . . always displays a ruling and ruled [element]."

7. See, e.g., 1254a34-36, where Aristotle says, "First of all, animal is constituted [*sunesteken*] out of soul and body, of which the former is by nature the ruler and the latter, the ruled." Cf. 1253a31-32: "The first one to constitute [the city] was the cause of the greatest of goods."

8. From the start the claim is that nature has produced the "slave" for a distinctive purpose, as much as woman. This is called into question by Aristotle himself when he turns to question the naturalness of a "natural slave."

9. Since every human being is either male or female *and*—supposedly—every human being is either ruler or ruled, several different possibilities arise that belie the simplicity of nature.

        Male and ruler   Male and ruled
        Female and ruler   Female and ruled

One might also speculate on one more set of possibilities:

        Male and potential ruler,   but actually ruled
        Female and potential ruler, but actually ruled

See Mary P. Nichols's discussion of nature's lack of simplicity in "The Origins of the City," in *Citizens and Statesmen: A Study of Aristotle's "Politics"* (Lanham, MD: Rowman & Littlefield, 1991).

10. Each of these three sets of terms has a different character. "Male" and "female" are biological terms, "man" and "woman" seem to be species distinctions, and "husband" and "wife" are political categories.

11. "Nature" here means what is given, what is natural *as opposed to* what comes to be through purposive action and choice.

12. Cf., e.g., 1254b4-5, where Aristotle speaks of the composite of *soul* and body. Oftentimes in his discussion, thought/body and soul/body seem to be equivalent.

13. In Book III, speaking of another whole—the regime—Aristotle says the regime is the governing body (1278b12). Perhaps the suggestion is that soul is to body as form is to matter, and insofar as soul provides the definition or form of the being, it may be identified with the whole. See *Metaphysics* VII.10, for example.

14. In the case of an individual human being, when body is separated from soul, the remaining body is a corpse and not a human being; what the separated soul is, is more problematic, although the problem of individuation suggests that at best the soul is the generic form and no longer an individual.

15. Consider the ox Aristotle mentions, quoting from Hesiod's poem (1252b11-13). See also 1254b16-21.

16. *Nicomachean Ethics* VI.12, 1144a9-10. See also I.7, I.13, and VI.1.

17. See *Nicomachean Ethics* I.7, 1097b33-1098a5, where these distinctions are introduced to account for the unique function (*ergon*) of human beings.

18. See *Nicomachean Ethics* I.7, 1097b33-1098a5; see also *Politics* 1253a9-10. In contrast, W. W. Fortenbaugh, for example, argues that "in denying slaves the capacity to deliberate (I.13.1260a12) Aristotle is not robbing them of their humanity." (W. W.

Fortenbaugh, "Aristotle on Slaves and Women," in *Articles on Aristotle, Vol 2: Ethics and Politics*, ed. Jonathan Barnes, Malcolm Schofield, and Richard Sorabji [New York: St. Martin's Press, 1977], 136).

19. An advocate of animal rights, for example, would want to dispute this claim as "speciesist." Because Aristotle's focus here is essentially the city, he is more concerned with what kinds of actions and relationships are justified among human beings than between human and nonhuman beings. Furthermore, the kind of purposive action necessary for an essentially political and human life requires the capacity for deliberation. Everything lacking such a capacity either belongs outside of the city or may justifiably be employed as a tool in the city.

20. See Plato's *Sophist* 229e1-230a3, where the Stranger identifies admonition as one kind of teaching—the kind fathers use especially on their sons. (The other kind of teaching is identified as refutation, the kind that results from self-examination.) Cf. Socrates' myth in the *Gorgias* (523a ff.), which raises the question of whether and how corporal punishment can transfer to the soul and translate into understanding.

21. Although Aristotle says, "mind rules over appetite with *politike and basilike*," his more common way of speaking is to say that, of the two, only *basilike* is intrinsically hierarchical, whereas *politike* is between free and equals. *Basilike*, therefore, emerges as the closer structural analog to *despotike*. Also, in moving from talking about natural slaves as if they were merely body to talking about them as if they were appetitive creatures able to perceive reason, Aristotle is either moving from presenting the master/slave relationship as a paradigm of *despotike*, to presenting it as a paradigm for *basilike*, or he is eroding the boundaries between *despotike* and *basilike*.

22. In Greek, *pais* may signify either "child" or "slave." According to Liddell and Scott, the correct translation depends upon the particular context or relation. They list *pais* as "child" in relation to descent and age, and as "slave" in relation to condition.

23. In *Republic* Book I, a similar move occurs in Socrates' discussion with Thrasymachus about the ruler as a knower. Whereas Thrasymachus wants to argue that the knowleg 'able ruler serves his own advantage, Socrates—using the doctor as a primary example—argues that insofar as the knower is a knower, he is complete and lacks nothing. The doctor as a knower, far from lording it over his patients, employs his knowledge to cure and hence serves his patients.

24. If slaves are little or no better than beasts or perpetual children, it would seem a master would be better off with a beast than a slave. At least with an animal one is not likely to feel compelled to treat it like a child. See Aristotle's follow-up to his quotation from Hesiod: "For an ox stands in the place of a servant for poor people" (1252b12). See also Aristotle's comment that, without virtue, human beings are the most savage of animals (1253a35-36).

25. See *Republic* Book IV's definitions of these virtues, both on the level of the city—where each virtue is assigned to a different kind of human being, and on the level of the individual—where each virtue is assigned to a different part of the soul. Both the *Republic* and the *Politics* seem to be confronting the same question: Is the city composed of different kinds of individuals, or does the city, in its desire to be a whole and a one, impose different kind distinctions on human beings?

26. See *Republic* Book IV. When moderation is introduced it is introduced as the virtue proper to the artisan class—the part of the city that represents desire—which supposedly lacks the mind necessary to rule and the spiritedness (*thumos*) necessary to safeguard the city's opinions, and presumably simply pursues desire after desire. And yet moderation is defined in part as ruling over or being in control of oneself, which is certainly a necessary prerequisite if one is to keep to and be successful in one's job in the

city, regardless of what that job is. To mind one's own business, therefore, and stick to one's own station—whether that requires ruling or obeying—would seem to require moderation. How then is the one who has moderated his desires *merely* a slave, or *merely* desire?

27. See Nicholas D. Smith, "Aristotle's Theory of Natural Slavery," in *A Companion to Aristotle's "Politics,"* ed. David Keyt and Fred D. Miller, Jr. (Cambridge, MA: Blackwell, 1991), 142-55, who arrives at a similar conclusion and, on this point, differs from Fortenbaugh. Cf. Fortenbaugh, "Aristotle on Slaves and Women."

28. "Child" in this context must mean male child, just as the only ruling parent Aristotle identifies is the father. It is interesting to note that in modern Greece, when a father of six is asked how many children he has, he might still be heard to say, "four, and two girls."

29. The relative equality of men and women was suggested with the first community Aristotle mentions—that of male and female. Recall that that community was juxtaposed and contrasted with the community of natural ruler and naturally ruled, which exemplified hierarchy. If one of the foundational elements of the city is hierarchy, the other element—embodied in the male/female community—must supply something else. Some have tried to dispute this, citing other texts of Aristotle's, especially biological texts (e.g., *Generation of Animals*, 728a18-20, 737a18-20, 765b10 ff., 766a30 ff.), where the male is supposed to provide the form and the female the matter, with the form being hierarchically superior to the matter. See, for example, Fortenbaugh, "Aristotle on Slaves and Women"; Susan Moller Okin, *Women in Western Political Thought* (Princeton: Princeton University Press, 1979).

30. Of course, there are specific exceptions, and if the justification for who should rule is strength, then, when a female is larger and stronger than a male, it would seem that the female should rule.

31. See, e.g., Hegel in the *Philosophy of Right*: Man is "powerful and active . . . [and] therefore has his actual substantial life in the state." Woman is "passive and subjective," and "has her substantial vocation in the family." (*Elements of the Philosophy of Right*, part 3: *Ethical Life*, section 1, "The Family," paragraphs 165, 166, ed. by Allen W. Wood [New York: Cambridge University Press, 1991].)

32. See Plato's *Theaetetus*, 197b3 ff., where Socrates speaks of the dovecote. There, Socrates draws a distinction between having and possessing. "To me, at any rate, to possess does not appear to be the same as to have. For example, if someone should purchase and hold on to a cloak but not wear it, we would say that he possesses it, but not that he has it."

33. On this conventional meaning of *akuron*, see Arlene Saxonhouse, *Women in the History of Political Thought* (Westport, CT: Praeger, 1985), 74.

34. See, e.g., Mary Nichols, who suggests two different kinds of ruling for men and women. Man goes "beyond what he possesses, or what he is . . . for the sake of bringing something new into being." Woman, on the other hand, serves, either "another human being or some undertaking or project. . . . Her work lies in trusting what is given and its natural development, guiding without imposing, accepting the limitations of what is nurtured even if that means rejecting new visions or goals that seem to hold more promise" (Nichols, *Citizens and Statesmen*, 32). This correlates with Hegel's assigning men to the city and women to the household and family.

35. Or, they are more passive, or nurturers as opposed to being hegemonic (see 1259b1-2).

36. See Plato's *Meno*, where Meno argues Gorgias's position of different virtues for different kinds of people (71e ff.), whereas Socrates argues, contra Meno, that virtue

consists not in *what* someone does, but in whether one does it *well*. According to Socrates, acting well is acting virtuously, and virtue is right use of one's resources, or acting with understanding (*nous*) and *phronesis* (88a-89a).

37. Aristotle suggests this when he calls the relationship between men and women "political." He also suggests that differences in soul are far more essential than differences in body when he says, "Nature wishes then to make the bodies of freemen and slaves different . . . but the opposite often occurs. . . . It is apparent, at any rate that those who were born as different in body alone as the images of the gods, everyone would say that everyone else was worthy to be their slave. And if this is true about the body, it is even more just to determine this about the soul." (1254b27-38).

38. See *Nicomachean Ethics* X.1181b12-15.

39. See *Politics* 1254a34 ff.: "The animal, first of all, is constituted of soul and body, of which the one is by nature ruler and the other, ruled. And one must investigate those whose nature is according to nature and not those who are defective. Therefore one must also examine that [human being] whose condition is best both with respect to body and with respect to soul, in whom this is clear. For in those who are corrupted or those who exist in a corrupted state, it is believed that the body often rules the soul on account of them being in a bad condition and contrary to nature."

40. See, e.g., Aristotle's remark that "It is clear then that the master must be responsible for this sort of virtue in the slave, but not with having the art of mastery that teaches a slave his tasks" (1260b3-5).

41. Consider both when Aristotle is speaking of virtue in the unqualified sense and ethical virtue. Regarding virtue in the unqualified sense, slaves lack the deliberative capacity altogether, women have it but it is *akuron* (see discussion above), and children have it but it is incomplete. "Therefore with respect to the ruler, intellectual virtue must be complete (for the work [*ergon*] belongs unqualifiedly to the master craftsman, and reason [*logos*] is the master craftsman)" (1260a12-17). Regarding ethical virtue, Aristotle says, "it is necessary that all share in it, but not in the same manner, but to each as much as is necessary for his own work [*ergon*]" (1260a19-20).

42. This is true even of masters, who supply the intellect, hence the direction necessary for the slaves' *praxis*. That is to say, if the goal is preservation, the preservation is not primarily of any particular individual or set of individuals, but rather of the household and the city. This renders particular individuals subordinate to both household and city, useful for whatever each has to offer toward the preservation of household and city.

43. See Michael Davis, "Cannibalism and Nature," chapter 1 of *The Politics of Philosophy* (Lanham, MD: Rowman & Littlefield, 1996). As he puts it, cannibalism is "the natural result of understanding other men solely in terms of their use" (24). Further, if the household is the highest community, incest is inevitable (see *Republic* Book V, the second wave, on the communism of women and children).

44. See 1258b25-27. There, Aristotle uses the phrase "those who are useful only for their bodies" to describe those who should be wage earners, which is reminiscent of his earlier description of natural slaves (1254b17-18). The politicization, hence emancipation, of slaves occurs when they are paid a wage. The question remains, however, whether this obviates *despotike*.

45. See *Nicomachean Ethics* VI.12-13, esp. 1144b14-21.

46. See the *Apology of Socrates*, 38a.

47. Either one is aiming at living or one is aiming at living well. Since these are essentially different goals and require essentially different actions, one may engage in them sequentially, but never simultaneously. The *Republic* comes to mind here as an example. There, whereas the interlocutors discuss and account for the provision of food (Book II), there is no indication that they themselves eat while the conversation is going on.

48. See Aristotle's comment that, without virtue, human beings are "the most unholy and the most savage, and the worst, especially with regard to sex and food" (1253a35-37). "Virtue" in this instance seems to refer to moral virtue. See *Nicomachean Ethics* III.10, 1117b23 ff.

49. It may not even be the case that all human beings share the same potential for being human in the highest sense—i.e., having virtue and *phronesis*.

50. For soul types cannot be discerned simply by look. See 1254b38-1255a1.

51. At least, the actual city as it *should* be.

52. The difference seems to be the difference between theory and practice, *theoria* or *gnosis* and *praxis*. See *Nicomachean Ethics* VI, on the difference between theoretical and practical wisdom, or *sophia* and *phronesis*. See also Plato's *Statesman*, which is one long argument about the togetherness and separateness of *gnosis* and *praxis* (see, e.g., 258e4-5).

53. See Aristotle's opening assertion about statesman, king, household-manager, and slave master (1252a7 ff.).

Chapter 5

Livy, Lucretia, and Rome's Republican Founding: A Reading of Female Rape and Masculine *Virtù*

Melissa Matthes

While often thought of as the original in the tradition of republican political theory, Livy's account of the rape of Lucretia in *Ab Urbe Condita* is by no means the only rendition. Other early accounts include those found in Ovid's *Fasti* and Dionysius of Halicarnassus's *Roman Antiquities*. Additional versions appear again centuries later in the Italian and English Renaissance. In Italy, in addition to Niccolo Machiavelli's satirical retelling of the rape in his comedy *Mandragola*, other popular versions included Coluccio Salutati's rhetorical treatise as chancellor of Florence, *Declamatio Lucretia*[1] and Giovanni Boccaccio's didactic rendition in *Concerning Famous Women*. And these were only the written accounts; there were numerous pictorial and other artistic Renaissance representations of Lucretia and her plight, among them a three-dimensional float paraded at the third wedding ceremony of her namesake, Lucretia Borgia. Assuming political significance again in the eighteenth century, primarily in France, Lucretia's story was recounted not only in Jean-Jacques Rousseau's unfinished tragic rendition, *La Mort de Lucrèce*, but also in Voltaire's tragedy *Brutus*.

Paradoxically, the tale itself does not seem to have the makings of trans-historical interest. It is, after all, only a story of a woman, and then a rather common story under patriarchy of a woman who is raped and then commits suicide after her violation. It is only when one recognizes that many of these renditions are inextricably linked to stories of the founding of republics that the entanglements and significance of the repetitions begin to develop for the political theorist.[2] That is, since republics are polities that value tradition[3] and consecutively imagine themselves in conversation with their republican ancestors,[4] it is not surprising that early stories of republican foundings would be repeated by their successors.[5] Nonetheless, the repetitions seem to suggest something else as well: the instability and fragility of republics; the repetitions are necessary, perhaps, to secure what does not quite seem able to be guaranteed. That is, although this foundational story seems to seek to delimit (indeed, perhaps to destroy) the feminine, the repetitions of the story suggest that the feminine is not finally obliterated but a feature of the republic that simultaneously enables and disrupts its founding. The feminine is, then, what might be named a "constitutive contradiction."[6] Not only are the variations in the historical incarnations of the story intriguing, but the logic that seems to necessitate the rape of a woman in order to found a republic is of especial interest.[7] Why is the sexual violation of a woman found at the origin of Livy's republic? That is, why is a republic, rather than a tyranny or monarchy, established as a result of the rape? Further, how does this sexual violence configure Livy's subsequent understandings of republican *virtù*? What does the rape signify that is integral to the forging of the initial community? In other words, how does Lucretia's rape in Livy's account secure a fraternal bond?

Split at its inception into public and private spheres that mimic the constitution of sexual difference, republics have been repeatedly decried for their foundational subordination of women.[8] And yet, in Livy's version, the feminine and femininity, if not Lucretia herself, continually oversteps the boundaries of this denial; and the effects of this transgression are manifest, partially, this essay argues, in Livy's anxiety that the fragile fraternal bond is both strengthened and strained by this incorporation and renunciation of the feminine.

Most dramatically, this negotiation, this struggle with the feminine other, is evident at the founding of Livy's republic. It is then with the violence of inauguration, when the boundaries are temporarily fixed and presumably stable, that that which must be banished or denied in order for the political community to begin is most visible. Not surprisingly then, the stories that explain and constitute the genesis of Livy's republic, its "founding stories," are also the stories of women, specifically of women's sexual violation and of men's intercession with femininity and feminine powers.

At its genesis, what must later be absent and silent—what is most destabilizing to and vulnerable about the incipient republic—is most exposed. What is manifest, most obviously, is the violence and deception at the very origin of the polity, but also, and perhaps more importantly, the radical contingency of the republican claim to political power as well as the fragility of the bond among republican actors who are united, in part, because of their failed masculinity.

And so it is here, at the founding, that a feminist political theorist can discover, reveal, and recreate how the parameters of the republic—in this case, Livy's conception of the Roman republic—are negotiated and defined. And that is what this essay pursues, not only the rather obvious gendering of the public and private spheres, but also the more subtle gendering of the very foundations of Livy's Roman republic.

Although Lucretia's founding story seems only to compound the feminist invective against republics, this essay argues that Livy's founding story augurs for something more complicated; namely, that the labor of Lucretia's body at the founding fulfills a cultural need. Rather than simply denying the feminine, a kind of authority is ascribed to the representations and spectacle of the female body. As Luce Irigaray has observed, the formation of the political is through and dependent upon the feminine.[9] In this case, Lucretia's body is the means by which a spectacle is constructed, a spectacle that inaugurates a political community founded upon seeing and being seen.

The story of the rape of Lucretia and the founding of the republic as Livy tells it in Book I of his history is as follows:

One day several men, among them Collatinus, Lucretia's husband, were drinking in the quarters of Sextus Tarquinius, the son of the then-ruling tyrant. Soon the subject of wives arose, and each man bragged that his wife was the most virtuous. Collatinus interrupted the rivalry, urging, "What need is there of words when in a few hours we can prove beyond doubt the incomparable superiority of my Lucretia?"[10] With this the men galloped off to Rome, where they found all of the other men's wives luxuriously enjoying themselves in their husband's absence while only Lucretia was found modestly dressed and "hard at work by lamplight upon her spinning" (Section 1.57).

During the subsequent dinner, Tarquin was inflamed with lust by Lucretia's beauty and proven chastity. Several nights later, he burst into her bedroom demanding she submit to him. Even when he threatened her with death, Lucretia refused. Finally, he reviled her, "If death will not move you, dishonor shall. I shall kill you first, then cut the throat of a slave and lay his naked body by your side. Will they not believe that you have been caught in adultery with a servant —and paid the price?" (Section 1.57). With this threat Lucretia yielded.

The following day she called her father, her husband, and Brutus, a family friend, around her. She recounted the rape and demanded revenge. She would testify to her innocence, she asserted, by killing herself: "My heart is innocent, and death will be my witness" (Section 1.57). Her family tried to dissuade her, arguing vehemently that only her body had been violated, not her honor; that without intention there could be no guilt. Lucretia refused to listen and plunged a dagger into her heart.

While her husband and father were lost in grief, Brutus pulled the dagger from Lucretia's breast and urged the men to join together to drive the despotic Tarquins from Rome. Roman men rallied around Brutus's call for vengeance, and Rome was subsequently liberated and Brutus named the founding father of the republic.

Perhaps this violence at the foundation could be dismissed as simply the necessity of any beginning; the violence imperative for the constitution of authority. As Niccolo Machiavelli asserts centuries later, innovations necessitate violence; and most certainly a republic is a dramatic innovation to a previously tyrannical state. Nonetheless, this narrative of sexual violence, present often at the republican foundings that look to Rome as their model, seems to be constitutive of the republic itself.

According to Livy, rape was among the "first steps to be taken to the founding of the mightiest empire the world has ever known":

The Vestal Virgin (Rhea Silvia) was raped and gave birth to twin boys. Mars, she declared, was their father; perhaps she believed it, perhaps she was merely hoping to by the pretence palliate her guilt. Whatever the truth of the matter, neither gods nor men could save her or her babes from the savage hands of the king. (Section 1.3)

The rest of the story is well known; the boys were ordered by the king to be drowned but were fortuitously found by a she-wolf and nursed by her until found by a herdsman whose wife, Larentia, raised them to adulthood.[11] These boys then grow up to become Romulus and Remus, founders of Rome.

The rape of Rhea Silvia highlights not only the premise that there is often violence at beginnings but that specifically *sexual* violence may be integral to Livy's rendition of the Roman founding. In the beginning it is a woman's sexual violation that spurs the founding. Further, there is the suggestion that Romulus and Remus are not of divine birth as Livy's rather intrusive, "perhaps she believed it, perhaps she was merely hoping to palliate her guilt," implies. The casting of this suspicion on the Vestal Virgin's credibility is, in part, Livy's attempt to make Romulus a figure with whom his contemporaries could more readily identify as mortal rather than divine. In this recasting of Romulus, Livy articulates his conception of history as mimetic, as a source for present-day imitation.

Nonetheless, although Romulus is held up as a figure for emulation, Rhea is disappeared from history: "The mother was bound and flung into prison" (Section 1.4). Nothing is known of her fate. What is known, however, is that the traditional punishment for vestal virgins who breached their code of virginity was to be buried alive at the Collantine Gate.[12] Thus, Rhea, the virgin mother, lies literally under the foundation; she, like Lucretia, is the foundation that makes the foundation possible. And, interestingly, it is she who also simultaneously threatens the stability of that foundation.

Another alternative might be to read the founding/rape story of Lucretia (and of Rhea Silvia)[13] as simply the consequence of a familial vendetta. In other words, because the woman of one community has been violated by a transgressor from another, the men of the violated woman seek revenge by conquering the rapist. Yet the complications and political consequences of the story defy this facile reading. First, men other than the kin of the raped woman are ignited to rebellion by the rape. The most telling example is Brutus himself. Although Brutus has a long-standing personal vendetta against the Tarquins—they murdered both his father and brother—the murder of his relatives does not stir him to action. The rape of Lucretia,—more than ten years later—has the power to enflame him, as a "true Roman" (Section 1.4). Further, this vengeance is not of the eye for an eye, tooth for a tooth variety. Collatinus, Lucretia's husband, does not want to rape Tarquin women, nor does Brutus seem bent on murder. Rather, what it means to avenge Lucretia's rape is not only to drive the tyrants from Rome but to establish a republic.

Finally, this explanation of the story as the culmination of a familial vendetta does not reveal the so-called logic of the narrative, i.e. why a *republic*, rather than a tyranny or monarchy, is established as a result of Lucretia's rape. Presumably, after the exile of the Tarquins, another tyranny could have been established; however, the story of Lucretia's rape/suicide seems, again, to spawn the founding specifically of a republic.

According to feminists Gayle Rubin, Carole Pateman, and others,[14] under patriarchy the ability to control the exchange of women is important because it guarantees the certainty of paternity. In other words, it is important that women do not have sexual intercourse with men to whom they do not legitimately "belong" so that the men to whom they do can be assured that the offspring are theirs. Paternity, as Pateman notes, has to be "discovered or invented. Unlike maternity, paternity is merely a social fact, a human invention."[15] Consequently, at its most fundamental level, rape jeopardizes the organization of paternal rights.

Under tyranny, as Tarquin's rape establishes, there is no legitimate control or exchange of women. All women belong, in effect, to the tyrant. Consequently, there can only be one legitimate father and he is the tyrant. Thus, Tarquin's rape of Lucretia is more than the exercise of his patriarchal power; it is also the wielding of his political power. Sextus, as son of the tyrant, hopes to establish his right of succession through the rape.[16] Lucretia's rape is a patriarchal repetition; just as Rhea's rape gave birth to a line of monarchs, Sextus, through his rape of Lucretia, is seeking to maintain that lineage. He is reenacting a founding claim to authority.

Under tyranny, both political and patriarchal powers are collapsed. Patriarchal power, the ability to guarantee the certainty of paternity, is in part what authorizes political power. In accordance with the traditional definition of patriarchy, power is located in fatherhood:

> Classical patriarchal argument was that sons were born into subjection to their fathers and therefore into political subjection. Political right was natural and not conventional, no consent or contract was involved and political power was paternal, having its origin in the procreative power of the father.[17]

The reign of the Tarquins itself begins with a confounding of patriarchal rights, thus highlighting early in Livy's narrative the dangers of fusing patriarchal and political power. The first Tarquin, Lucomo, is the sole inheritor of his father's property as a result of the premature death of his eldest brother, Arruns. However, what Lucomo's father did not realize when he bequeathed his patriarchal privileges was that Arruns's wife was pregnant at the time of his son's death. From the beginning, then, the Tarquins are usurpers. The legitimate heir, Egerius ("the needy one"), grows up to become the father of Collatinus, Lucretia's husband. Thus, Sextus's rape of Lucretia is designed in part to prevent the legitimate succession of the Collatine line, a lineage thwarted from the onset by the tyrannical Tarquin reign.

Lucretia's husband, then, is both literally and metaphorically the son in subjection to Tarquin's paternal and political power. Tarquin rapes Lucretia not only for her beauty but for her chastity. To violate Lucretia is in effect to violate her father and husband, to exert power over them, to demonstrate forcibly that they cannot control their women, cannot guarantee paternity, and therefore cannot assume political authority or power. The founding of the republic that Lucretia's rape ignites, however, is meant to change all that. The founding is the opportunity for the sons, the future republican citizens, to assume political authority without fathers and without guaranteed paternity. Lucretia's suicide ensures that she does not give birth to another line of tyrants. Rather, in the republic the sons will give birth to themselves. As a result of Lucretia's suicide, Collatinus is one of the early (although eventually expelled) republican leaders. Republican men understand cogently the danger of political power organized patriarchically and thus change the economy in which political power circulates. They will not rely on guaranteed paternity to secure political power. Rather, in the republic, they will become their own fathers.

In the story immediately preceding Lucretia's, two of Tarquin's sons, Titus and Arruns, along with Brutus, are sent by the king to consult the oracle at Delphi. After finishing the king's business at the oracle, the sons pose the question of who will succeed their father to the throne. The oracle's cryptic answer is, "He who shall be the first to kiss his mother shall hold in Rome supreme authority" (Section 1.57). Titus and Arruns decide to keep the prophecy secret and draw lots to determine which of them would, on their return, kiss their mother. Brutus, however, feigning clumsiness, falls to the ground and "his lips touched the Earth—the mother of all things" (Section 1.57).

This story is a potent illustration of the loss of paternal power in the transition to the republic. The tyrant father will not be able to bequeath his power to his legitimate sons. Rather, the transmission of patriarchal and political power is disrupted by the illegitimate son's deceptive kiss of the mother Earth. Brutus, through his kiss, conceives the republic without the father.

This story of Brutus and the foreshadowed founding is at some level the sanitized, desexualized mirror image of the sexually violent, ultimately fatal story of Lucretia's rape. This doubling of the story begins to expose the significance of the rape of a woman for the founding of the republic. The juxtaposition highlights, for example, both the insignificance of particular women, i.e., the Tarquins' mother and Lucretia herself, while simultaneously heralding the pervasiveness of "feminine power" through the symbol of the mother Earth and the desire to avenge Lucretia's lost innocence. Here symbols and metaphors are more real than bodies. The oracle's answer to the Tarquins' question desexualizes women; the kiss is not for a flesh-and-blood woman but rather for her symbolic replacement, the Earth. Nonetheless, the kiss is fruitful (i.e., giving birth to the republic), thus maintaining images of maternity and motherhood. The "dangerous" elements of woman's autonomous sexuality (her potential reproductive promiscuity and resistant independent subjectivity) are tamed while her generative potential is released. Brutus, through his kiss, conceives the Republic—the perfect emblem and fantasy of male solo procreation. Brutus has become both his own mother and his own father—the guarantee of paternity is self-generated.

This preface to the Lucretia story makes explicit the relation between the founding of the republic and metaphors of birth and motherhood. The story demonstrates the productive power of the male—his kiss initiates the republic. In a male assumption of the powers of the woman/mother, autonomous female sexuality and transgression under tyranny have been displaced. The reproductive powers of women are appropriated in this republican political birthing.

The transition to republicanism is an implicit challenge to patriarchal rule, traditionally conceived. The sons rebel and seize political rights, which they then share equally among themselves. All men, not just fathers, can now generate political life and political right. "Political creativity belongs not to paternity but to masculinity."[18] The bond among men is fraternal rather than paternal. Power is lateral, not hierarchical. And with the loss of paternal authority, masculinity assumes increased significance. Being a man, not a father, authorizes political right. How that masculinity/manhood is defined and maintained, however, will rest in part on the movement and exchange of Lucretia's body.

And this is the critical aspect of the story that Brutus's solo creation neglects—the very material role Lucretia's body plays in the founding. Although the fantasy is of solo procreation, it is a real woman—not the metaphorical Earth Mother—who is pivotal to the narrative. In multiple ways, Lucretia's body controls the narrative unfolding; in fact, her body generates the narrative. As Mieke Bal argues in another context regarding the Book of Judges, "The story is not told; it is done."[19] In other words, through the rape and suicide of Lucretia the founding of the republic is enacted. Once Lucretia becomes the answer to the brag of which man's wife is the most virtuous, "the only communicative function left open to her, as object, is to become speech, in body language."[20] This she does by literally taking in the seed of the tyrant Tarquin and then expunging it through her suicide. Her body contains the tyranny, both literally and metaphorically. Whereas for a man, his words have effect, for a woman, only her body does.

Further, Lucretia must die, literally forfeiting her body, in Livy's version, in order to testify to her innocence, her explicit motivation for committing suicide: "Never shall Lucretia provide a precedent for unchaste women to escape what they deserve" (Section 1.59). Apparently, in this economy, Lucretia's alive body cannot speak; her dead body, however, speaks volumes. Indeed, as Elisabeth Bronfen notes, "knowledge gained through a dead female body is ultimately analytic."[21] That is, knowledge achieved from a female corpse is contained and self-referential. Derived from a single point of view, it is not fecund, full of the ambivalence of the speaking female body. This is knowledge for and about the male gaze—his masculinity and his survival: "Over the dead woman's corpse, his status as subject will have been secured."[22] Thus, although female reproductive powers are displaced in the republican birthing, the female body, as corpse, is still integral to the formation of male identity.

Lucretia must die, then, for two reasons: first, because she is at risk of being pregnant with a monstrosity—the offspring of the tyrant.[23] The lineage of tyrants must be thwarted; the republic requires that the sons give birth to themselves in order to defy paternal power. And, secondly, she must die because her violation marks the failure of masculinity, specifically of her male kin to protect her. She reveals their failure to be men. With her death, Lucretia becomes the female pharmakon; she is the source both of disruption and of the return to order. Simultaneously the sign of what ails the community and its remedy, Lucretia is a paradoxical figure. Her rape both ensures the bond among the republican brothers and highlights the fragility of that bond. On the one hand, her rape codifies the bond because it is a reminder of the tyrant's violation of the men's political rights and their lack of political authority. The men band together against the usurpation of their power and rights by the tyrannical father/king. On the other hand, Lucretia's violation is also the talisman of what haunts the fraternal bond—the phantom of a failed masculinity. Her desecration is the vestige of a bravado that could display Lucretia's innocence but not preserve it. It was, after all, her own husband's bragging that precipitated her rape. Consequently, in the republic, notions of masculinity, rather than certainty of paternity, assume heightened political significance. Republics demand that their citizens be *men* within the parameters of a politically defined masculinity.

With the separation of political and patriarchal power in the republic, the public and private spheres are strictly delineated. Issues of paternity are confined to the private sphere and public life becomes the purview of men, the world of Brutus and his solo parthenogenesis. Nonetheless, there remains a tension among republicans about the possibility of a resurrected tyrant; that is, of the return of the father and his patriarchal privileges. Each republican citizen is perceived as potentially reinstating the tyrant. That is, each recalls that the patriarchal father was not only feared but envied.[24] This trepidation is fueled in part by the memory of their own "effeminacy"—a weakness so profound that the *virtù* of a woman was required to restore their manhood. Livy notes these heightened suspicions in the beginning of Book II:

> I cannot help wondering, myself, whether the precautions taken at this time to safeguard liberty even in the smallest details were not excessive: a notable instance concerned one of the consuls, Tarquinius Collatinus, whose sole offense was the fact that his name—Tarquin—was universally detested. (Section 2.1)

Livy argues throughout Book II that the primary threat to the early republic is internal discord, specifically the instability of the men themselves. True patriotism, he insists, takes time: "it is founded upon respect for the family and love of the soil. Premature liberty of this kind [i.e., republican] would have been a disaster. . . ." (Section 2.1). Apparently, men require a particular maturity before they are fit for republican liberty. Only after certain conditions of manhood are achieved are they capable of republicanism; a republic thus, for Livy, represents political adulthood.

This apprehension about the ability of men to be republicans is partially kindled by the homosociality[25] of the republic. Male citizens must rely on each other for the success and health of the state;[26] indeed, in a republic fraternity is more than a noble sentiment, it is a political imperative. Because republics privilege civil rather than blood relations, bonds within republics are fragile; citizens are joined together only by a spirit of fraternity rather than by the force of an ancestral inheritance. Consequently, the maintenance of republican stability depends in part on the crafting and then remembrance of a shared tradition; nonetheless, the authority of this tradition must not itself become ossified or so hegemonic that it thwarts the very political action vital to republics. Thus, republics struggle, always, to achieve a balance between the constitution of citizen identities that are performative and protean, and the cultivation of strong civic bonds forged through the recollection of a common and cooperatively generated tradition.

Republics thus celebrate public life—speech, performance, appearance, and reputation—which are pivotal to both their founding and their maintenance. Perhaps in no other political community is the intersection of speech and politics more integral to that community's political identity than in a republic. Republican actors, for example, understand themselves to be in *conversation* with the tradition of republicanism from which they conceive their origins. Machiavelli captured this moment of being in conversation with one's republican ancestors when at the end of a day of playing cards and chatting with the local merchants, he dons the garb of the ancients and receives their wisdom: "I am not ashamed to speak with them and to ask them the reasons for their actions."[27]

And yet, while speech is essential, republican citizenship is also, as this example illuminates, a visually and theatrically constituted epistemological field; as Machiavelli notes, "I take off the day's clothing, covered with mud and dust, and I put on garments regal and courtly; and reclothed appropriately, I enter the ancient courts of ancient men." Theatricality, too, is fundamental to republican politics.[28] Thus, republican politics is performative; it is dramatic, requiring both actors and spectators without a singular referent or fixed identity. Republican politics is the process of contesting meaning and creating identity in public. Here politics is clearly about the creation of meaning, rather than the search for truth.[29] Indeed, often the performance is more important than the truth itself.

Nonetheless, despite its garrulous and theatrical qualities, republican politics is also traditional; there is always both a nuanced texture and a specific context to republican conversations and their performance. In other words, these performances are not random play, but rather the stylized repetition of specific acts. Interestingly, it is these very repetitions that constitute the republic rather than represent it. This is, as Paul Ricoeur notes, "a quite strange brand of imitation which comprises and constructs the very thing it imitates!"[30] Indeed, the founding bonds of republics are often generated through the repetition of stories for which there are no stable originals.

This relation between the original and the repetition and between the real and representation is a frequent source of contestation in republican politics. For example, the "we" of the republic is constituted and maintained by a process of seeing and being seen by others; it is a process of repetitive re-presentation in the realm of appearances: "the reality of the world is guaranteed by the presence of others, by its appearing to all."[31] Fundamental to republics is this bond that joins each to the other in public fraternity through appearance, speech, and action.

Nonetheless, as important as this realm of appearance before others is to the security of the republic, there is also concurrently a desire to minimize, if not eliminate, dependence upon others. Thus, republican actors contend with the recognition of an identity constituted through representation with and before others, as well as with an anxiety of the contingency that this reliance upon others suggests; it is a struggle perhaps most aptly captured in the republican language of *virtù* and *fortuna*. Further, this struggle with autonomy and dependence, with sameness and difference, with public appearance and subjective essence complicates republican *virtù* as more than masculine heroics.

Thus, part of what it means to be a republican citizen is to perform for others. The "we" of the republic is constituted by the mutual recognition of each by the other. Fraternity is the acknowledgment of strangers as brothers. And this bond is partially safeguarded by seeing and being seen by others. That is, one is constituted as a citizen by the gaze of the other. Each performs for the other and with the knowledge of being seen. This confers three important qualities on republican citizenship: (1) a sociability of citizenship: one is not a citizen unless one acts in public *and* is seen to be acting by others; (2) one's actions are always performed with the knowledge that one is being looked at and therefore adjusted accordingly: the look of the other changes the act itself; and (3) the recognition of the power and responsibility of the spectator/audience, as well as the actors.

Nonetheless, this basis for community seems oddly to threaten the very rudiments of the republic; it is a dependence with shades of the effeminacy the men suffered under tyranny. Now, rather than being dependent upon the father, they are dependent upon one another. Consequently, in Livy's version, Lucretia's body is used to mediate this potential rivalry and fear that plagues the security of the republic. In other words, Lucretia's body defuses the homosocial elements of the republic and testifies to male aggression. Her body is the passive terrain that certifies masculine autonomy. Assuring the citizens that their interdependence is not passive submission to one another, her body signals guaranteed access to and control of women. Lucretia's corpse preserves femininity within the republican economy, although it is a femininity markedly without any of the power (and thus without any threat to the incipient republic's security) women were feared to wield under patriarchal tyranny.

Beginning with Aristotle through Machiavelli and including Rousseau, tyranny is criticized as the form of government under which women have the most power.[32] Repeatedly in political theory, republican women are symbolically depicted as the pinnacle of virtue and domesticity. With no suggestion of promiscuity, they are characterized as chaste mothers and monogamous wives. On the other hand, sexually transgressive women are usually at home in tyrannies, while suicidal virgins and modest wives are the representative emblems of republics. For example, in *The Politics* Aristotle warns that female power is dangerously increased under tyranny. "[Tyrannies] encourage feminine influence in the family in the hope that wives will tell tales of their husbands; and for a similar reason they [tyrants] are indulgent to slaves. Slaves and women are not likely to plot against tyrants: indeed they prosper under them."[33] Livy, too, tells several stories of the diabolical power women wield under tyranny; indeed, he narrates how women are themselves the cause of tyranny.[34] In the five-act tragedy of the reign of the Tarquins, tyrannical women ignite and maintain the despotic monarchy while the virtues of a chaste republican woman destroys the tyranny and spurs the founding of the republic.

In fact, the reign of the Tarquins begins with the maniacal ambition of a woman. Lucomo, who will become the first foreign king of Rome, leaves Tarquinii at the urging of his aristocratic wife, Tanaquil, to seek his fortune in Rome. During their journey she boldly interprets an omen of an eagle taking and then replacing the cap on Lucomo's head as a sign that the crown of Rome would eventually be his. Tanaquil's reading of the prophecy marks not only her ambition but her status as a foreign usurper. In Rome, the reading of auguries was confined to men, and amateurs did not divine without the assistance of a professional seer;[35] that Tanaquil assumes this role is itself an omen of her future trespasses.

Further, when Lucomo dies, it is Tanaquil who decides his successor; she chooses not one of her own sons but Servius, whom she had raised *as if* he were her own. Thus, her tyrannical power violates even the patriarchal right of paternal succession; she usurps political, as well as patriarchal, power when she does not permit her husband's children to succeed him.

Succeeding Tanaquil's dominion, however, is Tullia, who marries one of Lucomo's sons and is herself the daughter of Servius. Her ambition is to restore her husband's patriarchal rights as the former king's son. Thus she sets in motion a plot to assassinate her own father: "it was the woman," Livy notes, "who took the first step along the road to crime" (Section 1.46). Although seemingly restoring patriarchal succession, Tullia obviously violates patriarchal authority by killing her own father. And Livy is quite explicit as to who is Tullia's model: "To Tullia the thought of Tanaquil's success was torture. She was determined to emulate it" (Section 1.46). Part of the danger of tyranny, then, and the women who prosper under it, is that they perpetuate themselves as models for each other. Thus, Livy's republican Lucretia must disrupt the mimetic lure of tyrannical women; she must be simultaneously represented in a way that recalls to women their female *virtù*[36] as well as restores to men the masculinity they have forfeited under tyranny.

By winning the initial "best wife contest" when she is found at her spinning,[37] Lucretia sets the first parameter for female republican *virtù*; an ideal republican woman is sequestered in the domus, renounces the entertaining company of others, and is fulfilled by household work. Later, by thwarting the satisfaction of Sextus's patriarchal ambitions through her suicide, Lucretia repudiates the power offered women under tyranny.[38] Disrupting the collapse of patriarchal and political power, Lucretia's suicidal renunciation inaugurates a fundamental aspect of the republic—the autonomy of political power.

Her gesture also reflects a new economy in which women and their bodies will be replaced by *representations* of women and their bodies. This is one of the ways in which republics seek to contain the disruption of feminine power. Confined to the private sphere, republican women achieve more political potency as representations than as reality. The display of Lucretia's body after her suicide motivates the Roman citizenry against the despotic monarch and models the future for Livy's republican women. Lucretia's corpse is a representation of meaning elsewhere, signaling women's role in the future republic as silent signifiers who are the carriers of culture and cultural value but are not participants or makers of it.

In Livy's history, female republican *virtù*, unlike male *virtù*, requires that women become the compliant template for the projection of male representations. What women symbolize is more important than what they are; their seeming replaces their being. Lucretia kills herself so that she will be perceived as innocent. It is not sufficient that she *is* innocent. Lucretia's *virtù* is performative, not a manifestation of what she is, not a giving of her form to matter; rather, her *virtù* is a demonstration for others. Her suicide is a performance for a particular audience. Lucretia understands how her sexual violation will be understood and consequently orchestrates her death in order to try to ensure that her violation will be read the way she wants.[39] She does not kill herself because she believes herself guilty, as Augustine will argue centuries later, but because her reputation is more important than her self-knowledge. She cares not only that she is innocent but that she is *perceived* as innocent; in this way, she exemplifies Livy's conception of female *virtù*. As a republican woman, what she makes is less significant than what is made of her. In Livy's republic, women are the real who must become representations.

In Livy's republic, the rape and suicide of Lucretia celebrates female *virtù* that is not a threat to masculinity but is rather the very possibility for the achievement of male *virtù*. Femininity is reduced to a representation, a mirror for men and their relations with each other. Lucretia's corpse is a mirror into which men gaze and see themselves. Reflecting only the images men impose upon it, the female corpse at the founding, at the origin of history, serves as a source for unity among men. Forbidding dialogue with the Other, it is the source for stability, the only term that literally stays still at the otherwise chaotic founding. Consequently, a mirror (a female corpse) that reduces femininity to a reflection of sameness is the source of authority at the founding.

It is noteworthy that traditionally in fifth-century Rome nothing was said about women at their burial. Indeed, having praise given at a woman's funeral was a privilege, as Livy notes, that women were not accorded until 386 B.C.E., and even then it was granted only to a limited number of women:

> When it was found that there was not enough gold in the treasury to pay the Gauls the agreed sum [for the temple of Jupiter], contribution from the women had been accepted, to avoid touching what was consecrated. The women who had contributed were formally thanked and were further granted the privilege, hitherto confined to men, of having laudatory orations pronounced at their funerals. (Section 5.51)

At noble Roman male burials, on the other hand, the man's body was carried by members of the nobility into the forum where amid mourners wearing the clothes and death masks of the deceased ancestors, a son or a close relative pronounced an encomium (*laudatio funerbris*). The eulogy began with the life events of the deceased and included the exploits of the other dead ancestors represented at the gathering. These orations were preserved and eventually became an important source for history.[40]

Lucretia's burial, however, recalls the silence attendant at women's funerals. Although her body is carried into the forum, it is the display of her corpse and not her life deeds that inspires wonder; no words are spoken of her heroic suicide or of her *virtù*. Rather what Brutus cries while Lucretia's body is exhibited is that "it is time for deeds not tears"; Lucretia is barely mourned. In fact, after Lucretia dies, Brutus quickly withdraws the knife from her body and passes it from Collatinus's hands to Lucretius and then to Valerius (Section 1.59). This ritual bonding through the transfer of what Livy describes as the "knife dripping with blood" (*culturum manantem cruore*) begins the restoration of masculinity.

Reduced from real otherness to representational sameness, as well as confined to the private sphere, femininity is then valued only as a commodity signifying relations between and among men. Femininity is no longer an autonomous threat; "femininity [becomes] a role, an image, a value, imposed upon women by male systems of representation."[41] The real is lost in the representation. Or at least that is what the subordination of the feminine to the private sphere is intended to enact. What happens, however, is that femininity continues to overstep this confinement, which must then be repeatedly enacted. And this is another dimension of Lucretia's plight.

Although Lucretia's suicide reduces her to her body and to representational sameness as corpse, her decision to suffer the rape in order to be able to speak her own truth simultaneously defies a pivotal aspect of her prescribed cultural role. She steps outside her cultural role as body when she dares to speak of her violation: "The female herself must never control reproductions whether of cultural systems or of human beings. She must never see, and certainly never speak about, what she learns from her position."[42] That is, the story of Lucretia's rape details, on the one hand, the desire to reduce Lucretia to a nonspeaking, nonsignifying body *and,* on the other hand, Lucretia's simultaneous recognition and deployment of the fact that bodies do indeed speak and thus resist and destabilize unitary interpretations. By retelling her rape, Lucretia has revealed the cultural secret of male impotence; it is a transgression for which she accepts death. When her father and husband try to convince her not to commit suicide, she chides them that they can decide only what shall be done to Sextus, but that she will decide what is appropriate for herself. She defies her role as passive representation. Although she demands revenge, she does not trust her kin's ability to secure it: "He it is who last night came as my enemy disguised as my guest, and took his pleasure of me. That pleasure will be my death—and his, too, *if you are men*" (Section 1.59). That conditional "if" stresses her skepticism and is a challenge for her male kin to fulfill. Yet it is this very challenge that works to inaugurate their republican masculinity.

Lucretia's suicide is generative; her kin manage successfully to avenge her rape *and* to found the republic. In some odd way, Lucretia's suicide has taught them how to be men and republican citizens. Here is an apt illustration, again, of the complementary relation between the *display* of a woman's body and the *effects* of a man's words. With Lucretia's body and Brutus's words, the Romans are incited to action:

> Lucretia's body was carried from the house into the public square. Crowds gathered, as crowds will to gape and wonder—and the sight was unexpected enough and horrible enough to attract them . . . and when Brutus cried out that it was time for deeds not tears, and urged them, like true Romans, to take up arms against the tyrants who had dared to treat them as a vanquished enemy, not a *man* amongst them could resist the call. (Section 1.59)

This is a poignant illustration of the power of the spectacle of Lucretia's suicide. As spectacle, women are mirrors of value for men; the specularity of women's bodies make social and cultural life possible: "In order to serve as such, they [women] give up their bodies to men as the supporting material of specularization, of speculation. They yield up to him their natural and social values as a locus of imprints, marks and mirage for his activity."[43] In other words, women, as spectacle, help to constitute male identity; Lucretia's suicide is the material from which republican citizenship is fashioned. Her female corpse is the means by which a spectacle is constructed, a spectacle that inaugurates a political community founded upon seeing and being seen. It is the spectacle of the female body, both literally and metaphorically, that constitutes the initial political "we."

Of course, Lucretia's suicide can be read as an implicit submission to patriarchy, as her desire to protect her husband's honor as well as her own; she judges herself guilty by the terms of patriarchy, despite her resistance. Yet Lucretia's speech[44] demonstrates, oddly, that she is not completely passive. Although she is ultimately reduced to her body, Lucretia attempts to configure what the display of her body will mean.[45] She chooses to submit to the rape rather than to have her dead body read as guilty of adultery with a slave. She testifies to her innocence in a public space, in part revealing the autonomy of female generative powers as well as her own kin's failed masculinity. Lucretia's revenge is to speak of her violation: "By undoing her own body, she undoes the gender construction which places her in an inferior position. . . . Paradoxically, she can do so only by re-emphasizing the body in an act of disembodiment."[46] In other words, in Livy's founding narrative, female *virtù* is articulated through the very medium that seems most to deny women's agency—female corporeality.

This ambiguity, however, illuminates Livy's complicated conception of *fortuna/fatum*.[47] Although Livy believes that Rome is bound to succeed (i.e., fated by the gods), he also wants to demonstrate that Rome's success is due to the behavior of her citizens. Thus, on the one hand, Livy presupposes Roman fate (*fatum*)—the Stoic conception of determinism with its element of divine control. Yet, on the other hand, Livy wants to highlight the significance of Roman *virtù* and the importance of individual conduct. The elements of free will are necessary for the historian who crafts his history in order to spur the return of contemporary Rome to greatness. Consequently, Lucretia's rape and her deployment of that which has condemned her personifies Livy's conception of *fortuna/fatum*. Lucretia is destined for destruction, a victim of a fate she cannot control and did not choose, but she demonstrates the superiority of her *virtù* and exercises her autonomy within that destiny by attempting to control what her rape and death will signify. Despite the inevitability of Roman greatness (and republicanism) in which Livy believes, he nonetheless affords Lucretia some measure of autonomy in order to remind his readers that individual conduct matters. Even within a prescribed fate there is opportunity for the performance of *virtù*.

Livy's founding story of the rape of Lucretia demonstrates the relation between sexual violence and the inauguration of political order in Livy's rendition of the Roman founding. It is also tellingly a narrative about the constitution of masculinity and femininity; that is, the story is a recognition of the mediation politics and its concurrent formulation of masculinity has with conceptions of femininity.

Of course, this is not to deny that femininity is denigrated and subordinated in Livy's rendition of Lucretia, but rather to highlight that the articulation of the boundary between masculinity and femininity is itself integral to the formation of political life. Masculinity requires the feminine, the banished other, in order to found itself and in order to know and recognize itself. Consequently, the story of Lucretia is more than a tale of a passive woman who forfeits her life under patriarchy. Rather, it is a story designed to ignite political action; Lucretia's violation and suicide spurs a political founding. Lucretia is a cultural authority whose *virtù* stabilizes a chaotic founding by securing male identity and teaching men how to be republican citizens while she is also simultaneously an icongraphic figure whose repetitive return suggests the fragility and contingency of that republican bond and the failure, finally, for republican politics to be only about the masculine. Indeed, the story of Lucretia reveals that the feminine cannot finally be banished but rather that the feminine is a pharmakon; that is, Lucretia both makes the founding possible and remains the surfeit that threatens its stability.

Notes

1. See, for example, Stephanie Jed's *Chaste Thinking: The Rape of Lucretia and the Birth of Humanism* (Bloomington: Indiana University Press, 1989).

2. I want to offer a caution here. Although I am intrigued by the numerous repetitions of the story, I do not want to argue that there is a singular, transhistorical meaning to the story of the rape of Lucretia. Indeed, close examination of the various versions of the story reveals that the differences in the stories as well as the historical, political, and theoretical perspectives of the storytellers are more significant than any simple similarities among the tales. What is perhaps the only unifying claim I will make about the story is that it is repeated by republican theorists.

3. See Paul Rahe, *Republics Ancient and Modern: Classical Republicanism and the American Revolution* (Chapel Hill: University of North Carolina, 1992), and Hannah Arendt, *The Human Condition* (Chicago: University of Chicago Press, 1958).

4. J. G. A. Pocock, *The Machiavellian Moment: Florentine Political Thought and the Atlantic Republican Tradition* (Princeton: Princeton University Press, 1975).

5. It is interesting to note that at the American founding, there is no rendition of the story of the rape of Lucretia. There are at least two possible reasons for this: (1) America was ambivalent, in part, about whether ancient Rome had been an empire or a republic and whether the new republic should/could claim ancestral heritage. For discussion of America's complicated relation to the exemplar of ancient Rome, see both Hannah Arendt, *On Revolution* (New York: Viking, 1963) and Pocock's *The Machiavellian Moment*. (2) The story of the rape of Lucretia was replaced by narratives of the destruction of the Native American population. For a discussion of how both the slaughter of Native American peoples as well as the stories told of their destruction helped to secure the early republic, see Michael Rogin's *Fathers and Children: Andrew Jackson and the Subjugation of the American Indian* (New York: Knopf, 1975).

6. Gayatri Spivak, "Can the Subaltern Speak?" in *Marxism and the Interpretation of Culture*, ed. Cary Nelson and Lawrence Grossberg (Urbana: University of Illinois, 1988), 274.

7. Of course, since it is impossible to consider the significance of the variations in the historical incarnations of Lucretia's story here, this essay focuses on Livy's version while only occasionally gesturing toward the other renditions. Nonetheless, this work is part of a book-length project on the trope of the rape of Lucretia in Livy, Machiavelli, and Rousseau where such historical differences are pivotal to an understanding of each's conception of republican foundings.

8. There is a plethora of feminist work in this area. For a critique of the

public/private split in general, see Jean Bethke Elshtain, *Public Man/Private Woman: Women in Social and Political Thought* (Princeton: Princeton University Press, 1981); for critiques of the split of the public and private spheres in classical literature, see Adrienne Rich, "Conditions for Work: The Common World of Women," in *On Lies, Secrets, and Silence: Selected Prose* (New York: Norton, 1979) and Nancy Hartsock "The Erotic Dimension and the Homeris Ideal," in *Money, Sex and Power: Toward a Feminist Historic Materialism* (New York: Longman, 1983); and for a historical critique of the eighteenth-century banishment of women to the private realm of republican motherhood, see Joan Landes, *Women and the Public Sphere in the Age of the French Revolution* (Ithaca: Cornell University Press, 1988).

9. Luce Irigaray, *This Sex Which Is Not One*, trans. Catherine Porter (Ithaca: Cornell University Press, 1985).

10. Titus Livy, *The Early History of Rome*, trans. Aubrey De Selincourt (New York: Penguin Books, 1978), Section 1.57.

11. Livy notes at the end of this popular story that some believe that the origin of this fable was "the fact that Larentia was a common whore and was called Wolf by the shepherds." He makes no other comments on the story's veracity.

12. Michel Serres, *Rome: The Book of Foundations*, trans. Felicia McCarren (Stanford: Stanford University Press, 1991), 68.

13. N.B. Rhea Silvia was made a vestal virgin by her uncle, Amulius, after he murdered her brothers in order to ensure his right to the throne. Although Amulius claimed that he made Rhea a vestal virgin in order to honor her, it was actually done, as Livy notes, in order to preclude the possibility of her continuing her father's line. (Livy, *Early History of Rome*, 1.3, 37).

14. Gayle Rubin, "The Traffic in Women," in *Toward an Anthropology of Women*, ed. Rayna R. Reiter (New York: Monthly Review Press, 1975) and Carole Pateman, *The Sexual Contract* (Stanford: Stanford University Press, 1988).

15. Pateman, *The Sexual Contract*, 35.

16. Although kingship was not a matter of lineage in Rome at the time Livy was writing his history, Tarquin's rape can be understood as a manifestation of how he claims the authority of kingship belonging to his father. Here it is important to recall that Livy is telling a mythological story with the intent of offering an exemplum for the refounding of the republic. My analysis is reading the story as such, as Livy's *theory* of foundings, not Roman history.

17. Pateman, *The Sexual Contract*, 24.

18. Pateman, *The Sexual Contract*, 36.

19. Mieke Bal, "The Rape of Narrative and the Narrative of Rape: Speech Acts and Body Language in Judges," in *Literature and the Body: Essays on Populations and Persons*, ed. Elaine Scarry (Baltimore: Johns Hopkins University Press, 1988), 27.

20. Bal, "The Rape of Narrative and the Narrative of Rape," 27.

21. Elisabeth Bronfen, *Over Her Dead Body: Death, Femininity and the Aesthetic* (New York: Routledge, 1992), 101.

22. Bronfen, *Over Her Dead Body*, 101.

23. Interestingly, in Greek tragedy a woman's suicide by hanging was associated with marriage—or rather, with an excessive valuation of the status of a bride—while suicide that shed blood, like Lucretia's, was associated with maternity through which a wife, in her heroic pains of childbirth, found complete fulfillment. (Nicole Loraux, *Tragic*

Ways of Killing a Woman, trans. Anthony Forster [Cambridge, MA: Harvard University Press, 1987], 10). This would suggest that Lucretia kills herself not only to protect her husband's honor (because she is now violated chattel) but also because of the threat of pregnancy.

24. See Sigmund Freud, *Totem and Taboo,* trans. James Strachey (New York: Norton, 1950), for a further discussion of this identification and denunciation of the patriarchal father.

25. I use the term "homosociality" here rather than "homosexuality" because the fear is not of sexuality between men but of passivity and dependence among them. In the Roman republic homosexuality was neither illegal nor socially scorned. What was derided, however, was male passivity in sexual relationships. Sexual passivity was associated with political impotence in both republican and imperial Rome. See John Boswell, *Christianity, Social Tolerance and Homosexuality* (Chicago: University of Chicago Press, 1980).

26. Rahe, *Republics Ancient and Modern*, ch. 4.

27. "To Francesco Vettori," in *Letters of Machiavelli*, ed. and trans. Allan Gilbert (Chicago: University of Chicago Press, 1961) 142.

28. Indeed, scholars originally believed that Livy's rendition of the story of the rape of Lucretia had been a tragic play, so much did the five-part drama resemble theater. See Robert Oglivie, *A Commentary on Livy: Books 1-5* (Oxford: Clarendon Press, 1965).

29. Norman Jacobson, *Pride and Solace: The Functions and Limits of Political Theory* (New York: Methuen, 1978).

30. Paul Ricoeur, *Freud and Philosophy*, trans. Denis Savage (New Haven: Yale University Press, 1970).

31. Arendt, *The Human Condition*, 199.

32. These stories, of course, are not meant to detail whether historically women held more political power under tyranny. Rather, these are allegorical accounts of the dangers of tyranny; they are meant as cautionary tales to address male anxiety about the potency of feminine power if unrestrained.

33. Aristotle, *The Politics*, trans. Ernest Barker (Oxford: Oxford University Press, 1958), 245. Machiavelli echoes this concern in *The Discourses* when he mentions women as one of the first causes of the ruin of tyrants.

34. It is noteworthy that there are two Latin words for "female," *femina* and *mulier*, just as there are two words for "man," *vir* and *homo*. *Femina* and *vir* were used to signify the upper classes, while *mulier* and *homo* applied to everyone else. Since aristocratic life centered upon loyalty and service to the Republic, *femina* and *vir* became identified with its virtues, especially patriotism, frugality, generosity, and defense of the Senate and the conservative state religion. Conversely, *mulier* and *homo*, because of their use to indicate members of the lower order, came to connote foreign vices, avarice, luxury, association with the mob, and conspiracy. Thus, the women of the Tarquin reign are referred to throughout Livy's history as *mulier* while Lucretia is referred to only as *femina*. (Francesce Santoro L'Hoir, *The Rhetoric of Gender Terms: 'Man', 'Woman' and the Portrayal of Character in Latin Prose* [Leiden: E. J. Brill, 1992]).

35. Ogilvie, *A Commentary on Livy: Books 1-5*, 144.

36. Although *virtù* is usually applied only to men (the word being etymologically derived from *vir*), I am deliberating cultivating a conception of female *virtù* in order to suggest that the qualities and virtues of Lucretia are political; that is, her virtues are

necessary for the fulfillment of the political sphere. They are not merely "domestic virtues" for the preservation of the family. See also L'Hoir, *The Rhetoric of Gender Terms*.

37. So much was spinning considered a symbol of female republican virtue that Augustus actively encouraged his wives and daughters to learn to spin, presumably in order to cast a more "republican" aura on his reign.

38. This is made in explicit in Dionysius of Halicarnassus's version, in which Sextus tries to seduce Lucretia with promises of power, "For," he said, "if you will consent to gratify me, I will make you my wife and with me you shall reign, for the present, over the city my father had given me, and, after his death, over the Romans, the Latins, the Tyrrhenians, and all the other nations he rules; for I know that I shall succeed to my father's kingdom, as is right, since I am his eldest son." Dionysius of Halicarnassus, *The Roman Antiquities*, trans. Earnest Cary (Cambridge, MA: Harvard University Press, 1961), 2:475.

39. Gayatri Spivak notes the profound irony of women's attempts to locate their free will in suicide: "this text (i.e. story of self immolation) articulates the difficult task of rewriting its own conditions of impossibility as the conditions of its possibility" (Spivak, "Can the Subaltern Speak?" 285). In other words, Lucretia's suicide reinscribes her subordination while simultaneously seeking to displace it.

40. Andrew Lintott, "Roman Historians," in *The Roman World*, ed. John Boardman, Jasper Griffin, and Oswyn Murray (Oxford: Oxford University Press, 1986), 227.

41. Irigaray, *This Sex Which Is Not One*, 84.

42. Patricia Joplin, "Ritual Work on Human Flesh: Livy's Lucretia and the Rape of the Body Politic," *Helios* 17 (Spring 1990), 58.

43. Irigaray, *This Sex Which Is Not One*, 177.

44. It is noteworthy that only in Livy's version of the Lucretia story is there a record of Lucretia's words. For example, in Ovid's rendition the narrator only implies the rape, which Lucretia is reportedly too modest to recount.

45. For a contemporary account of the paradoxes of the colonial woman's ability to narrate and orchestrate her own life and death, see Gayatri Spivak's "Can the Subaltern Speak?" Consider also in this regard recent rape cases. Recall, for example, the rape trials (1992) involving the New York Central Park jogger and the St. John's University student. The nearly dead jogger, who was so badly beaten that she could not testify on her own behalf, was a better witness to her rape than the St. John's student, who, while not beaten and therefore able to give her own account of her experience, was unable to convince the court of her violation. The respective juries decided that the Central Park jogger was raped and that the St. John's University student was not.

46. Bronfen, *Over Her Dead Body*, 143.

47. Often the words *fatum* and *fortuna* are collapsed in Livy's extant work. See D. S. Levene, *Religion in Livy* (Leiden: E. J. Brill, 1993) for a full discussion of the history of Livy's use of these concepts.

Chapter 6

Plutarch on Philosophic *Eros* and Married Life

Matthew B. Crawford

> Women are ordinarily not capable of responding to this communion and fellowship, the nurse of this sacred bond; neither does their soul appear firm enough to support the strain of so hard and durable a knot. And truly, if that were not so, if such a free and voluntary familiarity could be established, where not only the souls might have their complete enjoyment, but the bodies also shared in the alliance, in which the entire man was engaged, it is certain that the friendship would be the fuller and more perfect. But the sex has never yet, by any example, been able to attain to it, and, by common agreement of the ancient schools, is shut out from it.
>
> — Montaigne, "On Friendship"

Montaigne holds out the possibility of a full-fledged friendship between men and women that would engage both the body and the soul, only to dismiss it on the authority of the ancients.[1] Yet the "common agreement of the ancient schools" Montaigne refers to is not quite complete. Though he was one of modernity's most devoted students of Plutarch, Montaigne seems to have overlooked Plutarch's work *Dialogue on Love* (*Moralia* 748e-771e). We find there an articulation of marriage as a species of body-and-soul friendship, one particularly well suited to the philosophic enterprise. Our approach to this work requires a fairly long propaedeutic, for Plutarch contends with a tradition, the "common agreement" Montaigne refers to, that associates philosophy only with friendship (and love) between males. Plutarch's revaluation of marriage as fertile ground for philosophic friendship is in large part a response to the pederastic tradition's long-standing polemic against marriage.

Introduction

In surveying the accounts ancient pederasts gave of their own activity we find conventionalized arguments for pederasty as a practice redounding to the good of the city, a linchpin of Greek republicanism. The tyrannicides Harmodius and Aristogeiton are central figures in this apologetic trope.[2]

Plutarch writes in a time when republican political life has been extinguished in the Greek world. The defense of pederasty as an incubator of republican virtue and spiritedness now falls somewhat flat. But there remains the association of pederasty with philosophy. This is surely not *only* a residual argument by which pederasts could put a highbrow interpretation on their desires. They were heirs to a tradition of reflection that had its serious origins in the Platonic corpus. Plutarch, well steeped in this corpus and familiar with its epigoni, takes up arguments for the philosophic character of pederasty, and the pederastic character of philosophy, and pushes them in various directions. He also introduces novel arguments for the possibility of incorporating philosophic *eros* into married life. Most broadly, he considers the relationship between philosophic *eros* and sexuality in the ordinary sense.

In the Platonic portrayal of Socrates we are given to understand that philosophy is a way of life centered on friendship, and that it is the most erotic way of life. Allan Bloom writes that while Rousseau is the most erotic of modern philosophers, Socrates is "the most erotic of philosophers, period." In general, the philosopher "longs for knowledge. If the need to know is what is most characteristically human, then such philosophical Eros would be the privileged form of Eros."[3] Thus, "Socrates' knowledge of ignorance is identical with his perfect knowledge of erotics."[4]

The Platonic conception of philosophy is erotic not only as presented in speech by his Socrates (longing for the Forms in the *Phaedrus*, climbing the ladder in the *Symposium*), but also as presented in deed by Plato; he shows Socrates in intimate conversation. Philosophy as apprehension of the Forms has its more human reflection in philosophy as dialectic; Socrates spends his life in conversation with human beings. Good-looking ones, often. Yet in Socrates' relations, with Alcibiades in particular, we see that it is a life from which the *aphrodisia* must be excluded; sexual consummation is incompatible with philosophic ascent. Philosophy is an erotic friendship in the first place because dialectical partners share a mutual *eros* for an elusive third thing, wisdom, outside the philosophic couple. To sleep with one another would then not be a consummation of that *eros*, but a confusion as to its object. Yet it is a confusion to which human beings are liable; witness Alcibiades' attempt to seduce Socrates.

Socrates married and had at least two children, but Nietzsche seems to get it just right (his malice notwithstanding) when he says that Socrates married ironically.[5] If Socrates feels no *eros* for his wife Xanthippe, then we cannot say that their union was a consummation of anything. If the philosophic *eros* strictly speaking is for Beauty Itself, but the plumage and aviary member needed for the ascent to beauty (*Phaedrus*) grow only in conversation, then it is in his relations with his dialectical partners that we must look for the philosopher's assessment of the proper relation between Eros and Aphrodite. That the exclusion of the *aphrodisia* from the philosophic life, or at least their partition from *eros* and dialectic, is a project rather than merely a lack of desire is indicated perhaps nowhere more clearly than by Socrates' reaction upon catching a glimpse inside Charmides' cloak: "I became inflamed" (ἐφλεγόμην, Plat. *Charm.* 155d).

Yet according to one theogony at least, to so partition Eros from Aphrodite is to dishonor his mother; Eros is born of Aphrodite.[6] There would be nothing novel in accusing Socrates of impiety. More important for our purposes is the question of whether he was really erotic. Xenophon gives us a Socrates who at times appears more Stoic than erotic, more interested in something like *ataraxia* (lack of perturbation) than beauty. "To need nothing is divine; and as the divine is best, what is closest to the divine is closest to the best."[7] Both the Platonic and Xenophonic Socrates present a question we must address to ourselves: how are we to understand our sexuality as students of philosophy? In speaking of philosophic *eros*, are we speaking merely metaphorically? The Greek word *eros*, like our word "love," captures something mysterious enough that it would be difficult to assign it a single literal meaning against which we may call other usages metaphorical. But we do well not to lose sight of its primary meaning of sexual longing.

Many of us, let me presume, are lovers of women (I hope the reader will indulge a male-centered point of view here). As such we are prone to fatherhood and economic (i.e., *oikos*-forming) life. What is the status of philosophy as a way of life for us whose *eros*, it seems, seeks immortality in the pedestrian, all-too-human form of procreation?[8] Here I presume an erotic origin to the impulse toward husbandry without presuming to answer the question of whether, once a man has become a husband and a father, his life may still properly be described as erotic. And in saying lovers of women are *prone to* fatherhood, I fudge the difference between being merely *liable* to become a father (a liability mitigated by modern contraception) and being *inclined* to become a father.

There is surely a tension between love of one's own and love of the good, and the commitments of the household are simply at odds with perfect freedom to pursue the good.[9] A related point is that philosophy as friendship and dialectic requires freedom of association and so, one could argue, bachelorhood. This is perhaps an argument in extremis, or a false dichotomy, but it raises a question: how are we to understand the relationship between our family lives and our philosophic activity? More particularly, how does marriage stand in relation to philosophic friendship? Among the fundamental differences between ancient and modern marriage, one is surely that a man is now more likely to regard his wife as his friend. The possibility of philosophic friendship in marriage thus presents itself. But Allan Bloom, with Montaigne, expresses some doubts about this possibility:

> Montaigne's view would clearly be that the common belief that one's wife should be one's best friend would ... corrupt both friendship and marriage. It would arouse unfulfillable expectations of what men and women would get from marriage, and it would set up arrangements that would make it impossible, and even immoral, to have a friend. It comes down to the choice of whom one would prefer to spend one's time with, and this choice must be made if one is to have friends. For Montaigne, it is clear that his wife has to accept that he prefers being with his friend to being with her, which would be almost impossible in our times.... In order for there to be friendship, there needs to be a rare leisure, and in addition, the institution of marriage has to have a limited status unlike our imperial version of marriage and the family. Montaigne would think that modern marriage demands the union of things that are almost impossible to unite, and therefore would fall of its own weight, except in the rarest of instances, where the gifts of husband and wife are high

and equal. It is simply intolerable for us to say that our friend is preferred to our spouse, both from the point of view of pleasure and that of virtue.[10]

On this view the modern conception and practice of marriage presents an even stronger case for the philosopher to remain a bachelor than ancient marriage did; the sham friendship of modern marriage comes at the expense of space for true friendship between males.

But in fact the compatibility of marriage and philosophy was a question of some currency in ancient thought as well, as reflected in the *peri gamou* literature and its antecedents. The authors of this literature, however, never conceived the question of philosophy's compatibility with marriage as turning on the prospects for *eros* and friendship within marriage. They were concerned rather with the tranquillity and leisure necessary for a theoretical life (is a wife a burden or a helper?) and the duty of a philosopher toward society.[11] Plutarch's innovation is to respond directly to the pederastic critique of marriage as unerotic and of women as incapable of friendship, and to make the compatibility of marriage and philosophy turn on this. He attempts to harmonize the Platonic conception of philosophy as dialectical friendship with the life of a householder, by reconceiving marriage as *itself* a variety of erotic friendship, rather than merely an economic partnership or procreative alliance that may or may not supply the *prerequisites* (leisure, tranquillity) to philosophy. The potential appeal of Plutarch's *Dialogue on Love* to modern readers is thus clear.[12] Our task is to determine whether in attempting this harmonization he is merely confused.

To provide some context for Plutarch's treatment of these themes, we first consider a non-Plutarchan argument for the affinity between philosophy and love of males.

Nature, Woman, and the Artifice of *Eros*

If the desire of one sex for the other is implanted in us by nature, and if natural compulsions are indeed compulsory, characterized by necessity or unfreedom, then perhaps an "unnatural" love that is free of compulsion and necessity better exemplifies the human capacity to reach beyond the merely given. Heterosexuality would then be more natural, homosexuality more akin to art, or artifice. Heterosexual unions must be given credit for preserving the species (one among many animal species), but homosexuality, on this view, gives better expression to what is distinctly human and is more distinctly erotic.

Philosophy has an ambiguous relationship to both nature and art. The philosophic impulse has its origin in the discovery of the variety of human opinions; it seeks to discover the natural and immutable as opposed to the conventional and various. But the philosophic pursuit of nature does not quite come naturally. Rather, it arises only under certain historical circumstances. Insofar as it is a self-conscious human project against what comes naturally, against the close horizon and comforting atmosphere of the familiar, it is akin to artifice. Because it seeks nature and, as Heraclitus says, "Nature loves to hide herself,"[13] it is erotic. Insofar as Nature, when she does allow herself to be uncovered, makes only ambiguous prescriptions for human beings, philosophy may be enlisted in the pursuit of liberation and experimentation.

The clearest statement along these lines is perhaps that of a character named Callicratidas in the dialogue *Amores* attributed to Lucian. I here reproduce the elegant translation of M. D. MacLeod:

> For marriage is a remedy invented to ensure man's necessary perpetuity, but only love for males is a noble duty enjoined by a philosophic spirit. Anything cultivated for aesthetic reasons in the midst of abundance is accompanied with greater honor than things which require for their existence immediate need, and beauty is in every way superior to necessity. Thus, as long as human life remained unsophisticated and the daily struggle for existence left it no leisure for improving itself, men were content to limit themselves to bare necessities, and the urgency of their day did not permit them to discover the proper way to live. But, once pressing needs were at an end and the thoughts of each succeeding generation had been released from the shackles of necessity so that they had leisure ever to devise higher things, from that time the arts gradually began to develop....
>
> Let no one expect love of males in early times. For intercourse with women was necessary so that our race might not utterly perish for lack of seed. But the manifold branches of wisdom and men's desire for this virtue that loves beauty were only with difficulty to be brought to light by time which leaves nothing unexplored, so that divine philosophy and with it love of boys might come to maturity. Do not then, Charicles, again censure this discovery as worthless because it wasn't made earlier, nor, because intercourse with women can be credited with greater antiquity than love of boys, must you think love of boys inferior. No, we must consider the pursuits that are old to be necessary, but assess as superior the later additions invented by human life when it had leisure for thought (33, 35).[14]

Further, Callicratidas goes on, the reason brutes have no desire for males is that they have not been provided with reason; "lions neither love nor philosophize." Human intention (*phronesis*) combined with exact knowledge (*episteme*) has, through experimentation, arrived at love of males as the finest and most stable (36).

Underwriting this anthropological, evolutionary account of Callicratidas there is a cosmogony: first there was only chaos, then Eros came into being. Eros "formed everything out of mute and piled-up formlessness," banishing chaos and bringing about likeness-of-mind, friendship, and goodwill (32). Callicratidas follows the Hesiodic account in positing Chaos first (*Th.* 116), and Eros prior to Aphrodite (*Th.* 201; cf. Phaedrus' speech at Pl. *Symp.* 178b).

We may contrast this cosmogony with that of Callicratidas's interlocutor Charicles, who loves women. According to him, Aphrodite is the first mother and cause of all things: the earth, the elements, living beings, etc. As a divine mechanic, she contrived the two sexes and their complementarity by which the species is preserved, with beings replacing one another. She instilled the mutual yearning for one another in the male and the female and ordained as a necessity that each retain its unique nature (*Amores* 19). Aphrodite is then prior to Eros;

Charicles is more in conformity with the tradition according to which Eros was born of Aphrodite (see note 6 above).

What is at stake in these competing cosmogonies? Like the biblical account, Charicles' story posits a divine providential intelligence that contrives the heterosexual order and lays a law upon human beings. For Callicratidas, on the other hand, the First Principle is not a law-giving mechanic, but chaos. Human life becomes possible only by the overcoming of chaos through *eros*. Further, human beings make laws for themselves, in political community. The impulse that drives them toward law drives them also toward love of males; both are discovered to be best through human intelligence. If Prometheus had given intelligence to other animals, Callicratidas says, they would not live in isolation but engage in political life under shared laws.[15] Presumably they would also discover male homosexuality.

Plutarch's *Dialogue on Love*

We turn finally to Plutarch's *Dialogue on Love* or *Erotikos*[16] (traditional Latin title, *Amatorius*). It is in the form of a dialogue narrated by Plutarch's son Autobulos to one Flavian and some others who are unnamed. Plutarch himself, author of the dialogue and father of its narrator, appears as a character in the dialogue; Autobulos is telling the story of what his father said and did before he was born. A third generation is represented too, as Plutarch the dramatic character recounts an anecdote in the life of his own father. The dramatic date of the speeches recounted by Autobulos is shortly after Plutarch's wedding. He has come with his new wife to the festival of Eros at Thespiae, to sacrifice to the god. The pilgrimage seems to have been inspired by the need to escape some dispute (διαφορᾶς καὶ στάσεως) between the newlyweds' parents (749b). Plutarch has also brought along some of his usual companions (συνήθεις, 749b). There is trouble in the city of Thespiae as well, however: a struggle has erupted among the festival's cithara players. To escape the fuss, Plutarch and his company decamp to Mount Helicon above the city and ensconce themselves in the shrine of the Muses. But a further controversy has sought them out. It seems a local widow, wealthy and beautiful, has fallen for a good-looking local youth and wants to marry him. The youth's older cousin counsels him to accept the match as an advantageous one, but his lover (*erastes*) is against it. The youth, unsure what to do, has left the decision to these two. They appeal to Plutarch and his company to serve as arbiters of the dispute, and each finds an ally there. The dialogue thus becomes a debate between advocates of pederasty and advocates of married love. The newly wed Plutarch himself makes a spirited contribution and attempts something like a synthesis of the two forms of love. This is but a sketch of the dramatic setting, which is rich with telling detail. Space does not allow me to undertake here a reading of this complex dialogue as a dramatic and literary whole, so my treatment is thematic and somewhat neglectful of the action that accompanies the argument. Because the work does not reside on the shelf of every classicist, much less every political theorist, I have undertaken to here translate substantial portions of Plutarch's text.[17]

Plutarch's character Protogenes[18] speaks for the same old-school pederastic tradition as Callicratidas:

> Since [marriage is] necessary for procreation, the law-givers, not indifferently, render it august and praise it greatly to the many. But nothing whatever of the true Eros is to be found among the women's quarters, and I deny that when you have felt affection for (προσπεπονθότας) women or girls, you *love* (ἐρᾶν), just as flies don't love milk and bees don't love honey and caterers and butchers don't feel friendship for the calves and birds they fatten in the dark. (*Am.* 750c)

According to Protogenes, natural compulsions such as bees feel for honey or men feel for women are not to be confused with genuine love.[19] In Protogenes' last analogy, the butcher fattening a calf in the dark seems to stand for a husband who keeps his wife locked up in the house, or even within the inner apartment, the women's quarters (γυναικωνίτιδι) of the house. No one could feel friendship (φιλοφρονοῦσι) for such a creature, and the potential for friendship seems to be an integral part of true love. Why is friendship impossible between husband and wife? Protogenes' argument requires some assistance, particularly for modern readers who do not share certain basic presuppositions that Plutarch might have presumed in his readers.

The city faces a constant, pressing need to produce citizen-soldiers. Presumably it is with an eye toward this necessity that lawgivers praise marriage to the many, not indifferently (οὐ φαύλως), as Protogenes says. But why marriage in particular? Won't any haphazard procreation suffice? The city, it seems, can reproduce itself only through the production of *legitimate* offspring, recognized as such by their fathers; children's participation in their paternal ancestor cult vouchsafes their obeisance to the gods of the city as well.[20] Further, every political community must prevent the confounding of descent lines, which may lead to disputes over property.

There is, then, a coherence to Protogenes' critique of marriage as a locus of *eros* if we but add a few of the missing links: the natural necessity of procreation coupled with the political necessity of legitimacy means that, given women's putative tendency toward licentiousness (which he elsewhere greatly expands upon), wives must be sequestered. This in turn means that there can be no friendship between husband and wife, not least because the domestic sphere offers such limited scope for the development of virtue, the potential for which is the basis for true friendship. Absent friendship there can be no *eros*, but only appetite or desire, Protogenes explains:

> The need for pleasure from one another is in women and men by nature, but they are incorrect to call the impulse that sets them on to this (τὴν δ' ἐπὶ τοῦτο κινοῦσαν ὁρμὴν), once it has become great and hard to restrain through vehemence and might, Eros. For Eros in fact it is who, by attaching himself to a well-natured young soul, initiates it (τελευτᾷ) into virtue through friendship. The net result of these desires for women, on the

other hand, is in the best cases only the harvesting of pleasure and enjoyment of a ripe body.... For the *telos* of desire is pleasure and enjoyment, whereas Eros, if he has lost the hope of friendship, refuses to hang around and cultivate toward fruition a sorry plant that has already reached its peak, if it can't yield the proper fruit of character directed toward friendship and virtue. (750d-e)

[T]he one legitimate Eros is of boys; ... you will see it unadorned and robust in schools of philosophy or, I suppose, around the gymnasia and wrestling schools, engaged in the eager pursuit of young men; with a great, piercing and noble cry [like the true mountain eagle] it cheers on to excellence those who are worthy of devoting attention to.

On the other hand is that [Eros, which is like a slow-flying, marsh-dwelling bird; it is] slack and a stay-at-home, spending its time in the (bosoms/folds/pockets/wombs [κόλποις]) of women, and in their little beds, always attaching itself to soft things; it is enervated amid pleasures that are devoid of manliness and friendship and inspiration... (751a-b).

Protogenes is answered by Daphnaeus,[21] who advances a complex of interwoven arguments against him. First he quotes some verses of Solon and Aeschylus that he takes to be examples of pederastic lechery, by way of debunking Protogenes' pretentious abhorrence of pleasure and intercourse. These supposedly august authors encourage lovers to view boys' bodies as priests view the hams and haunches they prepare for sacrifice (751c).

Daphnaeus goes on: If intercourse with males contrary to nature (ἡ παρὰ φύσιν ὁμιλία πρὸς ἄρρενας) doesn't destroy erotic goodwill (ἐρωτικὴν εὔνοιαν), how much more likely it is that the love experienced naturally by men and women arrives at friendship through *charis* (751c-d). Daphnaeus explains to Protogenes that the yielding of the female to the male was called *charis* (grace, favor) by the ancients. The yielding of male to male, on the other hand, entails either violence on the part of the active party if the passive one does not consent or cowardice and effeminacy on the part of the passive one if he does allow himself "to be mounted, as Plato says, and inseminated like a quadruped" (751d-e).[22] Plutarch's elaboration of *charis* is the central theoretical pivot on which turns his revaluation of marriage.

Female *charis* is something for which there exists no male counterpart; a woman can give herself graciously in a way that a male "playing the part of a woman" simply cannot. The submission of a male is an *acharis charis* (751e),[23] a gratification received (or given?) without gratitude, or an ill-favored favor, or a graceless gratuity, or a disagreeable agreement, or an unpleasant pleasure. A gratification *given* without gratitude because the pleasure in pederastic intercourse, unlike that between men and women, is not reciprocal.[24] A gratification *received* without gratitude because it can only be given by a youth who indicates, by his submission, that he is not after all what one had hoped; it is a gift that cannot be given without negating the youth's nascent manliness, the very virtue (*arete,* which shares its root with *arrhen*, male) the cultivation of which is supposed to be the focus of the relationship. Attraction to the masculine cannot be consummated without effeminizing the masculine.

But how can a woman give herself without also losing the virtue incumbent on her sex, namely, modesty? Protogenes' ally in attacking marriage, and more generally love of women, is Pisias, who declares that modest women cannot with propriety either love or be loved (752c; cf. 753b). Love of women is base then in part because it can only be of licentious women. We might expect the supreme value placed on female modesty to lead to the notion that a chaste love of women is a dignified form of love (like medieval courtly love), just as the supreme value placed on manliness led to the idea that chaste pederasty (which does not violate the youth's nascent manliness) is a dignified form of love. But the idea of a chaste love of women seems never to have occurred to the Greeks. The whole point of loving women is "the harvesting of pleasure and enjoyment of a ripe body," as Protogenes says, since women are incapable of virtue (750d-e). There is nothing toward which one would want to sublimate such pleasures.

Pisias's seems an oddly idealistic, insufficiently instrumental understanding of female modesty. He doesn't recognize the moment of female *charis*, graceful yielding, which is the delicate private thing shrouded by female modesty. All that modesty is stored social capital, and is pointless unless ultimately spent in the choice of some exclusive mate. Thus, as Herodotus has Gyges say, a wife lays aside her shame (*aidos*) along with her undergarment; Gyges' corollary is that as men we should look only upon what is our own, i.e., not at other men's naked wives (1.8). The pederasts' critique of marriage elides the distinction between public and private[25] and does not allow for the fact that the enveloping safety of the marriage bed relieves a woman of the other-regarding imperative of shame. One definition of *aidos* is "regard for others." But when husband and wife come together there is no other, unless there be some Gyges hiding behind the door. When Protogenes echoes Pisias by saying that anyone would flee and feel disgust at a woman's declaration of love, let alone found a marriage on such licentiousness (753b), Plutarch himself intervenes and says that Protogenes and Pisias are making their *hypothesis* public (*koine*).[26] Though the meaning of this statement is not perfectly transparent, we may conjecture something like the following: in applying the public, outdoor standard of pederastic love to conjugal love, Pisias and Protogenes fail to distinguish the graceful yielding of a wife in private from the come-on of a whore on the street. The pederasts are truly public spirited, in the sense that they explode the private. They are also trying to have it both ways in their polemic against marriage; recall that Protogenes earlier referred to the enervating effects of an indoor woman-love that is private or housebound (οἰκουρόν, 751a).

Yet the foregoing distinction between public and private is complicated by Plutarch's assertion in the *Marriage Precepts* that "Herodotus did not speak correctly [in saying] that a woman lays aside her shame along with her undergarment. On the contrary, a moderate woman puts on shame in its place, and [husband and wife] employ the greatest shame with one another as a token of the greatest friendship" (139c).

This requires some interpretation. Even absent a peeping Gyges, it seems, the erotic friendship of husband and wife requires that they retain a sense of the other as other, i.e., that they have mutual regard. Friendship, and the shame that accompanies it, places a limit on the instrumental use of another for our own pleasure. In heterosexual unions pleasure may be mutual, simultaneous, and even synergic. But pleasures that, on the contrary, are sought without regard to the other person's erotic subjectivity, without seeing oneself partially through her eyes, where one uses her as a mere instrument without regard for her reciprocal pleasure, would seem to place some strain on the bond of friendship. Now one hopes a robust friendship between lovers can accommodate moments of egocentric self-indulgence. Indeed, feeling that one has permission for such indulgence is one of the great luxuries of feeling that one is truly loved, and the permission one's lover grants may be experienced as an affirmation of that love. But Plutarch reminds us that such things can be experienced as affirmations precisely, and only, because they are departures from what must be the foundation: shame, or mutual regard in the sense of seeing oneself through the other's eyes. Liddel and Scott include among their primary definitions of *aidos* "respect for the feeling or opinion of others," and Homer uses the construction ἀλλήλους τ' αἰδεῖσθε to mean "show a sense of regard one for another" (Il. 5.530). For Plutarch, such regard is the token (*symbolos*) of friendship in marriage.

The character of the regard is different in pederastic intercourse, according to Xenophon: "For a youth does not share in the pleasure of the intercourse (τῶν ἐν τοῖς ἀφροδισίοις εὐφροσυνῶν) as a woman does, but looks on, sober, at another in love's intoxication. Consequently, it need not excite any surprise if contempt for the lover is engendered in him" (*Symp.* 8.21-22, trans. Todd, LCL). Due to the lack of reciprocity and hence lack of positive mutual regard, pederastic intercourse is necessarily shameless or instrumental. Hence for the lover to consummate his love of body is incompatible with love of soul (or friendship) in pederasty, but not in heterosexual relations, where the two forms of love may be mutually reinforcing.

Another important concept in the polemic against pederasty, both Daphnaeus's and Plutarch's, is *hubris*. The friendship of a pederastic couple depends crucially on the boy's never submitting to his lover's importunings, because that would constitute either hubris by the *erastes* against the *eromenos* or hubris against himself by the *eromenos*[27] that indicates his unworthiness for friendship. After relating a story of great devotion and heroic courage on the part of a wife who loved her husband, Plutarch says:

> Since many such things have occurred both among us [Greeks] and among barbarians, who could calmly endure it when men rail at Aphrodite, saying that friendship is prevented from coming into being when she joins with and attends Eros? However, concerning male-on-male intercourse (or intemperate assault, rather), one who has given it consideration might say that "these things are the work of hubris, not Cupris."[28] For this reason, classing those who take pleasure in pathicity in the lowest rank of vice, we give them no share of trust or respect or friendship, but as Sophocles says truly, "those who lose such friends rejoice; those who have them pray [for a chance] to flee." [Youths] who are not naturally cowardly, but have been deceived or forced into submitting themselves, continue to mistrust and hate no human being more than those who have so treated them, and take a bitter revenge when the right moment offers. Crateas killed Archelaus[29] after becoming his "beloved," and Pytholaus killed

Alexander of Therae. Periander, tyrant of Ambracia, asked his beloved whether he wasn't yet pregnant. Thus provoked, the boy killed him.[30]

But in the case of wedded wives these [sexual] things are the origin of friendship, a sort of sharing in great and sacred things. The pleasure is short [or small], but the respect and grace and affection for one another and trust that spring up day-by-day from this [sexual union] shows up neither the Delphians as foolish for calling Aphrodite "Harmony" nor Homer for designating this sort of intercourse "friendship." (*AM.* 768d-769a)

So while Protogenes had argued that there can be no *eros* between husband and wife because there can be no friendship, only desire, Plutarch here argues that friendship between husband and wife comes about precisely through their sexual union. The *aphrodisia*, rather than posing a danger to friendship and so to *eros*, as in the case of pederastic relationships, here underwrites the friendship between husband and wife.

A useful point of comparison here is Aristotle's idea of friendship between husband and wife, which he finds to be based on the division of labor necessary in child rearing; friendship is based on an economic partnership between husband and wife, centered on the children as a common good (*Ethics* 1162a16-33). Aristotle does say that "there appears to be pleasure as well as utility in this sort of friendship" (καὶ τὸ χρήσιμον εἶναι δοκεῖ καὶ τὸ ἡδὺ ἐν ταύτῃ τῇ φιλίᾳ, 1162a24-25), but he does not treat sexual union itself (as opposed to the care of its fruit) as the source of friendly feeling and union of hearts and minds. He is thus quite removed from the assertion we find in Plutarch's *Marriage Precepts* that it is "Aphrodite [who] crafts likemindedness and friendship of husbands toward wives, for while commingling their bodies under the influence of pleasure she welds together also their minds/souls" (156d).[31]

We might also juxtapose against Aristotle Plutarch's judgment, also in his *Marriage Precepts*, that marriages founded solely on procreation are deficient, compared to unions based on *eros*:

> The marriage of people in love is an organic union [like the union of elements in a living creature], but the marriage of those who marry for dowry or children is a marriage of elements joined together [like the elements in a house or ship], and the marriage of those who [merely] share a bed is that of separate elements [like a fleet or army], who might be regarded as sharing a house with one another, but not a life (142f).[32]

So simply sharing a bed is not sufficient for a true union, but neither is a marriage that is merely instrumental to procreation. The instrumental theme appears also in the *Dialogue on Love*, where Plutarch mentions two sorts of ill-tempered nonlovers: men who marry for a dowry and men who "stand more in need of children than of wives, just like cicadas"; they quickly inseminate any body they happen to come across, and once it bears its fruit they are glad to quit the marriage, or else, enduring it, they pay it no attention, thinking it worthwhile neither to love nor be loved (767d). To be fair, this criticism has little purchase on the Aristotelian model wherein husband and wife are united by their children; Aristotle in fact distinguishes humans from animals on this basis, that their sexual union is not just for the sake of making children, but also for the sake of providing them the necessities of life (*Ethics* 1162a20-21); unlike a cicada, the human male knows his children, sticks around, and educates them (provided the sexual contract is robust, we might add). Nevertheless, Plutarch's criticism does speak to the unerotic, instrumental character of any marriage founded solely on child rearing.

But is this aphrodisiac friendship of husband and wife capable of supporting the philosophic ascent? Can it be erotic in the Socratic sense? That would seem to depend on a wife's capacity for dialectic. Plutarch himself seems to have been acquainted with a number of highly educated women, to whom he addressed some of his works.[33] In the *Marriage Precepts*, addressed to a newlywed couple, Plutarch recommends to the groom that he seek out the company and instruction of philosophic teachers and, like a bee carrying pollen in its own body, bring the fruits home to share and discuss (μεταδίδου καὶ προσδιαλέγου) with his wife, making the best of the *logoi* he has gathered dear and familiar (φίλους . . . καὶ συνήθεις) to her (145b). Addressing himself to the bride, he recommends a treatise written by his own wife Timoxena (145a). Plutarch seems to have practiced what he preached; his *Consolation to My Wife* upon the death of their daughter, though tender in its opening, rises above sentimentality to the level of abstract principle. Theoretical dialectic seems to have been part of Plutarch's own marriage.

This no doubt reflects a change in the social landscape between Socrates' time and Plutarch's. One could speak of the spread of Roman mores in the Greek world or the generally higher assessment of women's capacities in Hellenistic and Imperial thought and practice, compared to classical thought and practice; wives are now more likely to be regarded by husbands as conversational partners.[34] But the harmony Plutarch posits between philosophy and married life has a different basis from that posited by his contemporaries. Musonius Rufus recommends marriage for the philosopher primarily as a political duty.[35] Though he does say that marriage is the one proper place for Eros and Aphrodite (75), the erotic character of marriage is unconnected to its goodness for the philosopher. For this moralist the philosopher is above all supposed to be good and just, and to serve as an example to others, "for it is quite apparent that to philosophize is nothing other than to seek out in speech the things that are fitting and proper (ἃ πρέπει καὶ ἃ προσήκει), and to practice them in deed" (76, lines 14-16). Musonius's Stoic predecessor Antipater, too, had recommended marriage as a matter of propriety, a duty enjoined by the necessity of perpetuating the fatherland (τὴν τῆς πατρίδος σωτηρίαν).[36] A similar view was expressed in a Pythagorean work contemporaneous with Antipater.[37]

For Musonius and his Stoic predecessors, philosophy is moral (i.e., political), whereas for Plutarch, who appears in the *Dialogue on Love* (though not in every work) to be above all a Platonist, philosophy is private and erotic. For Musonius, marriage is a civic duty and therefore good for the philosopher. For Plutarch, marriage is an erotic friendship ideally suited to the dialectical ascent toward Beauty, and therefore good for the philosopher.

The Platonic conception of philosophy is erotic not only as presented in speech by his Socrates (longing for the forms in the *Phaedrus*, climbing the ladder in the *Symposium*), but also as presented in deed by Plato; he shows Socrates in intimate conversation. We may oppose philosophy as private friendship to philosophy as politics[38] (the Platonic versus the Stoic conceptions), but philosophy as private friendship is nevertheless political, in a different sense. It must be politic in order to protect its privacy.

> The eros of souls for each other, experienced by two human beings who can share insights into the nature of man and of all other things, is much less palpable, and hence less believable, than the eros of bodies. . . .
>
> The rhetorical problem connected with explaining such friendship and making it attractive is thus very great: one has to give popularly accessible reasons for the sinister-appearing relation between two men to an audience that is not likely to grasp what it is that causes this relation. Such friends are suspect, for they seem to withdraw from the universal community of mankind in order to enjoy each other's company more perfectly and perhaps to be engaged in a conspiracy of one kind or another. This is the very problem of the Platonic dialogues, where Socrates seeks to make friends by way of conversation. . . .[39]

This problem of appearances would not obtain for a philosophic couple who also happen to be husband and wife. It's the perfect cover.

Second Thoughts

But are we satisfied that husband and wife can really attain such intimacy? That they can freely share insights into "the nature of man and of all other things?" What about all the usual objections, not really addressed by Plutarch? Even if "the gifts of husband and wife are high and equal" (Bloom, quoted above [5]), what about the screaming baby? The dirty dishes? And in addition to the lack of leisure that attends household management, there would seem to be a deeper problem posed by the potential indecency of free and open inquiry. Will the couple, upon the first menses of their daughter, have a searching conversation about the grounds for the incest prohibition? Will they indulge, even between themselves, the expression of wickedly funny insights into the rule of fathers and the nature of law while cohabiting with in-laws? Entertain the justice of father beating? The family is certainly an incubator of tender sentiments and natural attachments, but on the other hand

> the Greek philosophers argued that the family is only imperfectly natural because it, more than perhaps anything else in human life, requires myths, conventions, and prohibitions to hold it together, all of which stand in the way of the full development of man's powers, particularly the intellectual ones. . . . The family in principle prefers age to wisdom, and surrounds itself with all kinds of sacred terrors.[40]

In addition to the conflict between generations that Bloom here emphasizes, there would seem to be a threat posed more directly to the *couple* by philosophy's interrogation of the *nomoi*. Will husband and wife coolly consider together the merits of communism of women and children? Polyandry? Some manifestations of the love of beauty that a theoretical person (in the literal Greek sense of one prone to gazing) experiences are best shrouded in discretion. One is lucky if love of one's own constitutes a subset of the love of beauty, but even in the best case it is but a small part of the Whole. Isn't this grounds for offense to a spouse?

The exuberance of philosophy is at odds with decency in most human relationships, and seems to be fully at home only in friendship. Elsewhere it must employ a humane irony. Marriage can be made to include a sort of friendship, yet the other (economic, procreative, *nomos*-dependent) dimensions of the relationship would seem to attenuate the freedom of the friendship. And arguably freedom is the essence of friendship, radicalness of philosophy.

Conclusion

I have not come close to explicating Plutarch's last word on marital friendship. I am sure he does not envision the sort of suffocating "imperial" modern marriage lamented by Bloom that leaves little room for any other sort of friendship. I find appealing Plutarch's account of sexual pleasure united with friendship through *charis* and mutual regard. It goes behind the old dichotomy of love of body versus love of soul and points to the peculiar origin of that dichotomy in the predicament of pederasty.

Can Plutarch's brief for friendship and intellectual companionship in marriage be disentangled from his polemic against pederasty, the latter of which has little interest for us? Contemporary homosexuality has relatively little resemblance to ancient pederasty, the most crucial difference being its reciprocity of sexual desire.[41] The resemblance of the pederasty marriage debate in the *Dialogue on Love* to present-day cultural debates is then mostly superficial. One could even imagine contemporary advocates of gay marriage and other nonhubristic forms of mutual homosexuality appropriating Plutarch's analysis of friendship united with sexual pleasure; if gay culture (or the relevant part thereof) has relatively little of the *agon* for honor, or such honor does not attach to masculinity qua the active role, and pleasure can somehow be reciprocal even if not synergic, then perhaps the concept of *charis* can be extended from female to male pathicity. Or perhaps the dichotomy of active/ passive need not obtain at all.

Be that as it may, how is the work to be situated in the concerns of its own time? Plato's Puasanius speaks plausibly of the connection between free politics and robust friendships. One would have to consider, then, the consequences for friendship of Greece's subjugation to Rome in Plutarch's time. The demise of republican polis life must have meant the loss of an important arena for friendships based on speech-making (one thinks of the Athenian *hetaireiai* or political clubs of the classical era, which had also been a site of "laconizing" sexuality, or pederastic initiations). Also, insofar as political affairs are now more remote for the subject Greeks (the site of contention is now in the imperial center), men's access to the phenomena that are the beginning point for political philosophy is made more difficult. And indeed philosophy has arguably been coopted into something like ideology, serving the mission of Hellenistic cosmopolitanism and imperial assimilation (see note 38). Plutarch's expansion on the possibilities inherent in marriage may perhaps be understood as a turning inward, an attempt to theorize some consolation for the loss of genuine political life in the Greek world, and with it the loss of spirited friendship and philosophy. The demise of polis life must have meant that men were spending more time at home. Plutarch offers a humanizing reassessment of what that could offer and a corrective to the misogynistic opinions of his interlocutors: marriage may aspire to a species of intellectual companionship informed by decent mutual regard and enlivened by desire.

Yet such companionship rooted in domestic life seems necessarily to fall short of free philosophic friendship of the most radical or exuberant sort. Marriage cannot satisfy every human need and may even be in tension with the highest human need. Because the objections that lead us to this conclusion, though fairly obvious, are passed over silently by Plutarch, his *Dialogue on Love* might be regarded as a philosophical utopia, like Plato's *Republic*. As such it offers a spurious solution meant to clarify a genuine problem. If the sexual prescriptions of the *Republic* achieve this clarification through their manifestly tyrannical character, the sexual prescriptions of the *Dialogue on Love* are instead notably humane. The overly hopeful or insufficiently attentive among Plutarch's readers, the sort inclined to take up a utopian solution as a guide for living, will then come away with a salutary rather than a tyrannical teaching (salutary for Plutarch's time, that is, and perhaps merely innocuous for our own). Then as now, however, the philosophic alternative is to live not in the light of such solutions but rather in the shadow of the problem.

Notes

1. Montaigne, "On Friendship," in *The Essays of Montaigne*, trans. E. J. Trechmann (New York: Modern Library, 1946), 160.

2. The *locus classicus* for the assertion that pederasty was the "chief defense of equity and freedom," as exemplified by "the salutary loves of Harmodius and Aristogeiton" (Montaigne, "On Friendship," 161) is Pausanius's speech in Plato's *Symposium*. Late in the fourth century, the orator Aeschines refers to appeals to Harmodius and Aristogeiton as a standard defense tactic of pederasts (*Against Timarchus*, 140). Brought before the popular court for one reason or another, pederasts could find their sexual activities made an issue of by democratic-demagogic prosecutors such as Aeschines. Debunking accounts of the role played by the lovers in the liberation of Athens from the Peisistratid tyranny may be found at Thucydides 1.20, 6.54-59; Herodotus 5.55; Aristotle *Ath. Pol.* 19.1; Pausanius *Peri.* 23.1. See also [Ps.-] Plato, *Hipparchus*. For the enduring popularity of this trope, note Athenaeus's (fl. c. 200 C.E.) repetition of many positive references to the tyrannicides, indexed in the Loeb edition.

3. Allan Bloom, *Love and Friendship* (New York: Simon & Schuster, 1993), 431, 2;

cf. 411-4. See also Till Kinzel (Technische Universität Berlin, Institut für Englische & Amerikanische Literaturwissenschaft), "The Eroticism of Philosophy: Allan Bloom and Plato on Liberal Education," unpublished manuscript.

4. Allan Bloom, *The Closing of the American Mind* (New York: Simon & Schuster, 1987), 133.

5. "A married philosopher belongs *in comedy*, that is my proposition—and as for that exception, Socrates—the malicious Socrates, it would seem, married *ironically*, just to demonstrate *this* proposition" (Friedrich Nietzsche, *On the Genealogy of Morals*, trans. Walter Kaufmann and R. J. Hollingdale [New York: Vintage, 1989], Third Essay, sec. 7, 107, emphasis in original). Cf. Xen. *Symp.* 2.10 and Diog. Laer. 2.36-7, where Socrates concedes that his wife Xanthippe is a terrible shrew and says that he married her in order to build his endurance. At Xen. *Mem.* 2.2.7 Socrates chastises his son Lamprocles for also finding Xanthippe insufferable. He does get Lamprocles to admit that, unlike a wild beast, his mother has never tried to bite him.

6. The most popular view in classical and later times had Eros as the child of Aphrodite and Ares. A scholiast on Appollonius of Rhodes attributes this view to Simonides the lyric poet (D.L. Page, ed., *Poetae melici Graeci* [Oxford: The Clarendon Press, 1962], fr. 575, 296), which would make Simonides (c. 500 B.C.E.) its earliest exponent. Still earlier, Sappho (c. 600 B.C.E.) had Eros as the child of Aphrodite and Ouranos (Edgar Lobel and Denys Page, eds., *Poetarum Lesbiorum fragmenta* [Oxford: Clarendon Press, 1955], fr. 198, 105).

7. Xen. *Mem.* 1.6.10; cf. Seneca *de tranq.* 2.3: "est deoque vicinum, non concuti (to be unperturbed is close to [being a?] god."

8. The same question may be addressed to female students of philosophy, though for them pederastic *eros* would not be the alternative against which procreative sexuality is judged. Lesbianism has its own distinct features; I am not aware of any tradition that associates it with philosophic dialectic. Nevertheless, its freedom from child rearing and household management must confer some of the same advantages for theoretical reflection. It is also more akin to friendship, arguably, than heterosexual relations are.

9. Xenophon (*Mem.* 2.2.5-6) has Socrates extol to his son Lamprocles the sacrifices a mother makes for her children and the sacrifices a father is supposed to make, which include supporting his partner in parenting and providing beforehand (i.e., accumulating) as much as possible of what he thinks will be beneficial throughout life for his children. Given Socrates' extreme poverty and his days spent lurking around the gymnasia "whispering in a corner with three or four boys" (as Callicles says, Plat. *Gorg.* 485d), not charging for his conversation because that would compromise his cherished independence in choosing whom he consorts with (Xen. *Mem.* 1.6.5,13), how did Socrates understand the relationship between his philosophy and his fatherhood? Does he think that in his philosophic activity he is accumulating some resource more beneficial for his children than material prosperity? If so, how does he share this resource with his children? We do see Socrates, in the exchange with Lamprocles, practicing his usual sort of dialectic, getting him to recognize that his ingratitude to his mother is a form of injustice (Xen. *Mem.* 2.2.2-3). But we can't help wondering how pleasing an interlocutor Socrates found his own son. Socrates takes pride that for him it's not necessary to converse with anyone he doesn't want to (ἐμοὶ . . . οὐκ ἀνάγκη διαλέγεσθαι ᾧ ἂν μὴ βούλωμαι, Xen. *Mem.* 1.6.5). Yet we don't get to choose our children. If the paternity Socrates leaves his children is then unlikely to consist of philosophic conversation, and

he is otherwise dirt poor, then how good a father is he?

10. Bloom, *Love and Friendship*, 426. Bloom continues: "This can be seen from the practice of our time in the United States, where there is little time for friends and there are practically no facilities for the activity of friendship. Friends tend to be friends of the family, which means they are not friends in any sense intended by Montaigne. In countries like France and England, there are still reminiscences of the separateness of friends from marriage and the family. There are clubs and cafes where people meet who know each other very well but have hardly met the wife or children of their friends. These are two distinct kinds of relationship and, unfortunately, they are in conflict unless there is a natural rank order in which one takes precedence over the other" (426).

11. Socrates' contemporary Antiphon the sophist called marriage a great struggle (μέγας ἀγὼν). Even with a wife who is compatible, one's troubles are doubled compared to single life. And children increase one's anxiety still further (Antiphon fr. 49 [87 B49, Diels-Kranz]). Diogenes the Cynic (c. 400-c.325 B.C.E.) "appears to have advocated the practice of masturbation in place of all forms of sexuality that demanded a partner" (Will Deming, *Paul on Marriage and Celibacy: The Hellenistic Background of 1 Corinthians 7*, Society for New Testament Studies monograph series, no. 83 [Cambridge: Cambridge University Press, 1995], 64). Aristotle's student Theophrastus "held that married life and philosophy were incompatible with one another due to the cares and responsibilities imposed on a married man by his wife" (Deming, *Paul*, 65). Epicurus (341-270 B.C.E.) is reported to have said that "a wise man will not marry or have children" (Diog. Laer. 10.119). Antipater (2nd cent. B.C.E.) argued that having a wife skilled in household management would increase, rather than decrease, a man's leisure for liberal pursuits, since he would be undistracted with the necessities of life (περὶ τὰ ἀναγκαῖα ... ἀπερίσπαστον, Hans Friedrich August von Arnim, ed., *Stoicorum veterum fragmenta* [Leipzig: Teubner, 1903], v. 3, 257, lines 3-4, hereafter sited as SVF). The author of the *Cynic Epistle of Diogenes* disagrees with Antipater on this point (Deming, *Paul*, 71). The case of Musonius Rufus is taken up below. These various stances toward marriage are tied to various conceptions of philosophy, as we shall see. For a survey of ancient literature on the related topos *peri oikonomias* (on household management), see David L. Balch, *Let Wives Be Submissive: The Domestic Code in 1 Peter*, Society of Biblical Literature monograph series, no. 26 (Chico, CA: Scholars Press), 21-62.

12. Explications of this work have multiplied since the publication of Michel Foucault's interpretation in Michel Foucault, *Care of the Self: Volume 3 of The History of Sexuality*, trans. Robert Hurley (New York: Random House, 1986), 193-210. Foucault's remains the best philosophical treatment of the dialogue. I have made no effort here to situate my reading of the work against others', as the present chapter is meant only to survey some of the basic problems the work raises. It is a first approach to my planned larger treatment of the work

13. φύσις κρύπτεσθαι φιλεῖ (G. S. Kirk, J. E. Raven and M. Schofield, eds., *The Presocratic Philosophers*, 2nd ed. [Cambridge: Cambridge University Press, 1983], fr. 208, 192).

14. Lucian, *Amores*, vol. 8, trans. M. D. MacLeod, Loeb Classical Library (Cambridge, MA: Harvard University Press, 1913). Volumes in this series will hereafter be cited as LCL. Note the resemblance of this ancient statement to the "modern historical view" as characterized by Leo Strauss:

The adherents of the modern historical view ... reject as mythical the premise that nature is the norm; they reject the premise that nature is of higher dignity than any works of man. On the contrary, either they conceive of man and his works ... as equally natural as all other real things, or else they assert a basic dualism between the realm of nature and the realm of freedom or history. In the latter case they imply that the realm of man, of human creativity, is exalted far above nature. Accordingly, they do not conceive of the notions of right and wrong as fundamentally arbitrary. They try to discover their causes; they try to make intelligible their variety and sequence; in tracing them to acts of freedom, they insist on the fundamental difference between freedom and arbitrariness (Leo Strauss, *Natural Right and History* [Chicago: University of Chicago Press, 1953], 11).

15. The political character of male homosexual love is conceded by Callicratidas's woman-loving opponent Charicles (though with a different valence) when he says that the first person to consider using a male as a female did so "either tyrannically, using violence, or with shameless persuasion" (20). Violence and persuasion seem to be the basic constituents of politics for Charicles, whereas for Callicratidas it is law. Insofar as law depends on violence and persuasion, Charicles seems to be the more clear-sighted (or forthcoming) on this point. The pederast, like the lawgiver, must create the conditions for an assent that does not feel like submission. For Charicles, politics (and love of males) is a feature of our current state, which is a corruption and decline from original virtue, whereas for Callicratidas politics is part of the ascent, along with the arts, philosophy, and love of males, out of a primal chaos (on the cosmological level) and bestiality (on the evolutionary level).

16. Hubert Martin Jr. makes the case for understanding the implied noun in the title to be *logos*, thus "Erotic Speech" or, as he suggests, "The Conversation about Eros" (Hubert Martin Jr., "Amatorius (Moralia 748e-771e)" in *Plutarch's Ethical Writings and Early Christian Literature*, ed. Hans Dieter Betz, Studia ad corpus Hellenisticum novi testamenti [Leiden: E.J. Brill, 1978], vol. 4, 443-44). The date of the work is uncertain but on internal evidence appears to be after the death of Domitian in 96 C.E. The editor of the Teubner text gives us the circumstances of its publication: "*Libellus sub finem vitae a Plutarcho conscriptus, sed non iam expolitus et mortuo demum auctore videtur editus esse* (This little book was written by Plutarch near the end of his life, but was not yet polished; it seems to have been published by an executor upon his death)" (Curt Ernst Hermann Hubert, *Plutarchi moralia* [Leipzig: Teubner, 1971], vol. 4, 336). The manuscripts are discussed in Flaceliere's introduction to his edition and translation (Robert Flaceliere, *Plutarque: Dialogue sur l'Amour*, Annales de l'Université de Lyon, fasc. 21 [Paris: Société d'Édition Les Belles Lettres, 1952] 34-38) and in W. C. Helmbold's review of the first (1938) edition of the Teubner text (*Classical Philology* 36 [1941]: 85-88).

17. All translations of other authors, as well, are my own unless otherwise attributed.

18. His name means first-born or primeval. Speculatively, we note that primeval can imply *sui generis*, or independent of the chain of begetting. Note also Plato's use of the term *protogenes* at *Politicus* 288e.

19. Aristotle seems to concur that heterosexual attraction has its origin in the necessity of procreation: "necessity (ἀνάγκη) first couples those who are unable to exist without one another, the solitary female and the male, for the sake of generation, and this

is not out of deliberate choice (οὐκ ἐκ προαιρέσεως)," *Politics* 1252a26-31.

20. But see also Hannah Arendt's critique of this thesis as presented by Fustel de Coulanges in the Introduction to his *The Ancient City* (Hannah Arendt, *The Human Condition* [Garden City: Doubleday Anchor, 1959], 306).

21. We are told at 749b that Daphnaeus is in love with a certain woman, and the most successful of her suitors.

22. Plutarch here works extreme mischief on the Platonic passage, which is at *Phaedrus* 250e-251a. There Socrates makes an argument against merely procreative sex: those incapable of responding to Beauty Itself yield to pleasure, simply mount in the manner of quadrupeds, and inseminate. And this is a pleasure contrary to nature (παρὰ φύσιν ἡδονὴν)! Plutarch changes Plato's active verb *bainein* (to mount) to the passive *bainesthai* (to be mounted) and the active *paidosporein* (to inseminate) to the passive *paidosporeisthai* (to be inseminated). The argument against merely procreative sex is thus flipped by Plutarch's character Daphnaeus to become an argument against homosexual pathicity, by this very economical substitution.

23. The LSJ lexicographers inform us (vide ἄχαρις) that this phrase, or slight variations on it, occurs also at Aesch. *Prom.* 545 (the chorus calls Prometheus's gift of art to mankind an *acharis charis* apparently because of the suffering it brought upon him), *Agam.* 1545 (the chorus asks Clytemnestra if, having murdered her husband, she intends to offer him the *acharis charis* or graceless grace of lamenting him) and Eur. *Iph. Taur.* 566 (Iphigenia retrospectively calls her father's intended sacrifice of herself an *acharis charis*). Each is instructive, and Plutarch in his enormous erudition may very well have been aware of their resonances.

24. "But what consolation or what pleasure can he [the *erastes*] give the beloved? Must not this protracted intercourse bring him to the uttermost disgust, as he looks at the old, unlovely face, and other things to match, which it is not pleasant even to hear about, to say nothing of being constantly compelled to come into contact with them?" (Pl. *Phaedrus* 255d, trans. Fowler, LCL). Here Socrates makes the *erastes* out to be older, certainly, than was the norm; most men seem to have pursued boys only up until marriage, and then desisted (thus Jeffrey Henderson, *The Maculate Muse: Obscene Language in Attic Comedy*, 2nd ed. [Oxford: Oxford University Press, 1991], 206; and Kenneth James Dover, *Greek Homosexuality* [Cambridge, MA: Harvard University Press, 1989], 171-72, but see also Eva Cantarella, *Bisexuality in the Ancient World*, trans. Cormac ó Cuilleanáin [New Haven: Yale University Press, 1992], 40-42). Also, by Socrates' own poignantly subtle account of the *eromenos*' experience, the youth seems not to be entirely a passive spectator (*Phaedrus* 255a-256a). But the youth's putative lack of pleasure is a crucial premise for the exchange whereby pederasty is thought to be educative: the older partner can't offer beauty or pleasure, but he can offer wisdom instead. Montaigne, in his discussion of ancient pederasty, states the case aptly: "the lover studying to render himself acceptable by the good grace and beauty of his soul, that of his body being long decayed, and hoping, by this mental fellowship, to establish a firmer and more durable contract" (*On Friendship*, 161). Note that Montaigne calls even this refined version of pederasty, where there is no material exchange, a contract. See also David Halperin, "Plato and Erotic Reciprocity," *Classical Antiquity* 5 (1986): 60-80.

25. Recall also Pausanius's apparent conflation of public and private when he says that justice would ensue if lover and beloved each come to bed armed with a law, Pl. *Symp.* 184d4.

26. Prior to this declaration by Plutarch the dramatic character, Plutarch the writer of the dialogue makes the segue from Protogenes's speech to his own speech with a startling imitation of the assonant jingle with which Plato segues from Pausanius's speech to the place where Aristophanes was *supposed* (δεῖν) to speak; cf. Plato's Παυσανίου δὲ παυσαμένου (*Symp.* 185c4) with Plutarch's somewhat inferior παυσαμένου δὲ τοῦ Πρωτογένους (753b). In the arrangement of speeches, and by drawing our attention to the Platonic segue by imitating its assonant jingle, and by calling the pederasts' hypothesis public, Plutarch may intend to evoke the confrontation between Pausanius and Aristophanes. Paul Ludwig, "Eros and Ambition in Greek Political Thought," (Ph.D. diss., University of Chicago, 1997; cf. W. Robert Connor, *The New Politicians of Fifth-Century Athens* [Indianapolis: Hackett, 1992], 180-81) has argued convincingly that Plato's Aristophanes and the historical Aristophanes both offer a critique of the claims made by the public at the expense of the private, and that both offer a critique of pederasty as part of this critique of the political.

27. On homosexual submission as hubris against oneself, see Aeschines, *Against Timarchus* 29, 116 and the related point about shaming one's own body (καταισχύνων τὸ σῶμα τὸ ἑαυτοῦ) at 40.

28. Cupris, or Cypris, is an appellation of the goddess Aphrodite; Cypris is her traditional birthplace. Plutarch here quotes an anonymous tragedy that is extant only in fragments (Augustus Nauck, ed., *Tragicorum Graecorum fragmenta*, 2nd ed. [Leipzig: Teubner, 1889], fr. 409, 917).

29. In the *Alcibiades II*, Ps.-Plato attributes this murder to ambition rather than revenge. Like Plutarch, Aristotle attributes it to resentment at suffering shameful violation of the body (τὸ εἰς τὸ σῶμα αἰσχύνεσθαι, Politics 1311b8-9); the origin of Crateas's extreme alienation from his tyrant-lover was a feeling of being oppressed by the sexual gratification he gave (τῆς γε ἀλλοτριότητος ὑπῆρχεν ἀρχὴ τὸ βαρέως φέρειν πρὸς τὴν ἀφροδισιαστικὴν χάριν, Politics 1311b16-17). These examples of lovers who are literally tyrants seem calculated to emphasize the agonistic dimension of pederasty, on which see David Cohen, *Law, Sexuality, and Society: The Enforcement of Morals in Classical Athens* (Cambridge: Cambridge University Press, 1991), 171-202.

30. Cf. Ar. *Pol.* 1311a40-b2.

31. There is some semblance of such a thought in the *Laws*, where Plato's Athenian Stranger says that one effect of confining the sexual activities of men to intercourse with their lawful wives would be to make them "familiar with and friendly toward [or dear to] their wives" (839a-b). But it is primarily certain civic goods that are sought through the sexual legislation. In any case, the thought is not elaborated.

32. Plutarch seems to follow Antipater of Tarsus here in applying ideas from Stoic physics, specifically Chryssipus's classification of different degrees of mixing, to marriage. Cf. this passage with Antipater in Stobaeus, *Anthologium*, ed. Otto Hense (Berlin: Weidmannsche Verlagsbuchhandlung, 1958), v. 4, fr. 22.25, 508. For the Stoics' physical theory and its antecedents see Stobaeus, *Anthologium*, v. 1, fr. 17 *passim*, 152-55. See also Plutarch, *Moralia* 426a.

33. *On the Bravery of Women* is addressed to Plutarch's friend Clea, a high priestess at Delphi. He also dedicated his difficult work *On Isis and Osiris* to her. There is preserved among the works of Plutarch an essay, of questionable authorship, entitled *A Woman, Too, Should Be Educated*. The fragments of this work that have been preserved

by Stobaeus are assembled in v. 15 of the Loeb *Moralia*.

34. Xenophon has his Socrates ask Critobulus, "Is there anyone with whom you converse less than with your wife?" Critobulus answers, "No, or not many, at any rate," and the answer seems to be perfectly normal (*Oec.* 3.12). The prospects for that verbal or intellectual component of conjugal intimacy, *homophrosune*, which may be seen not only in Plutarch's milieu but also, very palpably, between Odysseus and Penelope, seem to be quite dim in the intervening classical period. Critobulus, who seems to represent a typical Athenian gentleman, will not lie with his wife and "revel in stories, speaking with one another" as Odysseus and Penelope did, apparently as part of their lovemaking (note the parallel repetition of the verb τέρπω at *Od.* 23.300-301). Penelope and Odysseus do not engage in theoretical discussions, but they do take delight in speeches with one another.

35. See the essay "On Whether Marriage Is an Impediment to Philosophizing" (εἰ ἐμπόδιον τῷ φιλοσοφεῖν γάμος) in *C. Musonii Rufi reliquiae*, ed. Otto Hense (Leipzig: Teubner, 1990), 70-76. Among other Stoic ethicists, Antipater and Hierocles both wrote books called *On Marriage*, substantial fragments of which are collected in Stobaeus, *Anthologium*, vol. 4, fr. 22.21-25, 502-12.

36. SVF, v. 3, 255, lines 7-8.

37. *On the Nature of the Universe*, falsely attributed to Ocellus Lucanus. This work is translated in Deming, *Paul,* 230-31. Deming also translates (226-29) the Stobaeus fragment of Antipater's *On Marriage*, which is otherwise not available in English. His discussion of "The Stoic-Cynic Marriage Debate" (ch. 2) is indispensable.

38. The public or political character of philosophy in later antiquity, or the blurring of the boundary between philosophy and professionalized rhetoric (one thinks of the Academic education of Rome's senatorial class, or Domitian's expulsion of the philosophers as *themselves* a class) may be contrasted with Plato's image of philosophy as discreet, intimate dialectic, and stands in even starker contrast to the essentially private conception of philosophy conveyed by Plato's image of the cave. "Philosophizing means to ascend from the cave to the light of the sun, that is, to the truth. The cave is the world of opinion as opposed to knowledge. Opinion is essentially variable. Men cannot live, that is, they cannot live together, if opinions are not stabilized by social fiat. Opinion thus becomes authoritative opinion or public dogma or Weltanschauung. Philosophizing means, then, to ascend from public dogma to essentially private knowledge" (Strauss, *Natural Right*, 11-12). Contrast this with the public-spirited, therapeutic moralism (Greek *diatribai*, Roman *sermones*) we associate with Plutarch's milieu (the so-called Second Sophistic, roughly). A vulgarized sort of philosophy is in this later epoch very much *part* of the Weltanschauung. One might question, then, Strauss's characterization of the "cave beneath the cave" phenomenon as distinctly modern. There seems to have been a sort of ancient Enlightenment. An attempt to characterize this enlightenment would entail an investigation of the efforts made by Hellenistic *philosophes* (first among whom would be the Cynics) to provide theoretical grounds for the new cosmopolitanism. By destroying polis life, the empire of Alexander seems to have prepared the way not only for the empire of Rome, but for the empire of reason and the first attempt at a universal moral system. The wedding of this system to the Jesus cult was perhaps only the final step in the movement whereby philosophy became dogmatic.

39. Bloom, *Love and Friendship*, 411-12.

40. Bloom, *Love and Friendship*, 441.

41. Ancient pederasty is in fact only ambiguously homosexual, since the lover's

attraction is to the feminine smoothness of an *immature* masculinity: "For boys are beautiful only for so long as and to the degree that they are similar to women in every way . . . (*Nam etiam pueri tum tantum pulchri sunt . . . quo usque mulieribus similes sunt . . .*)" (Clearchus fr. 36 in *Fragmenta historicorum Graecorum*, ed. Muller, v. 2, 314). Conversely, "[T]he older party is the more masculine of the two, yet precisely his masculinity makes him sexually undesirable to the younger beloved" (Ludwig, ch.1, 41-42).

Chapter 7

Women and/as Princes in Machiavelli's Comedies

Arlene W. Saxonhouse

In perhaps the most famous—and infamous—passage in Machiavelli's little pamphlet *The Prince*, from a chapter entitled "Of Those Things for Which Men and Especially Princes Are Praised or Blamed," Machiavelli writes:

> Since my intent is to write something useful to whoever understands it, it has appeared to me more fitting to go directly to the effectual truth of the thing than to the imagination of it. And many have imagined republics and principalities that have never been seen or known to exist in truth; for it is so far from how one lives to how one should live that he who lets go of what is done for what should be done learns his ruin rather than his preservation. For a man who wants to make a profession of good in all regards must come to ruin among so many who are not good. Hence it is necessary to a prince, if he wants to maintain himself to learn to be able not to be good, and to use this and not use it according to necessity.[1]

The last lines of this paragraph are the ones on which I will initially focus —the education in learning "not to be good." This, as I read it, is the real lesson of *The Prince,* and it is a lesson that is difficult to learn, but it is the lesson that best captures the radicalness of Machiavelli's political thought. The problem is that being "good" and not being "bad" is drummed into us from the earliest periods of our existence. Machiavelli suggests that those lessons in goodness are precisely what prevent us from being happy and that the task of the prince is to overcome those lessons, to overthrow the normative model that has guided our lives and release us for a happiness that is denied us by an antiquated value system, by a world that can look only to a future happiness rather than a happiness in this world, in the lives we live every day.

In the chapters that follow this famous warning to princes, Machiavelli explains to his readers how the traditional virtues in fact are meaningless, that bad is good, that good is bad and that those terms as traditionally used are meaningless—that what we thought was cruelty is in fact kindness, that what we thought was liberality and generosity in fact is a niggardliness, that being feared is better than being loved. Traditional virtues fade into vices while the vices in turn become virtues, for they become the foundation for human happiness. For instance, generosity—to give of one's possessions appears to be a virtue based on the Christian doctrines of grace, of imitating God who gives to us through the hope of salvation, but as Machiavelli analyzes the prince's ability to be generous he notes that generosity, the giving to some, also means taking away from some. Thus, he concludes: "a prince should esteem it little to incur a name for meanness, because this is one of those vices which enable him to rule." (*The Prince,* chap. 16, 64) This is because "if one wants to maintain a name for liberality among men, it is necessary not to leave out any kind of lavish display, so that a prince who has done this will always consume all his resources in such deeds. In the end, it will be necessary, if he wants to maintain a name for liberality, to burden the people excessively." (*The Prince,* chap. 16, 63) Or in comparing mercy and cruelty, he concludes: "A prince, therefore, so as to keep his subjects united and faithful, should not care about the infamy of cruelty, because with very few examples he will be more merciful than those who for the sake of too much mercy allow disorders to continue from which come killings and robberies; for these customarily harm a whole community, but the executions that come from the prince harm one particular person." (*The Prince,* chap. 17, 65)

In his comedies Machiavelli brings his political teachings from the public realm of cities and nations to the private realm of the family and the relations therein. At issue in the history of political theory has always been the relation between the public world of political life and the private world of the family and the household. Some of the great philosophers see analogies between the two; others find them profoundly distinct. Plato, for one, in his dialogue *The Statesman* presents an analogy between the ruler in the city and the ruler in the household, while Aristotle soundly rejects that analogy as equating institutions that have distinctly different ends or goals. In the medieval world, analogical thinking dominated and the microcosm was a vivid reflection of the macrocosm; the family governed by the father reflected the city governed by a prince and the universe governed by God. Machiavelli rejects analogies that impose order from one realm onto the other, because—simply—he rejects the idea that there is any inherent order in nature that can be translated from one realm to another. Whatever order there is, whether in the city or the family, arises from the human effort to impose an order on a natural world that of itself is chaotic, in need of a structuring that comes from human art and especially the art of politics. The tools of this artistry, tools that include learning how meaningless are the traditional terms of praise and blame, may require practicing what previously had been considered vices. The tools may be the same whether we are structuring the family or the city—or the world around us, but we do not look to one realm or another to discover therein the proper ordering of our world. There is no order in nature that defines the order of the regime—political or familial—in which we ought to live. We instead are the orderers of our environment, and therefore we ourselves are the ones responsible for bringing happiness to ourselves and those around us. The burden lies with us, and Machiavelli's lesson is that satisfying this goal may entail acting in ways that are opposed to what tradition has called "good" and in accordance with what tradition has called "bad," since those terms of praise and blame have no grounding in nature or truth and ought not act as limits on our actions. The goal is happiness and satisfaction of our desires.

In both the public and the private realms of human existence, happiness is hindered by old forms and models of behavior, models of the virtuous man and the virtuous woman who may be praised but whose supposed virtue leads to misery rather than happiness for the many. In particular, Machiavelli is eager to turn us away from the virtues that force us to attend to a life after death, to a future about which we can know nothing, rather than to a life in the current world, the world that we experience now with our senses and our passions, the world of the "effectual truth," not the imaginary truth of those who look beyond our senses, beyond the current world of everyday experiences, marked by the ambiguities of virtue and vice, not their adamantine structure. In Machiavelli's comedy *Mandragola,* on which I here focus most of my attention, the virtue that comes up for discussion is chastity, a female virtue that is often praised but makes everyone in the play unhappy; it is only when the main character, the wife Lucrezia, learns to be "bad" in the traditional sense of the term—just like the princes to whom Machiavelli speaks in *The Prince*—when adultery replaces chastity that the play can reach a happy conclusion for all the participants. The other characters all begin with their petty desires and try to figure out how to satisfy them; it is the wife, the beautiful but quiet Lucrezia, who listens and watches those around her and learns about the ambiguity of this virtue. It is she in this play who learns about human nature and becomes, in my mind, the true prince of Machiavelli's expectations by founding a new regime—albeit in the small confines of a Florentine home.

Machiavelli's writings portray a fluid world of uncertainties—that is, a world in which there are no sharp boundaries, where forms fade easily into one another and the successful prince is the one who can adapt and transform himself into a multitude of characters—into animals such as the lion and the fox, into godlike characters who deliver laws to their people, and even into women as they become fickle in order to match the fickleness of a Fortuna that "like a woman" (his image, not mine) is always changing. In his chapter 6 on the great heroes who have founded states on the basis of their manly excellence, in the Italian on their *virtù* alone, their own energies and skill without dependence on others or on Fortuna to help them out, Machiavelli moves swiftly between mythical and biblical and historical characters. They shade easily into one another, just as in other chapters—especially from his *Discourses on the First Ten Books of Livy*—women show that they become like men in their ability to found nations (Dido), to seek revenge, engage in plots to overthrow and kill emperors.[2] There is no prescribed form for a ruler, and as men rule, so too can women. Some of the examples that he introduces upset what others might have read as the natural order, a natural hierarchy between men and animals, old and young, male and female. But Machiavelli keeps presenting the stories that show that there is no such natural order or hierarchy upon which men can rely in the founding of states. We create our own hierarchies without a dependence on Nature. Men must learn from women just as they learn from animals and gods how to institute new regimes, create order out of chaos—and perhaps women too must learn the arts of rule from men, or at least some of them.

Machiavelli's corpus includes three comedies. Two of them, *Mandragola* and *Clizia,* come under discussion. These comedies, first performed in the 1520s, were part of a new genre in Italian literature and were differentiated from other comic performances in that they harked back to the Roman comedies of Terrence and Plautus—indeed *Clizia* is a modestly revised Roman comedy entitled *Casina* by Plautus, which Machiavelli translates into Italian and sets in contemporary Florence. Machiavelli has made some changes in the plot to give a more sympathetic role to the wife and the mother of the comedy, but it still draws heavily on the comedy from the third century B.C. The Roman comedies on which Machiavelli based his own comedies themselves derived from the New Comedy of ancient Athens, a theatrical form that rejected the openly political themes of Aristophanic Old Comedy, in which the events depicted took place in the open spaces of the agora and the assembly and the citadel of Athens and the characters often spewed forth satirical innuendo against actual political figures. New Comedy and Roman comedy focused inward—away from the public spaces and public concerns—and turned to life within the household as the venue for its comic action. Machiavelli takes over the form of New Comedy in his focus on the events of the household, but the events he portrays are hardly free from political implications, and the situations he presents capture well the Machiavellian vision of politics as a realm of creativity and novelty. In the comedies, though, it is the women who end up accomplishing the political acts of foundation and preservation in an uncertain world, while in his *Prince* and *Discourses* it is fair to say that the males dominate.

In Machiavelli's comedies we see women overthrowing the traditional princes, the husbands who officially ruled, according to custom and to what was perceived of as nature; the women as princes end the comedies by ruling over their households and the men within them. In *Mandragola*, once the character Lucrezia has learned to "be bad"—to exchange chastity for adultery, everyone in the play is happy, she most of all, as she can now enjoy the ardor of a young lover rather than endure the sterile lovemaking of an ugly old man. In *Clizia*, the wife and foster mother, upsetting the hierarchy of the family, begins by playing the Machiavellian role of an adviser to the ruler—but then overthrows the ruler and takes upon herself the governance of the household.

Let me turn first to *Mandragola*. It is Machiavelli's original comedy—a vibrant affirmation of his political thought that looks forward to a life of pleasure for all once they escape the burdens of religious virtue. Let me briefly summarize the plot and then turn to how it develops Machiavelli's themes. Callimaco, a young Florentine, is enamored of the beautiful Lucrezia, the young wife of a stupid old man, Nicia. Wracked by his desire to possess Lucrezia, he calls upon a certain Ligurio—a man who sponges off others, but does have a devious mind that enables him to hatch imaginative schemes to accomplish his ends. Nicia, the old husband, is disconsolate because of his wife's failure to conceive a child. This gives Ligurio the opening to hatch his plot, for he proposes that he assure Nicia that his wife will conceive if she drinks the mandrake, a drug that supposedly works like this: it will kill the first man with whom the woman sleeps after taking it, but thereafter will ensure fertility. Those planning on using this drug must, of course, supply the first man who will be sacrificed so that a child may be born to Lucrezia and Nicia. This supposed sacrifice will be a disguised Callimaco, who will then reveal his passion for Lucrezia. The only serious stumbling block to this plot is the resistance of Lucrezia, but with the encouragement of her mother, her husband, and a corrupt priest, Lucrezia yields, and after a night in the arms of Callimaco determines that his embraces are preferable to Nicia's. At the end of the comedy Callimaco is a permanent resident in the household, Nicia has a soon-to-be pregnant wife, Lucrezia's mother can expect grandchildren, and Ligurio is a welcome guest at the table of Nicia—and the priest is wealthier.

We can—and, given the themes of Machiavelli's political works, ought to—read the comedy as the establishment of a new order, the breaking down of the old regime of the family in order to found a new family structure with a new prince, one that will ensure the happiness of all. But in order to arrive at this new foundation, Lucrezia must be willing to reject the traditional virtue of chastity and accept a significant rereading of Christianity to which she was devoted at the beginning of the comedy. She must be willing to learn to be bad in order to achieve the happiness that awaits all at the end of the comedy. It is the quiet and reserved woman of this comedy who becomes the real founder of a new regime by learning and putting into practice this lesson. Let us delve a little more deeply into how all this comes about in Machiavelli's comedy.

To begin with, we need to take special note of Lucrezia's name. Machiavelli here is playing on the name of the most famous Lucretia from the stories of ancient Rome. The Roman Lucretia was a heroine whose concern with her own chastity and that of others led to the overthrow of the reign of the kings who had become tyrants and to the founding of the Roman republic. The story is well known—represented powerfully, for example, in Rembrandt's rendition of the suicide of Lucretia with her golden curls, bared breast, and threatening knife. Lucretia commits suicide after she is raped by Sextus Tarquinius, the son of the Roman king Tarquinius. The story goes that Sextus had been sitting around the fire in the military camp on the outskirts of Rome with the officers of the Roman army, and each of the officers praised the virtue of his wife. (In Machiavelli's presentation of the analogous scene in his comedy, the young men are praising women's beauty.) The young Roman officers decide to ride to Rome to see whose wife is indeed the most virtuous, and there Sextus sees Lucretia in all her beauty working at the spinning wheel by the hearth. He is smitten and returns later to seduce her. When she resists, he threatens to kill her and put the body of a naked slave by her and claim he had caught her in an adulterous act. Lucretia yields. Here, let me quote Livy:

> The unhappy girl wrote to her father in Rome and to her husband ... urging them both to come at once.... They found Lucretia sitting in her room, in deep distress. Tears rose to her eyes as they entered, and to her husband's question,

"is it well with you," she answered "no. What can be well with a woman who has lost her honor. . . . My body has been violated. My heart is innocent, and earth will be my witness. Give me your solemn promise that the adulterer shall be punished.". . . The promise was given. One after another they tried to comfort her. . . . It was the mind, they said, that sinned, not the body: without intention there could never be guilt. "What is due to *him*," Lucretia said, "is for you to decide. As for me I am innocent of fault, but I will take my punishment. Never shall Lucretia provide a precedent for unchaste women to escape what they deserve." With these words she drew a knife from under her robe, and drove it into her heart, and fell forward, dead.[3]

It is Lucretia's pleas and suicide that then lead to the overthrow of the kings and the founding of the Roman republic.

Obviously, the Lucrezia of Machiavelli's story plays a very different role. Like Livy's Lucretia she is violated by an ardent lover, but unlike Lucretia, Lucrezia does not resist and ends up accepting the new lover. Lucretia's resistance and suicide bring about the transformation of the political regime of Rome. On a much more modest scale, Lucrezia's acquiescence brings about the transformation of the regime within the family. Let us look a little more closely at what happens to Lucrezia in Machiavelli's play. Callimaco does not act as brutally as Tarquinius Sextus; he does not treat her as Machiavelli suggests the prince treat Fortuna—to conquer one must "hold her down, beat her and strike her down." (*The Prince*, chap. 25, 101) Instead, he engages the services of Ligurio—a character who in some ways appears very like Machiavelli himself, knowledgeable about human nature and how to manipulate others by playing on their fears and desires, himself an adviser to princes if not the prince himself, a role Machiavelli seemed to willing to play when he wrote to Lorenzo de' Medici in the dedicatory epistle of *The Prince* urging the prince of Florence to attend to the advice offered in his little pamphlet. It is Ligurio who hatches the plot about the mandrake that will cure Lucrezia of her infertility—not exactly as her husband imagines—by curing her of her chastity. Having devised this plot, though, Ligurio must also persuade Lucrezia to take the supposed medicine— and to sleep with a stranger who supposedly by drawing off the poisonous effects will himself die. In order to persuade her, he enlists the help of the friar, of the mother, of the stupid husband Nicia who does not understand the consequences, namely that he will become a cuckold and the object of laughter on the Florentine stage. Just as Ligurio had planned, they all, acting out of their own self-interest, persuade Lucrezia to yield, to drink the mandrake, and to sleep with a man who is not her husband and who will die as a consequence of that encounter. And that man, Callimaco, instead of dying persuades her to sleep with him again and again and again.

Thus, Lucrezia's chastity, in contrast to Lucretia's chastity, is cured; rather than a noble virtue to be preserved, a virtue that brings about the downfall of tyrants, something for which one might kill oneself, in Machiavelli's play chastity appears as a disease that needs medicine. Just as in *The Prince* the various virtues described in chapters 16-18 generosity, kindness, the keeping of faith, and so forth were shown not to be virtues, but rather the source of political disorder, so too in *Mandragola* the "virtue" of chastity appears not as a virtue but as a hindrance to happiness, as something to be overcome, not to be praised, but to be cured by the medicine administered by Ligurio. As Machiavelli develops it in this comedy, the happiness is great at the end. Lucrezia has a young and exciting lover rather than a boring old man; Callimaco can enjoy the object of his love. Nicia will have the children he desires (he may not know that they are not his, but there will be sons to inherit his wealth.) Ligurio can continue to sponge off both Nicia and Callimaco. The priest who was involved in persuasion has money for his church, and the mother has grandchildren.

To get to this point of happiness, there must be a violation, but the comedy teaches that the violation needs to be accepted, embraced rather than rejected as a source of happiness; once we learn to be "bad," an intolerable state of affairs can be overcome. In a manner similar to the princes of chapter 15 of *The Prince* and the passage with which I began, Lucrezia learns that she cannot be good and preserve her chastity; she cannot provide her husband with the offspring he desires nor her mother with the grandchildren she longs for by abiding by the old rules of chastity. She cannot make others happy by accepting the old rules of virtue. She is indeed the prince who has learned the lesson Machiavelli wrote his work to persuade. And having learned the Machiavellian lesson, she is the founder of a new regime. The lesson that she had to learn may be harsh and difficult, may invert the language of praise and blame, but those who reject the education that Machiavelli has for his princes will suffer and be oppressed; living in an imaginary world, they will ignore the "effectual truth."

The cure, the mandrake, the education in the Machiavellian understanding of the nature of the world in which we live transforms the ancient Lucretia into the modern Lucrezia. In antiquity, the preservation of virtue—the suicide of Lucretia so that other women could not use her as an excuse for promiscuity—could found new regimes; in the modern day, Machiavelli tells us, it is the denial of those virtues, it is their transcendence that becomes the foundation stone of new orders. The mandrake is a medication that supposedly gives life through death. Obviously in this play, it is a sham, a pretense, but the transformation of Lucrezia mimics the death and birth that the medicine is supposed to accomplish. Here we see dramatized the death of "the need to be good" and the birth of the assertion that by the will of seeking happiness Lucrezia will be able to cure the sickness that infects the characters at the beginning of the play. It does not come from the bottle that contains the mandrake, but from the transformation of the values—and it is the female character who in the end controls all in this comedy. She is the one who has learned the lesson, and all engaged in the activity of the play benefit from her education in the princely art of learning to be what was previously considered "bad."

In the Dedicatory Epistle to *The Prince*, Machiavelli portrays himself as an adviser to princes. In chapter 22 of *The Prince*, he warns the prince about the adviser who wishes to take over the city or state from the rulers, and in the famous last chapter of *The Prince* Machiavelli calls upon Lorenzo to be the new

Moses, using biblical images of manna falling from heaven and water pouring forth from the rock. But in the very use of this imagery, Machiavelli is raising questions about the relationship between himself and Lorenzo—Lorenzo as Moses is simply the servant or agent of God, thus Machiavelli as his "adviser" takes on the role of God whose will is to be carried out by his agent Lorenzo. It is easy to impose this model of the relationship between the prince and his adviser onto the *Mandragola*. According to this reading, Callimaco would be the "prince," the analog of Lorenzo, the one who succeeds in conquering and believes that he wins. But he does not do so through his own efforts. He is not a true prince, for he depends on the wiles of Ligurio, who divinely orchestrates the action of the comedy. It is Ligurio in this play who parallels Machiavelli, the sly shifty character who shows Callimaco how to conquer Fortuna—or at least gets access to the woman he desires. He does not help him do it by force or the brutal actions implied in chapter 25 of *The Prince,* where Machiavelli says that Fortuna is a woman and that "it is necessary, if one wants to hold her down, to beat her and strike her down. And one sees that she lets herself be won more by the impetuous than by those who proceed coldly." (*The Prince*, chap. 25, 101) Despite Callimaco's name, which means "beautiful battle," he avoids battles when he can and lives in Paris while his native country is ravished by the French, preferring the bed of beautiful women to the adventures of beautiful battles. He himself has no particular virtue—except that he knows to listen to Ligurio, who shows how Fortuna is to be conquered, by intrigue and trickery, not by force. Thus, I cannot agree with those who see in Callimaco anything of the prince whom one might regard with admiration for conquering the maiden Fortuna. Lucrezia herself is the one around whom the comedy revolves, the one who controls the final resolution. She, is in fact described in the comedy as one "who is fit to rule a nation,"[4] and at the beginning of the comedy Nicia is described as "allowing himself to be governed by her."[5] By the end of the play, it is clear that she does indeed rule and govern the regime she herself has founded by learning Machiavelli's lessons. Her ability to rise above her education in virtue, to learn to be able to be bad, is precisely what gives her this princely quality. The Machiavellian character Ligurio does not himself rule. He remains an adviser, controlling the fates of others from without and getting pleasure from the enactment and fulfillment of his plotlines.

The significance of *Clizia* for my discussion depends on attention to another famous passage from *The Prince*, this one from chapter 25 on Fortuna, to which I have already referred, where Machiavelli discusses the different ways in which Fortuna may be conquered. Above I cited the infamous passage that presents Fortuna as a woman, to be subdued by force and beaten back, but there is an alternative method that suits women (and indeed most men, especially men like Machiavelli who have been exiled and stripped of their direct influence in the political affairs of the day). The alternative method of conquering Fortuna is to learn from Fortuna herself the art of being fickle, of changing oneself, of not being confined to one character, unable to adapt to changing circumstances. The fickleness of Fortuna—and of the female—is a source of strength; masculinity may in fact be an indication of weakness. Machiavelli complains in chapter 25 of *The Prince*: "Nor may a man be found so prudent as to know how to accommodate himself to this, whether because he cannot deviate from what nature inclines him to or because, when one has always flourished by walking one path, he cannot be persuaded to depart from it. And so the cautious man, when it is time to come to impetuosity, does not know how to do it, hence comes to ruin." (*The Prince*, chap. 25, 100) Since most cannot so transform their own natures, the alternative method of force and the language of rape appear. *Clizia*, through the presentation of a princely woman—quite different from the character in *Mandragola*—illustrates the preferability of the female who can adapt to the situation at hand and manipulate others through trickery rather than rely on force, claims of natural hierarchies, or self-assertion.[6]

The story of *Clizia* is a bit more complicated than that of *Mandragola*, but let me try to quickly summarize the plot. Clizia is the name of a young girl of unknown origin raised by an aristocratic Florentine family. Both father, significantly named Nicomaco—capturing Machiavelli's two names—and son, Cleandro, fall in love with her, but for obvious reasons neither can marry her. The father plots to have Clizia marry his compliant servant so that he can have sexual access to her after the wedding, while the distraught son tries to stop that wedding by claiming that she ought to marry a less compliant servant. Amid a series of comic conflicts, the mother and wife of the family—Sofronia—arranges for the servants to draw lots as to who shall have the girl as a wife. The central character in the comedy is Sofronia, whose concern is not her husband's infidelity but his transformation from an upstanding citizen, father, and husband into a slobbering old fool. Fortuna shines on Nicomaco when the lottery assigns Clizia to his servant so that he can arrange to enjoy Clizia in the nuptial bed after the wedding; Sofronia, though, plots a magnificent countertrick and arranges for yet another servant to be in the bed instead. The ruse so shames Nicomaco that he agrees to mend his ways and leaves the rule of the household to Sofronia. Sofronia becoming the ruler of the household does not allow Cleandro to marry Clizia either, given their class difference, until—as always seems to happen in these plays—Clizia's father arrives and her aristocratic birth is discovered.

Sofronia stands firmly at the center of this play—guiding the action of others through her knowledge of human nature, controlling a Fortuna that seems to go against her by giving Clizia to Nicomaco's servant, and defying the traditional hierarchy of the family. In the prologue to the play, we are told that the comedy is to be "instructive to you," those eager to have Fortuna as their friend. But the young learn from watching Sofronia that neither youth nor masculinity is needed in order for Fortuna to smile—indeed, the young and the males of this comedy have no control over their destinies, and it is the female who structures the world around them. The skills that Sofronia demonstrates, even when Fortuna goes against her, include particularly the craftiness to make events turn out as she wishes, a craftiness that derives from her understanding of human motives and passions. The mistake both the young and the old males make is to assume that success comes from strength or violence, from a masculine assertion of power or from Fortuna's favoring you. The men provide images of love as analogous to war and conflate the two in their songs, but Sofronia shows that the female—even one who is no longer young—can overthrow the weak masculine rulers of her family and acquire rule for herself, by adapting to circumstances and not depending on the old orders. The males, again both old and young, produce only chaos and disorder because they rely on Fortuna and do not know how to conquer her in the subtle ways of the female. The son Cleandro in particular relies on Fortuna to favor him because of his youth; "Oh Fortuna," he laments after losing the lottery, "since you are a woman, you really ought to be the mistress of young men: but this time you are the old man's mistress." [7] He has built no dikes, and after his mother refuses to allow him to marry Clizia he cries: "Just when I thought my ship had come in, fortune blows me back out into the high seas, in the midst of darker and stormier waves." (*Clizia,* act 5, sc. 5, 391) Unlike his mother, he fails to act, to devise plots or tricks, and thus lets Fortuna govern him rather than conquering her.

In part, it is the inversion of power within the household between the male and the female that provides the play's comic force, but at the same time Machiavelli's characters also illustrate the permeability of the traditional lines of authority and the inadequacy of reliance on an old structure. The father-husband in this play is a fool—or rather becomes a fool because he does not control Fortuna, the sexual attraction to the young Clizia. He is smitten and changes from, in Sofronia's words, "a serious, resolute, considerate man, [one who] after lunch would converse with his son, . . . give him lessons and instruct him about men; using ancient and modern examples." (*Clizia,* act 2, sc. 4, 317) He insists that he wants to be master of his own house, he wants to have the wedding of Clizia as he planned it, and if this does not happen, he constructively comments, he will burn down the house. (*Clizia,* act 3, sc. 1, 327) In annoyance at his wife, he asks her: "But isn't it more sensible for you to do things my way than for me to do them your way?" (*Clizia,* act 3, sc. 4, 335) All in the audience will immediately recognize the foolishness of such a suggestion given the roles of the two characters, but in recognizing it they too accept the Machiavellian demonstration that traditional hierarchies are subject to question, that the control and order of regimes rests not on force or conquest or on Nature, but on the manipulation that derives from an understanding of human nature—an understanding as open to smart women as to smart men.

Nicomaco's decline and transformation from an upstanding citizen to an old fool supports the rule of Sofronia. There is no natural order that determines the rule of the male over the female. Since there is no natural order, humans—male or female—need to impose that order. That is *the* political challenge. Sofronia may function in the household realm, but it is there where she comes to play the part of the adviser who takes over rule, the secretary to the prince who becomes the prince him/herself. At the end of the play, Nicomaco is so completely overwhelmed by Sofronia's trickery that he yields and willingly transfers all power to her. "Sofronia, my darling," he says to her, "do whatever you want. I am ready to do anything you say." (*Clizia,* act 5, sc. 3, 387) Sofronia repeats

Nicomaco's words to her son: "He has given me carte blanche; and he wants me to manage [*io governi*] everything my way from now on." (*Clizia,* act 5, sc. 3, 387) And so she does. The differences between Sofronia and Nicomaco illustrate the necessity to transcend any notion of a natural hierarchy based on the natural distinction between male and female. The female, through wiles and adaptation, may be the far stronger prince than the male who relies only on the traditional hierarchy of a conventional view entailed in the natural world.

Sometimes people describe Machiavelli as separating public and private morality, of introducing two different moral universes, but the comedies illustrate that we cannot simply accept this view of Machiavelli, for the private world is governed—as is the political world—by the need to learn how to be "bad" or, indeed, that there is no such thing as good or bad independent of the "effectual truth," and how women need to trick their husbands in order to establish a new regime to replace one that has been corrupted by male foolishness. It is the women who act the part of the princes—who take over the role of founding and restructuring corrupt regimes; it is the women who illustrate that the principles Machiavelli teaches his princes in *The Prince* apply as well to the private world of the family. And it is these women who take on the role of princes who show us Machiavelli's ultimate view of the fluidity of nature and thus in turn the need for the princes who will impose some sort of form on the world.

Back in fourth-century Greece, Aristotle addressed the questions of generation and arrived at what one can call the flowerpot theory of generation—a theory we see in Athene's famous speech at the end of Aeschylus's *Oresteia*. According to that theory, the female provides the material or matter out of which the fetus is created, while the male provides the "form" that transforms that matter into Arial. Through their own actions and through their attention to the lessons Machiavelli teaches, they too can impose form on nature. They too can be the founders of political regimes—whether public or private. The comedies refer us to the private world of familial relations, but we learn there as well Machiavelli's lessons for those who create and found in the political world—and those lessons come from the wisdom that Machiavelli gives his female princes in his comedies as much as from his more famous political works.

I must add a postscript to the above discussion: Lest I appear to be encouraging adultery and presenting chastity as a disease, let me assure you that this is not my goal, but let me also use Machiavelli's discussion to point to the difficulty that he presents to us. Women in his analysis can be princes; they can become the rulers over their households and perhaps even over cities. This is because Machiavelli is willing to overthrow the traditional hierarchical models that had determined the "right" relationships between and identification of natural subordinates and superiors. Machiavelli is casting aside constricting modes of existence, and in his openness to a world of flux and of change, of uncertainties, of forms shifting from one realm into another, he opens us up to the questioning of traditional virtues at the same time that he opens us up to the questioning of our traditional hierarchies. In his mind, that all goes together, and the challenge that he poses for the modern world is whether the overthrow of a natural hierarchy also entails the overthrow of all traditions, including the traditional grounds for praise and blame. Machiavelli has used his comedies to set forth this challenge to the modern world, and it is not clear to me that the modern world has adequately been able to respond to the challenge he posed almost five hundred years ago.

Notes

1. Here and throughout I use Mansfield's new translation of *The Prince*. Niccolo Machiavelli, *The Prince*, trans. with an introduction by Harvey C. Mansfield (Chicago: University of Chicago Press, 1985), chap. 15, 61.

2. Niccolo Machiavelli, *Discourses on Livy*, trans. Harvey C. Mansfield Jr. and Nathan Tarcov (Chicago: University of Chicago Press, 1996), III.6.

3. Livy, *The Early History of Rome*, trans. Aubrey de Selincourt (Harmondsworth, Middlesex: Penguin Classics, 1960), 83.

4. Machiavelli, *Mandragola*, Ligurio in act 1, sc. 3. All quotes are from *Mandragola*, trans. by Mera J. Flaumenhaft (Prospect Heights, IL: Waveland Press, 1981).

5. Machiavelli, *Mandragola*, Callimaco in act 1, sc. 1.

6. Catherine Zuchert also connects *Clizia* to chapter 25 of *The Prince*. She identifies the relationship between Sofronia's willingness to conquer Fortuna with her rejection of a reliance on God to solve her problems ("Fortune Is a Woman—But So Is Prudence: Machiavelli's *Clizia*," in *Finding a New Feminism: Rethinking the Woman Question for Liberal Democracy*, ed. Pamela Grande Jensen [Lanham, MD: Rowman & Littlefield, 1996], 23-37). This too is the challenge that the prince must face, accomp-lishing his (her) ends through a reliance on his or her own *virtù* and not on Fortuna. See also chapter 6 of *The Prince*.

7. *Clizia*, act 4, sc. 1, 351. All quotes from *Clizia* are from the translation by David Sikes and James B. Atkinson in *The Comedies of Machiavelli* (Hanover, NH: University Press of New England, 1985).

Chapter 8

The Natural Rights Family: Locke on Women, Nature, and the Problem of Patriarchy

Lee Ward

In recent times, the thought of John Locke has been the subject of an intense debate involving both liberal and feminist commentators concerned with the position of women in Lockean natural rights theory. It has often been forgotten amid the din that liberalism and feminism derive their inspiration from a common source, the critique of patriarchy. Both liberalism and much of modern feminism rest on a foundation of individualism that is at the heart of this critique.[1] Some commentators, while remaining harsh critics of Locke, have still suggested that liberal individualism holds great promise of freedom and equality for women.[2] Locke's argument that human freedom and equality is consistent with beings whose "common Nature, Faculties and Powers, are in Nature equal, and ought to partake in the same common Rights and Privileges" rings through much of the modern debate about women's position in the family and political society (I:67, II:4).[3] The nature and status of women must be an issue for natural rights politics.

The current debate over the status of women in Lockean natural rights theory has pitted critics of Locke's argument concerning women against those who defend his natural rights argument as a clear, if partial, advance for sexual equality in the family and in political society. The contemporary critique of Locke is varied and has focused on many diverse elements of his thought, but there do seem to be a few common themes that recur throughout the literature. One theme has been that Locke's understanding of natural freedom and equality conceals a deeper argument for the natural inequality of men and women. It has been argued that Locke's conception of the family rests on a kind of natural male rule derived from his argument for men's natural superiority in strength and ability and on women's presumed natural disadvantage in reproduction.[4] Another theme holds that Locke's theory of property rights in the family constitutes a rejection of women's capacity to acquire property on equal terms with men and denies women the rationality required to participate in the forming of civil society.[5] A variant on this theme argues that Locke's entire theory of the family and political society systematically excludes the equality of women because it was intended to provide the theoretical justification of the absolute right of males to pass their property to their legitimate male heir.[6] A third criticism is that Locke maintains the constant subordination of married women through the terms of the marriage contract but does so under a thinly veiled "gloss of consent."[7] A fourth element of the argument among Locke's critics is that his theoretical distinction between conjugal and political society encourages a dichotomization of human life into a public, political sphere and a private, familial sphere. This dichotomy, it is argued, perpetuates the subjection of women in the private sphere of family life.[8] These four major streams of criticism all involve an argument that in one sense or another Locke's political teaching includes a violation of his own individualist principles when they are applied to women.

It may be unfair to generalize on the basis of an all too brief summary of what is an extremely complex criticism, but perhaps we can draw one principal conclusion from the major themes of Locke's contemporary critics: they see Locke's critique of patriarchy as, at best, a timid and incomplete attempt to extend the principles of natural freedom and equality to women and, in the worst case, a dismal sham systematically subordinating women in the family while extending his newly articulated freedom exclusively to men. What is common to all of these critics is the argument that though Locke sought to challenge patriarchy as a model and moral support for absolute monarchy, he did so without destabilizing the rule of husbands over wives in the family.[9] In this way Locke's critique of patriarchy may be seen as inadequate and demanding a critique of liberalism in that patriarchy, at least insofar as it provides a rationale for the natural inferiority of women, is a "constitutive part of the theory and practice of liberalism."[10]

Locke's defenders argue that the critique of his patriarchalist opponent Robert Filmer constitutes a partial, though significant, assertion of a natural ground for the equal rights of women in the family and in political society. This defense of Locke's argument concerning women rests on two main aspects of his thought. The first element of this defense points to the salutary consequences for women of a natural rights argument rooted in individual freedom and equality. It is argued that, though Locke retains some patriarchal assumptions regarding natural male superiority in the family and in political life, his individualist principles contain a logic of equality that can be extended through all familial relations and through the questions surrounding women's participation in politics and education. In being true to Lockean individualist principles, liberals "would be forced to bring their views on women into line with their theory of human nature."[11] Another strand of the contemporary defense of Locke's natural rights argument as it relates to women emphasizes the possibilities for greater equality and individual freedom inherent in Locke's theoretical distinction between the private and public realms of activities. According to this argument, Locke's view of society is comprised of a "multitude of interacting and partially integrated spheres" which promotes a greater degree of equality for women in each sphere by preventing the form of authority in one sphere from seeping into another.[12] Though many commentators have observed great caution in Locke's writings, perhaps due to his sensitivity to the prevailing prejudices of his time, even his defenders suggest that Locke failed to fully follow through on the implications of his natural rights argument as it pertains to the status of women.[13] Locke's general theory, in this view, established a more promising conceptual framework for sexual equality than his specific arguments would suggest.

This essay reexamines Locke's political teaching in light of this contemporary debate in order to determine whether Locke's claims to a new understanding of human freedom and equality can be seen as encouraging real sexual equality. It will be shown that there is a much greater harmony between Locke's specific arguments concerning women and his more general natural rights theory than has been supposed by both his critics and his defenders. Locke's reflections on nature led him to a radical reconceptualization of the family and politics. When the different strands of Locke's argument are connected we can recognize Locke's self-conscious awareness that the natural rights principles upon which he establishes his own political premises pervade his entire discussion of the family and politics. It will be argued that particularly in Locke's reformed version of the family, the natural rights family, we can see that his attack on patriarchy at its roots produced a radical, if often implicit, critique of the established conceptions of nature, religion, and the relations of men and women and parents and children. By considering Locke's treatment of conjugal society, the historical origins of patriarchy, the distinct but interrelated relations of the family and civil society, women's property rights, and the importance of educational reform, we will argue that Locke's destruction of the patriarchal family as a model for government ushered in the creation of a new understanding of the family and politics, one consistent with the natural freedom and equality of women. In reflecting on Locke's critique of patriarchy, the modern reader may come to appreciate the importance of this reformulation of the conception of women and the family for the origin of liberal politics.

Conjugal Society and the Problem of Nature

The state of nature is the theoretical grounding of Lockean individualism and the foundation for his conception of human nature. This prepolitical condition clearly develops Locke's view of the natural freedom and equality of humankind. This state is one of *"perfect Freedom"* wherein all individuals are able to "order their Actions, and dispose of their Possessions, and Persons as they think fit" (II:4). This freedom is not a mere contingent fact based on the hypothetical absence of civil law but is based on the natural equality of human beings as such. Nature is "a *State* also of *Equality*, wherein all the Power and Jurisdiction is reciprocal, no one having more than another" (II:4). As we are rational beings "promiscuously born to all the same advantages of Nature and the use of the same faculties," no individual is entitled to a natural authority over another (II:4). It would seem therefore that no source of authority, whether political or familial, may be derived from a natural inequality. It is from this perspective that determining women's place in the contractual family becomes pivotal.

The bulk of the contemporary debate over Locke's thought deals with the alleged subjection of women, either by nature or by contract, in the family. It seems fitting therefore to examine Locke's treatment of conjugal society. This discussion immediately follows the chapter dealing with paternal power and precedes his treatment of political society proper. By proceeding in this way Locke both clearly distinguishes the two kinds of power that the patriarchalists confounded, fatherly and political rule, and reminds us that the family neither derives from nor can be understood solely in light of the power of fathers or of political society.

Locke begins his consideration of the family with a quasi-biblical appeal: "God having made man such a Creature, that, in his own Judgement, it was not good for him to be alone, put him under strong Obligations of Necessity, Convenience and Inclination to drive him into Society" (II:77). Whereas the creation of Eve (Gen. 2:18-22) marks an expression of divine providence, in Locke's reformulation of the first society of man and woman the individual is "driven" by necessity and inclination to form a larger unit. The first society, Locke continues, was between "Man and Wife," which led to an expanding web of relations including parents and children and later that of "Master and Servant" (II:77). Soon Locke drops the scriptural rhetoric entirely when he reveals that "Conjugal Society is made by a voluntary Compact between Man and Woman" consisting in "such a Communion and Right in one another's Bodies, as is necessary to its chief End, Procreation" (II:78). The family must ensure "mutual Support, and Assistance" of the parents but also what is "necessary to their common Off-spring, who have a Right to be nourished and maintained by them" (II:78). When we realize that in Genesis—which was the authoritative source for Filmer—there is no talk of voluntary compacts or children having rights, and that in the biblical account of the curse of Eve procreation comes to be bound to humankind's fallen nature, then we begin to sense that Locke's new formulation of the family will differ greatly from traditional notions.

Locke's own account of the origins and structure of the family seems to follow from his observations of the natural world. Like the animals, the union of the human male and female is intended not simply for "Procreation, but the continuation of the Species," and as such it "ought to last, even after Procreation, so long as is necessary to the nourishment and support of the young Ones" (II:79). But Locke argues that human biology differs from that of the animals "because the female is capable of conceiving, and de facto is commonly with Child again, and Brings forth too a new Birth long before the former is out of a dependency for support on his Parents help" (II:80). The unique circumstances of extended infancy and female fertility explain "why the Male and Female in Mankind are tied to a longer conjunction than other creatures"(II:80). As a result, the human male "who is bound to take care of those he hath begot" is under greater "Obligation" than the males of most other species (II:80). The union of male and female is made "more lasting" than that of other animals so that "their Industry might be encouraged, and their Interests better united, to make Provision, and lay up Goods for their common Issue" (II:80). Locke's naturalistic account of the family concludes with a return to semireligious language as "the Wisdom of the great Creatour," who, to facilitate the biological needs of humanity, has "given to Man foresight and an Ability to lay up for the future" (II:80).

In contrast to the patriarchalist claims that scripture teaches the subjection of women and children to fathers (and especially Filmer's claim that all political rulers rule in the name of the first father, Adam), Locke argues for a naturalistic understanding of the origin of the family in the particular needs of human biology. This naturalistic argument deemphasizes the notion that parents, especially fathers, derive any natural authority over their children from being their source. Rather, humans, like the other animals, are to sustain their children until "they are able to shift and provide for themselves" (II:79). Yet Locke's account shows the human family to be distinguished from the animals in several ways. First, it originates in a voluntary compact between a man and a woman. The voluntary basis of human society is an expression of our natural freedom as conjugal society logically precedes the relation of parent and children. Also, only human offspring have a "Right" to be maintained (II:78). The logic of rights does not seem to operate in the nonhuman world. Another difference may be seen in how Locke argues that the human union "ought to last" long enough to support the young until maturity. Of this general rule "the Inferiour Creatures steadily obey," but Locke is strangely silent about human obedience to this rule (II:80). Instead, Locke argues that humans have been given "foresight" and an ability to accumulate property for future use. Whereas animals seem restricted to the supply of "present necessity," the human family reflects our unique futurity (II:80). As we may recall from Locke's chapter on property, it is this insecurity, which results from our desire to secure future pleasure and to avoid future pain, that is the spur to human labor and industry.[14] Contained in this notion of the importance of the human sense of futurity is Locke's identification of our relation to the external world as being one of a fundamental sense of lack of provision in the harsh necessity of nature. The human self is both conscious of its needs and of its inherent neediness. It is this future orientedness that most distinguishes humans from other creatures.

This naturalistic account of the origins of the family is revealed to be somewhat problematic when we glance back to the *First Treatise*. It is here, in the midst of his attack on Filmer's argument for paternal right through generation, that Locke argues that the simple "Act of begetting" imports no right to paternal dominion (I:50). This is at least partially based on Locke's observation that: "What Father of a Thousand, when he begets a Child, thinks farther then [sic] the satisfying his present Appetite?" (I:54). While the family may require foresight, the act of begetting requires none. Locke concedes that children are not produced in a manner involving reason and foresight but rather by "strong desires of Copulation" (I:54). The foresight required to preserve the young is not simply derived from the desire to copulate. In fact, the only mechanism to continue the species operates "without the intention, and often against the Consent and Will of the begetter" (I:54). How then are we to understand foresight as the ground of the family?

Locke's distinction between conjugal society, which requires foresight, and copulation, which implies none, raises a serious problem of consent. It is a central Lockean tenet that all human association derives its legitimacy and even its very existence from the consent of the contracting parties. Yet his argument that most parents do not consent to having children, and even those who "design and wish to beget them" have no actual control over whether and when conception will occur, raises the question of why parents are obligated to care for their children (I:54).[15] Beneath this discussion lie the roots of a potential human tragedy, in that we naturally free beings are produced by a process that violates the principle of consent that underlies all legitimate obligation. For Locke, reproduction seems to be a phenomenon that reminds us—as the patriarchalists have argued—of some inherent lack of freedom at the core of the human condition. We consent to marriage, government, and even language, but we can neither truly consent to begetting nor consent to being begotten.[16] Locke's distinction between conjugal society and copulation reveals that though the voluntary union of man and woman should precede the relation of parent and child, children are not the product of foresight but of a strong desire. Though this potential tragedy, which sees human reproduction as a phenomenon that undermines the moral validity of consent as the origin of legitimate obligation, has produced a tendency in the past to see the universal facts of human birth as a sign of our natural subjection, Locke implies that it is this desire rather than the "Act of begetting" that is the true natural beginning point for understanding the family.[17] To understand the way in which this potential tragedy is overcome in the family we must examine Locke's account of the principal human desires.

Locke's account of the principal human desires establishes a primary desire for self-preservation and a secondary desire to perpetuate oneself through one's children. As he explains:

> The first and strongest desire God planted in Men, and Wrought into the Very Principles of their Nature being that of Self-preservation, that is the Foundation of a right to the Creatures, for the particular support and use of each individual Person himself. But next to this, God planted in Men a strong desire also of propagating their Kind, and continuing themselves in their Posterity. (I:88)

The first desire grounds the right to property, while the second, subordinate desire points to family life.[18] The significance of this account of the desires is twofold. First, Locke makes it clear that the right to property is rooted in the universal desire for self-preservation. But children, being born weak and helpless, thus have a right to be "nourished and maintained by their Parents" (I:89).[19] Second, the hierarchy of human desires differs from that of the animals, for whom "the Preservation of their Young, as the strongest Principle in them overrules the Constitutions of their particular Natures" (I:56). The primacy of the particular, individualistic desires seems to result from the human rational nature. Locke argues that God directs humankind by their "Senses and Reason" as he does "the inferior Animals by their Sense and Instinct" (I: 86). The human lack of instinct seems to make their concern for their children somewhat more complex. Whereas animals "steadily obey" the rules of conjugal society necessary to preserve their young, humans, while possessing an "Intellectual Nature," are uniquely unprovided with instinct (II:80, I:30).[20] The human family is an institution that is both the most required and least provided for in nature.

The absence of a regular and stable instinct to govern family life presents Locke with two major problems. First, he has to make caring for the young compatible with the self-preservation of the parents.[21] Perhaps this is why the concern for property pervades Locke's discussion of the family. Conjugal society must encourage "their Industry . . . and lay up Goods for their common Issue" (II:78, 80). The good of the family, seen as accumulating property, will be consistent with the preservation of all its members. Locke's second problem is the insecurity of the male's attachment to his children. When Locke argues that concern for propagation derives from concern for self-preservation, he implies that this parental concern is activated only by the actual presence of one's offspring.[22] A mother who carries a child is more likely to effect such an attachment than a father who may not see his child or be certain that a child is his and thus may continue his self through his "Posterity."[23] We recall that it was particularly in respect to men that Locke argued, "What Father in a Thousand, when he begets a Child, thinks farther then [sic] the satisfying his present Appetite?" (I:54). Thus, we see that Locke's conjugal society is not an observation of natural human family behavior but a prescription of what ought to be a stable union that both secures the parents' attachment to their children and activates foresight to help secure the family needs without encouraging notions of natural or divinely sanctioned subjection of one over another.

Locke's discussion of conjugal society and the principal desires, which underlie it, makes the family appear as the epitome of what Locke calls a "complex idea."[24] The human family requires the synthesizing of many ideas and desires. It is because humans are rational that the family is a complex idea and not the product of unthinking instinct. The family is a rational response to natural necessity, but as a human contrivance and product of reason it is capable of better or worse formulation. By reconsidering the family in light of the ends of childrearing, Locke places the family on more rational grounds than traditionally held.[25] To look for the origin of political power in the family, Locke argues, is to misunderstand the purpose of both institutions. The great potential for tragedy and subjection, made manifest in patriarchy, may be overcome when we see the family as a human construction not simply determined by unfree necessity. Perhaps the true "foresight" underlying the family is that of the philosopher who devises a conception of it consistent with our natural freedom and equality. The family may, by satisfying the two strongest human desires, come to be an integral, constituent element of Locke's promise of the human conquest of nature and emancipation from necessity.

The account of conjugal society points to the problem of nature for the human family. On the one hand, the family originates in unthinking desires and the harsh necessities human biology imposes for child rearing. On the other hand, the human family, for Locke, is not, strictly speaking, natural and has important elements of consent in it, but these very elements of consent indicate that the human family is both the most required conjugal unit in nature and also a convention particularly unprovided for by physical and human nature. The family or conjugal society requires the application of reason in its actual formation by contracting individuals and for understanding the ends implied in this original construction. In this light, Locke's critique of patriarchy plays double duty as both a new analysis of what the family is, grounded on his theoretical understanding of nature, and as a new legislation for the family modeled on the practices that would conform to the standard of natural rights.

The Historical Origins of Patriarchy

When we turn to look at Locke's treatment of women in the family, we may begin to assess the criticism that Locke's argument for natural freedom and the voluntary, contractual basis of the family does not redress the traditional subjection of women.[26] This issue first emerges in the *First Treatise*. In the course of attacking Filmer's argument that scripture supports a husband's rule over his wife, Locke addresses the key scriptural passage regarding the curse of Eve (Gen. 3:16). Locke argues that any subjection implied in this passage may extend only to Eve or at least imports "no more but that subjection they (wives) should ordinarily be in to their Husbands" (I:47). Then he reveals that the curse is actually an act of "Providence," a kind of prediction that a woman "should be subject to her husband, as we see that generally the Laws of Mankind and the Customs of Nations have ordered it so" (I:47). Locke moves quickly to limit the effect of this traditional subjection as: "there is no more Law to oblige a Woman to such a subjection, if the circumstances either of her Condition or Contract with her Husband should exempt her from it" (I:47). On the surface Locke goes far to limit this subjection of women as he argues that husbandly power may be variable and limited by contract and does not include the political power over life and death, and he denies that this subjection extends to a woman's children or "all that should come of her" (I:47-49).[27] But wary readers are most struck by Locke's concession that, despite all his proposed limitations on husbandly power, there is "I grant, a Foundation in Nature for it" (I:47).

How are we to understand this "Foundation in Nature"? Is it something demanding our moral respect and obedience?[28] The first indication of Locke's attitude toward this natural foundation for female subjection may be seen in the context of his scriptural analysis. The discussion of the curse of Eve is preceded by Locke's treatment of biblical interpretation. Here Locke argues that God, "when he vouchsafes to speak to Men, I do not think, he speaks differently from them, in crossing the Rules of language in use amongst them" (I:46). Thus, the meaning of scripture is unambiguous. But when speaking of Eve, Locke argues that "*Thy desire shall be to thy Husband,* is too doubtful an expression, of whose signification Interpreters are not agreed, to build so confidently on, and in a Matter of such moment, and so great and general Concernment" (I:49). The position of women in the family becomes a crucial part of Locke's radical reinterpretation of scripture, for in the relation of husband and wife the Bible holds "too doubtful an expression" to build on confidently. Clearly, then, Locke's "Foundation in Nature" does not admit of scriptural support.

Locke suggests that the foundation for the traditional subjection of wives may be found in "the Laws of Mankind and Customs of Nations" (I:47). In this view God's providence as fact is almost equated with the general agreement of civilized men. This formulation of the "Foundation in Nature" raises two problems. The first is Locke's ambivalence toward looking to providence as a guide for human action: "If any one will say that what happens in Providence to be preserved, God is careful to preserve as a thing therefore to be esteemed by Men as necessary or useful, 'tis a peculiar Propriety of Speech, which every one will not think fit to imitate" (I:147).

By equating the curse on women with providence Locke implies that this subjection carries no paradigmatic or obligatory status.[29] The second problem for the natural subjection of women in law and custom is Locke's general criticism of making "the Example of what hath been done, be the Rule of what ought to be" (I:57). By such reasoning, Locke argues, one could justify not only subordinating wives but also cannibalism, adultery, incest, and every form of child abuse imaginable (I:57-59). The laws and customs of nations, which have often lacked a foundation in reason, which is humanity's "only Star and compass," cannot be said to establish a foundation in nature for anything in familial relations (I:58).

The context of this discussion, namely the curse of Eve, suggests that the foundation of inequality may involve the female role in reproduction. This has led some commentators to argue that Locke simply accepts the female reproductive capacity as a natural disadvantage codified in law.[30] But if Locke equates a wife's subjection with the "disadvantage" of childbirth, this is far from a simple subjection. Locke argues that there is no more law to oblige a woman to this subjection than "there is, that she should bring forth Children in Sorrow and Pain, if there could be found a remedy for it" (I:47). Locke's individualist principles suggest that just as a woman may improve the terms of conjugal society by contract, she may also blamelessly employ any device to reduce the pain of childbirth. Both the mutability of the marital contract and the potential for overcoming birth pains suggests that there is, for Locke, a certain malleability in human affairs that can allow for great improvement in the position of women in society.

When we examine Locke's treatment of the curse of Eve, we see that the traditional subjection of women lacks the character of a divine or natural law. Women are not strictly bound by necessity but rather may contract with their husbands on the best terms possible, just as they may seek medical aid to reduce the pain of childbirth. It may be significant that only three women are named in this crucial section, Eve and the two English queens, Mary and Elizabeth. Locke cites the last two as examples to show the absurdity of the patriarchalist argument for the subjection of wives: "And will any one say . . . that either of our Queens Mary or Elizabeth had they married any of their Subjects, had been by this Text put into a Political Subjection to him?" (I:47). Perhaps the contrast of Eve, denizen of the prepolitical Garden of Eden, and Mary and Elizabeth, both rulers of civil societies, suggests that the "Foundation in Nature" for wifely subjection may be changeable or improved to a large extent depending on the rationality of the form and laws of civil government. In a rational society the traditional subjection may be wholly anachronistic.

To identify the character of the "Foundation in Nature" for the subjection of wives we have to reexamine Locke's account of conjugal society in the *Second Treatise*. Here Locke argues that the structure of parental relations is not simply implied in the act of contracting. Though two free and equal beings may contract, this cannot ensure perfect agreement in all matters; therefore as it is necessary "that the last Determination, i.e., the Rule, should be placed somewhere, it naturally falls to the Man's share, as the abler and stronger" (II:82). Now the "Foundation in Nature" seems to embrace what Lorenne Clark calls a "natural male superiority in virtue."[31] Perhaps it is simply the inoperability of the principle of majority rule in the relation of only two contractors. Either way, Locke soon limits this exclusive male rule as "reaching but to the things of their common Interest and Property, leaves the Wife in full and free possession of what by Contract is her peculiar Right" (II:82). Thus, the husband's control over family property does not extend to the wife's particular property protected by contract, nor does it seem to assign the wife to some particular role or way of life.[32] As it appears that the husband's power does not include political power (over life and death) and reaches no wider than the family, perhaps the common concern over which the husband presides involves authority over the children.[33] At the very least we must presume that this power, like the curse of Eve, would not extend to a queen.[34] Nonetheless, Locke's argument that male rule in the family is natural seems to contradict the natural freedom and equality of all.

A crucial element in the contemporary critique of Locke is that the natural inequality implied in the rule of husbands as "abler and stronger" violates Locke's political principles. It creates a de facto inequality beneath a "gloss of consent."[35] Perhaps Locke's limitations on the husband's authority merely serve to undermine patriarchalist claims that husband's rule over wives is a model for absolute monarchy while retaining the natural subordination of women in the family. In this way Locke can separate the public and private spheres, thereby excluding women from the public realm, and demonstrate that public authority cannot be derived from authority in the family.[36] Some commentators have argued that even though Locke rests a husband's rule not on nature but on contract, he always assumes that married women will subject themselves.[37] Locke's discussion of male authority in the family leaves us to ponder at least these questions then: What is the status of a natural rule in an institution that is not simply natural? Is the natural subordination of women operable in all cases of conjugal society, both in nature and civil society? Can the "Foundation in Nature" for the subjection of wives be overcome by human contrivance?

In order to understand the status of married women, it will be useful to examine Locke's account of the historical origins of the patriarchal family. This account is interrupted by the chapter dealing with conjugal and political society (II:74-76, 105-12). By placing his argument for conjugal society between these two discussions, Locke distinguishes his conception of the family, a naturalistic one, from the traditional notions that have governed human thought. Locke argues that "in the first Ages of the World, . . . the Father of the Family" was "Prince of it" (II:74). This authority did not extend to power of life and death and was derived from the "express or tacit consent of the Children" and seems to have involved two distinct powers (II:74). First, the father alone in the family was permitted "that executive Power of the Law of Nature" which involves the right to punish other individuals in order to "preserve the innocent and restrain offenders" who would use force without right against any other individual (II:74,7-13,18). Second, paternal power extended to the settling of disputes and "controversies" over his children's property (II:75,107,108). Thus, Locke concedes that paternal power emerged as a model for family government rooted in the family's need for a recognized agent in the punishment of criminals and in the judging of property disputes.

It has been suggested that Locke's historical account of paternal power is a large concession to the patriarchalist argument.[38] Theresa Brennan and Carole Pateman argue that it represents Locke's legitimization of the exclusion of women from political life as his emphasis on the children's consent and his silence about the consent of a wife implies that the marriage contract contains a wife's implicit consent to the "transmogrification" of her husband.[39] Moreover, Locke's assumption of the natural inferiority of women precludes the possibility of matriarchy as the primitive form of government.[40] Nonetheless, reexamination of Locke's treatment of the historical origins of patriarchy shows that it does not constitute a concession to patriarchalism for a number of reasons. First, Locke demonstrates that the principle of consent can account for even the most patriarchal familial arrangement.[41] The consent of women to marriage and the consent of children to paternal rule maintains the principle of natural freedom even in an imperfect model of authority.[42] Second, though Locke does concede that the patriarchal family is historical, he does not concede that it is right. Locke explicitly links the emergence of one-man political rule to the structure of the patriarchal family as he argues, in the origin of commonwealths: "We shall generally find them under the Government and Administration of one man. I am also apt to believe, that where a Family was numerous to subsist by it self, . . . the Government commonly began in the Father" (II:105). This link of the patriarchal family and absolute monarchy reveals that the structure of the family—the first and most formative social relation for any human being—can be a source of habitual, unthinking submission in which women and adult children (or all subjects save the king) endanger their natural freedom. The establishment of legitimate government based on principles consistent with freedom and equality seems to require, in Locke's view, a reformation of the family.

Locke reminds us at the beginning of this discussion that even if patriarchy was the original form of the family this example is not authoritative now, as "An argument from what has been, to what should of right be, has no great force" (II:103).[43] We are reminded that the family is a complex idea requiring reason and experience, rather than simple instinct, to determine the structure consonant with freedom and equality. In the "innocence of the first Ages" patriarchy emerged, like monarchy, as a "simple" idea, one "most obvious to men"(II:94,107). Perhaps patriarchy suited that "poor but Virtuous Age" when there were few people and few possessions (II:110,105). Yet we may recall that in Locke's discussion of property it is precisely this age of poverty, in which patriarchy thrived, that Locke's teaching is trying to overcome (II:42).[44] Locke even suggests that this "Golden Age" may have had a seamier side, as some fathers might have lost their authority due to "Negligence, Cruelty, or any other defect of Mind" (II:111,105).[45] Far from being a concession to patriarchalism, this discussion suggests that the patriarchal family leads to faultily constructed governments that require people of greater experience to "examine more carefully the Original and Rights of Government, and to find out ways to restrain the Exorbitances, and prevent the Abuses of that Power" (II:111).[46] Human beings, lacking instinct or a natural political end, must use reason to lead to a goal not immediately apprehensible to reason as such. Herein lies Locke's promise for the improvement of family and government.

This account of the historical origins of patriarchy becomes more problematic when we turn to a curious passage in the heart of Locke's treatment of paternal power. In the course of his argument against Filmer's claim for absolute paternal dominion, Locke makes a revealing argument:

> And what will become of this *Paternal Power* in that part of the world where one Woman hath more than one Husband at a time? Or in those parts of America where when Husband and Wife part, which happens frequently, the Children are all left to the Mother, follow her, and are wholly under her Care and Provision? (II:65)

When we compare this statement with Locke's account of conjugal society, we can see that human relations are more complex than that discussion would lead us to believe. Here Locke suggests that there are parts of the world in which polyandry is accepted practice.[47] More importantly, we see that in some "parts of America" there is a conception of the family that violates Locke's argument against the "uncertain mixture, or easie and frequent Solutions of Conjugal Society" (II:80). The problem in the wastes of America, then, is not patriarchy but that there is no reliable paternal presence at all. The full significance of this statement comes to light only when we remember that "In the beginning all the World was America, and more so than it is now" (II:49).[48]

Locke's conception of conjugal society, we come to realize, is a highly conventional body because there is no natural support for the family, especially for the nomadic male who may never see his own child. Perhaps the mother may recognize the survival of her children as an expression of her desire to perpetuate herself through them, but as we recall from Locke's discussion of the principal human desires, it would seem that concern for offspring is elicited only by the actual presence of one's offspring (I:54-56, 88).[49] The frequent parting of husband and wife in America reminds us that Locke does not see in nature a reliable guarantee of a father's concern for his offspring.[50] Perhaps this is why Locke implied the possibility of matriarchy when he spoke of a "Family, wherein the Master or Mistress of it had some sort of Rule proper to a Family" (II:77).

When we consider Locke's account of the historical origins of patriarchy in light of his consideration of the infrequency of a lasting and reliable conjugal society in America, we come to see Locke's view of patriarchy somewhat differently. Patriarchy emerges as a later development in human relations and is a severely flawed response to the natural necessity to preserve offspring. The patriarchal family is a voluntary compact in which a woman submits to the authority of a husband by allowing him secure access to her body (which produces the vital corollary of ensuring paternal legitimacy) and in return gains a regular helper in securing the preservation of herself and her children. The male desire to copulate, as distinct from the desire to perpetuate himself through his offspring, becomes the grounding of spousal relations, and the particularizing of this desire through the regular cohabitation with a voluntary, contractual partner becomes the foundation for stable conjugal society. Though the patriarchal family may be seen as a deeply flawed improvement over the extreme penury of the natural state, Locke does go so far as to suggest that "Without such nursing Fathers tender and carefull of the publick weale, all Governments would have sunk under the Weakness and Infirmities of their Infancy" (II:110). The "Foundation in Nature" that explains the traditional subjection of wives seems to be rooted in a woman's voluntary subjection to a man to help secure her offspring. Locke suggests that this subordination is the product of a faulty familial arrangement that emerged in the poverty of the "first Ages" and is ultimately an inadequate attempt to overcome natural necessity and preserve the species. The question for us now is to determine whether Locke rests content with this patriarchal familial arrangement.

In light of Locke's account of the historical origins of patriarchy, it is necessary to investigate whether the state of nature actually contains the government of fathers and husbands and whether Locke's theoretical distinction between the state of nature and political society merely serves to show that, while supporting one-man rule in the family, he does not see it as a model for political life.[51] When we begin to analyze this "government of fathers," we see that the state of nature is deeply troubled by the "partiality and violence of Men" (II:13). Civil government emerges as the "proper remedy for the Inconveniences of the State of Nature, which must certainly be Great, where

Men may be Judges in their own Case" (II:13). Locke implies that the state of nature, wherein people lack a common judge or "Authority," is characterized by almost perpetual conflict (II:9,19, 21).[52] Locke later reveals that the state of nature is so insecure that "To avoid this State of War . . . is one great reason for Men's putting themselves into Society, and quitting the State of Nature" (II:21).[53]

The state of war implicit in the state of nature undermines the achievement of the ends of the family. Common property generated to preserve the young is radically insecure in a condition in which there is no common force to restrain "those Evils, which necessarily follow from Men's being Judges in their own Cases" (II:13). The natural desire for self-preservation ensures that this condition is "not to be endured" (II:13). Thus, the transition to political society implies the ultimate inadequacy of the patriarchal family as an institution designed to secure the lives and possessions of its members as well as an institution in serious tension with the natural rights of women and children. In light of the historical origins of patriarchy, we might also ask if the family is necessarily unchanged in the transition to Locke's conception of civil society.[54] When we begin to analyze the place of the family in civil society, we must recognize that Locke's stated aim is to distinguish these two institutions (II:2,58,61,76,77,82,87). The rule of fathers in the "first Ages" represents a simple and inadequate attempt to secure one end of the family, namely securing the property necessary for the preservation of all the family members (II:94,107). Though Locke argues that the family and civil society rest on a foundation of individual consent, they each involve consent to a different kind of institution. Civil society is not simply derived from the family, as the patriarchalists argue, because the "ends, tyes and bounds of each" are different (II:77,86). Locke argues that the family does not require civil society for its existence, as the ends of marriage may be "obtained under Politick Government, as well as in the State of Nature" (II:83). The family may be better able to secure its ends, even in the precarious natural condition, than under an absolute monarchy (II:13,92,93). When we try to determine the status of women in the family in civil society, we must recall that both institutions derive from individual consent as an attempt to secure through human contrivance what nature so sparingly supports.

In Locke's account of the historical origins of patriarchy we saw that wives and children consented to fatherly rule, which consisted in allowing one man to judge "controversies" regarding property and to punish transgressions of the rights of others (II:74,75,107,108). In Locke's conjugal society he makes a similar argument for paternal rule, as the male—"the abler and stronger"—has the "last Determination" regarding things "of their common Interest and Property" (II:82). Yet we must determine whether this apparently natural male rule over women binds them to a subjection in the private, familial sphere, thereby depriving them of their natural and public rights.[55] Even though Locke limits this paternal power in several ways, it still seems to raise problems for Locke's general teaching.[56] The relations of husband and wife cannot be governed by Locke's political principle of majority rule (II:96-98). The problem of majority rule in the family seems to lead us to that essential problem of the state of nature in which men, in this case fathers, "may be Judges in their own Case" (II:13). Locke's view of the family becomes even more grim when we recall that this condition encourages the "partiality and violence of Men" (II:13). Locke seems to imply that the rule of "abler and stronger" fathers, lacking a common judge in the family, hardly seems to be a recipe for good parenting. We must now consider if the common "Umpire" of civil society that remedies the "Inconvenience" of the natural state may also play a role in liberalizing or rationalizing the family.

The transition to civil society involves two crucial things. First, it is necessary "to quit everyone his Executive Power of the Law of Nature, and to resign it to the Publick, there and only there is a Political, or Civil Society" (II:89). Second, there must be the creation of a "common established Law and Judicature to appeal to, with Authority to decide Controversies between them" (II:87). Civil society requires common rules of judgment and punishment. The two functions that women and children have historically granted to the father, judgment and punishment, are now, Locke argues, the functions par excellence of civil government. Civil society is instituted to secure the property—including the lives—of all of its members and as such requires almost exclusive power of judgment and punishment.

The relation of the family to civil society is central to Locke's understanding of natural freedom and equality. In the relations of husband and wife, Locke argues, the "Civil Magistrate doth not abridge the Right" to the attainment of the ends of the family, but civil government does possess the power to decide "any Controversie, that may arise between Man and Wife about them" (II:83). But what of the man's rule as the "abler and stronger"? The problem of majority rule in spousal disputes is somewhat overcome when we consider that the deciding vote in such matters may be a civil judge. Moreover, the "natural" paternal rule over family property seems to be seriously qualified by the presence of civil government to settle marital disputes.[57] In light of this role of government, the claims of "abler and stronger" husbands appear highly contingent on prevailing conditions. What may be necessitated in the natural condition may have no reasonable ground for consent in an established legitimate regime. The government becomes the "abler and stronger" force that can best preserve the property of all its rights-bearing citizens. Perhaps the fullest expression of Locke's view of the proper spousal relations in the rationally ordered family would not involve any particular "Power in the Husband" but rather "might be varied and regulated by that Contract, which unites Man and Wife in that Society" (II:83).

Locke's discussion of conjugal and political society has serious implications for the status of women in the family. Locke argues that civil government may settle "any Controversie that may arise between Man and Wife." Because Man and Wife are "in Political Society together" and are thus "united into one body" they also have a "common ... Judicature to appeal to, with Authority to decide

Controversies between them" (II:83,87). Locke seems to suggest that men and women may be in conjugal and political society simultaneously. Beneath this suggestion may lie the notion that civil government established on the grounds of natural rights acts on individuals, including women, because it is individuals who form governments to protect their rights. The creation of conjugal and political society institutionalizes the public and private spheres of life, but rather than subjecting women to male rule in the domestic sphere, Locke seems to be distinguishing two areas of life the separation of which does not preclude the public activity of adult children. The private family, geared toward procreation and education, is primarily intended for the education and nurturing of children, whereas the public realm serves to facilitate the adult concerns of securing property and individual rights.[58] Locke's argument for the contractual understanding of spousal rights and duties suggests that it is not the separation of the public and private spheres that leads to the subjection of women but rather their confounding by the patriarchalists.

The complexity in Locke's account of the historical origins of the patriarchal family seems to be due to his attempt to give an account of what is and to provide a normative account of what by right should be. By distinguishing and contrasting what is from what should of right be, Locke is attempting, on the immediate level, to counter the prevailing providentialist account that tended to conflate these two. In separating the "is" from the "ought," Locke undermines the patriarchal argument of Filmer for the divine ordination of power in politics and in the family, which held that things are as they are because God made them that way, and since God made them that way that is how they should be.[59] Locke reveals patriarchy to be an erroneous principle animating a flawed conception of the family, which nonetheless proves to be a very common historical response to the penury of nature. On a more general level, Locke seems to be pointing the reader to the uniquely human capacity to equate truth with tradition. The argument for the patriarchal family, with its alleged supports in scripture and historical custom, provides Locke with a particular example to illustrate the broader danger to securing natural rights posed by the all-too-frequent human tendency to abandon reason, our "only Star and Compass" (I:58).

The Natural Rights Family

Though Locke does seem to recognize the subjection of women in the family as a feature of all previous thought, his new understanding of human freedom and equality suggests that this condition can and should be overcome.[60] The individualist principles that ground Locke's thought move him toward a view of the family consistent with this natural freedom and equality. While producing a "family safe for liberalism," Locke works to undermine the traditional supports for fatherly rule, such as arguments for greater strength and ability, and in the process opens room for the potential liberation of women.[61] Strength, Locke argues, does not give title to rule because people should not "live together by no other Rules but that of Beasts, where the Strongest carries it" (II:1).[62] All manner of inequalities of age, virtue, birth, and alliance may thrive in society without justifying the subjection of anyone "to the Will or Authority of any other Man" (II:54). Locke's new contractual family provides the theoretical framework for an arrangement in which the relations of husband and wife may be consistent with a political society based on natural freedom and equality.

One major criticism of Locke's natural rights theory is that women, being subsumed in the family, do not play a role in the original contract that begins civil society. In this view the individuals who enter civil society are fathers of families.[63] Yet when we consider Locke's treatment of conjugal and political society, this argument seems unfounded. Locke argues that a woman may protect her own "peculiar" property under the terms of the marriage contract (II:82). Also, civil government possesses the power to settle any "Controversie" between husband and wife (II:83). One plausible source of dispute may be over family property generated during the marriage. But why would a married couple require a human convention to decide what should easily be determined by nature, by man as "abler and stronger"? It seems that Locke is suggesting that a women's property rights are, like those of her husband, subject to a power beyond the limited sphere of the family, namely, civil law. If Locke recognizes women as individuals and property holders, they would have the same motive for entering civil society as men, namely, to secure their property. This is especially significant given Locke's identification of the natural right to property with the preservation of the individual's life and liberty. Property is both an end as an expression of human freedom, as this right is rooted in our self-ownership, and a means to the preservation of that freedom (II:27; 18, 131). Locke implies that the creation of a public sphere may allow women to preserve their property, and hence their freedom, in the event of a dispute with their husbands. Perhaps it is only in civil society that a woman would be able to protect both her particular and her family interests.

Locke's reconstitution of the family on a contractual basis implies that "the consent of every individual" needed to create civil society means more than merely that of fathers (II:96).[64] Perhaps it may be argued that a woman's consent to civil society is implied in her marriage contract.[65] Yet this argument is cast in doubt by Locke's suggestion that it would be absurd to think that a marriage contract would effect the political capacity of a reigning queen (I:47).[66] A woman may be obliged to enter civil society on the same grounds as a man. Women in the family may better secure their property in civil society, where they can appeal to the law, than in the state of nature, where the husband almost imperceptibly assumes executive power. The security offered by civil law would certainly be an incentive for a woman to contract into civil society in order to secure her "Life and Liberty," and as Locke argues: "No rational Creature can be supposed to change his condition with an intention to be worse" (II:131).

Locke's account of conjugal and civil society has been accused of creating a dichotomy of the public and private spheres that obscures the inequality of women in the family.[67] This argument suggests that Lockean liberalism systematically excludes women from the public sphere by encouraging their dependent position in the family. Yet the logic of Locke's reformulation of the family on the grounds of natural rights does not insulate the private sphere from the effects of the public principles of legitimate government; rather, the improved status of women in the family and political society seems to be crucial for reconstructing all social relations on the basis of these principles of legitimacy. To determine the depth of Locke's reformulation of the role of women in society, we will need to examine the status of women with respect to the key elements of political life. This will involve looking at the position of women relative to Locke's discussion of property rights in the marriage contract, labor, inheritance, and rationality.

A crucial question for determining the status of women in Lockean society is whether their property rights are recognized in the conjugal and political contract and whether the formal extension of such rights provides women with a meaningful control over their lives and their children's lives. Clearly, if men and women are not in a position of equality in the family Locke's support for a woman's freedom to contract as best she can is undermined by the subordination of women in the family to their husbands.[68] Yet one of the core patriarchalist arguments that Locke is attacking is the view that political authority originates in the universal childhood dependence on fathers. In this view human beings are neither competent nor entitled to actively improve their original condition.[69] Locke's entire theory of the family and government seems to make the argument that the improvement of a self-regarding individual's position with others is not simply possible but is necessary for protecting individual rights and releasing the productive capacities of a nation. A case in point is Locke's argument that the marital union is soluble. Locke argues that "the Wife has in many cases, a Liberty to separate from him (her husband); where Natural Right, or their Contract allow it" (II:82). Arguably, Locke's great innovation was in making the marriage contract negotiable, limited, and terminable.[70] The wife's natural right to separation seems to parallel the citizen's natural right to resist tyrannical government.[71] Locke argues that no one can consent to arbitrary rule or be required to honor a contract with a government that has become tyrannical (II:23, 24, 204-08). Likewise, a woman's natural freedom cannot be alienated by the first act of contract with her husband. The right to separation reaffirms her natural freedom. Locke's argument for a woman's right to resistance reminds us that the liberal ideals of consent and natural freedom can profoundly influence familial relations by providing the ground for a revolution in the relations of men and women that can lead to the establishment of families and governments consistent with human freedom and equality.[72]

A pivotal criticism of Locke's conception of conjugal society is that it denies women the natural right to acquire property through their labor. It has been argued that Locke's conjugal society violates this principle as a wife's right to the property generated by her labor is transferred to her husband.[73] The implication of this argument is that Locke cannot view women as naturally free beings because the ground of the property right through labor is the natural freedom of the human person. As Locke argues: "Man (by being master of himself, and *Proprietor of his own Person*, and the Actions or *Labour* of it) had still in himself the great Foundation of Property" (II:44). Private property derives from neither civil law, revelation, nor the consent of any other individual. Thus, if Locke does not extend the right to acquisition through labor to women, he has denied their very humanity by implying that women either do not appropriate through labor or have no claim to ownership.[74] To assess this argument we must carefully examine Locke's statements about women's capacity for acquisitive labor.

Locke's explicit references to the female capacity for labor are few but revealing. The first direct reference arises in Locke's refutation of Filmer's position that all title to property derives from God's grant of Dominion to Adam. Locke points out that God's grant of "Dominion over every Living thing that moveth on the Earth" (Gen. 1:28) was extended not solely to Adam but to "them," meaning him and Eve.[75] The significance of this for the position of all wives is revealed when Locke argues: "If it be said that *Eve* was subjected to *Adam*, it seems she was not so subjected to him, as to hinder her *Dominion* over the Creatures, or *Property* in them" (I:29). Locke disproves the absolute subjection of Eve on the grounds that it would be strange to "say that God ever made a joint Grant to two, and only one was to have the benefit of it" (I:29). The patriarchalist assumption that marriage places a woman entirely in service to her husband ignores the basic fact of nature that every person has the right to preserve his or her self (II:6). Buried in this patriarchalist assumption is the failure to recognize that though the family may involve an individual's concern extending to all the family members, *the root of property* is not in the service of others nor even in the service of the self, but in the very existence of the self. This, Locke argues, is as true of Eve as of all wives. The marriage contract cannot annul this natural right to acquisition because it is not in any individual's power to renounce the right to their own preservation, which is expressed in the natural right to property.

Locke's most explicit references to a woman's right to acquisition are contained in his discussion of conquest. This chapter is unique in two senses. First, it is Locke's only full treatment of what he considers to be a third hypothesis of the origin of political power besides that of consent and patriarchy.[76] Second, it is the only chapter in which Locke explicitly speaks of a wife's property acquired through her labor. We should examine the connection between these seemingly unrelated issues. Locke argues that the turbulence of human history has led many to "have mistaken the force of Arms, for the consent of the People; and reckon Conquest as one of the originals of Government" (II:175). Locke assures us that any argument proceeding from force cannot explain the origins of legitimate government. The rule of force is the way of "beasts of prey" and "savage ravenous," "noxious creatures" (II:1, 16, 181, 182). Force can certainly destroy a government, "but, without the consent of the People, can never erect a new one" (II:175). The link to Locke's theory of labor is in reminding us that just as only consent can create lawful government, it is only labor that creates the original title to property. Acorns may be bought, bartered, or inherited, but what first made them private and made a "distinction between them and the common" must have been someone's labor (II:28). Force can account for neither title to property nor the origins of lawful government.

The question of a woman's title to property emerges in the context of Locke's discussion of the rights of a lawful conqueror. The lawful power of such a conqueror—who has fought in retaliation against unprovoked aggression—is "perfectly despotical" over those responsible for the war (II:178-80). The one major restriction on the conqueror's rights is a "strange doctrine" whereby they do not extend to "the Innocent Wife and Children" (II:180, 182). The lawful conqueror "may appropriate to make himself reparation" from the goods of the unjust aggressor, but "he cannot take the Goods of his Wife and Children; they too had a Title to the goods he enjoy'd, and their shares in the Estate he possessed" (II:183). This "strange doctrine" may be Locke's attempt to define rules of conquest and occupation, but it also has implications for his view of the status of women.[77] The grounds for this restriction on the right of conquest differ as they relate to wives and children. Children have "a Title to their Father's estate for subsistence" (II:183). The natural right of children to be maintained—and the family's role in continuing the species—must not be interfered with even in a just war. But with respect to wives Locke argues that they have a title to property in their own right: "My Wife had a share in my estate, that neither could I forfeit . . . whether her own Labour or Compact gave her a Title to it, 'tis Plain, Her Husband could not forfeit what was hers" (II:183). A child has a right to his or her parents' property whether he or she labors or not, but a wife's sole title to property is through labor or contract. A wife's share in her husband's estate may even suggest that wives derive some title over family property generated during the marriage.

This discussion reveals that the property generated through a wife's own labor cannot be simply subsumed into her husband's estate. Locke employs the extreme case of foreign conquest to reveal the simplistic and unjust assumption underlying the patriarchal view of the family. When the paterfamilias loses a war, does his family lose their right to survive? This individual natural right can never be lost through the actions of others. Just as force is the way of "beasts," in forgetting that individual rights ground any human association, the patriarchalists regard women, children, and men as mere beasts. Locke also implies in this discussion that any family structure that denies women the right to the products of their own labor or denies them the contractual means to preserve their property is modeled on unjust conquest. Such a familial arrangement resembles the unfounded argument that force can provide title to property. This kind of argument contradicts natural rights and undermines the ground of any civilized society. In this view marriage would be like a perpetual state of war. Locke on the other hand sets a high standard for any legitimate familial arrangement: neither force nor paternity but only the consent of free and rational individuals can explain the origin of the family and civil society.

The issue of inheritance is crucial to Locke's theory of property and central to his reform of the family. As such, it is evident that real equality for women would require an equal right to the disposition of family property.[78] It has been argued that Locke's construction of the family simply provides the theoretical basis of the absolute right of males to pass on their property to their legitimate male heirs.[79] To assess this argument we will examine Locke's view of inheritance, particularly his attitude toward the practice of primogeniture. Locke's main treatment of primogeniture occurs in the *First Treatise* in his attack on Filmer's notion of the divinely ordained "monarchy by inheritance." Here Locke argues that in those "countries where their particular Municipal Laws give the Whole possession of Land entirely to the First Born, and descent of Power has gone so to Men by this Custom, some have been apt to be deceived into an Opinion, that there was a Natural or Divine Right of Primogeniture to both Estate and Power" (I:91).

Clearly, this passage is Locke's attempt to unlink the transmission of property through primogeniture from the patriarchal assumption of the transmission of power in the same way. As Locke argues, the distinct character of property and political rule are incommensurable, since government exists for "the good of the governed," whereas property is "for the benefit and Sole advantage of the Proprietor" (II:92).[80] Though the principal aim of this discussion may be to attack the patriarchalist tendency to confound the inheritance of property with that of title to rule, we cannot ignore that in the course of this assault Locke also questions the natural or scriptural justification for primogeniture (I:91, 111-18).[81] Locke even seems to imply that in those "Countries where their particular Municipal Laws" support primogeniture there is a tendency to structure the descent of political power on the same basis (or at least the two practices are often coeval), and this tendency may habituate people to support absolute monarchy. The unthinking, purely traditional practice of bequeathing property to the eldest son seems to mirror the dangerous condition in which ruler and ruled alike forget that all legitimate government rests on the consent of the governed and not on the birthright of an eldest son.

Locke's whole discussion of inheritance exposes a tension between a child's natural right to "inherit, with his Brethren, his Father's Goods" and the parent's right to freely dispose of his or her property (II:190). We recall that property exists for the "Sole Advantage of the Proprietor" and is the "unquestionable Property of the Labourer" (I:92, II:27). There seems to be a clash between the free, rational choice implied in the parents' right to dispose of their goods and the natural right of the children to inherit them. When we consider Locke's general teaching on property, it seems that he is not basing the child's natural right on any natural parental duty, as this would violate the sole proprietorship of the laborer, but rather is basing it on a parent's desire to continue his or her self through the child (I:88).[82] In this view a child's right to inherit is severely conditional on a parent's free will and not on a natural or divine argument for primogeniture.[83] Locke's rejection of primogeniture also seems to reflect his rejection of the premise that property belongs to a family as a whole and that the individual right—either of parents or children—is simply subsumed to serve its needs and interests.[84] We can begin to sense that inheritance will be a key element in Locke's reform of the family and civil society.

Locke's argument for the reform of inheritance law has profound implications for the position of women in the family. In the chapter "Of Paternal Power," Locke argues that this power does not extend to a natural dominion over a child's person, actions, possessions, or "whole Property" (II:57). By the law of nature, Locke argues, paternal power is actually "an obligation to preserve, nourish, and educate the children" (II:56). In return a child is bound to "that honour which he ought, by the Law of God and Nature, to pay to his *Parents*" (II:66). Significantly, Locke self-consciously asserts that the duty to educate, nourish, and preserve children is actually "parental" because "whatever obligation Nature and the right of Generation lays on Children, it must certainly bind them equally to both the concurrent Causes of it" (II:52).[85] Locke's assertion that parental honor must extend to mothers will have a serious impact on whether women may freely dispose of their property or come to inherit it themselves.

Through the course of Locke's discussion of parental power it becomes apparent that there is no natural guarantee of a child's duty to honor his or her parents. Locke makes a halfhearted appeal that "however it may become his Son in many things, not very inconvenient to him and his Family, to pay a deference to it" (II:69). Locke's less than enthusiastic endorsement of filial gratitude makes us aware that there is no natural law obligation as such for adult children to obey or honor their parents.[86] But Locke continues: "There is another *Power* ordinarily *in the Father*, whereby he has a tie on the Obedience of his Children: . . . And this is the Power Men generally have to bestow their Estates on those, who please them best" (II:72). Locke hints that "this is no small Tye on the Obedience of Children" (II:73). The parent's power to bequeath property on those children "who please them best" becomes the natural glue that—along with education—holds Locke's contractual family together.

Locke's theory would systematically discriminate against women if, though extending equality to women in the area of education, it did not extend this equality to the distribution of property. As such, maternal honor would simply depend on the arbitrary will of the male property holder, the father.[87] Locke's argument implies otherwise. Of maternal honor Locke argues: "The Father's authority cannot dispossess the mother of this Right, nor can any man discharge his Son from honouring her that bore him" (II:69; I:62). Locke continues that any honor due to a father "is owing to the Mother too" (II:70). If Locke has systematically deprived women of the right to transmit property to their heirs, we would have to ask if he is making an uncharacteristic appeal for an unconditional duty or is rather implying a mother's right to a share in the estate. The inalienability of the right to maternal honor suggests that the right to bequeath property is not invariably exercised by the father (Locke says it is a power "ordinarily" and "generally" in fathers) but may be delegated or even exercised by the mother in her own right (II:72).[88] It has been suggested that Locke never addresses the status of single women.[89] Yet the argument for a mother's need to possess property in order to secure the honor and support of her children must have serious implications for the position of separated women (I:62; II:82). The solubility of marriage in Locke's conception of the family makes any woman potentially a single woman (II:81,82). Locke is certainly encouraging women to protect their property under the terms of the marriage contract, but he may also be indicating that securing the right to generate property during the marriage would be any sensible woman's condition for entering marriage. Without such a secure holding it is unclear why any woman would diligently nourish and educate children who would never be obliged to support or honor her later.

Inheritance is central to Locke's reform of the family. The reduction of the Fifth Commandment to a child's calculated self-interest to inherit parental goods emerges as a great incentive for parents (especially women) to accumulate property, but it also frees industrious children from filial obligations to lazy, unproductive parents.[90] One crucial consequence of Locke's natural rights argument as it pertains to inheritance is the stimulation of the acquisitive talents of the family members. When the enjoyment of inherited goods is a source of political obligation, inheritance also becomes a stabilizing force in political society (II:73). This discussion has particularly profound implications for women's equality. Locke's equating of parental honor with securing property provides a rationale for the extension of property rights to women, particularly in the case of widowed or separated women. Moreover, Locke's attack on primogeniture may extend the right of inheritance to daughters, allowing them to negotiate their own marriage contracts more freely and on better terms. It may be a daughter, rather than an eldest son, who most comports with the "Will and Humour" of her parents (II:72). By making favoritism rather than primogeniture the basis of inheritance law, Locke seeks to counter the stultifying resignation of individuals to their economic condition and the dictates of custom.[91] Rather, Locke aims to unleash the productive capacities of individuals who, relying on their own industry, are brought to a recognition of the true misery and insecurity of the natural condition.

The thrust of Locke's teaching may be summed up in the statement: "Thus we are born *free*, as we are born Rational" (II:61). This simple but beautiful line rests at the heart of Locke's understanding of human nature and is an argument antithetical to patriarchy. Of children's dependence on parents, Locke argues: "Age and Reason as they grow up, loosen them till at length they drop quite off, and leave a Man at his free Disposal" (II:55). It has been argued that Locke's treatment of women excludes them from his conception of rationality. But, for Locke, individual rationality is tied, though not limited, to the powerful desire for self-preservation common to all human beings. Diana Coole and others have argued that Locke prevents the full development of female rationality by restricting women to the private sphere, yet this ignores the degree to which Locke prevents the insulation of the family from the public principles of legitimacy.[92] If women lacked the reason characteristic of full human relations, they would be what Locke calls "Lunaticks," "Ideots," "Innocents," or "Madmen" (II:60). If Locke believed this he never said so. Rather, we saw that in America, children are often left wholly under the "Care and Provision" of their mother (II:65). Granted, Locke implies that women often require men to help secure their children, but clearly Locke does not argue that women by nature require men to preserve themselves (II:77-80). In Locke's view of nature, reason, like necessity, is not gender specific.

A key aspect of the issue surrounding female rationality is the act of contracting. To be a party to a contract implies rationality because the "Brutes" do not contract. Contracting is an expression of human freedom and reason, which consists of two distinct principles: the freedom *to* contract, regarding whether and with whom to contract, and the freedom of contract regarding the choice of terms.[93] Though a woman in the natural condition may be under strong necessity to contract with a man to secure her children, Locke clearly argues that in principle it is ultimately her free choice that will decide, whether in nature or civil society. Locke also goes very far in arguing for a woman's freedom of negotiating the terms of the marriage contract (II:82, 83, 183). The inherent rationality of the contractual act suggests a political contract that can legitimately support monarchy, aristocracy, or democracy as well as a marriage contract that supports a number of familial arrangements (II:81-83).[94] The family may be ruled by a "Master" or "Mistress," or the spousal affairs may be "varied and regulated" entirely by contract (II:77, 83). The mutability and adaptability of either contract is restricted only to the impossibility of legitimately consenting to arbitrary rule (II:23, 82). Neither absolute monarchy nor the extreme patriarchal family à la Filmer are justified by Locke's account of human reason.

Perhaps one of the most striking features of Locke's reformation of the family is his emphasis on its educative role in the formation of free and equal citizens. The family, so long an enemy of liberty, will have the responsibility of educating children, consistent with their natural freedom, and do so independent of political supervision.[95] Of this important role, Locke continually emphasizes that "the mother hath an equal share" (II:52, 53, 55, 58, 66, 67). In one fell swoop Locke undermines the patriarchalist inference of political obligation from paternal power and redistributes the remaining "parental" power—education—into the hands of the father and mother equally. Though it may appear that Locke's argument for parental education serves to limit a father's absolute control over his children but still leaves men, not women, ruling the family, this fails to recognize the way in which Locke's treatment of education undermines paternal claims to rule.[96] By extending the duty of education to mothers, Locke places women in the very crown of the family's virtues. Women as powerful agents in achieving the chief moral goal of the family is a stark contrast with the patriarchal family, which encouraged unthinking submission and obedience to the father alone. In failing to recognize the distinction between the family and political society, patriarchy failed to recognize that politics is the realm of mature, self-regarding adults while the family is characterized by the relations of parent, as educator, to child. The family, for Locke, is not meant to institutionalize the unequal power relations of the adult male and female but rather is intended to provide for the maintenance and education of the young through the institutionalization of the relations of parent and child.[97] If the family were ordered on the basis of Locke's proposal, there is nothing to suggest that it would preclude the political participation of women.

The mother's role in education reaffirms Locke's argument for the inherent rationality of women. The very essence of Lockean education is the inculcation of the principles of reason in children. Parents should make the mind of the child "pliant to Reason" and encourage "such vigour and rectitude to their minds, as may best fit the children to be most useful to themselves and others" (II:64, STCE:34).[98] Parental relations wherein two free and equal beings work together for a common end, without the subjection of either party, may also provide an example for the moral development of future citizens of a liberal society, thus showing the enormous public importance of the private family.[99] Perhaps the full extent of Locke's argument for women's rationality is seen in his contradiction of one of the long-cherished tenets of Aristotelian biology: "The Rational Soul . . . (of the yet Unformed Embrio) . . . if it must be supposed to derive anything from the Parents, it must certainly owe most to the Mother" (I:55). Though Locke's materialism predisposes him to reject the superiority of form over matter, he seems to argue that even if one proceeds from Aristotelian terms, the generation of the rational soul would indicate the natural superiority of women, not men. Locke's reinterpretation of the generation of animals, like his reformation of family education, reaffirms his argument for the natural equality of beings "promiscuously born to all the same advantages of Nature" (II:4).

Having examined the impact of Locke's educational reform on mothers, we should now look at the status of daughters. Near the beginning of Locke's *Some Thoughts Concerning Education,* he reveals a telling ambiguity: "I have said He here, because the principal Aim of my Discourse is, how a young Gentleman should be brought up from his Infancy . . . , though where the Difference of Sex requires different treatment 'twill be no hard Matter to distinguish" (STCE: 6).

A few sections later Locke reveals the essential similarity of the proper education of boys and girls as he proposes that, of the education of daughters, "the nearer they come to the Hardships of their Brothers in their Education, the greater Advantage will they receive from it all the remaining Part of their Lives" (STCE:9). The significance of Locke's views on the education of girls is twofold. First, his encouragement of physical training for girls suggests that the presumed physical weakness of the "softer sex" may be overcome by individual effort.[100] It implies that much of the concern for female fragility is the result of convention, the product of a poor education rather than any natural cause. The suggestion that girls can strengthen their bodies reminds us of Locke's argument that women may relieve the pain of childbirth "if there could be found a Remedy for it" (I:47). As Melissa Butler has pointed out, Locke's individualist principles encourage women to resist succumbing to complacency in their current condition and stresses the ability of individual women to overcome their particular obstacles.[101] Perhaps more importantly, Locke's reform of family education makes the encouragement of this belief in daughters a parental duty.

The second and perhaps most significant implication of Locke's view of the education of girls may be seen in that, in a book intended for the education of young gentlemen to prepare them for careers in business and politics, Locke retains only minor, nonintellectual differences for girls.[102] It is in his *Letter to Mrs. Clarke* that Locke reveals the source of his argument for the essential commonality of the method required for the mental development of boys and girls: "I acknowledge no difference of sex in your mind relating ... to truth, virtue, and obedience, I think well to have no thing altered in it from what is (writ for the son)."[103] Clearly both girls and boys should be schooled in the use of reason. Locke's argument that the native intellectual potential of girls should be developed in childhood seems to mark a revolution in thinking from the patriarchal assumptions of the natural and irremediable inequality of father and child, male and female.

Locke's argument for the equal education of girls and boys casts a critical light on traditional notions of conventional sex roles in the family and politics. Locke's thoughts on education, like so much else in his work, reflects his belief that there is a pliancy in human nature that is obscured by procrustean efforts to design a rigid, differentiated education for girls and boys. Locke encourages parents toward a deeper reflection on the influences of a conventional education and the misguided assignment of individual rights and duties on the basis of sexual difference.[104] His own theory of education raises new possibilities for an understanding of the moral and intellectual development of children that would reduce the inequality of men and women in the public and private spheres.[105] Locke hints at the potential for revolutionary change in human relations near the end of this work when he expresses his hope that "it may give some small light to those, whose Concern for their dear little Ones makes them so irregularly bold, that they dare venture to consult their own Reason, in the Education of their Children, rather than wholly to rely upon Old Custom" (STCE:216).

Though Locke points to the natural rights family as the end product of his critique of patriarchy, it is necessary to engage in the debate over the thorny question of Locke's reluctance to explicitly follow through on the more radical implications of his natural rights argument. The first possible explanation is rooted in the political and historical context in which Locke worked. The *Two Treatises*, which contains his clearest attack on patriarchy, is a work of constitutional theory as well as a work of political philosophy. Because it is on the immediate level a constitutional tract intended to combat the promonarchy arguments in the Exclusion Crisis, Locke presumably had to be cautious in illuminating the full implications of his natural rights theory for fear of losing support for the Whig constitutional position from men concerned primarily with the political balance of power that was the focus of the immediate controversy.[106] Locke addresses this very particular feature of the argument in the preface to the *Two Treatises* when he appeals to any "Englishman, much less a Gentleman" who would display the "generous Temper and Courage of our Nation" (I.1). It is unclear whether the typical "Englishman, much less a Gentleman" of Locke's time would wholly support his radical vision for the reformulation of the family and of women's role in society.

The second explanation for Locke's reluctance to explicitly follow through on the more radical elements of his argument is rooted in his philosophy itself. His conception of nature holds the promise of sexual equality but also reveals a certain fragility at the core of the family. Locke seems to recognize that the extreme individualism that could be extrapolated from his theory would actually undermine liberal rights. The need to preserve a stable conjugal unit in the face of the harshness of nature is rooted in the notion that human biology makes children vulnerable longer than the young of other animals, but Locke also suggests that a properly structured family can act as a spur to economic growth, which will redound to the benefit of all. For example, the stable conjugal union encourages the industry of parents to accumulate property in order to pass it on to their children.[107] The family can become a vehicle for the conquest of nature, which by itself provides "little more than nothing." (II:42) Yet Locke's vision of the family as a spur to economic growth does not depreciate from his conception of the reformed family as the primary school for teaching the respect for rights. The conquest of physical nature through human labor and technology does not require the conquest of or the liberation from the family, but rather it requires the destruction of the patriarchal model of the family. Locke's vision of the moral purpose of the family as the inculcator of respect for rights in the young makes the reformed family a cornerstone of natural rights citizenship for men and women.

Conclusion

It is hoped that this examination of Locke's treatment of women in the family and political society may uncover some of the generally obscured points of harmony between Locke and many of his contemporary critics. Commentators drawn to the defense of Locke's argument as it pertains to the status of women may also more fully appreciate the extent to which Locke's radical reformulation of the family and political society on the ground of natural rights serves the aim of sexual equality. His critique of patriarchy in the name of natural freedom and equality both undercuts previous claims to male dominance on the grounds of a natural or divinely sanctioned superiority and bases the family and government on individual consent. In arguing that the traditional sources of the subjection of women, namely the family and civil society, are human institutions capable of improvement, Locke desanctifies and denaturalizes the inequality of women. Locke's discussion of the natural rights family and the property rights and education of women presents a conception of women as rights-bearing individuals free to control their lives. Political society, for Locke, is not a natural association in which the position of women is simply determined by the interweaving of lower natural associations, such as the family. The poverty of nature provides no such natural order or set "boundaries ... giving exactly the same real internal constitution to each individual which we rank under one general name."[108] Locke's conception of the self-actualizing individual encourages both the improvement of women's lot and the creation of families and political societies consistent with natural freedom and equality.[109] Nature will be both the problem and the solution for the establishment of liberal politics.

In many ways, Locke's critique of patriarchy began a revolution in thinking that made modern feminism possible. He systematically undercut the core patriarchalist assumptions that had marked, to varying degrees, all premodern thought. Like many feminists today, Locke recognized the importance of language and custom as either a source of subjection or a vehicle for liberation. Perhaps Locke laid the foundation for the rhetoric of women's liberation when he argued of the distinction between paternal and parental conceptions of authority, that finding "fault with words and names that have obtained in the World ... it may not be amiss to offer new ones when the old are apt to lead Men into mistakes" (II:52-53). In the end, though, Locke may not have been too sanguine about the immediate prospects for change implied in all areas of his teaching as "this mistake of words ... charm men into notions far remote from the truth ... remaining firm in their minds, it is no wonder that the wrong notions annexed to them should not be removed."[110] Locke suggests that it will take a long time to overcome the poverty and error of the past. At one point in the *Second Treatise,* Locke compares the "Humane" tenderness of parents to God's chastisement of the Israelites in Deuteronomy 8:5 (II:67). When we look at this biblical passage we realize that God's tenderness involved the death of an entire generation of people after forty years in the desert before reaching the Promised Land. Perhaps Locke's promise may also require many years and much pain before women can reach his view of the land of plenty and justice for all.

Notes

The author would like to thank the Lynde and Harry Bradley Foundation for their generous support during work on this chapter.

1. Carole Pateman, *The Disorder of Women* (Stanford: Stanford University Press, 1989) 118.
2. Theresa Brennan and Carole Pateman, "Mere Auxiliaries of the Commonwealth: Women and the Origins of Liberalism," *Political Studies* 27, no. 2, (June 1979): 187.
3. I cite from the *First* and *Second Treatises.* See John Locke, *Two Treatises of Government*, ed. Peter Laslet (Cambridge: Cambridge University Press, 1965).

4. Lorenne Clark, "Women and Locke: Who Owns the Apples in the Garden of Eden?" in *The Sexism of Social and Political Theory*, ed. Lorene Clark and Lynda Lange, (Toronto: University of Toronto Press, 1979), 16, 19, 25, 36; Diana Coole, *Women in Political Theory* (Boulder: Lynne Rienner, 1993) 64; Pateman, *Disorder*, 121.

5. Brennan and Pateman, "Mere Auxiliaries," 193, 195; Clark, "Women in Locke" 32; Coole, *Women in Political Theory*, 73, 75.

6. Clark, "Women in Locke," 16; Coole, *Women in Political Theory*, 70.

7. Brennan and Pateman, "Mere Auxiliaries," 183-84, 191-93.

8. Jean B. Elshtain, *Public Man, Private Woman* (Princeton: Princeton University Press, 1981), 122, 127; Susan Moller Okin, *Justice, Gender and the Family* (New York: Basic Books, 1989), 111; Pateman, *Disorder*, 120.

9. Coole, *Women in Political Theory*, 68; Carole Pateman, *The Sexual Contract* (Stanford: Stanford University Press, 1988), 3, 22.

10. Pateman, *Disorder*, 123.

11. Melissa Butler, "Early Liberal Roots of Feminism: John Locke and His Attack on Patriarchy," *American Political Science Review* 72 (March 1978): 135.

12. Mary Walsh, "Locke and Feminism on Private and Public Realms of Activities," *Review of Politics* 57 (Spring 1995): 252.

13. For good discussions of Locke's famous caution, see Butler, "Early Liberal Roots," 147; Richard Cox, *Locke on War and Peace* (London: Oxford University Press, 1960), 1-44; Elshtain, *Public Man*, 121-22; Thomas Pangle, *The Spirit of Modern Republicanism* (Chicago: University of Chicago Press, 1987), 132-38; Leo Strauss, *Natural Right and History* (Chicago: University of Chicago Press, 1953), 206-09, 220, 246; and Michael Zuckert "Fools and Knaves: Reflections on Locke's Theory of Philosophical Discourse," *Review of Politics* 36, no. 2 (1974): 544-64 and his "Of Wary Physicians and Weary Readers: The Debate on Locke's Way of Writing," *Independent Journal of Philosophy* 2 (1977): 55-66.

14. Nathan Tarcov, *Locke's Education for Liberty* (Chicago: University of Chicago Press, 1984) 97.

15. David Foster, "Taming the Father: John Locke's Critique of Patriarchal Fatherhood," *Review of Politics* (Fall 1994): 659; and Ingrid Makus, *Women, Politics and Reproduction* (Toronto: University of Toronto Press, 1996), 67.

16. For consent to language, see John Locke's *Essay Concerning Human Understanding*, ed. Peter H. Nidditch (Oxford: Oxford University Press, 1975) III.2.8. (Hereafter ECHU III.2.8).

17. Foster, "Taming the Father," 659.

18. Foster, "Taming the Father," 646.

19. Tarcov, *Locke's Education*, 67.

20. Tarcov, *Locke's Education*, 69.

21. Foster, "Taming the Father," 647.

22. Tarcov, *Locke's Education*, 68.

23. Pangle, *The Spirit*, 174.

24. For complex ideas, see ECHU III.iii.1-7, III.x.22-33; For thinking separates us from animals, see ECHU II.ix.11, 15.

25. Pangle, *The Spirit*, 230-32.

26. Brennan and Pateman, "Mere Auxiliaries," 183; Coole, *Women in Political Theory*, 64-65.

27. Tarcov, *Locke's Education*, 59.

28. Pangle, *The Spirit*, 173.

29. Tarcov, *Locke's Education*, 64.

30. Clark, "Women and Locke," 17; Coole, *Women in Political Theory,* 64; Elshtain, *Public Man, Private Woman,* 125.
31. Clark, , "Women and Locke," 19.
32. Coole, *Women in Political Theory,* 66.
33. Gordon Schochet, *Patriarchalism in Political Thought* (Oxford: Oxford University Press, 1975), 249-50.
34. Tarcov, *Locke's Education,* 70.
35. Brennan and Pateman, "Mere Auxiliaries," 191.
36. Coole, *Women in Political Theory,* 65; Pateman, *Disorder,* 121.
37. Brennan and Pateman, "Mere Auxiliaries," 183-84, 192-93.
38. Laslett, 316 note lines 14-37; Foster, "Taming the Father," 651; Pateman, *Sexual Contract,* 92-93.
39. Brennan and Pateman, "Mere Auxiliaries," 194.
40. Coole, *Women in Political Theory,* 69.
41. Foster, "Taming the Father," 652.
42. Tarcov, *Locke's Education,* 75.
43. Foster, "Taming the Father," 651.
44. Foster, "Taming the Father," 652.
45. Foster, "Taming the Father," 652.
46. Tarcov, *Locke's Education,* 75.
47. Walsh, "Locke and Feminism on Private and Public Realms of Activities," 265.
48. Pangle, *The Spirit,* 236.
49. Tarcov, *Locke's Education,* 68.
50. Pangle, *The Spirit,* 236.
51. Brennan and Pateman, "Mere Auxiliaries," 193.
52. Strauss, *Natural Right and History,* 228.
53. Strauss, *Natural Right and History,* 224-25.
54. Clark, "Women and Locke," 16, 33; Pateman, *Disorder,* 193.
55. Brennan and Pateman, "Mere Auxiliaries," 191; Clark, 19; Pateman, *Disorder,* 120.
56. Butler, "Early Liberal Roots of Feminism," 145.
57. Compare with Brennan and Pateman, "Mere Auxiliaries," 193; Butler, "Early Liberal Roots of Feminism," 147; Coole, *Women in Political Theory,* 66.
58. Walsh, "Locke and Feminism on Private and Public Realms of Activities," 262.
59. See especially Robert Filmer, *Patriarcha and Other Writings,* ed. Johann Somerville (Cambridge: Cambridge University Press, 1991), 6-7 (sect. 3), 11 (sect.9).
60. Butler, "Early Liberal Roots of Feminism," 143.
61. Foster, "Taming the Father," 641; Tarcov, *Locke's Education,* 76.
62. Mary Shanley, "Marriage Contract and Social Contract in Seventeenth Century English Political Thought," *Western Political Quarterly* 32, no. 1 (March 1979): 90.
63. Brennan and Pateman, "Mere Auxiliaries," 185; Pateman, *Sexual Contract,* 52-53.
64. Strauss, *Natural Right and History,* 229; Tarcov, *Locke's Education,* 71.
65. Brennan and Pateman, "Mere Auxiliaries," 185; Coole, *Women in Political Theory,* 72.
66. Butler, "Early Liberal Roots of Feminism," 147.
67. Okin, *Justice, Gender and the Family,* 111.
68. Coole, *Women in Political Theory,* 64-65.
69. Tarcov, *Locke's Education,* 19.

70. Butler, "Early Liberal Roots of Feminism,"144; Shanley, "Marriage Contract and Social Contract in Seventeenth Century English Political Thought," 89.

71. Shanley, "Marriage Contract and Social Contract in Seventeenth Century English Political Thought," 83.

72. Walsh, "Locke and Feminism on Private and Public Realms of Activities," 268-69.

73. Brennan and Pateman, "Mere Auxiliaries," 192; Coole, *Women in Political Theory,* 73.

74. Clark, "Women and Locke," 32.

75. Butler, "Early Liberal Roots of Feminism," 142.

76. Tarcov, *Locke's Education,* 214 n.5.

77. Locke's other *strange doctrine* was the executive power of the Law of Nature (II:9).

78. Clark, "Women and Locke," 27.

79. Clark, "Women and Locke," 16; Coole, *Women in Political Theory,* 70.

80. Tarcov, *Locke's Education,* 60.

81. Tarcov, *Locke's Education,* 61.

82. Pangle, *The Spirit,* 232-33.

83. Pangle, *The Spirit,* 233.

84. Foster, "Taming the Father," 649.

85. Shanley, "Marriage Contract and Social Contract in Seventeenth Century English Political Thought," 89.

86. Strauss, *Natural Right and History,* 218.

87. Clark, "Women and Locke," 27, 30.

88. Martin Seliger, *The Liberal Politics of John Locke* (New York: Praeger, 1969), 216.

89. Clark, "Women and Locke," 20.

90. Foster, "Taming the Father," 667; Pangle, *The Spirit,* 238.

91. Pangle, *The Spirit,* 242; Michael Zuckert, "An Introduction to Locke's First Treatise," *Interpretation* 8 (January 1979): 73-74.

92. Brennan and Pateman, "Mere Auxiliaries," 195; Coole, *Women in Political Theory,* 75.

93. Okin, *Justice, Gender and the Family,* 120; Shanley, "Marriage Contract and Social Contract in Seventeenth Century English Political Thought," 79.

94. Pateman, *Disorder,* 129; Walsh, 267.

95. Foster, "Taming the Father," 646; Tarcov, *Locke's Education,* 72.

96. Clark, "Women and Locke," 22.

97. Walsh, "Locke and Feminism on Private and Public Realms of Activities," 276; Makus, 56.

98. See also Walsh, "Locke and Feminism on Private and Public Realms of Activities," 276. All references to John Locke's "Some Thoughts Con-cerning Education" are from *Locke's Educational Writings,* ed. James L. Axtel, (New York: Cambridge University Press, 1968). Hereafter, this will be cited as STCE:34.

99. Tarcov, *Locke's Education,* 100.

100. John Locke's "Letter to Mrs. Clarke, February 1685," *Locke's Educational Writings,* ed. Axtell, 344.

101. Butler, "Early Liberal Roots of Feminism," 149.

102. Axtell, *Locke's Educational Writings,* 344-45.

103. Axtell, *Locke's Educational Writings,* 344-45.

104. Butler, "Early Liberal Roots of Feminism," 149.

105. Walsh, "Locke and Feminism on Private and Public Realms of Activities," 277.

106. For a good discussion of the historical and political context of the *Two Treatises* in the Exclusion Crisis, see Richard Ashcraft, *Revolutionary Politics and Locke's Two Treatises of Government* (Princeton: Princeton University Press, 1986), especially chapter 5, "The Formation of Whig Ideology."

107. Makus, 81.

108. ECHU III, x, 20.

109. For a discussion of Locke's concept of the self see Michael Zuckert, *Natural Rights and the New Republicanism* (Princeton: Princeton University Press, 1994), 275-86.

110. ECHU III, x, 16.

Chapter 9

Convention and Constraint in the Education of Rousseau's "Natural Woman"

Deborah L. Winkle

Rousseau is surely the modern philosopher of nature par excellence. The goodness of nature is both the mainspring of Rousseau's philosophy and the thread unifying all of his disparate writings. "Everything is good as it leaves the hands of the Author of things; everything degenerates in the hands of man," he says simply.[1] Thus begins Rousseau's most profound and ambitious work, *Emile*, which aims at demonstrating what it might mean to reconcile nature and society on the level of the individual. Yet Rousseau was well aware of the difficulty, if not the impossibility, of attempting such a reconciliation. For he contends that social or political life requires human beings to be unnatural in two specific ways. First, because we must forsake our natural independence in order to enter into the web of dependent relationships that constitutes human society; and second, because in becoming social we must necessarily learn to become moral as well. In *Emile*, Rousseau attempts to negotiate this complex transformation without alienating the natural inclinations of his young pupil, meaning more precisely without ushering in the twin specters of dependence and *amour-propre* that together account for the viciousness and corruption that Rousseau regards as the hallmarks of civil society. By dint of the most painstaking care, he succeeds in bringing Emile to late adolescence with only the most cursory knowledge and experience of human sociality and thus staving off the birth of *amour-propre*. But in so doing his task is only half finished. Since Emile is not "a savage to be relegated to the desert [but] a savage made to inhabit cities," he must also be made fit for social life.[2] In other words, Emile must be brought to the point where he desires to quit his independent and largely asocial life in order to become a husband, father, and citizen.[3] Rousseau completes this difficult and delicate task in Book V, in which, not coincidentally, we are introduced to Sophie, the young girl intended for Emile who also personifies woman as such.[4] In this way, we learn that Emile's passage from "natural man" to civil man cannot be effected without the intercession of a woman. Sophie socializes Emile; if he does not precisely lose his physical independence, he nonetheless loses his emotional and moral independence when he falls in love with her. Moreover, his relation to Sophie transforms him from one who was good simply because of the absence of passions to one who freely and consciously chooses to be bound by the laws of virtue.[5] For Rousseau, then, women occupy a unique position at the juncture between nature and society.

Yet in one of the many paradoxes surrounding his discussion of women, Rousseau appears to identify women as being both more natural *and* more the product of artifice than men. In other words, women represent both nature and what is for Rousseau the enemy of nature, culture or society. This is especially apparent in the education of Sophie, who, unlike Emile, is exposed to the conventions and opinions of society from birth but who nonetheless exemplifies "natural woman" just as Emile represents "natural man."[6] The role women play, then, in laying the necessary foundation for political and social life cannot be understood apart from a consideration of how the twin themes of nature and artifice come to light in Rousseau's discussion of women. And what such a consideration reveals is that ultimately, for Rousseau, art—meaning in particular education, which is the philosopher's art—is indispensable not simply for fulfilling nature's design but indeed for "perfecting" it.[7] Rousseau's education of Sophie and her education of Emile in turn perfect the natural relation between men and women and thereby transform it into the only proper basis for society.

I

Book V of Rousseau's *Emile* opens with Rousseau echoing God's pronouncement in Genesis that "It is not good for man to be alone."[8] And like God, he will create an Eve for his new Adam.[9] As Emile's future beloved, Sophie "ought to be a woman as Emile is a man." "That is to say," Rousseau explains, "she ought to have everything which suits the constitution of her species and her sex in order to fill her place in the physical and moral order."[10] Yet those who hope to find here an educational program for women as radical as the one proposed for Emile will be disappointed. We quickly learn that while Emile's entire education is founded on practices contrary to those of society, Sophie's appears to be completely in conformity with them. Indeed, in some ways, Sophie's education appears to serve principally as a foil to that of Emile, since the two are opposed in almost every conceivable way. Emile is taken from his parents and reared in such complete isolation that at the beginning of adolescence he resembles a "savage" who has little understanding or experience of human sociality.[11] Sophie, on the other hand, is raised by her parents in the midst of society and acquires early on all the passions of a social being. Emile's early education aims at recreating in him the independence of natural man, while Sophie's aims at reconciling her to lifelong dependence on others. Perhaps most significantly, while Emile is taught never to bow to the empire of opinion, Sophie learns that heeding the dictates of public opinion is not only one of the chief duties of a decent woman but indeed constitutes the "throne" of woman's virtue. Nevertheless, Rousseau maintains that Sophie is "a pupil of nature just as Emile is" and that her education is likewise in conformity with its dictates.[12]

Yet if what is "natural" is associated with independence, asociality, and indifference to opinion, as the entire thrust of Emile's education indicates, then what are we to make of Sophie's education? To suggest that the same conventions that would warp the natural development of Emile are nonetheless in complete harmony with Sophie's natural disposition makes sense only if one begins with the premise that men and women possess radically different natures.[13] And indeed that is the argument Rousseau appears to make in Book V of *Emile*. Yet there are at least two reasons for pausing before concluding that Rousseau is purveying a rather simplistic essentialism here. First is Rousseau's own bold exposition in the *Second Discourse* of the problem with discerning what is natural in a being who is as much marked by history and civilization as man. There, Rousseau's radical archaeological excavation of the human soul reveals that thousands of years of civilization have obscured its original form in the same way that "time, sea and storms" disfigured the statue of the sea god Glaucus.[14] Moreover, in a work ostensibly devoted to laying an unshakable foundation for the primacy of nature over society and the claims of natural right, Rousseau succeeds in calling into question the very idea of "nature" as something capable of providing human beings with an absolute and unchanging standard. The second reason arises from the ambiguity surrounding Rousseau's use of the word "nature," an ambiguity I believe is deliberate on his part. In the *Second Discourse*, we learn that the only natural attributes of human beings are self-love and pity; our sole natural needs are for food, water, and sleep. Significantly, the sexual impulse is equivocal, described more as a fleeting desire than a need.[15] However, in *Emile*, Rousseau cautions that "One must not confound what is natural in the savage state with what is natural in the civil state."[16] In other words, the life of the savage that is so vividly described in the *Second Discourse* has only the most attenuated relation to the lives of the civilized men and women for whom Rousseau is writing and cannot be taken literally as a standard for the latter. With both of these caveats in mind, then, let us briefly examine Rousseau's discussion of the natural status of women and relations between the sexes which prefaces his description of Sophie.

Perhaps the first thing to note about this discussion is that it is both unabashedly materialist and emphatically complementary.[17] Rousseau takes his bearings from the physical differences between male and female bodies and finds that "In everything connected with sex, woman and man are in every respect related and in every respect different."[18] Admitting the difficulty of discerning what in their constitutions is connected with sex, Rousseau nonetheless concludes that "These relations and these differences must have a moral influence."[19] This means in the first place that women will be considered not in and of themselves, but as they relate to men. It is not sufficiently noticed that the entire discussion of women here proceeds from a consideration of the respective roles each sex plays in contributing to what Rousseau calls the "common aim," meaning, presumably, sexual union and the preservation of the species, and that in so doing he locates the fundamental paradigm for relations between the sexes in the act of sexual intercourse. He begins by observing that the physical differences between men and women contribute to the diverse roles men and women play in the union of the sexes. "From this diversity," he continues, "arises the first assignable difference in the moral relations of the two sexes. One ought to be active and strong; the other passive and weak. One must necessarily will and be able; it suffices that the other put up little resistance."[20] Following these indications of nature, Rousseau then proceeds to construe *all* relations between the sexes in light of their complementary roles in promoting the "common aim." "Observe how the physical leads us unawares to the moral, and how the sweetest laws of love are born little by little from the coarse union of the sexes," he hints.[21] Rousseau thus signals that his analysis begins with the body and grounds even the most seemingly arbitrary distinctions between men and women in the physical facts of their sexual union.[22]

The most significant and irreducible fact of the female body, of course, is that it is capable of bearing children, and from this simple fact Rousseau deduces all of the duties of wife and mother that ought to order the lives of women. In other words, women live in conformity with nature by tending to their families, according to Rousseau. He acknowledges that the duties this imposes on women constitute a severe and unequal burden. To those who complain of such inequality, however, he replies that "This inequality is not a human institution—or, at least it is the work not of prejudice but of reason. It is up to the sex that nature has charged with the bearing of children to be responsible for them to the other sex."[23] This passage is telling, for it again alerts us to Rousseau's ambiguous use of the term "nature," in particular with regard to women. For he tacitly admits here that the inequality between men and women that exists in society is not given by nature and thus reaffirms the argument of the *Second Discourse*. Yet it is precisely on the basis of this work that questions arise concerning Rousseau's presentation of women's natural status in *Emile*. For the *Second Discourse* offers a radical view of relations between the sexes in the state of nature: Rousseau argues there that savage men and women lived in equal independence; that families were not present in the original state of nature; and that the sexual union between men and women does not constitute necessary grounds for any permanent society. In the original state of nature it was only by degrees and after much progress in enlightenment that the first families were formed and savage men and women assumed in them their now familiar roles.[24] As we note above, Rousseau seeks to resolve this paradox by claiming that the original state of nature depicted in the *Second Discourse* does not represent the standard by which he judges what is natural for Emile and Sophie, who are social creatures living in civilized society.[25] What is natural in civil society, then, seems to be that which finds some support in our fundamental impulses, or is "in accord with" nature. Guided by this more expansive view of nature, Rousseau claims that the family is natural, and this serves as the starting point for his discussion of women in *Emile*.[26]

Within the family (as well as in society), there exists a clear hierarchy of authority. The man serves as head of the family and is the sole link between it and the rest of society; he represents its public face.[27] The woman, on the other hand, possesses no public or formally acknowledged authority. Rather, in what Rousseau insists to be the model intended by nature, she is meant to serve as man's helpmate and support.[28] To the everlasting indignation of his feminist readers, Rousseau even goes so far as to wax poetic in *Emile* about the joys of the "patriarchal and rustic life" and refer bluntly to women as the sex that is "made to obey."[29] In *Political Economy* we find Rousseau's only explicit justification for this arrangement within the household. "For several reasons derived from the nature of things, the father should command in the family," he declares and then proceeds to enumerate them.[30] He begins by noting that children should obey their father, first through necessity and later through gratitude; and that domestic servants owe him their services in return for the livelihood he gives them. More importantly, he claims that the authority of the mother and father should not be equal and that a "single government" must obtain so that when opinions are divided a single voice predominates. Rousseau simply asserts this, without showing why a shared authority between men and women along a democratic model is harmful to the family. He confers this authority on the man, then, with the following justification: "however slight the incapacitations peculiar to the wife are thought to be, since they are always an inactive period for her, this is sufficient reason to exclude her from primacy, because when the balance is *perfectly equal*, a straw is enough to tip it."[31] What ends up being noteworthy about this passage, then, is not so much Rousseau's assertion of the man's natural primacy as his acknowledgment that within the family, the "balance of power" between the man and the woman is "perfectly equal." Thus, Rousseau at once asserts the natural authority of the male and reveals the tenuousness of its foundation. Is it possible, then, that his advocacy of male authority is more rhetorical than sincere?

On first blush, it might appear that Rousseau's endorsement of the social inequality between men and women is based on the differences between men's and women's physical strength. Echoing the argument for a father's right to exercise authority over his children, he could claim that men's superior strength gives them the title to rule women as well; women, being weaker, must naturally submit. Yet whereas the right and need for paternal authority over children is more easily and logically defended by pointing to their evident inability to care for themselves, Rousseau himself casts this proposition into doubt in the case of men and women by depicting both sexes as naturally autonomous and self-sufficient in the *Second Discourse*. Moreover, this formulation appears strikingly inconsistent with his political teachings.[32] For Rousseau refuses to recognize a legitimate title to rule based on force in other contexts. Indeed, in the *Social Contract* he makes perfectly clear that such a claim utterly fails to meet any principled standard of political right.[33] Thus, if in fact men's title to rule women is based on their superior strength, we must answer the question of why this is legitimate in the private realm but not in the political. But is it really true that men's title to rule is based on their physical superiority to women? Book V of *Emile* seems to offer contradictory evidence. On the one hand, Rousseau writes there that "woman is made to please and to be subjugated."[34] While the woman ought to please the man, he is under a "less direct necessity" to please her. Rather, "His merit is in his power; he pleases by the sole fact of his strength."[35] Nature itself has indicated the proper relations between the male and female, Rousseau contends, since "dependence is a condition natural to women and thus girls feel themselves made to obey."[36] Yet we should recall that the context for the entire discussion of women's nature and education in Book V proceeds from Rousseau's initial consideration of the nature of the physical union between men and women and the requirements it places upon each sex. Crucial to his analysis is the following proposition: that in order for sexual union to occur "One ought to be active and strong; the other passive and weak. One must necessarily will and be able; it suffices that the other put up little resistance."[37] From this fact Rousseau draws perhaps his most important conclusion regarding the proper role and status of women: "Once this principle is established," he asserts, "it follows that woman is made specially to please man."[38]

If indeed woman is made to please man and "be subjugated," then it appears that there is something pleasing to men about ruling women. One commentator suggests that it is crucial to male *amour-propre* that men see themselves as "dominating" their partners and alludes to the following passage from *Emile*:

> If woman is made to please and to be subjugated, she ought to make herself agreeable to man instead of arousing him. Her own violence is in her charms. It is by these that she ought to constrain him to find his strength and make use of it. The surest art for animating that strength is to make it necessary by resistance. Then, *amour-propre* unites with desire, and the one triumphs in the victory that the other has made him win.[39]

In other words, male desire is inseparable from a man's sense of his own superior strength. What Rousseau depicts here, then, is not a crude "will to power" on the part of the male, but a subtle interplay of male and female desire, which he asserts is ultimately grounded in the physiological differences between men and women. And his analysis of it suggests that for men to perceive themselves as being subjected to women, as power*less* vis-à-vis women, has disastrous consequences for male desire.[40] Once again, however, Rousseau complicates the picture a mere two pages later by observing that the superior strength of the male is a fiction in which the female willingly participates. The male is stronger in appearance, but in fact depends on the weaker, who "consent[s] to let him be the stronger."[41] Indeed, far from naturally desiring to assert his superior strength, the woman must "constrain [the man] to find his strength and make use of it."[42] Rousseau adds that in savoring his "triumph" over the woman, what is "sweetest" for man is not knowing whether she yields because of her weakness or whether she merely uses this weakness as a subterfuge to disguise the complicity of her will. In actuality, then, there is a parity of strength *and* desire, yet this truth must be concealed from men. Why? Most simply, I believe, because it is only in asserting their strength that men clearly establish their *difference* from women. In other words, it is in some sense only by bringing to light this fundamental disparity (or inequality) that men and women perceive their mutuality and are able to function in the complementary way that "nature" intended, according to Rousseau.[43] Thus, the superior strength of the male (or perhaps more accurately, his natural ability to dominate the female) may well be a fiction, but it is one Rousseau regards as necessary to preserve and reinforce the complementarity of the sexes.

II

If, then, the inequality between men and women in society is more a product of convention than natural necessity, on what grounds can Rousseau justify it? For clearly social life imposes much greater restraints on women than on men. It is in this respect that Sophie's unfreedom is most apparent, and it is precisely what most contemporary readers of this work find especially galling: that the freedom and independence we modern democrats prize so highly appears to be reserved for men alone.[44] Indeed, it might even be regarded as the essence of masculinity since Rousseau sums up the whole object of Emile's education with the simple injunction, "Be a man."[45] Conversely, Rousseau maintains that "dependence is a condition natural to women."[46] Keeping in mind the capaciousness (and elasticity) of the term "nature" for Rousseau, what might he mean by insisting on the "naturalness" of women's dependence?

He begins with the premise that the mere fact of society entails a certain physical and social (what Rousseau would call "moral") dependence on the part of both men and women, a dependence he loudly laments. For him, the loss of our primitive independence is the first and greatest sacrifice we make in moving away from the state of nature and toward society.[47] Even so, Rousseau's writing is animated by the desire to show us how to minimize the dependence we experience in society. To this end, he educates Emile to be as self-sufficient as possible and urges others to emulate the isolated and independent life he so touchingly depicts in works such as *Emile* and *Julie*. The less we need others—be it their money, their aid, or their esteem—the less prone we are to vice, according to Rousseau. Now, one important respect in which men can regain their independence is in their habits of thought. Thus, by teaching men to rely on themselves and their own judgment rather than that of others, Rousseau helps them regain a small measure of their primitive independence and, more importantly, offers a means to escape from the clamor of artificial needs and passions. A certain dependence cannot be avoided; it is in the nature of society itself. Yet by urging men to free themselves from dependence on public opinion and extricate themselves as much as possible from the "entanglements" of society, Rousseau holds out the promise that they can recapture some of the sweetness of their primitive and independent existence.

Yet for women the case appears to be quite different. The prospect of reclaiming a measure of their primitive independence seems neither possible nor desirable. Rather, by arguing that that the family represents the natural locus of women, Rousseau presents women as being "naturally" more dependent than men. If we recur to Rousseau's distinction between what is natural in the primitive state and what is natural in civil society, women's dependence can be considered natural insofar as it proceeds from the initial division of labor between men and women, which results in a kind of sexual segregation.[48] Once dwellings and nascent families are established, women inevitably become subject to more frequent pregnancies. Increasingly more occupied with the tasks of child care and child rearing, they also become more dependent on men to supply them with the necessary food and shelter for themselves and their children. Insofar as families are natural, so too is women's dependence on men for the necessities of life. Thus, though the union between men and women entails mutual emotional dependence, social life by its very nature imposes a greater dependence on women. Rousseau elaborates:

> Woman and man are made for one another, but their mutual dependence is not equal. Men depend on women because of their desires; women depend on men because of both their desires and their needs. We would survive more easily without them than they would without us. For them to have what is necessary for their station, they depend on us to give it to them, to want to give it to them, to esteem them worthy of it. They depend on our sentiments, on the value we set on their merit, on the importance we attach to their charms and their virtues.[49]

In other words, men may seek to please women in order to satisfy their desire, but women need to please men out of both desire and necessity. This seems to mean, in practice, that while both men and women are constrained to some extent by the opposite sex's opinions about their sexual desirability, these constraints weigh much more heavily on women. One might be able to live without sex, Rousseau seems to be saying, but one cannot live without the necessities of food and shelter, which women depend on men to give them.[50] Thus, women's dependence in society is (and ought to be, according to Rousseau) more thoroughgoing than that of men. But if this dependence is not to render them miserable, it must, paradoxically, be made absolute. This conclusion seems to lie behind his somewhat cryptic remark regarding women's subjection to opinion in general and the proprieties in particular: "This misfortune, if it is one for them, is inseparable from their sex, and they are never delivered from it without suffering far more cruel misfortunes."[51]

Acknowledging both the necessity (social and economic) and merits of a "traditional" ordering of relations between men and women, one that has some foundation in nature, Rousseau approves the historic tendency to assimilate women into the private, and men into the public, sphere. As long as opinion reinforces the notion that women's proper role is a domestic and subservient one, then women's subjection to the iron rule of the proprieties is salutary, both for them and for society at large. "What is, is good," he pronounces.[52]

Yet the exact nature of the relation between women and opinion is one of the most vexing issues in Rousseau's discussion of women. For while it would be hard to overemphasize the significance of this relation, Rousseau's account of it is both complex and seemingly contradictory. On the one hand, he identifies women as society's true opinion makers. In concluding his critique of dueling in the *Letter to d'Alembert*, for example, Rousseau warns that efforts to change public opinion on this matter "will never succeed . . . without bringing about the intervention of women, on whom men's way of thinking in large measure depends."[53] Moreover, by highlighting the link between women and *moeurs* (morals and manners), Rousseau signals the influence women exercise not simply over men's opinions but over public opinion in general. Noting that "Men will always be what is pleasing to women," he underlines the necessity of enlisting women in any project aimed at changing public *moeurs*: "if you want [men] to become great and virtuous, teach women what greatness of soul and virtue are."[54] Opinion itself is feminized; it is the "queen of the world" to whom even kings are subject, or rather are themselves "her first slaves."[55]

On the other hand, as we see above, Rousseau also depicts women as being severely constrained by opinion. Enjoined always to observe the proprieties and defer to the unspoken rules of public opinion regarding their behavior, they are in some sense the slaves of opinion. The word is a strong one, but rather surprisingly it is Rousseau's own. "All their lives [women] will be enslaved to the most continual and severe of constraints—that of the proprieties," he bluntly announces.[56] Similarly, in discussing women's religious faith, Rousseau emphasizes how thoroughly women are subjected both in their behavior and in matters of conscience: "Due to the very fact that in her conduct woman is enslaved by public opinion, in her belief she is enslaved by authority."[57] Opinion has (at least) two faces for Rousseau: one reflects the need for rules prescribing what constitutes acceptable behavior in society—the "proprieties"—and the other announces society's judgment about how particular individuals conform to these rules.[58] This idea of public judgment is implicit in the notion of a "reputation," and if learning to heed public opinion about what is proper and becoming to her intended station as wife and mother is an essential part of woman's moral education, then having a reputation for such circumspection is at least equally important. Indeed, for Rousseau, opinion—meaning the good opinion of her neighbors—is nothing less than the "throne" of woman's virtue.[59] "It is not enough that [women] be estimable; they must be esteemed. . . . It is not enough for them to be temperate; they must be recognized as such."[60] More perplexing still, perhaps, is the way in which Rousseau seems to regard both of these apparently contradictory positions as true: women are both the opinion makers of society and its slaves. Surely, if women exercised as much influence over opinion as Rousseau seems to claim for them, they would be quick to discard those aspects they find constraining and devote themselves to extolling opinions more favorable to their own interests.

The key to this puzzle might lie in considering how this issue bears on Rousseau's account of sexual politics. For one way women shape opinion is by the mere fact that men wish to win their sexual favors. By aiming to please women, by seeking their approval, men fall under the sway of women's opinions. This apparently immutable fact of existence is one Rousseau regards with a good deal of ambivalence. In the *First Discourse*, for example, he decries the tendency of artists, writers, and intellectuals to sacrifice their true genius in order to flatter the insipid tastes of the time, tastes that have largely been dictated by women. "Tell us, famed Arouet, how many vigorous and strong beauties have you sacrificed to our false delicacy, and how many great things has the spirit of gallantry, so fertile in small things, cost you?" Rousseau laments.[61] According to him, those who pride themselves on being the arbiters of public opinion are no less under the spell of women's siren song than any other man; indeed they are perhaps more so. For their *amour-propre* demands not mere acclaim but also and especially the acclaim of "the fair sex."[62] Yet men's desire to win the good opinion of women is not always viewed so harshly by Rousseau. In the first place, he concedes that women are the proper judges of men's merit. Acknowledging the "intimate sentiment we all have that women are the natural judges of men's merit," he goes on to ask "and I who tell them such harsh truths, do you believe that their judgments are indifferent to me? No, their approval is dearer to me than yours, readers—you who are often more womanish than they are. In despising their morals, I still wish to honor their justice."[63] Moreover, when women are virtuous their effect on opinion redounds to the benefit of all society. Rousseau's bold proclamation in the *First Discourse* that the reeducation of women could confer almost unimagined benefits on society is evidence of the tremendous power for good that this motive represents.[64]

Just as women exercise a formidable influence over public opinion by means of men's desire to please them, men likewise have a similar motive at their disposal. For Rousseau does not simply argue that women should judge men's merit but that this is a right they mutually share: "Women are the natural judges of men's merit as men are of women's merit. That is their reciprocal right, and neither men nor women are ignorant of it."[65] Thus, his characterization of women as both the opinion makers of society and those who are most in its thrall can be read as one aspect of a sexual relation in which men and women engage in a mutual exchange of rule. In describing the partnership between men and women, Rousseau declares that "Each follows the prompting of the other; each obeys, and both are masters."[66] Thus, although men rule women publicly, women in turn rule men privately, an arrangement Rousseau finds both equitable and eminently desirable. While most feminist commentators have emphasized—and deplored—Rousseau's unabashed endorsement of the formal rule of men over women, they often overlook the fact that at the same time he encourages the informal or private rule of women over men. Rousseau permits men and women to rule one another in different spheres according to their proper roles; thus, the purposes and nature of their rule are tailored to the requirements of their sex. As one commentator puts it, Rousseau is actually in considerable agreement with the feminist goal of attaining equality between the sexes; he disagrees, however, about the means to achieve this end.[67] Thus, in possessing the right to judge each other's merit, men and women are both subject to the opinions (the "rule") of the opposite sex.

Nonetheless, one may wonder whether this fully explains the need for women to be so thoroughly subjected, not just to the opinion of their beloved, but to opinion as such, or indeed why they must be "enslaved" to the proprieties. While Rousseau admits to some ambivalence about men being ruled by women's opinions, he is characteristically uncompromising in asserting the necessity of women's subjection to the judgment of men. "If it is important that a father love his children, it is important that he esteem their mother. These are the reasons which put even appearances among the duties of women, and make honor and reputation no less indispensable to them than chastity."[68] Even more emphatically, he asserts that women "never cease to be subjected either to a man or to the judgments of men and they are never permitted to put themselves above these judgments."[69] And "since she is subject to the judgment of men, she ought to merit their esteem," Rousseau concludes.[70] Thus, Rousseau seems implicitly to distinguish between the subjection of men to *individual* women's opinions and to *opinion* per se.[71] And while he may somewhat reluctantly accept the former, he resolutely opposes the latter.[72] However, not only does Rousseau maintain both the desirability and necessity of women's subjection to men's opinions but he also urges their subjection to "opinion" as such. Why this distinction? The answer seems to lie in the importance Rousseau attaches to female modesty. For it would appear that what men desire most in women is their modesty or, in other words, their sexual continence. The proprieties to which women are "enslaved" (and that constitute "the most continual and severe of constraints")[73] all conspire to limit the expression of female desire. Woman's modesty is the public badge of her sexual continence. In order for a man to care about his children and, no small thing for Rousseau, to ensure the ordered and legitimate inheritance of property, he must be assured that his children are indeed his flesh and blood. It is for this reason that Rousseau reserves especially harsh criticism for the female adulterer. An unfaithful wife not only violates her vows, he intones, but also "dissolves the family and breaks all the bonds of nature. In giving the man children which are not his, she betrays both. She joins perfidy to infidelity. I have difficulty seeing what disorders and what crimes do not flow from this one."[74]

I am not arguing here that Rousseau equates the whole of female virtue with chastity alone. In an instructive passage from *Julie*, for example, we find Claire seeking to console the despondent Julie by assuring her that although she has lost her "virtue" in the specific sense of her virginity, she nonetheless remains a virtuous and admirable young woman, a judgment Rousseau himself seems to share.[75] Nonetheless, Rousseau makes clear that he regards sexual continence as woman's *preeminent* virtue. And, in a certain sense, a woman's "virtue" (meaning her chastity) is indeed a matter of opinion. If this is the "greatest prize" a woman has to offer a man, as Rousseau avers, then an unsullied reputation is the chief guarantor of the value of this prize.[76] For this reason alone, women, much more than men, are forced to bow down before the altar of public opinion. To free women from their "enslavement" to public opinion, then, would mean removing the single most important restraint on female desire. Rousseau warns of this danger in an intriguing footnote in *Emile* in which he defends supposedly outdated notions of female modesty against the ridicule of the *philosophes* and other progressive thinkers of his day. He protests that by denigrating female modesty one takes from women the last bit of honor remaining to them and goes on to argue that if one removes this, the "greatest curb on their sex," women will find that "Once having put their passions at ease, they no longer have any interest in resisting."[77] What is noteworthy here is Rousseau's emphasis on the crucial role of women's "resistance" to men, a resistance that apparently is essential to male desire. Once again we see Rousseau's insistence on the necessity of constructing an elaborate social edifice in order to sustain the ostensible fragility of male desire. And once again we are reminded that the moral aspects of social relations between men and women proceed ineluctably from Rousseau's understanding of the nature (and specifically the dialectic) of male and female desire. The key here seems to be the role of modesty in maintaining sexual desire between men and women, which for Rousseau depends largely on woman's explicit resistance to the man, a resistance that nonetheless conceals her tacit acquiescence. Modesty, which forces a woman to veil her desires and "touch the heart of man without appearing to think of him," is, whether men realize it or not, what they truly desire of women.[78] For it serves two specific functions: first, it flatters men's *amour-propre* by signaling the exclusivity of the favors they are about to enjoy; and second, it reassures them that the children they will be asked to nurture and support are indeed their own. Thus, insofar as the demands of modesty coincide with the demands of propriety, women *are* necessarily more subject to them than men are. Rousseau strives mightily to show that opinion is not simply arbitrary in the case of relations between the sexes, but rather, like these relations themselves, is grounded in certain natural verities. Women cannot free themselves from the male preference for female modesty simply because they wish it, for in the end this preference proceeds from a fundamental "law of nature." Opinion, then, serves as the accomplice to nature and helps to fulfill its aim.

And yet the careful reader can, I think, detect a certain ambivalence on Rousseau's part here. The very strength of his language regarding women's "enslavement" to opinion and its repetition throughout Book V suggest that Rousseau was well aware of the dangers inherent in giving women public opinion as the sole guide and rule for their conduct. In so doing, one leaves them without a moral compass, vulnerable to the vagaries of opinion. Book V of *Emile*, then, presents a curiously mixed message, offering up both the most emphatic endorsements of women's subjection to opinion along with hints that Rousseau nonetheless regards this subjection with some unease.[79] Clearly, Rousseau perceives both the wisdom and necessity of female desire being constrained by public opinion to a large extent. Yet his repeated references to women's "enslavement" give us pause. For Rousseau especially, it would be surprising if the prospect of any sort of enslavement, either of body or spirit, could be viewed with complete equanimity.[80] Some suggest that Rousseau's materialism necessarily leads to the conclusion that women are naturally more social than men, either because they are physically weaker and therefore dependent on men for subsistence or because of their capacity to bear and nurture children.[81] Accordingly, one could argue that the dependence and constraints they endure in society to support that role are less burdensome to them. Yet even if one grants the premise, the conclusion does not necessarily follow. Women may be more naturally more social, more other-directed than men on the basis of biology alone, but that statement alone says nothing about what *kind* of social life women are oriented toward. Nor does it consider whether this orientation simply makes women more irrevocably divided than men: fitted by nature with an inclination for social life but as subject as men to its debilitating effects. Moreover, Rousseau's own description of the proper education for women subverts his initial protestation that the dependence women suffer in society is any more "natural" for them than it is for men. For if in fact "dependence is a condition natural to women,"[82] then why go to such great lengths and take such extraordinary measures to school women to become accustomed to it? "Do not allow for a single instant in their lives that [girls] no longer know any restraint," Rousseau admonishes. Why? Because "From this habitual constraint comes a docility which women need all their lives, since they never cease to be subjected either to a man or to the judgments of men."[83] Yet it is curious that such rigorous constraints would be necessary if indeed "girls feel themselves made to obey."[84] The entire education Rousseau prescribes for girls is directed toward two ends: first, constantly reminding them of their duties as decent women and wives; and second, cultivating in them the tastes and sentiments proper to that end. This means, in practice, habituating them to the necessity of being subjected to men and the opinions of men. Far from being easily achieved, this habituation—or "domestication" of women—comes about only as the result of the most vigilant care and painstaking efforts. "It is not a question of making her dependence painful for her; it suffices to make her feel it," Rousseau explains.[85] As one learns in reading Book V, a great deal is required to make her "feel it" in such a way that she no longer attempts to resist it.

III

Essential to this end is the moral education Rousseau prescribes for women. If women can be taught to love virtue, he argues, then the very constraints they suffer paradoxically offer the path to moral freedom insofar as they become a law that is *self-imposed*. Just as Emile learns to accept natural necessity, so too must Sophie learn to accept social necessity. In so doing, she comes to understand that giving law to one's own desires—which is the definition of virtue for Rousseau—is the most elevated and noble form of freedom. Accordingly, the practice of virtue secures a certain freedom on the level of individual conscience in the same way that the essence of freedom within a republican regime lies in each citizen's willingness to ratify the general will and thus obey only the law each prescribes for himself. One cannot dismiss or ignore Rousseau's abiding ambivalence about our passage from the state of nature to civil society, yet it is noteworthy that he speaks with singular eloquence about perhaps the most significant advantage it confers, namely, the possibility of morality. In the following section of the *Social Contract*, both his ambivalence and his appreciation for the moral freedom our humanity gives us are strikingly on display:

> This passage from the state of nature to the civil state produces a remarkable change in man, by substituting justice for instinct in his behavior and giving his actions the morality they previously lacked. . . . Although in this state he deprives himself of several advantages given him by nature, he gains such great ones, his faculties are exercised and developed, his ideas broadened, his feelings ennobled and his whole soul elevated to such a point that if the abuses of this new condition did not often degrade him beneath the condition he left, he ought ceaselessly to bless the happy moment that tore him away from it forever, and that changed him from a stupid, limited animal into an intelligent being and a man. . . . To the foregoing acquisitions of the civil state could be added moral freedom, which alone makes man truly the master of himself. For the impulse of appetite alone is slavery and obedience to the law one has prescribed for oneself is freedom.[86]

Thus, the freedom one can enjoy in society is the freedom of not being ruled by others or by one's own appetite or impulses; it is the freedom of self-legislation. At bottom, then, Rousseau's concern with social and political reform is a concern for moral reform on the part of individual men and women.[87] In

Emile, all of these concerns are treated as a seamless whole. Let us then turn to a brief consideration of what we might call the moral education of Sophie.

To begin, it is clear that the two very different educations of Emile and Sophie show us two paths toward moral autonomy. In both instances, however, Rousseau conceives of the problem of morality in the same way: in order for human beings to be capable of acting morally, they must learn how to oppose will to desire. Thus, for both Emile and Sophie, virtue is defined as giving the law to their passions. Rousseau's innovation, however, is to demonstrate that it is on the basis of these very passions that they are made to sense their moral duties—most particularly, the passion of love. According to Rousseau, our most enduring and immediate experience of love is our primitive and innate sentiment of self-love. In society, however, this sentiment is soon modified so that we are not content with preferring ourselves, but desire that others prefer us as well. When this desire to obtain preference is particularized and joined with ideas of goodness, beauty, and merit, it becomes romantic love. Thus, the desire to love and be loved is somehow natural for social beings. And Rousseau perceives in this desire a powerful motive for morality.[88]

As he envisions it, the romantic relationship between men and women culminating in marriage encompasses all the most important principles of morality. First, it requires that one not use others merely as objects to satisfy one's own desires. Because love implies reciprocity, it means that one must care for one's beloved in some sense for his or her own sake. Next, the marriage tie requires the faithful keeping of one's promise and the capacity to honor a contract. It implies a respect for others' rights, especially the rights of one's partner to be free and equal within this union. The fidelity demanded of each partner to the marriage imposes on them respect for the rights of others in another sense as well, insofar as one is thereby forbidden from usurping the exclusive sexual pleasures promised to another's husband or wife. Finally, all of the duties one owes to humanity are implied in the care, nurturing, and protection that parents are required to give to their children.

In the original state of nature it was only by degrees and after much progress in enlightenment that the first families were formed and savage men and women assumed in them their now familiar roles. Yet for Rousseau the family still represents the most natural association of human beings, even though it is not a necessary one. It is within the family that the primitive sexual union between men and women is deepened and made permanent by means of the sentiments, and there that the children of that union come to be cherished and cared for as the symbol of their parents' love. Thus, the family represents a kind of resting place on the path from the isolation and brutishness of savage life to the invidious sociality and corruption of civilized life. Rousseau looks back and pronounces the era of the first families the happiest time in human history. He believes it possible (or at least worthy of the attempt) to recapture for modern human beings the happiness of this earlier time by reinvigorating the sentiments that constitute its foundation: conjugal and paternal love, which he calls "the sweetest sentiments known to men."[89] Rousseau's emphasis on the importance of the family can be understood, then, at least in part as a response to the increasing anomie of bourgeois society and its lack of any real possibility for civic involvement. The family thus becomes the one viable ground for genuine community and the practice of virtue. In order for his project to succeed, however, women must be persuaded that they will find both their interest and greatest pleasures in caring for their families. The burden necessarily falls on women, Rousseau asserts, because they are the mainstay of the family. A woman is "the link between [children] and their father; she alone makes him love them and gives him the confidence to call them his own."[90] Thus, the entire education he prescribes for women is aimed at teaching them to know and love the duties of wife and mother, the first of which are chastity and fidelity. This points to an obvious difference between the moral educations of Emile and Sophie: insofar as there is something moral involved as soon as we begin to consider ourselves in relation to others, Sophie's entire education must be considered a moral education, whereas that of Emile properly begins only with puberty.

Since Sophie is a social creature from the outset, reared in the midst of family and society, she will not enjoy the healthy unity of self-love that characterizes Emile. In Book IV, we see Rousseau go to great lengths to assure that the passions are born in Emile "according to the order of nature," in order that they confirm and enhance rather than divide his self-love. No similar precautions are taken in the case of Sophie's education, however. Rather, she is subject to all of the unruly passions arising from the uninhibited development of *amour-propre* and as a result will be divided in her self-love. Unlike Emile, she is alienated from herself in some sense, since she, like every social creature, lives in the opinions of others. "Remember that as soon as *amour-propre* has developed, the relative *I* is constantly in play, and [one] never observes others without returning to himself and comparing himself with them," Rousseau cautions.[91] All of Emile's early education was aimed at ensuring that he would always return to himself with a sense of pleasure since he would see himself so advantageously placed among men, enjoying the goods that constitute true happiness. Yet without such similar and elaborate artifice in the education of Sophie, there is no way to preserve in her the original wholeness of her self-love. The task at hand, then, as Rousseau conceives it, is to create a unity out of the passions themselves. In other words, he will show how to subordinate all the passions to a single overriding one: the passion for virtue. How will he do so? By means of the passions themselves, Rousseau replies. "One has a hold on the passions only by means of the passions. It is by their empire that their tyranny must be combated," he asserts.[92] In other words, by guiding Sophie's principal passions toward an enthusiasm for virtue, he provides her with the very means to triumph over these passions and creates in her a kind of psychic unity.[93] As we shall see in what follows, Rousseau relies on three passions in particular to achieve this goal: Sophie's desire for love, her pride, and her desire to rule.

To begin, Sophie's desire for love, which awakens with her *amour-propre*, will be interpreted to her as the means to secure her happiness. Just as he does with Emile, Rousseau dons his Romantic garb and unabashedly proclaims that the greatest human happiness consists in loving and being loved. "I do not conceive how someone who loves nothing can be happy," he declares emphatically.[94] Sophie will be taught that all the happiness to be hoped for in this life can be found in the love she will share with her husband and family. Her desire for love, however, will be tempered by the understanding that happiness is inseparable from virtue. Only a worthy and estimable man can make her happy; and he, in turn, will love her more for her virtue than her person. A great part of her education, then, will be devoted to teaching her how to recognize this man.

Next, Rousseau appeals to women's pride by emphasizing that virtue alone confers true honor and dignity on human beings. He urges them to find in their virtue, rather than their beauty or talents, the true source of their merit. Moreover, he tells women that by dedicating themselves to virtue they can aspire to a kind of heroic greatness of soul. The rather puzzling story Rousseau tells about the real Sophie who languished to the point of death for the love of virtue seems intended at least in part to prove this point—to show that a noble enthusiasm for virtue is just as much the province of contemporary women as of ancient heroes.[95] At the same time, Rousseau teaches that the virtue women honor in themselves necessarily commands the honor of others. The virtuous woman, he says, enjoys the admiration, respect, love, and esteem of all who surround her; she basks continually in the warmth of others' good opinion of her. While Emile is raised to be indifferent to the opinions of others and suspicious of worldly honor, Sophie, like all social creatures, lives in the opinions of others and seeks to distinguish herself in their eyes. Rousseau's argument here demonstrates how, properly enlightened, this desire can be a powerful support to virtue.

Yet for all his lofty rhetoric, Rousseau is hardheaded about what motivates human beings and realizes that he must convince women that virtue is in their interest in a more tangible sense as well.[96] To this end, he urges women to regard their duties as not only the source of their pleasures, but also the foundation of what he terms their "empire." He argues to this effect in a passage that typically blends touching sentiment with a *sotto voce* appeal to self-interest:

> Is it so hard to love in order to be loved, to make oneself lovable in order to be happy, to make oneself estimable in order to be obeyed, to honor oneself in order to be honored? How fine these rights are! How respectable they are! How dear they are to the heart of man when woman knows how to turn them to account! To enjoy them, she does not have to await the passage of the years or the coming of old age. Her empire begins with her virtues.[97]

This theme of women's rule—their "empire" or "ascendancy"—recurs throughout Rousseau's writings and occupies an important, though ambiguous, place in his thought.[98] To better understand its meaning and foundation, we must again turn to his discussion of relations between the sexes at the beginning of Book V. In analyzing the mechanics of male and female sexual desire, he concludes that nature grants women greater facility to excite the desires than men have to satisfy them.[99] Likewise, the very modesty that Rousseau describes as a gift of nature given to women to moderate and dissimulate their own desire serves merely to enhance that of men. Thus, men are always in some sense at the mercy of women and their willingness to satisfy men's desires, and this constitutes what Rousseau calls the natural ascendancy of women.[100] Earlier in *Emile*, Rousseau had boasted that he could lead armies of children to the ends of the earth with promises of sweets; here, he implies that women can lead men in the same way by means of sexual desire.[101] Although Rousseau claims that women's empire is given to them by nature, his rhetorical position seems to be that the only way to secure this empire is by basing it on virtue. This may reflect a certain hedging on his part concerning the natural status of modesty. For if modesty is not simply natural, then women's empire is more tenuous or at least more dependent on social practices than Rousseau indicates above.[102] Hence his emphasis on the importance of virtue. According to Rousseau's sexual psychology, it is the very modesty and reserve imposed on women by virtue that paradoxically serve to inflame men's desires and keep them in thrall to women. Thus, he seeks to persuade women that it is in giving the law to their own desire that they acquire their right to rule men. Sophie will be taught that her "empire" depends on her morals and good conduct, and that "a man will serve his mistress no better than he serves virtue."[103]

IV

There is, then, a clear rhetorical purpose behind Rousseau's analysis of woman's "nature" and the natural relations that obtain between men and women, one that aims at persuading individuals of both sexes to understand themselves and their place in the social and political order in the terms provided for them by Rousseau. This, in turn, entails a tacit recognition on Rousseau's part of the essential malleability of women as well as men, a malleability he appears to deny them. For upon closer examination much of what Rousseau presents in Book V as being in accord with the "nature" of women comes to light as being deliberately contrived in order to exaggerate whatever natural differences do exist between men and women, differences he then uses to justify his ordering of relations between the sexes.[104] Rousseau's depiction of women as "naturally" more interested in adornment, less chafed by constraint, more prone to dissembling and coquetry can just as easily and with more reason be explained as the result of an education that gives them as their principal object a desire to please others, especially men.[105] Thus his extended discussion purporting to limn woman's "nature" ultimately reveals that it is no less a product of human artifice than that of "natural man," for we should not forget that Emile's entire education results from the hidden but elaborate contrivances of his tutor. While ostensibly purveying a kind of biological determinism with regard to women, *Emile* in fact reprises the inescapable conclusion of the *Second Discourse*: namely, that nature and especially human nature is neither fixed nor even readily apparent amid the profound changes human beings have undergone in the course of their evolution. Despite Rousseau's constant recurrence to nature and "the natural" as the touchstone of his own philosophy, then, his reflections on the subject demonstrate in fact that "nature" can be glimpsed and recaptured on the level of society only with the greatest *human* art. Indeed, as he observes in a telling quote from *Emile*, "One must use a great deal of art to prevent social man from being totally artificial."[106]

Rousseau teaches that it is with regard to relations between the sexes that human art is both most necessary and of greatest import. For while nature indicates that men and women are meant to come together to perpetuate and preserve the species, it tells us little about precisely *how* they are to do so. Indeed, Rousseau even hints that our efforts to moralize and make permanent the attachment between an individual man and woman is perhaps the most unnatural thing that could be attempted. Nevertheless, it is necessary for the very existence of society, since "marriage . . . being a civil contract has civil effects without which society could not even subsist."[107] Moreover, if social life is not to alienate us completely from our natural sentiments, then relations between the sexes must be grounded insofar as possible on the "natural" sex differences that Rousseau outlines, all the while betraying just how much these supposedly natural differences in fact depend on human artifice. As one commentator puts it, "natural sex roles are, perhaps, what Rousseau might consider a noble lie."[108] Women thus embody and problematize in an especially dramatic fashion the question that lies at the heart of all Rousseau's writings: whether it is possible to reconcile nature and society and in so doing regain for humanity a measure of our original happiness.

Notes

1. Jean-Jacques Rousseau, *Emile or On Education*, trans. Allan Bloom (New York: Basic Books, 1979), 37.

2. Rousseau, *Emile*, 205.

3. When Rousseau uses the term "citizen," he generally means a member of a republic. For example, when he refers to the impossibility of educating Emile to be both a man who is whole and "entirely for himself" and a citizen, who is "a fractional unity dependent on the denominator," it is this specific sense of the word he has in mind (see *Emile*, 39-40). I am using the term here to refer simply to any member of a political community, regardless of regime.

4. Book V is subtitled "Sophie or the Woman."

5. While recent and especially feminist scholarship has focused attention on Rousseau's discussions of relations between the sexes and rightly established their significance in his thought, less study has been given to the standpoint from which he considers this subject, which I believe is primarily a moral one. On this understanding, it is important to ask *why* Rousseau regards it as morally salutary for women to play a private and essentially domestic role. Some of the most useful works to address this theme are Allan Bloom, *Love and Friendship* (New York: Simon & Schuster, 1993); Nicole Fermon, *Domesticating Passions: Rousseau, Woman and Nation* (Hanover, NH: University Press of New England, 1997); Joel Schwartz, *The Sexual Politics of Jean-Jacques Rousseau* (Chicago: University of Chicago Press, 1984); and Penny A. Weiss, *Gendered Community: Rousseau, Sex and Politics* (New York: New York University Press, 1993). Judith Shklar's *Men and Citizens* (Cambridge: Cambridge University Press, 1969) offers many insights into Rousseau's moral teaching but does not explore in any detail the role women play in upholding or transforming social morality. Other noteworthy works to take up this issue as well as Rousseau's account of relations between the sexes in general include: Jean H. Bloch, "Women and the Reform of the Nation," in *Woman and Society in Eighteenth-Century France*, ed. Eva Jacobs, W. H. Barber, and Jean H. Bloch (London: Athlone Press, 1979); Ann Charney Colmo, "What Sophie Knew," in *Finding a New Feminism*, ed. Pamela Grande Jensen (New York: Rowman & Littlefield, 1996), 67-91; M. B. Ellis, *Julie or La Nouvelle Héloïse: A Synthesis of Rousseau's Thought* (Toronto: University of Toronto Press, 1949); Jean Bethke Elshtain, *Public Man, Private Woman* (Princeton: Princeton University Press, 1981); Claude Habib, *Pensées Sur la Prostitution* (Paris: Belin, 1994); Lynda Lange, "Rousseau and Modern Feminism," in *Feminist Interpretations and Political Theory*, ed. Mary Lyndon Shanley and Carole Pateman (University Park: Pennsylvania State University Press, 1991); Susan Moller Okin, *Women in Western Political Thought* (Princeton: Princeton University Press, 1979); and Tracy B. Strong, *Jean-Jacques Rousseau: The Politics of the Ordinary* (London: Sage Publications, 1994).

6. Rousseau, *Emile,* 357, 410.

7. In a discussion of the moral or social relation between the sexes, Rousseau emphasizes the perfect complementarity of the sexes and observes: "And this is how art can constantly tend to the perfection of the instrument given by nature" (*Emile,* 387).

8. Rousseau, *Emile*, 357.

9. Bloom speaks of Emile as Adam in the introduction to his translation of the *Emile* (13). For Rousseau to envision himself as the creator of a new Adam and Eve implies that he sees himself as in some sense a rival of God; specifically, as one who is capable of improving upon God's natural creation.

10. Rousseau, *Emile,* 357.

11. Rousseau, *Emile,* 208, 222.

12. Rousseau, *Emile,* 410. This suggests that there is perhaps a disjunction between what women (and men) *are* by nature and what they *ought to be.*

13. For two recent considerations of the question of natural sex differences from a social science perspective, see Nancy Holstrom, "Do Women Have a Distinct Nature?" and Sherry Ortner, "Is Female to Male as Nature Is to Culture?" in *Women and Values,* ed. Marilyn Pearsall (Belmont, CA: Wadsworth Publishing, 1993), 48-72.

14. Jean-Jacques Rousseau, *The First and Second Discourses,* trans. Roger D. Masters and Judith R. Masters (New York: St. Martin's Press, 1964), 91.

15. *Second Discourse*, 95, 105, 120-21, 135. In *Emile*, Rousseau is even more emphatic that sexual desire is wholly a result of the activity of the imagination. "As for me," he writes, ". . . I am persuaded that a solitary man raised in a desert, without books, without instruction, and without women, would die there a virgin at whatever age he had reached" (333). Moreover, even though Rousseau limits the "first and simplest operations of the human soul" to self-love and pity in the *Second Discourse*, the latter quickly becomes problematic, leaving self-love as the only truly natural attribute of human beings. On the question of Rousseau's discussion of pity in this work, see Marc F. Plattner, *Rousseau's State of Nature* (DeKalb: Northern Illinois University Press, 1979).

16. Rousseau, *Emile,* 406.

17. Schwartz stresses the importance of Rousseau's materialism to his argument for sexual differentiation. See especially chapters 1 and 2. It is important, however, to distinguish Rousseau's materialism from what could be called a kind of biological determinism. Rousseau clearly begins with the body but does not consider that alone to be determinative.

18. Rousseau, *Emile*, 357.

19. Rousseau, *Emile*, 358.

20. Rousseau, *Emile*, 358.

21. Rousseau, *Emile*, 360.

22. Not only does Rousseau appear to derive all moral relations between the sexes from the physical facts of their union, but morality itself comes to light as inextricably bound to our bodily and specifically our sexual development. In the earliest draft of *Emile*, for instance, Rousseau had written and then crossed out the following lines: "If I am asked how it is possible for the morality of human life to emerge from a purely physical revolution, I will answer that I do not know. . . . I do not know what connection there may be between the seminal spirits and the soul's affects, between sexual development and the sentiment of good and evil. I see that these connections exist. I reason not to explain them but to draw out their consequences" (488-89, note 2).

23. Rousseau, *Emile,* 361.

24. Rousseau, *Second Discourse,* 120-21,135, 141-47.

25. Rousseau, *Emile,* 406.

26. While the family sets the parameters in the discussion of what is natural in women, this does not seem to be the case for men. Rather, the independence and self-sufficiency of savage man in the original state of nature serve as the model for Emile as "natural man." Thus, while Emile's early education is designed to recapture the autarky of savage man, Sophie is never permitted to aspire to similar independence. It is possible that, just as with Sophie, the model for Emile is the savage who lived during the time of the first families, since he still retained most of his independence and self-sufficiency. In this regard, the establishment of the family clearly altered the lives of women more than men by making them depend on men for their survival. However, this would seem to be a problematic position for Rousseau inasmuch as it still implies a kind of (natural) other-directedness in human beings that he is at such pains to deny in the *Second Discourse*. It is possible that Rousseau believed that women are "naturally" more social than men and therefore did not regard his two different standards of nature as being in tension with each other. For a discussion of this view see, Schwartz, *The Sexual Politics,* 84-88.

27. Rousseau, *Emile,* 407.

28. This model has also traditionally been understood to be supported by Christian

teachings as well.

29. Rousseau, *Emile*, 370, 407, 474, 478. Some contemporary readers of Rousseau who are most exasperated by his supposedly misogynist views include Susan Moller Okin; Nannerl Keohance, "'But for Her Sex...' The Domestication of Sophie," *University of Ottawa Quarterly* 49 3-4 (1979): 390-400; and Victor Wexler, "Made for Man's Delight: Rousseau as Antifeminist," *The American Historical Review* 81 (April 1976): 266-91. Rousseau's writings about women provoked similarly strong reactions from some female readers of his own time as well. On this subject, see Mary Seidman Trouille, *Sexual Politics in the Enlightenment* (Albany: State University of New York Press, 1997). For a contrasting view regarding Rousseau's contemporary readers, see Gita May, "Rousseau's 'Anti-Feminism' Reconsidered," in *French Women and the Age of Enlightenment,* ed. Samia I. Spencer (Bloomington: Indiana University Press, 1984).

30. Jean-Jacques Rousseau, *On the Social Contract, with Geneva Manuscript and Political Economy*, ed. Roger D. Masters, trans. Judith R. Masters (New York: St. Martin's Press, 1978), 210.

31. Rousseau, *Social Contract*, 210, emphasis added. Rousseau adds that the husband has the right to oversee his wife's conduct in order to be assured that the children she bears are indeed his own; the wife, on the other hand, has no need for similar rights over her husband.

32. This is one of Okin's principal criticisms of Rousseau. See especially Okin, *Women in Western Political Theory*, chapter 7.

33. Rousscau, *Social Contract*, 48-49.

34. Rousseau, *Emile*, 358.

35. Rousseau, *Emile*, 358.

36. Rousseau, *Emile*, 370.

37. Rousseau, *Emile*, 358.

38. Rousseau, *Emile*, 358.

39. Schwartz, *The Sexual Politics*, 43-44; Rousseau, *Emile,* 358.

40. Schwartz concludes that Rousseau regards male desire as something that is in fact naturally weak and thus requires the elaborate social and sexual artifice he prescribes in order to support it. See especially Schwartz, *The Sexual Politics*, 34-6.

41. Rousseau, *Emile*, 360.

42. Rousseau, *Emile*, 358.

43. Both Schwartz and Weiss pay careful attention to Rousseau's arguments for sexual differentiation and emphasize his conviction that they are both necessary and beneficial for society. According to Weiss, however, they differ on the question of whether these differences are natural (meaning necessary) or, as she argues and I agree, largely the (intentional) product of the different educations Rousseau prescribes for men and women.

44. A concern for "authenticity" and "individuality" is one of Rousseau's many legacies, and it would seem that freedom is their necessary precondition. For this reason, too, modern readers of Rousseau find his account of women so objectionable, for he appears to deny them the possibility of freely creating such an "authentic" self. On the issue of Rousseau and authenticity, see Arthur M. Melzer, "Rousseau and the Modern Cult of Sincerity," in *The Legacy of Rousseau,* ed. Clifford Orwin and Nathan Tarcov (Chicago: University of Chicago Press, 1997), 274-95.

45. Rousseau, *Emile*, 445. See also pages 41-42.

46. Rousseau, *Emile*, 370.

47. In the *Second Discourse*, Rousseau writes that one can trace the ills of civilization back to the necessity of a division of labor. "[F]rom the moment one man needed the help of another," he writes there, "equality disappeared, property was introduced, labor became necessary; and vast forests were changed into smiling fields which had to be watered with the sweat of men and in which slavery and misery were soon seen to germinate and grow with the crops" (151-52). For an explanation of how personal dependence leads to what Rousseau calls the "contradiction of society," see Arthur M. Melzer, *The Natural Goodness of Man* (Chicago: University of Chicago Press, 1990), chapter 5.

48. The establishment of the family, then, constitutes the *first* division of labor, which is a sexual one.

49. Rousseau, *Emile*, 364. Rousseau's reasoning that men could survive more easily without women than women without men perhaps makes sense given a particular set of social and economic circumstances, but seems curiously short-sighted. For instance, Schwartz points out that it would certainly be easier for a community to reproduce itself if there were one man and fifty women, rather than fifty men and one woman. Viewed in this light, individual women's lives are intrinsically more valuable to the preservation of the political community than are men's. Schwartz raises this issue in the context of a discussion about why women are not permitted to be citizens of a republic, arguing that since one of the requirements of citizenship is military participation, the fear of losing women in battle could be an important reason for Rousseau's insistence that citizenship remain an exclusively male privilege. See Schwartz, *The Sexual Politics*, 159, note 3.

50. The extent to which Rousseau's argument appears to be directed solely toward middle- and upper-class women here is striking. Surely, the poor and working-class women of the eighteenth century did not have the luxury of waiting for a man to provide them with the necessities of food and shelter. On the different social conditions faced by women of different classes during this time, see Cissie Fairchilds, "Women and Family," and Elizabeth Fox-Genovese, "Women and Work," in *French Women and the Age of Enlightenment,* ed. Samia I. Spencer (Bloomington: Indiana University Press, 1984), 97-127.

51. Rousseau, *Emile*, 369.

52. Rousseau, *Emile*, 371, 383. On the meaning and consequences of the public/private distinction in political theory, see Jean Bethke Elshtain, *Public Man, Private Woman.*

53. Jean-Jacques Rousseau, "Letter to M. d'Alembert on the Theatre," trans. Allan Bloom, in *Politics and the Arts* (Ithaca: Cornell University Press, Agora Editions, 1960), 71-2.

54. Rousseau, *First Discourse,* 52-53, note.

55. Rousseau, "Letter to d'Alembert," 73-74.

56. Rousseau, *Emile*, 369.

57. Rousseau, *Emile*, 377.

58. Rousseau also appears to distinguish between "opinion"—which he views as salutary or not depending upon the circumstances and which particular opinions are at issue—and what he calls "public prejudices," a term he always uses pejoratively and that presumably refers to false or harmful opinions.

59. Rousseau, *Emile*, 365. Significantly, the quote ends with Rousseau claiming that

it is the "grave" of man's virtue.

60. Rousseau, *Emile*, 364.

61. Rousseau, *First Discourse*, 53.

62. On this point, it is interesting to note how often Rousseau himself is at pains to point out that unlike the gallants of his time, he eschews the custom of basely flattering women. Admitting that what he writes may very well provoke and enrage them, he insists that he does so only out of a genuine love and regard for them, for their happiness and their honor.

63. Rousseau, *Emile*, 390.

64. Rousseau, *First Discourse*, 52-53, note.

65. Rousseau, *Emile*, 398.

66. Rousseau, *Emile*, 377.

67. Schwartz, *The Sexual Politics*, 85.

68. Rousseau, *Emile*, 361.

69. Rousseau, *Emile*, 370.

70. Rousseau, *Emile*, 383.

71. Rousseau also seems to make a subtle distinction between "public opinion," which can be reformed and made to serve philosophic ends, and "public prejudices," which are simply wrong-headed notions inimical to society's well-being.

72. It is possible, too, that Rousseau deliberately refrains from emphasizing the extent to which men also are dependent on women. He has already loudly lamented the "slavishness" of his contemporaries in other contexts, and perhaps sees no reason to draw their attention to another sort of enslavement from which, perhaps, it is impossible to free themselves.

73. Rousseau, *Emile*, 369.

74. Rousseau, *Emile*, 361.

75. Jean-Jacques Rousseau, *Julie or the New Heloise,* trans. Philip Stewart and Jean Vaché (Hanover, NH., and London: University Press of New England, 1997), 79-81.

76. Rousseau, *Emile*, 393, note.

77. Rousseau, *Emile*, 386, note.

78. Rousseau, *Emile*, 385.

79. We may find a clue to Rousseau's true intentions here by noting that he ends the passage regarding the need for women's subjection to the proprieties with the following equivocal statement: "Amidst our senseless arrangements a decent woman's life is a perpetual combat against herself. It is just that this sex share the pain of the evils it has caused us" (*Emile*, 369). This last line appears to be an allusion to the biblical account of Eve's role in bringing about the Fall and the eternal banishment of humanity from the Garden of Eden. Interestingly, the other notable reference to the biblical depiction of relations between the sexes occurs in the brief introduction to Book V, where Rousseau proclaims, as God himself does, that "It is not good for man to be alone." Rousseau's allusions to the Christian understanding of relations between the sexes are, I believe, not insignificant in this context. "It is not good for man to be alone": it is both a moral judgment and the announcement of a resolutely male-oriented point of view. Moreover, it contrasts strikingly with Rousseau's approach in the *Second Discourse*, where he announces his intention to begin by "setting all the facts aside," the "facts" in this case being the biblical account of human origins (*Second Discourse*, 103). Here, however, Rousseau seems to signal from the outset that what follows in Book V of *Emile* will not

constitute a scientific inquiry into human sexuality as such, but rather a *moral* one, meaning as well a social one. It also alerts us to the possibility that there may exist behind or beneath the surface teaching another one that questions the very tenets Rousseau purports to uphold. For in fact, he does not hesitate to attack the Christian teaching about sexuality for its corrosive effects on marriage and its tendency to stifle even the most innocent of pleasures. "By forbidding women song, dance, and all the entertainments of the world, [Christianity] makes them sullen, shrewish and unbearable in their homes," Rousseau fulminates. "There is no other religion," he continues, "in which marriage is subjected to such severe duties and none in which so holy an obligation is so despised" (*Emile*, 374). Rousseau's explicit recurrence to Christian dogma, then, is perhaps both a ruse and a clue. On the one hand, it serves the rhetorical purpose of reinforcing a certain understanding of relations between the sexes that emphasizes women's subordinate and essentially domestic role. Insofar as Rousseau's project entails teaching women about how they can both enhance and deploy most effectively the power they possess vis-à-vis men, it may very well be necessary for him to do so from a position that unequivocally asserts male authority, an observation made by Schwartz, *The Sexual Politics,* 147. Thus, Rousseau upholds the convention that equates formal and public authority with men, a convention supported by Christian teachings. On the other hand, it serves notice to his careful readers that there is an important ambiguity in Rousseau's position. For he also undermines the Christian understanding of human sexuality in order to replace it with one he believes to be less censorious of sexuality and more in accord with human nature. Moreover, a careful reading of this section discloses that Rousseau subsequently modifies his position and quietly offers women a way to flee the prison of public opinion by stressing that conscience must take precedence over opinion when the two conflict, and appealing to reason to mediate between the two.

80. Note, however, Melzer's interesting argument that Rousseau does not unconditionally condemn oppression or even slavery. "In the very rare cases where injustice, violence or oppression does not cause corruption but rather prevents it, he *does not condemn it,*" (Melzer, *The Natural History of Man,* 63). It might be possible to view women's inequality in society, along with the "enslavement" to opinion and the proprieties Rousseau recommends for them, in this light. If so, then Rousseau's defense of this inequality would seem to rest on surprisingly utilitarian grounds—its usefulness for society. Yet Rousseau tries to deflect that criticism, I believe, by arguing that such an arrangement benefits women as well by securing for them the greatest happiness social life has to offer: namely, the sentimental pleasures of romantic, conjugal, and parental love.

81. Schwartz, for example, claims that while nature grants men the possibility of leading a completely independent, autarkic existence, it denies women that same possibility. "Women, being physically weaker, are naturally and necessarily social; they inescapably depend upon men, so they must also induce men to depend upon them" (Schwartz, *The Sexual Politics,* 6). Likewise, one might conclude that women's capacity to bear children renders them more naturally "other-directed" than men.

82. Rousseau, *Emile,* 370.
83. Rousseau, *Emile,* 370.
84. Rousseau, *Emile,* 370.
85. Rousseau, *Emile,* 370.
86. Rousseau, *Social Contract,* I:8, 55-56.

87. Fermon puts it this way: "The political and pedagogical enterprise is about forming the heart and then appealing to sentiment," 2. Melzer, in the *Natural Goodness of Man,* makes a similar argument in his chapter entitled "Curing Humanity."

88. On the moral implications of romantic love and its significance in Rousseau's thought, see Bloom, *Love and Friendship.*

89. Rousseau, *Second Discourse,* 146-47.

90. Rousseau, *Emile,* 361.

91. Rousseau, *Emile,* 243.

92. Rousseau, *Emile,* 327.

93. For a discussion of the significance of this idea of psychic unity or "wholeness" in Rousseau's thought, see Melzer, *The Natural Goodness of Man.*

94. Rousseau, *Emile,* 221. This is the happiness of an imperfect creature, however. In the preceding sentence, Rousseau writes: "A truly happy being is a solitary being. God alone enjoys an absolute happiness." Perfect happiness would consist in complete self-sufficiency. Social beings, who are dependent on others, must seek their happiness in loving and being loved by those on whom they depend.

95. Rousseau, *Emile,* 402-06. This is the interpretation Rousseau himself supplies at the end of the story. A less sanguine interpretation might regard it as a warning about the dangers of the imagination. For while the imagination might be indispensable to romantic love and thus play a vital role in both the establishment and maintenance of society, Rousseau demonstrates that it also can drive us away from society when its pleasures are greater than the real pleasures society has to offer.

96. In an earlier draft of *Emile,* one finds the sentence, "Lead [girls] to virtue by means of *amour-propre.*" In place of *amour-propre,* Rousseau had first written "vanity," then "pride." The final version of this sentence that appears in *Emile* reads: "Lead them to virtue by means of reason." All of these motives seem to play a role in the moral education of Sophie. Jean-Jacques Rousseau, *Oeuvres Complètes,* 4 vols., ed. Bernard Gagnebin and Marcel Raymond (Paris: Gallimard, Bibliothèque de la Pléiade, 1959-69), vol. 4:1654.

97. Rousseau, *Emile,* 390.

98. After all, women's desire to rule can at least partly (and perhaps largely) be construed as proceeding from their greater dependence on men, a dependence Rousseau carefully cultivates through the program of education laid out for women in Book V of *Emile.* It is only when one is weak that one does evil, Rousseau writes, and it is only when one needs to put the hands of another at the end of one's own arms that one acquires the desire to rule or manipulate others. If in society women are made dependent on men for the necessities of life, they naturally have a great interest in capturing men's wills to ensure that they are always willing to provide these things for them.

99. Rousseau, *Emile,* 360.

100. In the context of this discussion, Rousseau condemns rape as "the most brutal of all acts," and the one most contrary to both nature and reason.

101. Rousseau, *Emile,* 153. For an entertaining and instructive analysis of the role of food in Emile's early education, see Bloom, *Love and Friendship,* 60-61.

102. Insofar as modesty is associated with women's resistance to men's sexual advances, then as we saw above, there are good grounds for doubting its naturalness. See notes 11-12 and 21-23.

103. Rousseau, *Emile,* 392. Rousseau also joins desire to rule with pride. By praising

the "noble ambition" of the women of Sparta to rule over "great and strong souls," he hopes to inspire a similar ambition in modern women (392-93). Finally, two other principles of Sophie's education that support and encourage her virtue deserve brief consideration. First is the training of her taste. Instructing Sophie's tastes early and continually means enlightening her about the difference between true and false pleasures. It is particularly important that Sophie's tastes be guided toward those occupations and amusements that are compatible with the domestic life for which she is destined, for in this way her habits and inclinations will be in conformity with her duties. Second, Rousseau calls upon conscience to confirm to Sophie her moral duties. Sophie's religious instruction will be much more limited than that of Emile since she will adopt her husband's religion upon marriage. Nonetheless, she, too, will be taught that the "inner sentiment," or conscience, provides an independent moral guide. Conscience enables her to judge opinion, and she will follow the latter only insofar as it accords with her sentiments. Yet here conscience becomes more ambiguous, for Rousseau claims that both conscience (or sentiment) and opinion must cooperate in Sophie's education. But since conscience can go astray and opinion is subject to errors, she needs an arbiter between them. That arbiter is reason. Reason will confirm to Sophie her duties as a wife and mother, duties that are "so natural and easily sensed that she cannot without bad faith refuse her consent to the inner sentiment that guides her, nor fail to recognize her duty if her inclinations are still uncorrupted" (*Emile*, 382).

104. Weiss, *Gendered Community*, does a good job of detailing just how this comes to light in the education of Sophie.

105. See Rousseau, *Emile*, 365-76.

106. Rousseau, *Emile*, 317.

107. Rousseau, *Social Contract*, 131, note.

108. Weiss, *Gendered Community*, 52. In this regard, we should not forget that the name of Rousseau's heroine derives from *sophia*, the Greek word for wisdom.

Chapter 10

Honor, Civility, and Civilization: David Hume on the Refinement of Sexual, Moral, and Civic Relations

Eduardo A. Velásquez

> Honour occupies about the same place in contemporary usage as chastity.
> —Peter Berger

"The age that saw the decline of honour," argues Peter Berger, "also saw the rise of new moralities and of a new humanism, and most specifically of a historically unprecedented concern for the dignity and rights of the individual."[1] Lost in the ascendancy of rights is a world of "stable institutions, a world in which individuals can with subjective certainty attach their identities to the institutional roles that society assigns to them."[2] Berger does greet this transition with an appreciation for the benefits that accrue to those enslaved, oppressed, and otherwise tyrannized peoples around the globe who courageously undertake to reform their respective societies by appeals to universal human rights. Yet the movement to the new regime of rights is not without costs. Community-minded critics argue that the new rights dispensation engenders the "unen-cumbered," "abstracted," "solitary" "self" or "individual."[3] Stripped of all the necessary civic and moral attachments that give life meaning, depth, and stability, "Modern man," Berger concludes, "is ever in search of himself."[4]

This, of course, is not a new story. Modernity's discontents are numerous. Before the more recent communitarian revival, for example, advocates of "Classical Republicanism"[5] and/or "Civic Humanism"[6] reminded us of a tradition reaching back to Aristotle that properly locates the human being in the context of the political community from which she or he emerges. Whatever the equivalent of "bowling" might have been in those days, people were certainly not doing it "alone."[7] On this broad view of the relationship between the individual and the community, it is understandable why honor assumes the sovereign place among civic virtues. Honor is the political version of pride that takes its bearings from the things a community prizes and shuns. It is aristocratic in that it distinguishes between abilities, endowments, and contributions to the good of the "whole" above the "part." It is martial in that the highest honors are accorded to those who are most able to take up arms to preserve and secure the community against domestic and foreign threats. Consequently, it is "manly" in that civic affairs fall within the province of men, the domestic of women.[8] Not that today's advocates of community would rush to implement the austere requirements of honor, although some would if given the opportunity. Theirs is for the most part a kinder, gentler community, a critique of which is not proposed here. We can, however, learn much about the modern age by coming to terms with the nature and displacement of honor.[9] This is what is proposed here. I return to the difficult question of the relative merits and demerits of the shift from the old to the new at the conclusion of this essay.

I seek to advance two interrelated arguments here. I do so by engaging David Hume's essay "Of the Rise and Progress of the Arts and Sciences."[10] First, I show that Hume's intention is to partially deflate the aristocratic virtue of honor and to elevate the democratic virtue of civility.[11] The deflation of honor and the ascendancy of civility coincide with the collapse of feudalism and the rise of modern, commercial republics. Commercial and dynamic societies may require something other than honor to sustain the diversity and leveling that are partly the fruits of the emerging economy. This diversity and leveling are connected to the opportunities and problems Christianity brings to political life. Civility is the virtue that allows society to cope with and mute religious sectarianism, zealotry, and tyranny. To the extent that the church is seen as increasingly less authoritative in defining and cultivating public morals, and human life is increasingly understood as inhabiting the separate spheres of "private" and "public," "church" and "state," the prospects for public engagement, reconciliation, and improvement increasingly depend on civility. Civility is akin to, and is perhaps a secularized version of, "toleration."[12] Together, these arguments inform the author's larger case on behalf of "civilization."

Second, the deprecation of honor and the elevation of civility depend for their success on the calling into question of the patriarchal structure that characterized the relations between men and women in the age of honor. The flip side of this critique is a reconception of relations between the sexes on the basis of the twin principles of liberty and equality. A brief anticipation of what follows must suffice. Honor (often, not always) becomes suspect when it fosters an excessive love of self, especially when linked to inherited wealth and social status, and not to individual accomplishments. Aristocratic presumptuousness in the guise of honor is not favorable to civility. The obverse of this excessive self-love is humility, also potentially pernicious because it tends to foster self-debasement, servility, and otherworldliness, all of which are at odds with the proper recognition and defense of liberty.[13] The potential excesses and deficiencies of self-love are entangled with Christianity, in a manner not always favorable to or in harmony with a peaceful and productive human coexistence. "Enthusiasm" and "superstition" are the words Hume uses to describe these two pernicious mutations of self-love.[14] Now, according to Hume, the excesses and deficiencies of self-love find expression in the most basic of all relationships, with enormous consequences for society at large. "Manly honor" is a virtue not infrequently attached to the male's sexual prowess (*vir*-tue and *vir*-ility are of a piece) and to his rule or government over his wife and dependents. The female complement is sexual "modesty" and "chastity," from which follow a host of "deferential" virtues appropriate to the so-called fair sex. The assertive "masculine" and the deferential "feminine" virtues are based on assumptions about the relative physical and intellectual endowments of each sex. Man's concession to woman's supposed weaknesses are exercised in "gallantry." It is precisely honor and its complements that Hume sets out to reform. We thus get to civility by way of a curious marriage and reformation of opinions and habits that were once seen as falling within distinctly male and female spheres. Civility is androgyny.[15]

Monarchs and Barbarians

That Hume anticipates and grapples with the some of the concerns of contemporary feminists is nowhere more forcefully, persuasively, and eloquently stated than in the essays of Annette Baier.[16] I propose a modest reconsideration of Baier's lucid and persuasive interpretation of Hume. I do so by returning to one of Hume's most important essays, "Of the Rise and Progress of the Arts and Sciences." Baier does indeed bring this essay to our attention, noting that it contains some of Hume's most blatantly misogynist remarks.[17] She proceeds to contrast these remarks with other statements of Hume's from his vast philosophic, literary, and historical corpus. The contrast is revealing, Baier shows, for it suggests that Hume's thinking in "Of the Rise and Progress of the Arts and Sciences" must be qualified. But Baier's qualifications do not stem from an analysis of the essay itself.[18] What remains in doubt is the status of Hume's apparent misogyny *within* the context of the argument in that essay. Unpacking Hume's argument and reflecting on the place of his apparent misogyny within the discussion of the rise and progress of the arts and sciences is important for several reasons.[19]

Baier reads Hume's essay as a "'natural history' of learning."[20] While I would not reject this characterization, I suggest that there are two additional arguments advanced simultaneously in "Of the Rise and Progress of the Arts and Sciences" that may be equally revealing of Hume's intentions. To begin, the essay shows a progression from "barbarism" to "civilization." Hume brings under scrutiny tyrannies of various kinds, chief among them the tyranny of a single monarch. He also accounts for the historical evolution from tyranny/monarchy to liberty/republicanism. Let us call this argument the "history of civility and civilization." Mirroring this argument is another on the "history of sexual relations." This argument reveals the equivalents to barbarism and tyranny, civilization and liberty, in the relations between the sexes. The patriarch is to the domestic sphere what the monarch is to the political. Presumption in the guise of manly honor and excessive deference in the guise of female modesty are potentially linked to tyranny. There is an intimate connection between what we today call the "private" and "public" spheres, the reform of the latter requiring the reform of the former. Although reading Hume in light of a history of learning is important and revealing, the prospects of learning fall under the larger considerations of civilization and reconstituted sexual relations. In the most decisive and comprehensive respects, "Of the Rise and Progress of the Arts and Sciences" is a history of morals or manners. [21]

"Of the Rise and Progress of the Arts and Sciences" is introduced with a digression, a series of reflections on the relationship between "chance" and "causes" that seem to bear little on the essay's primary concerns. But upon closer scrutiny the opening is apt. A great number of human beings, not least some prominent writers, Hume argues, are inclined to the opinion that human events are generally "derived from chance" (111). Hume might as easily used the word "Providence." The human propensity, under the sway of religious opinions, is to view their affairs as falling largely outside of their control and thus subject to the unintelligible will, caprice, or justice of God or the gods. To hold this view ultimately arrests further inquiry into the workings of the human world and also hampers our proper engagement within it. The gods are mysterious, some might say. The alternative proposed by Hume is not for all human endeavors to be brought before the light of reason, thus removing all doubt as to their causes. Rather, Hume's moderate claim is that much more is subject to our comprehension and thus to our *control* than previously thought. If I correctly read "Of the Rise and Progress of the Arts and Sciences" as an essay partly devoted to the "history of sexual relations," then Hume suggests that those relations are themselves not merely subject to chance or historical accident.

With regard, then, to the world of causes and effects, Hume makes four "observations." Let us examine each in turn, and attempt to elucidate the complicated and less than obvious connections between them. The first observation, "*That it is impossible for the arts and sciences to arise, at first, among any people unless that people enjoy the blessings of a free government*," sets into motion Hume's history (115).

> In the first ages of the world, when men are as yet barbarous and ignorant, they seek no farther security against mutual violence and injustice, than the choice of some rulers, few or many, in whom they place an implicit obedience, without providing any security, by laws or political institutions, against the violence and injustice of these rulers (115).

Hume will subsequently develop the argument according to which "barbarous and ignorant" ages are defined by the *absence* of security, laws, and political institutions. Rule of the law is a necessary but insufficient condition for civilization. Before we turn to Hume's negative formulation leading to law, it is important to pause on his positive one. Ignorance, mutual violence, injustice, and the implicit obedience of the citizenry, on the one hand, and the violence and injustice of rulers against the citizenry, on the other, define the "first ages of the world." Violent assertion and deference characterize rulers and subjects, attributes that will occupy much of Hume's attention throughout his essay. Initially, Hume leaves open the possibility that the one, few, or many can exercise tyranny. However, a few steps further we learn that the first ages of the world lend themselves to the rule of one man. It is only when populations increase "either by conquest, or by the ordinary course of propagation" that the "monarch, finding it impossible, in his own person, to execute every sovereignty, in every place, must delegate his authority to inferior magistrates, who preserve peace and order in their respective districts" (115-16). Hume's ensuing discussion is devoted to the character of a monarch and to the habits he propagates among his subjects.[22]

It is important to examine tyranny for its own sake, but also in anticipation of Hume's discussion of the rule of men over women. This examination also sheds light on the connections Hume sees between political forms and human character. I grant at the outset that this relation is suspect in the case of tyranny, where rule is arbitrary. But even arbitrary rule *in*forms the character of the person who exercises power, and the persons who are subjected to it. "Arbitrary power, in all cases," Hume posits, "is somewhat oppressive and debasing." When it is "contracted in a small compass," it is "altogether ruinous and intolerable." It becomes "still worse, when the person, who possesses it, knows that the time of his authority is limited and uncertain" (116-17). As for a people "governed in such a manner," Hume says that they "are slaves in the full and proper sense of the word." It is impossible that such a people "can ever aspire to any refinement of taste or reason." This is the heart of Hume's thesis on the effects of arbitrary power.

There is an immediate objection to Hume's thesis, one that echoes the teachings of classical antiquity, or at least some version of that teaching. What of benevolent and just rulers, "statesmen" as we are fond of saying, or a "philosopher-king"? It is arguable that the rule of a monarch need not result in the ills Hume describes. In response to this objection, Hume develops an argument for the importance of the rule of law and its connections to liberty, equality, and civilization. Just before his account of the debasing qualities of unadulterated power, Hume brings to our attention the example of Peter I of Russia (1689-1725). "We are told," Hume writes, "that the late Czar, though actuated with a noble genius, and smit with love and admiration of EUROPEAN arts . . . approved of such summary decisions of causes, as are practiced in that barbarous [Turkish] monarchy, where judges are not restrained by any methods, forms, or laws" (116). Why is the noble genius of a czar or monarch not sufficient to restrain his admiration for barbarous monarchy? Why is not the private virtue of a king a sufficient motive to promote public virtue? Hume argues that general laws are by their very nature "attended with inconveniences, when applied to particular cases." Accordingly, it "requires great penetration and experience," he continues, "both to perceive that these inconveniences are fewer than what would result from full discretionary powers in each magistrate; and also to discern what general laws are, upon the whole, attended with the fewest inconveniences." This is, Hume argues,

> a matter of so great difficulty, that men may have made advances, even in the sublime arts of poetry and eloquence, where rapidity of genius and imagination assists their progress, before they have arrived at any great refinement in their municipal laws, where frequent trials and diligent observation can alone direct their improvements. It is not, therefore, to be supposed, that a barbarous monarch, unrestrained and uninstructed, will ever become a *legislator* . . . ." (116, emphasis added)

Hume's first reference to a "legislator" points to requirements of the rule of law, and to a distinct kind of rule. The private virtue of a king, monarch, or tyrant is not sufficient to guarantee the impartial and equitable rule of law. Those requirements are the result of time, experience, trial and error, in short, of accumulated wisdom. Later in the essay, Hume argues that the attempt to "balance a large state, whether monarchical or republican, on general laws, is a work of so great difficulty, that no human genius, however comprehensive, is able, by the mere dint of reason and reflection, to effect it" (124). Hume anticipates the need for a distinct kind of "enlightenment" that makes the rule of law possible. This enlightenment would need to be comprehensive.

I grant that Hume's critique of monarchy leaves the reader with numerous unresolved questions, chief among them the sources of the *prerequisite* judgment and experience that seem to be curiously the *effects* of law. Hume compounds this problem himself. He argues that to expect "that the arts and sciences should take their first rise in a monarchy, is to expect a contradiction." Before the "refinements" of the arts and sciences have taken hold, "the monarch is ignorant and uninstructed; and not having knowledge sufficient to make him sensible of the necessity of balancing his government upon general laws, he delegates his full power to all inferior magistrates." The necessary consequence is that "this barbarous policy debases the people, and for ever prevents all improvements" (117). How then will the arts and sciences *arise*? Which comes first, refinement or law? Do the various refinements, of human beings and of the law, coincide? Has chance made a clandestine appearance? In his critique of arbitrary power, Hume has established a probable connection between law and civilization, although, as noted, this connection is first presented negatively. But Hume's various qualifications do not allow the reader to reverse his account of tyranny. Initially, the reader is tempted to conclude that if arbitrary power leads to debasement, then to be governed by laws or republican forms would lead to virtue. Hume, however, argues that refinement of the arts and sciences is necessary before we can properly speak of civilization. The reasons for Hume's qualifications come to light as we turn to his analysis of the *transition* from monarchic to republican forms of government.[23]

Hume argues that "the necessity of restraining the magistrates, in order to preserve liberty," must at some point appear in the minds of an enslaved people. Necessity coupled with the desire for liberty gives rise to general laws and statutes (117). Hume takes us back to the example of the Roman republic to locate the genesis of freedom, although ancient Greece has much to teach us in this regard, as we shall see. Yet Hume's appeals to antiquity are hardly flattering. He speaks of republics in their "infant state" as if they were almost indistinguishable from "barbarous monarch[ies]" (117). "The ROMAN consuls," he argues, "decided all causes, without being confined by any positive statutes, till the people, bearing their yoke with impatience, created the *decemvirs*, who promulgated the *twelve tables*" (117-18). He grants that this "body of laws" was indeed "sufficient, together with other forms of free government, to secure the lives and properties of the citizens, to exempt one man from the dominion of another; and to protect every one against the violence or tyranny of his fellow citizens." We should not underestimate or under-appreciate the contributions of antiquity to our experience of liberty and civilization. Even so, Hume insists that there is something barbarous about antiquity. Initially, turning us to the example of Rome does not clarify the relation between law and civilization, but rather shows how law may be coincident with barbarism. At this stage of Hume's argument we encounter his famous formulation on the relation of freedom, law, and learning. He writes:

> Here then are the advantages of free states. Though a republic should be barbarous, it necessarily, by an infallible operation, gives rise to LAW, even before mankind have made any considerable advances in the other sciences. From law arises security: from security curiosity: And from curiosity knowledge. The latter steps of this progress may be more accidental; but the former are altogether necessary (118).

Instead of speaking as he did previously of barbarous monarchies, Hume attaches the epithet to *republics*. Republican forms may be barbarous, perhaps as barbarous as monarchies. The law is insufficient. But the law is necessary to set in motion a process by which citizens acquire the learning Hume argues is necessary to and suited for the sustenance of republican forms of government. It seems that if we are to speak comprehensively and accurately about civilization, we need to take into account not just law and liberty, but the entire "infallible operation" leading to enlightenment. The interconnection among the various parts of this operation comes to light as we examine the second observation.

The Physical and Moral Geography of Politeness and Learning

Hume's second observation is "*That nothing is more favorable to the rise of politeness and learning, than a number of neighboring and independent states, connected together by commerce and policy*" (119). This is an unexpected turn of events. The preceding section anticipates and prepares us for a discussion of the "infallible operation," the transition from monarchy to law, to learning, and then to manners or politeness, or so we are led to think. But Hume turns toward what we call "international relations."[24] He provides a justification for this apparent digression. Immediately following his second observation, Hume says that "The emulation, which naturally arises among those neighboring states, is an obvious source of improvement: But what I would chiefly insist is the stop, which such limited territories give both to *power* and to *authority*" (119). We have not strayed, but return to the problem of the extent and form of power, in a word, to *empire*. Empire is at odds with politeness and learning. A critique of emperors, kings, or monarchs is implied. Empire also prevents the kind of *emulation* that would be fostered by many independent but interconnected states. So we thus return to the question of learning, or enlightenment, by way of a discussion of the *methods* of education. We are creatures who learn by example, and are thus improved or depraved by the models before us. Hume's introduction to the second observation weaves together a variety of connected elements the meaning and significance of which cannot be understood except in reference to their respective connections.

"Extended governments, where a single person has great influence, soon become absolute," Hume argues, "but small ones change naturally into commonwealths" (119). The configuration of political power affects the dispositions of citizens and rulers. Large governments are "accustomed by degrees to tyranny" because "each act of violence is at first performed upon a part, which, being distant from the majority, is not taken notice of, nor excites any violent ferment." In a large government the various parts are disconnected. Ignorant of the resolutions of the rest, each part is thus "afraid to begin any commotion or insurrection." Hume adds that among humans there is a "superstitious reverence for princes," a habit they "naturally contract when they do not often see the sovereign, and when many of them become not acquainted with him so as to perceive his weaknesses." Hume's psychology of liberty and dominion takes another peculiar turn. Not only should we ascribe to humankind the love of liberty and the love of dominion, we should note that there is an inclination to submit to dominion. This inclination is inflamed when "large states can afford a great expense, in order to support the pomp of majesty." All the glitter and gold fuels a peculiar "kind of fascination" that takes hold of humankind "and naturally contributes to the enslaving of them" (119).

Proximity to political power, the extent of empire, and the dispositions of the populace are all intertwined. The same connections are apparent when the sphere of government is contracted, but with consequences more favorable to liberty and to virtue. "In a small government," Hume argues, "any act of oppression is immediately known throughout the whole." When "murmurs and discontents" are more easily communicated among a people, the level of indignation rises because "subjects are not apt to apprehend in such states, that the distance is wide between themselves and their sovereigns" (119-20). In a statement that is bound to complicate our understanding of Hume's argument on behalf of the didactic effects of emulation, he immediately follows his ruminations on small states with the claim that "admiration and acquaintance are altogether incompatible toward any mortal creature." Hume argues that sleep and love convinced even Alexander the Great that "he was not a God." Were the opportunities available to us, acquaintance with the great would reveal their "numberless weaknesses" and provide "convincing proofs" of their "humanity" (120). How then ought we to parse Hume's account of emulation, acquaintance/ proximity, and admiration? What is implied in the claim that our acquaintance with the so-called great tempers admiration? Are we all equally frail, equally human? But what then of models worthy of imitation or emulation? What of emulation simply?

In Hume's peculiar way, he brings us back to the central concern of his essay, namely, the nature, variations, contradictions, and government of self-love. In this case, Hume's concern is with the human propensity to take our bearings from others. In other words, emulation, admiration, learning, self-improvement are all entangled with our *vanity*. "Reputation," Hume writes, "is as great a fascination upon men as sovereignty, and is *equally* destructive to the freedom of thought and examination" (120, emphasis added). We learn through emulation partly because we are taken in by opinions of others and by the charms of sovereignty. At the same time, such aping of the great stands in the way of our ever acquiring the self-understanding that befits a genuinely enlightened, liberal, and self-governing human being. Paradoxically, then, emulation may lead one to aspire toward greatness at the same time that it may lead to ignorance. Honor is not too far away. According to Hume, a constellation of small, interdependent states helps us to soften some of the potentially debilitating effects of vanity. Hume argues:

> Where a number of neighbouring states have a great intercourse of arts and commerce, their mutual jealousy keeps them from receiving too lightly the law from each other, in matters of taste and reasoning, and makes them examine every work of art with the greatest care and accuracy. The contagion of popular opinion spreads not so easily from one place to another. It readily receives a check in some state or other, where it concurs not with the prevailing prejudices. And nothing but nature and reason, or, at least, what bears them a strong resemblance, can force its way through all obstacles, and unite the most rival nations into an esteem and admiration of it (120).[25]

Greece provides us a noteworthy example of the government of vanity, mutual jealousy, and excessive admiration. Greece was a "cluster of little principalities," Hume writes, and was thus divided in a way imperial Rome was not. To a favorable geography, Hume notes that there also "concurred a happy climate, a soil not infertile, and a most harmonious and comprehensive language." As a consequence, "Each city produced its several artists and philosophers, who refused to yield the preference of those of the neighboring republics." Hume argues that the inevitable contention and debate that arises out of differences sharpened the wits of men. The diversity of republics is preferable to the homogeneity of empires. When a "variety of objects were presented to the judgment," as they were in Greece, each "challenged the preference to the rest." Thus citizens, "not being dwarfed by the restraint of authority, were enabled to make such considerable shoots, as are, even at this time, the objects of our admiration" (120-21). We cannot ignore the role of chance. The Greeks enjoyed the happy coincidence of geography, language, and climate. But this happy coincidence made for competition and debate, for challenges that aroused the pride, vanity, and thinking of citizens. It is hard to be persuaded that Hume thinks the desire for self-improvement and learning suffice as the means toward human betterment. The goal is more likely to be secured if the most basic human passion can be coopted in the service of human improvement. To this end, diversity and division are preferable to homogeneity, as a means to arouse our curiosity and to arrest our pretensions. Self-love is given expression at the same time that it is moderated by the self-love of others.

The virtues of the Greek model are all the more striking in the contrast Hume draws to the Roman empire. The Rome Hume brings to our attention is the one conquered by Christianity, or, more precisely, by Christian Aristotelianism. And for important reasons. Hume aims to show the pernicious effects of this hegemony over the human mind:

> After the *christian*, or *catholic* church had spread itself over the civilized world, and had engrossed all the learning of the times; being really one large state within itself, and united under one head; this variety of sects immediately disappeared, and the PERIPATETIC philosophy was alone admitted into the schools, to the utter depravation of every kind of learning (121).

Empire depraves the mind of its proper nourishment. It leads to complacency and stagnation. Most pernicious is the marriage of territory and ideology. Hume makes a case for the liberty of thought and of conscience. Whether Hume's reservations about engulfing humankind under one comprehensive understanding indicate the salutary consequences of his skepticism is a question too large for us to entertain here. What is apparent in this instance is that empires over bodies and minds extinguish diversity and division and, as a consequence, halt the process of examination, assessment, and correction necessary to moderation and to learning.

In keeping with comparisons, Hume asks us to look at the Europe of his day through the lenses of the ancient Greek example. "EUROPE is at present a copy at large," Hume writes, "of what GREECE was formerly a pattern in miniature." Hume continues to move his analysis from the physical to the intellectual and moral world. "What checked the progress of the CARTESIAN philosophy, to which the FRENCH nation shewed a strong propensity towards the end of the last century," Hume continues, was the "opposition made to it by the other nations of EUROPE, who soon discovered the weak sides of that philosophy." The "severest scrutiny, which NEWTON'S theory has undergone, proceeded not from his own countrymen, but from foreigners" (121). Such self-scrutiny that is at the heart of self-understanding and self-improvement also takes place in the realm of morals. On the one hand, Hume argues, "The ENGLISH are become sensible of the scandalous licentiousness of their stage, from the example of FRENCH decency and morals." On the other hand, "The FRENCH are convinced that their theatre has become effeminate, by too much love and gallantry; and begin to approve of the more masculine tastes of some neighboring nations" (122). Hume now introduces the balance of character, born of the mutual appropriation of the "effeminate" and the "masculine."

Hume has brought us closer to an understanding of civilization. Arbitrary power is corrupting not just of the ruler but of the ruled. Private virtue alone will not suffice in moderating such power. We are left to wonder about the means by which imperial power can be transformed into the rule of law. Necessity and liberty intrude. There are, of course, numerous examples where the demands of necessity and liberty are thwarted. But as some monarchs extend their dominions, as they tend to do, the need to delegate power is impressed upon them. However barbarous the delegation of power remains, the division of power itself anticipates or even partakes of something republican. Coincidentally, the desire for liberty makes itself felt by way of citizens' demands for the protection of their lives and property. Hume sees in these various developments the origins of the law. Law has a constancy to it that the judgments of men do not. We seek order and protection. And if the law is in some measure an expression of the *public* will on behalf of liberty, the restraints it imposes and the freedoms it makes possible are more likely to be *equitable*. Liberty and equality are twins. But though it preserves lives and property as in the Roman empire, Hume contends that law alone does not make for civilization. It is at this point in the analysis that Hume introduces the "infallible operation" from liberty, to law, to learning. The introduction of this operation takes a peculiar turn as Hume first directs us to the good fortune of geography and circumstances that make for enlightenment. In so doing, he reveals much about the less-than-noble motives at the heart of self-improvement, chief among them our vain self-love. We wonder if the turn to international relations is Hume's rejoinder to "state of nature" theorists. But instead of treating the permanent and necessary passions of our nature as sins fit for purgation (Christianity), or as suited for the government of the almighty Leviathan (Hobbes), Hume ponders the manner in which they might be put to use consistent with what is fitting and proper for human beings. Allowing humans free rein to gravitate to the variety of objects to which the human dispositions incline, Hume sees potentially ennobling results. Those results are found in the various improvements in the arts and sciences, as well as in human character. A keen awareness of the various claims and opinions of our fellow citizens, which emerge concurrent with but also in opposition to our own claims and opinions, generates a process of examination that is friendly to moderation. Though in a language Hume himself might reject, he presents to the reader something not too far removed from what liberals today call the "mutual recognition of rights."[26] Just how we understand the connection between the mutual recognition of rights and his provoking statement that the nations of Europe moderate their morals by an appeal to the "masculine" and "effeminate," Hume leaves to his third observation. As we shall see, the reference to masculine and feminine virtues, and to the prospects of conflation or synthesis, are neither fortuitous nor unconnected to Hume's argument on behalf of moderation, enlightenment, civility, and civilization.

Culture, Cultivation, and Cultivators

Before directly confronting Hume's discussion of masculine and feminine qualities or habits, we must revisit one difficulty that continues to haunt Hume's analysis thus far. The manner in which Hume first frames his history invites us to think about *how* the intrusion of liberty, understood largely in terms of the rule of law, affects the arbitrary rule of tyrant, monarch, or head of state. Arbitrary power is transformed by the demands for liberty into the rule of law, to the general benefit of humankind, or so we are led to think. But precisely this somewhat sanguine or naïve discussion of "progress" obscures questions born out of the very amalgamation of regimes Hume's history presents to the reader. For example, let us turn Hume's history upside down. Are there residues of monarchism in republicanism? If so, what are they? If Hume is intent on arresting the view that the republicanism is simply coincident with or the same as civilization, then could we argue that there are qualities in monarchy itself that make for civilization? These questions are demanded by the admixture of regimes Hume sets before us in his history, but also by his own very complicated and not always lucid discussion of the relation between liberty and dominion. We do well to recall that liberty is not license, and Hume demonstrates as much by arguing that civilization when viewed in the light of human character depends on enlightenment and *moderation*. The restraints required for moderation are not born of the corrupting and debilitating effects of imperial power, but they are restraints nonetheless, the fruits of diversity, difference, enlightenment, and, curiously, maybe even skepticism. Whether of the self, by the self, or for the self, government or administration does require a kind of dominion, or at least something authoritative by which liberty is kept within proper bounds. Before turning to the "history of sexual relations," Hume sees fit to explain the relation between monarchism and republicanism as a way of further developing the tensions between power and freedom, authority and liberty. This tension is by no means absent in the relations between the sexes, both in the context of historical precedent and the propriety of manners.

Hume's third observation is "*That though the only proper* Nursery *of these noble plants be a free state; yet may they be transplanted into any government; and that a republic is most favorable to the growth of the sciences, a civilized monarchy to that of the polite arts*" (124). The gardening metaphors continue. Free states provide the "nursery," but Hume also claims that any government provides soil for the arts and sciences. At first glance, it is not clear what we should make of the prospects for transplantation. There is little if anything to explain why Hume draws distinctions in the third observation among the *nursery* of the arts and sciences, their *transplant*, and their *growth*. But we are now aware that Hume's history is replete with examples that belie the notion that progress is simply linear. Even while Hume identifies direction to history informed by and pointing toward liberty, let us say a *philosophical* history, there is another *empirical* history that reveals a host of different regimes situated between the extremes of monarchy and republicanism, dominion and freedom. Since in *practice* each regime is a curious amalgamation of monarchic and republican forms, questions arise as to the composition and relation of the parts. For the first time in the essay, Hume divides the "sciences" from the "arts," indicating that a "republic is most *favourable* to the *growth* of the sciences," and a "civilized monarchy to that of the polite arts" (emphasis added).[27] Now, if civilization requires *both* the arts and the sciences, and if a civilized regime falls within a spectrum and thus partakes of a mixture, Hume's division of the arts and sciences and their respective connections to monarchic and republican forms might reveal to the reader how the various parts might be put together in a manner favorable to *growth* or *progress* of liberty and civilization. Hume may be showing us the benefits, deficiencies, tensions, and contradictions attending civilization, and the means by which it can be either nurtured or destroyed. Bear in mind that further down the road we come to Hume's final observation that states "necessarily decline" once they have perfected the arts and sciences. (135) Thus, for all of the hints and allusions to, even assertions on behalf of, historical progress or determinism, it seems as if Hume has a few words for "gardeners."[28]

What then are the advantages and deficiencies attending republics and civilized monarchies that may help account for, support, and/or undermine civilization? In both of these regimes, Hume argues, "those who possess the supreme authority have the disposal of many honours and advantages, which excite the ambition and avarice of mankind" (125-26). A republic is not the same as a pure democracy. Although supported by a popular base, representatives are distinguished from the populace by the offices they hold. Republican government does not dispense with the need to exercise political authority in some form. Accordingly, honor remains effective as an animating political principle. We examined earlier how Hume, in a discussion of interstate relations, finds ways in which self-love is channeled to the general betterment of each respective regime. Hume now turns to a discussion of self-love in the context of intrastate relations. The means to citizen moderation and to the taming of honor differ. In a republic, Hume argues, "the candidates for office must look downward, to gain the suffrages of the people." In a monarchy, "they must turn their attention upwards, to court the good graces and favour of the great." In order to be "successful in the former way, it is necessary for a man to make himself *useful*, by his industry, capacity, and knowledge." To be "prosperous in the latter way, it is requisite for him to render himself *agreeable*, by his wit, complaisance, or civility." Accordingly, a "strong genius succeeds best in republics," and "a refined taste in monarchies." The consequence is that "the sciences are the more natural growth of one, and the polite arts of another" (126).[29]

It is not difficult to imagine why courts and monarchs esteem the agreeable arts. Less obvious is the connection Hume makes among utility, science, and republicanism. Simply put, the appeal to utility is most effective in a republic because *equality* is one of its animating principles. While distinctions between rulers and ruled are necessary for government and governing, republicans do not tolerate these distinctions very well. They violate equality. For this reason social or political rank must be *legitimized*, we say, by an appeal to the citizenry at large. Since republicans must make their appeals to legitimacy to a broad and diverse audience, the prospects for agreement must rest on what is readily apparent, visible, and immediately felt. If asked to choose between medicine and art history, to judge between these in light of the benefits that would accrue to the citizenry writ large, one would be hard-pressed to choose art history. Hume invites the reader back to the opening of his essay. There we learned that the "principles or causes, which are fitted to operate on a multitude, are always of a grosser and more stubborn nature" (112). There is something base about utility. This is not to say that it is bad. After all, Hume links the useful to industry, capacity, and knowledge. Yet there is a coarseness to republicanism that requires a peculiar kind of refinement, one that curiously brings us back to enlightenment, but this time by way of a reflection on the virtues cultivated in a civilized monarchy. Hume speaks specifically of the "arts" of "conversation." The contrast here to the competition, mutual jealousy, and the ubiquitous desire for preeminence among states (or individuals?) is revealing. Hume is pointing us to the virtues of cooperation, to moderation with a different motive. Do we require both? If so, how? As we shall see, we are but a short step from the discussion of reconstituted sexual morals, from which republics can draw the refinement necessary to them.

"Among the arts of conversation," Hume argues, "no one pleases more than mutual deference or civility, which leads us to resign our own inclination to those of our companion, and to curb and conceal that presumption and arrogance, so natural to the human mind." A person who is good-natured and who is well educated is said to practice "this civility to every mortal, without premeditation or interest." Note the deprecation of presumption in favor of mutual respect founded on equality. Curiously, though, Hume argues that in regimes where the "power rises upwards from the people to the great, as in all republics, such refinements of civility are apt to be little practiced." I say *curiously* because one would think that the old aristocratic regime of honor is not favorable to civility, since it is not founded on equality. This is a fruitful tension worth pondering, the meaning of which emerges slowly as we proceed. At this point, Hume seems to be concerned with the defects engendered by republicanism that work against civility. In republics, Hume argues, "the whole state is . . . brought near to a level, and every member of it is rendered, in great measure, independent of another." (126) For all of the virtues of competition, diversity, and difference, republics may be prone to what we today might call excesses of "individualism." Individualism should not be mistaken for the capacity to separate oneself from the crowd by virtue of one's superior excellence. Although Hume does not use this word himself, he seems to be referring to a condition identified by Alexis de Tocqueville, who speaks of an impoverished isolation among citizens of a democracy.[30] The ameliorating effects on human character that are the product of mutual engagement and exchange are threatened by the very conditions and the very principles that make republicanism effective in the first place. According to Hume, there is a connection among citizens in a civilized monarchy that alerts republicans to the potential deficiencies of their own regime. In a *civilized* monarchy, Hume argues, "there is a long train of dependence from the prince to the peasant," which, if "not great enough to render property precarious, or depress the minds of the people," is "sufficient to beget in every one an inclination to please his superiors, and to form himself upon those models, which are most acceptable to people of condition and education" (126-27). We begin to see something of the erosion of authority in republican practices, an important point to which we return more fully in the conclusion.

The foregoing would seem to suggest that the train of dependencies that characterize relations in a civilized monarchy are preferable to the equality and independence of citizens in a republic, at least when viewed in light of the prospects for polite conversation and civility. But this is not simply so. After a digression that examines Greek and Roman manners, Hume concludes that "No advantages in this world are pure and unmixed." As "modern politeness," Hume continues, is "naturally so ornamental, runs often into affectation and foppery, disguise and insincerity," the "ancient simplicity, which is naturally so amiable and affecting, often degenerates into rusticity and abuse, scurrility and obscenity" (131-32). The manners of courts and monarchies are prone to degenerate into insincerity, while ancient manners may demand too much honesty. Hume says that he is "bold to affirm, that among the ancients, there was not much delicacy of breeding, or that polite deference and respect, which civility obliges us either to express or *counterfeit* towards the persons with whom we converse" (128, emphasis added). After taking us through ancient and modern examples none of which fully captures the posture human beings should assume toward one another, Hume turns to a discussion of gallantry. In a highly tentative and conditional statement, he writes:

If the superiority in politeness should be allowed to modern times, the modern notions of gallantry, the natural produce of courts and monarchies, will probably be assigned as the causes of this refinement. No one denies this invention to be modern: But some of the more zealous partizans of the ancients, have asserted it to be foppish and ridiculous, and a reproach, rather than a credit, to the present age. It may here be proper to examine this question (131).

Hume is about to turn from the discussion of politeness and civility to what I suggested at the outset is a "history of sexual relations" or manners. The focus is on the modern invention of gallantry, which refines and gives to modern politeness a superiority over ancient rusticity. In a series of cryptic footnotes to his discussion of ancient manners, Hume has quietly but firmly alerted us to the relation between the rudeness of ancients and their treatment of women.[31] Conversely, the prospects of an improvement in politeness, civility, and learning rests on properly configuring the relations between the sexes. The discussion of gallantry is not fortuitous.

On the Nature of Gallantry

Hume's examination of the refinements gallantry brings to modern manners begins by taking us back to nature. Hume argues that "nature has implanted in all living creatures an affection between the sexes, which, even in the fiercest and most rapacious animals, is not merely confined to the satisfaction of bodily appetite" (131). The affection between the sexes often "begets a friendship and mutual sympathy, which runs through the whole tenor of their lives." This is true even of those species in which "nature limits the indulgence of this appetite to one season and to one object," or where nature "forms a kind of marriage or association between a single male and female." Even in those cases in which *nature* restricts bodily appetite, Hume argues, "there is a visible complacency and benevolence, which extends farther, and mutually softens the affections of the sexes toward each other." Hume's opening is striking. For the first time in his history we come across living creatures engaged in friendship, mutual sympathy, benevolence, complacency toward one another and, in some cases, bound to lifetime associations according to nature. While the possibility of such attachments was foreshadowed by Hume's account of civilized monarchies, the ties of *nature*, not those of *convention*, are the most compelling here. Also, if contrasted with the foregoing accounts of competition and conflict, the ties of nature presented here allow for a qualitatively different bond than those previously described by Hume. But Hume has not yet spoken of *humans* specifically.

In turning from "living creatures" in general to "man" in particular, Hume advances a *question*. "How much more must this [friendship, mutual sympathy, visible complacency, benevolence, etc.] have a place in man, where the confinement of the appetite is *not natural*; but either is derived accidentally from some strong charm of love, or arises from reflections on duty and convenience?"

(emphasis added). The question is rhetorical, but not for obvious reasons. While *nature* has "implanted" in all living creatures something *more* than the desire to satisfy bodily appetite, and while *nature* in some living creatures "limits the indulgence to one season and one object," the human bond seems not to profit from the same endowments. Love, duty, and convenience are not simply natural. The latter two stem from "reflection." Hume says that "Nothing . . . can proceed less from affection than the passion of gallantry." Nothing. The emphasis seems squarely on convention, not on the natural passions. But then Hume immediately follows up the emphasis on convention by saying that gallantry is thus "*natural* in the highest degree." The explanation he gives for the naturalness of gallantry is that "*Art* and *education*, in the most elegant courts, make no more alteration on it, than on all the other laudable passions. They only turn the mind more towards it; they refine it; they polish it; and give it proper grace and expression" (131, emphasis added). Again convention, not nature.

Hume is deliberately mischievous and playful. He is also deliberately ironic and misleading. Hume does not deny sexual, physical attraction grounded in nature. In fact, he indicates that humans are *more* sexually promiscuous than other living creatures. The confinement of sexual appetite is "not natural" in "man."[32] But in contrast to other living creatures, humans are distinguished by the *restraints* they place on nature. While living creatures find in *nature* the sources of friendship, mutual sympathy, benevolence, and the affections necessary for association, humans cannot rely merely on nature. We must grant that humans are part of "all living creatures." But they are distinguished from the animals precisely in their posture toward and/or *against* nature. Hume begins his digression to nature by rendering suspect the appeal to nature as a standard for *human* behavior.

It first appears that this is as far as Hume goes in his account of the supposed "naturalness" of gallantry. For Hume follows his cryptic remarks on the nature of gallantry with the no less ambiguous claim that "gallantry is as *generous* as it is *natural*" (132). From the "natural" we turn to the "generous." However, as we shall see, the "generous" will illumine the "natural." As for gallantry's generosity, Hume offers the following explanation. He must be quoted at length.

> To correct such gross vices, as lead us to commit real injury on others, is the part of morals, and the object of the most ordinary education. Where *that* is not attended to, in some degree, no human society can subsist. But in order to render conversation, and the intercourse of minds more easy and agreeable, good manners have been invented, and have carried the matter somewhat farther. Wherever nature has given the mind a propensity to any vice, or to any passion disagreeable to others, refined breeding has taught men to throw the biass [sic] on the opposite side, and to preserve, in all their behaviour, the appearance of sentiments different from those to which they naturally incline. Thus, as we are commonly proud and selfish, and apt to assume the preference over others, a polite man learns to behave with deference towards his

companions, and to yield the superiority to them in all the common incidents of society (132).

If by generous Hume means liberal or free in giving, it is not clear how the passage just cited explains the *liberality* of gallantry. The examples Hume provides there and in the subsequent passages speak to the necessity for restraints on the natural passions, uncultured biases, selfishness, and the other so-called *natural* vices. The generous is thus at odds with the natural, and more akin to the conventional. Lest we forget, Hume says that manners are "inventions." Moreover, on Hume's account, generous does not mean giving. He implies that generosity means not taking.[33] Again, restraint or convention makes up for the failings of nature. Perhaps there is some light to be found in the older meaning of generous, understood as noble or magnanimous. But gallantry as generosity thus understood would also mean restraint, with the added implication that gallantry means the restraint of superiors over inferiors. Magnanimity is a distinctly classical or aristocratic virtue. There is yet a third possible meaning to generous. It comes from the root *genus*. Seen in this light, Hume may be referring to generosity, and thus to gallantry, as the ability to "generate" or "procreate." Generosity may be a reference to birth, race, and stock. Hume's concern for the "intercourse of minds" as the product of good manners may very well be intended as a way of contrasting the "intercourse of bodies." Gallantry may be liberal or generous, but not in the most obvious way.[34]

There is good reason to suspect that all three accounts of generosity are at work here, all of which shed light on Hume's account of nature. Up to this point, much of Hume's history focuses on dominion and subjection. Hume's analysis is very much about force, or power, to put the matter in the crudest terms. It is also about the legitimate use of power, or what we might call authority. Even when Hume led us to the virtues of division, diversity, and competition as a means to temper the enlargement and abuse of power, we discovered the less than edifying motives in the hearts of competitors. Mutual jealousy and the desire for preeminence are only two of the most salient. The spirit of dominion is not easily separated from the competitive, perhaps not from liberty itself. As a whole, then, Hume's analysis brings to our attention the less than edifying foundations of political life. What I have here called Hume's "history of sexual relations" mirrors the discussion in the first and second observations, even while Hume gives the impression that nature is beneficent. We have to wonder if sexual metaphors have not been present throughout the essay. In turning directly to the relations between the sexes, we just learned that nature gives to "man" unlimited sexual desire. Monogamy is not natural, though it has a natural foundation in sexual attraction. By implication, neither is marriage and its corresponding duties.[35] We are thus tempted to say that "nature" is akin to untamed force or power, which is not to say that this is Hume's full account of nature. It must soon occur to us that, in regard to the sexes, nature gives to the male superior physical strength. In the absence of culture, art, and education, what is present between the sexes is the dominion of force, sexual force or tyranny. In the most primitive state, the rule of men over women can be accounted for by the physical or anatomical distinctions of nature. Hume's explication of the claim that "gallantry is as *generous* as it is *natural*" begins with a reference to the "gross vices" that lead "us" to "commit real injury to others." Hume has specific vices in mind, and these vices are not too far beneath the thin veneer of gallantry. They are the vices of male presumption, and the abuse of power or superior strength.

This reading is supported by the numerous examples Hume marshals to elucidate the relation between nature and force, on the one hand, and convention and gentility, on the other. In the midst of his discussion of gallantry, Hume speaks of the relations between the old and the young, strangers and foreigners, or generally those "without protection." He draws us to the example of the "man who is lord in his own family," and of the well-mannered deference required of him toward those "subject to his authority" (132). In all cases it is clear that the moderation and civility required of civilized life proceed from the artifices of various conventions, not from the spontaneous hand of nature. Precisely at this junction—amid the doubts Hume introduces about the beneficence of nature, and the importance of human conventions—we encounter one of the most condescending remarks Hume directs at women. Hume writes:

> Gallantry is nothing but an instance of the same generous attention. As nature has given *man* the superiority over *woman*, by endowing him with greater strength both of mind and body; it is his part to alleviate that superiority, as much as possible, by the generosity of his behavior, and by a studied deference and complaisance for all her inclinations and opinions (132-33).

In light of the foregoing observations, we would have to think very hard about what Hume means by man's *natural* superiority and *generous* attention. As Annette Baier has persuasively demonstrated, there is no indication that Hume believes women are any less capable than or are inferior to men in the exercise of their *moral* and *intellectual* faculties.[36] And from our own careful parsing of the analysis as it unfolds in "Of the Rise and Progress of the Arts and Sciences," one would have to be very careful about ascribing misogynist intentions to Hume. What then leads Hume to speak in this manner?

In reflecting on why Hume would make the apparently sexist remarks that do appear prominently throughout his writings, Baier offers the following explanation. She rightly observes that women in Hume's day "*were* inferior in bodily strength and in intellectual achievement." When Hume, for example, says women are passive, timorous, pious, and deferential, Baier argues that this is intended as a *criticism*. Since Hume "ties these characteristics with powerlessness, his diagnoses here are of a piece with his more direct discussions of how much power women have." The questions for Hume are about potential and fact, principle and practice, Baier suggests, and the reader must be attentive to where the emphases rest. Hume, she argues, is "at pains not just to point out the subordination of [women's] . . . interest to those of men in the existing institutions (marriage in particular) but also to show women where their power lies, should they want to change their situation."[37] Baier argues that Hume writes for the attentive female reader. And she is right up to a point. But in my estimation, this does not capture the breadth of Hume's intentions.

Baier is correct in directing our attention to women's practical, political, social, and economic circumstances in the eighteenth century. Given the limited opportunities available to women for improvement, independence, and liberty, women *were* indeed inferior in bodily strength and intellectual achievement. Conversely, and no less significantly, then, men of Hume's day *were* superior in bodily strength and intellectual achievement. To be effective, Hume's rhetoric must address his female audience, *and* a male audience that holds to the opinion that men are superior to women "by nature."[38] These tasks cannot be divorced. But there is an additional problem a partisan of reform would have to take into account. According to Hume, gallantry conceals and in some cases restrains a host of "gross vices." While not entirely laudable (or honest), gallantry is not entirely contemptible (or dishonest) either. To return to Hume's analysis: In "Barbarous nations," he argues, men display their "superiority, by reducing their females to the most abject slavery; by confining them, by beating them, by selling them, by killing them." Though conventional, and though founded on an *opinion* about the relative endowments or capacities of men and women, gallantry does constitute an advance toward civilization that can be exploited by Hume. He argues that the "male sex, among a polite people, discover their authority in a more generous, though not a less evident manner; by civility, by respect, by complaisance, and, in a word, by gallantry." Gallantry does not grant to women the liberty and equality that is appropriate to them. It reveals an "authority" over women that may be no "less evident" than the authority of barbarians. But at the very least, it allows men to "discover" their supposed authority by civility, respect, and complaisance. This is a long way from confining, beating, selling, and killing. Moreover, that Hume says gallantry is the product of *civilized* monarchies suggests that it is a practice informed or even partly constituted by the same principles of liberty and equality that once worked to tame the monarch or despot. As the practice of civilized *monarchies*, we must acknowledge that gallantry remains aristocratic. It is founded on a comprehensive and political inequality, which men take to be by nature. But Hume is not above writing in a way that flatters the pride or honor of males. He knows only too well the extent of males' investment in virtue and virility. Hume's flattery is in the service of turning that pride toward civility, mutual respect, and a visible deference or complaisance. Hume suggests to his male audience that their "authority" is best displayed by voluntarily *yielding* political space to their female counterparts.

But this is hardly satisfactory. From the point of view of a liberating feminism, Hume is potentially misogynist. It is not clear just how Hume's qualified praise of gallantry is meant to square with the message of liberation Baier claims is one of the principal aims of Hume's work. Moreover, to sustain gallantry requires the perpetuation not only of men's misguided opinions about their superiority, but women's misguided opinions about their own inferiority. The authority of "nature" sustains both of these opinions. It is by no means obvious that an enlightened woman taking note of Hume's ironic suggestions will find an interest in perpetuating her subordination. Perhaps to our astonishment, we discover that Hume is keenly aware of these concerns. He is by no means unaware of the inequity of his proposals, and of the potential dangers in perpetuating these inequities. In drawing the "history of sexual relations" to a close, Hume says, first, that "Gallantry is not less compatible with *wisdom* and *prudence*, than with *nature* and *generosity*" (133), and, second, when "under the proper regulations," gallantry "contributes more than any other invention, to the *entertainment* and *improvement* of both sexes" (133-34). In other words, gallantry is in some peculiar way compatible with wisdom and prudence, with enlightenment generally. More than any other invention, it serves the pleasure and the *benefit* of *both* sexes. What is wise, prudent, and enlightened about gallantry? What is enlightened about sustaining the very inequality Hume himself brings to our attention? While we can imagine the benefits that accrue to men, what do women have to gain from this arrangement? We must not ignore that for Hume the relations between the sexes must be properly regulated. He speaks of the importance of law. Hume engages these questions by way of yet another digression.

Immediately following the observation that gallantry contributes to the pleasure and betterment of men and women, Hume ruminates on what humans share with the animals. Hume sees fit to reflect on the endowments of *nature*— again. He argues that among every species "nature has founded on the love between the sexes their sweetest and best enjoyment." We are tempted to think that Hume is providing a summary of the preceding discussion of nature and convention.[39] But Hume's retelling is not quite the same as the original. We recall that the human bond in the original account is cemented by accidents of love, or by reflections on duty and convenience. Convention there held the day. In the present account, "love between the sexes" is natural. Hume's reversals continue. He argues that "the satisfaction of the bodily appetite is not *alone* sufficient to gratify the mind; and *even* among brute creatures, we find, their play and dalliance, and other expressions of fondness, form the greatest part of the entertainment" (emphasis added). Whether "brute creatures" participate in "mind" is not perfectly clear, although Hume is more than suggestive that they do. The animal and the human world, let us say also the "natural" and the "conventional," are here conflated, whereas in the original account Hume was at pains to separate them. Mind, reason, and nature all seem to be of a piece. "In rational beings," Hume says, "we must certainly admit the mind for a considerable *share*" in all of the pleasures that go beyond the satisfaction of the bodily appetite (emphasis added). We are tempted to say that humans are the "rational beings" we distinguish from the "brute creatures," but the distinction cannot be strictly drawn here. A human being *shares* the same endowments of the animal or natural world. We cannot forget that Hume's curious conflation of the animal and the human takes place in the context of the "proper regulations" that make gallantry compatible with wisdom, prudence, entertainment, and improvement. He is not sanguine about the beneficence or endowment of nature, and reminds us of the importance of law or convention. Yet even while alerting us to the requirements of the law, Hume reasserts the power of nature to endow human beings (as well as "brute creatures") with all the virtues that extend beyond the "satisfaction of bodily appetite." It is in this context that Hume speaks of female softness, an echo of and contrast to the assertive and supposedly superior male qualities ascribed to nature. "What better school of manners," Hume asks, "than the company of virtuous women; where the mutual endeavor to please must insensibly polish the mind, where the example of female softness and modesty must communicate itself to their admirers, and where the delicacy of that sex puts every one on his guard, lest he give offense by any breach of decency?" (134).

There are several very important reasons for conflating nature and custom when speaking about "female virtues." The first points to the female's proximity to the child-bearing process. In this sense, women could be said to be "closer to nature." The implications of this proximity are too extensive for discussion here, though they are by no means unrelated to the general thrust of Hume's argument.[40] Of more pressing concern in the context of this analysis is the manner in which Hume thinks women can exploit their supposed "weakness" on behalf of the civilizing process. For all of the injustices practiced under the aegis of gallantry, and for all of the misguided, unfounded, and pernicious opinions advanced in its name, gallantry and its corresponding virtues and vices prove useful in allowing *women* to govern men. For all that Hume ascribes to convention, he is keenly aware that nature is never smothered altogether, that the violence of nature can very easily overwhelm the frail conventions that make for decent human relations. Anatomical and physical distinctions between men and women forever remain. So too persists male presumption. And in the worst cases, so too persists the threat and the reality of rape. Not even the staunchest advocate of civility and civilization, not least in our own century amid unprecedented enlightenment, material progress, and terror, can responsibly say that all of the accoutrements of civilization have succeeded forever in burying the barbaric in us all. At the same time, sexual attraction (i.e., nature) is always with us. Hume's very suggestive remarks about the importance of "play and dalliance" among the sexes is, on the one hand, light-hearted, but, on the other, so very grave. Female modesty allows for the arousal and the government of male sexual desire. Female modesty is the means by which men come to believe, or rather "discover," what they think is their authority. There may be much gained by men thinking (or learning to think) that gentility is appropriately directed toward women, that their "nature" somehow demands it. As they learn how to be *gentle*-men, men might cement habits that would lead to a more general and comprehensive civility.

Now, none of this is to say that Hume does not see room for improvement. After all, manners qua manners are conventional. This is no less true of the modest, supposedly "female" virtues. Hume never underestimates the native endowments, qualities, and capacities of women.[41] We should note that Hume follows his account of the virtues of female softness and modesty by noting, "Among the ancients, the character of the fair-sex was considered as altogether *domestic*; nor were they regarded as part of the polite world or of good company" (134, emphasis added). For this reason, the ancients have left us with not "one piece of pleasantry that is excellent" (134). By confining women to the domestic sphere, the ancients are unable to produce the refinements of character necessary to civilized life. The virtue of the moderns is that the principles of liberty and equality have extended in some considerable degree to women, to the benefit of both sexes. Hume does see the potential for a well-governed equity among the sexes. We must also consider that Hume's account of the propriety of softness is not restricted to the female sex. It is appropriate to human beings as such. Reason, discourse, sympathy, friendship, and gaiety—in short, all of the highest aspirations of and possibilities available to both sexes—require a softening of manners, mutual deference, and complaisance. We recall Hume's praise of competition, born of jealousy, partiality, and a strong concern for one's own. We do not relinquish the competitive spirit. But it is not enough given our needs and possibilities, nor is the aggressive, competitive spirit appropriate in all circumstances. Just as he had turned earlier from the ills of unity and to the virtues of division and competition, Hume now turns from the ills of division and to the virtues of cooperation and union. Our deepest longings and enjoyments, the possibilities for betterment that come from enlightenment, are so very often the fruits of the acquired capacity to listen, defer, reflect upon the opinions and concerns of others, sympathize or harmonize with the sentiments of our fellow human beings. The desire to assert and to have it our own way will not allow for the necessary "intercourse of minds" that allows us to understand the other person for whom we care, and to correct our misguided opinions and presumptions. The moderation Hume speaks so highly of may result from our humiliation, from the overwhelming strength of others coupled with our weakness. But it can also be the fruit of a just self-deprecation consistent with self-respect and self-understanding. Wisdom and prudence are the fruits of the well-regulated "intercourse of minds" Hume proposes. Wisdom and prudence also inhere in the arrangement itself.[42]

Conclusion: The End/Ends of History?

Just as we are about to draw our conclusions about the various claims of and prescriptions throughout Hume's very complicated and multilayered essay, we are arrested from doing so by Hume's final observation on the *decline* of civilization. Before we are permitted to think through the virtues and vices of the traditions we inherit and the prospects of a more equitable liberty, Hume invites us to think about the defects of civilization. Is decline the product of a faulty inheritance? Or is decline the product of the attempt to advance the principles of liberty and equality? Partisans and patriots beware.

Hume's fourth observation is *"That when the arts and science come to perfection in any state, from that moment they naturally, or rather necessarily decline, and seldom or never revive in that nation, where they formerly flourished"* (135). Hume acknowledges that this observation is "at first sight ... esteemed contrary to reason." It is, however, "conformable to experience." That the things of the world do indeed change, decay, and often perish is a truth available to anyone with sufficient experience. The *reasons* why they naturally or necessarily decline are less so. Why is progress in the arts and sciences not infinite? Note that Hume speaks of "perfection," and this would seem to be a clear indication that there are ends or limits to each activity. Are those ends or limits imposed by the "nature" of the activity itself? Or by something extrinsic to the thing itself? When speaking of the limits, ends, perfection, decline of the arts and sciences, we cannot but include civilization itself. All regimes perish, even civilized ones. So why does civilization as Hume understands it "naturally, or rather necessarily decline"?

With these questions in mind, Hume first turns us back to *nature*—again. "If the natural genius of mankind be the same in all ages, and in almost all countries, (as seems to be the truth)," Hume writes, "it must very much forward and cultivate this genius, to be possessed of patterns in every art, which may regulate the taste, and fix the objects of imitation" (135). As we might expect, the statement is conditional. The truth "seems" to be that humankind is equally possessed with a "natural genius," which if pointed to the right objects and cultivated by the right arts can flourish equally. We return to the virtues of emulation and enlightenment. Hume begins by suggesting that "civilization" falls within the compass and the possibilities of humankind broadly understood. Hume extends what began as an observation of the decline of civilization to a consideration of why civilization does *not* arise in the first place, or, as we shall see later, why civilization in the context of Hume's own time (the age of enlightenment) exhausts itself. "The models left to us by the ancients gave birth to all the arts about 200 years ago, and might have advanced their progress in every country of EUROPE." But they did not. Why, Hume asks, "had they not a like effect during the reign of TRAJAN and his successors; when they were much more entire, and were still admired and studied by the whole world?" (135) The seeds of civilization's own destruction are sown within.

The trajectory of a single human being illumines the trajectory of civilization as a whole. Hume says that a "man's genius is always, in the beginning of life, as much unknown to himself as to others." Again, the play on "genius" and its connections to "genus" and "generation" hover in the background. We begin in ignorance. It is only after "frequent trials, attended with success," Hume continues, that a person "dares think himself equal to those undertakings, in which those, who have succeeded, have fixed the admiration of mankind." But having arrived at the heights proposed to us by the civilizing process, Hume encounters a problem. "If his own nation be already possessed of many models of eloquence," a person will "naturally" compare our own "juvenile exercise with these; and being sensible of the great disproportion, is discouraged from any farther attempts and never aims at a rivalship with those authors, who he so much admires." Enlightenment depends on emulation. And emulation depends on admiration. According to Hume, "*noble* emulation is the source of every excellence" (135, emphasis added). The problem facing civilization is that it seems to extinguish the admiration necessary for emulation. A civilized regime lacks the resources to "generate" and to "re-generate" the very virtues that define and sustain it.

What we may call civilization's *genetic* defect thus turns on the problems of self-love.[43] The perfection of models "extinguishes emulation, and sinks the ardour of the generous youth" (136). However problematic admiration of the great undoubtedly is, Hume argues that it must be allowed to hold sway. Yet the gradual refinement of a populace makes it harder and harder for pride and vanity to show their wares. This is an odd turn of events, not least in light of Hume's concern for the debilitating effects of excessive self-estimation. At this junction we are compelled to wonder just how sound Hume's entire argument is. What reason have we to believe that an increasingly refined society, making ample and comprehensive use of the arts and sciences, naturally or necessarily extinguishes emulation and its corresponding motives? Has Hume himself not offered sufficient reasons to the contrary? His account of Greece and Europe is intended to show the enlightening effects of competition. While moderation may follow from our engagement with diversity in the public sphere, there is no reason to think that enlightened self-deprecation and mutual regard are naturally and necessarily at odds with human improvement and excellence. Indeed, Hume's arguments show that they are mutually supporting and consistent. Or are they? Following the claim that noble emulation is the source of every excellence, Hume argues that "Admiration *and* modesty naturally extinguish this emulation" (135, emphasis added). We are reminded of the potentially *debilitating* effects of admiration, and now of modesty as well. To make matters worse, it also turns out that "no one is so liable to an excess of admiration and modesty, as a truly great genius." In other words, there is something about the "truly great genius" that makes him or her liable to the *excesses* of admiration and modesty. The problem is not merely focused on the prospects for improvement within the reach or desire of those who do not yet possess excellence. The problem rests with the character of the excellent themselves. At the pinnacle of civilization, the person who ascends to these heights is for some reason plagued with a defect that leads to his or her own demise.

Hume the philosopher squarely and unsentimentally faces the problems of modernity, problems that we are tempted to link to our own liberal modernity. Modern liberal societies rest their political institutions and social arrangements on the principles of freedom and equality. And for this many of us should be grateful. But one has to wonder whether these principles, however good, are self-sustaining. Modernity is defined by a taming of honor in favor of a less austere and less political virtue we call civility. Lest we forget (perhaps the most modern of all modern books), Hobbes's *Leviathan* is a reference to the "god of the proud." Honor is not a principle that sits well with the love of equality, with the view that we are all "by nature" equal and free, that no one has a political claim over anyone else save what follows from consent. But does the gradual erosion of distinctions upon which honor must rest (perhaps including the distinction between nature and convention) begin to debilitate the desire for and eventually even call into question the objects of excellence? And does not the erosion of the standards also mean that nothing remains authoritative for the "modern liberal individual" save his own arbitrary judgment? Conflation of habits and opinions, and the smoothing out of rough edges, requires some dilution of the extremes. Does dilution also mean dissolution?

Consider how Hume brings "Of the Rise and Progress of the Arts and Sciences" to a close. He reflects on the models left to us by the ancients. He compares ancient and modern "wits," and then draws the following conclusion:

> the comparison is not so perfect or entire between modern wits, and those who lived in so remote an age. Had WALLER been born in ROME, during the age of TIBERIUS, his first productions had been despised, when compared to the finished odes of HORACE. But in this island the superiority of the ROMAN poet diminished nothing from the fame of the ENGLISH. We esteemed ourselves sufficiently happy, that our climate and language could produce such a faint copy of so excellent an original (137).

Does the gradual perfection of equality and liberty account for the complacency of the English, and of "modern wits" in general? Does "modern" self-satisfaction born out of the benefits of freedom and equality hamper our capacity to admire what is truly great? Is the flip side of the incapacity for admiration an "excess" of modesty? Does modesty animated by the love of equality temper the spirit that makes for excellence? In failing to admire what is truly great, do we sell ourselves short? A host of related questions emerge as we extend our reflections from equality to liberty. As Hume notes, the civilizing process allows for a measure of independence and freedom, which by necessity severs our connections to our fellow citizens. We are compelled to wonder just how far such freedom extends or, rather, ought to extend. To return to Berger and the opening of this chapter: to be perfectly free might come to mean that we are perfectly without a place in the world, perfectly without attachments that give meaning and stability to our lives, perfectly without the authority of tradition, history, and custom, and thus perfectly without obligations toward one another. History begins at the barbaric, at the *arbitrary* rule of the tyrant. In pursuing the principles of liberty and equality, does barbarism make an unexpected appearance? Does the extension of liberty and equality not end up abolishing all distinctions, making the choice between the noble and ignoble nothing short of arbitrary?

Let us turn these questions onto the differences and relationships between the sexes. Our civic and civil androgyny is consistent with a respect for equal rights, irrespective of the differences in sex. But does the love of liberty and equality distort the phenomena? Is there a nobility peculiar to each sex that no convention should ever transgress? If so, what does this mean for our view of the law, or what we call "equality before the law?" What of the "proper regulations" Hume invites us to ponder but in the end does not discuss? How do we square equality before the law with sexual difference? Are there limits to equality? But what of our liberty? The intrusion of liberty and equality into our understanding of the sexual manners ultimately undermines the habits of gallantry and modesty that, for Hume, allow an accommodation between the sexes. Under the aegis of modern principles, the old gallant and modest engagements, if not the arts of *court*-ship itself, must of necessity come to be viewed as vestiges of a bygone era, repressive, patriarchal, and unjust. For Hume the old arts of sexual engagement and courtship kept the violence of nature at bay, at the same time that they gave it proper expression. We are left to wonder what happens when the old conventions are no longer authoritative for us. Most of us will agree that under the old dispensation some gross injustices were perpetrated against women in the name of the justice and the so-called order of nature. Under the new dispensation of perfect equity and liberty, do we have cause to fear from the erosion or deconstruction of all "oppressive" conventions? The questions abound. We do well to remember that for Hume "No advantages in this world are pure and unmixed" (130). Whether we in this time and in this place will have more of the good and less of the bad would seem to depend on good gardeners. Has modernity not set into motion the conditions for their disappearance? Even if gardeners could be found, they need a fertile ground and seeds to cultivate. A gaze over our political landscape reveals a barren ground. And the cool breezes anticipate a long winter.

Notes

Funding for this study was provided by a Fellowship for College Teachers and Independent Scholars, from the National Endowment for the Humanities, by a Fellowship

Research Grant, from the Earhart Foundation, and by a Glenn Grant from Washington and Lee University. I thank them all for such generous support. Scott Sundby of the Frances Lewis Law Center at the Washington and Lee School of Law provided a quiet place to hang my hat during leave. The careful reading, editing, and suggestions of Marc Conner, Deborah Winkle, and Scott Yenor saved me from myself. The errors that remain are, of course, my own.

1. Peter Berger, "On the Obsolescence of the Concept of Honour," in *Liberalism and Its Critics*, ed. Michael Sandel (New York: New York University Press, 1984), 150.

2. Berger, "On the Obsolescence," 156.

3. See Michael J. Sandel, *Liberalism and the Limits of Justice* (New York: Cambridge University Press, 1982); Michael Walzer, *Spheres of Justice: A Defense of Pluralism and Equality* (New York: Basic Books, 1983); Alasdair MacIntyre, *After Virtue*, 2nd ed. (Notre Dame: University of Notre Dame Press, 1984); Robert N. Bellah, Richard Madsen, William M. Sullivan, Ann Swidler, and Steven M. Tipton, *Habits of the Heart: Individualism and Commitment in American Life* (New York: Harper & Row, 1985); Charles Taylor, *Sources of the Self: The Making of the Modern Identity* (Cambridge, MA: Harvard University Press, 1989); and Michael J. Sandel, *Democracy's Discontent: America in Search of a Public Philosophy* (Cambridge, MA: Harvard University Press, 1996).

4. Berger, "On the Obsolescence," 156.

5. See Hanna Arendt, *On Revolution* (New York: Penguin Books, 1965); Gordon S. Wood, *The Creation of the American Republic, 1776-1787* (New York: Norton, 1972); Lance Banning, *The Jeffersonian Persuasion: Evolution of Party Ideology* (Ithaca: Cornell University Press, 1978); Gordon S. Wood, *The Radicalism of the American Revolution* (New York: Knopf, 1992); and Carl J. Richard, *The Founders and the Classics: Greece, Rome, and the American Enlightenment* (Cambridge, MA: Harvard University Press, 1994).

6. See J. G. A. Pocock, *The Machiavellian Moment: Florentine Political Thought and the Atlantic Republican Tradition* (Princeton: Princeton University Press, 1975) and J. G. A. Pocock, *Politics, Language and Time: Essays on Political Thought and History* (Chicago: University of Chicago Press, 1989).

7. The reference here is to Robert D. Putnam's controversial and much discussed "Bowling Alone: America's Declining Social Capital," *Journal of Democracy* 6, no. 1 (1995): 65-78. See also his *Making Democracy Work: Civic Traditions in Modern Italy* (Princeton: Princeton University Press, 1993).

8. An excellent and detailed account of the classical virtues that supports the foregoing characterization is Paul A. Rahe, *Republics Ancient and Modern: Classical Republicanism and the American Revolution* (Chapel Hill: University of North Carolina Press, 1992), 15-218.

9. A strong case can be made that the distinction between antiquity and modernity rests on the respective attachments to honor and civility. See, for example, Thomas Hobbes, *Leviathan*, ed. with introduction and notes by Edwin Curley (Indianapolis: Hackett Publishing, 1994), chap. 15, sec. 17, 95, on the fifth law of nature, on complaisance. The reader might also consider the contrast between "classical" and "modern" theories of education in Lorraine Smith Pangle and Thomas L. Pangle, *The Learning of Liberty: The Educational Ideas of the America Founders* (Lawrence:

University Press of Kansas, 1993), 32-72. In discussing the centrality of civility to John Locke's political philosophy, and to the modern project as a whole, the Pangles write: "Civility . . . does not refer to political leadership, statecraft, or even citizenship: it is a social rather than civic or political virtue . . . civility embodies [the] egalitarian sentiment of humanity," 70. The Pangles go on to argue that the failure of modernity consists largely in its incapacity to properly cultivate greatness of mind, or the classical virtue of magnanimity, 262-64.

10. David Hume, "Of the Rise and Progress of the Arts and Sciences," in *Essays Moral, Political, and Literary*, ed. Eugene F. Miller, rev. ed.' (Indianapolis: Liberty Classics, 1987), 111-37. Of the various interpretations of Hume, few if any take seriously the importance of *Essays* to an understanding of his political philosophy as a whole. The notable exceptions are John W. Danford, *David Hume and the Problem of Reason: Recovering the Human Sciences* (New Haven: Yale University Press, 1990), and, more recently, Donald W. Livingston, *Philosophical Melancholy and Delirium: Hume's Pathology of Philosophy* (Chicago: University of Chicago Press, 1998).

11. This reading of Hume is bound to startle those familiar with his account of virtue. It has "always been found," Hume writes, "that the virtuous are far from being indifferent to praise; and therefore that they have been represented as a set of vain-glorious men, who had nothing in view but the applauses of others. But this is also a fallacy. It is very unjust in the world, when they find any tincture of vanity in a laudable action, to depreciate it upon that account, or ascribe it entirely to that motive. The case is not the same with vanity, as with other passions. Where avarice or revenge enters into any seemingly virtuous action, it is difficult for us to determine how far it enters, and it is natural to suppose it the sole actuating principle. But vanity is so closely allied to virtue, and to love the fame of laudable actions approaches so near the love of laudable actions for their own sake, that these passions are more capable of mixture, than any other kinds of affection; and it is almost impossible to have the latter without some degree of the former. Accordingly, we find, that this passion for glory is always warped and varied according to the particular taste or disposition of the mind on which it falls. NERO had the same vanity in driving a chariot, that TRAJAN had in governing the empire with justice and ability. To love glory of virtuous deeds is sure proof of the love of virtue." See Hume, "Of the Dignity and Meanness of Human Nature," in *Essays*, 86. For elaborations on this theme, see Douglass Adair, *Fame and the Founding Fathers: Essays of Douglass Adair*, ed. Trevor Colburn, reprint of the 1974 edition by W. W. Norton (Indianapolis: Liberty Fund, 1998). As we can appreciate, if only partially here, Hume's account of self-love with all of its various modifications is complex, to say the least. While it is important to draw distinctions between the various kinds of self-love—pride, vanity, honor, love of fame—they are easily conflated. Howsoever noble, the love of honest fame, pride, and honor are reflexive, and thus very close to vanity. Although attentive to the various modifications of self-love, this essay focuses on the qualifications that Hume makes on an exalted self-love—honor, glory, the love of fame—qualifications that are necessary to the success of civility. We must recall that even while recognizing the close connection between an exalted sense of oneself and virtue, Hume is also a *qualified* partisan of liberty and equality. He is keenly aware of ills that accompany an excessive self-estimation founded on praise, even virtue. At the same time, he guards against the excesses of self-deprecation, or modesty. I take "Of the Rise and Progress of

the Arts and Sciences" as Hume's attempt to articulate what the proper regulation of self-love requires. He charts a course between vanity, grandeur, and aristocratic presumption, on the one hand, and debilitating humility, servility, and slavishness, on the other. Hume's aim is neither the exaltation of self-love nor its eradication. Hume's intention turns on the possibilities and methods for the proper government of self-love. For a judicious parsing of pride and the love of fame, see Robert A. Manzer, "Hume on Pride and Love of Fame," *Polity* 18, no. 3 (Spring 1996), 333-55. See also Livingston, *Philosophical Melancholy and Delirium*, who argues that Hume's political philosophy as a whole charts a course between the "greatness of mind" (ancients) and "benevolence" or "humanity" (moderns), 141-42.

12. In my estimation, there is no more lucid examination of the relationship between toleration and civility than Clifford Orwin, "Citizenship and Civility as Components of Liberal Democracy," in *Civility and Citizenship in Liberal Democratic Societies*, ed. Edward C. Banfield (New York: Paragon House, 1992), 75-94. Also of note, see David Heyd, ed., *Toleration: An Elusive Virtue* (Princeton: Princeton University Press, 1996); Susan Mendus, ed., *Justifying Toleration: Conceptual and Historical Perspectives* (Cambridge: Cambridge University Press, 1998); and Edward Shils, *The Virtue of Civility: Selected Essays on Liberalism, Tradition, and Civil Society*, ed. Steven Grosby (Indianapolis: Liberty Fund, 1997).

13. The initial focus on self-love is by no means to deny the other-regarding sentiments of our nature, all of which are important to Hume's political thinking. But the government of self-love proves to be the most important to political life. We arrive at a discussion of the benevolent affections later in this chapter.

14. See Hume, "Of Superstition and Enthusiasm," in *Essays*, 73-79.

15. The statement that "civility is androgyny" is intended to raise questions concerning the nature of and relationship between the "masculine" and the "feminine." In the first instance, I use the word literally. Androgyny combines the Greek word for man, male (*andro, aner*) and the Greek word for woman, female (*gyne*). The reference to androgyny does not imply either the "masculinization" or "femininization" of political space. Civility is both. Just how civility is both is the burden of this essay. Second, as we proceed, the "nature" of the "masculine" and "feminine," the grounding of those distinctions in artifice or convention, will become clear.

16. Annette C. Baier, *Moral Prejudices: Essays on Ethics* (Cambridge, MA: Harvard University Press, 1995), especially "What Do Women Want in a Moral Theory?" 1-17, "Hume the Women's Moral Theorist?" 51-75, and "Hume, the Reflective Women's Epistemologist?" 76-94. Also noteworthy is Annette C. Baier, "Hume on Women's Complexion," in *The Science of Man in the Scottish Enlightenment: Hume, Reid and Their Contemporaries*, ed. Peter Jones (Edinburgh: Edinburgh University Press, 1989), 33-53; and Annette Baier, "Good Men's Women: Hume on Chastity and Trust," in *Hume: Great Political Thinkers, 10*, ed. John Dunn and Ian Harris (Cheltenham, England, and Lyme, NH: Edward Elgar Publishing, 1997), 59-77. For alternative readings of Hume's feminism, see Steven A. Macleod Burns, "The Humean Female," and Louise Marcil-Lacoste, "Hume's Method of Moral Reasoning," in *The Sexism of Social and Political Theory: Women and Reproduction from Plato to Nietzsche*, ed. Lorenne M. G. Clark and Lynda Lange (Toronto: University of Toronto Press, 1993), 53-60, and 60-73. Baier's thesis stands in sharp contrast to Adair's. Baier sees Hume as a partisan of equality, with important qualifications. She also sees Hume as a liberal, though providing

a corrective to a rational, deductive, social contract theory. By noting the virtues and vices associated with an elevated and deficient self-love as I do here, my study could be understood as charting a course between Adair and Baier. Again, my reading provides a vantage point from which to assess *both* Hume's praise of honor, on the one hand, and his liberality, on the other.

17. Baier, "Hume on Women's Complexion," 33, and "Hume, the Reflective Epistemologist?" 90.

18. Baier points to two small openings Hume provides in "Of the Rise and Progress of the Arts and Sciences" that, if extended and supported by other statements of Hume's, make the essay appear less misogynist. But this is as far as she goes. See Baier, "Hume on Women's Complexion," 36, and "Hume, the Reflective Epistemologist?" 92.

19. I ask for the reader's indulgence in advance. Hume is a careful, playful, and ironic writer. He writes in puzzles; indeed, Hume's essay is a puzzle. More importantly, Hume's arguments are not easily disentangled from his mode of presentation. Hume's essays are philosophic, not merely historical. For these reasons, the interpreter of Hume must be faithful to his mode of presentation, to the structure of the argument, to its unfolding, to the juxtaposition of parts and how the parts complement and contradict each other. This study is thus necessarily far more exegetical than is generally tolerable. Later in this discussion we come to a fuller engagement of the reasons for and character of Hume's peculiar rhetoric.

20. Baier, "Hume, the Reflective Epistemologist?" 90.

21. The reasons Hume theorizes in the context of history is a question well beyond the scope of this essay. A few provisional remarks are warranted, however. It is a mistake to think that Hume's "turn" to a more historic and literary approach is prompted by the cool reception to his *Treatise of Human Nature*. (On this score, see Donald Livingston, "Introduction," in *Hume as Philosopher of Society, Politics and History)*, ed. Donald Livingston, (Rochester, NY: University of Rochester Press, 1991), ix-xix. The juxtapositions of the historical and the philosophical, experience and principle, practice and reflection speak to Hume's comprehensive understanding of the proper ways to inquire about the character of society. For Hume, human beings are "social" beings, which is not to say that they are simply animated by love for one another. Rather, Hume's point is that we are not "abstracted" beings as depicted in, say, the philosophies of Hobbes and Locke. We are born in society, in a regime of laws, subject to the demands of conventions. When speaking to or about the "nature" of human beings, Hume's approach reminds us that "nature" must be interpreted in light of the conventions that give it expression. As strange as this may sound, "nature" is always "conventional," or at least subject to the artifices of human design and accidents. Theorizing human society must of necessity incorporate the historical. But there is an additional reason for the various conflations and juxtapositions. As we are about to see, to say that human beings are born into society means that they are all subject to an inheritance. But this inheritance and the hold it has on us raises some very important questions about human agency. Now, Hume is very much a partisan of and an advocate for liberty, properly understood. Yet the prospects for reform (as opposed to, say, revolution) depend on a judicious appreciation of the political circumstances and possibilities open to human beings at a particular time and place, and of what the native endowment is at that time. Just how the requirements of practice are to be blended with the natural capacities and natural aspirations is not something left exclusively to chance. To make a long story short, the proper blend of custom and nature

is the task of rhetoric. Hume is the master rhetorician. I have already suggested why we must pay attention to his mode of presentation.

22. Cf. David Hume, *A Treatise of Human Nature*, ed. P. H. Nidditch (Oxford: Clarendon Press, 1990), Bk. III, pt. II, sec. VIII, 540-41.

23. Cf. Hume, *Essays*, "Of the First Principles of Government," 32-36, and "Of the Origin of Government," 37-41. See also "Of Justice and Injustice," in *A Treatise of Human Nature*, Bk. III, pt. II, 477-573, and *An Enquiry Concerning the Principles of Morals*; "Of Justice," in *Enquiries Concerning Human Understanding and Concerning the Principles of Morals*, ed. P. H. Nidditch (Oxford: Clarendon Press, 1989), sec. III, 183-204.

24. It must strike the reader that the salient characteristic of international relations is the absence of a sovereign. Now, in this context, this fact may seem trivial, if not entirely irrelevant. Or it may seem misplaced, since the discussion thus far has been about nothing but sovereignty, particularly a monarch, king, and/or tyrant. But if we take a quick glance ahead to Hume's third observation, several arguments there invite us to pause on Hume's turn to international relations. In the third observation, Hume *explicitly* takes up the question of "nature" as it relates to the larger discussion of sexual natures and relations. I say explicitly because I think the question of nature is implicit throughout. Against the competitive motivations that emerge in the discussion of international relations, Hume contrasts the virtues of cooperation, civility, mutual deference, and polite conversation. Are these all natural capacities? Are these capacities founded on different emphases one gives to self-love, one allowing it free reign, the other calling for its moderation? Which is preferable, unity or diversity, division or cooperation? This glance ahead might lead us to wonder if Hume is in this instance using "international relations" to mean the "state of nature," that is, to describe the motives that impel humans to action in "nature." Students of Hume are, of course, aware that if this Scotsman is known for anything, it is for his critique of social contract theory derived from a prepolitical "state of nature." I am not saying that on this score Hume is a Hobbist or a Lockean. I am suggesting that Hume is using the second observation as a vehicle to describe some of "man's" natural motivations, which, as we shall see, prove on inspection to be far more robust than the motivations Thomas Hobbes and John Locke would ascribe to human beings. This section may be Hume's critique of "state of nature" thesis. I qualify "man's" because I am also persuaded that not far beneath Hume's argument as a whole is a consideration of "masculine" and "feminine" characteristics. In light of the third observation and the restraints women will necessarily place upon men, one has to wonder if Hume is in the second observation speaking more about the distinctly masculine. Later, we will have occasion to reflect on how the various approaches to human engagement and to self-love harmonize, or are at least accommodated.

25. The reader should keep in mind that there are "things" that "resemble" both "nature" and "reason." What we take to be natural may not be natural; what we take to be reasonable may not be reasonable. The purpose of this obfuscation becomes evident when we turn to Hume's third observation.

26. The question of whether Hume's political philosophy is more properly termed "conservative" or "liberal" has generated much heat in the academy. The most authoritative statement on behalf of Hume's conservatism is perhaps Frederick G. Whelan, *Order and Artifice in Hume's Political Philosophy* (Princeton: Princeton University Press, 1985). A most persuasive rejoinder and critique is found in John B.

Stewart, *Opinion and Reform in Hume's Political Philosophy* (Princeton: Princeton University Press, 1992). For the dangers of reading "conservatism" and "liberalism" back into Hume, see Livingston, *Philosophical Melancholy and Delirium*, 371-73.

27. The second observation did provide us with a hint to this division, as Hume there speaks of politeness and learning as qualities pertaining to the arts and sciences respectively. But this is the first time the division become explicit. The arts and sciences are now objects of separate but related analyses, connected to specific regimes.

28. We should keep in mind that the third observation compares republics with *civilized* monarchies, not monarchies proper or simply. There may be at least three good reasons for this. First, Hume argues, "However perfect . . . the monarchical form may appear to some politicians, it owes all its perfection to the republican; nor is it possible, that a pure despotism, established among a barbarous people, can ever, by its native force and energy, refine and polish itself. It must borrow its laws, and methods, and institutions, and consequently its stability and order, from free governments. These advantages are the sole growth of republics. The extensive despotism of a barbarous monarchy, by entering into the detail of the government, as well as into the principal points of administration, for ever prevents all such improvements" (125). Only at the point at which monarchy ceases to be completely despotic, that is, once power begins to be delegated broadly, do the prospects for civilization emerge. They may not emerge. If they do not, discussion ends and reform is no longer possible. But if reform is possible, then gardeners are required. Hume does not use the word "gardener," but his references to nurseries, transplants, cultivation, and the like imply one. Whether the gardener is the legislator or philosopher is a question for the conclusion. Second, Hume may also have his contemporary circumstances in mind when he speaks of "civilized monarchies." The question of how to combine monarchism with republicanism was perhaps nowhere more salient than in Hume's Great Britain. Finally, regimes in Hume's "history" partake of a curious mixture of authority and liberty, each of which varies as a matter of degree. As noted earlier, Hume's conflation of "regime types" is intended to alert us to this tension.

29. Hume's critique of organized, extensive religion surfaces again in connection with emulation and learning. He argues that "monarchies, receiving their chief stability from a superstitious reverence to priests and princes, have commonly abridged the liberty of reasoning, with regard to religion, and politics, and consequently metaphysics and morals. All these form the most considerable branches of science. Mathematics and natural philosophy, which only remain, are not half so valuable" (126). This is not to say that Hume is an atheist. Hume's concern is with the "abridged liberty" that does not allow for "reasoning . . . with regard to religion" and other branches of knowledge. Always, Hume's concern is moderation, and a radical skepticism may be as dogmatic and as pernicious as an overly enthusiastic and superstitious religion, supported by tyrannical power. For a lucid account of Hume's moderate posture toward religion, see John W. Danford, "'The Surest Foundation of Morality': The Political Teaching of Hume's *Dialogues Concerning Natural Religion*," in *Hume, Great Political Thinkers, 10*, vol. II, ed. John Dunn and Ian Harris (Cheltenham, England, and Lyme, NH: Edward Elgar Publishing, 1997), 209-32.

30. Alexis de Tocqueville, *Democracy in America*, trans. George Lawrence and ed. J. P. Mayer (New York: Harper Perennial, A division of Harper Collins, 1969), vol. II, pt. II, 561-664, *passim*.

31. Eugene Miller's notes to Hume's references to Sallust, Horace, Ovid, Lucretius,

Lord Rochester, and Juvenal are extremely helpful in elucidating Hume's less than explicit condemnation of the ancients' treatment of women. See Hume, "Of the Rise and Progress of the Arts and Sciences," 127-28, n. 18-22.

32. In this context, one is tempted to say that Hume's discussion of "man" is not generic but rather gender specific. But we cannot be certain. The obfuscation is deliberate. Later Hume will parse "man" and "woman."

33. Hume may be alerting us to the modern critique of charity, one of the Christian virtues par excellence. This critique is of a piece with the requirements of toleration. For a helpful exploration of this large question, see Clifford Orwin, "Machiavelli's Unchristian Charity," *American Political Science Review* 72 (1978), 1217-28.

34. Cf. Hume, *Enquiry Concerning the Principles of Morals*, sec. IV, "Of Political Society," 205-11.

35. Cf. Hume, "Of Polygamy and Divorces," 181-90. Hume there shows that the forms of union among men and women vary substantially. Now, this is not to say Hume does not endorse monogamous marriage. He does. But the question for us here is the extent to which that specific union is sanctioned by nature alone. For a comprehensive discussion of Hume on marriage, see Baier, "Good Men's Women: Hume on Chastity and Trust," 59-77.

36. This is not the occasion to rehearse Baier's arguments. What is proposed here is an amendment to Baier's claim that Hume is a theorist friendly to feminists, or at least some feminists. I aim to show that Hume's friendliness is present within the context of the argument as it unfolds in "Of the Rise and Progress of the Arts and Sciences"—what Baier has not shown. Moreover, Baier extends Hume's sympathies farther than Hume seems willing to go. "As a friend to truth," Baier argues, "Hume challenges his female contemporaries' perceptions of their interests and of their opinions. He challenges the entrenched doctrine of the 'nobler' male sex with its intrinsic authority. He challenges the assumption that the husband must be 'head' of a family, that it needs any one such head. His vote is for 'perfect equality.'" See Baier, "Hume on Women's Complexion," 49-50. Hume has some important qualifications to the "perfect equality" thesis, which turns on the revival of honor, as we shall see at the conclusion of this essay. Hume's proposals are not as immodest as Baier's.

37. Baier, "Hume, the Women's Moral Theorist?" 72-73.

38. There are good reasons for calling a convention natural as Hume does. Human beings are generally inclined to take what is most familiar or common as "natural." We call "natural" not only what is most convenient, but also what we think is most authoritative. Throughout the discussion of gallantry, Hume flatters the pretension of those who think it is natural. But, at the same time, Hume shows us that our *opinions* of "nature" are themselves malleable. And this is of enormous consequence to political life, chiefly because we take the supposed "authority" of "nature" as a "guide." Hume reveals the harshness of nature at the same time that he tries to preserve its authority as good or beneficent. Cf. Hume, *A Treatise of Human Nature*, Bk. III, pt. II, sec. 1, 477-84. See note 22.

39. See Notes, 18-21.

40. In the context of the *Treatise*'s larger argument on justice, Hume argues that chastity and modesty are manners employed by women to secure the attachment of men to their families and to ensure the education and protection of the young. Hume writes: "Whoever considers the length and feebleness of human infancy, with the concern which

both sexes naturally have for their offspring, will easily perceive, that there must be an union of male and female for the education of the young, and that this union must be of considerable duration. But in order to induce the men to impose on themselves this restraint, and undergo chearfully all the fatigues and expences, to which it subjects them, they must believe, that the children are their own, and that their natural instinct is not directed to a wrong object, when they give a loose to love and tenderness. Now if we examine the structure of the human body, we shall find, that this security is very difficult to be attain'd on our part; and that since, in the copulation of the sexes, the principle of generation goes from the man to the woman, an error may easily take place on the side of the former, tho' it be utterly impossible with regard to the latter. From this trivial and anatomical observation is deriv'd that vast difference betwixt the education and duties of the two sexes." There is no indication here that the sexual drive is any less powerful in women than it is in men, only that convention has found ways of checking it in women. Appearances, however important, may be deceiving. See *A Treatise of Hume Nature*, Bk. III, sec. XII, pt. II, 570-73.

41. Hume does not underestimate the competitive spirit in women, nor does he underestimate their capacity for and love of dominion. See Hume, *Essays*, "Of Love and Marriage," 558-59.

42. To claim that Hume thinks a reform of sexual manners *alone* provides the basis for civilization is an exaggeration. This is not my claim here. Hume's argument for the reformation of sexual manners consistent with liberty and equality must be connected to the larger argument on behalf of commerce and republicanism. Commerce and republican self-government are mostly responsible for taming and redirecting the impulses of men. Unfortunately, the scope of this essay does not allow for a just and proper engagement with the whole of Hume's philosophic corpus or teaching. I thank Scott Yenor for reminding me of the limits of Hume's claims on behalf of the effects of reformed sexual manners on the populace of a republic at large.

43. Hume argues that "Next to emulation, the greatest encourager of the noble arts is praise and glory." Speaking of the arts of eloquence, and of writers (perhaps himself?), Hume argues that the practitioners of these arts are "animated with a new force, when [they] hear the applauses of the world." Being "roused by such a motive," the eloquent artist "often reaches a pitch of perfection, which is equally surprising to himself and to his readers." Again, the prospects of self-improvement and self-knowledge depend in some measure on pride, honor, maybe even vanity. "But when the posts of honour are all occupied," Hume continues, "his first attempts are but coldy received by the public; being compared to productions, which are both in themselves more excellent, and have already the advantage of an established reputation" (136).

Chapter 11

When Vanity Leads to Virtue:
Self-Regard in Jane Austen and Adam Smith

Inger Sigrun Brodey

> For one's own dear self, one ascertains & remembers everything.
> —Jane Austen

> The great secret of education is to direct vanity to proper objects.
> —Adam Smith

Young ladies' conduct books, popular throughout the eighteenth century in England, focused on the supreme importance of modesty and humility. John Essex, for example, warned in *The Young Ladies Conduct*, that "Happiness is Vain and Dangerous, except that only which proceeds from a Sense of Modesty, Obedience, Humility, and such like Virtue...."[1] Heather Chapone carried his point even further in *Letters on the Improvement of the Mind*: "Pride and vanity, the vices opposite to humility, are the sources of almost all the worst faults, both of men and women."[2] Other conduct books from the period, however, reveal the occasional hypocrisy of the moral psychology underlying the denunciation of pride and vanity. Consider, for example, the following admonition from *The Lady's Preceptor*: Having established that "[W]omen not... blessed with a sufficient Degree of Modesty... give themselves up to Vanity," the author warns that "[modesty] is so very necessary, that all who would make themselves pleasing and acceptable, are obliged to call in either the Virtue itself or the resemblance of it, to their Assistance."[3] The passage suggests, in other words, that self-interest and concern with appearances will drive young ladies to feign modesty. In his attempt to emphasize the value of modesty, the author unwittingly points to the benefits of vanity, revealing exactly the sort of dynamic that became quite interesting to moral philosophers in the latter half of the eighteenth century. A century after La Rochefoucauld remarked that "Hypocrisy is the homage vice pays to virtue," some conduct books tacitly acknowledged the frequently theatrical, social, and even self-interested underpinnings of virtue.

This brings us to the other strain of thought regarding vanity and pride that was also prevalent during Jane Austen's lifetime: eighteenth-century moral philosophers, especially Bernard Mandeville, David Hume, and Adam Smith, all engaged in a heated philosophical debate about the possibility that all passions, including even pride and vanity, could form the basis of virtue and thereby benefit humanity. The new evaluation of self-regard, pride, and vanity in the philosophy of the time marked a radical turn away from many Christian theologians[4] who had called pride the worst of the deadly sins, but many of whom also had to admit the difficulty of "performing any good action, without some secret applause."[5] In fact, the pride of self-regard formed, together with sympathy, the two "keystones" in eighteenth-century theories of motivation.[6]

The terms "vanity" and "pride" need some clarification, since, as Arthur Lovejoy has shown, they were used rather inconsistently, and frequently interchangeably, in eighteenth-century philosophical discourse. The 1775 edition of Samuel Johnson's *Dictionary of the English Language* defines both "pride" and "vanity" as "ostentation," but "pride" primarily as "inordinate and unreasonable self-esteem"; however, since Dr. Johnson defines "vanity" as "petty pride" or "pride exerted upon slight grounds," he suggests that the difference between pride and vanity is one of degree or context rather than any distinct difference of kind.[7] Adam Smith, in his *Theory of Moral Sentiments*, uses the distinction that seems most prevalent within eighteenth-century philosophical discourse when he says that, unlike the vain man, the proud man "disdains to court your esteem." The proud man is happy with the knowledge of his own superiority, whereas the vain man relies upon the opinions of others. The proud man may feel "offended" where the vain man will feel "mortified."[8] When Jane Austen's character Mary Bennet defines the difference between vanity and pride in *Pride and Prejudice*, she almost seems to be quoting Adam Smith:

> "Pride," observed Mary, who piqued herself upon the solidity of her reflections, "is a very common failing.... [H]uman nature is particularly prone to it, and... there are very few of us who do not cherish a feeling of self-complacency on the score of some quality or other, real or imaginary. Vanity and pride are different things, though the words are often used synonymously [sic].... Pride relates more to *our opinion of ourselves*, vanity to *what we would have others think of us*." (*P*, 20, emphasis added)[9]

The generally accepted distinction seems to have been that pride is high self-estimation, while vanity involves the desire for high estimation by others. We will return below to a more thorough explication of the role of these characteristics in Smith's theory as well as its application to Austen's novels.

In actuality, pride and vanity may not be quite as distinct as Mary suggests. We will see that within Austen's last novel *Persuasion*, Sir Walter Elliot is both the very model of "Elliot pride" and the epitome of vanity. Pride and vanity share a self-regarding, self-evaluative quality as well as a tendency to desire praise and to notice others' opinions of oneself. Both are, in the words of Smith, "modifications of excessive self-estimation" (*TMS*, 255), and self-estimation is rarely entirely free of external comparison. We can see, however, from these definitions that whether it is for the sake of others' opinions or for the sake of one's own opinion of others (including one's opinion of their opinions), *both* pride and vanity are dependent upon an awareness of how one ranks in relation to others. The mirror is therefore an appropriate symbol for both traits: the difference is that the proud person has internalized the mirror to a greater degree, while the vain person needs the constant, external mirroring of others. Thus it is that vanity has been called both more "slavish" and also more "social" than pride.[10]

In the course of these philosophical debates, the nature of woman also underwent considerable redefinition as characteristics commonly associated with women such as vanity, sensibility, subjectivity, and fancy (or imagination) gained in ethical status. These characteristics started to be seen by a growing number of authors as important keys to virtue rather than as inhibitors of it. Perhaps in response to this cultural and philosophical interest in vanity, self-regard, and other "selfish passions," Jane Austen developed a psychology of virtue in her novels that reveals an interrelation of self-regard, sympathy, and virtue, and resembles the moral psychology discussed by eighteenth-century moral philosophers, especially Adam Smith. Like Smith, she is keenly aware of the strongly selfish passions inherent in human nature, but sees that they can also help lead human beings to virtue. As a result, Austen participates in the regeneration of vanity, subjectivity, and the imagination.

A concern with the selfish passions—and with the dangers, inescapability, and unexpected benefits of subjectivity and self-regard—permeates Austen's novels from the strong partialities of Elizabeth Bennet to the willful blindness of Emma Woodhouse. The culmination of her treatment of these themes, however, seems to occur in her last complete novel, *Persuasion*, which opens with a stark depiction of obsessive self-regard: Sir Walter Elliot reads and rereads his own entry in the Baronetage "with an interest which never fail[s]" until the book begins to open automatically to the page that features his name (*P*, 3). In Sir Walter's case, Austen does not call it "self-regard"; instead she gives his leading characteristic a far more potent name. "Vanity," the narrator informs us with unusual directness, "was the beginning and the end of Sir Walter Elliot's character; vanity of person and of situation" (*P*, 4).[11] "He considered the blessing of his beauty," we learn, "as inferior only to the blessing of a baronetcy; and the Sir Walter Elliot, who united these gifts, was the constant object of his warmest respect and devotion" (*P*, 4). Within the first two pages, we witness the portrayal not only of a man who is deeply vain, but also of the vanity—the "nothingness"—of his life as a whole.

However well Sir Walter embodies the novel's resources of vanity and "Elliot pride," he does not exhaust them.[12] There are very few characters who are not called either vain or proud in the course of the novel. In the rare moment when his eldest daughter, Elizabeth, "struggle[s] between propriety and vanity," the reader is not surprised when "vanity [gets] the better" of her (*P*, 219). Her sister Mary, too, has "inherit[ed] a considerable share of the Elliot self-importance" and constantly "fanc[ies] herself neglected and ill-used" (*P*, 37): as her sister-in-law Louisa remarks, "She has a great deal too much of the Elliot pride" (*P*, 88). With Mary as with her father, the preoccupation with rank or "place" presumes vanity: Mary is not satisfied with her social superiority unless it is acknowledged by all around her. Mr. Elliot, too, the heir to Sir Walter's estate, admits to Anne that he is thought to be proud and does not seek to deny it (*P*, 151). Even the hero, Wentworth, when he finally realizes that he is to blame for at least six years of his separation from Anne, admits: "I was proud, too proud to ask again" (*P*, 247). Villains and heroes alike, in other words, are blinded by excessive self-estimation and the desire for approbation. Lady Russell is characterized as having a "more tempered and pardonable pride" (*P*, 26), and although she is not an official member of the family, Elliot pride it remains nonetheless: "Their respectability was as dear to her as her own" (*P*, 36).

The new philosophical estimation of pride and vanity, or of self-regard and the desire for esteem, was perhaps made most (in)famous by Bernard Mandeville, whose *Fable of the Bees: Private Vices, Publick Benefits* shocked many indignant readers. One of Mandeville's most inflammatory formulations of his main thesis—that society encourages private vice for the sake of its own peace and stability—is that "the moral Virtues are the Political Offspring which Flattery begot upon Pride."[13] He suggests that only by flattering and encouraging vices, especially vanity and pride, at an early age can society cajole human beings into action that is called moral (and whatever is convenient to society is called moral). His examples include the pedagogical techniques commonly and unreflectively used upon children, such as the way parents (and nursemaids) flatter children into better behavior: "There's a delicate Curt'sy! O fine Miss! There's a pretty Lady! Mama! Miss can make a better Curt'sy than her Sister *Molly*!"[14] Today we call it "positive reinforcement," "scaffolding," or Kohutian "mirroring." It is interesting that we can find a passage in *Persuasion* that exhibits this same technique. The lawyer, Mr. Shepherd, uses it on Sir Walter: "Sir Walter ... had ... been flattered into his very best and most polished behavior by Mr. Shepherd's assurances of his being known, by report, to the Admiral, as a model of good breeding" (*P*, 32). Sir Walter's vanity leads him to be treated as a child; however, the passage also shows that vanity can be used to achieve better ends—in this case, civility.[15] We will see that this "civilizing" power of vanity was of great interest to Adam Smith as well as Jane Austen.

It was the Scottish philosophers of "Moral Sentiments," and most notably David Hume and Adam Smith, who gave the new moral psychology the popular shape that, I would argue, most likely influenced Jane Austen.[16] Where Mandeville seeks to reduce all motives to vanity and imply that vanity is always a (private) vice, Hume and Smith draw much more subtle distinctions and allow for a vanity that can be more virtuous. Hume writes, "It is very unjust in the world, when they feel any tincture of vanity in a laudable action, to depreciate it on that account, or ascribe it entirely to that motive," and again he remarks: "Vanity is so closely allied to virtue, and [the love of] the fame of laudable actions approaches so near the love of laudable actions for their own sake, that ... it is almost impossible to have the latter without some degree of the former."[17] Hume uses the images of self-regarding and mirroring[18] that Smith later takes up and that Austen depicts thematically in *Persuasion*. In the following passage, Hume shows how external mirrors (the eyes of others upon us), which Smith later calls the "mirror of Society," help encourage or correct our internal mirror (or conscience):

> By continual and earnest pursuit of a character, a name, a *reputation* in the world, we bring our own... conduct frequently in review, and consider how [it] appear[s] in the eyes of those who approach and regard us. This constant habit of *surveying ourselves* ... keeps alive all the sentiments of right and wrong, and begets, in noble natures, a certain reverence for *themselves* as well as for others, which is the surest guardian of every virtue.[19]

By "surveying ourselves" imaginatively, we may come to "reverence" others by reverencing ourselves. It is interesting to note his subtle disclaimer as well: it seems that only "noble natures" can be trusted to benefit from this dynamic. We will return to this point later.

In his extremely influential first work, *The Theory of Moral Sentiments*, Adam Smith personifies this internal mirror and places it squarely in the center of his entire moral psychology, calling it "the impartial spectator" (sometimes the "Demigod within the breast" or "the great inmate of the soul"). We automatically imagine this "impartial spectator," says Smith, in all our daily actions, and more particularly, we imagine how the spectator would think and feel about our responses to any given situation. By approximating their feelings, we can imaginatively enter into the experiences of others around us, from whom we would otherwise be hopelessly separated. Since "[t]he compassion of the spectator must arise altogether from the consideration of what he himself would feel if he were reduced to the same unhappy situation" (*TMS*, 12), the degree of sympathy we can feel for others is directly proportional to both our self-interest and the degree to which we can imagine ourselves feeling the same pain we witness in others: self-interest, sensibility, and imagination are all necessary for achieving sympathy with others. It is an imaginative way of describing an ethically and socially useful union of self-approbation or self-regard and sympathy for others that seeks to avoid both solipsism, on the one hand, and heroic and generally unattainable altruistic ideals, on the other. We will see that Austen shares an interest in at least part of this same goal of balancing the demands of self-perfection with the need for social cooperation.

In *Persuasion*, the theme of self-regard appears most literally in the number of references to mirrors scattered throughout the novel. For example, Austen chooses the image of mirrors to characterize Sir Walter's vanity, beginning with the Baronetage that includes his entry. Not only is his "book of books" (*P,*7) a verbal mirror of himself (and only of the part he most wishes to see), but we also find that he has an unabashed love of mirrors in general. His tenant, Admiral Croft, is dismayed at the inordinate number of very large looking glasses in Kellynch Hall—especially in Sir Walter's dressing room: "Such a number of looking-glasses! oh Lord! there was no getting away from oneself. ... [N]ow I am quite snug, with my little shaving glass in one corner, and another great thing that I never go near" (*P*, 128).

Sir Walter's desire for admiration leads him to assume that even outside his dressing room, in the wide expanses of Bath or even London, all eyes are constantly observing him and his minutest actions. Of course the joke is that, just like in his dressing room, all the eyes are his own. "[He] was the constant object of his [own] warmest respect and devotion" (*P*, 4), as the narrator informs us early on. He is terribly conscious of his public appearances—to the point that one suspects he must think they are recorded in an appendix to his book of books. Even the offensive behavior of the young Mr. Elliot is a greater blow to his *vanity* than to his sense of propriety or justice, "'for they *must have been seen together*,' he observed, 'once at Tattersal's, and twice in the lobby of the House of Commons" (*P*, 8, emphasis added). His lawyer knows how to use Sir Walter's vanity to achieve his own ends: "Consequence has its tax—," he says fawningly, "I, John Shepherd, might conceal any family matter that I chose, for nobody would think it worth their while to observe me, but Sir Walter Elliot has eyes upon him which it may be very difficult to elude" (*P*, 17).

The reader knows of his delusion, largely through the help of the heroine, Anne Elliot, who early on reveals a keen awareness of the *absence* of eyes on matters of Elliot importance:

> Anne had not wanted this visit to Uppercross to learn that a removal from one set of people to another, though at a distance of only three miles, will often include a total change of conversation, opinion, and idea. She had never been staying there before, without being struck by it, or without wishing that other Elliots could have the advantage in seeing how unknown, or unconsidered there, were the affairs which at Kellynch Hall were treated as of such general publicity and pervading interest. (*P*, 42)

This "art of knowing our own nothingness" (*P*, 42) entails the ability to regard both oneself and others from a spectatorial distance. Adam Smith uses a landscape description to represent just such an ethically desirable, spectatorly stance: "I can form a just comparison between those great objects and the little objects around me, in no other way, than by transporting myself, at least in fancy, to a different station, from whence I can survey both at nearly equal distances" (*TMS*, 135). Our ability to imagine and our desire to please this impartial spectator allow us, even when we are biased by our own involvement in a situation, to distance ourselves from our situation and view it as another might from afar. The success of this dynamic is directly related to one's sensibility and powers of imagination. Rather than leading us astray, imagination and strong feelings are actually the *key* to virtue (*TMS*, 9). These issues become quite central to the plot and character development of *Persuasion* as well.

But are pride and vanity entirely foreign to the heart of Anne Elliot, that heroine whom Austen remarked was "almost *too* good"?[20] A reader's initial response would almost certainly be to assert Anne's modesty and claim that her nature is the very opposite of her father's. We may be misled by Austen's technique of using a deceased parent to answer the kinship riddles of children who bear seemingly no resemblance to their surviving, inferior parent. One of the Miss Musgroves supports this opinion by remarking to Anne: "I have no scruple of observing to *you*, how nonsensical some persons are about their place [i.e. rank], because, all the world knows how easy and indifferent you are about it. . . ." (*P*, 46). Even Mr. Elliot, master of flattery though he is, has difficulty "kindl[ing] his modest cousin's vanity" (*P*, 214).

If pride is high self-estimation, and vanity is concern for how one is seen by others, however, then Anne may have greater pride and vanity than both Sir Walter and Elizabeth. Just as Anne is the repository of memories that others have forgotten, she is also the one who feels vanity and pride when Sir Walter and her sisters forget to. For example, when her father shows himself swayed and delighted by the attention and flattery of the society in Bath, "[Anne] must sigh that her father should feel no *degradation* in his change; should see nothing to regret in the duties and *dignity* of the resident landholder" (*P*, 138, emphasis added). Austen here seems to support Smith's claim that the ability to feel shame and mortification is intimately connected with the ability to feel pride and vanity, respectively (*TMS*, 255). Anne feels not only the shame of which he is entirely incapable, but also *more pride* than Sir Walter over his former position of responsibility in the social order. She keenly senses both "dignity" and "degradation" where her father and sister are oblivious. In fact, the narrator informs us that Anne "saw no dignity in anything short of [expediently clearing away the claims of all Sir Walter's creditors]" (*P*, 12-13).

In the ludicrous scenes surrounding the Dowager Viscountess Dalrymple, Anne again exhibits more pride than her haughty father and sister. She wishes that they would refrain from attempting to ingratiate themselves with their high-ranking relatives: Anne "had hoped better things from their high ideas of their own situation in life, and was reduced to form a wish she had never foreseen—a wish that they had more pride" (*P*, 148).[21] Anne had hoped, in other words, that their pride (and vanity) would lead them to have higher standards for their own behavior. A little later she confides to Mr. Elliot: "I suppose I have more pride than any of you; . . . I certainly am proud, too proud to enjoy a welcome which depends upon place" (*P*, 151)—that is, which depends upon an esteem for rank rather than character. There are other clues that Anne's self-assessment is accurate. In a couple of striking passages, we witness Anne's high self-regard, such as the passage where Anne *almost* envies the Miss Musgroves' importance at home: "they were of consequence at home, and favorites abroad. Anne always contemplated them as some of the happiest creatures of her acquaintance; but still, saved as we all are *by some comfortable feeling of superiority* from wishing for the possibility of exchange, she would not have given up her own more elegant and cultivated mind for all their enjoyments" (*P*, 41, emphasis added).[22] Later in the novel, Anne again implies that she deserves more "sympathy and goodwill" than Captain Benwick but receives less (*P*, 97). Since it is actually through Anne's own thoughts that we learn of her superiority, it is additionally remarkable that the reader does not censure her as proud or vain; instead, her remarks encourage readerly sympathy and tend to place the reader in the position of impartial spectator.

Anne not only has more pride, but if vanity is the concern for reputation and the desire for admiration, then she has a considerable degree of vanity as well. Throughout the novel, Anne displays a constant longing to be loved, to be wanted, to be useful—in other words, to *please* and to be *important*. A variety of passages reveal this motivation as central to her character. In some cases, Anne does not seem to need external, adult recognition of her importance, such as when she reflects on her visit to Uppercross: "Her usefulness to little Charles would always give her some sweetness to the memory of her two months' visit" (*P*, 93). At other times, it is clear that she longs for more external recognition: "To be claimed for a good . . . is at least better than being rejected as no good at all; and Anne, glad to be thought of some use . . . readily agreed to stay" (*P*, 33). Such external recogniton clearly motivates many of Anne's actions: "their mutual friend answered for the *satisfaction* which a visit from Miss Elliot would give Mrs. Smith, and Anne *therefore* lost no time in going" (*P*, 53, emphasis added). Finally, Anne reveals the major reason why she does not wish to go to Bath: "for who would be glad to see her when she arrived?" (*P*, 135).

Anne relishes the company of good listeners such as Mr. Elliot and Lady Russell, both of whom are uniquely similar in wishing to hear Anne's account of events: they shared "the wish of really comprehending what had passed, and . . . [a] degree of concern for what she must have suffered" (*P*, 144). In leaving Kellynch, she regrets only her separation from Lady Russell as she recognizes "the extraordinary blessing of having one such truly sympathizing friend as Lady Russell" (*P*, 42). The irony is, of course, that it is precisely this friend who is the cause of (much of) Anne's unhappiness, by having convinced Anne to break off her engagement to Wentworth seven years earlier. Anne, in short, longs to be heard, seen, understood, needed, and loved. This sounds like "vanity" in the sense that it is a desire for admiration and a great concern about others' opinions—but is it a flaw?

It seems that Austen is eager to show that self-regard and even the desire for external approbation can be a key to virtue. Anne, who was "only Anne," whose "word had no weight," who knows her own "nothingness" (*P*, 5,42), is also the *same* Anne who is greatly concerned about "dignity," her reputation, and how the family is seen. Only Anne cares enough to protect the family name and reputation by taking leave of "almost every house in the parish" because, she says, "I was told that [the parishioners] wished it" (*P*, 45). Just as her mother had "concealed [Sir Walter's] failings and promoted his real respectibility for seventeen years" (*P*, 4), we learn that Anne, too, works to promote the "real respectability" of the Elliot family and name. Even Anne's ability to understand Elliot "nothingness" from afar actually suggests a greater concern for *how* (and whether) she and her family are *seen* than we saw in her father.

The scheme that in the first few pages of *Persuasion* seems so starkly delineated—namely that Sir Walter embodies vanity while Anne retreats in pure modesty—actually shows itself to be much more subtle; it reflects the heated eighteenth-century philosophical debate about the possibility that all passions, including pride and vanity, could be the basis of virtue and benefit humanity.

Austen characteristically moves beyond standard definitions of vices and virtues and makes us question the terms themselves. Just as Wentworth learns that the virtue of "resolution" may sometimes camouflage stubbornness and wilfulness, the reader is asked to consider whether vices like "pride" and "vanity" may not sometimes lead to virtue.

The question remains, Why is it then that we approve of Anne's pride and vanity, her self-consciousness and desire for dignity, while we disapprove of Sir Walter's and Elizabeth's? Why does Anne's vanity end in virtue, while Sir Walter's ends in vice and folly? Why does Sir Walter's self-regard and concern with his public image not lead him to virtue? Is it true, as Hume implied, that only "noble natures" can be trusted to transform self-regard into sympathy? Does Smith's moral psychology help give insight into this issue, or is Austen's view of human nature simply bleaker than Smith's, suggesting the frequent failure of the majority of people, who are less than "noble"?

The juxtaposition of Sir Walter and Anne shows a central problem in the regeneration of vanity and self-regard: it is more apparent that vanity can lead to the desire for praise, and thereby smooth social relations and improve civility, than it is that vanity would tend to lead to virtue. Austen is here illustrating a central difficulty that preoccupied Smith in *The Theory of Moral Sentiments* as well. Insofar as they are both involved in portraying moral education, Austen would agree with Smith that "the great secret of education is to *direct* vanity to proper objects" (*TMS*, 259): the object is not to extinguish but to channel the "selfish" passions. If we return to the initial description of Sir Walter's flaw with this in mind, we can better understand the role of vanity in the novel as a whole. "Vanity was the beginning and the end of Sir Walter Elliot's character" (*P*, 4): this formulation is crucial for the moral psychology presented through the novel, for Sir Walter's fault is not so much that he *begins* in vanity, but that that is where he *ends*. However, neither Austen nor Smith seems to have a clear solution to the temptation to substitute the love of praise for the love of praiseworthiness.

This problem occupies Smith throughout *Theory*. Smith does not underestimate the centrality of vanity as we have been defining it, for he claims that "the chief part of human happiness arises from a consciousness of being beloved" (*TMS*, 41), as we saw in Anne Elliot of *Persuasion*. In fact, he even goes so far as to say that people pursue wealth primarily neither out of necessity, for material comfort, nor even for pleasure, but rather for social approval (*TMS*, 50).[23] However, one of the major ways in which Smith tries to distinguish himself from Mandeville's argument about the primacy of the love of praise is by trying to assert that "Man naturally desires, not only to be loved, but to be lovely," without necessarily demonstrating why that is the case. On occasion, Smith goes so far as to claim that the love of praise actually stems from the love of praiseworthiness (turning Mandeville's claim on its head),[24] but more often Smith tries to establish a delicate balance between the two, as in the following passage, where he discusses the necessity for both the love of praise and the desire for praiseworthiness:

> [The love of praise] could only have made [man] wish to appear to be fit for society. The [desire for praiseworthiness] was necessary in order to render him anxious to be really fit. The first would only have prompted him to the affectation of virtue, and to the concealment of vice. The second was necessary in order to inspire him with the real love of virtue, and with the real abhorrence of vice. (*TMS*, 117)[25]

Smith leaves the question open as to whether the love of praise alone is sufficient to achieve the demands of civility, as demonstrated in Austen by Mr. Shepherd's deft manipulation of Sir Walter; however, it does not seem to suffice for virtue, since it has no sway over the internal, invisible world of thoughts and motives. Alternating between description and prescription, Smith claims that only those who entertain both of these loves are capable of "self-approbation" properly understood, and only those who are capable of self-approbation are in the end capable of full happiness.[26] Smith uses the connection between "self-approbation" and happiness to keep human beings interested in praiseworthiness; however, in order to preserve society and the possibility of friendship, he claims that human happiness must also depend upon praise. The concern for praise saves us from solipsism, while care for praiseworthiness enables us to strive for virtue even when it is invisible to others, providing Smith's response to Plato's story of the ring of Gyges.

According to Smith's terms, the problem with Sir Walter may be that he is incapable of true self-approbation because he is incapable of spectatorship. This may seem an odd claim when Sir Walter is frequently portrayed as watching others as well as himself,[27] and when he seems to think very highly of himself. But while Sir Walter frequently watches others, even more frequently watches himself, and generally wants others' good opinion, he is missing the ability to see himself through others' eyes and therefore the ability to spectate, as Smith defines it. Sir Walter's mistake is that he limits his desire to regard himself to the mirror in his dressing room rather than extending it to the parishioners, for example, or to the worthier members of his family: he observes himself neither through what Smith calls the "mirror of Society" (*TMS*,110), nor through an "inward eye" (*TMS*, 113), in which and through which Anne regards herself, and therefore limits his ability to receive praise and entirely prevents him from striving for praiseworthiness.

It is Anne's combination of love of praise and love of praiseworthiness that enables her both to become a spectator and also to achieve greater self-approbation and happiness than her father. Anne gradually strengthens her self-esteem by acting virtuously and caring for and observing others around her. Her habit of self-regarding gives Anne the strength (eventually) to become her own judge, to maintain her own judgments even when her faulty external spectators disapprove. Consider the following passage:

> I have been thinking over the past, and trying impartially to judge of the right and wrong, I mean with regard to myself; and I must believe I was right, much as I suffered from it.... I should have suffered more in continuing the engagement than I did even in giving it up, because I should have suffered in

my conscience. I have now, as far as such a sentiment is allowable in human nature, nothing to reproach myself with. (*P*, 246)

Anne's combination of love of praise and love of praiseworthiness enables her to see herself through others and also to see herself through an internal mirror when her external mirrors fail. Her love of praiseworthiness sustains her in the absence of praise, while her desire for praise assists her in forming friendships, performing good deeds, pursuing social concord, and aspiring to love and virtue.

The third element of Smithian moral psychology that separates Anne from her father, and which enables her vanity to lead her to virtue, is her ability to achieve spectatorly detachment. As Smith describes spectatorship, human beings turn their eyes inward to divide each individual into two: a subject and an object, an I and a me, a spectator and an agent. This purely human self-consciousness is what enables us to judge, and to measure ourselves against, the standard of the impartial spectator. The keenness with which we can imagine the impartial spectator will determine how well our internal eye or what Smith calls the "Eye of Mankind"[28] functions. Only when we gain the distance from ourselves, which sympathy with, or love for, the impartial spectator enables us to achieve, do we become capable of seeing ourselves with others' eyes. It is this very distance that, in turn, is essential to the impartiality of the spectator lodged in our breast.[29]

Anne's ability to sympathize and her powers of imagination both enable her to gain the spectatorly detachment necessary for virtue. Within the novel, these characteristics are relayed through the metaphor of the *traveler* in the passage that I will repeat for convenience:

> Anne had not wanted this visit to Uppercross to learn that a removal from one set of people to another, though at a distance of only three miles, will often include a total change of conversation, opinion, and idea. She had never been staying there before, without being struck by it, or without wishing that other Elliots could have the advantage in seeing how unknown, or unconsidered there, were the affairs which at Kellynch Hall were treated as of such general publicity and pervading interest. (*P*, 42)

Even though the passage concerns the small distance of three miles, her travel entails "a total change of conversation, opinion, and idea." Anne's travel is presented with the grandeur of a naval expedition, a movement from "commonwealth" to "commonwealth" (*P*, 42). In this crucial passage, where Anne has traveled just far enough away from Kellynch to practice once again "the art of knowing our own nothingness," she describes how differently the Musgroves live: "She acknowledge[s] it to be very fitting that every little social commonwealth should dictate its own matters of discourse." Saying this much would have demonstrated Anne's powers of sympathetic imagination, but she continues: "[She] hoped, ere long, to become a not unworthy member of the one she was now transplanted into" (*P*, 45). This moving passage signifies Anne's willingness to empathize, give domestic comfort, and carry her "home" with her wherever she goes. In a sense, it is the "art of pleasing" that she describes, and yet it is entirely different from the art of Mrs. Clay, to whom that phrase is applied in the novel (*P*, 20). It is the kind of conforming to others' ways that takes an extraordinary amount of observation and strength. Anne can understand the various languages of the little commonwealths and speak them without hypocrisy. She can monitor her linguistic progress, for she has an internal standard from which to judge—that is, she gains a clear enough sense of herself, by seeing herself from afar, as the impartial spectator would, to be aware of her harmony or disharmony with her surroundings. This dynamic of self-regarding, "measuring oneself up" in the "mirror of society," or using the "inward eye," is the type of social vanity that leads to virtue. Sir Walter's more selfish vanity, on the other hand, involves an inability to travel or to imagine, and therefore to spectate: his lack of awareness of what others think of him prevents his vanity from leading him to desire their better opinion.

The impartial spectator and Smithian moral psychology may be especially appropriate in the democratized, secularized, decentralized society described in *Persuasion*. Could it be that the impartial spectator is particularly critical when external standards of moral authority are corrupt? In a world particularly devoid of "authority", as Tony Tanner has observed in *Persuasion*, Anne, the traveling heroine, homeless yet always carrying her "center" with her, functions as a model for moral agents in a changing world.[30] This changing, decentralized, and atomizing context is part of the essential need to have self-regard. It is this self-regard, finally, that gives Anne the "resources for solitude," which, we are told, her sisters so decidedly lack (*P*, 14, 39): "I know you do not mind being left alone," says Mary, and for once she observes correctly (*P*, 58). When Anne plays the piano, she is little attended to: "She knew that when she played she was giving pleasure only to herself; but this was no new sensation." She functions as the central moral authority of the novel, and gradually some of the others unconsciously acknowledge this. When Louisa falls, for example, Charles and Wentworth look to Anne for leadership: "'Anne, Anne,' cried Charles, 'what is to be done next? What in heaven's name, is to be done next?' Captain Wentworth's eyes were also turned towards her" (*P*, 106). The irony of this scene, of course, is that the brave, strapping young naval officer is helpless in the crisis, while the woman he has been criticizing as weak single-handedly sustains them with her courage and presence of mind. Similarly, Anne's pride does not suffer the blow that Wentworth's does, when he must endure the humbling experience of admitting his errors at the end of the novel.

There have been many attempts to explain Austen's use of such strong, proud female characters. Anne Crippen Ruderman notes, for example, that "For a Christian, Austen talks a surprising amount about the merits of pride. Far from considering pride a chief human vice, it is not clear that she considers it, when justified, to be a vice at all." Ruderman considers this to be "one of the chief signs of the classical bearing in her writing" and therefore a token of Austen's deep-seated Aristotelian tendencies.[31] Claudia Johnson takes Austen's preoccupation with pride and self-regard to show her radical feminist tendencies: "In endowing attractive female characters... with rich and unapologetic senses of self-consequence, Austen defies every dictum about female propriety and deference propounded in the sermons and conduct books which have been thought to shape her opinions on all important matters."[32] What neither Ruderman nor Johnson sees is the eighteenth-century philosophic tradition, which did indeed borrow notions from Aristotle, through the well-known philosophical writings of such authors as Shaftesbury and Smith, and which must have indirectly shaped Austen's conception of human nature. Austen's treatment of vanity and vice show her to be more philosophical than many have thought, while not necessarily as politically radical as others have wanted to claim.

And while there are many resemblances between Austen's moral psychology and Smith's, there are perhaps some central differences between their conceptions of human nature. Smith seems, particularly in Parts I and II of *The Theory of Moral Sentiments*, to have a very optimistic view of human nature, to think that our selfish urges transform themselves into sympathy for others' suffering almost as soon as we learn to observe the world around us and start recognizing others as separate from ourselves. Societal functioning seems to be quite smooth, facilitated by the well-oiled wheels of the "Great Machine of the Universe." (We will remember that Smith's well-known phrase "the Invisible Hand" first appeared in *The Theory of Moral Sentiments* long before he wrote *The Wealth of Nations*.)

Austen, on the other hand, shows an amused preoccupation with the weaknesses of human nature and the inescapability of human subjectivity or partiality, making notions such as an idealized and "*impartial* spectator" harder to accept. Phrases that remind us of this human frailty permeate her letters, not only the passage chosen for the epigraph of this essay,[33] but also numerous passages in her novels. In *Persuasion* alone, the narrator makes many remarks on our tendencies toward subjectivity and solipsism: "How quick come the reasons for approving what we like" (*P*, 19); "[It was] soon sufficient to convince..., where conviction was at least very agreeeable" (*P*, 58); "What wild imaginations one forms, where dear self is concerned!" (*P*, 201); and the encapsulating comment "Self will intrude" (*P*, 208). The question follows, of course, whether these intrusions of self can lead to greater virtue and objectivity.

It could be argued that Smith is equally convinced of the inescapability of human subjectivity and even that this limitation of human experience is essential to the moral psychology he describes. It is the inability to escape our private experience and to feel others' pain that first awakens our imagination to attempt to approximate what others must feel. The failure of complete identification between sufferer and spectator leads to the possibility of cooperation, in Smith's scheme, and to the very possibility of society and virtue. "Unison" is impossible, Smith notes in his memorable musical metaphor, but that is why we strive for "harmony" and "concord." Imagination and memory allow us to transcend our own private experiences and help provide the "constant need for compromise in... mundane social interactions" (*TMS*, 22-23). Smith's emphasis, however, especially in the first half of *Theory of Moral Sentiments*, is clearly on the natural ease with which such "harmony" and "concord" are achieved.

Critics who wish to emphasize the darker side of Austen often mention the passage near the end of *Emma*, in which the narrator remarks, "Seldom, very seldom, does complete truth belong to any human disclosure; seldom can it happen that something is not a little disguised, or a little mistaken. . . ." These critics, however, seldom cite the second half of this sentence, in which the narrator concludes that "where, as in this case, though the conduct is mistaken, the feelings are not, it may not be very material."[34] The passage does reveal a potentially isolating factor of human existence, yet the ending of *Emma* is still comic, and the lack of perfect communication, of perfect transparency, and therefore of complete intimacy does not cause bitterness, regret, or a sense of tragedy in Austen's novels. While Austen recognizes the inescapable gap between individual experience and its potentially isolating results, she is not bitter about this human inability to attain perfect objectivity. Subjectivity, like Smith's "harmony," is indeed a token of human frailty, but the fact that our partiality controls our reasoning capabilities is the very basis of love, just as it is the source of many mistaken judgments.

In the course of reading *Theory of Moral Sentiments*, the reader may notice that Smith's Enlightenment confidence in the "Great Machine of the Universe" seems to falter. Part III, which suggests that the impartial spectator governs how we feel and think, wavers increasingly between prescription and description. Smith even acknowledges in Part III that "the passions . . . justify themselves" (*TMS*, 157), which is clearly a problem for attaining a corrective image of the impartial spectator through our sentiments. In Part IV, Smith starts to suggests the importance of customs and tradition in educating our notion of the impartial spectator, and in preventing it from degenerating into a justification of our petty desires and vices. Eventually, it seems that we need rules of conduct to ensure the continuance of the "natural" moral sentiments, since self-love turns out to be such a strong force in human relations.

While the content of Smith's and Austen's moral psychologies are quite similar, they differ primarily in tone. Smith begins confidently and ends tragically, admitting greater and greater difficulties with the prospect of basing virtue or even sympathy on natural sentiments. He also begins to distinguish more and more between the kinds of happiness and virtue accessible to the masses versus the ones accessible only to the rare, philosophical few. Austen's approach is in some ways the reverse. She begins with a recognition of many of the same human limitations that Smith ends with, and yet each novel achieves a comic ending. For Austen as well as Smith, it is clear that subjectivity and partiality are never overcome: the better one chooses one's partialities, the closer one comes to attaining love, sympathy, and virtue. Moral education, therefore, consists in directing our potentially selfish sentiments to the worthiest objects. Smith and Austen agree that the way to virtue is through sentimental education—rather than through law, discipline, or reason alone. Smith's moral psychology, like Austen's, substitutes a warm affection for the impartial spectator, for a cold, rational obedience to the law, whether natural or civil.

In the context of this regenerative approach to subjectivity and self-regard, Austen's focus on love and courtship becomes increasingly interesting. As we have seen, one of the crucial factors for achieving moral sentiments in Smith's *Theory* is arriving at a proper conception of the impartial spectator and a desire to please him. A recent critic, David Marshall, correctly identifies a central danger in this dynamic. Marshall warns that the impartial spectator—or rather one's private conception of the impartial spectator—can easily become a substitute for real spectators,[35] leaving an individual open to the danger of solipsism. It is clear that Smith intended to counteract this difficulty with the awakening and corrective force of not only traditions and customs, but also of the "mirror of Society" and the flesh-and-blood spectators that one encounters in daily life. However, it is not clear that Smith ever fully surmounts this difficulty. We see this problem with Sir Walter, in a sense, for it is not the case that Sir Walter has no vanity—that he has no concern for external spectators and their opinions. Rather, the problem is twofold: first of all, Sir Walter cares only about the most foolish and superficial of spectators, such as the Dowager Viscountess Dalrymple, and second, he lacks the imagination to see himself from a distance, with the result that he cannot understand others well enough to know their opinions of him. If Sir Walter has the ability to conceive of an internal spectator that he would consider "impartial," chances are that it would think remarkably well of all of Sir Walter's thoughts and actions. The two factors above prevent Sir Walter's vanity from leading him to virtue or even to the appearance of virtue.

Another way of describing Sir Walter's difficulty is to say that he is incapable of any love other than self-love. As Austen depicts it, one of the most reliable tokens of love is being able to see oneself with the eyes of the beloved. Her early novel *Pride and Prejudice* reveals how subjectivity or partiality can lead to virtue and even to greater objectivity when the beloved is virtuous. Love entails the selection of an external mirror that helps shape one's notion of the impartial spectator. Just as one desires to please one's beloved, one learns to please the "demigod" within the breast. Examples of this dynamic are particularly prevalent in the three Austen novels that depict the maturation of a heroine, including *Pride and Prejudice*. These heroines are frequently plagued by a certain kind of vanity that ultimately aids them in fulfilling their potential by the end of the novel, albeit often only after having experienced "mortification," a word favored by Austen and an experience that Smith calls the counterpart of vanity. Mortification, however, does not mean that the vanity of these heroines is extinguished; rather it means that it is redirected, channeled in a new direction, more in line with the "impartial spectator," as they grow more capable of seeing themselves through the eyes of their beloved.

In *Pride and Prejudice*, Elizabeth Bennet at first shows herself to be one of the most acute judges of character in the novel; she is also very aware of her prowess and is eager to display it publicly. However, the reader eventually learns of certain areas where she is less reliable—in particular, opinions regarding the man who has wounded her vanity: Mr. Darcy. In fact, the effect of flattery and wounded vanity upon powers of observation and objectivity quickly becomes a central theme of the novel. If we consider the public responses to the arrival of Mr. Bingley, Mr. Darcy, and their retinue, we will see that Austen uses the narrative voice to describe the quickly shifting opinions of the newcomers. Within two sentences, the narrator shows: that the crowd assembled at the ball desire to gratify their vanity by being liked by a wealthy man; that Darcy's coldness subsequently mortifies their vanity; and that, in response to their shifting opinions, even the description of his physical appearance shifts in the course of a few hours.

> Mr. Bingley was good looking and gentlemanlike; he had a pleasant countenance, and easy, unaffected manners . . . but . . . Mr. Darcy soon drew the attention of the room by his fine, tall person, handsome features, noble mien; and the report which was in general circulation within five minutes of his entrance, of his having ten thousand a year. The gentlemen pronounced him to be a fine figure of a man, the ladies declared he was much handsomer than Mr. Bingley, and he was looked at with great admiration for about half the evening, till his manners gave a disgust which turned the tide of his popularity; for he was discovered to be proud, to be above his company, and *above being pleased*; and not all his large estate in Derbyshire could then save him from having *a most forbidding, disagreeable countenance*, and being unworthy to be compared with his friend.[36]

There are no fewer than three stages of group opinion about Darcy, and the third directly contradicts the first. Not only Darcy's character but even his actual physical appearance improves as news of his wealth fires the ambition of those around him, and declines as he subsequently wounds their pride. Darcy's "handsome features" metamorphose within just two sentences (and a few hours) into a "forbidding, disagreeable countenance." Notice also that these changes of opinion are referred to as "the tide of his popularity," and indeed it ebbs and flows like the tide, describing the group dynamics of the fickle audience at the assembly. These features emphasize the eventual polarity of opinion caused by thwarted ambition and wounded pride and vanity. To complete the picture, Austen also makes it clear that gratified vanity, as well as disappointed vanity, will distort one's perceptions, using Jane Bennet as an example: "with more quickness of observation and less pliancy of temper than [Jane], and with *a judgment too unassailed by any attention to herself*, [Elizabeth] was very little disposed to approve [of Mr. Bingley's sisters]."[37]

Gradually, and somewhat paradoxically, Elizabeth's objectivity regarding Mr. Darcy grows alongside her love of him, or her "partiality" for him. In an interesting passage when Elizabeth visits Pemberly, Darcy's estate, she encounters his portrait on a wall. The narrator informs us that after studying this portrait for a while, Elizabeth "fixe[s] his eyes upon herself."[38] This formulation is significant because it suggests her internalization of his opinion; her desire to see herself as he might see her, warts and all; and a growing ability to achieve spectatorly distance on her own assumptions and actions, regardless of the outcome of her romantic attachment. It may be that Austen believes that moral education entails a recognition of the radical separation that exists between ourselves and others, before we can gain the maturity to feel true sympathy or love. Perhaps this is why the climax of the heroines' growth in *Pride and Prejudice*, *Emma*, and *Northanger Abbey*, as well as of Marianne Dashwood in *Sense and Sensibility*, occurs with a mortifying recognition at the time when the return or outcome of her love is most unsure. Austen seems to think that if we are not socially reminded of this separation, our imaginations may be lulled to sleep, and we may begin to assume (as Sir Walter does) that others are merely narcissistic projections of ourselves.

Contemporary critics are often struck by the "modern" tone of Austen's recognition of the "darker" sides of human nature, such as her recognition of the power of subjectivity and the limits of rationalism, by the pervasive "intrusions" of self, or by the fact that the world she depicts seems to provide neither certainty nor rosy, idealized pictures of humanity. As a result of this seeming kinship with modern relativistic thought, they often will emphasize her irony, her anger, her "hatred," or even her relativism in critical studies of Austen. Considering the philosophical discourses of her time will help us see that such critics are not considering the full import of her thoughts. Adam Smith's *Theory of Moral Sentiments*, for example, helps us see that the depiction of darker or "selfish" aspects of human nature is crucial to the moral education both of her heroines and of her readers. Austen embeds her sharp recognition of human frailty within a generally comic, hopeful, and deeply religious worldview. It is also her sense of human frailty that makes Austen emphasize the importance of civility in the absence of virtue. Although she understands the natural limitations that can be brought about through self-regard and subjectivity, the import of her novels is still that we must be responsible for the directions in which we channel our vanity, and we must still persist in the search for objectivity and truth.

Notes

This essay is based partly on a presentation made to the Jane Austen Society of North America in Alberta, Canada, in September 1993 and later published as "Persuasion and Persuadability: When Vanity Is a Virtue," in Persuasions *15 (December 1993): 235-44. I would like to thank Stuart Warner, Francis DuVinage, and Douglas Den Uyl for their helpful criticism of an earlier draft of this essay.*

1. John Essex, *The Young Ladies Conduct* [sic]: *Or Rules for Education, Under Several Heads; with Instructions upon Dress, both before and after Marriage, and Advice to Young Wives* (London, 1722), 20, quoted in Penelope Joan Fritzer, *Jane Austen and Eighteenth-Century Courtesy Books* (Westport, CT: Greenwood Press, 1997), 82.

2. Heather Chapone, *Letters of the Improvement of the Mind Addressed to a Young Lady* (London, 1772), 105, quoted in Fritzer, *Jane Austen*, 82.

3. Abbe D'Ancourt, *The Lady's Preceptor: Or, a Letter to a Young Lady of Distinction upon Politeness. Taken from the French and Adapted to the Religion,*

Customs, and Manners of the English nation By a Gentleman of Cambridge (London, 1743), 47, quoted in Fritzer, *Jane Austen*, 82.

4. This was not true of all theologians, of course. Joseph Butler, for example, showed an interest in how self-love teaches the limits of self-regard (Joseph Butler, *The Works of Joseph Butler* [Oxford: Clarendon Press, 1896], 7,13). See also note 14.

5. Arthur O. Lovejoy, *Reflections on Human Nature* (Baltimore: Johns Hopkins University Press, 1961), 154-55.

6. Eric Rothstein, *Systems of Order and Inquiry in Later Eighteenth Century Fiction* (Berkeley: University of California Press, 1975), 314.

7. Samuel Johnson, *A Dictionary of the English Language* (Dublin: Thomas Ewing, 1775).

8. Adam Smith, *The Theory of Moral Sentiments* (Indianapolis: Liberty Press, 1976), 255. Henceforth references to this text will be abbreviated as *TMS*.

9. Jane Austen, *Persuasion* (Oxford and New York: Oxford University Press, 1988), 4. All references to Jane Austen's novels are from this same six-volume edition. Henceforth references to *Persuasion* in the text will be abbreviated as *P*.

10. Cf. Lovejoy on becoming "slaves to mankind" through vanity (Lovejoy, *Reflections on Human Nature*, 200) and Smith on vanity's social side: "vanity is almost always a sprightly and gay, and very often a good-natured passion. Pride is always a grave, a sullen, and a severe one" (*TMS*, 257).

11. The description also reveals the traditional association between vanity and women: "Few women could think more of their personal appearance than he did" (Austen, *Persuasion*, 4).

12. Since there is little distinction made between the two traits in Sir Walter's case, and since Elliot pride involves an assumption of external admiration, it seems to be Elliot vanity as well.

13. Bernard Mandeville, *The Fable of the Bees* (Indianapolis: Liberty Press, 1988), i.51. According to the Smithian definitions we are using, Mandeville's saying should actually be "The Moral Virtues are the Political Offspring which Flattery begot upon Vanity."

14. Mandeville, *The Fable of the Bees*, i.53.

15. Mandeville's was not the only voice in praise of vanity's public benefits. As I mentioned above, similar points were being made in much more orthodox Christian corners of the debate: Bishop Butler, for example, called "the desire for esteem" beneficial because it "regulate[s] our behaviour": "[The desire for esteem] can no more be gratified, without contributing to the good of society, than [hunger] can be gratified without contributing to the preservation of the individual" (quoted in Lovejoy, *Reflections on Human Nature*, 178-80).

16. It is unknown what books Jane Austen actually read. However, these philosophical themes would have figured not only in the sermons of the day, but also in the books and journals studied by her father and brothers and frequently read aloud at family gatherings. It is not my purpose to assert any direct historical influence of Adam Smith upon Jane Austen, but rather to suggest an affinity that could have been partially influenced by their shared historical moment.

17. David Hume, *Essays: Moral, Political, and Literary* (Indianapolis: Liberty Press, 1985), 86.

18. Cf. "The minds of men are mirrors to one another" (David Hume, *A Treatise of Human Nature* [Oxford: Clarendon Press, 1992], 365).

19. David Hume, *Enquiries Concerning Human Understanding and Concerning the Principles of Morals* (Oxford: Clarendon Press, 1975), 75.

20. Jane Austen, *Jane Austen's Letters* (London and Oxford: Oxford University Press, 1952), 487, emphasis added.

21. This is a recurring theme in Austen's novels: "Of pride, indeed, there was perhaps scarcely enough" (Jane Austen, *Emma* [Oxford and New York: Oxford University Press, 1988], 210).

22. Anne's comments here bear a striking resemblance to Hobbes's second argument for equality among men in Book 13 of *Leviathan*: "For such is the nature of men, that howsoever they may acknowledge many others to be more witty, or more eloquent, or more learned; yet they will hardly believe there be man so wise as themselves; for they see their own wit at hand, and other men's at a distance" (Thomas Hobbes, *Leviathan* [New York: Collier, 1962], 98). The impartial spectator is Smith's device for allowing human beings to see themselves "at a distance" as well.

23. Douglas Den Uyl and Charles Griswold, "Adam Smith on Friendship and Love," *Review of Metaphysics* 49 (March 1996): 618. This article has been very helpful on Smith's understanding of the role of self-approbation in love and friendship.

24. See *TMS*, 114.

25. See Den Uyl and Griswold, "Adam Smith on Friendship," 619.

26. See Den Uyl and Griswold, "Adam Smith on Friendship," 631.

27. For example, in Bath, Sir Walter stands by a window counting "eighty-seven women go by, one after another, without there being a tolerable face among them" (*P*, 134). When he does watch others, he bases his interest in others on their appearance or on their location between "A" and "Z" (*P*, 8)—that is, on the location (and length) of their entry in the "book of books." He counts people; he alphabetizes them, purely according to external, extrinsic qualities.

28. Cf. *TMS*, 109-13, 153.

29. Compare with Freud's notion of ego and superego: the eighteenth-century philosophical discourse describes the dynamic as love, rather than as a power struggle.

30. Tony Tanner, *Jane Austen* (Cambridge, MA: Harvard University Press, 1986).

31. Anne Crippen Ruderman, *The Pleasures of Virtue* (Lanham, MD: Rowman & Littlefield, 1995), 99.

32. Claudia Johnson, *Jane Austen: Women, Politics, and the Novel* (Chicago: University of Chicago Press, 1988), xxiii.

33. Austen, *Letters*, 262.

34. Austen, *Emma*, 431.

35. David Marshall, "Adam Smith and the Theatricality of Moral Sentiments," *Critical Inquiry* 10, no. 4 (June 1984): 608.

36. Austen, *Pride and Prejudice* (Oxford and New York: Oxford University Press, 1988), 10, emphasis added.

37. Austen, *Pride and Prejudice*, 15.

38. Austen, *Pride and Prejudice*, 251.

Chapter 12

Virtue and Friendship in *Persuasion*: Jane Austen's "Aristotelian" Understanding of Happiness

Germaine Paulo Walsh

The novels of Jane Austen never have been wholly out of fashion, but recently there has been a renewal of interest in her work. Within the last few years, three of Austen's novels—*Sense and Sensibility*, *Emma*, and *Persuasion*—have been made into feature films (the first two succeeding quite well, even by Hollywood standards), and a television miniseries of *Pride and Prejudice* garnered very high ratings among both English and American audiences. Furthermore, many bookstores report that sales of Austen's novels have increased dramatically, and sightings of people, especially young women and girls, reading Austen's novels, have been on the rise.[1] In seeking to account for Austen's popularity, reviewers with feminist sympathies have tended to argue that her stories appeal to today's young women primarily because they offer a kind of "escapism." That is, women are attracted to Austen's novels and the films based on the novels because Austen's stories present an image of life in a simpler time, a time in which social roles were clearer. In particular, the social expectations for women differed from those for men, and both were more easily understood. Such reviewers maintain that there is a kind of "Cinderella" quality about Austen's stories, in that her central female characters are virtually guaranteed a happy ending, one in which the heroine marries the man she loves and rides off into the sunset.

The comments of Elayne Rapping illustrate this view. She contrasts the films based on Austen's novels with the television show *Melrose Place*, maintaining that the Austen films appeal to female viewers because of their "fairy tale" quality. In Austen's stories, those young women who are able to live up to society's expectations for women's conduct are ultimately rewarded by wedding their conventionally upright, though distinctly male, counterparts. The lives of Austen's women contrast sharply with the lives of the liberated and independent women depicted in *Melrose Place*, who seem to embody the modern ideals of self-expression, self-creation, and power. These women have overcome the limits of essentialist assumptions about gender traits. Women and men share similarly rapacious, individualistic, conniving genes—tempor-arily anyway—and then they morph, male and female alike, into the opposites, suddenly becoming caring, loving, vulnerable, sensitive, and altruistic. For even in the realm of psychology and personality, there are no rules or limits on what one may become.[2]

According to Rapping, women who are attracted to Austen's stories mistakenly believe that the frustrations and disappointments they experience in contemporary society are in some sense caused by the fact that sexual equality has been achieved. Although Rapping sympathizes with those women who know through experience that "all the gender equity in the world can do little to calm our nerves or fulfill our deepest needs and desires,"[3] she maintains that it is not gender equality per se that is the cause of women's dissatisfaction and anxiety, but rather the dominance of "marketplace values and dynamics."[4]

However each of us ultimately determines just what will "calm our nerves or fulfill our deepest needs and desires," Rapping's insistence that Austen's stories support conventional moral standards (i.e., those of late eighteenth- and early nineteenth-century England) places her squarely into one of the two dominant camps of literary criticism regarding Austen's novels. According to one line of interpretation, that with which Rapping's argument coincides, Austen's novels support conventional morality; i.e., she is a defender of English bourgeois society, and thus may rightly be designated as a conservative.[5] According to a second line of interpretation, rather than supporting conventional moral standards, Austen's novels in fact undermine them; i.e., she is a defender of individual happiness, and thus may rightly be designated as a Romantic.[6]

It is important to note that critics in both camps are in agreement regarding two important points. First, they maintain that in her novels, Austen addresses both the issue of conventional morality or "society," and the issue of individual happiness or the "self." Second, and more importantly, critics in both camps accept the modern philosophic position that these two—conventional morality and individual happiness, or "society" and "self"—are necessarily in conflict.[7] The chief task of interpretation regarding Austen, then, is to determine which side she supports. That is, insofar as Austen can be shown to defend the claims of conventional morality or "society," she is understood as undermining the claims of individual happiness or the "self," and vice versa.

While the tendency to interpret Austen in one of these two ways predates contemporary feminist critique, most feminist critics tend to follow similar lines of interpretation.[8] Some feminist scholars maintain that the central female characters in Austen's novels submit to conventional morality, and thus conclude that there is ultimately little or nothing in Austen's novels that supports feminist claims.[9] Others, however, maintain that the central female characters in Austen's novels rise above conventional morality in their quest for individual happiness. For these critics, Austen's novels ultimately do provide support for feminist claims.[10]

Apart from these two dominant approaches to Austen's novels, there is another approach to Austen's work that has some adherents. According to those who support this third interpretation, the entire debate over whether Austen's novels support conventional morality or individual happiness, "society" or "self," is based on a mistaken assumption: that Austen accepts the modern philosophic position that human beings are by nature individualistic and void of any naturally directed ends. However, careful attention to Austen's novels shows that her understanding of human nature and human fulfillment is in many respects fundamentally at odds with the modern view and is in fact closer to the classical view.

The most thorough and persuasive defense of this approach is given by Anne Crippen Ruderman, who argues that Austen's understanding of human nature and happiness is in many respects similar to the classical view, specifically, that of Aristotle.[11] Rather than portraying individual happiness and traditional morality as being inherently at odds, as is commonly assumed by critics, Austen recognizes them as being deeply interconnected. This stems from the fact that, rejecting the premises of modern philosophy, Austen understands human beings to be social or political by nature. Her heroes and heroines seek to achieve happiness or fulfillment through a life of attachment to others, guided by certain objective moral principles. Hence, like Aristotle, Austen associates happiness with the achievement of virtue. Her well-known and much-admired portrayal of character illustrates her understanding of the various ways that men and women succeed, and often fail, in achieving virtue.

In this essay, I examine Austen's understanding of happiness in *Persuasion*, focusing specifically on her depiction of the role of virtue and friendship in the achievement of happiness. My analysis supports Ruderman's claim that Austen's outlook is in many respects "Aristotelian."[12] While I think that a similar case could be made by examining any one of Austen's novels, I have chosen to focus on *Persuasion* for two reasons. First, some scholars argue that Austen's viewpoint in *Persuasion*, the last novel she completed, is markedly different from that of her earlier novels.[13] They claim that *Persuasion* conveys in the sharpest and clearest way Austen's view of the inherent contradictions between "self" and "society." According to this view, Austen's portrayal of Anne Elliot, the heroine of the story, is the closest Austen comes to advocating the Romantic ideal of the self. Anne is able to reach this ideal only by rejecting conventional morality, rather than submitting to it, as Austen's earlier heroines supposedly do. In light of this common interpretation, one might think that of all of Austen's novels, it would be most difficult to associate *Persuasion* with the Aristotelian view of happiness, yet that is precisely what I attempt to do. Second, it is in *Persuasion* that Austen presents her most explicit treatment of the differences between men and women, addressing the issue of the different "natures" of men and women.

Happiness

In the *Nicomachean Ethics*, Aristotle acknowledges that happiness[14] is defined in different ways by different persons. In examining the various opinions about happiness, he concludes that there is some truth in each view.

> Happiness is thought to be 1) virtue by some, 2) prudence by others, 3) a sort of wisdom by others, or all of these or some of them, together with 4) pleasure or not without pleasure by still others; and there are some who also include 5) material prosperity . . . and it is reasonable that none of them should be

altogether mistaken but should be right at least in one or even in most respects.[15]

While Aristotle defines happiness as including each of these components or features, he identifies happiness most fundamentally with virtue or, perhaps more accurately, with actions or activities in accord with a virtuous character or disposition. He includes pleasure in happiness by arguing that, for virtuous persons, the performance of virtuous acts is inherently pleasurable. In explaining how pleasure accompanies virtue, he touches on the question of human nature, suggesting that there must be something about the way we are constructed, the nature of our being, that makes certain actions or, more precisely, a certain kind of life, pleasurable for us (*NE*, 1103a24-27). Such a life, for Aristotle, is objectively superior to a life that deviates from or falls short of virtue in one respect or another.

While Aristotle argues that what is most fundamental to happiness is the achievement of virtue, he explains that happiness also requires some degree of material prosperity. It is "impossible or at least not easy," he states, to engage in virtuous activity without possessing at least some degree of external goods, such as wealth, friends, or political power. Furthermore, he remarks that human beings may fall short of achieving the most supreme or perfect kind of happiness if they lack such blessings as good birth, good children, or beauty. In considering the need for external goods, Aristotle acknowledges that chance or luck plays some role in happiness, and this raises some difficulties. If happiness requires good luck, or at least avoidance of bad luck, then is happiness something beyond human control? Might the achievement of virtue in itself be insufficient for happiness, if misfortune, at least in certain cases, may destroy the pleasure we take in life? While Aristotle acknowledges this possibility by referring in particular to the fate of Priam,[16] he maintains that the happiness that comes through a life of virtue is something enduring, even in the face of misfortune. In his account of prudence, which is in a sense the central or guiding virtue of life, Aristotle emphasizes how the truly prudent person is successful in attaining her ends (*NE*, 1142b28-33). Though the power of chance never can be wholly overcome in life, the prudent person directs her life in such a way that she is able to foresee many potential difficulties or obstacles, making it very unlikely that her happiness might be ruined by misfortune. Although Aristotle acknowledges that human life is always in some sense dependent on chance, he maintains that a virtuous person, even were she to experience great misfortune, would recover in time, since such a person would have the resources of soul to endure and rebuild her life again, to the point that pleasure and fulfillment would return.

In examining *Persuasion*, we see that Austen's understanding of happiness is in many respects very similar to Aristotle's. While Austen depicts nearly all of the characters in the novel as having experienced misfortune of one kind or another, their differing responses reveal much about their disposition and hence their potential to achieve genuine happiness. At the opening of the novel, we are informed that Anne Elliot, the twenty-seven-year-old central female character, has experienced a good deal of "bad luck" in her life, which has contributed to her rather melancholy situation. While she is well-born, with "an elegance of mind and sweetness of character, which must have placed her high with any people of real understanding" (*P*, 5),[17] she has very few true friends, certainly none among the members of her own family. To her vain father and older sister, Sir Walter and Elizabeth, she is "nobody," "her word [having] no weight" (*P*, 5). To her hypochondriac younger sister, Mary Musgrove, though not quite a "nobody," Anne is valued only as a means of relief from Mary's imagined afflictions. The only family member with whom she had a relationship of true friendship was her mother, Lady Elliot, who died when Anne was fourteen. Furthermore, her greatest misfortune occurred when, at the age of nineteen, she reluctantly broke off her engagement to Captain Frederick Wentworth, and thereby lost the only man she ever loved. In the eight years since that event, she has not met any other man whom she could love. Yet Anne, despite these very heavy misfortunes, responds in a way that mirrors what Aristotle expects of the truly virtuous person, whose happiness in some sense endures despite misfortune. Though it is clear at the beginning of the novel that Anne in many ways does not enjoy her life, she nevertheless strives to engage in virtuous actions, and she does take pleasure in such actions, though this is not always something that she experiences immediately. Yet as the novel proceeds, we see that Anne's efforts to be of use to others—i.e., to provide some genuine service to those with whom she associates—does bring her pleasure, and as others begin to recognize and appreciate her goodness, her enjoyment of life increases.

Austen sheds further light on her understanding of happiness through her treatment of the interaction between Anne and Captain Benwick. Like Anne, Benwick's hopes for happiness have been marred by the loss of his beloved. In Benwick's case, he and his fiancé, Fanny Harville, postponed marriage for nearly two years, until Benwick had achieved "fortune and promotion" (*P*, 65). Yet while his luck was good in regard to earning sufficient wealth and promotion, Fanny died shortly before he returned from sea. Benwick, whom Austen portrays as almost a caricature of the Romantic lover, responds to this misfortune in a way that contrasts sharply with Anne's response to her misfortune. Benwick becomes virtually despondent, spending much of his time in a kind of indulgent self-pity, reading the "tenderest songs" and "the impassioned descriptions of hopeless agony" (*P*, 67) of the Romantic poets of the day. While Anne is both familiar with and appreciative of such poetry, she urges Benwick to turn his mind away from so much attention to writings that inevitably keep his loss fresh and foremost in his mind.

In recommending that he turn his attention toward other writings that will help him to overcome his suffering, writings "calculated to rouse and fortify the mind by the highest precepts, and the strongest examples of moral and religious endurances" (*P*, 68), she implies that through his own efforts, and perhaps the grace of God, he can overcome his suffering and eventually be restored to happiness. But lest we presume that Anne thereby believes that all suffering can be overcome by diligent effort and a prayerful attitude, Austen almost immediately softens this impression, describing Anne's reflections as she thinks back over the evening.

> When the evening was over, Anne could not help but be amused at the idea of her coming to Lyme, to preach patience and resignation to a young man whom she had never seen before; nor could she help fearing, on more serious reflection, that, like many other great moralists and preachers, she had been eloquent on a point in which her own conduct would ill bear examination (*P*, 66).

Like Aristotle, Austen acknowledges, through the character of Anne Elliot, the role of chance in human affairs. Indeed, Anne has directly experienced great suffering as a result of misfortune. But as Aristotle argues, Anne's attitude suggests that human beings, at least in part through their own agency, can direct themselves toward certain virtuous activities that enable them, over time, to regain some meaning and some enjoyment from life. While Anne may take herself to task for failing to sufficiently "practice what she preaches," we see by this point in the novel that she has put into practice much of what she recommends to Benwick, and in doing so has improved her life. Austen emphasizes this by commenting on how Anne's external appearance improves along with her inner being. Upon arriving in Lyme, Austen states that Anne's "early loss of bloom and spirits" (*P*, 20) has been "restored," so much so that her "face" and "animation of eye" draw the admiration of her as-yet-unknown cousin, Mr. Elliot, as well as her former suitor, Captain Wentworth (*P*, 70).

Another aspect of the novel through which Austen conveys her understanding of happiness is her description of Anne's impressions on meeting the Harvilles in Lyme. Captain Harville, one of Wentworth's closest friends (and the brother of Benwick's late fiancé, Fanny) has been in ill health since being wounded in battle and, at least in part as a result of his medical condition, has little money with which to support himself and his family. When Anne, along with the others in the party visiting Lyme, is first introduced to the Harvilles, she is struck by their very deep affection for Wentworth and the generous hospitality they wish to bestow on him and all those in the visiting party. Upon hearing that the visitors already have made plans to dine at the inn where they are staying, she notices that the Harvilles "seemed almost hurt that Captain Wentworth should have brought any party to Lyme, without considering it as a thing of course that they should dine with them" (*P*, 66). When Anne actually sees how small and simple the Harvilles' home is, she is astonished that the couple would have expected, much less wished, to provide a meal to so many people. But almost immediately Anne's astonishment is "lost in the pleasanter feelings which sprang from the sight of all the ingenious contrivances and nice arrangements of Captain Harville" (*P*, 66). Anne notices the many ways in which Captain Harville has "[turned] the actual space to the best possible account" and in so doing made the home more comfortable for himself and his family. In particular, Anne notices that Harville has engaged in some domestic endeavors designed specifically to serve others: for his wife, "he fashioned new netting-needles and pins with improvements"; for his children, "he made toys";

and, though not a reader himself, he "fashioned very pretty shelves, for a tolerable collection of well-bound volumes, the property of Captain Benwick," who has lived with the Harvilles since his fiancé's death (*P*, 66).[18] Hence despite the bad luck he has experienced, Anne recognizes the many ways in which Harville's virtuous activity on behalf of his loved ones has enabled him to achieve a happy life. Indeed, Austen writes that in leaving the Harville home, "Anne thought she left great happiness behind her" (*P*, 66).

Virtue

Habituation, Education, and Character Formation

Aristotle maintains that human beings have by nature the potential to develop various ethical or moral virtues, such as courage, self-control, generosity, and truthfulness. In claiming that we have a natural potential to develop such virtues, Aristotle does not mean that they arise in us without any kind of effort or direction on our part, as, for example, sight and hearing develop naturally, apart from our having to do anything to acquire them. The ethical virtues, in contrast to natural abilities like sight and hearing, are acquired through a kind of learning or training that involves habituation, through the repeated performance of certain actions that conform to specific virtues. Developing an ethical virtue is in some ways analogous to learning an art. Just as a person becomes a builder by building, or a pianist by playing the piano, so too a person becomes courageous by performing courageous actions, generous by performing generous actions, and so on (*NE*, 1103a15-1103b2).

Yet what is required to develop a virtue goes beyond what is required to develop an art in that developing virtue involves the training of one's passions or emotions, so that one not only performs the right actions but also wishes to perform them, i.e., one "feels rightly" in regard to actions. Hence a person who possesses the virtue of good temper responds rightly to situations that arouse feelings of anger; a person who has the virtue of courage responds rightly to situations that arouse feelings of fear, and so on. In general, according to Aristotle, the ethical virtues involve our responses to situations wherein we tend to experience certain kinds of passions or emotions that, if they involve immediate pleasure, move us to act or, if they involve immediate pain, to refrain from acting.[19] Aristotle defines each of the ethical virtues as a mean between extremes, the extremes being vices. For example, courage is the mean between the extremes of cowardice and rashness; generosity is the mean between the extremes of extravagance and stinginess. Hence in a sense there are more vices than virtues, more ways of going wrong or being mistaken, than of being right.

In order to succeed in hitting the mean and, in general, developing the various ethical virtues, Aristotle maintains that one must also develop the intellectual virtue of prudence.[20] Aristotle argues that one must be trained rightly in one's youth. One must have someone external to oneself who possesses "right reason" as a teacher or guide, though eventually this guidance or direction must come from within oneself. That is, a person becomes truly virtuous when she no longer relies on another for guidance, but rather understands for herself why she should perform or not perform certain actions. While habituation from youth makes the ultimate achievement of the ethical virtues possible, such habituation in and of itself is not sufficient for the achievement of virtue. One also needs prudence. Prudence is a virtue of intellect, but one that is combined with emotive disposition or character. That is, prudence entails both intellectual virtue in regard to directing action—in particular, prudence is associated with the ability to deliberate well in achieving one's ends—and ethical virtue in regard to feeling as one should.[21]

Through her depiction of character, Austen conveys a view of virtue and vice that in many respects parallels Aristotle's. Like Aristotle, Austen recognizes the importance of the education or training one receives in youth for the formation of character. For example, upon arriving at her younger sister's home in Uppercross, Anne is pressed to listen to the criticisms, which she knows to be justified, made by her brother-in-law, Charles, and his mother, Mrs. Musgrove, regarding Mary's mismanagement of the children (P, 30). Mary herself acknowledges that her children are "unmanageable" (P, 26), but she blames her husband and mother-in-law. Austen later contrasts the rearing of the Musgrove children with that of the Harville children. The Harville children, who are well behaved and, one is led to believe, conscientiously educated by their parents, must be "sedulously [guarded]" by Mrs. Harville during their visit to Uppercross over the Christmas holidays from "the tyranny" of the two Musgrove children (P, 88).

While Austen acknowledges the importance of early education for the achievement of virtue, she shows that such education may not be sufficient. Although none of her virtuous characters could have become so without the guidance of some parent or parental figure, such guidance does not guarantee virtue. For example, Austen points to the influence of Lady Elliot, and after her death, Lady Russell, on the development of Anne's character. However, the guidance of these two good women proves to be insufficient in the case of Anne's elder sister Elizabeth, who develops a number of vices rather than virtues. While Austen gives no definitive answer as to why these sisters, having similar influences in both the direction of virtue (from Lady Elliot and later Lady Russell) and vice (from their father, Sir Walter), end up being so different in character, she suggests two possibilities, both of which correspond to arguments Aristotle makes.

First, she suggests that differences in natural or inherent tendencies among individuals play a significant role in the development of character, for good or ill (NE, 1109b2-4 and 1144b1-7). For example, though Austen portrays Lady Russell as a virtuous person, she indicates that Lady Russell's intellectual abilities do not, and cannot ever, equal Anne's.

> There is a quickness of perception in some, a nicety in the discernment of character, a natural penetration, in short, which no experience in others can equal, and Lady Russell had been less gifted in this part of understanding than her young friend (P, 166).

Also, in introducing Mrs. Smith, "an old school-fellow" (*P*, 100) of Anne's who had been especially kind to Anne after her mother's death, Austen again points out that natural tendencies play some role in the development of character. Upon first visiting Mrs. Smith, Anne is struck by the terrible misfortunes her old friend has had to endure. Upon leaving the school they had attended together, Mrs. Smith (then Miss Hamilton) had married a fairly wealthy man and had lived a rather carefree life with him. However, several years into the marriage, Mr. Smith had died, and, due to their extravagant lifestyle, his estate was left in financial ruin. Shortly thereafter, Mrs. Smith became seriously ill, and eventually became a permanent invalid. As Anne becomes reacquainted with Mrs. Smith upon moving to Bath, she is astonished that Mrs. Smith is still a rather cheerful person despite her misfortunes. As Austen writes,

> [Anne] could scarcely imagine a more cheerless situation in itself than Mrs. Smith's. She had been very fond of her husband,—she had buried him. She had been used to affluence,—it was gone. She had no child to connect her with life and happiness again, no relations to assist in the arrangement of perplexed affairs, no health to make all the rest supportable. . . . Yet in spite of all of this, Anne had reason to believe that she had moments only of languor and depression, to hours of occupation and enjoyment. How could it be? She watched—observed—reflected—and finally determined that this was not a case of fortitude or of resignation only.—A submissive spirit might be patient, a strong understanding would supply resolution, but here was something more; here was that elasticity of mind, that disposition to be comforted, that power of turning readily from evil to good, and of finding employment which carried her out of herself, which was *from Nature alone*. It was the choicest gift of Heaven. (*P*, 101-02, emphasis added)

Similarly, Austen suggests that Elizabeth Elliot's "natural" disposition inclines her toward thinking and acting like her father rather than her mother. In remarking that Elizabeth won her father's affection by being "very like himself" (*P*, 5), Austen points to a likeness both in terms of external appearance—Elizabeth looks like her father—and internal disposition—Elizabeth is more naturally inclined to her father's character. Similarly, Lady Russell's reference to Anne's likeness to her mother points to a likeness both of physical appearance and of natural disposition (*P*, 5).

Second, Austen suggests that the development of character involves an element of freedom or self-determination (*NE*, 1095b8-13 and 1111b4-12a17). That is, at some point in life, even those still relatively young (e.g., Elizabeth and Anne as teenagers) make choices about whom to listen to and how to behave. Being taught sound principles is not sufficient, since one must in a sense internalize them. For example, in describing Elizabeth's character, Austen mentions that Lady Russell "had endeavoured to give Elizabeth the advantage of her own better judgment and experience—but always in vain," as Elizabeth chose not to listen to her, but only to her father. For Anne, of course, the reverse is true.

Furthermore, Austen suggests that human beings have the ability to reflect back on their lives and, recognizing mistakes they have made, endeavor to change their character. For example, Austen portrays Mrs. Smith as someone whose experience of life has led her not only to regret some of the habits she had fallen into, particularly that of extravagance, but also as able to change. In thinking back over her life, Mrs. Smith remarks to Anne that "there are so many who forget to think seriously till it is almost too late," (*P*, 103) indicating that for those who do come "to think seriously before it is too late," some kind of change is possible. Hence like Aristotle, Austen suggests that character development involves some combination of natural inclination and choice.

Despite acknowledging the role of choice in character development, and the possibility of change, Austen emphasizes, like Aristotle, that once one's disposition or character, be it virtuous or vicious, is formed, it cannot be altered quickly or easily (*NE*, 1152a29-33). We see particular evidence of this in Austen's portrayal of Mr. William Walter Elliot, the man who is the nearest male relative to Sir Walter, and the heir to his title and property. In the opening pages of *Persuasion*, we learn that Sir Walter and Elizabeth resent Mr. Elliot. Shortly after the death of Lady Elliot (which occurred about thirteen years before the action of the novel takes place), Sir Walter, who has no living son, decided to seek the acquaintance of Mr. Elliot, who was then in his early twenties. Sir Walter's principal design in seeking the acquaintance of Mr. Elliot was to induce him to marry Elizabeth, who herself was eager for the match, having come to "[like] the man for himself, and still more for being her father's heir" (*P*, 7). However, Mr. Elliot did not respond as Sir Walter and Elizabeth wished. To the contrary, instead of conforming to their plan, he "purchased independence for himself by uniting himself [in marriage] to a rich woman of inferior birth" (*P*, 7). To add insult to injury, in the years that followed, it was reported to Sir Walter and Elizabeth that Mr. Elliot had "spoken disrespectfully" and "contemptuously" about them and about the baronet's title he would one day inherit (*P*, 7). In the decade that followed these events, there was no communication between Mr. Elliot and Sir Walter. However, in the course of the action that takes place in the novel, we learn that Mr. Elliot eventually wishes to be on friendly terms with Sir Walter and his family. His circumstances have changed, as his wife recently died, leaving no children. Initially Sir Walter and Elizabeth are resistant to renewing the acquaintance, but they accept him with open arms after he assures them that he never spoke contemptuously about them or the honor of the baronet's title, and once again they set their sights on his marrying Elizabeth.

Upon becoming acquainted with Mr. Elliot, Anne, like her father and sister, as well as Lady Russell, is impressed by his good manners and intelligence. However, unlike the others, she is wary of believing that he is what he appears to be. Lady Russell comes to think that it is "perfectly natural that Mr. Elliot, at a mature time of life," should come to recognize that he had erred "in the heyday of youth" and now value his prospective title and wish to be on good terms with his relations (*P*, 97). Anne, however, is suspicious of him. She perceives that he developed many bad habits in his younger years, and she believes that such habits, forming one's character, cannot easily be changed. While she does think it possible that a person might change his character for the better, she knows that such a change would require a great deal of time and effort. Furthermore, she wonders whether, rather than truly seeking to improve himself, Mr. Elliot has simply learned how to disguise his true character in order to ingratiate himself with Sir Walter's family, and perhaps with society in general. As Austen writes,

> [Mr. Elliot] certainly knew what was right, nor could [Anne] fix on any one article of moral duty evidently transgressed; but yet she would have been afraid to answer for his conduct. She distrusted the past, if not the present. The names which occasionally dropt of former associates, the allusions to former practices and pursuits, suggested suspicions not favourable of what he had been. She saw that there had been bad habits; that Sunday-traveling had been a common thing; that there had been a period of his life (and probably not a short one) when he had been, at least, careless on all serious matters; and, though he might now think very differently, who could answer for the true sentiments of a clever, cautious man, grown old enough to appreciate a fair character? How could it ever be ascertained that his mind was truly cleansed? (*P*, 106)

The similarity of Austen's view of virtue to Aristotle's is further shown in considering another ground upon which Anne is suspicious of Mr. Elliot. In attempting to understand his character, she looks to his passions or emotions, as well as to his actions. Believing that emotions reveal something fundamental about one's judgment and character, Anne distrusts Mr. Elliot because he is so wholly lacking in "openness," i.e., in revealing his emotions. This fact, even apart from his habits of the past, leads Anne to question the seeming goodness of his character. As Austen writes,

> Mr. Elliot was rational, discreet, polished—but he was not open. There was never any burst of feeling, any warmth of indignation or delight, at the evil or good of others. This, to Anne, was a decided imperfection (*P*, 106).

In the end, of course, Anne's suspicions prove to be well-founded. We learn that Mr. Elliot has lied to Sir Walter and his family on a number of points, and has devised a crafty plan to deceive Sir Walter. Having heard from Colonel Wallis that Mrs. Clay has been residing in Sir Walter's household, and believing it possible that she might insinuate herself sufficiently into Sir Walter's affections to get him to marry her, Mr. Elliot fears that he may not inherit the baronetcy after all. That is, if Sir Walter marries again and has a son, Mr. Elliot will be supplanted as heir. Eventually Mrs. Smith, who has known Mr. Elliott for many years, reveals the truth about him to Anne, and Anne learns that the extent of his vice goes even beyond her suspicions.

Virtues and Vices

Another point on which we notice similarities between Aristotle's and Austen's understanding of virtue is in their respective treatment of the relation between prudence and ethical virtue. That is, both maintain that those persons who display various ethical virtues also possess the intellectual virtue of prudence (as in the case of Anne Elliot), while those who display various ethical vices either lack intelligence in some important respects (as in the case of Sir Walter) or else possess a kind of intellectual vice known as cleverness (as in the case of Mr. Elliot and Mrs. Clay). While it would be impossible in the space of this essay to discuss all of the virtues and vices of the various characters in *Persuasion*, we may learn something of Austen's views by examining some notable qualities of a few characters in the novel.

Austen's depiction of the character of Mrs. Clay parallels Aristotle's discussion of the virtue of "friendliness" and its corresponding vices. In introducing this virtue, Aristotle remarks that it has to do with actions in the sphere of social relations, i.e., with how human beings should speak and act in living and associating together. Friendliness,[22] Aristotle argues, is the mean between the extremes of obsequiousness—which refers to the behavior of those who never object to what others say or do, out of a desire to give others pleasure and avoid giving pain—and quarrelsomeness—which refers to the behavior of those who object to everything others say and do, without caring in the least whether they give others pain. There is a particular type of obsequiousness, Aristotle remarks, that characterizes one who has an ulterior motive in seeking to give pleasure and avoid giving pain to another. If the real motive of such a person is to receive some kind of personal benefit in the form of wealth or whatever is attainable by means of wealth, this person is a "flatterer," which is worse than being simply obsequious. The worst or most serious vices, Aristotle indicates, are those that involve a kind of perverse use of one's practical intelligence, which Aristotle refers to as "cleverness."[23]

Austen depicts Mrs. Clay as being quite an accomplished flatterer. Being the widowed daughter of a solicitor, rather plain-looking, and without much in the way of material means, Mrs. Clay seeks to improve her situation by achieving a degree of intimacy with Sir Walter and Elizabeth. She begins by seeking the friendship of Elizabeth, but as an ultimate goal has in mind winning the affections of Sir Walter. In introducing Mrs. Clay's character, Austen refers both to her ethical disposition and to her intelligence.

> She was a clever young woman, who understood the art of pleasing; the art of pleasing, at least, at Kellynch-hall; and who had made herself so acceptable to Miss Elliot, as to have been already staying there more than once, in spite of all that Lady Russell, who thought it a friendship quite out of place, could hint of caution and reserve (*P*, 11-12).

Mrs. Clay's "cleverness" is evident in her understanding of Sir Walter and Elizabeth's character, especially their vanity, and in her ability to communicate with them in ways that flatter their opinions about their own consequence. For example, in considering the suggestion of Mr. Shepherd (who is Sir Walter's solicitor and Mrs. Clay's father) that it might be possible to rent Kellynch Hall to a naval officer, Sir Walter remarks on how repulsed he is by most men who have served in the Navy, given that they become "deplorable looking" (*P*, 14). Mrs. Clay responds to Sir Walter's argument in a way that lends support to her father's suggestion, but simultaneously appeals to Sir Walter's vanity. That is, she expresses appreciation for those "poor men" who must engage in occupations that damage their looks, while acknowledging that only those men "not obliged to follow any [profession]," like Sir Walter, "hold the blessings of health and good appearance to the utmost" (*P*, 15).

Unlike Sir Walter and Elizabeth, Anne is not deceived by Mrs. Clay's behavior, and she recognizes that her father's character may indeed make him susceptible to the clever flattery of Mrs. Clay. As Austen writes,

> With a great deal of quiet observation, and a knowledge, which she often wished less, of her father's character, [Anne] was sensible that results the most serious to his family from the intimacy, were more than possible. She did not imagine that her father had at present an idea of the kind. Mrs. Clay had freckles, and a projecting tooth, and a clumsy wrist, which he was continually making severe remarks upon, in her absence; but she was young, and certainly altogether well-looking, and possessed, in an acute mind and assiduous pleasing manners, infinitely more dangerous attractions than any merely personal might have been. (*P*, 23)

In her judgment of Mrs. Clay, as in her judgment of Mr. Elliot, Anne proves to be right. Upon Anne's joining her family in Bath after her visit with Mary in Uppercross, we see that Sir Walter's opinion of Mrs. Clay has been improving, to the point where he seems to be becoming more and more fond of her. When Mrs. Clay suggests that she should leave Sir Walter's household, now that Anne is present, Sir Walter joins Elizabeth in urging her to remain, even going so far as to praise her "fine mind" (*P*, 96). Moreover, in commenting to Anne on how the lotion he recommended to Mrs. Clay has "carried away her freckles" (*P*, 96), he indicates that he thinks her looks are improving.

Austen's treatment of pride also, in many respects, parallels that of Aristotle. Aristotle defines pride[24] as a virtue that has to do with belief about one's own worthiness or goodness, and concern that one's worthiness be recognized by others. The proud person "thinks he deserves great things and actually deserves them" (*NE*, 1123b2-3). While Aristotle contrasts pride with two vices, vanity and meekness, he devotes more of his analysis to contrasting pride with vanity—i.e., thinking that one deserves great things when one does not—than with meekness. Austen follows a similar procedure. Like Aristotle, she defines pride as a virtue and contrasts it with the vice of "vanity," which she sometimes refers to by the synonym "conceit."

Austen's portrayal of this vice resembles Aristotle's, in that both present the vain person as being mistaken about his own worthiness or goodness. Austen often refers to the "vanity" of various characters in *Persuasion*, and she always uses this term to express criticism. However, she uses the term "pride" in an equivocal way. That is, when referring to a character's "pride," Austen sometimes expresses criticism, sometimes praise. At times Austen uses "pride" to refer to a quality that is like vanity, but that goes beyond vanity in that the person's understanding of her worth leads her to have little or no concern for the feelings of others.[25] In this sense, Austen suggests that pride can become a vice if it is not balanced with other virtues, such as justice and friendliness.[26] For example, in *Persuasion*, Austen refers to the "Elliot pride" (*P*, 59), which is the tendency of the Elliots to insist that their superiority over others always be recognized. The only exception is Anne, who is praised by one of the Miss Musgroves because, unlike Mary, Anne does not insist that her superiority, as the daughter of a baronet, be acknowledged. Mary, however, is insistent, even to the point of wishing to be accorded precedence over her mother-in-law, Mrs. Musgrove.

However, at other times Austen refers to "pride" in a positive way, i.e., as a virtue. For example, in lamenting how her father and elder sister seek to ingratiate themselves with their highborn relative, the Dowager Viscountess Dalrymple, despite the fact that this lady has "no superiority of manner, accomplishment, or understanding," Anne wishes that they had "more pride" (*P*, 98-99). In explaining her thinking on this subject to Mr. Elliot, who supports Sir Walter and Elizabeth's behavior, Anne states, "I suppose (smiling) I have more pride than any of you" (*P*, 99).[27] Ironically, Austen maintains that Anne, the only member of the Elliot family who does not exhibit the "Elliot pride," is in fact the only truly proud member, or perhaps more accurately, is the only member of the family who possesses a kind of proper pride, which is a virtue.[28]

The other members of the Elliot family, particularly Sir Walter and Elizabeth, are said repeatedly by Austen to be vain. In illustrating Sir Walter's vanity in particular, Austen conveys how those who think themselves worthy of great things, while misunderstanding what is truly great or most valuable in life, tend to go astray. She shows that Sir Walter's vanity is, to use Aristotelian terms, both an "ethical" and an "intellectual" defect, calling him at various times "vain" or "conceited," as well as "silly" or "foolish" (*P*, 4, 165).[29] Sir Walter's vanity is a kind of "foolishness" insofar as it relates to his belief that people's worthiness or goodness lies not in their virtue or character, but rather in their rank and beauty. In the opening lines of *Persuasion*, we are introduced to Sir Walter as he takes up the only book he ever reads, the history of the Kellynch Baronetage. There is something ironic in his fondness for this book, Austen shows, since he thinks that he is reading "his own history," while in fact he has done nothing to add to the dignity of this "ancient and respectable family" (*P*, 3). This is Austen's first indication of Sir Walter's lack of self-understanding. He takes pleasure in reading about the various honorable actions taken by his ancestors, which, presumably, made them worthy of their noble rank, such as serving as High Sheriff or in Parliament, although he himself engages in no honorable actions whatsoever. To illustrate Sir Walter's empty existence, Austen states that

> vanity was the beginning and the end of Sir Walter Elliot's character; vanity of person and of situation. He had been remarkably handsome in his youth; and, at fifty-four, was still a very fine man. Few women could think more of their personal appearance than he did; nor could the valet of any new made lord be

more delighted with the place he held in society. He considered the blessing of beauty as inferior only to the blessing of the baronetcy; and the Sir Walter Elliot, who united these gifts, was the constant object of his warmest respect and devotion (*P*, 4).

Sir Walter thus makes the mistake that, according to Aristotle, is common among those who have received various gifts of fortune, such as good birth, power, wealth, or beauty. Because "without virtue it is not easy to bear the gifts of fortune with propriety," such persons "think themselves superior to others," and become "disdainful and insulting." Since only one with "complete virtue" is truly worthy of honor, vain people have no just claim to great things or to being called proud, but they "imitate the proud person without being like him," showing "contempt for others, and [doing] whatever chances to please themselves" (*NE*, 1124a28-b3). Even Aristotle's description of the way vain people dress seems directly applicable to Sir Walter. Aristotle remarks that the vain are conspicuously foolish, adorning themselves in showy dress and talking about their good fortune out of a desire "to publicize what fortune has given them" (*NE*, 1125a30-33). When Anne visits the Crofts in Kellynch Hall after they take up residence there, Admiral Croft informs her that they have made only minor alterations in the home. One change he speaks of, however, is his having had the mirrors removed from Sir Walter's room, which the Admiral now uses. As he says to Anne, "I should think [Sir Walter] must be rather a dressy man for his time of life.—Such a number of looking-glasses! oh Lord! there was no getting away from oneself" (*P*, 84).

As Austen shows, Sir Walter's "pride" is in fact empty. He possesses the vice of vanity rather than the virtue of pride, because he has no qualities of which one could be truly proud. To the contrary, he possesses a number of vices, even apart from vanity. In particular, Austen depicts Sir Walter as being extravagant, lacking in self-control, and unjust. First, in regard to his extravagance, Sir Walter does precisely what Aristotle says is characteristic of the extravagant person, i.e., he "causes his own ruin" by wasting his wealth (*NE*, 1120a1-3). As we learn at the beginning of the novel, Sir Walter has been exceeding his income, and becoming more and more in debt, since the death of his wife, Lady Elliot, some twelve years before. Although he has attempted to ignore this fact and even to conceal it from his favorite daughter, Elizabeth, as the action of the novel begins, we learn that his creditors are becoming more and more determined to be repaid, and Sir Walter reluctantly accepts the fact that he must in some way "retrench" (*P*, 7).[30] As we learn why Sir Walter has exceeded his income, we see that his extravagance is not the result of some kind of misguided impulse of generosity.[31] To the contrary, it is connected to other vices, and thus is a sign of his more generally vicious character.[32] That is, Sir Walter's financial difficulties are connected both to his vanity, which prevents him from taking any action that would cause his financial situation to become known publicly, and to his lack of self-control, which prevents him from taking any action that would result in his losing the comforts of life.

Austen makes a point of contrasting Sir Walter's vices quite sharply with the virtues of others. For example, as mentioned previously, his vanity contrasts with Anne's pride, and his extravagance contrasts with the Harvilles' generosity.[33] Furthermore, in considering his situation, we see that Sir Walter is also unjust. The money he has been spending so freely is not his own, but that of businessmen and creditors with whom he has been dealing. Hence Sir Walter's financial actions have been injurious not only to himself and his own family, but to others as well. This fact is perceived quite clearly by both Lady Russell and Anne as they consider what actions Sir Walter should begin to take. While Lady Russell has some sympathy for Sir Walter's wish to save his "dignity," she maintains that he should act "like a man of principle," and repay the debts he has contracted (*P*, 9). Similarly, Anne considers it "an act of indispensable duty to clear away the claims of the creditors," believing that all his other concerns should now be subordinate to the claims of "justice and equity" (*P*, 9).

Friendship and Marriage

In introducing the subject of friendship, Aristotle immediately refers to its importance in the happy life, remarking that, "friendship is [either] a virtue or involves virtue," and that "it is most necessary to life, for no one would choose to live without friends, though he were to have all other goods" (*NE*, 1155a4-6). Furthermore, Aristotle alludes to the fact that, as in regard to happiness, different people define friendship in different ways. In particular, there is disagreement as to whether friendship involves some sort of likeness or similarity, or some sort of unlikeness or difference (*NE*, 1155a31-b7). As he proceeds in his discussion, Aristotle places greater emphasis on the ways in which friendship requires similarity among the friends, though he acknowledges that friendship also involves difference.

Aristotle identifies three kinds or types of friendships, which are distinguished on the basis of the grounds for which the friends care for one another: friendships of virtue, of pleasure, and of use. Although Aristotle defines friendship broadly enough to include virtually any association between persons wherein there is some degree of reciprocal affection and goodwill, he maintains that only the type of friendship he calls "virtue" friendship is friendship in the complete or perfect sense.[34] Hence pleasure and use friendships are friendships only insofar as they resemble virtue friendship. In defining virtue friendship, Aristotle emphasizes that the partners care for each other for what they truly are, which he identifies most centrally with their practical intelligence and ethical virtues.[35] That is, unlike use and pleasure friendships, wherein each partner cares for the other "not for what he is, but insofar as he provides some use or pleasure," (*NE*, 1156a17-18) in virtue friendships each partner cares for the other "because of what he is" rather than incidentally, and wishes the other's good "for the other's sake" rather than his own. While virtue friendships are characterized by their permanence, use and pleasure friendships are "easily dissolved" once the partners in such friendships are no longer pleasant or useful to each other (*NE*, 1156a20-22 and 1164a9-13).

In discussing virtue friendship, Aristotle does not pose an ideal of friendship that demands some kind of superhuman purity of motive, by which the friends overcome any appreciation of each other on the basis of pleasure or use. To the contrary, Aristotle maintains that virtue friends do experience pleasure and use in their friendship (*NE*, 1156b14-18), though those are not the primary motives for which the partners are friends. Indeed, in the course of his discussion of friendship, Aristotle indicates that the culmination of happiness occurs in the context of the shared life of virtue friends, who care for each other on the basis of their respective virtuous character, and find pleasure and use in their association. What is most characteristic of friendship, according to Aristotle, is "living together," and the most perfect expression of "living together" entails "sharing in conversation and thoughts" (*NE*, 1170b11-12).[36]

In considering the friendships of the various characters in *Persuasion,* we see that Austen's depiction of friendships mirrors Aristotle's assessment. She suggests, like Aristotle, that the kind of friendships a person has or seeks is a reflection of that person's beliefs about what is most important in life. For example, her virtuous characters, like Anne Elliot and Captain Wentworth, seek friendships with other persons primarily on the basis of their character, i.e., their virtue.[37] However, many of her characters seem to seek friends for other reasons. Those who most value some useful good, such as wealth, or some pleasure, such as being honored, seek friends who can assist them in achieving their ends. In exchange, they provide whatever use or pleasure is desired by their friend. We see this in the friendship between Mrs. Clay and Elizabeth. Friendship with Elizabeth provides Mrs. Clay with access to a more comfortable and enjoyable way of life than she would otherwise have, as well as the potential to cultivate the favor of Sir Walter, while friendship with Mrs. Clay provides Elizabeth with the servile flattery that she values. According to Aristotle, such a friendship, given that it is grounded in use and pleasure rather than virtue, cannot be enduring. Confirming this view, at the end of the novel Austen depicts the simultaneous dissolution of this friendship with the unraveling of Mrs. Clay's and Mr. Elliot's respective schemes to achieve a greater degree of intimacy in Sir Walter's family. In her characteristically ironic way, Austen ends the novel with Mrs. Clay sneaking off to become the mistress of Mr. Elliot.

Hence among the vicious, former foes (Mrs. Clay and Mr. Elliot) may become "friends" as soon as their circumstances differ and they become useful or pleasant to each other. Similarly, former "friends" (Mrs. Clay and Elizabeth) may become foes once their circumstances change and they are no longer useful or pleasant to each other. While remarking that Elizabeth was "shocked and mortified by the loss of [her] companion" (*P*, 167), Austen indicates that what Elizabeth really missed was not Mrs. Clay per se, but rather the sycophantic role she played in Elizabeth's life. In describing how Elizabeth and Sir Walter dealt with the loss of Mrs. Clay, Austen remarks that although they still had "their great cousins, to be sure, to resort to for comfort," they come to realize that "to flatter and follow others, without being flattered and followed in turn, is but a state of half enjoyment" (*P*, 167).

There is one aspect or type of friendship that Austen addresses in a much lengthier and more explicit fashion than Aristotle does, i.e., friendship between men and women. Regarding friendships that involve women, and the capacities of women in general, Aristotle provides relatively brief commentary. Nevertheless, his remarks are significant, and, as a growing number of scholars argue, however brief his commentary may be, Aristotle argues that women are capable of virtue, and hence of virtue friendship.[38] Aristotle explicitly raises the possibility of women participating in the highest form of friendship in commenting on the type of friendship that is possible between men and women within marriage,[39] which I shall refer to as marital friendship. As with all friendships, he maintains that marital friendship is based on both similarity and difference, but, given that there are "natural" differences between men and women, difference plays a more significant role in marital friendship than in friendships more generally. That is, there is a natural basis for marital friendship, according to Aristotle, that is unique to such friendships, since "human beings are by nature pairing or coupling beings [even] more than they are political beings" (*NE*, 1162a17-18). Marital friendship thus is based in part on the aspect of human nature that involves what Aristotle identifies as the different and complementary functions of men and women, paralleling their different roles in reproduction.[40] Yet the friendship between them need not be limited to the ends of use and pleasure. As he states, "human beings live together not only for the sake of reproduction, but for other things in life as well" (*NE*, 1162a20-22).[41] "Living together," as discussed previously, is perfected by "sharing in conversation and thoughts." Hence marital friendship is "both useful and pleasant, and if both partners are good, it may also be a friendship of virtue" (*NE*, 1162a24-26).

In all of Austen's novels, the central male and female characters are drawn together in large part by an appreciation of each other's virtues. Their love for each other, while certainly based in part on sexual attraction,[42] is rooted principally in the goodness each recognizes in the other. Thus their marriages fulfill both the "higher" and "lower" ends that Aristotle identifies. In regard to the "higher" ends, Austen indicates that each couple is well matched insofar as both partners are equally virtuous and equally intelligent, particularly concerning their capacity for moral judgment. However, like Aristotle, Austen suggests that there are some important natural differences that lead to their having somewhat different functions in life, and, perhaps more importantly, she maintains that these differences play a part in their respective practical reasoning and in their exercise of the ethical virtues. Specifically, she attributes greater "spirit" or daring to men and greater "gentleness" and "constancy" to women.[43]

Spirit, as Austen defines it, is a combination of boldness and resolution, even in the face of great risk. Gentleness, by contrast, is a tendency to yield to the wishes of others ahead of one's own. Given that Austen attributes greater gentleness to women, one might think that she supports a kind of submissiveness of women to men, but this is not the case. Austen's heroines do not simply bow to the wishes of others. They accede to the wishes of others only in matters that are morally inconsequential, given that their gentleness is yoked with an adherence to principle. Constancy, the other quality Austen attributes to women, is a deeper expression of this adherence to principle. In one sense, Austen defines constancy as loyalty to loved ones, but in another, more fundamental sense, she defines constancy as loyalty to one's moral principles.

Austen depicts Wentworth as an extraordinarily spirited man. In recounting the history of Anne's brief engagement to Wentworth near the beginning of the novel, Austen describes him as having "spirit and brilliancy" (P, 18), as well as "confidence," a "sanguine temper," and "fearlessness of mind" (P, 19). He does not see any risks involved in becoming engaged to Anne, either for himself or for her, despite his having insufficient money at present to support her. He is certain that they have a bright future ahead of them. While Anne initially is overjoyed at his proposal, and willing to become engaged for an indefinite period of time, she eventually is persuaded by Lady Russell to break off the engagement. Wentworth's reaction to Anne's decision is one of injured pride. Feeling "ill-used" (P, 19), and being, as he later acknowledges, "too proud to ask again" (P, 169), he decides to make a permanent break with her.

Through the character of Wentworth, Austen shows that excessive spirit, or spirit that is not balanced with other qualities, can lead to certain flaws in character. First, she associates spirit with the belief that one is not limited by chance. Wentworth believes that he can achieve virtually anything he sets out to do, solely on the basis of his own efforts. Although he speaks on several occasions of having benefited from good luck (P, 19 and 43-44), Austen shows that he does not actually believe that luck has played any significant role in his life. To some extent, Austen maintains, Wentworth is correct in believing that his success is due to his own efforts. As she writes,

> All his sanguine expectations, all his confidence, had been justified. His genius and ardour had seemed to foresee and to command his prosperous path. He had, very soon after their engagement ceased, got employ; and all that he had told her would follow, had taken place (P, 21).

Nevertheless, Austen also shows that, however much intelligence, foresight, and exertion Wentworth exhibited, his success is at least in part due to chance, i.e., to good luck. It is only at the end of the novel, after having come to understand Anne's decision to break off their engagement, that he finally is able to acknowledge this. That is, it is only after admitting to himself that he still loves her, and learning that she would have married him had he asked again after making his fortune, that he truly grasps the role of chance in his own life. As he tells Anne,

> Six years of separation and suffering might have been spared. It is a sort of pain, too, which is new to me. I have been used to the gratification of believing myself to earn every blessing that I enjoyed. I have valued myself on honourable toils and just rewards. Like other great men under reverses, . . . I

must endeavour to subdue my mind to my fortune. I must learn to brook being happier than I deserve (*P*, 164-165).

Second, Austen associates spirit with the belief that, in virtually all circumstances, one should be resolute in maintaining one's opinions and decisions, even when presented with sound judgment in opposition to one's own. That is, Wentworth's spirit leads him to value "firmness of character" (*P*, 78) above all other qualities, and thus to have contempt for those whom he deems to be "easily persuaded" to change their minds (*P*, 58). It is for this reason, of course, that he refuses even to consider forgiving Anne for breaking off their engagement. In his mind, she has revealed a weakness of character that he cannot respect. This becomes evident in his conversation with Louisa Musgrove during their walk to Winthrop. Louisa has persuaded her sister, Henrietta, to seek a reconciliation with her former suitor, Charles Hayter. After Louisa explains how she urged Henrietta to action, Wentworth responds by telling her,

> Woe betide [Charles Hayter], and [Henrietta] too, when it comes to things of consequence, when they are placed in circumstances, requiring fortitude and strength of mind, if she have not resolution enough to resist idle interference in such a trifle as this. Your sister is an amiable creature, but *yours* is the character of decision and firmness, I see. If you value her conduct or happiness, infuse as much of your own spirit into her, as you can (*P*, 58-59).

In overhearing this conversation, Anne knows it to be his assessment of "her own character" (*P*, 59). Wentworth acknowledges that he is mistaken in so highly valuing "firmness of character" only after Louisa's terrible accident, when she jumps off the seawall at Lyme, despite Wentworth's urging her not to. As he waits along with all of her friends and family to hear whether she will survive her injuries, he feels responsible, since he had encouraged in her that very quality that led her to take such a foolish risk, contrary to his sound objections. Only with this event does he learn that in his assessment of "firmness of character," and thus in his reaction to Anne's decision to break off their engagement, he may have been mistaken. He learns, as Anne reflects he will, that "firmness of character," "like all other qualities of mind, should have its proportions and limits," and "that a persuadable temper might sometimes be as much in favour of happiness as a very resolute character" (*P*, 79). Austen informs us that his lesson is complete when he acknowledges that Anne's character is "fixed in his mind as perfection itself, maintaining the loveliest medium of fortitude and gentleness" (*P*, 161).

In recognizing his own character faults and mistaken judgments in the aftermath of Louisa's accident, Wentworth acknowledges his own incompleteness and neediness. Only after acknowledging this can he admit that he wronged Anne, and that he needs her love and friendship. Throughout the novel, Austen shows that his association with Anne brings out the gentleness in him that softens and perfects his spirit.[44] Perhaps most importantly, immediately after Louisa's fall, Austen depicts Wentworth as being, for once, at a loss as to what to do. "As if all of his own strength were gone," he cries out, in a "tone of despair, 'Is there no one to help me?'" (*P*, 74). Anne, of course, who has continued to love him all these years, is the very one who can help him, in this situation and in his life in general. She responds to his plea by rousing her own spirit, as it were, and, giving orders to everyone, sees that Louisa is taken care of as well as circumstances allow.

In contrast to Wentworth, Austen emphasizes Anne's "gentleness" and "modesty" (*P*, 18), as well as her "constancy" (*P*, 155-57). Just as Austen points out various flaws toward which men are more prone due to their tendency toward spirit, so too she points out various flaws toward which women are more prone due to their tendency toward gentleness and constancy. Although clearly Austen portrays the character of Anne Elliot as being extraordinarily virtuous—superior even to Wentworth, at least at the time that the action of the novel begins—even Anne is not without any flaw. Anne's flaw is, in a sense, a lack of sufficient spirit, which is, in a sense, the opposite of Wentworth's. While Wentworth fails to sufficiently acknowledge the role of chance in his life, believing himself able to determine his own future, Anne tends to believe that her chances have already passed her by, and that there is virtually nothing she can do to bring love back into her life again.

In the years since Anne's parting with Wentworth, although she continues to seek the fulfillment that comes through a life of virtuous attachment to others, in which she can at least "be useful," she does not entertain much hope of ever again loving and being loved as she was during her brief engagement to Wentworth. This lack of hope, Austen subtly suggests, is a fault. However, just as Wentworth begins to understand his faults through associating again with Anne, so too she begins to understand hers in associating with him. As each gains in self-knowledge, each becomes better able to correct his or her respective flaws.[45] Even though she believes that Wentworth's love is lost to her forever, Anne's association with him reminds her of what it is to love and be loved, and this reanimates her. Just as Wentworth's gentleness comes to the fore more and more by associating with Anne, so too Anne's spirit comes to the fore more and more by associating with Wentworth. We see this in her more bold attempts to communicate her enduring love to Wentworth in speech and in deed, as in her statement that she is "not yet so much changed" (*P*, 150), and her attempt at the concert in Bath to be closer to Wentworth by moving to the end of the bench (*P*, 126).

Austen suggests that in their marriage, Wentworth's characteristic spirit will be balanced with Anne's characteristic gentleness, and vice versa. The Crofts' marriage, Austen hints, will serve as a kind of model in this regard. While Admiral Croft and Mrs. Croft each exhibit the distinctively male and female qualities Austen identifies, each also exhibits something of the qualities more generally attributed to the other sex. For example, Admiral Croft, exhibiting his greater spirit, drives them about in their carriage in a rather daring way, but, when appropriate, Mrs. Croft instructs him on how to drive, and, exhibiting her own spirit, even goes so far as to "coolly give the reins a better direction herself," by taking them into her own hands (*P*, 62).[46] In witnessing their style of driving, Anne considers it to be "no bad representation of the general guidance of their affairs."

Near the end of the novel, Austen explicitly addresses the issue of the differences between men and women in regard to constancy. Captain Harville, distressed that his friend, Captain Benwick, has become engaged to Louisa Musgrove so soon after his former fiancé's (Harville's sister Fanny's) death, begins a conversation with Anne concerning the respective constancy of men and women. While Anne's arguments suggest that Austen attributes greater constancy to women than to men, it is unclear as to whether she believes that this difference is due to nature or to circumstance, or perhaps to some combination of the two. Despite the fact that the conversation is triggered by the seeming inconstancy of a man, i.e., Benwick, Harville claims that men exhibit greater constancy than do women, and he maintains that this difference is due to nature rather than circumstance. Anne claims that in fact women are more constant, but she provides two different, seemingly contradictory arguments to account for this difference.

She first argues that women's greater constancy is due to their circumstance in life, that it is "our fate" to be more constant, "rather than our merit" (*P*, 155). That is, the fact that women lead more narrow and constrained lives, rather than any difference in their nature, accounts for women's greater constancy. Since women, Anne states, must remain "at home, quiet, confined," they are preyed upon by their "feelings" (*P*, 155). By contrast, men "are forced on exertion," having "a profession, pursuits, business of some sort or other," to take them "back into the world immediately, and continual occupation and change soon weaken impressions" (*P*, 155). If Austen believes this argument to be true, then of course she is suggesting that women's greater constancy could be altered by their becoming involved in pursuits outside of the domestic realm. That is, if they had professions or business pursuits, as men do, they could more readily overcome their attachments. At this point, Austen is silent as to whether she believes this change would be beneficial to women. However, the next line of argument Anne presents suggests that Austen doubts whether such change would be beneficial to women. Perhaps more accurately, through Anne's next argument, Austen suggests that widening the sphere of women's activities, however many advantages it might bring, would also bring disadvantages to women.

In her next argument, Anne claims that it is in fact nature, rather than circumstance, that accounts for the differences in men's and women's constancy. While men's attachments may be, as Harville claims, "more robust" than women's, women's attachments, Anne responds, are "the most tender" and "longer-lived" (*P*, 155). While acknowledging that a change of circumstances— e.g., having some type of profession outside the home—may well have a diminishing effect on both men's and women's constancy, Anne nevertheless states that even if such change were to occur, women still would remain more constant, given their nature. "It would be too hard indeed," Anne tells Harville, if, in addition to all of the difficulties men face in their professions, "women's feelings were to be added to all this" (*P*, 155). If Austen believes this argument to be true, then, as previously stated, she suggests that if women were to take on the tasks currently reserved for men, women would not necessarily become more fulfilled in life, but rather face even more difficulties.[47]

In considering this argument, it seems that Austen supports some type of division of labor between men and women, with women's activities centered in the domestic sphere and men's activities centered in professions of some sort. Yet Austen does not thereby argue that men's and women's duties and activities are to be wholly different. While Wentworth will return to his naval career, Austen takes care to show that his greatest source of happiness will come through his domestic life with Anne.[48] Similarly, while Anne's activities will center around fulfilling the duties of wife, and probably mother, she will go to sea with her husband. Thus she will have new opportunities to widen her experience of the world and improve her mind through more extensive travel with her husband.[49]

For Austen, as for Aristotle, happiness comes through a life of virtue within the context of the shared life of true friends. In illustrating the differences between men and women, Austen shows that, although these differences may be sources of contention and misunderstanding, they are also grounds for mutual admiration and attachment. Her presentation of the relationship between Anne and Wentworth indicates her belief that it is within the context of marital friendship that men and women, given their natural complementarity, may best perfect their capacity for prudence and ethical virtue, and thereby achieve happiness.

Notes

I wish to thank the Lynde and Harry Bradley Foundation for a generous grant that enabled me to complete this paper.

1. Elayne Rapping discusses this trend in "The Jane Austen Thing," *The Progressive* 60 (July 1996): 37-38.

2. Rapping, "The Jane Austen Thing," 38. For a similar argument, see Susan Lee, "A Tale of Two Movies," *Forbes* 158 (November 4, 1996): 391, who contrasts the films based on Austen's novels with the film *The First Wives Club*. Lee maintains that Austen's stories emphasize polite manners and refined language in a hypocritical way, disguising the "back-stabbing," "betrayal," and "humble marriages" so common in her day. Regarding the main female characters, Lee states that "the quiet acceptance required of Austen's heroines is rather repellent."

3. Rapping, "The Jane Austen Thing," 38.

4. Rapping, "The Jane Austen Thing," 38.

5. Some notable supporters of this line of interpretation are Marilyn Butler, *Jane Austen and the War of Ideas*, 2nd ed. (Oxford: Clarendon Press, 1987); Alistair M. Duckworth, *The Improvement of the Estate* (Baltimore: Johns Hopkins University Press); and Jane Nardin, *Those Elegant Decorums: The Concept of Propriety in Jane Austen's Novels* (Albany: State University of New York Press, 1973).

6. Some notable supporters of this line of interpretation are Claudia Johnson, *Jane Austen: Women, Politics and the Novel* (Chicago: University of Chicago Press, 1988); Marvin Mudrik, *Jane Austen: Irony as Defense and Discovery* (Princeton: Princeton University Press, 1952); and Alison G. Sulloway, *Jane Austen and the Province of Womanhood* (Philadelphia: University of Pennsylvania Press, 1989).

7. Evidence of the acceptance of this belief is revealed in the fact that critics of Austen's works commonly center their analysis on what they see as the characters' power struggles and conflicts of will, often describing how various characters strive to "construct" their identity or "self." Among those who see Austen as defending individual happiness, see Harold Bloom, "Introduction," *Modern Critical Views: Jane Austen*, ed. Harold Bloom (New York: Chelsea House Publishers, 1986), and Johnson, *Jane Austen: Women, Politics and the Novel*. Among those who see Austen as defending conventional morality, see Duckworth; Mary Poovey, *The Proper Lady and the Woman Writer: Ideology as Style in the Works of Mary Wollstonecraft, Mary Shelley, and Jane Austen* (Chicago: University of Chicago Press, 1984); and Lionel Trilling, *The Opposing Self* (New York: Viking Press, 1955). For an argument that explicitly links Austen's novels with Hobbes's philosophy, see Avrom Fleishman, *A Reading of Mansfield Park* (Minneapolis: University of Minnesota Press, 1967), 80, who states that for Austen, as for Hobbes, "society is permanent organized hostility" that is "carried on by each against all," such that "for better or worse it is the only permanence we can attain."

8. Poovey and Johnson, for example, though they evaluate Austen's compatibility with feminist claims quite differently, nevertheless agree that Austen's novels focus on conflicts between "female power" or "autonomy" and "male oppression" or "patriarchalism."

9. This is the position of Mary Poovey. It is also the position that Butler generally takes. See especially Butler, *Jane Austen and the War of Ideas*, 298, where, in commenting on Austen's "conservative morality," she questions Austen's modern relevance and even asks whether we are "right to call her a great novelist at all."

10. This is the position of Johnson and of Mary Evans, *Jane Austen and the State* (London: Tavistock Publications, 1987).

11. Anne C. Ruderman, *The Pleasures of Virtue: Political Thought in the Novels of Jane Austen* (Lanham, MD: Rowman & Littlefield, 1995). While this claim that Austen's understanding of human nature and human happiness is in many respects "Aristotelian" is not widely accepted, it is not something new. Archbishop Richard Whateley, in a review of *Persuasion* and *Northanger Abbey* published in the early nineteenth century, *Quarterly Review* 24 (1821): 352-75, points to a number of connections between Austen's and Aristotle's views of morality, prudence, and human nature. He states explicitly that "we know not whether Miss Austen ever had access to the precepts of Aristotle, but there are few, if any, writers of fiction who have illustrated them more successfully" (360). Like Whateley, Ruderman acknowledges that there is no evidence suggesting Austen had any direct exposure to Aristotle's writings. However, Gilbert Ryle, in "Jane Austen and the Moralists," in *Critical Essays on Jane Austen*, ed. B. C. Southam (London: Routledge & Kegan Paul, 1968), argues that Austen very likely had a kind of indirect exposure to Aristotelian philosophy, through reading the works of Lord Shaftesbury. He remarks that "Shaftesbury had opened a window through which a relatively few people in the eighteenth century inhaled some air with Aristotelian oxygen in it. Jane Austen had sniffed this oxygen" (122).

12. Ruderman claims that Austen's and Aristotle's outlooks on human nature and happiness are in many respects similar, though certainly not identical, insofar as Austen, accepting certain Christian beliefs, tends to find the happiness available in this life to be

in some respects inevitably limited or incomplete. As Ruderman states, "[Anne Elliot's] virtue makes her more completely happy. Nonetheless, Austen seems ultimately to think that the perfection or completeness aimed at by virtue is not available in this life. Although the novels are generally quite reticent about religion, certain topics—such as the need for good luck or hope or a kind of humility—show that a religious belief underlies them" (Ruderman, *The Pleasures of Virtue*, 122). In considering some lines from a prayer written by Austen, we notice support for Ruderman's assessment: "Give us grace to endeavour after a truly Christian spirit to seek to attain that temper of forbearance and patience of which our blessed saviour has set us the highest example; and which, *while it prepares us for the spiritual happiness of the life to come, will secure to us the best enjoyment of what this world can give*" (*The Works of Jane Austen*, vol. VI, *Minor Works*, ed. R. W. Chapman [Oxford: Oxford University Press, 1988], 456, emphasis added).

13. This argument was first suggested by Virginia Woolf, *The Common Reader* (New York: Harcourt, Brace 1925), 204, who writes that in *Persuasion*, Austen was "beginning to discover that the world is larger, more mysterious, and more romantic than she had supposed." The argument is more fully expressed and refined by Nina Auerbach, "O Brave New World: Evolution and Revolution in *Persuasion*," *ELH* 39 (1972): 112-28, reprinted in *Romantic Imprisonment*, ed. Nina Auerbach (New York: Columbia University Press, 1985). See also Butler, *Jane Austen and the War of Ideas*, who maintains that in this novel alone Austen struggles, and ultimately fails, "to integrate the novel's two planes of reality": one plane supporting "inward interest" or "subjectivism" (i.e., individual happiness or the "self") and one plane supporting "objective existence" or "the old ethical certainties" (i.e., conventional morality or "society"). For two excellent though quite different rebuttals of this argument that *Persuasion* is significantly different in outlook from Austen's other novels, see Johnson, *Jane Austen*, 144-48, and Ruderman, *The Pleasures of Virtue*, 60-81.

14. *Eudaimonia* is generally rendered as "happiness," despite the fact that "happiness" can connote a feeling, which may be fleeting. For Aristotle, however, *eudaimonia* is the highest good that human beings may achieve, and it is an enduring good. He associates *eudaimonia* with "living well" and "doing well."

15. Aristotle, *Nicomachean Ethics* (1098b23-29). All references to Aristotle's writings are to the *Nicomachean Ethics*, hereafter referred to as *NE* unless otherwise noted. Translations of the *NE* in this essay are for the most part those of Hippocrates G. Apostle, trans., *Aristotle's Nicomachean Ethics* (Grinnel, IA: Peripatetic Press, 1984), although in some instances I make alterations.

16. Aristotle twice cites the fate of Priam, the king of Troy whose city was eventually destroyed by the Greeks during the legendary Trojan War, as an example of the most dramatic reversal of fortune (*NE*, 1096a1 and 1100a5-9).

17. All references to *Persuasion* in this essay, and cited hereafter as *P*, are to the Norton Critical Edition, ed. Patricia Meyer Spacks (New York: Norton, 1995).

18. It is important to note that Austen would agree with Aristotle that, had the Harvilles been utterly destitute—e.g., unable to afford a home or enough food—they certainly could not be happy. But given that they possess at least the minimum degree of wealth necessary to support themselves, happiness is possible for them, insofar as they live a life of virtue, which Austen takes care to show.

19. For example, developing the virtue of good temper requires that a person refrain from engaging in violent action despite his anger, while developing the virtue of courage

requires that a person act despite her fear.

20. Aristotle introduces the subject of virtue by distinguishing between ethical and intellectual virtue, each of which corresponds to the proper development of one "part" or "aspect" of the soul: the "desiring part" of the soul, which "has reason in the sense that it obeys reason," and the "rational part" of the soul, which "has reason in the sense that it engages in thinking" (*NE*, 1098a4-5). Despite making this distinction between ethical and intellectual virtue, however, Aristotle eventually explains that the development of the ethical virtues requires, along with habituation, a kind of knowledge or intelligence, to which he refers as prudence.

21. This becomes especially clear in Aristotle's discussion of the difference between prudence and "cleverness" (*NE*, 1144a23-37). While cleverness is a kind of knowledge or intelligence that very much resembles prudence, it falls short of prudence. Cleverness involves knowing how to secure whatever ends one wishes, but prudence entails knowing and ascribing to the proper human end.

22. Actually, Aristotle states that this is a "nameless" virtue that "resembles friendship most of all" (*NE*, 1126b19-20). Translators generally have deemed the virtue "friendliness."

23. See note 21.

24. The word is *megalopsychia*, which is rendered variously as "pride," "magnanimity," "high-mindedness," "dignity," or, most literally, "greatness of soul."

25. For example, after learning that Captain Wentworth, her former fiancé, will be coming to visit his sister and brother-in-law, Colonel and Mrs. Croft, Anne fears that their former relationship may become a matter of public knowledge. But as she considers this possibility, she concludes that it is unlikely to happen, given that "the pride of some," i.e., of her father and elder sister, will make them unlikely to disclose it, while "the delicacy of [another]," i.e., Lady Russell, will make her unlikely to disclose it. That is, Sir Walter and Elizabeth will keep quiet out of a selfish concern that no connection between their family and Captain Wentworth, whom they consider beneath them, be known, while Lady Russell will keep quiet because of her concern for Anne's feelings.

26. Austen's line of reasoning is similar to Aristotle's. While praising "pride" as a virtue, Aristotle indicates that it may become a vice if it is not balanced with other virtues. In particular, Aristotle questions the justice of proud persons, who "remember the good deeds they have done, but not those they have received" (*NE*, 1124b12-13), as well as their capacity for friendship (*NE*, 1124b31-25a1).

27. Austen uses "pride" in a similar way in her other novels. For example, in *Pride and Prejudice*, ed. Donald Gray (New York: Norton, 1993), Elizabeth Bennet at first is critical of Mr. Darcy for being proud, which is associated with his being "above his company and above being pleased" (8). However, her friend Charlotte Lucas defends Mr. Darcy's pride, remarking that, "One cannot wonder that so very fine a young man, with family, fortune, every thing in his favour, should think highly of himself. If I may so express it, he has a *right* to be proud." Elizabeth responds by remarking that pride goes too far if it leads one to be unconcerned with the feelings of others. She states, "I could easily forgive *his* pride, if he had not mortified *mine*" (14). Eventually, however, upon getting to know him well, Elizabeth concludes that he has "no improper pride" (242).

28. This seems to be related to the fact that Anne is prudent as well as proud. Aristotle states that pride "is the crown, as it were, of the [ethical] virtues, for it makes them greater and it cannot exist without them," (*NE*, 1124a1-2). One would be legitimately proud, as is Anne, only if one practiced ethical virtue in general, which requires self-knowledge and prudence.

29. Similarly, in his discussion of pride, Aristotle states twice that vain people are "fools," in that they "do not know themselves" (*NE*, 1123b4 and 1125a28-29).

30. Near the end of the novel, Austen again mentions his extravagance, referring to him as "a foolish, spendthrift baronet, who had not had the principle or sense enough to maintain himself in the situation in which Providence placed him" (*P*, 165).

31. There are, according to Aristotle, at least two types of extravagance. One type is characteristic of those who exceed in spending their wealth out of a desire to please or see to the needs of others. That is, such persons are like the truly generous person in that they seek to give to others rather than to take for themselves. This type of extravagance, Aristotle maintains, is more easily curable than another type, which in fact is more like stinginess. Such extravagance is characteristic of those who, like Sir Walter, upon exhausting their wealth, seek to replenish it by taking more from the wrong sources. Such persons are prone to giving wrongly as well, giving nothing to those who are virtuous, but enriching those who flatter them or give them pleasure in some way, thereby exhibiting lack of self-control as well as extravagance (*NE*, 1121a31-b10). Sir Walter exhibits precisely these tendencies in his behavior toward his own daughter Anne, whose virtue prevents her from speaking and behaving in ways that please him, compared with his behavior toward Mrs. Clay, whose speech and behavior are designed to flatter him.

32. As Aristotle states, while extravagance is a particular vice, distinct from others, it is often connected with certain other vices as well. This is reflected in the fact that "we sometimes apply the term 'extravagance' to a combination of vices, for we call 'extravagant' also the incontinent and those who spend money due to lack of self-control. [Such persons are] thought to be the worst, for they have many vices at the same time" (*NE*, 1119b31-34).

33. Austen depicts the efforts of the Harvilles to share all that they have with Captain Wentworth and his friends, despite their relative poverty, as an expression of the highest form of generosity. As Aristotle argues, generosity is not determined by the amount that one gives to others, but by the extent to which one is willing to give whatever one has. As he states, "Generosity is attributed to a man by taking into account the extent of his wealth. For generosity depends not on the quantity of what is given but on the disposition of the giver. . . . Accordingly, it is possible that a man who gives less is more generous, if he has less to give" (*NE*, 1120b7-11).

34. Aristotle refers to this form of friendship in various ways. For example, he calls it "friendship of those who are good and alike in virtue" (*NE*, 11567-8 and 1158b8-10), and "friendship of the good," (*NE*, 1157a21, b25, and 58a1). On two occasions Aristotle refers to this type of friendship as "perfect" (*NE*, 1156b7 and b34). Furthermore, he calls it "friendship in the primary and principal sense" (*NE*, 1157a31).

35. See especially *NE*, 1166a1-66b29 and 1169b3-70b19.

36. Aristotle also defines "concord" as one of the fundamental marks of virtue friendship, which refers to a similarity of practical judgment. That is, for virtue friendship to exist, the friends must have similar thoughts as to how human beings should act in various situations, i.e., in regard to exercise of the ethical virtues (*NE*, 1167a21-67b16).

37. Contrary to the assessment of some critics, it is not Anne's "romantic" nature that accounts for her inwardness and rather melancholy attitude, but her lack of the deepest friendship. While she does have a true friend in Lady Russell, Anne cannot totally confide in her, since she has come to believe that it was a mistake to break off her engagement to Wentworth.

38. While traditionally Aristotle's views on women have been viewed as being sexist, even misogynist, there is a growing group of scholars who have challenged this view, arguing that Aristotle recognizes men and women as being fundamentally equal in

their respective capacities for virtue, though somewhat different in their characteristic expressions of virtue. See Darrell Dobbs, "Family Matters: Aristotle's Appreciation of Women and the Plural Structure of Society," *American Political Science Review* 90 (March 1996): 74-89; Harold L. Levy, "Does Aristotle Exclude Women from Politics?" *Review of Politics* 52 (1990): 397-416; Mary P. Nichols, *Citizens and Statesmen: A Study of Aristotle's Politics* (Savage, MD: Rowman & Littlefield, 1992), and "Toward a New—and Old—Feminism for Liberal Democracy," in *Finding a New Feminism: Rethinking the Woman Question for Liberal Democracy*, ed. Pamela Grande Jensen (Savage, MD: Rowman & Littlefield, 1996); Stephen G. Salkever, *Finding the Mean: Theory and Practice in Aristotelian Political Philosophy* (Princeton: Princeton University Press, 1990); Arlene Saxonhouse, *Women in the History of Political Thought: Ancient Greece to Machiavelli* (New York: Praeger, 1985); and Daryl Tress, "The Metaphysical Science of Aristotle's *Generation of Animals* and Its Feminist Critics," *Review of Metaphysics* 46 (December 1992): 307-41.

39. Paralleling Aristotle's assessment, Austen presents an array of male and female characters who possess various virtues and as well as vices. For example, both Sir Walter and Elizabeth are vain and extravagant, both Mrs. Clay and Mr. Elliot are obsequious and boastful, and both Anne and Captain Wentworth are proud and truthful. Moreover, Austen clearly maintains that men and women are equally intelligent, as in the cases of Anne and Wentworth, and equally able to misuse their intelligence, as in the cases of Mrs. Clay and Mr. Elliot.

40. Aristotle states, "There is division of labor from the very beginning, and those of a husband are different from those of a wife, and so by contributing to the common stock whatever is proper to each they supply each other's needs" (*NE*, 1162a 222-24).

41. As Apostle argues in regards to Aristotle's remarks here, "Men live together not only for the sake of living, which includes the necessary pleasures or pleasures of the senses, but also for the sake of living well, which includes the pleasures of the intellect also" (Apostle, *Aristotle's Nichomachean Ethics*, 329, note 6).

42. For example, in explaining how Anne and Wentworth first came to fall in love, she refers to their respective good looks and their recognition of each other's physical attractions (*P*, 18). However, she maintains that, for virtuous persons like Anne and Wentworth, the aspect of physical attraction in romantic love is always subordinate to regard for the character of the beloved. For example, Anne certainly finds Mr. Elliot to be very handsome, but her inability to admire his character prevents her from growing to love him, despite his obvious wish to marry her and thereby establish her as mistress of her beloved Kellynch Hall (*P*, 70, 94, and 105-106). Similarly, Wentworth finds Louisa Musgrove attractive, but when he finally recognizes her true character, he knows he never could love her.

43. Austen's view of the differences between men and women parallels Aristotle's. While acknowledging that men and women are equal in their capacity for intelligence, he associates men with greater "spiritedness" and courage, and women with greater self-control and modesty (*Politics* 1177b21-25).

44. For example, while Anne attempts to care for her older nephew who has broken his arm, Wentworth removes the younger nephew from clinging to Anne's neck (*P*, 54); noticing that Anne is weary after a long walk, Wentworth asks the Crofts to take her home in their carriage (*P*, 61); thinking that Anne must walk home in the rain, Wentworth offers her his umbrella (*P*, 117).

45. Austen's depiction of the way in which Anne and Wentworth's association assists in the perfection of their respective characters is in agreement with Aristotle's view. As he states, "The friendship of good persons . . . is good, and it grows as their

companionship continues; and they seem to become even better persons by acting together and correcting each other, for each models himself on what he approves of the other" (*NE*, 1172a11-14).

46. Similarly, Mrs. Croft brings out Admiral Croft's gentleness, as is suggested in the scene near the end of the novel where Anne meets Admiral Croft on a street in Bath, and enters into conversation with him regarding Wentworth's reaction to Louisa's engagement to Benwick. In his characteristic way, Admiral Croft guides the direction of both their walk and their conversation. Anne, though she wishes to change his direction, reflects that she cannot, since, not being his wife Mrs. Croft, the only person for whom Admiral Croft will always curb his spirit, "she must let him have his own way" (*P*, 113).

47. For a similar argument, see Ruderman, *The Pleasures of Virtue*, 150.

48. Austen ends the novel by praising the naval profession as being even "more distinguished in its *domestic* virtues than its national importance" (*P*, 168, emphasis added).

49. It is significant that a chief benefit of marriage for many of Austen's heroines is more extensive travel and knowledge of the world. When Elizabeth Bennet, in *Pride and Prejudice*, finally realizes that she loves Mr. Darcy, she reflects that, in marrying him, she would benefit from "his judgment, information, and knowledge of the world," (199). In *Emma*, ed. Stephen M. Parrish (New York: Norton, 1993), 312, Emma Woodhouse, who has been confined to life in the small village of Highbury all her life, is to spend her honeymoon with Mr. Knightley by traveling to the sea.

Chapter 13

Evolving Conceptions of Women in Modern Liberal Culture: From Hegel to Mill

Nicholas Capaldi

The writings of Hegel and John Stuart Mill on women are important for two reasons. First, both authors contribute significantly to the clarification of the meaning of autonomy for women in liberal culture. Second, both authors use the discussion of the evolving relation between men and women to solve the key problem within liberal culture, namely, reconciling individual autonomy with a communal good.[1]

Liberal Culture versus Liberal Social Theory

It is necessary to distinguish between liberal culture and liberal social theory.[2] By *liberal culture* is meant the culture that emerged in Western Europe in the post-Renaissance and post-Reformation period and eventually spread to the Western Hemisphere and beyond. The most distinctive institutions of liberal culture are personal autonomy, individual rights, the rule of law, a republican (or limited) form of government, a free market economy, and toleration. By *liberal social theory* is meant those attempts to understand, to justify, or to resolve tensions within the practices of liberal culture.[3]

There are two sets of disputes that must be carefully separated: (1) whose understanding of liberal culture is correct and (2) whether liberal culture is a good thing. At the moment we are concerned with the former question. Failure to make the distinction between liberal culture and liberal social theory leads to a misunderstanding of key cultural practices. Liberal culture was not a conscious construct. Hobbes did not invent individuality; Locke did not invent representative government; Smith did not invent the free market economy; Hume did not invent the rule of law, and so on. What these and other social thinkers (including but not limited to Machiavelli, Montesquieu, Rousseau, Kant, Constant, and Marx) do is to call attention to a set of new and interrelated social practices that have superseded the practices of the ancient and medieval world, most especially feudalism. In addition to calling attention to such practices, the social thinkers attempt to explicate the implicit norms within the practices in order to extract from previous practice a set of norms that can be used reflectively to guide future practice.

The accuracy of the respective explications varies with the perspicacity of the individual thinker. Not everyone gets everything right, nor does any one theorist see the whole ensemble with total clarity. We should not be surprised by this. Nor should we attribute dubious motives or hidden agendas to their lacunae.

There are three factors that help to explain the difficulties in explicating the norms embedded in cultural practices. To begin with, cultural practices are historical entities—that is, they emerge over time and not full blown. A certain amount of time must pass before one can discern the shape of a practice with clarity.[4] In addition, individual social practices form part of a network of practices and therefore can rarely be understood apart from other evolving practices.

There is a second factor. In their endeavor to conceptualize these emerging practices (and to hold on to the notion of some kind of universal truth embedded in those practices), early modern thinkers continued to appeal to classical intellectual models that for the most part invoked allegedly timeless entities (reason, nature, revelation, a covenant, etc.). That is, they poured the wine of the newly emerging practices into old conceptual bottles. The limitation of this approach is that in attempting to articulate the new in timeless terms one is always in danger of hypostatizing accidental features. One example of this is the tacit identification in Locke of property with real estate. This identification of property with land is part of the feudal legacy but hardly a useful model for an economy of finance capital. The richest and most complete explications of liberal culture had to await social thinkers who combined the search for universals with a constitutive account of historical development. It is no accident that such accounts occur in Hegel and Mill.

Finally, in a post-Wittgensteinian and post-Oakeshottean world, we have come to take for granted that it is not possible to conceptualize fully the pre-theoretical world of cultural practice including theoretical activity itself.[5] The norms implicit in such practices do not form a neat axiomatic structure from which all their future permutations and applications can be deduced in algorhythmic fashion. We discover in time what our practices mean. Any adequate account of cultural practice requires not only the recognition of a larger historical context but an account of how individuals come in time to grasp the norms. Again, it is no accident that Hegel and Mill play key roles in the explication of liberal culture, because in addition to the macro sense of historical development both were concerned with the phenomenological development of the recognition of norms in the lives of individuals. Mill's *Autobiography* is not an account of the intimate details of his life as much as it is an account of the phenomenological development in the individual of the grasp of the larger cultural context.

Key Concepts in Liberal Culture: Autonomy, Private Property, and Representative Government

Liberal culture is a form of modernity. As such it rejects two important classical doctrines. It rejects the notion of a collective good over and above the good of the individual. It rejects as well the notion that the individual good is the fulfillment of a telos dictated by nature. What it replaces these doctrines with is the notion of autonomy. The concept of autonomy is a controversial one. As I understand it, the psychological origin of autonomy lies in the Christian doctrine of free will as enunciated by St. Augustine and revived in modern times by the Protestant Reformation, Rousseau, and Kant. Human beings cannot be understood simply as natural beings, organic or otherwise. Human beings are free to choose. This is the fundamental truth about them and in a logical sense constitutes their nature, but it is not a nature in an Aristotelian sense. Human fulfillment results from the exercise of this capacity for choice as long as the choices do not compromise or undermine that capacity itself. It is not a form of self-assertion, for the latter easily leads to the destruction of the capacity for choice. The social origin of autonomy lies in the classical doctrine that the collective good of the polis is freedom understood as self-government. Once the collective good is replaced by the individual good, then autonomy means the self-government of the individual. All this is packed into Rousseau's assertion that freedom is living a life of self-imposed rules. Personal autonomy, then, within liberal culture means self-rule. It does not mean self-assertion or self-definition.

An autonomous individual is one who accepts personal responsibility. In order to accept responsibility, one must be aware of oneself as the author of one's acts. That discovery is not a matter of introspection, for our capacity to choose is not a natural object. Nor is that capacity learned from the outside. The capacity for responsible action is learned by its exercise through self-discipline and self-control. Kant spelled out the implications of the recognition of this freedom or autonomy in his discussion of the categorical imperative.

Hegel absorbed all of this but rejected what he considered its overly abstract formulation. Hegel distinguishes between consciousness and self-consciousness. He was concerned with how we become self-conscious, specifically conscious of our freedom. Self-consciousness is neither innate (introspectively apprehended) nor externally induced. There is an aspect of consciousness, however, that we project outward, namely, the will. To be apprehended, the will must give itself content by putting itself into something outside itself. The exercise of the will is always contextual, and we do not have complete control of context. Labor is an example of how we gain insight into our own agency or subjectivity. There is a second source, namely, recognition by another conscious will. When we unite these two perspectives, we become fully self-conscious.

The moral categories and forms of social interaction and customs through which we live our lives are not natural but a product of will. But they are not the product of an arbitrary will; rather, they reflect the historical growth of the self-consciousness of freedom. History is the development toward the consciousness of freedom as expressed in the political, cultural, and religious institutions of a community. The institutions of modern liberal culture are necessarily the way they are because they represent the only way, according to Hegel, in which human wills can coherently interact.[6]

Mill attaches the same importance to autonomy. The Kantian doctrine of autonomy comes to Mill via Humboldt.[7] As Mill states in his essay *On Liberty*, he is utilitarian who advocates utility in the largest sense, grounded on the permanent interests of man as a progressive being.[8] The most important ingredient in our happiness is choosing for ourselves. This is what is meant by individuality.

This conception of personal autonomy is the metaphysical, epistemological, and axiological ground of liberal culture. It is in terms of autonomy that economics and politics are to be understood, that intermediate institutions such as the family are to be understood, and even personal relationships reoriented.

The two important macro implications of personal autonomy are economic and political. If personal autonomy requires that individuals acquire as much responsibility and control as possible over their lives, then this requires the protection and extension of private property. Private property, of course, is a necessary condition for a free market economy. Locke, Hume, Kant, and Hegel all stressed the extent to which the ownership of private property was instrumental in the human conception of self-worth. Those individuals either unable or unwilling to acquire private property through self-discipline lacked the requisite qualities of citizenship and were not entitled to vote. Such individuals remained dependent upon others.

Human fulfillment comes from personal endeavor and not political activity. The origin of this belief lies in St. Augustine's doctrine of the two cities that dedivinized the state. The purpose of government is negative, that is, to discourage evil and not to promote good. Modern liberal culture embodies this belief along with the positive function of providing the legal conditions for the pursuit of fulfillment in one's private life. This is the message of Constant's essay on the difference between ancient and modern liberty. Even the positive function is construed as an extension of the negative role in protecting individual rights.

Rights, so understood, are absolute, do not conflict, and are possessed only by individual human beings. Rights are morally absolute or fundamental because they are derived from human nature and God (or later the categorical imperative) and as such cannot be overridden; the role of these rights is to protect the human capacity to choose. Finally, such rights impose only duties of noninterference. The purpose of political activity is both to ensure that government provides those conditions of the rule of law in the form of a constitution with an enumeration of individual rights and to check the abuse of governmental power. Individual participation in politics is designed to protect rights and not to create new privileges. The purpose of political activity then is to limit the government to its rightful role.

The logic of this argument is as follows:

1. Autonomous individuals require private property and limited government.

2. Individuals cannot be made autonomous from the outside in. Social and legal conditions can only permit the growth of internal self-discipline, not cause it.

3. Therefore, one cannot argue for political participation as a means to acquire private property (i.e., redistribution of wealth).

4. As a free market economy and other social conditions permit more individuals to become economically self-sufficient (in the sense of controlling one's own finances), the franchise or right to vote is extended.

5. Women will receive the franchise only after their right to own their own property is recognized.

6. Changes in the conception of the family will lead to the recognition of the right of women to own their own property. These changes will lead, in time, to the right to vote. It will be Hegel who calls attention to the changing conception of the family. It will be Mill who presses the case for economic and political independence.

The remainder of this section focuses on the case of how economic independence leads to political independence, and the next section indicates the social circumstances that fostered economic independence. James Mill, the father of John Stuart Mill, wrote a highly influential essay entitled "Government" for the *Encyclopaedia Britannica* in 1820. James Mill maintained that the interests of children and women were included within the interests of their fathers or husbands and therefore did not require representation.

> If one man has power over others placed in his hands, he will make use of it for an evil purpose—for the purpose of rendering those other men the abject instruments of his will. . . . It is very evident that, if the community itself were the choosing body, the interest of the community and that of the choosing body [representative body] would be the same. . . . One thing is pretty clear, that all those individuals whose interests are indisputably included in those of other individuals may be struck off without inconvenience. In this light may be viewed all children, up to a certain age, whose interests are involved in those of their parents. In this light, also, women may be regarded, the interest of almost all of whom is involved either in that of their fathers or in that of their husbands.

There is an evident inconsistency here as Thomas Babington Macaulay pointed out in his critique of James Mill's essay. Macaulay asks James Mill why, if a monarch cannot always share the interests of his subjects, should we assume that a father or husband always shares the interests of his wife or daughter? Without adducing one fact, without taking the trouble to perplex the question by one sophism, Mill placidly dogmatizes away the interests of one half of the human race.[9]

It was precisely this Macaulay critique of his father that John Stuart Mill cites in his *Autobiography*[10] as leading him to question his father's position.

> It was my father's opinions which gave the distinguishing character to the Benthamic or utilitarian propagandism of that time. . . . But indeed there was by no means complete unanimity among any portion of us, nor had any of us adopted implicitly all my father's opinions. For example, although his Essay on Government was regarded probably by all of us as a masterpiece of political wisdom, our adhesion by no means extended to the paragraph of it, in which he maintains that women may consistently with good government, be excluded from the suffrage, because their interest is the same with that of men. From this

doctrine, I, and all of those who formed my chosen associates, most positively dissented. It is due to my father to say that he denied having intended to affirm that women *should* be excluded, any more than men under the age of forty, concerning whom he maintained, in the very next paragraph, an exactly similar thesis. He was, as he truly said, not discussing whether the suffrage had better be restricted, but only (assuming that it is to be restricted) what is the utmost limit of restriction, which does not necessarily involve a sacrifice of the securities of good government. But I thought then, as I have always thought since, that the opinion which he acknowledged, no less than that which he disclaimed, is as great an error as any of those against which the Essay was directed; that the interest of women is included in that of men exactly as much and no more, as the interest of subjects is included in that of kings; and that every reason which exists for giving the suffrage to anybody, demands that it should not be withheld from women. This was also the general opinion of the younger proselytes; and it is pleasant to be able to say that Mr. Bentham, on this important point, was wholly on our side.[11]

One specific area in which coincidence of interest cannot always be assumed concerned property. It was still the case in Mill's time that married women could not own property or have a right to the proceeds of their labor. Even Mill's conservative critics agreed that this was an unacceptable anomaly. It is easy to see why. Not only did it violate the notion that an autonomous person is entitled to the fruits of her labor (Locke's argument), but fathers were rightly concerned to see inheritances given to daughters passing into the hands of other men. Not long after the publication of Mill's essay "The Subjection of Women," the Married Women's Property Bill was passed, giving women the legal right to own property.[12] In due course this was followed by the granting of the franchise to women.

One other aspect of the importance of private property in a free market economy for the emancipation of women deserves mention. The free market economy is not only one of the spheres in which individuals seek fulfillment through the exercise of their autonomy, but it is the market economy that expands the possibilities for becoming autonomous. During his tenure in Parliament, Mill opposed a bill intended to limit the number of hours that women could be employed. The backers of the bill intended it to protect women and children from exploitation. Mill, on the other hand, pointed out that the opportunity to work and to accumulate capital was one of the ways in which women could become autonomous. Limiting the amount of time they could work, while well intentioned, was in the end paternalistic and counterproductive to their opportunity to become autonomous. We might add the following insight as well. Whereas the feudal economy constrained thought in terms of a fixed economic pie, the market economy of finance capital thinks in terms of an expanding pie. In an expanding economy, women do not enter the marketplace to take jobs from men but contribute to an ever-expanding context in which opportunities are maximized for everyone.

The Communion of Autonomous Individuals: Romantic Love and the Family in Hegel

In this section I will address the transformation in family life made possible by the concept of autonomy. To be autonomous, for Hegel, is to be self-governing or self-limiting. To be self-governing, one needs to be self-conscious. Self-consciousness requires that our self is projected back onto ourselves, specifically through our reflection on our activity and through the recognition of others. Our greatest sense of fulfillment comes not through the acquisition of things or even control over nature but from the conscious control of ourselves exercised in that process. That fulfillment cannot be reflected back by others who themselves lack that sense. Hence, what an autonomous person needs is recognition, and what a fully autonomous person needs is the recognition of other fully autonomous persons.

This helps us to understand the importance of Hegel's discussion of the master/slave relationship. Historically, the master achieves recognition of his superior status by the willingness to risk death and the self-discipline that requires; the slave loses because of the fear of death. The master's sense of the recognition of his dignity depends upon slaves who are lacking. Hence, the master's sense of dignity is forever deficient. The master needs the slave more than the slave needs the master. To the extent that the master needs the slave, the master is not fully in control of himself. There is, then, an inherent sense of dissatisfaction with the kind of recognition available in aristocratic societies. In liberal culture, on the other hand, autonomous individuals achieve a complete sense of recognition. Such individuals demand conditions such as the rule of law that not only serve everyone's quest for dignity and recognition but also lead to an increase in the number of others who reciprocally extend the recognition of the special dignity attaching to autonomous individuals.

The relationship between two fully autonomous individuals who bring out what is best in each other is, of course, Aristotle's conception of friendship. It is precisely this kind of fulfilling relationship that men and women demand of each other in modern liberal culture. The relationship between men and women in a family can no longer be the feudal one of functional hierarchy, nor is a socially defined role of comradeship sufficient. Autonomous men and women in a liberal culture demand a form of recognition that can only come from another autonomous person.

> Love means in general the consciousness of my unity with another, so that I am not isolated on my own, but gain my self-consciousness only through renunciation of my independent existence and through knowing myself as the unity of myself with another and of the other with me.... The first moment in love is that I do not wish to be an independent person in my own right.... The second moment is that I find myself in another person, that I gain recognition in this person, who in turn gains recognition in me.... Love is both the production and the resolution of this contradiction.[13]

It is this foregoing conception of human relationships that Hegel uses to illuminate the relationship between men and women in liberal culture.

1. Neither biology nor the contingent attraction of two individuals is the essential element in marriage. What is required is the coincidence of the wills (volition) of the partners. It is the attempt to create a real and enduring community of wills. The union of the natural sexes is transformed into a *spiritual* union, into self-conscious love.[14]

2. Within the family, individuals are bonded together immediately through love and affection. Family relationships, unlike those in civil society, are emotional and altruistic, not calculating or instrumental; or, if they are, there is something wrong with the family.

3. Because, through love, individuals' wills are merged with others, rights as such—the expression of a single will in such a way as to exclude other wills—do not appear within the healthy family.

4. Marriage is not really a contract so much as an agreement to transcend contract. It is equally crude to interpret marriage as merely a civil contract, a notion that is still to be found even in Kant. On this interpretation, marriage gives contractual form to the arbitrary relations between individuals and is thus debased to a contract entitling the parties concerned to use one another.[15] Marriage differs from concubinage inasmuch as the latter is chiefly concerned with the satisfaction of the natural drive, whereas this drive is made subordinate in marriage.[16]

5. The recognition of this community of wills by friends, family, and society gives marriage its true ethical significance (hence, merely living together is not enough). The perfect manifestation of this community are children—but only if unified in love.

6. Having children is not an obstacle to marriage; it can create a greater common bond.

7. True ethical behavior involves treating others as ends in themselves, not merely as means to one's own will; in a family one needs to respect others as ends and not merely as means, and one needs a sense of community—shared ends. One without the other will not suffice.

The reader will, of course, recognize that what Hegel is describing is romantic love. Hegel did not invent or create romantic love. Nor was he the first to call attention to it, for novelists such as Jane Austen and Benjamin Constant (in *Adolphe*) had already done so. They had identified the key ingredients of a spiritual union between autonomous equals, and they had promoted the notion of marriage based upon such love as opposed to feudal patriarchy. Romantic love, as opposed to lust, chivalry, friendship, or infatuation, only comes into existence with the rise of liberal culture. It is only within liberal culture that both men and women cultivated and were encouraged to cultivate the kind of individual autonomy that permitted such a romantic relationship. Specifically, it is a form of modern friendship (similar to but different from Aristotle's classical teleological version) in which love is a way in which the will finds fulfillment in creation and re-creation with another self.

Romantic love also transforms the nature of family life in four important respects.

First, there is the rise of the nuclear family as opposed to the clan. The wife is part of the creation of a new unit and no longer belongs to her kinfolk. Two important aspects of this nuclear family are that marriage is essentially monogamous in which there is a mutual and undivided surrender[17] and that, focused as they are on their own nuclear family, children love their parents less than their parents love them.[18]

Second, a prominent function of family life is the socialization of children to become autonomous beings. Until this point in history, until the rise of liberal culture, children had not been treated as candidates for autonomy. In modern liberal cultures, the attitude of the family to its members is remarkably different: one looks very differently on a child perceived as a subject of cultivation as opposed to a child perceived as the inadvertent product of a biological process or as an object of utility. Parents do not, strictly speaking, have personal rights over their children; rather, they have obligations to educate them out of childishness and into the world of ethical culture. This requires a certain measure of authority that is indeed irresistible, but it is also limited, and forfeitable if abused. Children are free and cannot be claimed or treated as property, but they do not have the right to resist instruction in becoming free and responsible beings.

Third, marriage based upon the romantic love of autonomous individuals transforms our understanding of inheritance. Although insisting that the husband is still the head of the family, Hegel recognizes that the assets of a nuclear family do not belong to the husband/father per se. Family property is common property, so that no member of the family has particular property, although each has a right to what is held in common.[19] The purpose of inheritance is to respect the autonomy of each and every member of the family.

> That institution of the laws of inheritance which, in order to preserve the *family* and to enhance its *renown* by means of *substitutions* and *family testamentary trusts*, either favours the sons by excluding the daughters from inheritance or favours the eldest son by excluding the remaining children (or allows any other kind of inequality to arise) on the one hand infringes the principle of the freedom of property (see #62), and on the other depends on an arbitrariness which in and for itself has no right to recognition. . . . *the family as such* is the Idea which has this right [to recognition], and freedom [to dispose] of resources and equality of inheritance are much more likely than their opposites to preserve both the shape of ethics and the *families* themselves.[20]

In his discussion of inheritance, Hegel made reference to his earlier discussion of the relationship among freedom, autonomy, and property. It is worth quoting here both because it identifies why personal autonomy as the foundation of liberal culture entails that women among others should be allowed to own property and because it underscores the gradual nature of the historical process by which we come to understand what is implicit in our fundamental norms.

It must be nearly one and a half millennia since the freedom of personality began to flourish under Christianity and became a universal principle for part— if only a small part—of the human race. But it is only since yesterday, so to speak, that the freedom of property has been recognized here and there as a principle—an example from world history of the length of time which the spirit requires in order to progress in its self-consciousness, and a caution against the impatience of opinion.[21]

The fourth respect in which the romantic love of autonomous individuals as the basis of marriage transforms family life is with regard to divorce. A number of things will destroy a marriage; most important are the failure to achieve a community of wills (usually subverted by private agendas individuals bring to a marriage—i.e., not really sharing the same values or the prioritizing of those values, or seeing the partner as a means to a private agenda) and the presence of children who are allowed to resist instruction (i.e., allowed to act as if they are outside of or in opposition to the community of wills). As a consequence, divorce is permitted.

There can be no merely legal or positive bond which could keep the partners together once their dispositions and actions have become antagonistic and hostile. A third ethical authority is, however, required in order to uphold the right of marriage . . . against their mere opinion that a hostile disposition is present, and against the contingency of merely transient moods, etc., to distinguish these from total estrangement. . . . Since marriage is based only on subjective and contingent feeling, it may be dissolved. . . . Marriage certainly *ought* to be indissoluble, but this indissolubility remains no more than an *obligation*. Since, however, marriage is an ethical institution, it cannot be dissolved by the arbitrary will but only by an ethical authority, whether this be the Church or a court of law. If a total estrangement has occurred—e.g. through adultery—then even the religious authority must permit divorce.[22]

Having gone this far, one is prepared to see Hegel advocate the complete emancipation and equality of women. But this expectation is not realized. Hegel insists that (1) women achieve fulfillment only in their family role and that (2) women lack the capacity for achievement in the higher sciences, for philosophy, and certain artistic productions[23] as well as politics. When women are in charge of government, the state is in danger, for their actions are based not on the demands of universality but on contingent inclination and opinion.[24] Hegel even goes so far as to invoke Sophocles' *Antigone* in support of his claim that "Woman . . . has her substantial vocation in the family, and her ethical disposition consists in this piety."[25] The conflict between Antigone and, presumably, Cleon is represented as the opposition between the feminine and the masculine, between the ancient religious law and the law of the state:

In one of the most sublime presentations of piety—the *Antigone* of Sophocles—this quality is therefore declared to be primarily the law of woman, and it is presented as the law of emotive and subjective substantiality, of inwardness which has not yet been fully actualized . . . as the law of the ancient gods . . . and in opposition to the public law, the law of the state—an opposition of the highest order in ethics and therefore in tragedy, and one which is individualized in femininity and masculinity in the same play.[26]

There are a number of tensions in Hegel's position.[27] Our interest here lies in two of them. First, if there is a substantial difference in kind (as opposed to degree) between men and women, for it remains unclear how recognition form a woman can be sufficient for the unity required in marriage. Second, if mothers are charged with rearing children and promoting the autonomy of the latter, it again remains unclear how this can occur if there remain substantial differences in kind.

Mill and the Liberation of Women

It fell to Mill to spell out the full implications of liberal culture for women.

1. Women are as fully capable as men of achieving autonomy. The first chapter of *The Subjection of Women* argues that the current subordinate status of women is not based in nature but in historical accident. Mill does not maintain in any dogmatic or a priori fashion that all human beings are totally a product of their environment. In fact, it is important to his thesis about individuality in *On Liberty*, and as buttressed by arguments in the *Logic*,[28] that human beings are capable of molding their own character. Differences there may be, but whatever differences there are either between the sexes or among individuals are (1) a matter for empirical determination and (2) irrelevant to each individual's capacity for personal autonomy. In the third chapter he presents evidence of the accomplishments of women as an indication of what they are capable of achieving. In his correspondence he cites the achievements of Elizabeth I, thereby challenging the notion that women lack the capacity for politics (and, indirectly, the judgment to exercise the franchise).[29]

2. Women should be permitted to achieve financial autonomy. As a member of Parliament, Mill supported the Married Women's Property Bill.[30] Such bills had been introduced since 1857 but did not finally gain passage until 1870. He advocated the opening of higher education and the professions to women.

3. Women should have equality before the law and thereby gain the protection of the rule of law. The purpose of *The Subjection of Women* was to maintain the claim of women, whether in marriage or out of it, to perfect equality in all rights with the male sex.[31] This means, among other things, that women should have a right to control their own resources; that women should share the guardianship of their children as opposed to the exclusive guardianship of the husband; that women should be protected from domestic violence and have the right to refuse the last familiarity; that divorce should be permitted. As Mill pointed out, the wife's position under the common law of England is worse than that of slaves in the laws of many countries.[32]

One aspect of this notion of equality before the law deserves special mention. Between 1864 and 1869, Parliament passed the Contagious Diseases

Acts. The Acts permitted compulsory medical inspection of women suspected of being prostitutes in garrison towns. Mill objected to the Acts on the ground that they applied police powers to women but not to men.[33]

4. Mill advocated that women be given the right to vote and full political participation, most significantly during the debate of the 1867 Reform Bill. He was supported by seventy-three members of Parliament, including Bright, Disraeli, and Salisbury.[34] Mill considered this amendment by far the most important, perhaps the only really important public service he performed in the capacity of a member of Parliament.[35] This was followed by active leadership, along with Helen Taylor, in the establishment of the National Society for Women's Suffrage.

The most significant feature of the argument in *The Subjection of Women* is the claim that the autonomy of men is corrupted by the then present conception of the relationship between men and women. In a now classic restatement of the Hegelian master/slave thesis,[36] Mill maintained that there remain no legal slaves except the mistress of every house.[37] He emphasized the extent to which the relation of superiors to dependents is the nursery of such male vices as willfulness, overbearingness, unbounded self-indulgence, and a double-dyed and idealized selfishness.[38] In the end, anyone who tyrannizes another cannot achieve or retain personal autonomy. For the love of power and the love of liberty are in eternal antagonism. The desire of power over others [is a] depraving agency among mankind.[39] The future of liberal culture requires overcoming this obstacle. The moral regeneration of mankind will really commence only when the most fundamental of the social relations is placed under the rule of equal justice and when human beings learn to cultivate their strongest sympathy with an equal in rights and in cultivation.[40]

Another dimension of this is worth stressing. An autonomous man who marries a woman who is less than autonomous is stunted by the relationship, and it affects the children as well. We see this obliquely by the fact that Mill never mentioned his mother in his *Autobiography* and explained his father as follows:

> In this period of my father's life there are two things which it is impossible not to be struck with: one of them, unfortunately, a very common circumstance. . . . The first is, that in his position, with no resource but the precarious one of writing periodicals, he married and had a large family; conduct, than which nothing could be more opposed, both in point of good sense and of morality, to the opinions which, at least at a later period of life, he strenuously upheld.[41]

More important was the section Mill eliminated from the final version:

> That rarity in England, a really warm-hearted mother would in the first place have made my father a totally different being and in the second would have made the children grow up loving and being loved. But my mother with the very best intentions only knew how to pass her life in drudging for them. . . . many and indelible are the effects of this bringing up in the stunting of my moral growth.[42]

Like Hegel before him, Mill (1) recognized the centrality of the nuclear family; (2) understood that parents were responsible for initiating children into autonomous adulthood (even reminding us that one should not be a parent or teacher of the same individuals forever because of the corrupting influence on the mentor);[43] (3) was concerned with the corrupting effect of inherited wealth; in *The Principles of Political Economy* he distinguished between the right of disposing of one's own wealth (not the government confiscation of wealth) and limiting the amount that could be inherited by a single individual;[44] and (4) explained what divorce means in a community of autonomous individuals.

In November 1855, his opinion on divorce was that though any relaxation of the irrevocability of marriage would be an improvement, nothing ought to be ultimately rested in, short of entire freedom on both sides to dissolve this like any other partnership.[45] But in *On Liberty* he rejected Humboldt's view that marriage is a contract that could be terminated by the declared will of either party to dissolve it. Marriage created a new series of moral obligations that may possibly be overruled, but cannot be ignored.[46] In 1870, he reiterated that there could be no proper divorce law until women have an equal voice in making it; he went on to deny having advocated dissolution at the will of either party.[47]

Personal autonomy can never mean the overriding of someone else's autonomy and always carries some degree of responsibility.

The Basic Challenge to Liberal Culture

Liberal culture, as a form of modernity, superseded the classical and medieval worldview, specifically the notion of a collective (teleological) good over and above and inclusive and constitutive of individual good. What liberal culture substitutes for a collective good is a common good. This raises the basic problem with which modern political theorists have had to grapple: what is the common good and how are we to understand the relationship between the individual good of autonomous individuals and a common good?

The common good consists of the conditions (procedural norms) that promote individual flourishing. Here arises the potential conflict: what guarantees are there that some individuals will not perceive their own flourishing in terms of the domination of others and/or practices that undermine the conditions for universal flourishing? Hegel answered this best when he asserted that the supreme form of flourishing requires interaction with and the recognition of other autonomous individuals. No society, no institution (e.g., the family), and no relationship (male/female, parent/child, etc.) can promote individual flourishing if it is based on a permanent relationship of domination or subjection. Autonomous individuals cannot sympathize with perceived inferiors; they can, at best, only pity them. Even sympathy is transformed in a society of autonomous beings.

Mill carries the point further. He agrues that

> The desire to be in unity with our fellow creatures, . . . is already a powerful principle in human nature, and happily one of those which tend to become stronger, even without express inculcation, from the influences of advancing

civilization. The social state is at once so natural, so necessary, and so habitual to man, that, except in some unusual circumstances or by an effort of voluntary abstraction, he never conceives himself otherwise than as a member of a body.... In this way people grow up unable to conceive as possible to them a state of total disregard of other people's interests.... He comes, as though instinctively, to be conscious of himself as a being who *of course* pays regard to others. The good of others becomes to him a thing naturally and necessarily to be attended to.[48]

In the culmination and achievement of autonomy in family relationships, in the true friendship of husband and wife, we have the model of the solution of liberal culture's greatest challenge.

The equality of married persons before the law is not only the sole mode in which that particular relation can be made consistent with justice to both sides, and conducive to the happiness of both, but it is the only means of rendering the daily life of mankind, in any high sense, a school of moral cultivation. Though the truth may not be felt or generally acknowledged for generations to come, the only school of genuine moral sentiment is society between equals.... We have had the morality of submission, and the morality of chivalry and generosity; the time is now come for the morality of justice.... The family, justly constituted, would be the real school of freedom.... The moral training of mankind will never be adapted to the conditions of the life for which all other human progress is a preparation, until they practice in the family the same moral rule which is adapted to the normal constitution of human society.[49]

Hence, Mill's *Subjection of Women* is not just about women but about the fundamental issue in liberal culture. Collini was right to point out that this work offers the whole of Mill's characteristic political and moral arguments in microcosm; themes whose best known *loci* are in the *Principles*, *On Liberty*, or *Representative Government* are here drawn together and focused on a single issue.[50]

Note

1. Mary Shanley has called attention to some of the parallels between Hegel and Mill in her article "Marital Slavery and Friendship," *Political Theory* 9, no. 2 (May 1981): 229-47. My interpretation of Mill is very much in agreement with her positive and constructively critical reading. Stefan Collini has also noted the similarities (see note 36). There is no evidence of Mill's having read Hegel's *Philosophy of Right*. All references to Hegel in Mill's writings are to issues in metaphysics and epistemology, often identifying Hegel with Schelling and French Hegelians. Mill did read James Hutchinson Sterling's *The Secret of Hegel* (1865) but was not impressed. My argument is not that Mill thought of what he did as a development of Hegel's thought; it is that Hegel and Mill were both explicating the implicit norms of liberal culture. That Mill did not get the idea directly from Hegel is confirmation of my thesis.

2. For an elaboration of the distinction, see Nicholas Capaldi, "J. S. Mill's Defense of Liberal Culture," *The Political Science Reviewer* 24 (1995): 205-50—a special issue

on Mill's Place in Liberalism. Wendy Donner has also noted this distinction in "John Stuart Mill's Liberal Feminism," *Ethics* 106 (1996): 621-32. Both of these articles have been republished in the anthology *Mill and the Moral Character of Liberalism*, ed. Eldon J. Eisenach (University Park: Pennsylvania State University Press, 1998).

3. Although the model of liberal culture has achieved hegemonic status, most of the world's practice, most of the people in the world, and probably most of the people who write about it are hostile to liberal culture. Liberal culture is not only by many outside of the "West" (Islamic nations, China, etc.), but is also opposed by those within the "West" who either want to see a return to some version of classical culture or medieval culture or who, like socialists and Marxists, want to see liberal culture evolve into or be replaced by another set of institutions (e.g., command economy, participatory democracy, dictatorship); or it is opposed by the countercultures who disdain the moral practices necessary to sustain it, or by those who see the tensions within liberal culture and want something without those tensions but are not clear on what that could be.

4. Implicit in this account is a rejection of the traditional view of social science as modeled after physical science. That is, we reject the notion that social practices are informed by rigid hidden structures analogous to the way in which entities that cannot be seen by the unaided eye, such as molecules or genes, explain surface phenomena in the physical sciences. The notion of unified science, in which the social sciences are based upon the physical sciences, is a product of the Enlightenment. It is important to note that Hegel, following Kant, rejected this view and opted for a conception of *geisteswissenschaften* that is fundamentally different from and prior to the physical sciences. Mill as well spent much of Book VI of the *Logic* trying to overcome the Enlightenment conception of the social sciences.

5. Retrieving our tradition is not a simple matter of an uncritical return to the past. Instead, it is the reidentifying of something that is a permanent part of the human condition even though it is always expressed in specific historical contexts. The fact that these universal truths are always contextualized means that the act of retrieval inevitably involves a reformulation. To encompass the past is to make it our own in some fashion. A tradition is not a rigid structure but a fertile source of adaptation that not only evolves but expands to incorporate things that might from an earlier perspective even seem alien. Philosophers are intellectually and morally obligated to engage in a perpetual retrieval of their tradition. Since the universal truths are moral truths, and since their apprehension is not solely an intellectual act, we should not be surprised that there is no definitive articulation of the cosmic order and there is inevitable controversy over its articulation and a necessary act of faith in its continuing apprehension.

The clearest and most fundamental example of this is natural language. Language has an inherent structure that was not planned but whose rules we can articulate. That is why philosophy *always* begins with what we assume when we begin to speak and rightfully takes to task those who insist upon using language to deny that language has meaning. It is hopelessly misguided to offer an explanation of language in terms of its structure since all such speculation would have to be judged by intuitions about what the language really meant. Plato's Socratic notion of reminiscence, Aristotle's conception of teleology, Hume's notion of custom, Kant's conception of the synthetic a priori, Wittgenstein's notion of practice, and Heidegger's "retrieval" are all examples of explication. See Nicholas Capaldi, *The Enlightenment Project in the Analytic Conversation* (Dordrecht: Kluwer, 1998), for a further account of explication.

6. For a good brief summary of Hegel, see the article on Hegel by Shlomo Avineri in

The Blackwell Encyclopedia of Political Thought, ed. David Miller (Oxford: Blackwell, 1987).

7. Capaldi, "J. S. Mill's Defense of Liberal Culture."

8. John Stuart Mill, "Essays on Politics and Society," *On Liberty*, in *The Collected Works of John Stuart Mill*, ed. John M. Robson (Toronto: University of Toronto Press, 1977) vol. XVIII, 217-27. All references to John Stuart Mill are from this Collected Works, hereafter cited as CW.

9. Thomas Babington Macaulay, "Utilitarian Logic and Politics," *Edinburgh Review* 49 (March 1829): 159-89.

10. J. S. Mill, *Autobiography and Literary Essays*, CW I, 165-66: "gave me much to think about."

11. Mill, *Autobiography*, 107.

12. See Lee Holcombe, *Wives and Property: Reform of the Married Women's Property Law in Nineteenth Century England* (Oxford: Martin Robinson, 1983).

13. G. W. F. Hegel, *Philosophy of Right*, Part III (Ethical Life), Section 1 (The Family), Paragraph 158, Addition (H, G), 199 of *Elements of the Philosophy of Right*, ed. Allen Wood (Cambridge: Cambridge University Press, 1991).

14. Hegel, *Philosophy of Right*, paragraph 161, 201.

15. Hegel, *Philosophy of Right*, addition (G), 201.

16. Hegel, *Philosophy of Right*, paragraph 163, Addition (H, G), 203. Mill expressed a similar view: "I think it most probable that this particular passion will become with men, as it already is with a large number of women, completely under the control of the reason," in a letter to Lord Amberley, *Later Letters*, CW XVII, 1693 (February 2, 1870). Mill's contemporary biographer Alexander Bain reacted to Mill's views with the following comment: "It was the opinion of many, that while his estimate of pure sentimental affection was more than enough, his estimate of the sexual passion was too low," in *John Stuart Mill, A Criticism with Personal Recollections* (London: Longmans, Green and Co., 1882), 89-90.

17. Hegel, *Philosophy of Right*, paragraph 167, 207.

18. Hegel, *Philosophy of Right*, paragraph 175, addition (H,G), 213.

19. Hegel, *Philosophy of Right*, paragraph 171, 209.

20. Hegel, *Philosophy of Right*, paragraph 180, 217-18.

21. Hegel, *Philosophy of Right*, paragraph 62, page 92.

22. Hegel, *Philosophy of Right*, paragraph 176, addition (H), 213-14.

23. Hegel, *Philosophy of Right*, paragraph 166, addition (H,G), 207.

24. Hegel, *Philosophy of Right,* paragraph 166, addition (H,G), 207.

25. Hegel, *Philosophy of Right,* paragraph 166, addition (H,G), 207.

26. Hegel, *Philosophy of Right,* paragraph 166, addition (H,G), 207.

27. One issue we shall not be discussing here is whether Hegel is entitled to invoke Sophocles as identifying a permanent truth as opposed merely to identifying a truth in a preliberal culture.

28. Mill, *System of Logic*, VI, chap. 2, sec. 3; CW, VIII (1974), 839-42.

29. Mill, *Later Letters*, CW XVII, 1632-4 (letter to John Nichol, August 18, 1869).

30. Mill, *Public and Parliamentary Speeches,* CW XXVIII (1988), 283-86 (June 10, 1868).

31. Mill, Letter to Henry Keylock Rusden, *Later Letters*, CW XVII, 1751 (July 22, 1870).

32. Mill, *Subjection of Women, Essays on Equality, Law, and Education, CW* XXI (1984), 323; see also 284-86.

33. An even more fundamental reason given by Mill is that "I do not think it is part of the business of the Government to provide securities beforehand against the consequences of immoralities of any kind," *CW* XXI, 353.
34. Gladstone and Queen Victoria, among others, opposed women's suffrage.
35. Mill, *Autobiography, CW*, I, 285.
36. Stefan Collini notes this in his introduction to *CW*, XXI, xxxiv.
37. Mill, *Subjection of Women, CW* XXI, 323.
38. Mill, *Subjection of Women*, 288-89.
39. Mill, *Subjection of Women*, 338.
40. Mill, *Subjection of Women*, 336.
41. Mill, *Autobiography, CW*, I, 7.
42. Mill, *CW*, I, 612.
43. In connection with this, it is important to note that Mill was largely educated by his father and that, despite criticisms of that education, John Stuart Mill took for granted a world in which parents, including fathers, were personally involved and invested a great deal of time in their children's education. This should be kept in mind by those critics who point out that Mill still expected the traditional division of labor between men (work in the economic world) and women (responsibilities at home). Like Hegel, Mill was also very critical of education that pandered to children and made no demands on them, thereby "training up a race of men who will be incapable of doing anything which is disagreeable to them." *Autobiography, CW*, I, 55.
44. Mill, *CW*, II, 225.
45. *Later Letters,CW*, XIV, 500 (unidentified correspondent).
46. Mill, *CW*, XVIII, 300.
47. Mill, Letter to Henry Rusden July 1870 (*Later Letters,CW*, XVII, 1750-51).
48. Mill, *Utilitarianism, Essays on Ethics, Religion, and Society, CW*, X (1969), 231-32. Both Hegel and Mill recognize what we now call a social epistemology. That is, individuals are socialized in their learning right from the beginning. However, the recognition that individuals require a social context in order to become autonomous does not entail a social or historical determinism. Once autonomous, the individual is free to critique his or her society to become more consistent and coherent.
49. Mill, *Subjection of Women, CW*, XXI, 293-295. Mill also anticipated that the emancipation of women and their rise to personal autonomy would alleviate the problems of overpopulation and poverty. Autonomous women would, presumably, neither need to nor permit themselves to be treated as objects of sexual pleasure.
50. Collini, xxxiii of the introduction, *CW*, XXI.

Chapter 14

Nietzsche's Woman as Friend: The Paradox of Distance and Proximity

Denise Schaeffer

"Has the dialectic of marriage and friendship ever been explicated?" Nietzsche poses this question in Book I of *The Gay Science*.[1] In raising this question, he suggests that marriage and friendship have a relationship, but that the nature of this relationship is not obvious. That they even have a relationship is a point worth emphasizing in light of many commentaries on Nietzsche that present his understanding of the relationship between men and women as fundamentally misogynist.[2] Such an oversimplification of Nietzsche's views has been challenged, both by those such as Derrida who read his comments on women metaphorically[3] and by those who focus on the middle period works in which we find Nietzsche at his least misogynist and most sensitive to contingency.[4] But even defenders of Nietzsche's middle works acknowledge that there are many inconsistencies in his treatment of the woman question.[5] These "inconsistencies," if they are inconsistencies, point us back toward Derrida's reading, which holds that the impossibility of pinning down woman generates emancipatory potential. However, Derrida's reading has been criticized as politically naive by scholars who wish to confront seriously and literally Nietzsche's direct statements on the practical issue of women's social position.[6]

Whatever flaws we find in *Spurs*, we are challenged to investigate Nietzsche's suggestion that truth is a woman. Commentaries that address Nietzsche's statements regarding women's social position tend to focus on determining whether (or to what degree) Nietzsche is useful for contemporary feminism, and do not confront the fact that Nietzsche uses the idea of woman as a metaphor to indicate something about the possibility and nature of truth. In taking on the question of truth, however, Derrida focuses only on woman as an erotic being.[7] Therefore, commentaries that engage the possibility of male/female friendship in the middle works are a useful addition to our understanding of Nietzsche's "woman," even if they do not address what it might mean for truth to be this woman. We must combine these two approaches and investigate the implications for woman as truth once friendship, and not just sexual love, is considered. Analyzed together, *The Gay Science* (*GS*) and *Human, All Too Human* (*HAH*), the two principal middle works, offer a good starting point for this inquiry.[8] *The Gay Science* poses the question of marriage and friendship in a list of several examples of the kinds of questions that need to be raised before a new (gay) science can emerge. He does not, however, explicate marriage and friendship in this book, although he does intersperse aphorisms about friendship among a concentration of aphorisms about women. *Human, All Too Human* is where Nietzsche has answered his own challenge, offering an explication of the dialectic of marriage and friendship.[9]

An investigation of woman as a candidate for friendship and not only as an erotic being is necessary if we are to understand more fully Nietzsche's positioning of truth as a woman, specifically with regard to the truth of a text, or the question of whether and how meaning is conveyed through writing. Derrida emphasizes passages in which woman is figured as an erotic being, acting at a distance to weave the illusions that operate in sexual seduction. While this woman arouses the yearning to possess, she defies possession. Derrida takes the elusiveness of woman as evidence of the elusiveness of the meaning or truth of a text. The fact that "woman" defies any fixed interpretation in Nietzsche's text is paradigmatic of the unfixed character of the text as a whole. Thus Derrida uses woman's distance to challenge the logocentric "metaphysics of presence" that informs the traditional approach to interpretation as the decoding of the meaning or "truth" of a text. "The hermeneutic project which postulates a true sense of the text is disqualified under this regime."[10]

In reading Nietzsche, however, the issue of truth inevitably runs up against the issue of rank.[11] The question that must be raised is whether any and every interpretation of a text is as good as any other, once it is determined that the text, like a woman, is undecidable.[12] Alan Schrift addresses this dilemma in *Nietzsche and the Question of Interpretation*, noting that Nietzsche maintained a distinction between reading well and reading badly, "insofar as the reader is cautioned to *respect* the text and remain open to that which the text presents."[13] Seeking to forge a middle ground between hermeneutics and deconstruction, Schrift concludes that Nietzsche adjudicates interpretive activity in terms of value rather than correctness or correspondence. The character of this adjudicating standard as Schrift presents it is twofold: an interpretation must both open the text and respond to the text. Thus interpretations that generate greater possibilities for other interpretations are valuable, but the "forging of meaning must respond to and fit with the text."[14] Just precisely what it means to "fit" with the text is left somewhat unclear by Schrift, who acknowledges the difficulty of formulating protocols of reading once the idea of faithful representation of the meaning of a text is suspended. He goes so far as to say that the fitness of any interpretation "will have to be decided *in practice*, in terms of the strength and value of the interpretation(s) that can be generated from it."[15] But this formulation doesn't quite capture the connotation of authenticity that we detect in Nietzsche's call for honesty, justice, and responsibility in reading. While we cannot (and should not try to) derive a "method" from Nietzsche, a metaphor might be the best way to apprehend what it would mean for an interpretation to "fit" with the text. Friendship, I will argue, is an apt metaphor.[16]

The metaphor of friendship does not supersede the metaphor of woman but rather incorporates it. Both metaphors entail an understanding of distance that is crucial to the question of the accessibility of the "truth" of a text. If woman is pure distance, if she is indeed the "perennial empty set"[17] that Derrida's interpretation suggests, then it is impossible to connect with her, and any responsibility toward her (and thus the text) vanishes into a field of infinite possibilities. But one possible "woman" in Nietzsche's text has been overlooked by deconstructive readings: the possibility of woman as friend. Friendship does not destroy distance—indeed it requires it—but distance in friendship has a different character from distance in sexual love. And if friendship between men and women is possible, an alternative model of the relationship between reader and text is also possible; if truth is like *this* woman, Derrida's use of woman as paradigmatic for the elusiveness of all meaning is misleading.

Distance in Love and Friendship

Nietzsche is well known for arguing that the purported "love of wisdom" that is taken to be the basis for the traditional understanding of the pursuit of truth (in philosophy or science) is actually a will to power—a will to dominate and possess. And Book I of GS, which challenges the prevailing understanding of science in order to set the stage for a new, more "joyful" science, contains passages that indicate that this self-imposing quality belongs not only to "love of wisdom" but to "love" itself, even (especially) romantic love. Nietzsche states that while people tend to think of love and avarice as opposites, they really amount to the same thing: the desire for possession. "Our love of our neighbor—is it not a lust for new possessions? And likewise our love of knowledge, of truth, and altogether any lust for what is new?" While this is true of various kinds of love, he goes on to say that "sexual love betrays itself most clearly as a lust for possession" (*GS,* 14).

Nietzsche reveals this lust to be misguided, for we love what we love only because it remains distant from us, and the moment that distance is destroyed by possession, the object desired loses its appeal. In *GS,* 15, he gives the following illustration: we see the mountain from a distance and appreciate its charm; we climb the mountain and it loses its charm. Possession and desire are treated as incompatible in these two passages; one precludes the other.

There is one ray of hope offered for the transcendence of this antagonism: friendship. Nietzsche ends the aphorism on love by referring to

> a kind of continuation of love in which this possessive craving of two people for each other gives way to a new desire and lust for possession—a *shared* higher thirst for an ideal above them. But who knows such love? Who has experienced it? Its right name is friendship. (*GS,* 14)

Friendship is not immune to the desire for possession, but that desire is directed toward a higher ideal rather than directly toward another individual.[18] Thus there is an indirectness to friendship that is essential and that distinguishes it from sexual attraction. Two friends are united in their love of a higher ideal, but their love does not threaten their individuality because they are not consumed with and by each other. This means that friendship can sustain itself in a way that sexual love cannot, since the latter leads to the destruction of distance through possession. In contrast, a connection between friends is achieved by their shared desire for an ideal above them, but that ideal also serves to maintain a separation between them.

In *GS*, 16, Nietzsche continues the theme of separation and connection in friendship. He writes of a time "when we were so close that nothing seemed to obstruct our friendship and brotherhood, and only a small footbridge separated us." Even as he points out the footbridge separating the friends, Nietzsche stresses how close the two friends were and says that nothing was obstructing the friendship. This suggests that the existence of the footbridge is necessary to the friendship rather than a hindrance to it. However, it is a *small* (*kleine*) footbridge. It is important to pay attention to how Nietzsche qualifies the distance between individuals, even as he is insisting on the importance of maintaining some distance.

This is true even when Nietzsche turns to the question of woman in *GS* Book II. In the extended metaphor of *GS*, 60, woman is figured as a sailboat that glides past a man in the midst of a raging surf. Looking at the sailboat, the man sees taciturnity and calm, and supposes that his happiness lies on that boat. But according to Nietzsche, the man is mistaken; he has been led into fantasies. "All great noise leads us to move happiness into some quiet distance." Nietzsche corrects the male perspective by pointing out that "even on the most beautiful sailboat there is a lot of noise, and unfortunately much small and petty noise." The taciturnity is revealed to be an illusion that can only be maintained at a distance.

This aphorism is crucial to many readings of Nietzsche's woman as thoroughly elusive. But although it is entitled "Women and their action at a distance,"[19] we must not essentialize woman as distance, for Nietzsche says that "man *moves* happiness into some quiet distance." The distance is created, or at least augmented, by the man himself, even as he supposedly longs to approach the sailboat. His desire aims at reducing and expanding the distance simultaneously. But how distant is woman, really? "Only [*nur*] a few [*wenige*] fathoms away," says Nietzsche. Nietzsche's use of "only" and "few" invites us to believe that the distance is not vast. At the same time that he is emphasizing the importance of distance, Nietzsche mitigates that distance with qualifiers that diminish the gap. Woman is not unapproachable; she is only a few fathoms away. But man pushes her away so that he can imagine her as he wishes, as his "better self." He pushes her away in order impose his own vision upon her. This is not a healthy distance that serves the cause of independence and openness. It springs from the desire for possession and does nothing to mitigate it. Indeed, when woman might appear the most distant, she is the most subject to man's possession.

What the man sees in the sailboat that causes him to romanticize it is in fact women's supposed achievement of distance—not from man, but from the world. The man sees the sailboat "quietly observing, gliding, floating" and believes woman has achieved a comfortable detachment from the pains of human existence. "Yes! To move *over* existence! That's it! That would be something!" (*GS*, 60) This may be what leads Derrida to take this parable to mean that woman does not only act at a distance; she is "distance's very chasm . . . distance itself."[20] But Nietzsche corrects this view of woman, a move that Derrida fails to take into account. In identifying woman with distance itself, Derrida falls into the same error as the man in the parable. While the man believes woman has distanced herself from existence, Nietzsche dispels the illusion and thus brings her back to earth.

This is not the only time Nietzsche undermines the effect of woman at a distance by dispelling certain illusions. For example, he exposes women's physical weakness to be a carefully calculated ruse to manipulate men (*GS*, 66). He also counsels a woman who looks upon her beloved "with quiet confidence—like a cow" to simulate mysteriousness, since "what bewitched him was precisely that she seemed utterly changeable and unfathomable" (*GS*, 67). Clearly, Nietzsche's advice encourages the cultivation of some distance between the woman and her beloved in order to enhance her mysteriousness and hence her power over him. However, by revealing that her mysteriousness is a matter of dissimulation, Nietzsche also weakens the effect of that dissimulation, which would be most effective if taken to be real. If Nietzsche is concerned about preserving the distance necessary to protect the feminine illusion, why does he expose so much about women to his readers?

Nietzsche is cultivating what he deems to be a proper attitude toward such illusions, and therefore must "educate" men.[21] This education may be what the sage has in mind when he responds to the crowd's cry that "women need to be educated better" with the retort that "men need to be educated better" (*GS*, 68). Both points have some merit, and Nietzsche (who should not be identified with the sage) does a little of both. He counsels women to simulate unfathomability (rather than loving with quiet confidence like a cow); he simultaneously reveals the fact of that dissimulation to men. The result is that man knows both less and more about woman.

This corrects the two tendencies that we find in the absence of Nietzsche's reeducation: either men persist in the delusion that they can fully possess and know a woman (i.e., penetrate reality), or they realize that everything they thought about women was only illusion and this causes them to despair—sexual nihilism, as it were. Nietzsche helps men move beyond the poles of delusion and disillusion so that they can understand illusion and become conscious participants in it. This is the case not only with regard to women, but generally. This emerges explicitly in *GS,* 54, titled "The consciousness of appearance," where Nietzsche describes a somnambulist waking just to the point of realizing that he is dreaming, and knowing that he must go on dreaming lest he fall. But he does not denigrate the dream state as "unreal" in opposition to a waking state. What then does it mean to "know"? It means

> that among all these dreamers, I, too, who "know," am dancing my dance; that the knower is a means for prolonging the earthly dance and thus belongs to the masters of ceremony of existence; and that the sublime consistency and interrelatedness of all knowledge perhaps is and will be the highest means to *preserve* the universality of dreaming and the mutual comprehension of all dreamers and thus also *the continuation of the dream.* (*GS,* 54, emphasis in original)

We are left with a dream, but only those with a misleading traditional standard of complete possession (of knowledge, of woman) would be disappointed. Those who have been freed from this error can embrace this state of affairs—and understand it. The somnambulist knows he is dreaming and knows he must go on dreaming. To know this is to know something about human nature and reality. This is a paradox more than a contradiction. It captures the overriding tension in Nietzsche's work, which appears to present certain "truths" about how there is no "truth," a tension that has preoccupied many scholarly interpreters of Nietzsche.[22]

Derrida, however, uses the question of woman to deny this tension in Nietzsche's work. "There is no such thing as the truth of woman"[23] and "there is no such thing either as the truth of Nietzsche, or of Nietzsche's text. . . . Indeed there is no such thing as a truth in itself."[24] Such formulas threaten to turn into dogmas. And it is precisely dogmatism that Nietzsche challenges, especially philosophical dogmatism. When Nietzsche is most emphatic about the requirement of distance, he puts it, he says, "in philosophical language" (*GS,* 60). Philosophers are notorious for reducing ideas to formulas, and for this Nietzsche reproaches them. Woman at a distance is such a formula, as it captures only what Nietzsche says, and not what he does, which is to undermine the effect of the illusion and thus move woman closer rather than simply farther away. It may be odd that the traditional philosophical position would require correction by increased proximity, since too much emphasis on proximity (the belief that the truth is there to be grasped, possessed) is part of its problem. By thinking they had grasped everything they grasped nothing; but by grasping the limits of what cannot be grasped, they are not left empty-handed.

Friendship is presented as part of the correction to the dogmatic philosophical position in the next aphorism, "In honor of friendship" (*GS,* 61). Here Nietzsche explains that in antiquity, friendship was honored even higher than the pride of the self-sufficient sage. He recounts the story of a Macedonian king who gave an Athenian philosopher some money as a gift. The philosopher returns the gift and the king asks, "Has he no friend?" Nietzsche explains that the king meant to criticize the philosopher because "he does not know one of the two highest feelings—and the higher one at that" (*GS*, 61). The designation of friendship as "higher" (*hochere*) echoes aphorism 14, where Nietzsche uses the same word to characterize friendship as a higher thirst than the erotic lust for possession. Friendship is presented as higher than the self-destructive proximity of love's lust for possession, and as higher than the absolute distance required for complete self-sufficiency.[25]

The philosopher is corrected not only *in* the story of the Macedonian king, but also *by* the story of the Macedonian king. The story is told in the aphorism immediately following Nietzsche's affirmation—in "philosophical language"—of distance "first of all and above all" (*GS*, 60). The juxtaposition suggests that the story corrects the philosophical perspective that distance is above all, given Nietzsche's praise of the story as well told. The story indicates that in fact friendship is above all. Friendship incorporates distance, but it is a distance that connects rather than simply separates. Thus the independent individual can be a good friend, and true friendship does not destroy one's independence.

Women and Friendship

The juxtaposition of *GS*, 60 and 61 invites us to consider the questions of women and friendship in tandem. Up to this point, we have discussed women and we have discussed friends, but we have not discussed women as friends. Nietzsche does entertain the possibility of a higher relationship between men and women. In *Human, All Too Human* (*HAH*), he meets his own challenge to explicate the dialectic between marriage and friendship. The first time marriage is mentioned in *HAH*, Nietzsche states that "the best friend will probably acquire the best wife, because a good marriage is founded on a talent for friendship" (*HAH*, 378). Indeed, the entire chapter about women immediately follows a long aphorism on friendship, suggesting that the one issue leads into the other. Nietzsche also advises that "When entering into a marriage one ought to ask oneself: do you believe you are going to enjoy talking with this woman up into your old age? Everything else in marriage is transitory, but most of the time you are together will be devoted to conversation" (*HAH*, 406).

Nietzsche also discusses friendship between a man and a woman who are not married. However, here he adds that "to preserve such a friendship no doubt requires the assistance of a slight physical antipathy" (*HAH*, 390). The sexual longing and desire to possess that would exist in a relationship between those who do not share a slight physical antipathy could undermine their friendship. Physical antipathy serves to preserve the necessary distance between them. However, we must notice that once again, the distance is not presented by Nietzsche as overwhelming; a slight (*kleine*) physical antipathy is all that is required. Repulsion might completely sever the connection, just as overwhelming attraction might strain it. Some unquantifiable but necessary balance between proximity and distance seems necessary to maintain the proper tension that keeps a relationship alive.

That tension may be harder to maintain in marriage, where cohabitation can cause it to collapse from sheer monotony. When Nietzsche is most critical of marriage, it is for its ossifying tendency. In *HAH*, 427, he criticizes the habituation that accompanies most marriages, and remarks in *HAH*, 402 that the test of a good marriage is whether it is "able to endure an occasional 'exception'" (*HAH*, 402). It is possible that by "exception" he means sexual infidelity, and this may be the first thing that comes to mind. But Nietzsche does not specify, and his ambiguity invites us to take his point much more literally. There are many rules, routines, and habits in married life; an "exception" in any form disrupts the monotony.

Nietzsche distinguishes between higher and lower types of marriages, just as he distinguishes between higher and lower types of human beings.[26] The majority of marriages are of the lower type, just as the majority of women (and men!) earn Nietzsche's derision. Thus he refers to the "usual consequences of marriage" as diminishing to individuality. But this is the usual, not inevitable, consequence. He also describes a "higher conception of marriage as the soul-friendship of two people of differing sexes," one in which the wife is "a friend, assistant, mother, family head and housekeeper, and may indeed have to run her own business or job quite apart from that of her husband." He concludes, however, that such a marriage will probably require the coexistence of concubinage, for if men are to be expected to rely on only one woman for their sexual satisfaction, "then in the choice of a wife the decisive consideration will be one hostile to the objectives of the marriage just indicated" (*HAH*, 424). Nietzsche does not argue that a man cannot be sexually attracted to a woman who is his equal, only that a man who is choosing a marriage partner based *only* on physical attraction will probably not take into consideration other characteristics that would be necessary in order to achieve a "soul-friendship." Nietzsche neither underestimates the power of sexual desire fueled by a beautiful illusion nor rules out the possibility of getting beyond such illusions and experiencing a "soul-friendship." In actuality, such friendships are rare, and "all human institutions such as marriage permit only a moderate degree of practical idealization . . ." (*HAH*, 424). Following this resignation, Nietzsche devotes the rest of the chapter "On Woman and Child" to warning free spirits away from marriage. But even here, Nietzsche's language admits of exceptions. He states that *in general* free spirits should avoid marriage and fly alone (*HAH*, 426,. emphasis added). Later, in the chapter entitled "Man Alone With Himself," we are warned against taking this rejection of marriage to the level of dogma. "He who protests against marriage, in the way Catholic priests do, will try to think of it in its lowest and most vulgar form" (*HAH*, 598). Like marriage, a life of solitude must be open to the possibilities of exceptions to the rule.

Higher forms of marriage incorporate openness in another sense as well. Nietzsche criticizes marriages that engender too much closeness. "If married couples did not live together good marriages would be more common" (*HAH*, 393). Too much closeness leads to the loss of individuality; the individual becomes caught like a spider in its web. This is certainly true in marriage, but the principle extends to any relationship. In an aphorism entitled "Too Close," Nietzsche explains:

> If we live together with another person too closely, what happens is similar to when we repeatedly handle a good engraving with our bare hands: one day all we have left is a piece of dirty paper. The soul of a human being too can finally become tattered by being handled continually; and that is how it finally appears to us—we never see the beauty of its original design again.—One always loses by too familiar association with friends and women; and sometimes what one loses is the pearl of one's life. (*HAH*, 428)

While "Too Close" argues that excessively familiar association with *anyone* is detrimental, Nietzsche singles out women as posing a special risk to a man's independence. One reason he thinks women pose this risk is that they exhibit a tendency "towards a quiet, calm, happily harmonious existence" that "unwittingly works against the heroic impulse in the heart of the free spirit" (*HAH*, 431). For the sake of a comfortable present, women inhibit their husbands' striving for the future (*HAH*, 433) and attach themselves to free spirits in order to hold them back and prevent them from disrupting accepted authorities (*HAH*, 435). However, even here Nietzsche recognizes the occasional exception. In the midst of these various aphorisms denigrating women's conservatism, he praises Socrates' wife Xanthippe, who "made his house uncomfortable and unhomely to him: she taught him to live in the street and everywhere where one could chatter and be idle" and thus fashioned him into the gadfly that he was (*HAH*, 433).

Nietzsche is critical of a womanly love that is all-encompassing and smothering not only because of its detrimental effect on a man's spirit, but also because such self-abnegation lowers the woman as well. He refers to a woman's passion as a renunciation of her self (*GS*, 363), which is of course incompatible with human nobility. But he also provides quite an astute analysis of the social causes of this self-renunciation. In *GS*, 71, Nietzsche comments upon the "monstrous" quality of the education of upper-class women, who are kept ignorant of sexual matters until they are married and then are thrust, "as by a gruesome lightning bolt, into reality and knowledge." Having been told that their ignorance is a matter of virtue, it must be somewhat disconcerting to have that virtue annihilated "precisely by the man they love and esteem most!" This places "love and shame in a contradiction," according to Nietzsche, and leads to a "psychic knot . . . that may have no equal." A woman responds, Nietzsche adds, by "closing her eyes to herself."

If "one cannot be too kind about woman" (*GS*, 71), it may be due to these circumstances, which make independence much more difficult for a woman than for a man. If women cling to family life in a stifling way, it is because the social construction of their sexuality causes them to experience their husbands "as a question mark concerning their honor, and their children as an apology or atonement" (*GS*, 71). Moreover, even a woman who would foster independence, like Xanthippe, would not necessarily be sought out as a wife. Nietzsche says Socrates "would not have sought her if he had known her well enough: the heroism of even this free spirit would not have extended to that" (*HAH*, 433). It is not only women, then, who are to blame for the prevalence of bad marriages. Even a man with the potential to be a free spirit may choose a wife who makes him comfortable rather than uncomfortable. In light of all these factors, it is no wonder that Nietzsche counsels free spirits to avoid marriage. They may not make good choices, even though good choices are available (if rare). Nietzsche recognizes not only the limits of perfecting the institution of marriage but also the limits of perfecting the individual.

Friendship, Woman, and Truth

As we have seen, in friendship the distance between two individuals does not rule out the possibility of mutual understanding. *GS*, 279 makes this all the more explicit. In this aphorism, Nietzsche speaks again in the first person plural to his friend, from whom he has become estranged. He does not lament the estrangement. "But this was right, and we do not want to conceal and obscure it from ourselves as if we had reason to feel ashamed. We are two ships each of which has its goal and course." Individuals grow and change; their experiences are radically different and may even make it almost impossible for them to know each other. "[P]erhaps we shall meet again but fail to recognize each other: our exposure to different seas and suns has changed us" (*GS*, 279). Until this point, this aphorism might seem to support a view of human existence as radically isolated, marked by insurmountable distance. However, the positive view of friendship as the highest sentiment, put forward in *GS*, 14, is echoed here.

> That we have to become estranged is the law above us; by the same token we should also become more venerable for each other—and the memory of our former friendship more sacred. There is probably a tremendous but invisible stellar orbit in which our very different ways and goals may be included as small parts of this path; let us rise up to this thought. But our life is too short and our power of vision too small for us to be more than friends in the sense of this sublime possibility.—Let us then *believe* in our star friendship even if we should be compelled to be earth enemies. (*GS*, 279)

Nietzsche calls into question the permanence of human friendship, but not the possibility. To become estranged after being so close is a higher law, because human beings who are alive grow and change. But the differences between two individuals need not preclude a strong bond; indeed, respect for those differences can strengthen a bond and make the individuals "more venerable for each other." Moreover, in the face of enormous difference, the "sublime possibility" of a future commonality is affirmed. They have connected before; they may connect again. The "invisible stellar orbit" is the counterpart to the small footbridge of *GS*, 14. While the footbridge introduced distance into a close connection, the stellar orbit introduces some connection into vast distance. The image of the stellar orbit suggests an indirect connection, reminding us of the shared thirst for a higher ideal that was described in *GS*, 14.

The necessary tension between proximity and distance, when properly preserved, produces a dynamic rather than static friendship. Human beings change, so one cannot hold another to some strict "rule" of identity. We should cherish the friend who surprises us, even if that surprise is not a pleasant one. A friend should be a moving target. This helps make sense of the affinity between friendship and enmity that we find throughout Nietzsche's writings; Zarathustra's admonition to "honor the enemy" in one's friend comes to mind.[27] In *GS*, Nietzsche elaborates the concept of the worthy opponent; "An easy prey is something contemptible for proud natures. They feel good only at the sight of unbroken men who might become their enemies . . . " (*GS*, 13). There is some mutual recognition and understanding between higher types that mitigates the ultimate unknowability of one human being to another. Indeed, human difference is presented not as an obstacle to, but rather as the basis for, such veneration.

Women are not excluded from this measure. Nietzsche makes a distinction between strong women and weak women. Weak women and slaves can only suffer (*GS*, 325), but those women (and men) whom we respect can defend themselves and possess the capacity for revenge, the capacity to inflict suffering. "If someone cannot defend himself and therefore does not want to, we do not consider this a disgrace; but we have little respect for anyone who lacks both the capacity and the good will for revenge—regardless of whether it is a man or a woman" (*GS*, 69). Nietzsche respects a woman who can inflict suffering as well as experience it. The capacity to inflict suffering is a sign of greatness, a capacity that *weak* women lack (*GS*, 325).

Enmity, otherness, distance—these aspects of a friend reflect that kernel of unknowability of each unique individual, "the pearl one's life" that is threatened by overly close association (*HAH*, 428). And while one way to protect the pearl of one's life may be to live a life of isolation, it is worth noting that even when advocating isolation Nietzsche includes the possibility of friendship. In an aphorism condemning the notion of pity, he advises: "Live in seclusion so that you *can* live for yourself" (*GS*, 338). But he follows this statement with the instruction to help "only those whose distress you *understand* entirely because they share with you one suffering and one hope—your friends—and only in the manner in which you help yourself" (*GS*, 338). The challenge is to reconcile the needs of self with the needs of the other, respecting both the possibility that that reconciliation may be impossible (even when it seems possible) and that it may be possible (even when it seems impossible).

It is necessary to cultivate distance like a true friend, rather than like a deluded lover. Nietzsche makes a distinction between a kernel of unknowability that is authentic and one that is illusory. When man pushes woman away, moving the sailboat into the distance, he projects an unknowability that serves his own weakness and inability to confront his own "noise." This is echoed in *GS*, 363, in which Nietzsche discusses "how each sex has its own prejudices about love." In this aphorism, Nietzsche refers to the self-abnegating character of feminine love, contrasting woman's desire to be possessed with man's desire to possess. He concludes the aphorism by pointing out that while "wanting always comes to an end with having," it is possible for man's love to increase after surrender, for "he will not readily concede that a woman should have nothing more to give him." This is man's prejudice about love. It maintains a distance that is not real and precludes respecting any distance that is real. Both dispositions may appear the same from the outside. Ultimately, an individual has to be honest with himself or herself. Nietzsche's standards involve a level of serious confrontation that Derrida's emphasis on playfulness misses. Respect for the other, and for the text, requires it.

Only a few women, and only a few men, are capable of the kind of friendship that can preserve the "pearl of one's life." A true friendship respects true distance, avoiding the kind of handling of another's soul that ruins its "original design" (*HAH*, 428). Nietzsche spends much more time discussing the majority of women who are not up to these demands than he does the few who are. But, again, if we are going to notice that there are multiple women in Nietzsche, we should take note of which women he praises and which he criticizes. He praises those who are capable of maintaining distance, but he distinguishes between respectful and self-serving distance. The latter turns into its opposite. In other words, the women he praises are capable of being friends. If woman is capable of friendship, and if friendship involves connection as well as separation, then woman as truth is not pure elusiveness. When Nietzsche likens truth to a woman in the preface of *GS*, he proposes that truth is a woman "who has reasons for not letting us see her reasons."

Conclusion

If the question is one of style, then friendship is a better model for understanding Nietzsche, at least in the middle period. The indirectness of his writing parallels the indirectness of friendship, which generates the paradoxical combination of proximity and distance. Nietzsche's analysis of "the question of being understandable" toward the end of *The Gay Science* expresses a similar paradox: "One does not only wish to be understood when one writes; one wishes just as surely not to be understood" (*GS*, 381). His claim indicates that the tensions, apparent contradictions, and paradoxes we find in his work are intentional.

Nietzsche describes a kind of writing that has a double goal: to connect with and be understood by some readers while shutting out others (most, in fact). "All the more subtle laws of any style have their origin at this point: they at the same time keep away, create a distance, forbid 'entrance,' understanding . . . while they open the ears of those whose ears are related to ours" (*GS*, 381). Meaning must be conveyed and covered up at the same time. This is necessary for two reasons; Nietzsche's double goal reflects a double actuality. There is, of course, the matter of the mixed character of one's audience. But indirect writing is not only a political decision on Nietzsche's part; it has also to do with the nature of that which is conveyed. Part of his indirectness is his brevity. In contrast to long plodding arguments, his brief aphorisms only *hint*. The reason is that "there are truths that are singularly shy and ticklish and cannot be caught except suddenly—that must be *surprised* or left alone" (*GS*, 381). One must sneak up on these truths, come at them indirectly. Nietzsche thus supplies two reasons why he must write in such an ambiguous fashion. The indirectness of his writing is intended to reach only certain readers who are prepared to think for themselves, but he constructs his text to get them to think about *particular* questions, to pursue a particular line of questioning that demands indirect pursuit. Therefore his readers—"my friends," as he often calls them—are connected to the text even as they are freed by the possibilities it generates.

Like a woman, Nietzsche has reasons for not letting us see his reasons. The woman that he conjures does not allow us to impose just any interpretation on her; she commands respect, like a friend. Nor does she impose dogmatic restrictions on our ability to think for ourselves; she respects us, like a friend.

Notes

I would like to thank the Lynde and Harry Bradley Foundation for their generous support of this research.

1. Friedrich Wilhelm Nietzsche, *The Gay Science*, trans. Walter Kaufmann (New York: Random House, 1974), section 7.

2. Examples of interpretations that charge Nietzsche with misogyny include Ofelia Schutte, *Beyond Nihilism: Nihilism Without Masks* (Chicago: University of Chicago Press, 1984), and Carol Diethe, "Nietzsche and the Woman Question," *History of European Ideas* 11 (1989): 865-75.

3. Jacques Derrida, *Spurs: Nietzsche's Styles*, trans. Barbara Harlow (Chicago: University of Chicago Press, 1979). See also Sarah Kofman, *Nietzsche et la Scène Philosophique* (Paris: Union Générale d'Editions, 1979); David Farrell Krell, *Postponements: Women, Sensuality, and Death in Nietzsche* (Bloomington: Indiana University Press, 1986); and Kelly Oliver, "Woman as Truth in Nietzsche's Writing," in *Feminist Interpretations of Friedrich Nietzsche*, ed. Kelly Oliver and Marilyn Pearsall (University Park: Pennsylvania State University Press, 1998).

4. See, for example, Ruth Abbey, "Beyond Misogyny and Metaphor: Women in Nietzsche's Middle Period," *Journal of the History of Philosophy* 34 (April 1996): 233-

56; Kathleen Marie Higgins, "Gender in the Gay Science," in *Feminist Interpretations*, 130-51; and Lynne Tirrell, "Sexual Dualism and Women's Self-Creation: On the Advantages and Disadvantages of Reading Nietzsche for Feminists" in *Nietzsche and the Feminine*, ed. Peter J. Burgard (Charlottesville and London: University Press of Virginia, 1994), 158-84.

5. Abbey argues that these inconsistencies allow us "to set Nietzsche's different statements against one another, challenging his essentialist claims with his own historicist ones" (Abbey, "Beyond Misogyny and Metaphor," 236). Tirrell also determines that the positive outweighs the negative, concluding that Nietzsche's "misogyny is tempered by a surprising understanding of the situation of the (white, European, upper-class) women of his day" (Tirrell, "Sexual Dualism and Women's Self-Creation," 176).

6. See Keith Ansell-Pearson, "Nietzsche, Woman and Political Theory," in *Nietzsche, Feminism and Political Theory*, ed. Paul Patton (London: Allen & Unwin, 1993), 27-48, and Erik Parens, "Derrida, 'Woman,' and Politics: A Reading of *Spurs*," *Philosophy Today* (Winter 1989): 291-301.

7. Even in his more recent book on friendship, woman are virtually absent, although he does critically note the "androcentric" character of the treatment of friendship in the Western tradition. Jacques Derrida, *Politics of Friendship*, trans. George Collins (London and New York: Verso, 1997).

8. I will refer to Nietzsche's texts with these acronyms, followed by the section number. Citations are from the following translations: *The Gay Science*, trans. Walter Kaufmann (New York: Random House, 1974) and *Human, All Too Human: A Book for Free Spirits*, trans. R. J. Hollingdale (Cambridge: Cambridge University Press, 1996).

9. It is not my intention to present an exhaustive survey of Nietzsche's various remarks on women or on friendship. It is always dangerous, in writing about Nietzsche, to draw conclusions after grazing through various works and thereby undercutting the integrity of each work. But there is good reason to consider *HAH* and *GS* in tandem. As Kaufmann points out, Nietzsche had the following statement printed on the back cover of the first edition of *The Gay Science*: "This book marks the conclusion of a series of writings by FRIEDRICH NIETZSCHE whose common goal is to erect *a new image and ideal of the free spirit*." He then lists the works of the "series," which begins with *HAH* and ends with *GS*. See Kaufmann, *GS*, 30. This reference to a common goal is more definitive, in my opinion, than the position of these works in the "middle" of Nietzsche's chronology. For this reason, I will include Book V and the Preface of *GS* in my analysis, even though they were added by Nietzsche after he wrote *Thus Spoke Zarathustra* and *Beyond Good and Evil* and thus are not part of the "middle period," strictly speaking. Obviously, Nietzsche thought these additions belonged to *The Gay Science*, and I will treat them that way.

10. Derrida, *Spurs*, 107.

11. For an excellent discussion of the problem of reconciling Nietzsche's "perspectivism" with his insistence on the importance of rank, see Ted Sadler, "The Postmodernist Politicization of Nietzsche" in *Nietzsche, Feminism and Political Theory*, ed. Paul Patton (London and New York: Routledge, 1993), 225-43.

12. Derrida's answer to this question is ultimately undecidable.

13. Alan D. Schrift, *Nietzsche and the Question of Interpretation: Between Hermeneutics and Deconstruction* (New York and London: Routledge, 1990), 163.

14. Schrift, *Nietzsche and the Question of Interpretation*, 189.

15. Schrift, *Nietzsche and the Question of Interpretation*, 189.

16. Schrift mentions Nietzsche's reference in *Daybreak* to philologists as goldsmiths, "who know the limits of their material and yet can forge this raw material into ever-new and creative forms . . ." (Schrift, 189). Schrift continually emphasizes the potential of the text as raw material to take on new and ever-changing forms and downplays the limits that the inherent properties of any raw material place on the forms that it could take. In other words, Schrift turns Nietzsche's goldsmith into an alchemist. While goldsmithing is one metaphor to describe the relationship of the reader to the text, we can also work with Nietzsche's reference to truth as a woman, and his constant reference to his readers as "my friends," to further explore this question.

17. Rosi Braidotti, *Patterns of Dissonance* (New York: Routledge, 1991), 102.

18. Nietzsche does not indicate the gender of the friends he is describing in this passage, referring only to two *Personen*. Although he implies that friendship as he describes it is exceedingly rare, women are certainly not ruled out from participating in friendship.

19. Jean Graybeal points out that "Kaufmann's translation . . . does not fully convey the active sense suggested by the construction 'Wirkung *in* die Ferne.' 'In' with an object in the accusative case implies movement into or toward, not static presence in or at." Jean Graybeal, *Language and "The Feminine" in Nietzsche and Heidegger* (Bloomington and Indianapolis: Indiana University Press, 1990), 31. Graybeal goes on to argue that "woman" is moved into the distance in the process of the self-creation of the subject in relation to language, and concludes that Section 60 is ultimately about the effects of language (Graybeal, 38).

20. Derrida, *Spurs*, 49.

21. Higgins also reads the passages on women in *GS* to have an educative function. "Nietzsche insists that women's reality is quite different from traditional male fabrications, and he jars his readers into sensing the discrepancy between their habitual thinking and actual women's points of view" (Higgins, "Gender in The Gay Science," 145).

22. Maudemarie Clark offers a clear exposition of this tension in Nietzsche's work and provides an overview of the various strands of interpretation of this tension, in *Nietzsche on Truth and Philosophy* (Cambridge: Cambridge University Press, 1990).

23. Derrida, *Spurs*, 53.

24. Derrida, *Spurs*, 103.

25. Peter Berkowitz argues that in *Thus Spoke Zarathustra*, the point of friendship is to learn to overcome the need for it. Thus friendship can serve the cause of radical self-sufficiency; we learn self-love from other-love. Berkowitz notes that Zarathustra "seems unable to account for the moment of intimacy and melting of barriers in friendship." Peter Berkowitz, *Nietzsche: The Ethics of an Immoralist* (Cambridge, MA: Harvard University Press, 1995), 173. However, while it is true that Zarathustra criticizes the longing for a friend as a lack of faith in ourselves, he appears to direct this criticism at the common type of friendship that contains no distance. He goes on to elaborate a view of friendship that is indeed compatible with independence. As to whether women are capable of this elevated notion of friendship, Zarathustra argues: not yet. Woman is not essentially incapable of friendship, but as she presently exists, it is unlikely. The same, however, is true for most men. "Woman is not yet capable of friendship. But tell me, you men, who among you is capable of friendship?" *The Portable Nietzsche*, ed. Walter

Kaufmann (New York: Viking Press, 1968), 169.

26. On the ranking of types of marriages, see also *Thus Spoke Zarathustra*, I:20. *Daybreak*, 403 suggests a distinction between higher and lower types of both sexes.

27. See *Thus Spoke Zarathustra*, I,14.

Chapter 15

What Death Will Buy: Escaping Gender in Emily Dickinson

Lesley Wheeler

The contemporary definition of gender as a social or cultural category of identity (as opposed to sex, a biological one) arose during the 1960s. Nevertheless, the mid-nineteenth-century poetry of Emily Dickinson represents a similar distinction between nature, or the biological fact of femaleness, and the cultural meanings attached to womanhood. Dickinson expresses the difference between sex and gender through her contrast between, respectively, women's freedom in eternity, where social prescriptions no longer apply, and their limited lives on earth, where they are profoundly constrained by their relegation to the separate sphere of domesticity.

In their influential study of nineteenth-century literature by women, *The Madwoman in the Attic*, Sandra Gilbert and Susan Gubar suggest that the "angel in the house," the era's ideal of womanhood, "having died to her own desires, her own self, her own life, leads a posthumous existence in her own lifetime . . . for to be selfless is not only to be noble, it is to be dead."[1] A significant subset of Emily Dickinson's lyric poems treat the death-in-life of the Victorian housewife: for Dickinson, the separate sphere of the home becomes equivalent to the confinement of the grave. In fact, Dickinson argues, real death offers women release from the constrictions of gender; therefore, physical death extends distinctive advantages over figurative burial in domesticity.

In the poems I will discuss, Dickinson rejects passivity and self-sacrifice as woman's nature. Instead, these attributes belong to the feminine gender, a social construction. The Protestant tradition in which Dickinson was schooled (Dickinson's family practiced New England Congregationalism) predicts resurrection in glorified versions of mortal, and therefore sexed, bodies; although Dickinson remains well known for her religious unorthodoxy, the freedom she anticipates coincides with this doctrine.[2] In the afterlife Dickinson imagines, her speakers apparently continue to be female, but escape the socially prescribed death-in-life she attributes to gender.

Dickinson propounds this argument in the literary genre perceived to be least hospitable to social critique: the lyric poem. Dickinson's poems, in fact, epitomize lyric brevity and intensity, characterized as they are by short ballad stanzas and syntactic elisions. Further, they seem unmoored from real-world referents, difficult to pin to biographical events, much less to the larger issues and conflicts her work might have recorded. Nonetheless, many scholars have successfully shown that Dickinson's elliptic poems do engage with timely questions: for instance, Shira Wolosky demonstrates the influence of the Civil War on Dickinson's poems, and Karen Sanchez-Eppler shows the famously reclusive poet's participation in feminist-abolitionist rhetoric.[3] Dickinson studies promise more such revelations, especially since readers can now place the poems within Dickinson's original groupings, the forty hand-sewn fascicles found in her bureau drawer after her death. Such sequences, although not strictly narrative, increase the information about each narrow lyric in potentially productive ways, as Sharon Cameron and Martha Nell Smith, for instance, have already shown in their book-length studies about Dickinson's fascicle groupings.

However, this essay seeks to show how a subset of Dickinson's poems criticizes prevailing definitions of femininity not despite but through her practice of the lyric.[4] Dickinson uses the limited space of the lyric, which she often depicts as a kind of house, to mimic and subvert qualities of modesty and reserve conventionally associated with femininity; as Joanne Dobson shows, she works within the "code of reticence" imposed on women of her culture.[5] In the poems treated here, the presence of a third image, namely the tomb, grave, or coffin to which the lyric-house is compared, clarifies her critique: Dickinson compares the positions of women in houses, writers in lyric poems, and corpses in graves in order to dramatize how women may be oppressed by and/or transcend conventions of femininity.

My argument begins with two frequently anthologized poems, "The Soul selects her own Society—" (*P*. 303)[6] and "One need not be a Chamber—to be Haunted" (*P*. 670), in order to demonstrate the centrality of the lyric-house-grave figure to Dickinson's work. Later, through four less familiar works about, and in some cases assuming the perspective of, dead and dying women, I show how Dickinson uses this liminal experience to highlight the pain endured by some women as a result of tightly prescribed gender roles. These readings reveal a nineteenth-century poet's subtle interrogations of her culture's doctrines concerning woman's nature, and her rejection of those formulations. Well before contemporary feminist definitions, Dickinson uses death's transformation to signal what is, for her, a crucial distinction between sex and gender.

I

American women poets of Dickinson's time reacted to social pressures toward domesticity by employing the lyric poem as yet another vehicle of womanly duty: in it they either pursued the charitable causes that were felt to be part of the feminine sphere (as Helen Hunt Jackson wrote about Native America) or consoled, moralized, or inspired their readers. Although Dickinson rejects, even despises, this metaphor to describe her enterprise, domesticity and its defining structure, the private home, have powerful meanings for Dickinson as a nineteenth-century woman. In fact, the house, whose stability facilitates Dickinson's retreat even as its associated cultural values seem to trap her, figures the enclosed nature of Dickinson's poetry, famous for its secrecy and stylistic difficulty.

Dickinson was, or became, housebound. She may have been agoraphobic, probably saw the career advantages of seclusion, and certainly perceived herself to be constrained by her society and class's expectations of women.[7] Increasing industrialization in the nineteenth century strengthened Anglo-America's pairing of women with domestic and men with public spaces; much of the literature Dickinson encountered, including works like Coventry Patmore's then popular, now notorious 1854 poem sequence *The Angel in the House*, reinforces these stereotypes.[8] Alternate models for feminine identity were available; Helen Hunt Jackson, a commercially successful writer and career-oriented woman, came from a background nearly identical to Dickinson's. Nonetheless, the most powerful example in Dickinson's life remained her mother, the other Emily Dickinson, who conformed to the type of the quiet, nonintellectual domestic angel. Dickinson's ambivalence toward her mother and her occasional denial of her mother's very existence correspond with the poet's distaste for many of the domestic activities expected of a woman.[9] She felt, correctly, that her main gifts were other than housewifely, and yet this fact was not necessarily appreciated by those around her.

Although Dickinson stayed in her father's house for nearly her entire life, eventually refusing to leave its grounds or, often, accept visitors, she did not resemble a dutiful daughter in all respects. She baked bread for her father, in fact using his dependence on her skill as an excuse not to travel, and nursed her sick mother; on the other hand, she would not go to church, avoided chores in favor of reading and writing, and kept an unorthodox late-night schedule; and neighbors believed that fights with her father had resulted in her voluntary seclusion.[10] Her poetic railings against a heavenly father reinforce an impression of intense feeling but less than perfect harmony between the imposing, successful public man Edward Dickinson and his eldest daughter. Her poetry and letters also document a feeling of alienation and difference from her family, immediate society, larger culture, or all three. Dickinson represents herself alternately as an orphan, an outcast, or even a thief; very often, she is a prisoner, a potentially explosive "Vesuvius at Home" (*P*. 1705).

Dickinson's houses can be protective but often imprison; they exist as emblems of privacy, a condition Dickinson seems to have valued tremendously, but also represent her culture's insistent identification of women with domesticity. This doubleness produces Dickinson's mixed feelings about houses, played out in numerous poems. Dickinson's ambivalence intensifies when the house becomes a metaphor describing the female body, as it does in certain poems from the twentieth fascicle, which concerns renunciation, specifically the renunciation of earthly love until heavenly reward.[11]

"The Soul selects her own Society—" (*P.* 303), a well-known poem of renunciation since Dickinson's first editors (Mabel Loomis Todd and Thomas Wentworth Higginson) published it as "Exclusion" in 1890, writes the house both as a site of valuable privacy and as a woman's body. This "Soul" regally elects one companion and then refuses to be available, even to "an Emperor." Her selectivity equals Dickinson's own, possibly in romance but certainly in daily affairs: the poet lived reclusively enough to turn away friends who had made long journeys to visit her. Dickinson, like other women of her status, was expected to be always accessible to others, always in the parlor to graciously receive callers. Her retreat may have been a result of illness, or a strategy to avoid these interruptions, but it is not surprising that to others this choice seemed odd or remarkable. Dickinson was struggling for the luxury of house as refuge, a luxury the woman-as-caretaker enables but does not always enjoy. "The Soul selects" compares this imperious figure controlling access to her house to the soul within the body; only a few, sometimes only one, break into the soul's circle of attention. The mechanisms that keep strangers out of the home—the familiar doors and gates—give way in this poem to "Valves," a word with a different valence. Valves are more mechanical, or more anatomical than doors. The "Valves of her attention" must be the whorled ears, the lidded eyes, passageways of communication; here Dickinson brings us back from the house metaphor to the body as a neater, tighter enclosure. This link suggests a disturbing alienation of mind from body: it also evokes Dickinson's agoraphobia through the soul's inability to move freely. "The Soul selects" depicts an intelligence inhabiting a shell of a body that is dumb, helpless against the soul's mandates, although its desires may be betrayed by them. Most disturbing is the final clang of the last line, "Like Stone," as if the door has been shut on a tomb. This fastidiousness or singlemindedness about companions (or lovers) leads to a self-imposed burial alive.

Also in Fascicle 20, "One need not be a Chamber—to be Haunted" (*P.* 670) repeats this metaphor but emphasizes the murderousness of the denied self. As Gilbert and Gubar note, this poem exemplifies how Dickinson dramatizes interior schisms: "she felt herself the victim to be haunted by herself the villain."[12] The metaphor is gothic, with its Abbey and Assassin and Ghosts and even its Scottish accent ("one's a'self"), straight out of Sir Walter Scott. Perhaps more than any other poem, this one indicates that she was living (or, more accurately, constructing) her life as if it were a gothic romance, and it comments upon the real significance of the gothic genre, especially for women: its usefulness in providing metaphors describing those turbulent psychological states into which the divided selves of the nineteenth century so often fell.[13] It compares the relatively trivial danger of "an Abbey gallop, / The Stones a'chase—," in which dangers are external and "outside of the integral 'I,'" to the total peril of a self divided in desire.[14] Whether or not the fascicles offer a record of personal experience, they tell a conventional story with familiar tropes and even allusions to similar works, like those of Poe or Hawthorne.

Again, the house becomes a type of the body, its passageways resembling the corridors of the brain. This particular body-house is haunted; the poem conveys an ominous sense of extra presence, frightening materializations of things that should be dead and buried. Dickinson encodes here both the results of her own renunciations and those expected of domestic angels. Women "haunt" houses as mothers and maids and cooks, nearly invisible in their constant labor; women themselves are haunted by desires and ambitions these roles do not allow for. Finally, any poem must be haunted, however faintly, by the circumstances of the poet's life; haunting offers an effective metaphor to describe how the world around Dickinson filters into her work, through echoes and apparitions.

"One need not be a Chamber" demonstrates extreme interiority, the specter inside the body inside the room inside the house, furious at her confinement. These nesting boxes do not suggest entombment as strongly as "The Soul selects," although references to assassins and revolvers threaten death throughout the piece. Both poems, however, draw attention to the lyric's formal constrictions by resisting them. The only perfect rhyme in "The Soul selects" is door / more in the first stanza, a rhyme repeated in the last stanza of "One need not be a Chamber." Both poems slant-rhyme two stanzas, and both end prematurely with a shortened final line. Dickinson's evasions of formal enclosure, here and elsewhere, suggest the pains caused by thematic constrictions in both pieces.

II

Throughout Dickinson's work, life itself means renunciation, an imprisonment in houses that are not homes; imagining more satisfying companionship with a loved one, Dickinson writes, "This [the imagined relationship] seems a Home— / And Home is not—" (P. 944). In poems about houses that are not homes, in particular, Dickinson's critique of domesticity possesses an undertone of excluded longing. In other poems, her female body resembles another kind of house, unhappily, but temporarily, inhabited. In contrast stand eternity and freedom; for Dickinson the narrow "house" of the grave is paradoxically roomier, even homier, than the above-ground kind. This can be especially the case for the wives in Dickinson's poems. Although Dickinson can declare her wifeliness with defiant exuberance, as in "Title divine—is mine!" (P. 1072), even there she demonstrates ambivalence about the union she elsewhere feels deprived of. Wives are "Born—Bridalled—Shrouded— / In a Day—," robbed of an old life, delivered into a new one that can be fatally imprisoning.

Dickinson drives home the confinements of the nineteenth-century wife in "How many times these low feet staggered—" (P. 187). This poem occurs in Fascicle 9, a playful sequence apparently addressed to a beloved, in which Dickinson assumes a childlike voice, alternately asking religious questions to which she already possesses personal answers, and demanding reassurance of her lover's devotion. These may be persona poems, exploring a role Dickinson is interested in but does not mean to undertake in any way, or, as William Shurr controversially suggests, Dickinson may be referring by her "marriage" to a private compact of love made with another person, an alternative connection to the impossible legal one. Shurr misses, however, the negativity about marriage or at least housewifery that permeates all the wife poems. Whatever or whomever Dickinson desired, she did not want to become entangled in her culture's intimate association of married women with the houses they labored to maintain. In the same fascicle, "I'm wife—I've finished that—" (*P*. 199) compares married life, which is supposed to be "comfort," to girlhood, which was supposed to be "pain," with a definite wistfulness. The speaker's decision to marry is "safer," conventional, and by the end of the poem she decides she dare not look back and make real comparisons. Further, her ascension into marriage is equated with heaven, as if, again, marrying is dying.

"How many times these low feet staggered—" figures death as an escape from drudgery for the nineteenth-century woman, dying as somehow an "indolent" thing for a woman to do. The poem begins by trying to open the heavy lid of the housewife's coffin, to investigate the woman's situation: "Try— can you stir the awful rivet— / Try—can you lift the hasps of steel!" The sealed casket, this woman's new house, strongly resembles the sealed lips of the corpse, called a "soldered mouth." "Solder" explicitly links the metallic rivets and hasps with the dead body, as if the body itself constitutes a sort of coffin. Dickinson encloses the housewife in multiple ways: the first box is the unspeaking corpse, the second the coffin, the third the chamber where the body is laid out, the last the poem itself.

Further, the poem behaves in a housewifely manner. It tends the housewife, strokes her forehead, arranges her hair and fingers the way the housewife may have laid out other corpses in her time. The word "feet" here, as always in Dickinson, possesses an extra resonance. Elsewhere she describes her meter as barefoot, deliberately at variance with the constricting "feet" of traditional stress patterns (L. 265).[15] Here "these low feet stagger" the way the housewife's had under the burden of her chores, as if the subject burdens the prosody, or as if the speaker of the poem has to take on the duties the deceased can no longer perform. This poem possesses no clearly defined speaker, like many of Dickinson's poems; instead, it speaks in the second person, directing its imperatives to the lyric's audience. The reader occupies the position of one invited to view the body, a strange but apt metaphor: readers of poetry examine, in a less corporeal way, the remains of the dead. Further, while the coffin lid seems to have been raised successfully, the final enclosure of the dead body is permanently incommunicado, lips sealed, the housewife refusing to make herself available for any more needy questions.

"How many times" identifies the living housewifely speaker with the actual dead housewife. It also comments upon the posthumousness-in-life of the Victorian lady. Nineteenth-century women were already profoundly linked with death through their roles as childbearers, midwives, nurses, and sitters of watches. For these angel-women, as Gilbert and Gubar argue in the quote introducing this essay, this link became a lethal fusion. Edgar Allan Poe's dubious theory that the death of a beautiful woman "is unquestionably the most poetical topic in the world" is only the logical extension of this association.[16] Living female *objets d'art* are dangerously prone to moving, speaking, aging, and otherwise disrupting the male artist's adoration; the dead lady becomes the perfect blank page for imaginative projection. Dickinson's housewife poem parodies this aesthetic: if its object already possesses less erotic potential than the funeral of a wasted maiden, the ordinariness of the thimbles and flies and daisies Dickinson depicts renders romanticization impossible. Further, for Dickinson's housewife death is not tragic or even particularly sentimental; instead, she must prefer real death to the living death of faithful drudgery. Compared to the tedium of her life, "real" death offers a "Gay, Ghastly, Holiday" (*P.* 281). In "For Death—or rather" (*P.* 382), a poem in this line of argument that occurs much later in the fascicles (the thirty-first), Dickinson darkly advises that although "With Gifts of Life / How Death's Gifts may compare— / We know not—," there is certainly good reason to consider putting away "Life's Opportunity."

> The Things that Death will buy
> Are Room—
> Escape from Circumstances—
> And a Name— (*P.* 382)

These amenities would not be inconsiderable to someone like Dickinson. She did indeed possess a room of her own, as Virginia Woolf famously requires that a woman writer should, although many duties pressed upon her and she may often have craved real solitude; room in the sense of perceived freedom remained less available. The last valuable item death provides, according to the poem, "name," suggests, among other things, fame (posthumous, as Dickinson's was).

Biographer Cynthia Griffin Wolff writes about Dickinson's difficult relationship with her family name, her experiments with it, and her desire to claim it:

> The entire Dickinson family was obsessed with the importance of "name." Edward [Emily's father] hovered over his only son anxiously—eager that he marry, settle in Amherst, and produce a son of his own. This was not affection, but a strain of entrenched fanaticism concerning the "House of Dickinson." He expended no similar concern about his daughters' future: one or the other might marry and produce children, but if she did, these would carry their own father's name; the daughters might retain the Dickinson name and remain at home, but then they would be childless and be unable to perpetuate "Dickinson."[17]

Edward considered his son Austin to be his only significant heir, even though the family name ultimately only continued in his line of descent through his daughter's literary productions (Austin's sons died before they had children of their own). Wolff's explanation of the connotation of "name" for Dickinson also adds to the significance of the word "house" to the poet. "House" can mean family or line of descent, masculine power and its traditional transfer, something Emily Dickinson both designs to usurp and feels hopelessly excluded by.

"For Death—or rather" is, ultimately, a hardheaded look at a woman writer's situation, based on an economic metaphor. The phrase "Life's Opportunity" here acquires a distinctly ironic ring. Perhaps death, offering seclusion in a tomb and one's name on a headstone, is really a proper lady's only chance of freedom, dignity, "escape." However, this poem's position within the fascicles suggests another reading: "circumstances" could mean Dickinson's distance from a beloved, and one of the things death might "buy" is a reunion.

Similar poems appear in Fascicle 26, which expresses particular impatience for death and its associated freedoms; this sequence contains an elegy and perhaps other poems for Elizabeth Barrett Browning (P. 312). One extraordinary lyric watches the moon rise enviously; Dickinson compares it to a guillotined head "independent" of a lady's body, and regrets being unable to follow its intellectual vault (*P*. 629). In the same vein (and fascicle), "I am alive—I guess—" (*P*. 470) unfavorably compares the speaker's earthly home to entombment, her lifeless life to the advantages of death. Physical life, as elsewhere, stands in strong contrast to real "Life," which would entail happiness and that impossible companionship with her absent lover (*P*. 640).

"I am alive—" gradually assembles evidence affirming the speaker's mortal state. She notes the warm color of her hands and fingertips, even holds a glass before her mouth to see if it will collect the moisture of breath. Still tentative, she notes optimistically that she is not in the parlor, where the dead would be laid out and also where the angel in the house, herself a kind of zombie, would dutifully receive her visitors. The clincher, the best proof, is

> I am alive—because
> I do not own a House
> Entitled to myself—precise—
> And fitting no one else—
>
> And marked my Girlhood's name—
> So Visitors may know
> Which Door is mine—and not mistake—
> And try another Key—

The speaker finally knows that she is a living woman because she does not possess property, privacy, or her born (not her married) name marking the (lockable) door as her own. The speaker's confusion about her own condition conveys a grim joke about the always posthumous nineteenth-century woman, who does not experience what a man would call "life," as well as about her own loneliness. The image of the parlor helps to blur the dead with the living lady, but the whole poem is concerned with proving that it's almost impossible to tell them apart. The most significant difference, at least here, is that the dead lady has some rights.

Dickinson writes a great many poems imagining what happens after death; some are satires, others ghost stories. Fascicle 16 also occupies itself with mortality; to its speaker, a woman in breakdown after a terrible but unnamed loss, there exist no clear distinctions between death and life. The dead are alive to her, and she is dead. She can write so vividly from a corpse's perspective, as she does in the final poem this essay treats, because she is experiencing death-in-life, an existence apparently without the power to seize happiness.

"Twas just this time, last year, I died" (P. 445) offers a first-person account of death in this sequence. Like the rest of the undead in Dickinson's poetry, this speaker experiences paralysis: she has "wanted to get out, / But something held my will." She can hear and imagine what occurs in the outer world—for example, she heard the tasseled corn waving as she was carried to her grave, and is still able to follow the passing of the seasons—but cannot speak or move. Instead, she rehearses her memories of the colors and textures of things, and imagines how her family spends the holidays without her.

An aspect of malevolence poisons these fantasies, apparently those of a daughter who has died early. "I wondered which would miss me," she thinks, "least." She isn't sure her death will affect anyone's holiday cheer. In the last stanza, however, she brightens spookily; she turns from grieving that she may have been forgotten, to looking forward to when, "some perfect year—/ Themself, should come to me."

Dickinson's dead daughter, although as unspeaking as the housewife, is hungry. This speaker died at harvest time and can't stop thinking about what she's missing. Corn, apples, and pumpkins occupy her mind; she wonders whether her father might accidentally set a plate for her on Thanksgiving. Her eagerness for her family to join her, somewhat insensitive to what their own wishes might be, also seems hungry, even greedy. This poem presents a dark version of the angel in the house who has become a ghost in a grave: her passivity becomes paralysis, renunciation becomes starvation, decorous silence and attention to male need become frustrated eavesdropping on father and brother, and of course the house becomes a tomb. Instead of devoting her labor and imagination to tending other people's lives, she wishes for their deaths. This extreme version of the domestic daughter is speechless and powerless, but thinking dangerous things. As the housewife parodies it, the daughter stands as the nightmare answer to Poe's idea that "a dead lady is the most poetical topic in the world."

"Twas just this time" portrays a daughter set apart from the rest of her family and from their sheltering house; it reverses Dickinson's claim in other poems to be an orphan, but creates the same effect of alienation. Dickinson repeats this motif, emphasizing that while her life seems housebound, in other ways she remains a stranger to domesticity and all the values that would seem to be associated with her nunlike seclusion. In this version of domestic confinement, the daughter never achieves even the relative freedom Dickinson locates in poetry, the airy house of "Possibility" in Poem 657. Instead, a culturally prescribed gender role oppresses the girl into murderous resentment.

Dickinson continually subverts versions of the domestic angel: nunlike recluses act imperially, busy housewives prefer indolence, virgins express greedy hunger. However, she does not or cannot hypothesize about woman's nature without reference to the separate sphere nineteenth-century American society designs middle-class white women to inhabit. Instead, she looks to death, the unimaginable state of resurrection, for release from stultifying expectations. The lyric poem offers the chief forum for this stretch of her imagination: as women find eternity through confinement in tombs, the artful box of the poem can contain some portion of freedom.

Notes

1. Sandra M. Gilbert and Susan Gubar, *The Madwoman in the Attic: The Woman Writer and the Nineteenth-Century Literary Imagination* (New Haven: Yale University Press, 1979), 25.

2. *The Encyclopedia of Religion* describes the Christian doctrine of resurrection, although "the least coherent aspect of Christian theological tradition" (459), as follows: "Every man and woman of the Christian way who truly believes in the power of Christ will rise with ... in a body that will be like Christ's 'glorious' body" (457). Roger Lundin, author of *Emily Dickinson and the Art of Belief*, also observed in correspondence to me that "the imagery of consummation figures in some of her poems about death, so it would not seem likely that she would consider it to be, definitively, a state without sexuality," although he rightly emphasizes the mystery of the afterlife for Dickinson. Many thanks to Alex Brown, my colleague in the Religion Department at Washington and Lee University, for her insight on these issues.

3. Karen Sanchez-Eppler, *Touching Liberty: Abolition, Feminism, and the Politics of the Body* (Berkeley: University of California Press, 1993), and Shira Wolosky, *Emily Dickinson: A Voice of War* (New Haven: Yale University Press, 1984).

4. For a fuller discussion of such strategies as employed by Dickinson and subsequent American women poets, see Lesley Wheeler, *The Poetics of Enclosure: Emily Dickinson, Marianne Moore, H.D., and Gwendolyn Brooks* (Ph.D. diss., Princeton University, 1994).

5. Joanne Dobson, *Dickinson and the Strategies of Reticence: The Woman Writer in Nineteenth-Century America* (Bloomington: Indiana University Press, 1989), xii.

6. My numbering of the poems refers to *The Poems of Emily Dickinson*, ed. Thomas H. Johnson, 3 vols. (Cambridge, MA: Belknap Press, 1955). My numbering of the fascicles will refer to the valuable reproductions of the reassembled books in *The Manuscript Notebooks of Emily Dickinson*, ed. R. W. Franklin (Cambridge, MA: Belknap Press, 1981).

7. For a discussion of Dickinson's agoraphobia, see Maryanne M. Garbowsky, *The House Without the Door: A Study of Emily Dickinson and the Illness of Agoraphobia* (Teaneck: Fairleigh Dickinson University Press, 1989).

8. See, for instance, Nancy Woloch, *Women and the American Experience* (New York: Knopf, 1984), 114-20. In Dickinson's time, at least in the Northeast, the home was ceasing to be a center for production by all family members. Men started working outside the home to earn the salaries that supported it; women stayed at home, assuming full responsibility for the running of the household and the raising of children. *Home* was beginning to acquire its meaning as *refuge*.

9. See Thomas H. Johnson and Theodora Ward, eds., *The Letters of Emily Dickinson*, 3 vols. (Cambridge, MA: Harvard University Press, 1958), especially her comment that "My Mother does not care for thought" (II: 404), or Higginson's quoting of Dickinson in the same volume, "I never had a mother" (II: 475).

10. See the reminiscences gathered in Jay Leyda, *The Years and Hours of Emily Dickinson*, 2 vols. (New Haven: Yale University Press, 1960), 478-80.

11. The fascicle conveys this subject partly through allusions to Hawthorne's *The Scarlet Letter* (1850), another story of thwarted love and dangerous temptation: burning red is transformed by internal struggle into a refined blaze in "dare you see a soul at the White Heat?" (*P*. 365); "Mine—by the Right of the White Election!" (*P*. 528) refers to a "Scarlet prison," and one poem even calls renunciation "the Scarlet way" (*P* 527).

12. Gilbert and Gubar, *The Madwoman in the Attic*, 624.

13. Ibid., 624-25.

14. Cynthia Griffin Wolff, *Emily Dickinson* (New York: Knopf, 1986), 464.

15. *Letters*, 265.

16. Edgar Allan Poe, "The Philosophy of Composition," in *The Complete Poems and Stories of Edgar Allan Poe, with Selections from his Critical Writings*, ed. A. H. Quinn (New York: Knopf, 1981), 982.

17. Wolff, *Emily Dickinson*, 201.

Chapter 16

Wild Women and Graceful Girls: Toni Morrison's Winter's Tale

Marc Conner

The role of music, or more generally of sound, in the written word forms the principal aesthetic concern of Toni Morrison. She has stated that she wants "to break away from certain assumptions that are inherent in the conception of the novel form to make a truly aural novel," a novel that would be modeled upon "the one other art form in which black people have always excelled and that is music."[1] Morrison's 1992 novel, *Jazz*, emerges out of these aesthetic concerns, and as a result the novel presents two problems that scholars have been unable to resolve: who, or what, is the narrator of this novel? and what is the actual role of music in this novel's structure? Most critics have combined these two problems by identifying the narrator with the novel's titular concern with music: as one critic asserts, "jazz *is* the mysterious narrator of the novel," and another, "Morrison seeks to create the very rhythms of jazz" in the narrative voice; the narrative is "like a jazz performance," states a third, and another, "just as in jazz, the story and the telling of the story are one."[2] Thus the novel is reduced to a simple proposition: it is about jazz, and it is like jazz—indeed, it *is* jazz.

Yet while it is surely true that this novel engages, and is in many ways structured by, jazz music, this is only the first thing—and really the most obvious and least interesting thing—to say about *Jazz*. Yes, music lies at the heart of Morrison's work, and the complex and uncanny narrator of the novel is quite aware of this; but the music in question is not—or is not merely—the music of clarinets and pianos and Harlem nightclubs, the music of a historical time and place. On the contrary, what appears to be a human and temporal art develops into an inhuman, eternal, and in some sense even maternal art that both transcends and unites its various human representations. The novel becomes an aesthetic quest, moving beyond the constrictions and reductions of race, gender, politics, and history, and gesturing finally toward an aesthetic realm that is far more ancient, fundamental, and redemptive than any earthly corollary could be. Morrison thereby offers a new direction for the African-American novel, which heretofore has been dominated by either a realist/ naturalist aesthetic (exemplified by Richard Wright, Zora Neale Hurston, James Baldwin) or a modernist aesthetic (as in the work of Ralph Ellison, Charles Johnson, Ishmael Reed, and Morrison's earlier novels): in *Jazz* Morrison imagines the African-

American novel as Romance. In this composition, *Jazz* becomes its own rejection and its own fulfillment, a complex quest tale for a fundamental mothering figure who harmonizes the human, the natural, and the supernatural. In this figure, Morrison finds the source of healing for which her tortured characters yearn throughout each of her novels, and she discovers the source for her own art.

I

A sad tale's best for winter.
—*The Winter's Tale,* 2.1.25

In its most elemental form, *Jazz* is a quest tale, with the motif of the journey at its heart. The movement from south to north is the fundamental journey of the novel—the great migration of African-American peoples at the end of the nineteenth and beginning of the twentieth centuries from the rural, agrarian south to the urban, industrial north. When Joe and Violet Trace undergo this migration in 1906, they experience it with a rush of pleasure, anticipation, and excitement that matches the music that announces their arrival:

> entering the lip of the City dancing all the way. Her hip bones rubbed his thigh as they stood in the aisle unable to stop smiling. They weren't even there yet and already the City was speaking to them. They were dancing. And like a million others, chests pounding, tracks controlling their feet, they stared out the windows for first sight of the City that danced with them, proving already how much it loved them. Like a million more they could hardly wait to get there and love it back.[3]

The music embodies the promise of the City: the jazz of early-twentieth-century New York expresses the hope of the great migration. As one critic has described it, this music "jazzifies the history of a people," giving in its rhythm "the theme of migration, of people on the move, on the go," expressing "the joy and the abandon of a million people entering a land where the cities of the North dissolve into one big City, Harlem."[4] Upon arriving, Joe and Violet—and all the migrants for whom they stand as emblems—are enchanted by "a City seeping music" (67).

The unidentified narrator expresses the allure of this City and its music early in the novel. After a brief prelude—the first four pages set out the basic story—the narrator turns to what can be considered the novel's chief interest and main character:

> I'm crazy about this City. . . .
> Below is shadow where any blasé thing takes place: clarinets and lovemaking, fists and the voices of sorrowful women. A city like this one makes me dream tall and feel in on things. . . . I'm strong. Alone, yes, but top-notch and indestructible—like the City in 1926 when all the wars are over and there will never be another one. The people down there in the shadow are happy about

that. At last, at last, everything's ahead. . . . Here comes the new. Look out. There goes the sad stuff. The bad stuff. The things-nobody-could-help stuff. The way everybody was then and there. Forget that. History is over, you all, and everything's ahead at last. (7)

This is our initial impression of the City, just as it is Joe and Violet's: a place of endless possibility, of new and intoxicating music, where the dwellers are alive and in control of their destinies for the first time in their lives. This City embodies the quintessential Modernist gesture of rejecting the past, discarding history in favor of the new, an ethos that Nietzsche identifies with the "modern spirit."[5] And all of this occurs to the restless rhythm of the new music, the jazz that pervades these early pages—as the narrator states, "you could hear it everywhere" (56).[6]

All characters who come to the City are scarred in physical or psychic ways that leave them in need of healing. In the South they leave behind murdered parents, lynch mobs, lost land, beatings, humiliations; in the City they hope to find the respite and the ministering they need. Urged on by the reports of others who have been there, the migrants arrive and "knew right away that it was for them, this City and no other," precisely because it allows them to abandon their old, ravaged selves: "Part of why they loved it was the specter they left behind." Upon arriving they "surrendered themselves to the City" and become "not so much new as themselves: their stronger, riskier selves" (32-33).

These characters all feel that the City's music—underground, anti-establishment, quintessentially black—provides the tonic for the oppressed lives they flee. Its erotic qualities—"dirty, get-on-down music the women sang and the men played and both danced to, close and shameless or apart and wild"—mark it as potentially liberating and empowering, full of "a complicated anger" and urging its listeners to "do unwise disorderly things. Just hearing it was like violating the law" (58-59). Most readers of *Jazz* see the City and its music as providing the very nurturing these fragmented characters seek: as Richard Hardack argues, "[T]he disconnection between print and child, parent and child, word and meaning, self and body, self and other, are all staged as *in need of jazz*. . . . It is only the music . . . which ultimately transcends double-consciousness and restores nature to itself."[7] Thus the music is viewed as "Dionysian," a rebellious expression of energy that promises liberation and revelation.[8]

Yet there is abundant evidence to make us suspect that the effects of the City and its music upon its new inhabitants is hardly overwhelmingly positive; indeed, we might even wonder if, far from being what the characters need, the City and its music are precisely the cause of their splintered, fragmented lives. The most obviously ravaged figure is Violet, who is split into two separate selves, one of whom is nicknamed "Violent" because she takes a knife to the body of the girl with whom her husband had an affair. Words elude Violet's control; she is psychically fragmented, possessing "private cracks," "dark fissures in the globe light of the day" (22-23). These cracks are the signs of

Violet's inability to maintain a stable sense of self in the City that disrupts her. For neither Joe's affair nor his murder of his young lover drives Violet apart; rather, her cracking began years ago, when she left her home in Virginia to come to the City. Violet tells Alice that she "never gave a speck of trouble. . . . Till I got here. City make you tighten up" (81). And toward the conclusion she confesses to Felice that the movement north caused her fragmentation: "I messed up my own life. . . . Before I came North I made sense and so did the world" (207).

Joe too has been harrowed by his movement north. At the beginning of the novel, he is presented to us as a drained, wasted man, recalling only in loss what his past had been: "For when Joe tries to remember the way it was when he and Violet were young, when they got married, decided to . . . move up North to the City almost nothing comes to mind. . . . it was drained of everything but the language to say it in" (29). The City is a place of early aging, where the vital force is stripped away; as the narrator reveals, "The young are not so young here, and there is no such thing as midlife" (11). Even more than aging him, the City takes away Joe's moral commitment. Alice Manfred cannot forgive him for taking the life of her niece because Joe "*knew* wrong wasn't right, and he did it anyway" (74). When Joe stalks Dorcas the night he kills her, he wonders if the evil he is thinking comes from him or if it comes from the music that no one in the City can escape: "I dismissed the evil in my thoughts because I wasn't sure that the sooty music the blind twins were playing wasn't the cause. . . . they confused me, made me doubt myself, and I lost the trail" (132). Living in the City even makes Joe forget the fundamental lesson that Hunters Hunter taught him in the Virginia woods of his youth: "never kill the tender and nothing female" (175).

Dorcas, Joe's young lover, is not of the older generation, like the Traces, nor did she leave a world where she experienced a wholeness of being, as they did. When Dorcas's parents were killed in the St. Louis riots, her aunt Alice took her to live in New York, and so she left a childhood of violence and death to come to the City and its promise of vitality. And for Dorcas, despite her aunt's efforts to keep her rigidly disciplined and safe from temptation, the City and its music promise to satisfy all her desires:

> While her aunt worried about how to keep the heart ignorant of the hips and the head in charge of both, Dorcas lay on a chenille bedspread, tickled and happy knowing that there was no place to be where somewhere, close by, somebody was not licking his licorice stick, tickling the ivories, beating his skins, blowing off his horn while a knowing woman sang. . . . (60)

The stories the older women tell of loves lost and the desperate sacrifices they have made for passion convince Dorcas that sensual love is exactly "the Paradise" she has dreamed of: "Paradise. All for Paradise," she marvels (63).[9] Yet life in the City fragments Dorcas, too: Felice reports that Dorcas "had all the ingredients of pretty," but "all together it didn't fit" (201). Alice is aware of the danger of the music, of "what it did to the children" (56)—desire for a jazz record prompts a girl to abandon her baby sister to a stranger (20-21)—and Dorcas represents the fate suffered by all the novel's children: for just as the City "is not the place for old men" (192), so too is it not the place for children. Hence when Joe and Violet arrive, they agree that they do not want children to complicate their new, jazzy world—"citylife would be so much better without them" (107).

Only the young can thrive in the City, only those between childhood and adulthood, caught in the throes of first passion for whom music and dancing and the intoxicating rhythms of the City are irresistible. Yet as the narrator informs us, "Little of that makes for love, but it does pump desire" (34). Desire is the law of the City, a desire that makes people want to fix themselves in the flush of their first youth. But this desire carries a cost—"they love that part of themselves so much *they forget what loving other people was like*" (33, emphasis added)—a cost that even the narrator comes to realize near the story's end: "It was loving the City that distracted me and gave me ideas. Made me think I could speak its loud voice and make that sound sound human. I missed the people altogether" (220). The narrator learns that the voice of the City is *not* human, that indeed it is opposed to the human principle altogether.

Not only does the City oppose human sympathy and human cares, it overwhelms the human will; indeed, the "illusion" that the human characters control their own fates "is the music's secret drive: the control it tricks them into believing is theirs" (65). When Joe comes to Dorcas, "he thinks he is free," the narrator states, but in fact the City itself, and its unceasing music, propels him on a "track" that is determined:

> Take my word for it, he is bound to the track. It pulls him like a needle through the groove of a Bluebird record. Round and round about the town. That's the way the city spins you. Makes you do what it wants, go where the laid-out roads say to. All the while letting you think you're free. . . . You can't get off the track a City lays for you. Whatever happens, whether you get rich or stay poor, ruin your health or live to old age, you always end up back where you started: hungry for the one thing everybody loses—young loving. (120)

"Young loving" rules the City, but this "loving" is actually the site of violence and death. Alice senses the City's capacity for violence, "its appetite," its "longing for the bash, the slit" (59); and when Joe finally finds Dorcas at the party, she is enmeshed in blood and warfare: "Everything is now. It's like a war. Everyone is handsome, shining just thinking about other people's blood. As though the red wash flying from veins not theirs is facial makeup patented for its glow" (191).

When Joe shoots Dorcas there is no mention of her pain, not one word describing suffering or bodily harm. What is mentioned, repeatedly, is her "blood": blood on Acton's coat, handkerchief, and shirt; blood seeping all the way through the sheets and into the bed on which Dorcas is lying (192). Felice later reveals that Dorcas "bled to death," and that "all they talked about" at the party was "the blood" (210). Dorcas's blood is the price exacted by the City, the blood sacrifice it demands whereby youth itself is offered up to the world of sensuality and desire. Thus, readers who have described the City and its music as "Dionysian" are more accurate than perhaps they realize: the City is the place of *true* Dionysian revelry, which Nietzsche describes as "the annihil-ation of the individual."[10] The Dionysian principle, as Walter Kaufmann explains, is "that drunken frenzy which threatens to destroy all forms and codes; the ceaseless striving which apparently defies all limitations; the ultimate abandonment *we sometimes sense in music.*"[11] Joe's winter murder of Dorcas—his killing of the very girl he adores on "an icy day in January" (180), "the awful January one that ended everything" (73)—most forcefully expresses this pervasive, destructive energy.

II

The storm begins; poor wretch,
That for thy mother's fault art thus expos'd
To loss, and what may follow!
—*The Winter's Tale*, 3.2.48-50

Each character in *Jazz* longs for something the City does not and cannot provide, and ultimately each searches for the same thing. Violet seeks to mother a child: despite her stated desire not to have children, and despite her three intentional miscarriages, she finds herself overcome with "a panting, unmanageable craving," a longing "heavier than sex," which she identifies as "mother-hunger" (108). She buys a doll to sleep with, and her fantasies of a child grow so powerful that she walks halfway home with a neighbor's baby before the crowd stops her. This desire to become a mother reveals Violet's deeper desire to be reconciled with her own mother, who committed suicide when Violet was sixteen by jumping into a well.

This well—"a place so narrow, so dark it was pure, breathing relief to see her stretched in a wooden box" (101)—becomes for Violet an image of the womb as place of death; she thinks of her own womb, where three babies died before they were ever born, as "so violent a home," and thoughts of her mother's experience teach Violet "to never never have children" (102). To be a mother, for Violet, is to carry death within you. Yet her craving for a child ultimately overcomes this loathing, for at some level she hopes a baby could heal her wound of having lost her mother when she herself was a child. The narrator muses that Violet's dreams of a baby offer her "a brightness that could be carried in her arms. Distributed, if need be, into places dark as the bottom of a well" (22). Hence Violet at the novel's beginning insists that "she didn't want to be like" her own mother (97); but by the close her chief desire is "to be the woman my mother didn't stay around long enough to see. That one. The one she would have liked" (208). Violet's primary desire is to be reconciled with the lost figure of her mother.

Joe's desire follows a similar pattern. Like so many archetypal American literary figures—Fitzgerald's Gatsby, Faulkner's Thomas Sutpen, Ellison's Invisible Man—Joe names himself and so becomes, or would like to become, his own progenitor. Yet he names himself precisely after what he lacks—his true parents. Before he is three years old, he asks his stepmother "where my real parents were. She looked down at me . . . and told me, O honey they disappeared without a trace. The way I heard it I understood her to mean the 'trace' they disappeared without was me" (123-24). Thus Joe christens himself "Joe Trace," suggesting that he contains within himself the track that would lead him back to these lost parents. He is convinced that someday his lost mother is "coming back for me" (124).

When Hunters Hunter makes it clear that Joe's mother is Wild, the feral woman who lurks in the cane fields near their town, Joe "wrestled with the notion of a wildwoman for a mother" (175-76) and concludes that he must track her down and make her acknowledge his status as her son. Yet Wild is chiefly characterized by her refusal to be a mother: when Hunters Hunter first enters his cabin and finds Wild about to give birth, he realizes that "his house was full of motherlessness—and the chief unmothering was Wild's" (167). When her baby, presumably Joe,[12] is born, Wild "was of practically no help," and "would not hold the baby or look at it" (170). Thus Joe thinks of her later as "too brain-blasted to do what the meanest sow managed: nurse what she birthed" (179).[13]

Yet Joe, like Violet, is unable to rest without reconciling with this figure of a vanished, or rejecting, mother. Before he leaves Virginia, he determines to find her and have his status as son, and hers as mother, either confirmed or rejected. He discovers her lair, a womblike place in the rock above a river, and he waits patiently for a sign from her:

> what makes him think he can see her hand even if she did decide to shove it through the bushes and confirm, for once and for all, that she was indeed his mother? And even though the confirmation would shame him, it would make him the happiest boy in Virginia. If she decided, that is, to show him it, to listen for once to what he was saying to her and then do it, say some kind of yes, even if it was no, so he would know. And how he was willing to take that chance of being humiliated and grateful at the same time, because the confirmation would mean both. (36-37)

Though Joe waits for hours, and though he eventually enters into the burrow (from the top, head-first, as if reentering the womb from which he hopes he once emerged), the sign is never given (183). This event makes Joe give up the woods and take Violet to the City—and if we find it difficult to reconcile the fifty-year-old cosmetics salesman with the magnificent hunter and tracker Joe once was in Virginia, perhaps this is Morrison's point. When he fails to receive the sign of confirmation from his mother, Joe leaves behind the natural world in which he is literally at home.

Joe's search for Dorcas on the night he kills her is conflated with his never-ceasing search for Wild: the figures at the party look to him like "the flock of redwings" (130) that always accompanies Wild's appearances, and when he arrives at the party and asks himself, "where is *she*?" (184), it is unclear if he thinks he is in a borough apartment or Wild's home in the rocks. "I had the gun," Joe recalls, "but it was not the gun—it was my hand I wanted to touch you with" (130-31); he thinks he is still stretching out to touch Wild, when in fact he is destroying Dorcas. Thus in his love for Dorcas, Joe is re-enacting his love for his mother, the love he could never confirm and finally can only express through death.

This longing for the lost mother fills Dorcas, too. Joe becomes her lover because she "knew better than people his own age what that inside nothing was like. And who filled it for him, just as he filled it for her, *because she had it too*"; indeed, Joe speculates, "[m]aybe her nothing was worse since she knew her mother" (38, emphasis added). The house in which Dorcas's mother burns to death is her equivalent of Violet's dark well in which Violet's mother drowns. Whether by fire or by water, both women lose their mothers in a womblike space of death.

The result for Dorcas is a desperate desire to be loved and accepted. She temporarily satisfies this desire with Joe, and she comes to him because of her cruel rejection by the dancing brothers at one of her first teen parties. This rejection is a kind of death for Dorcas, and like her later, literal death, it occurs to the accompaniment of the jazz music:

> just as the music, slow and smoky, loads up the air, his smile bright as ever, he wrinkles his nose and turns away.
> Dorcas has been acknowledged, appraised and dismissed in the time it takes for a needle to find its opening groove. (67)

The narrator tells us that "by the time Joe Trace whispered to her through the crack of a closing door her life had become almost unbearable" (67); the desire she transfers to Joe replaces the desire for love she had crushed by her peers; and this desire emerges from the pain of separation she feels when her mother is taken from her.

Even the novel's narrator partakes of this desire for the mother. While relating the desire both Joe and Violet feel toward their lost mothers, the narrator confesses to knowing nothing about their particular losses; yet, the narrator adds, "it's not hard to imagine what it must have been like" (137)—not hard at all, because the narrator shares this same longing. This is why the narrator is so drawn to the character of Golden Gray, the half-white, half-black man who travels back to Virginia to murder his father and ends up witnessing Wild's delivery of Joe. Golden Gray has little relation to the main plot of the story, yet the narrator becomes increasingly interested in his situation, precisely because Golden Gray also suffers the amputation of a missing parent. Golden Gray imagines he will confess this pain to his father, Hunters Hunter, when he sees him, but his words as he imagines this meeting could well be the narrator's, or those of any other character in this novel: "When I see him . . . I will tell him all about the missing part of me and listen for his crying shame. I will exchange then; let him have mine and take his as my own and we will both be free, arm-tangled and whole" (159). *This* is the desire of Violet, and of Joe, and of Dorcas: that reuniting with the lost parent will heal their wounds and make them whole.

Thus the narrator becomes most self-revealing, and most concerned with the artifice of narration and the fidelity of the story, when approaching the climax of Golden Gray's tale; here the narrator confesses to a need "to think this through carefully," even "to alter things" in the story, in order to achieve the necessary end:

> I have to be a shadow who wishes him well, like the smiles of the dead left over from their lives. I want to dream a nice dream for him, and another of him. Lie down next to him, a wrinkle in the sheet, and contemplate his pain and by doing so ease it, diminish it. I want to be the language that wishes him well, speaks his name, wakes him when his eyes need to be open. I want him to stand next to a well dug quite clear from trees so twigs and leaves will not fall into the deep water. . . . where the light does not reach, a collection of leftover smiles stirs, some brief benevolent love rises from the darkness and there is nothing for him to see or hear, and there is no reason to stay but he does. For the safety at first, then for the company. Then for himself—with a kind of confident, enabling, serene power that flicks like a razor and then hides. But he has felt it now, and it may come again. . . . he will remember it, and if he remembers it he can recall it. That is to say, he has it at his disposal. (161)

In a passage that recalls Violet's loss ("a well dug quite clear") and Joe's loss ("where the light does not reach"), the narrator reveals a desire to ease the pain of loss of these characters, to "dream a dream" (tell a story) wherein and whereby they can find comfort, healing ("some brief benevolent love"), and the power to recall the dream or the story for themselves when the pain returns.[14]

Ultimately, the narrator wants to do this for the narrator, as well. In the closing pages the narrator seems to realize what the attentive reader has suspected for some time: that Joe's tears throughout the novel "were for more than Dorcas," that while he was searching for her, he was also—perhaps primarily—searching for "Wild's chamber of gold" (221). Then, the narrator confesses to sharing this desire:

> That home in the rock; that place sunlight got into most of the day. Nothing to be proud of, to show anybody or to want to be in. *But I do.* I want to be in a place already made for me, both snug and wide open. With a doorway

never needing to be closed, a view slanted for light and bright autumn leaves but not rain. Where moonlight can be counted on if the sky is clear and stars no matter what. And below, just yonder, a river called Treason to rely on. (221, emphasis added)

This remarkable passage, barely eight pages from the novel's ending, expresses the sum of every character's yearning, and the yearning of the narrator, too: for a primal source of love, comfort, and security that they locate somewhere in the distant past, in the natural world, and associate with a lost mother-figure. In *Jazz* all figures long for their mothers, and they long for home.

But is the South they leave behind truly such an idyllic place? Joe and Violet flee brutal lynchings, burnings, starvation, disenfranchisement—their fond recollections of this awful place recall Sethe's musings in *Beloved* about "Sweet Home," the plantation so brutal she would rather murder her own children than see them returned to it; yet in her memory it is still a place of beauty, "as though Sweet Home really was one."[15] All of Morrison's novels have some kind of return to the South, either in recollection (*The Bluest Eye, Beloved, Paradise*) or actual journey (*Song of Solomon, Tar Baby, Sula*); and in each novel the sense of the South is akin to that expressed by Langston Hughes in his 1922 poem, "The South":

> The lazy, laughing South
> With blood on its mouth.
> ....
> Beautiful, like a woman,
> Seductive as a dark-eyed whore,
> ....
> And I, who am black, would love her
> But she spits in my face.
> And I, who am black,
> Would give her many rare gifts
> but she turns her back upon me.
>   So now I seek the North—
>   The cold-faced North,
>   For she, they say,
>   Is a kinder mistress,
> And in her house my children
> May escape the spell of the South.[16]

The final six lines, in particular, could stand as the epigraph to *Jazz*: despite the lingering affection the characters feel for the South, they must leave her for the colder North in hopes of greater opportunity and more humane treatment. Yet the novel attests to the futility of this vision, just as it gives witness to the illusion of the South as the loving, nurturing home for which the characters yearn. Whatever constitutes home in this novel, the ultimate fulfillment of the characters' longing, it is not, nor can it be, an earthly location.

III

We were as twinned lambs, that did frisk I' th' sun,
And bleat the one at th' other; what we changed
Was innocence for innocence; we knew not
The doctrine of ill-doing . . . —The Winter's Tale, 1.2.67-70

How do the characters of the novel imagine the world they have left behind? Or, put differently, what is the content of their imaginings when they think back on this home they have lost? For Joe, this "home" is the woods and fields he roamed as a boy and young man, when he was "picked out and trained to be a man" (125) by "the man so expert in the woods he'd become a hunter's hunter" (168). Joe is figuratively the child of these woods, since his mother is (likely) Wild, who is more an emblem of nature than a human mother. Thus, like Faulkner's Isaac McCaslin, Joe is at heart "more comfortable in the woods than in a town"; "Piled-up buildings? Cement paths? . . . Not me" he states (126). Joe's lost home is the realm of nature.

For Violet, the City has not only cracked her, it causes her to waste away. She has become "pick thin" (206), quaffing "Dr. Dee's Nerve and Flesh Builder" (93), and "cooking pork [Joe] can't eat" (49), trying desperately, as Joe puts it, "to grow an ass she swore she once owned" (69). As with Joe, city life softens and weakens Violet: "twenty years doing hair in the city had softened her arms and melted the shield that once covered her palms and fingers." But the Violet of Virginia was strong: "she loaded hay and handled the mule wagon like a full-grown man" (92). Violet's strongest recollections of this home are of a land of plenty: she brags to Alice about Joe's hunting prowess in Virginia, how they feasted on rabbits, deer, possum, and pheasant, how they "ate good down home" (81). Thus her sense of home is a land of fruitfulness and plenty, where every herb-bearing seed, every beast of the earth, and every fowl of the air is available to give humans strength and fullness of being.[17]

This home is also the site of a passionate and pure love between Joe and Violet. In the closing pages, the narrator strangely slips back in time to describe a scene in 1906—the year Joe and Violet depart for the City—when Violet left the field on a scorching day, bathed herself in their cabin, and fell asleep naked on the bed. Joe came home to find her "dark girl-body limp on the bed," gently eased off her last work boot, and stroked her head and thigh while she slept on. "It must have helped something in her dream," the narrator muses, "for she laughed then, a light happy laugh that he had never heard before, but which seemed to belong to her" (225-26). This is the only glimpse in the novel of the young, intimate lovers Joe and Violet were before coming to the City; indeed, this scene is unique in all of Morrison's fiction: in no other novel does she depict a love that is so suffused with peace and harmony, so absent of pain and scars that need to be touched, without violence or rivalry or hidden rage. Only in this lost home that Joe and Violet dimly recall, and that the narrator invokes near the novel's close, is such a love intimated. That Violet falls asleep with the singing of "Go Down Moses" echoing in her ears reinforces the motif of exile and return that pervades the entire novel—here, in some sense, is a homecoming.

Finally—and crucially—this home provides a different kind of music in the novel, a more fundamental and healing music than what the City provides. When Joe searches for his mother in rural Virginia, he hears the sound of "some combination of running water and wind in high trees." The alternative music of the novel is precisely these elemental sounds of nature: "The music the world makes, familiar to fishermen and shepherds, woodsmen have also heard. It hypnotizes animals. Bucks raise their heads and gophers freeze. Attentive woodsmen smile and close their eyes" (176). With this description, the narrator overtly shifts the form of the narrative from the genre of the novel to the mythos of romance: for although this novel has woodsmen and fishermen, there are no shepherds to be found in the Virginia woods, and none in the world of the realistic novel.[18] Only in the world of pastoral romance does music emanate from nature itself. The pastoral world, with its sense of timelessness, tranquillity, and perfect harmony between humanity and nature, is a poetic rendering of Eden, the archetype of the pastoral in postclassical literature. And it is, of course, an Edenic world that Morrison's characters long for throughout *Jazz*: an idyllic realm of nature; a land of plenty, where humanity is strong and without blemish; a site of pure and passionate love; a place of maternal comfort, prior to the separation of mother and child; and a domain where the music of the world is intelligible to humans. That this music is definitively inhuman is confirmed by the narrator's statement that "the music the world makes has no words" (177)—the source of this music is prelinguistic, prior to human creativity.

Such Edenic imaginings are nothing new to Morrison's fiction. In *Song of Solomon*, Milkman begins to locate his authentic self only when he journeys into the woods (again, of rural Virginia) and attends to the communication between the woodsmen and their animals, and realizes that, like Blake's ancient Poets, they are conversing on a level somehow prior to language:

> No, it was not language; it was what there was before language. Before things were written down. Language in the time when men and animals did talk to one another, when a man could sit down with an ape and the two converse; when a tiger and a man could share the same tree, and each understood the other; when men ran *with* wolves, not from or after them.[19]

Only by attending to this mythic sound, by hearing "what ... the earth had to say" (278), can Milkman realize his true self and bring that self into an authentic relation with the earth, the supernatural world, and his past.

Similarly, in *Beloved*, when the women gather at Sethe's home to exorcize the demonic figure Beloved has become, they reach back to a primal chant that resists language and comes before human words:

> They stopped praying and took a step back to the beginning. In the beginning there were no words. In the beginning was the sound, and they all knew what that sound sounded like.... the voices of the women searched for the right combination, the key, the code, the sound that broke the back of words. (259)

The sound emitted by the company resists representation and thus cannot be written down; it renders the sublime power that precedes human existence, and reaches back toward the source of all creation, the pure, uttering sound of being.[20]

In *Jazz*, this intimation of the prehuman is given the explicitly pastoral setting of romance, associated with the natural world and, beyond that, with the supernatural spirit that pervades that world. This spirit is what each character longs for, and the further the characters get from this pastoral setting, the further they get from the source of their being and the only comfort they have known. The music of the City fools the characters into believing they have found their Paradise at last—as Joe muses on coming to the City, "perfect was not the word. It was better than that" (107)—but in fact the City serves as a whited sepulchre, exhibiting a clean and lovely exterior but hiding within only suffering and death. Thus Joe mistakenly associates his love for Dorcas with Adam's love for Eve in the Garden: "I told you again that you were the reason Adam ate the apple and its core. That when he left Eden, he left a rich man. Not only did he have Eve, but he had the taste of the first apple in the world in his mouth for the rest of his life" (133). But what Joe invokes is not the love of Eden but the desire that resulted in the loss of Eden; Joe himself realizes that he only "thought it really was Eden" (133), when in fact, on his death-hunt for Dorcas, he is dimly aware that "he is a long way from Virginia, and even longer from Eden" (180). The error made by each figure in this novel is trying to find the Paradisal in the Earthly, trying to reconstruct a paradise that is already lost in a new world that beckons to them with such alluring promise. In this prideful gesture, the characters assure their inevitable fall.[21]

IV

Now bless thyself; thou met'st with things dying, I with things new born.
  —*The Winter's Tale*, 3.3.112-13

This is the main story of *Jazz*: a tragic story of lost, frustrated love; of opposition between the old and the young; of desire, sin, and death; of the loss of home, belonging, and the sense of place; of the fragmentation of identity; and of the archetypal human tragedy, the fall itself. Yet another, subterranean story lurks throughout the novel, a story that rises to the surface in the final two chapters, where the emotional direction of the novel shifts in rather startling ways and the narrator reveals a different, and greater, purpose than has been suggested before.

By placing the recollection of young, passionate love between Joe and Violet so near the very end of the novel, the narrator suggests that this love may yet linger, that it may be restored before the final page. Indeed, this becomes the aim of the narrator, and perhaps the whole point of the book: to recover and resuscitate the love between Joe and Violet. But their love has exacted a sacrifice—Dorcas—and so any reconciliation requires something external to Joe and Violet: youth, the one thing they have lost, what Joe seeks in Dorcas, what Violet seeks in her mother-hunger and daydreams of the always-young Golden Gray. The figure of Felice, Dorcas's wiser friend, offers youth again to Joe and Violet and, by extension, to the entire world of *Jazz*.

Felice is an exceptional character in the novel, for she is the only person who grew up with a living mother and father. (Indeed, this makes her an exceptional character throughout Morrison's *oeuvre*, which she peoples with more orphans and broken families than Dickens ever conceived.)[22] Dorcas tells Felice that she is lucky, because, even though Felice's parents worked in another town and saw Felice only a handful of days throughout the year, "at least they were there, somewhere" (200). Because she is not the product of a broken, shattered, or destroyed marriage, but rather the offspring of parents who have survived and stayed married, Felice does not harbor the same desperate need for parental love and a lost home that haunts the other characters. Though Felice is not entirely complete, the yearning desire that haunts Joe, Violet, and Dorcas does not possess her. Hence, even though when Violet first sees Felice she thinks it is "another true-as-life Dorcas" (197), in fact Felice insists that "I'm not like her!" (209).

As a result, Felice is able to see the Traces more clearly than anyone else in the novel can, including the narrator. When Felice goes to see Violet, she realizes that "they're wrong about her. . . . there is nothing crazy about her at all" (202). In a novel that is nearly defined by the rift between the old and the young, Felice sees in Violet a difference: "She doesn't lie, Mrs. Trace. Nothing she says is a lie the way it is with most older people" (205). Felice also perceives Violet's beauty, the beauty that we see only in the Violet of the past: "I didn't expect her to be pretty, but she is. You'd never get tired looking at her face" (206). Similarly, Felice sees Joe not as a pathetic killer of the young, but as someone "kind," "handsome," who "likes women" with respect and admiration, and who is "like a kid when he laughs." With Joe, Felice feels the worth of her own self: "Mr. Trace looks at you. . . . I like when he looks at me. I feel, I don't know, interesting" (206).

The effect of the Traces upon Felice is as important as her accurate vision of them. Violet tells Felice that the movement north was what "messed up" Violet's life and made the world stop making sense; Felice is astonished, convinced as she naturally is that "living in the City was the best thing in the world. What can you do in the country?" But Violet implies that it is not the trees or the hills that make the countryside what it is, but rather one's ability to see in nature the image, or source, of the human: "She said it wasn't like that, looking at a bunch of trees. She said for me to go to 143rd Street and look at the big one on the corner and see if it was a man or a woman or a child" (207-08). The point, Violet urges, is to be able to "make [the world] up the way you want it," to allow it "to be something more than what it is." "If you don't," she tells Felice, "it will change you and it'll be your fault cause you let it" (208). This was Violet's error: allowing her desire for what was lost to make her "[wish] I was somebody else." Now, Violet insists, all she wants is "Me." This insistence on a strong sense of self is exactly what every character in the novel lacks, and it so powerfully impresses Felice that she determines to emulate it: "The way she said it. Not like the me was some tough somebody, or somebody she had put together for show. But like, like somebody she favored and could count on. A secret somebody you didn't have to feel sorry for or have to fight for" (210). Violet's sense of self replaces the false sense of self Felice's mother bequeathed to her, false because it was stolen, "a present taken from whitefolks" (211). Thus Violet becomes a kind of substitute mother for Felice, just as Felice provides for Violet the daughter-figure Violet never had.[23]

Felice cries over Dorcas, for the first and only time, only in the presence of Joe and Violet (210). And just as Violet comes to stand as Felice's mother, so too Joe becomes a father for her. Joe speaks Felice's name repeatedly, and he pronounces it "with two syllables, not one like most people do, including my father" (214). Joe tells her, "Felice. They named you right. Remember that" (215). Felice's name—*felicitas*, happiness, and also fertility—functions much as the names of the young girls do in Shakespeare's late romances: like Miranda (wonder), Perdita (little lost girl), Marina (daughter of the sea), Felice functions as an allegory for the reconciliation and regeneration that comes about seemingly with her very presence. For as Felice begins to gain a stronger sense of self through her relation with the Traces, they begin to heal themselves through the influx of youth and vitality that Felice brings. When Felice asks Joe how he and Violet are doing, he responds, "We working on it. Faster now, since you stopped by and told us what you did" (212). When Violet complains that people are "plain mean"—voicing the tragic vision that dominates the main story of this novel—Joe softly corrects her and voices the wisdom of the second, hidden story of the novel: "No. Comic is what they are" (214).[24] As Felice watches, Joe and Violet break into a dance as music floats through the window, and Felice laughs and promises to "bring some records" the next time she comes.

This promised gift of music is, of course, ambiguous. Will Felice bring the records of jazz back into the house and begin the cycle of unrest and deadly desire all over again? This hardly seems likely, for the music itself changes in the last part of the novel. Felice's entrance into the novel—like the entrance of Perdita into *The Winter's Tale*—is marked by the advent of spring, and a gradual transformation of the world of the City:

Sweetheart. That's what that weather was called. Sweetheart weather, the prettiest day of the year. And that's when it started. On a day so pure and steady trees preened.... I could see Lenox widening itself, and men coming out of their shops to look at it, to stand with their hands under their aprons or stuck in their back pockets and just look around at a street that spread itself wider to hold the day.... And the women tip-tapping their heels on the pavement tripped sometimes on the sidewalk cracks because they were glancing at the trees to see where that pure, soft but steady light was coming from. (195-96)

The transformation of the cityscape by the regenerating power of nature affects the music as well: "The clarinets had trouble because the brass was cut so fine, not lowdown the way they love to do it, but high and fine *like a young girl singing by the side of a creek*, passing the time, her ankles cold in the water" (196, emphasis added). Just as in Shakespeare's late romances, the music of nature, embodied in the figure of a young girl, brings regeneration and reconciliation to the wasted human world of winter and of death. Thus the music brought by Felice to the Traces is hardly the same deadly jazz that dominates so much of the novel; rather, it is the music the world makes, the music of nature and perhaps of something beyond nature, bringing transformation to an otherwise dying world.

V

Please you to interpose, fair madam; kneel,
And pray your mother's blessing.
    —*The Winter's Tale*, 5.3.119-20

This effort toward restoring the love between Joe and Violet, and through them regenerating the world of the novel, helps explain the intriguing twists and turns taken by the narrative voice in the novel's final chapter, when the narrator confesses to having gotten the story wrong. The narrator shares the same desire as the rest of the characters, and falls victim to the same enchantment of the City's music, causing the narrator to miss the essential human drama suggested through the story: "I missed it altogether," the narrator confesses. "I got so aroused while meddling, while finger-shaping, I overreached and missed the obvious. I was watching the streets, thrilled by the buildings pressing and pressed by stone; so glad to be looking out and in on things I dismissed what went on in heart-pockets closed to me" (220-21). The narrator realizes in the final pages the gravity of this error, and its tragic effect of separating the storyteller from the human world it tries to narrate: "I ought to get out of this place.... It was loving the City that distracted me and gave me ideas. Made me think I could speak its loud voice and make that sound sound human. I missed the people altogether" (220). The narrator implies that the one thing needful for each figure in this novel—to be restored with the spiritual presence that speaks through nature—has been granted to the narrator by the story's end, perhaps through the very telling of the story:

> I'd love to close myself in the peace left by the woman who lived there and scared everybody. Unseen because she knows better than to be seen. . . . She has seen me and is not afraid of me. She hugs me. Understands me. *Has given me her hand. I am touched by her. Released in secret.*
> *Now I know.* (221, emphasis added)

The secret of Wild, the music made by nature, the spiritual home longed for by each character and denied to all, is granted to the narrator by the story's end.

This may explain the novel's enigmatic epigraph, taken from the "Thunder: Perfect Mind" section of the *Nag Hammadi*, the Coptic text of Gnostic writings discovered in 1945:

> I am the name of the sound
> and the sound of the name.
> I am the sign of the letter
> and the designation of the division.[25]

This utterance is "a revelation discourse by a female figure" who is never identified, but whose style in the *Nag Hammadi* text certainly describes the narrator of *Jazz*: "written throughout in the first person, interweaving and combining three types of statement: self-proclamation in the 'I am' style, exhortations to heed the speaker, and reproaches for failures to heed or love."[26] The "Thunder" narrator can be ultimately understood as "the extension of the divine into the world," thereby "asserting the totally otherworldly transcendence of the revealer."[27] This description of an omnipotent female transmitter of divine wisdom expresses the narrative goal of *Jazz*: to make heard a nurturing voice from beyond the world, and in that voice to heal and restore the shattered figures who have indeed failed to heed, failed to love. Thus, as Craig Werner has glossed the epigraph, "this African voice provides renewed access to the gospel foundation, the vision of community and possible salvation, lost as the village became the city."[28] Like the narrative voice of *Jazz*, this remarkable "narrator" claims to be both "the mother and the daughter," and to speak "the silence that is incomprehensible." And, just as *Jazz* promises to reconcile those who are lost and regenerate those who have passed away, the narrator of "Thunder: Perfect Mind" promises that those who attend to her utterance will find her presence when they "go up to their resting-place," "and they will live / and they will not die again."[29]

After suggesting that Wild has offered her touch, the narrator of *Jazz* quickly summarizes each character's fate with a storylike brevity ("like an old tale still," as the final plots of *The Winter's Tale* are described [5.2.65]): "Alice Manfred moved away," "Felice still buys Okeh records," "Joe found work at Paydirt," and so on; then moves to Joe and Violet and tells how they "stay home figuring things out" (222-23). Their love is now quiet, muted, and cool, and though they still see in the dark the shapes of their distorted past (images of

Dorcas bleeding and Wild's redwings for Joe, of True Belle's well for Violet), they touch under the sheets and comfort each other.

The narrator then describes the scene of their young love from 1906—again as if, like the ravaged love of Leontes and Hermione in *The Winter's Tale*, it has been resurrected, restored, though with the intervening years having made their difference—and then arrives at the final, meditative conclusion, revealing that the novel's climactic vision of love ("the mystery of love" that the narrator has been seeking from the novel's third page) is not that of youthful desire, fashionable music, nor dusky speakeasies, but rather the "whispering, old-time love" of "grown people," whose "ecstasy is more leaf-sigh than bray" and for whom "the body is the vehicle, not the point" (228). This love is the timeless love that the City and its music distorts, but that nature and the music of the world recovers. The narrator longs for this love, longs to understand it, possess it, and ultimately pass it on to the reader:

> I envy them their public love. I myself have only known it in secret, shared it in secret and longed, aw longed to show it—to be able to say out loud what they have no need to say at all: *That I have loved only you, surrendered my whole self reckless to you and nobody else. That I want you to love me back and show it to me. That I love the way you hold me, how close you let me be to you. I like your fingers on and on, lifting, turning. I have watched your face for a long time now, and missed your eyes when you went away from me. Talking to you and hearing you answer—that's the kick.* (229)

As numerous critics have noted, the narrator here turns to the reader holding this book, "lifting" and "turning" the pages, the reader who at times will answer back, and who is the one person who can proffer this love back to the narrator. Thus the narrator's final, enigmatic words—"make me, remake me. You are free to do it and I am free to let you because look, look. Look where your hands are. Now."—seek to bring the reader into the narrator's world and to pass on to that reader the narrator's own quest for love, home, and peace.[30]

VI

> *It is required*
> *You do awake your faith . . .*
> *. . . Music, awake her: strike.*
> *'Tis time; descend; be stone no more; approach;*
> *Strike all that look upon you with marvel.*
> —*The Winter's Tale*, 5.3. 94-95, 98-100

The final chapters of *Jazz* signal a radical shift in the novel's narrative structure, in which we veer away from the tragic mode, leaving Dorcas's death behind—by the novel's close it seems distant, hardly remarkable, strangely unviolent—and move toward the mode of romance. The reconciliation of old and young, the healing presence of a young girl, the celebration of the restored love of old people, the narrator's Prospero-like address to the reader at the end, and the yearning for the signal element in romance—grace—all mark this shift. Indeed, grace is the dominant mode of the novel's final pages, that "divine influence which operates in men to regenerate and sanctify, to inspire virtuous impulses, and to impart strength to endure trial and resist temptation."[31] The grace invoked in the final pages is akin to that in *The Winter's Tale*, as described by Northrop Frye: "such grace is not Christian or theological grace, which is superior to the order of nature, but *a secular analogy of Christian grace which is identical with nature*."[32] Such a conclusion is remarkable and unique among Morrison's novels (though there is some hint of a similar movement in the closing pages of *Beloved*, when Sethe and Paul D reconcile and Denver emerges as an independent self)[33]; and by extending the spirit of healing and reconciliation that defines romance to the reader in the final paragraphs, the novel expands the restored community beyond its own pages.

This is the import of my claim that the mystery of the novel's narrative voice actually is linked inseparably to music, though hardly the music of the novel's title. The sense of music that *Jazz* finally invokes, and that the narrator hopes to preserve, is "the music the world makes," the music of nature, of the elements, even of the gods. This music aspires to the eerie, wonderful harmonies that pervade *The Tempest*,[34] or the strains that accompany Hermione's quickening at the end of *The Winter's Tale*. The narrator becomes the singer of this music, and thereby resembles the model for the poet as singer: Orpheus, the greatest of musicians whose lyre could soothe even the god of death and who could charm the very creation with his music. This is the music toward which the narrator of *Jazz* aspires, a music that "hypnotizes animals" and can even, perhaps, defeat death. For at the novel's end, Joe, who has most clearly heard this music, has Violet restored to him—Orpheus does not lose his Eurydice, as if the narrator has sung their love back into life.

The movement toward regeneration extends even to Dorcas, who for so much of the novel is present only as the absent lover, the corpse who marks the text as a world of death. I have described Dorcas as a sacrificial figure in the novel, the young girl who must die in order to make possible the survival and restoration of Joe and Violet. In this respect she functions as a Persephone figure, the daughter who stays in the underworld but who returns annually with the spring to ensure the regeneration of the world above (and whom Perdita invokes in act 4 of *The Winter's Tale*). There is a hint that Dorcas is saved by the elemental music just before she dies: although she is shot to the accompaniment of the deadly jazz music, in her dying thoughts she attends to a different music: "The record playing is over," she muses. "Somebody they have been waiting for is playing the piano. A woman is singing too. The music is faint but I know the words by heart. . . . Listen. I don't know who is that woman singing but I know the words by heart" (192-93). The woman singing may be Wild; it may be the murmur of the world's music; it may be the music of the narrator. Regardless, this shift in the music is remarkable, for in her final breaths Dorcas moves away from the music of death and attends to the music of life, the music that dominates the novel's final pages and that offers regeneration to those who hear it. Thus Dorcas too can be resurrected before the novel ends.

This is what we would expect of a young girl named Dorcas. Morrison takes the name from the ninth chapter of the Book of Acts, wherein Peter restores to life a young girl who has just died:

> Now there was at Joppa a certain disciple named Tabitha, which by interpretation is called Dorcas: this woman was full of good works and almsdeeds which she did. And it came to pass in those days, that she was sick, and died. . . . Then Peter arose and went with them. When he was come, they brought him into the upper chamber: and all the widows stood by him weeping, and shewing the coats and garments which Dorcas made, while she was with them. But Peter put them all forth, and kneeled down, and prayed; and turning him to the body said, Tabitha, arise. And she opened her eyes . . . (Acts 9:36-40)

This connection between the Dorcas of *Jazz* and the Dorcas who is resurrected in Acts is the signal element in *Jazz*, for it underscores the movement toward regeneration that drives the novel in its concluding pages.[35]

Morrison has famously stated that her writing is not "like" Joyce, Hardy, Faulkner, or other male modernist precursors; her effort, she insists, "is to be *like* something that has probably only been fully expressed in music."[36] Most critics have claimed that she demonstrates this in *Jazz*, where the writing itself is a representation on the page of jazz musical techniques. Though there is some effort in the novel to echo in writing what jazz does in music, it must be evident that *Jazz* is a densely *written* work, wrought with extreme complexity and interweaving elements, probably more comparable to a classical prelude and fugue than to the improvisatory, unstable quality of true jazz music.[37] And though no reader of this novel would want to assert that in its pages Morrison fully rejects jazz, the novel demonstrates that jazz music is not the transcendent music toward which the narrator aims, and is only redemptive to the extent that it partakes of this grander music, as it seems to in the closing pages.

Similarly, the race, sex, and identity of the narrator has occasioned much debate. But as soon as we ask these sorts of questions of the narrator, we fail to understand what this narrator is, and what this narrator is trying to accomplish. This narrator is faceless, nameless, even bodiless ("I haven't got any muscles," the narrator confesses [8]), seems to float with ease in and out of every character's mind, past, and dreams, yet is not all-knowing, but actually learns as the novel goes on, learns through the telling of the story that is simultaneously transmitted and created. The narrator is not individual but rather is communal; and Morrison's model for a communal narrator is again an ancient musical one, the chorus of Greek drama, the definitive voice of a community. Morrison has often stated that Greek tragedy bears a strong "similarity to Afro-American communal structures," especially in "the function of song and chorus."[38] By invoking such a communal narration in *Jazz*, Morrison again demonstrates an engagement with the music of the novel's title, and, like Prospero, puts into her art a subtle questioning of her own aesthetic heritage.

Hence *Jazz* is a quest narrative, but its dominant journey is not a geographical one; rather, the novel travels backward through time and ultimately journeys from the physical to the metaphysical, to invoke a spirit that was once present and is now painfully absent. In her 1981 essay "City Limits, Village Values: Concepts of the Neighborhood in Black Fiction," Morrison argues that such an ancient invocation is at the heart of contemporary African-American experience, and of African-American literature, in the late twentieth century. The attraction of the urban world for African-American writers, Morrison argues, is not for the city itself, but rather "for the village within it: the neighborhoods and the population of those neighborhoods." The great example of the African-American village within the larger American city is "Harlem, the closest thing in American life as well as literature to a Black city, and a mecca for generations of Blacks," where "this village quality" was exemplified, and where "the relationships were clannish because there was joy and protection in the clan."[39] By turning to Harlem as both theme and setting for *Jazz*, Morrison focuses upon the primary example of a black village within the white urban world in American history.

But by showing the cracks in Harlem, by exposing the grim reality of the idealized, romanticized jazz city of the 1920's, Morrison suggests what went wrong in the movement to the cities: the "village values" of the rural world are left behind when the City takes over. "What is missing in city fiction and present in village fiction," she argues, "is the ancestor. The advising, benevolent, protective, wise Black ancestor is imagined as *surviving in the village but not in the city*." This, in effect, is the problem of *Jazz*: the ancestor figure, presented throughout the novel as a maternal love, is lost in the City, and must be sought in the country. Morrison states, "when the Black American writer experiences the country of the village, he does so . . . to *touch the ancestor*," for "the ancestor is the matrix of his yearning."[40] This "matrix"—female, motherly, a place of origin—is lost in the story of *Jazz*, but is recovered through the telling of that story.

The method of reconciliation, then, is the method of memory, or what Morrison calls in *Beloved* "rememory," the process of recalling something and thereby making it live once more. In an essay written nearly twenty years before *Jazz*, Morrison argues that this is the essence of the "Black History" movement:

> The point [of recovering black history] is not to soak in some warm bath of nostalgia about the good old days—*there were none!*—but to recognize and rescue those qualities of resistance, excellence and integrity that were so much a part of our past and so useful to us and to the generations of blacks now growing up.[41]

Much of Morrison's work—from her championing of young African-American writers while an editor at Random House, to her publishing *The Black Book* in 1974, to her increasing presence as a writer on issues of politics, social justice, and cultural studies, to her fiction—can be understood as an effort to accomplish this "rescuing" of the moments of "resistance, excellence and integrity" in the black past, and to make those moments live again. But—as *Jazz* so powerfully depicts—this project is not, or is not merely, cultural anthropology. Rather, Morrison seeks to bring back to life what she has called "the only mythic quality unique to Black people: presence."[42]

This effort to make the past live in the present recalls what Walter Benjamin terms "the involuntary recollection," in which a dead object thought to be devoid of meaning suddenly appears luminous in its revelation of the past, and makes apparent the vital importance of that past to the present. Benjamin sees this expressed most powerfully in Proust, where sudden recollection serves as a "rejuvenating force" for the present moment.[43] Michael Jennings describes Benjamin's theory as expressing "the conviction that truth, the hint of redemption, is present to the modern world in hidden and fragmentary form."[44] This captures the function of the ancestor, or the presence of the village, in *Jazz*: to shock the characters into recalling, at first dimly and later with more clarity and understanding, the source from which they emerge and to which they long to return. In this recollection is the key to their redemption.[45]

This entire project of restoring the past through its spiritual recollection shows Morrison reworking (consciously or not) one of the more remarkable moments in Ellison's *Invisible Man*, when another nameless narrator witnesses the eviction of an old black couple in Harlem. Ellison's Invisible Man turns aside from the evicted couple and looks at "the clutter of household objects" that have been taken out of their tenement and deposited on the sidewalk, "feeling strange memories awakening that began an echoing in my head." The objects he sees—a faded photograph, minstrel instruments, the Ethiopian flag, a portrait of Lincoln, a baseball scorecard, a yellowed breast pump, and, most poignant of all, faded free papers from 1859—constitute the relics of history of this black couple, and of a legion of African-Americans who made the journey north in search of a home, only to be thrown from that home into the winter night. The effect on the Invisible Man is precisely the effect wrought by *Jazz*—to remind him of his own past, what he has left behind and what he must find again in order to be whole:

> I turned and stared again at the jumble, no longer looking at what was before my eyes, but inwardly-outwardly, around a corner into the dark, far-away-and-long-ago, not so much of my own memory as of remembered words, of linked verbal echoes, images, heard even when not listening at home. And it was as though I myself was being dispossessed of some painful yet precious thing which I could not bear to lose.... And with this sense of dispossession came a pang of vague recognition: this junk, these shabby chairs, these heavy, old-

fashioned pressing irons, zinc wash tubs with dented bottoms—all throbbed within me with more meaning than there should have been. *And why did I, standing in the crowd, see like a vision my mother hanging wash on a cold windy day... why were they causing me discomfort so far beyond their intrinsic meaning as objects? And why did I see them now, as behind a veil that threatened to lift, stirred by the cold wind in the narrow street?*[46]

Like each of the characters in *Jazz*, the Invisible Man is reminded involuntarily of his village past, which he too links with images of his mother, in a way that both upsets and comforts him. But unlike Ellison, who cannot resolve in 1952 the dilemma of the dispossessed, Morrison works in *Jazz* to move beyond the emotions of loss, fragmentation, and isolation, and to find a sense of comfort and meaning in the reconstructed lives of her characters.

Thus the music to which Morrison finally turns is hardly Dionysian but instead its contrary, the music of Apollo that, in Nietzsche's understanding, offers not the dissolution of the individual, but rather represents "the *principium individuationis*," the principle of individuation, the constituted self that resists the "self-forgetfulness" of Dionysus.[47] This principle is, as Kaufmann argues, "the form-giving force" that offers "the power to create harmonious and measured beauty; the strength to shape one's own character no less than works of art."[48] Consequently, the aesthetic domain of the conclusion of *Jazz* is Kant's category of the beautiful, an aesthetic "directly attended with a feeling of the furtherance of life."[49] The narrator of *Jazz* makes clear in the opening pages that its guiding interest is "the mystery of love" (5) —that is, the domain of the beautiful, for as Burke defines it, beauty is "that quality or those qualities in bodies by which they cause love." The beautiful is also a distinctly maternal realm, evoking the emotions of "the mother's fondness and indulgence."[50] And finally it is the realm where society and the individual are brought together in harmony: "the beautiful," Frances Ferguson argues, "registers human sensation as a susceptibility to all the experiences that draw an individual into society."[51] The general movement toward reconciliation and regeneration that dominates the close of *Jazz*—a movement that is difficult, incomplete, and at risk, but nevertheless attempted—is a movement toward the realm of beauty. As Thomas Weiskel has written—in a sentence that captures the conclusion of *Jazz*—"the beautiful intimates reconciliation, however precariously and ambiguously."[52]

The final reconciliation and regeneration offered by *Jazz* reaches toward a broad community indeed: Joe and Violet stand for the restoration of all African-Americans who fled the violence of Reconstruction for the promise of the northern cities; for all who lived the fleeting hope of the Harlem Renaissance in the 1920's; and further, for those today who struggle in the benighted world of America's inner cities (it is no accident that this is the only novel of Morrison's that is set in an urban location, making it a contemporary allegory of sorts). Beyond these connections, the novel seeks a redemption not limited to time, place, or race, a satisfying of a universal human hunger for an original home and a metaphysical sense of peace. In this respect the mysterious figure of Golden Gray may actually be the most important in the novel (again despite—or perhaps because of—the odd manner in which he simply vanishes from the text): neither wholly white nor black, city nor country, northern nor southern, prodigal son nor savior, he is a liminal figure, occupying the boundaries between all of these limiting and restrictive categories, and offering a point of connection for all figures in—and all readers of—this novel. For finally the music of *Jazz* is a transcendent music that issues from beyond the world and promises—even if only in its fleeting grace notes—to gather that world back home.

Notes

1. Charles Ruas, "Toni Morrison," in *Conversations with Toni Morrison*, ed. Danille Taylor-Guthrie (Jackson: University Press of Mississippi, 1994), 108; Robert Stepto, "Intimate Things in Place: A Conversation with Toni Morrison," in Taylor-Guthrie, *Conversations* , 28.

2. Quoted from, respectively, Paula Gallant Eckard, "The Interplay of Music, Language, and Narrative in Toni Morrison's *Jazz*," *College Language Association Journal* 38:1 (1994): 11; Eusebio L. Rodrigues, "Experiencing *Jazz*," *Modern Fiction Studies* 39:3-4 (1993): 735; Philip Page, *Dangerous Freedom: Fusion and Fragmentation in Toni Morrison's Novels* (Jackson: University Press of Mississippi, 1995), 168; Doreatha Drummond Mbalia, "Women Who Run With Wild: The Need for Sisterhoods in *Jazz*," *Modern Fiction Studies* 39:3-4 (1993): 623.

3. Toni Morrison, *Jazz* (New York: Knopf, 1992), 32. Subsequent citations will be noted parenthetically in the text by page number.

4. Rodrigues, "Experiencing *Jazz*," 742-43.

5. Nietzsche's argument about the need for "the destruction of the past" occurs in his early essay, "Of the Use and Misuse of History for Life," discussed at length in Paul deMan's seminal essay, "Literary History and Literary Modernity," in his *Blindness and Insight: Essays in the Rhetoric of Contemporary Criticism*, 2nd ed., revised, introduction by Wlad Godzich (Minneapolis: University of Minnesota Press, 1983), 142-65. Nietzsche's ambivalence about the possibility of truly forgetting one's past relates to Morrison's desire to reject a past that has been horrifying and brutalizing to African-Americans, yet at the same time to recall what in that past can be useful and healing to her people.

6. Thus, as Eckard remarks, the narrator's very language alters when the scenes shift to the urban, as the narrator's words become marked by "musical language" and "jazz imagery" to mirror the City, which "like a beckoning jazz instrument . . . speaks to them" (Ekard, "The Interplay of Music," 15).

7. Richard Hardack, "'A Music Seeking Its Words': Double-Timing and Double-Consciousness in Toni Morrison's *Jazz*," *Callaloo* 18:2 (1995): 457, emphasis added.

8. The term "Dionysian" is Hardack's (462). Similar readings of the music as a positive, liberating force for the African-American characters, in addition to those readings cited above, can be found in Betty Fussell, "All That Jazz," in Taylor-Guthrie, *Conversations*, 280-87; John Leonard, "Her Soul's High Song," *The Nation* 25 (May

1992): 706-18; Alan J. Rice, "Jazzing It Up a Storm: The Execution and Meaning of Toni Morrison's Jazzy Prose Style," *Journal of American Studies* 28:3 (1994): 423-32; Katherine J. Mayberry, "The Problem of Narrative in Toni Morrison's *Jazz*," in *Toni Morrison's Fiction: Contemporary Criticism*, ed. David L. Middleton (New York: Garland, 1997), 297-309.

9. With this word, and its deceptive implication of bliss that conceals death beneath, Morrison foretells the drama of her next novel, *Paradise*, in which the quest for an earthly locale that will be free of greed, gluttony, anger, pride, lust, sloth, and envy is shown to be impossible and leads only to death and destruction.

10. Friedrich Nietzsche, *The Birth of Tragedy*, trans. by Walter Kaufmann (New York: Random House, 1967), 104. Hardack emphasizes this effect: "This music," he concludes, "locates the site of the involuntary in the text . . . which nullifies the very concept of a self-contained individual will" (Hardack, "A Music," 462). However, Hardack continues to read this loss of self as a positive event in the novel, a reading quite contrary to what I will suggest.

11. Walter Kaufmann, *Nietzsche: Philosopher, Psychologist, Antichrist* (Princeton: Princeton University Press, 1974), 128, emphasis added.

12. Morrison leaves Joe's parentage intentionally uncertain. The novel is very careful about its dating and chronology, but the crucial information that would establish Joe's birth—the year in which Golden Gray goes in search of his father—is never clearly revealed. Morrison has suggested elsewhere that the year is 1873, the same year that, in *Beloved*, Beloved flees the cabin for the Ohio wilderness, implying that Beloved could well be Wild. See Angels Carabi's interview with Morrison in *Belles Lettres* 10:2 (1995): 40-43. Roberta Rubenstein discusses this element of the novel in her "History and Story, Sign and Design: Faulknerian and Postmodern Voices in *Jazz*," in *Unflinching Gaze: Morrison and Faulkner Re-Envisioned*, ed. Carol A. Kolmerten, Stephen M. Ross, and Judith Bryant Wittenberg (Jackson: University Press of Mississippi, 1997).

13. The motif of the failed mother in Morrison's work merits an essay to itself. Suffice it to say here that the general reading of Morrison's work as matrilineal, offering a kind of nurturing and mothering to its characters and its readers, is deeply suspect. Morrison's mothers reject their children for the children of others (Pauline in *The Bluest Eye*); they burn their children alive, and admit to not liking their daughters (Eva and Hannah in *Sula*); they try to drown their daughters in quicksand (the swamp women in *Tar Baby*); they lock their babies in smothering cars on summer days (Mavis in *Paradise*); and, most spectacularly, they cut the throats of their newborn babies (Sethe in *Beloved*). Morrison's view of motherhood is, indeed, complex, and more closely related to the death urge than to the life principle. For a reading of the mother figure in *Jazz* that sees it as the healthy and nurturing force typical of Morrison scholarship, see Andrea O'Reilly, "In Search of My Mother's Garden, I Found My Own: Mother-Love, Healing, and Identity in Toni Morrison's *Jazz*," *African-American Review* 30:3 (Fall 1996): 367-79.

14. This, I think, may explain why Golden Gray rather mysteriously vanishes from the narrative soon after this. His story is the story of the father and the son, which is not the main concern of *Jazz*; the narrator uses him to get to the position of ministering to the fragmented characters who dominate the rest of the novel—including the narrator. Once this point has been reached, the narrator has no further use for Golden Gray, and so discards him.

15. Toni Morrison, *Beloved* (New York: Knopf, 1987), 23. Subsequent citations will be noted parenthetically in the text by page number.

16. Langston Hughes, *Selected Poems of Langston Hughes* (New York: Vintage, 1990), 173.

17. The language here, of course, is from Genesis 1:28-31.

18. For a fascinating study of the tensions between the novelist and the romancer in Morrison's work, see Maria DiBattista, "Contentions in the House of Chloe: Morrison's Tar Baby," in *Speaking the Unspeakable: The Aesthetic Dimensions of Toni Morrison*, ed. Marc C. Conner (Jackson: University Press of Mississippi, in press).

19. Toni Morrison, *Song of Solomon* (New York: Knopf, 1977), 278. Subsequent citations will be noted parenthetically in the text by page number. For Blake's comparable idea of "the ancient Poets" who "animated all sensible objects with Gods or Geniuses, calling them by the names and adorning them with the properties of woods, rivers, mountains, lakes, cities, nations, and whatever their enlarged and numerous senses could perceive," see his "The Marriage of Heaven and Hell" in *The Complete Poetry and Prose of William Blake*, revised edition, ed. David V. Erdman with commentary by Harold Bloom (New York: Doubleday, 1988), 38. Blake's concept derives from Genesis 2:19-20, in which Adam names every living creature.

20. For a detailed analysis of Morrison's use of the sublime in her writing, see Marc C. Conner, "From the Sublime to the Beautiful: The Aesthetic Progression of Toni Morrison," in Conner, *Speaking the Unspeakable*.

21. Through this theme, Morrison aligns her writing with perhaps the archetypal American story, one that begins at least with Winthrop's desire for the Puritans to construct "a city upon a hill" and continues through Fitzgerald's vision of "the last and greatest of all human dreams" that "flowered once for Dutch sailors' eyes—a fresh, green breast of the new world." Indeed, the novel that follows *Jazz* is the aptly titled *Paradise*, which is defined by this very problem of seeking to make one's paradise on earth. At the same time that she invokes this definitive American myth, Morrison also shifts it to an African-American milieu, thereby complicating and enriching the myth itself.

22. Though no critic that I have found has remarked on this, it seems to me that Morrison's catalog of shattered families arises to an extent from her own experience. She has stated that her first novel arose out of her own efforts to recover from her divorce and her need to raise two young children on her own, and that writing was precisely the method by which she reclaimed her identity and sense of worth:

> at that moment [of first writing] I had no choice. . . . I was really in a corner. And whatever was being threatened by the circumstances in which I found myself, alone with two children in a town where I didn't know anybody, I knew that I would not deliver to my children a parent that was of no use to them. . . . And as I began to [write], I began to pick up scraps of things that I had seen or felt, or didn't see or didn't feel, but imagined. And speculated about and wondered about. And I fell in love with myself. I reclaimed myself and the world—a real revelation. (Gloria Naylor, "A Conversation: Gloria Naylor and Toni Morrison," in Taylor-Guthrie, *Conversations*, 198).

Thus, Morrison's depictions of shattered families, and in particular the failed and failing mothers and the broken, haunted children, may be an imaginative working-through of her own most elemental fears as a single mother and hopeful writer. (See also Betty Fussell's

1992 interview, in which Morrison remarks that "if she'd stayed married, she might never have begun to write," in Taylor-Guthrie, *Conversations*, 284.) In this sense, *Jazz*—the first Morrison novel to depict the reconciliation between broken families—represents the first successful vision in Morrison's effort to minister both to herself and to her communities.

23. Violet's refusal to surrender her desire for selfhood, and Felice's determination to seek this same autonomy, refutes the reading of the novel offered by Hardack, who claims that "throughout *Jazz*, no character, male or female, can or would want to be self-reliant and self-created" (460). To be sure, the characters are often denied the opportunity for self-reliance; but, as with Ellison's Invisible Man, the impossibility of self-reliance in no way equates with its undesirability—indeed, the blocks to selfhood only serve to underscore the need for identity and strength, as Violet's experience makes clear.

24. The importance of the regenerative power of comedy to this novel is also emphasized when Alice and Violet break into peals of laughter in the very midst of their litany of complaints about their plight: "Violet learned then what she had forgotten until this moment: that laughter is serious. More complicated, more serious, than tears" (113).

25. Epigraph to *Jazz*. Morrison in all likelihood learned of the *Nag Hammadi* texts through her Princeton colleague Elaine Pagels, with whom Morrison is reportedly good friends. Pagels is author of *The Gnostic Gospels* and one of the contributors to *The Nag Hammadi Library in English*, from which the epigraph is taken.

26. George W. MacRae, "Introduction," "The Thunder: Perfect Mind," *The Nag Hammadi Library in English*, third, completely revised edition, ed. James M. Robinson (New York: Harper & Row, 1988), 295.

27. Douglas M. Parrot, commentary, in MacRae, *Nag Hammadi Library*, 296; MacRae, *Nag Hammadi Library*, 296.

28. Craig Werner, "*Jazz*: Morrison and the Music of Tradition," in *Approaches to Teaching the Novels of Toni Morrison*, ed. Nellie McKay and Kathryn Earle (New York: MLA, 1997), 92. Rodrigues also briefly discusses the novel's epigraph ("Experiencing Jazz," 748-49).

29. "The Thunder: Perfect Mind," in Robinson, *Nag Hammadi Library*, 297, 303.

30. This is one of the central elements in Morrison's aesthetic, what I have elsewhere described as her commitment to a "reader-response" or "communal" narration. Morrison has stated that "one of the major characteristics of black literature is the participation of the *other*, that is, the audience, the reader" (Christina Davis, "An Interview with Toni Morrison," in Taylor-Guthrie, *Conversations*, 231). Her own writing, she insists, "demands participatory reading. . . . My language has to have holes and spaces so the reader can come into it" (Claudia Tate, "Toni Morrison," in Taylor-Guthrie, *Conversations*, 164). In her Nobel acceptance speech, this is the aim of the story told about the blind old woman, who concludes by turning to the young audience and exclaiming, "Look. How lovely it is, this thing we have done—together" (Toni Morrison, *The Nobel Lecture: 1993* [New York: Norton, 1994], 13). See Marc C. Conner, "Aesthetics and the African-American Novel: The Example of Toni Morrison," in Conner, *Speaking the Unspeakable*.

31. As defined in *The Oxford English Dictionary*, vol. IV (Oxford: Clarendon Press, 1933), 327.

32. Northrop Frye, *Fables of Identity: Studies in Poetic Mythology* (New York: Harcourt, Brace, Jovanovich, 1986) 111, emphasis added.

33. On the conclusion of *Beloved*, see Conner, "From the Sublime to the Beautiful," in Conner, *Speaking the Unspeakable*.

34. Caliban's achingly lovely description of the music of Prospero's island could well be applied to the music that Joe has heard at moments in the wild:

> Be not afeard, the isle is full of noises,
> Sounds, and sweet airs, that give delight and hurt not.
> Sometimes a thousand twangling instruments
> Will hum about mine ears; and sometime voices,
> That if I then had wak'd after long sleep,
> Will make me sleep again, and then in dreaming,
> The clouds methought would open, and show riches
> Ready to drop upon me, that when I wak'd
> I cried to dream again. (*The Tempest* 3.2.135-43)

I do not know if Morrison had this passage in mind when she wrote about the otherworldly music of *Jazz*, but I am convinced that this describes the same realm toward which her novel gestures.

35. In this allusion to resurrection in Acts (a connection that, to my knowledge, has gone oddly unnoticed in the scholarship on this novel), Morrison may also be calling our attention to the even more famous moment of transformation and regeneration that occurs in the ninth chapter of Acts, the conversion of Paul. Intriguingly, this conversion is precisely what Lucy ponders on her deathbed (though she thinks of its description in the twenty-sixth chapter) in Zora Neale Hurston's *Jonah's Gourd Vine*, one of the crucial novels to emerge from the Harlem Renaissance and a key precursor text to *Jazz*, just as Hurston is one of the key precursor writers to Morrison. See *Jonah's Gourd Vine* (New York: HarperCollins, 1990), 130.

36. Nellie McKay, "An Interview with Toni Morrison," in Taylor-Guthrie, *Conversations*, 152.

37. Hence Michael Wood has rightly stated that "This is not a novel about jazz, or based on jazz, and I think reviewers' comments about the improvisatory quality of the writing underestimated what feels like the careful premeditation of the work." Michael Wood, *Children of Silence: On Contemporary Fiction* (New York: Columbia University Press, 1998), 127. If the narrative form has a true ancestor, it is likely the "Sirens" chapter of Joyce's *Ulysses*, which attempts a similar rendering of music in language. On the complex question of Morrison's relation to Joyce, see David Cowart, "Faulkner and Joyce in Morrison's *Song of Solomon*," *American Literature* 62:1 (1990): 87-100; and Marc C. Conner, "Aesthetics and the African-American Novel, in Conner, *Speaking the Unspeakable*.

38. Toni Morrison, "Unspeakable Things Unspoken: The Afro-American Presence in American Literature," *Michigan Quarterly Review* 28:1 (Winter 1989), 2-3.

39. Toni Morrison, "City Limits, Village Values: Concepts of the Neighborhood in Black Fiction," in *Literature and the Urban Experience: Essays on the City and Literature*, ed. Michael C. Jaye and Ann Chalmers Watts (New Brunswick: Rutgers University Press, 1981), 38.

40. Morrison, "City Limits," 39.

41. Toni Morrison, "Rediscovering Black History," *The New York Times Magazine*, 11 August 1974, 14.

42. Toni Morrison, "Behind the Making of the Black Book," *Black World* 23 (February 1974): 89.

43. Walter Benjamin, "The Image of Proust," in *Illuminations*, ed. Hannah Arendt, trans. Harry Zohn (New York: Schocken, 1968), 211.

44. Michael Jennings, *Dialectical Images: Walter Benjamin's Theory of Literary Criticism* (Ithaca: Cornell University Press, 1987), 12.

45. Jennings discusses Benjamin's aesthetics alongside Benjamin's politics and argues that the moment of recollection is the first step in "a destructive process that purges the cultural object of its mythical, or dehumanized, character" (*Dialectical Images*, 12). But Morrison parts company with Benjamin, or at least Jennings, at this point, for in *Jazz* (as in her other writings) she clearly commits herself to the mythical world as the realm where the human finds its proper home. For a view more parallel to Morrison's elevation of the mythic past, see Benjamin's "The Storyteller" (*Illuminations*, 83-109)—an essay that is much more difficult for scholars to accommodate to Benjamin's reputedly revolutionary politics. (Jennings, for example, in a book devoted to Benjamin's ideas of literature, mentions this seminal essay only once.)

46. Ralph Ellison, *Invisible Man* (New York: Vintage, 1989), 270-73. Intriguingly, Morrison has indicated that much of the story of *Jazz* emerged from her recollections of the tales and experiences of her own grandparents, thereby echoing the process of rememory that she, Ellison, and Benjamin all seem to be addressing. See Dana Micucci, "An Inspired Life: Toni Morrison Writes and a Nation Listens," in Taylor-Guthrie, *Conversations*, 275. In general, Morrison's significant debt to Ellison has not been sufficiently stressed.

47. Nietzsche, *Birth of Tragedy*, 36, 72.

48. Kaufmann, *Nietzsche*, 128.

49. Immanuel Kant, *The Critique of Judgement*, trans. James Creed Meredith (Oxford: Clarendon Press, 1991), 91. Kaufmann points out that Nietzsche's theory of Apollo parallels Kant's theory of the beautiful (Kaufmann, *Nietzsche*, 133).

50. Edmund Burke, *A Philosophical Enquiry into the Origin of Our Ideas of the Sublime and Beautiful*, ed. James T. Boulton (Notre Dame, Indiana: University of Notre Dame Press, 91, 111).

51. Frances Ferguson, *Solitude and the Sublime* (New York: Routledge, 1992), 8.

52. Thomas Weiskel, *The Romantic Sublime: Studies in the Structure and Psychology of Transcendence* (Baltimore: Johns Hopkins University Press, 1976), 48. I have argued elsewhere that the shift from the sublime to the beautiful defines the general movement of Morrison's career. See Conner, "From the Sublime to the Beautiful," in Conner, *Speaking the Unspeakable*.

Index

Adam, xv, 1, 5, 6, 8-13, 33, 153, 167, 182, 245-50, 261, 353
adultery, 32, 38, 97, 109, 139, 140, 148, 157, 304,
aesthetic, 26, 119, 335, 341, 361, 363
affection, 27, 121, 125, 224, 225, 259, 270, 273, 280, 302, 335, 350
agreement, 73, 115, 122, 157, 158, 191, 222, 266, 302, 309
amour-propre, 181, 186, 190, 192, 196, 197
ancient, 2, 19, 25, 26, 28, 29, 34, 39, 40, 41, 46, 103, 115, 117, 118, 128, 140, 141, 143, 146, 197, 215, 218, 223, 224, 234, 278, 295, 298, 304, 341, 352, 360, 361
animal, xvii, 5, 12, 55, 57, 60, 74, 75, 76, 78, 81, 82, 85, 87, 88, 97, 118, 120, 125, 139, 150, 152, 153, 154, 173, 175, 194, 224, 225, 229, 230, 352, 359
Antigone, 304
Aphrodite, 4, 28, 37, 116, 119, 124, 125, 126
Apollo, 3, 31, 33, 37, 363
Arendt, 236
Aristophanes, 2, 3, 4, 7, 12, 13, 57, 61, 66, 68
Aristotle, xiii, xvi, 26, 28, 66, 68, 73-89, 92, 93, 95, 96, 97, 105, 125, 138, 147, 209, 257, 267, 268, 270, 271, 272, 274, 275, 276, 277, 279, 280, 281, 282, 287, 301, 302,
art, xi, xv, xvi, 12, 23, 35, 36, 40, 41, 58, 59, 60, 61, 62, 64, 65, 66, 67, 74, 77, 80, 118, 119, 138, 140, 143, 144, 182, 186, 199, 211, 212, 213, 214, 217, 219, 221, 222, 227, 232, 233, 235, 250, 255, 271, 276, 335, 341, 346, 361, 363
artifice, 118, 182, 196, 199, 349
Augustine, 106, 297, 298
authority, xiii, 8, 9, 10, 11, 42, 82, 96, 97, 99, 100, 101, 102, 103, 105, 107, 110, 115, 146, 150, 151, 153, 158, 159, 160, 161, 166, 170, 176, 185, 189, 213, 216, 218, 220, 221, 223, 226, 227, 228, 229, 231, 235, 256, 303, 304
autonomy, xii, 77, 88, 104, 106, 109, 195, 295, 297, 298, 300, 301, 302, 303, 305, 306, 307, 308

Baier, 211, 227, 228, 229
barbarian, 23, 32, 33, 34, 39, 124, 228
barbaric, 22, 23, 32, 43, 231, 235
beasts, 5, 6, 10, 77, 80, 88, 95, 167, 168, 351
beauty, xiv, 56, 97, 100, 116, 117, 119, 128, 141, 195, 197, 247, 268, 278, 279, 321, 350, 354, 363
belief, 19, 35, 41, 117, 174, 189, 277, 278, 283, 284, 287, 298, 318
benevolent, 213, 349, 361
Bloom, 116, 117, 127, 128, 200
brave, 40, 256
Brutus, 97, 98, 100, 101, 102, 107, 108

Camus, 26
cause, 11, 25, 29, 34, 36, 68, 79, 97, 105, 119, 173, 235, 252, 258, 266, 279, 298, 316, 320, 343, 344, 355, 363
chance, 26, 62, 124, 212, 214, 218, 268, 270, 283, 285, 336, 347
character, xvi, 6, 8, 9, 10, 19, 20, 21, 23, 25, 27, 29, 30, 32, 34, 42, 44, 54, 55, 58, 59, 62, 67, 69, 116, 119, 120, 121, 122, 124, 126, 129, 139, 140, 142, 143, 144, 145, 157, 158, 169, 213, 219, 220, 223, 231, 234, 246, 247, 249-53, 259, 260, 267, 268, 270, 272-79, 281, 283, 284, 285, 299, 305, 314, 315, 324, 325, 342, 346, 348, 350, 353, 354, 355, 357, 360, 363
characteristic, 1, 9, 21, 77, 84, 172, 228, 246, 247, 279, 281, 285, 308, 320
chaste, 105, 123
chastity, xv, 60, 97, 100, 139, 140, 141, 142, 143, 148, 191, 192, 196, 209, 211
children, xiv, xv, 20, 23, 24, 29, 31, 32,

33, 34, 36, 42, 43, 44, 53, 55, 58, 61, 63, 66, 68, 73, 78, 79, 80, 82-9, 95, 96, 105, 116, 121, 125, 126, 128, 140, 143, 151-59, 161, 162, 163, 164, 166, 168-75, 184, 185, 188, 191, 192, 193, 195, 198, 248, 250, 268, 270, 272, 273, 274, 299, 300, 302-7, 322, 335, 336, 343, 345, 346, 350, 351, 352, 355
Christian, 137, 218, 246, 256, 297, 338, 359
Christianity, 141, 210, 218, 219, 304
city, 2, 3, 12, 25, 30, 32, 33, 35, 40, 46, 53-60, 62-69, 74, 75, 76, 80-89, 94, 95, 96, 97, 115, 120, 121, 138, 143, 148, 181, 217, 342, 345, 351, 357, 361, 364
civil, 103, 149, 151, 158, 159, 162, 163, 165, 167, 169, 170, 172, 175, 181, 183, 184, 188, 194, 199, 235, 259, 302
civility, 210, 211, 220, 222, 223, 224, 227, 228, 230, 234, 248, 253, 254, 261
civilization, 183, 210, 211, 212, 213, 214, 215, 219, 220, 221, 228, 230, 232, 233, 308
civil society, 149, 151, 158, 159, 162, 163, 165, 169, 170, 172, 175, 181, 184, 188, 194, 302
classical, 37, 41, 44, 45, 52, 126, 128, 213, 226, 256, 267, 296, 302, 307, 309, 360
Cleon, 304
comedy, 56, 95, 138, 139, 140, 141, 143, 144, 145, 147, 148
companion, 23, 222, 281, 332
companionship, 1, 128, 129, 333, 336
compassion, 249
concord, 255, 257
conflict, 7, 30, 43, 127, 162, 224, 266, 298, 304, 307
conjugal, 123, 150, 151, 152, 153, 154, 155, 156, 157, 158, 159, 160, 161, 162, 163, 165, 166, 175, 196
conscious, xii, 7, 34, 153, 250, 295, 297, 301, 308, 317
consent, 99, 122, 150, 154, 156, 158, 159, 162, 163, 165, 166, 167, 169, 175, 150, 186, 234
contract, 99, 126, 150, 152, 156, 157, 158, 159, 165, 166, 167, 168, 171, 172, 195, 199, 216, 302, 307

contractual, 151, 156, 161, 164, 165, 168, 170, 172, 302
control, 10, 64, 83, , 99, 100, 104, 108, 109, 145, 146, 154, 158, 166, 172, 176, 212, 268, 297, 298, 301, 305, 343, 345
convention, xvii, 10, 59, 82, 156, 165, 173, 187, 224, 225, 226, 227, 229, 230, 234, 235
conventional, xv, 10, 56, 60, 68, 75, 82, 99, 118, 147, 161, 174, 226, 228, 230, 231, 266, 267, 332, 334
couple, 88, 116, 124, 126, 127, 165, 251, 270, 282, 321, 362
creation, 1, 5, 6, 11, 12, 21, 34, 40, 42, 103, 151, 152, 163, 164, 165, 176, 236, 302, 303, 353, 359
cruel, 28, 31, 32, 45, 188, 348
cruelty, 45, 137
cultivate, 122, 232, 236, 281, 302, 306, 324
cultivated, 119, 222, 232, 251, 302
cultivation, 103, 122, 303, 306, 308, 317
cultural, xi, 32, 38, 41, 96, 106, 107, 108, 110, 128, 247, 295, 296, 297, 329, 331, 362
culture, xii, 22, 34, 106, 128, 182, 227, 295, 296, 297, 298, 301, 302, 303, 305, 306, 307, 308, 309, 330, 331, 334
custom, xiii, xviii, 11, 29, 56, 57, 60, 140, 157, 164, 171, 176, 230, 235, 258, 259, 297

Dante, 23, 37, 46
daughter, 23, 24, 25, 26, 33, 42, 44, 63, 105, 126, 127, 171, 247, 276, 278, 279, 299, 331, 336, 337, 355, 357, 359
death, 1, 3, 4, 6, 11, 12, 25, 29, 30, 32, 42, 43, 97, 99, 102, 106, 107, 108, 109, 126, 139, 143, 156, 158, 159, 176, 197, 271, 272, 273, 274, 279, 286, 301, 329, 330, 333, 334, 335, 336, 337, 338, 344, 345, 346, 348, 353, 356, 358, 359
democracy, 172, 221, 223, 309
democratic, 32, 34, 69, 185, 210
Derrida, 313-18, 324, 316
desire, xiii, xiv, xv, xvi , 1, 3, 4, 9, 10, 11, 12, 28, 40, 65, 66, 68, 100, 104, 108, 116, 118, 119, 121, 122, 125, 128,

Index

129, 139, 142, 143, 144, 153-57, 161, 162, 169, 171, 181, 183, 186, 187, 188, 190-95, 197, 198, 215, 218, 219, 222, 225, 226, 231, 234, 246, 248, 250, 252, 253, 254, 255, 256, 258, 259, 260, 266, 276, 279, 306, 307, 315, 316, 319, 320, 324, 329, 332, 333, 335, 344-49, 353, 354, 355, 356, 358
despot, 228
despotic, 79, 97, 105, 106
despotism, 87
destiny, xiv, 23, 26, 27, 29, 30, 35, 42, 45, 109
difference, xiv, xv, 9, 32, 37, 58, 59, 60, 63, 75, 76, 79, 80, 82, 83, 84, 89, 104, 110, 117, 128, 145, 147, 153, 174, 183-87, 196, 197, 198, 199, 218, 220, 223, 235, 246, 247, 257, 267, 272, 280, 282, 286, 287, 298, 305, 322, 323, 329, 331, 337, 354, 358
different, xiii, xiv, xvii, xviii, 1, 5, 9, 20, 26, 30, 33, 36, 43, 58, 73, 74, 75, 82, 83, 84, 85, 86, 88, 89, 124, 126, 127, 138, 142, 144, 147, 151, 162, 173, 183, 188, 191, 195, 221, 222, 224, 226, 246, 250, 256, 267, 272, 280, 282, 286, 287, 302, 303, 306, 309, 315, 322, 316, 332, 352, 353, 359
dignity, 33, 197, 209, 251, 252, 253, 278, 280, 301, 336
Dionysian, 343, 346, 363
Dionysius, 95
divorce, 6, 13, 30, 304, 305, 307
domain, 82, 86, 352, 363
domestic, 121, 129, 164, 185, 189, 200, 210, 211, 231, 255, 270, 286, 287, 305, 331, 333, 337, 338
domesticity, 105, 329, 330, 331, 333, 338
dominion, 1, 6, 10, 105, 153, 160, 170, 215, 216, 220, 221, 226
duties, 79, 118, 119, 126, 156, 164, 169, 170, 172, 174, 182, 184, 191, 193, 195, 196, 197, 225, 227, 229, 251, 275, 280, 287, 298, 330, 334, 335

economic, 34, 117, 118, 125, 128, 171, 175, 189, 228, 298, 299, 300, 336
economy, 100, 101, 104, 106, 210, 295, 296, 298, 299, 300, 309

educate, xiv, 170, 171, 303, 317
educated, 126, 222, 272, 317
education, 56, 65, 86, 137, 143, 144, 150, 164, 170, 172, 173, 174, 176, 182, 183, 186, 187, 189, 193, 194, 195, 196, 197, 198, 216, 223, 225, 227, 245, 253, 258, 261, 272, 305, 317, 321
educator, 173
effeminate, 219, 220
emotion, 27
empire, 34, 37, 97, 182, 196, 197, 198, 216, 218, 219
enjoyment, 115, 122, 123, 171, 229, 269, 270, 273, 282
enlightened, xii, 197, 217, 229, 233
enlightenment, 184, 195, 214, 215, 216, 219, 220, 222, 229, 230, 231, 232
Enlightenment, 233, 236, 258, 309
equal, xvii, 19, 57, 80, 86, 88, 96, 118, 127, 149, 150, 158, 169, 172, 173, 174, 184, 185, 188, 195, 233, 234, 235, 250, 272, 306, 307, 320, 321
equality, xv, 57, 59, 65, 81, 86, 149, 150, 151, 155, 158, 160, 163, 164, 166, 169, 170, 171, 173, 175, 191, 210, 213, 219, 222, 223, 228, 231, 232, 234, 235, 266, 303, 304, 305, 308
erotic, 4, 38, 60, 61, 68, 116, 117, 118, 122, 123, 126, 127, 313, 314, 319, 335, 343
eroticism, 42
essence, xi, 11, 35, 76, 104, 128, 173, 187, 194, 361
ethical, 247, 271, 276, 278, 280, 282, 287, 302, 303, 304
ethics, 35, 303, 305
ethos, 343
Eve, xv, 11, 12, 33, 152, 156, 157, 158, 167, 182, 353
existence, xv, 1, 4, 29, 61, 68, 85, 119, 137, 139, 148, 154, 162, 167, 188, 190, 199, 258, 278, 301, 302, 316, 317, 318, 321, 322, 329, 331, 337, 353

faith, 40, 143, 189, 358
faithful, 138, 195, 314, 335
family, xiv, 10, 22, 23, 30, 63, 66, 67, 85, 97, 102, 105, 117, 127, 138, 140, 141, 142, 145, 147, 149-76, 184, 185, 188, 191, 195, 196, 197, 227, 248, 250,

252, 254, 269, 270, 274, 275, 277, 278, 280, 281, 284, 298, 299, 301, 302, 303, 304, 306, 307, 308, 320, 322, 329, 331, 335, 336, 337, 354
fantasies, 101, 316, 337, 346
father, 6, 22, 24, 25, 26, 27, 28, 32, 35, 36, 37, 63, 64, 73, 78, 80, 82, 84, 85, 86, 89, 97, 98, 99, 100, 101, 102, 104, 105, 108, 117, 120, 121, 127, 138, 141, 145, 152, 153, 155, 159, 160, 161, 162, 163, 165, 166, 170, 171, 172, 174, 181, 185, 191, 196, 247, 250, 251, 252, 254, 255, 269, 272, 273, 274, 276, 277, 278, 299, 303, 306, 331, 335, 337, 348, 354, 355
fatherhood, 99, 117
fear, 1, 9, 11, 12, 19, 20, 21, 22, 28, 29, 33, 34, 38, 40, 55, 104, 174, 236, 271, 301
feeling, 124, 125, 246, 249, 251, 272, 275, 304, 331, 362, 363
female, xi, xv, 1, 3, 5, 19, 20, 21, 22, 23, 26, 29, 30, 33, 37, 39, 40, 41, 42, 43, 44, 45, 56, 57, 59, 74, 75, 76, 81, 86, 97, 96, 101, 102, 105, 106, 108, 109, 119, 122, 123, 128, 139, 143, 144, 145, 146, 147, 152, 156, 157, 167, 171, 172, 173, 174, 183, 184, 186, 191, 192, 193, 198, 211, 212, 224, 228, 230, 231, 256, 265, 266, 268, 282, 285, 269, 307, 313, 329, 331, 333, 335, 344, 357, 361
feminine, xv, xvi, 38, 43, 45, 95, 96, 100, 105, 106, 107, 110, 211, 220, 304, 317, 324, 329, 330, 331
femininity, xi, 39, 45, 96, 104, 107, 110, 305, 330
feminism, 37, 149, 176, 229, 313
feminist, 21, 40, 41, 45, 96, 149, 185, 191, 200, 256, 265, 266, 330
fidelity, 195, 196, 349
Filmer, 150, 152, 153, 156, 160, 164, 167, 169, 172, 151
fortune, 22, 23, 26, 28, 30, 105, 146, 219, 269, 279, 283, 284
foundation, 37, 58, 86, 97, 98, 124, 137, 140, 141, 143, 149, 151, 156, 157, 161, 162, 176, 182, 183, 185, 189, 196, 197, 198, 227, 303, 357
free will, 28, 29, 109, 169, 297

friends, 20, 29, 35, 39, 54, 62, 65, 89, 97, 117, 124, 127, 145, 252, 268, 269, 270, 272, 273, 280, 281, 284, 286, 287, 302, 315, 316, 319, 321, 322, 323, 324, 325, 332
friendship, 115, 116, 117, 118, 119, 121, 122, 123, 124, 125, 126, 127, 128, 129, 224, 225, 231, 254, 267, 269, 276, 280, 281, 282, 284, 287, 301, 302, 308, 313, 314, 315, 316, 318, 319-25, 332, 354
fundamental, xi, 1, 5, 6, 7, 12, 34, 38, 41, 42, 57, 59, 60, 61, 66, 67, 74, 78, 86, 93, 99, 103, 106, 117, 153, 184, 187, 193, 268, 275, 283, 297, 298, 303, 306, 308, 341, 342, 344, 352

Garden of Eden, 11, 158, 150
gender, xii, xvii, 21, 22, 30, 31, 33, 34, 37, 39, 42, 45, 109, 172, 265, 266, 329, 330, 338, 341
generation, 3, 4, 64, 119, 120, 147, 153, 173, 176, 233, 344,
generation gap, 64
generosity, 137, 142, 225, 226, 227, 229, 271, 279, 280, 308
Genesis, xv, 1, 2, 4, 5, 6, 7, 8, 10, 12, 13, 152, 182
girls, 31, 121, 141, 145, 173, 174, 181, 186, 193, 265, 338, 343, 345, 346, 355, 356, 358, 359, 360
God, 1, 2, 4-12, 20, 137, 138, 144, 148, 152, 154, 155, 156, 157, 164, 167, 170, 176, 182, 212, 217, 269, 298
gods, xii, 2, 3, 4, 8, 12, 22, 27, 28, 31, 33, 36, 40, 41, 44, 63, 88, 98, 109, 120, 121, 139, 183, 212, 234, 305, 359
goodness, xi, xiv, 55, 61, 126, 137, 181, 195, 269, 275, 277, 278, 282
grace, 122, 125, 137, 225, 269, 359, 364
Greece, 19, 28, 128, 147, 215, 217, 233, 236
Greek, xvii, 19, 20, 22, 23, 24, 25, 26, 27, 28, 30, 31, 32, 33, 34, 35, 36, 37, 39, 41, 44, 56, 115, 117, 126, 127, 128, 129, 218, 223, 360

habit, 21, 25, 216, 249, 254
Hades, 4
harmonious, 217, 321, 363

harmonize, 118, 231
harmony, 66, 126, 151, 175, 183, 210, 256, 257, 258, 331, 351, 352, 363
hate, 42, 124
hatred, 20, 261
heart, 23, 27, 29, 32, 38, 46, 85, 142, 149, 160, 171, 192, 197, 199, 213, 219, 250, 321, 341, 342, 344, 351, 359, 361
Hellenic, 34
history, xiii, xvii, 40, 45, 97, 98, 106, 107, 109, 138, 167, 183, 195, 211, 212, 220, 221, 222, 224, 226, 229, 235, 278, 283, 303, 304, 341, 342, 343, 361, 362
Hobbes, xiii, 219, 234, 295
home, 23, 24, 25, 26, 28-33, 35, 36, 43, 82, 105, 126, 128, 129, 139, 251, 255, 270, 272, 279, 286, 329, 331, 332, 333, 335, 336, 344, 346, 348-54, 357, 358, 362, 364
Homer, 4, 24, 65, 124, 125
homosexuality, 118, 120, 128
honor, xiv, 40, 97, 108, 119, 128, 142, 166, 170, 171, 190, 191, 192, 195, 197, 209, 210, 212, 221, 223, 228, 234, 274, 279, 318, 322, 323
household, 10, 59, 61, 63, 73, 74, 81, 82, 83, 85, 86, 88, 89, 95, 96, 97, 106, 117, 127, 138, 140, 141, 145, 146, 148, 185, 275, 277, 362
human being, xiii, xiv, xv, xvii, 1, 2, 4-8, 10, 12, 13, 20, 21, 27, 34, 42, 43, 57, 61, 65, 73-8, 80, 81, 83-89,108, 116, 119, 120, 124, 127, 151, 159, 166, 171, 181, 183, 195, 197, 199, 209, 212, 214, 217, 219, 223, 230, 231, 233, 247, 248, 254, 255, 266, 267, 268, 270, 271, 274, 276, 282, 298, 305, 306, 320, 321, 322, 323
human, xii, xiii, xiv, xv, xvii , 1-13, 19, 20, 21, 22, 27, 31, 33, 34, 36, 38, 41-45, 53, 55, 57, 59, 60, 61, 62, 65-69, 73, 74-89, 95, 96 99, 108, 116, 118, 119, 120, 124, 126, 127, 128, 129, 137, 138, 139, 142, 145, 146, 149, 150-57, 159, 160, 161, 162, 164-68, 171, 172, 174, 175, 181, 182, 183, 184, 195, 197, 199, 209, 210, 212, 213, 214, 217, 218, 219, 220, 222, 223, 225, 227, 229, 230, 231, 233, 247, 248, 253-58, 261, 266, 267, 268, 270, 271, 274, 276, 282, 297, 298, 299, 302, 304-9, 317, 318, 320, 321, 322, 323, 341, 345, 351, 352, 353, 355, 356, 363, 364
humanity, 1, 12, 33, 89, 153, 157, 167, 194, 195, 199, 217, 246, 252, 261, 352
human nature, xiv, xv, 3, 20, 21, 22, 43, 48, 53, 63, 87, 96, 139, 142, 145, 146, 150, 151, 156, 171, 174, 199, 247, 253, 255, 257, 261, 267, 268, 282, 298, 307, 318
humankind, 5, 151, 152, 155, 216, 218, 220, 232
human rights, xii, 209
Hume, xvii
humility, 210, 245
husband, 10, 11, 23, 29, 31, 32, 33, 34, 38, 75, 81, 89, 97, 98, 99, 102, 105, 108, 117, 121, 123, 124, 125, 126, 127, 128, 140, 141, 142, 143, 145, 147, 150, 156, 157, 158, 159, 161, 162, 163, 165, 166, 167, 168, 181, 195, 197, 272, 273, 287, 299, 303, 305, 308, 320, 321, 322, 343

identical, 66, 69
imagination, xii, 9, 19, 21, 34, 40, 137, 214, 247, 249, 250, 255, 257, 259, 337, 338
independent, 7, 20, 21, 56 , 100, 147, 172, 181, 187, 215, 223, 265, 301, 319, 336, 359
individual, xii, xiii, 3, 5, 11, 54, 57, 62, 66, 73, 76, 79, 80, 84, 85, 86, 88, 109, 150, 151, 152, 154, 156, 159, 162, 164-71, 173, 174, 175, 176, 181, 189, 191, 194, 198, 199, 209, 210, 222, 234, 255, 258, 259, 266, 267, 272, 295-307, 316, 319, 321, 322, 323, 324, 346, 360, 363
individualism, 149, 151, 175, 223
individualist, 150, 157, 164, 174
individuality, xx, 4, 295, 298, 305, 316, 320, 321
infidelity, 145, 192, 320
inherent, xvi, 129, 138, 150, 153, 154, 172, 173, 193, 247, 267, 272, 301, 341
inheritance, 103, 166, 169, 170, 171, 191, 232, 303

inhuman, 31, 40, 341, 352
innate, 195, 297
intelligent, 21, 40, 43, 194, 282
intercourse, 7, 61, 62, 63, 99, 119, 122, 124, 125, 184, 217, 225, 226, 231

judging, xvii
judgment, xiii
justification, 75, 81, 82, 149, 169, 185, 216, 258

Kant, xii, 295, 297, 298, 302, 309, 363
kind, xiv, xvi, xvii, 65
king, 23, 24, 25, 26, 29, 43, 44, 73, 85, 98, 100, 102, 105, 141, 159, 213, 214, 318, 319
King, 24, 25, 29, 30, 31, 33, 34, 36, 43
kingdom, 31, 32, 36, 43, 81
know, xv, xvi, 1, 4, 7, 29, 41, 44, 81, 110, 116, 139, 143, 145, 146, 193, 196, 256, 259, 266, 317, 318, 319, 322, 335, 336, 347, 354, 357, 359
knowing, 12, 187, 250, 255, 301, 318, 344, 348
knowledge, 54, 65

labor, 10, 11, 12, 59, 60, 61, 67, 68, 79, 83, 96, 125, 153, 166, 167, 168, 175, 188, 287, 300, 333, 337
law, xii, xiii, xvii, 3, 6, 8, 12, 34, 45, 54, 55, 56, 57, 59, 60, 62, 63, 66, 67, 68, 69, 120, 127, 139, 151, 157, 158, 165, 167, 168, 170, 171, 182, 184, 193, 194, 195, 198, 212-17, 219, 220, 229, 230, 235, 258, 295, 298, 301, 303, 304, 305, 307, 308, 322, 325, 343, 345
law of nature, 170, 193
learn, xvi, 29, 62, 137, 139, 141, 143, 144, 145, 147, 181, 182, 183, 194, 195, 210, 213, 216, 217, 231, 247, 250, 251, 252, 255, 257, 274, 275, 276, 279, 284, 306
legitimacy, 121, 154, 161, 166, 172, 222
legitimate, 59, 82, 99, 100, 121, 122, 149, 154, 160, 163, 166, 167, 168, 169, 185, 191, 226
life, xiv, 1-5, 8-12, 20, 22, 23, 28-33, 35, 39, 40, 42, 61, 63, 66, 85, 86, 87, 88, 101, 102, 103, 107, 108, 110, 115-20, 125-29, 137, 138, 139, 140, 143, 144, 150, 154, 155, 156, 158, 159, 161-66, 176, 181-85, 187, 188, 189, 193, 195, 196, 197, 199, 209, 210, 215, 219, 224, 226, 227, 231, 233, 235, 247, 251, 259, 265, 267-71, 273, 274, 275, 278-83, 285, 286, 287, 296, 297, 298, 301, 303, 304, 306, 308, 320-24, 329, 331-38, 344, 348, 349, 351, 353, 354, 359-63
living, 1, 10, 11, 42, 76, 77, 85, 86, 87, 119, 125, 129, 143, 184, 224, 225, 274, 276, 281, 297, 302, 332, 334, 336, 354
Locke, xii, xiii
love, 9, 10, 20, 22, 23, 24, 25, 27, 28, 31, 33, 34, 35, 37, 42, 43, 58, 102, 115, 117-25, 128, 143, 145, 146, 181, 184, 191, 194, 195, 197, 210, 213, 216, 217, 219, 225, 229, 234, 235, 248, 249, 253, 254, 255, 258, 259, 260, 269, 282, 284, 285, 301, 302, 303, 306, 313, 315, 316, 319, 321, 324, 331, 334, 342, 344, 345, 348-54, 356-61, 363
lover, 4, 7, 33, 37, 38, 66, 117, 120, 122, 124, 140, 142, 143, 269, 324, 332, 334, 336, 344, 348, 351, 359
loyalty, 20, 39, 283
Lucretia, 95, 96, 97, 98, 99, 100, 101, 102, 104, 105, 106, 107, 108, 109, 110, 139, 140, 141, 142, 143, 144, 141, 142, 143

Machiavelli, xiii
Maimonides, 5, 8
male, xi, xv, 20, 21, 29, 30, 33, 34, 37, 39, 40, 41, 43, 45, 56, 57, 59, 74, 75, 76, 81, 86, 97, 101, 102, 104, 106, 107, 108, 110, 119, 120, 122, 126, 128, 139, 146, 147, 149, 150, 152, 155, 158, 161, 162, 164, 169, 170, 173, 174, 175, 183, 185, 186, 192, 198, 211, 224, 227, 228, 230, 265, 274, 282, 285, 305, 306, 307, 313, 316, 335, 337, 360
mankind, 127, 215, 221, 232, 233, 306, 308
manner, 29, 31, 34, 37, 39, 40, 46, 143, 153, 165, 189, 210, 212, 213, 216, 219, 220, 221, 223-28, 230, 231, 235,

260, 269, 274, 277, 278, 323, 334, 364
marriage, xv, 3, 6, 23, 24, 30, 32, 61, 115-26, 128, 129, 145, 146, 149, 150, 154, 158, 159, 162, 165, 166, 167, 168, 171, 172, 195, 199, 211, 218, 224, 227, 228, 269, 273, 274, 275, 282, 283, 285, 300, 302-8, 313, 314, 319, 320, 321, 322, 334, 335, 336, 344, 354
masculine, 38, 104, 110, 122, 146, 211, 219, 220, 304, 336
masculinity, xi, 96, 101, 102, 106, 107, 108, 109, 110, 128, 144, 145, 187, 305
master, 29, 61, 62, 64, 65, 73, 74, 75, 76, 77, 78, 79, 80, 81, 82, 83, 85, 86, 88, 89, 97, 146, 167, 194, 251, 301, 306
maternal, 170, 341, 352, 361, 363
maternity, 42, 45, 99, 100
men, xi, xv, xvi, 1-13, 19, 20, 21, 24, 25, 29, 30, 32, 33, 34, 37-41, 43, 45, 53, 54, 56, 57, 58, 59, 60, 61, 63, 64, 66, 73, 74, 75, 80-86, 89, 96-108, 110, 115, 117, 119, 121-25, 127, 129, 137-46, 149-57, 159-66, 168, 170, 172-76, 182-200, 209, 210, 212, 213, 214, 215, 217, 218, 219, 222, 224-30, 233, 245, 246, 247, 254, 260, 265, 267, 269, 270, 273, 274, 275, 276, 278-83, 285, 286, 287, 295, 298-302, 305, 306, 308, 313, 315, 316, 317, 319, 320, 323, 324, 331, 337, 338, 343, 344, 345, 348, 351, 352, 353, 355, 356, 359
metaphor, 56, 255, 257, 313, 314, 315, 316, 330, 331, 332, 333, 334, 336
moderate, 65, 123, 198, 212, 220, 320
moderation, 3, 53, 56, 65, 79, 84, 218, 220, 221, 222, 227, 231, 233
modern, xi, 23, 28, 29, 37, 110, 116, 117, 118, 121, 128, 129, 143, 146, 148, 149, 150, 151, 176, 181, 187, 195, 200, 209, 210, 223, 224, 234, 235, 236, 261, 265, 266, 267, 295, 296, 297, 298, 301, 302, 303, 307, 343, 362, 364
modernist, 341, 360
modernity, xii, 115, 234, 236, 296, 307
modesty, xv, 122, 123, 191, 192, 198, 211, 212, 230, 231, 233, 234, 235, 245, 250, 252, 285, 330
monarch, 99, 106, 211, 213, 214, 215, 216, 219, 220, 222, 228, 299
monogamous, 7, 105, 303
moral, xi, xii, xiii, xiv, xv, 21, 22, 42, 53, 57, 78, 87, 126, 147, 150, 154, 156, 172, 173, 174, 175, 181, 182, 183, 187, 189, 192-96, 200, 209, 210, 212, 218, 219, 220, 222, 225, 227, 245, 247, 248, 249, 253, 255-59, 261, 266, 267, 269, 271, 275, 282, 283, 297, 306, 307, 308, 309, 344
morality, 147, 194, 195, 200, 266, 267, 306, 308
Morrison, xvii
mother, 6, 11, 28, 31, 36, 37, 39, 42, 44, 63, 82, 98, 100, 101, 116, 119, 140, 141, 142, 143, 145, 146, 155, 161, 170, 172, 173, 184, 185, 189, 191, 196, 252, 269, 272, 273, 287, 306, 320, 331, 346, 347, 348, 351, 352, 354, 355, 356, 357, 363
motherhood, 24, 29, 39, 100, 101
motive, 6, 25, 32, 45, 165, 190, 195, 213, 222, 248, 276, 281
music, 56, 59, 65
myth, 11, 19, 20, 21, 23, 24, 25, 26, 29, 30, 35, 36, 42, 43, 44, 46, 127
mythical, 22, 25, 43, 44, 139
mythological, 7, 11, 19, 23
mythology, 31, 33, 40, 44
myths, 19, 127

nature, xi, xii, xiii, xiv, xv, xvi, xvii, xviii, 2, 3, 6, 8, 10, 12, 19, 20, 21, 26, 29, 30, 33, 35, 38, 41, 45, 57, 58, 59, 60, 61, 62, 64, 65, 67, 73, 74, 75, 76, 77, 81, 82, 83, 85, 97, 118, 119, 121, 122, 127, 138, 139, 140, 143, 145, 146, 147, 149, 151, 152, 153, 154, 155, 156, 157, 158, 159, 161, 162, 163, 164, 165, 167, 170, 172, 173, 175, 176, 181, 182, 183, 184, 185, 186, 187, 188, 189, 191, 192, 193, 194, 196, 198, 199, 210, 213, 217, 219, 222, 224, 225, 226, 227, 228, 229, 230, 232, 234, 235, 246, 247, 250, 257, 261, 266, 267, 268, 271, 273, 282, 286, 296, 301, 303, 305, 313, 325, 329, 330, 331, 338, 343, 351, 352, 355, 356, 357, 358, 359
natural law, 157, 170

natural rights, xii, 149, 150, 151, 156, 162, 164, 165, 166, 168, 171, 174, 175
necessity, xi, xiii, xvii, 54, 61, 66, 68
Nietzsche, xvi
noble, 27, 36, 103, 107, 119, 122, 142, 194, 197, 199, 213, 221, 226, 233, 235, 249, 253, 260, 278, 329
nuclear family, 303, 307

obedience, 8, 12, 13, 153, 156, 173, 174, 194, 212, 213, 259
obey, 78, 79, 153, 155, 170, 185, 186, 193, 194
obligation, 154, 170, 171, 172, 304
Oedipus, 25, 44, 63, 64
Okin, 150, 152, 200
opinions, xiv, 26, 65, 87, 118, 124, 129, 182, 183, 185, 188-94, 196, 197, 211, 212, 217, 219, 227-31, 234, 246, 250, 251, 252, 254, 255, 257, 259, 260, 267, 276, 277, 284, 299, 300, 304, 306, 307
origin, 23, 64, 96, 99, 106, 117, 118, 125, 128, 145, 151, 153, 154, 155, 159, 167, 169, 297, 298, 325, 361
Ovid, 22, 23, 24, 30, 37, 46

parents, xiv, 63, 79, 120, 151-55, 168, 169, 170, 171, 173, 174, 175, 176, 182, 195, 248, 250, 272, 299, 303, 307, 343, 344, 347, 349, 354
partners, 6, 10, 43, 86, 116, 126, 161, 186, 195, 280, 281, 282, 302, 304, 320
partnership, 1, 118, 125, 190, 307
Pascal, 26
passion, 141, 195, 196, 218, 225, 321, 344, 345
passionate, 38, 351, 352, 354
Pateman, 99, 159, 154, 150, 151, 152, 200
paternal, 99, 100, 101, 102, 105, 121, 152, 153, 159, 160, 161, 162, 163, 170, 172, 176, 185, 196
paternity, 99, 100, 101, 102, 169
patriarchal, 10, 21, 25, 29, 41, 99, 100, 101, 102, 105, 106, 150, 151, 159, 160, 161, 162, 164, 168, 169, 172, 174, 175, 185, 210, 235
patriarchy, 95, 99, 108, 110, 149, 150, 151, 155, 156, 159, 160, 161, 162, 164, 167, 171, 173, 174, 175, 176, 302

person, xii, 78, 87, 124, 128, 138, 167, 170, 197, 213, 216, 222, 231, 233, 234, 247, 260, 268, 269, 271, 272, 273, 275, 276, 277, 278, 279, 281, 300, 301, 321, 322, 334, 354, 357, 358
personality, 265, 304
philosopher, xiii, xvi, xviii, 11, 53, 54, 60, 63, 68, 69, 87, 88, 116, 118, 126, 127, 138, 155, 181, 182, 218, 234, 245, 247, 248, 319
philosophy, xiii, xvii, 35, 53, 54, 55, 56, 60, 62, 63, 65, 66, 67, 68, 69, 88, 115, 116, 117, 118, 119, 122, 126, 127, 128, 129, 174, 175, 181, 199, 218, 246, 267, 304, 315
pity, 3, 27, 34, 37, 183, 307, 323
Plato, xiii, xvii, 2, 4, 13, 26, 53, 54, 55, 66, 69, 89, 116, 122, 126, 127, 128, 129, 138, 254
pleasure, 3, 9, 54, 77, 78, 108, 118, 121, 122, 123, 124, 125, 128, 140, 144, 153, 196, 229, 253, 256, 267, 268, 269, 271, 276, 278, 280, 281, 282, 342
poet, 2, 22, 23, 24, 30, 37, 38, 43, 44, 45, 46, 56, 57, 58, 59, 60, 63, 234, 269, 330, 331, 332, 333, 336, 338, 359
poetic, 65, 185, 331, 352
poetry, 19, 23, 24, 41, 44, 56, 214, 269, 329, 331, 334, 337, 338
polis, xvii, 35, 128, 297
polite, 221, 222, 223, 226, 228, 231, 269
politeness, 215, 223, 224
political, xi, xii, xiii, xv, xvii, 21, 23, 25, 26, 29, 32, 41, 44, 45, 53, 58, 59, 60, 62-69, 73, 74, 75, 81-89, 95, 96, 98-103, 105, 106, 108, 109, 110, 115, 120, 121, 126, 127, 128, 137, 138, 140-44, 146, 147, 149-53, 155, 156, 158-63, 165, 166, 167, 169, 171, 172, 174, 175, 153, 181, 182, 185, 194, 198, 200, 209-13, 216, 221, 222, 226, 228, 234, 236, 267, 268, 282, 297, 298, 299, 306, 307, 308, 325
politics, xi, xii, xv, 20, 25, 44, 45, 103, 104, 110, 127, 128, 138, 140, 149, 150, 151, 164, 173, 174, 176, 190, 298, 304, 305, 341, 362
pregnant, 99, 102, 125, 141
pride, 3, 13, 31, 190, 197, 209, 218, 228, 233, 245, 246, 247, 248, 250, 251,

252, 253, 256, 260, 277, 278, 279, 280, 283, 318
principle, 6, 12, 56, 58, 61, 62, 67, 69, 86, 126, 127, 147, 150, 151, 154, 157, 158, 159, 160, 163, 164, 166, 172, 173, 174, 186, 195, 220, 221, 222, 223, 228, 231, 232, 234, 235, 267, 273, 280, 283, 303, 304, 307, 321, 345, 346, 363
privacy, 69, 127, 331, 332, 336
private, 59, 61, 68, 96, 102, 106, 107, 123, 126, 127, 138, 139, 147, 150, 158, 162, 164, 165, 168, 172, 173, 174, 186, 189, 191, 200, 210, 212, 213, 214, 248, 257, 259, 298, 300, 304, 331, 334, 343
Prometheus, 120
promiscuity, 100, 105, 143, 225
proper, xi, xii, xv, xvii, 11, 14, 54, 57, 61, 65, 67, 78, 80, 82, 83, 84, 86, 116, 119, 122, 126, 138, 152, 161, 163, 173, 182, 186, 189, 190, 191, 193, 210, 212, 213, 218, 219, 220, 221, 224, 225, 229, 230, 235, 245, 253, 259, 278, 307, 317, 320, 336
property, 99, 121, 149, 151, 153, 154, 155, 158, 159, 160, 162, 163, 164, 165, 166, 167, 168, 169, 170, 171, 175, 176, 191, 219, 223, 271, 274, 296, 298, 299, 300, 303, 304, 336
Providence, 156, 157, 212
prudence, 62, 69, 87, 229, 230, 232, 267, 268, 271, 276, 287
public, 32, 54, 55, 56, 59, 60, 62, 68, 96, 102, 103, 104, 108, 109, 123, 138, 139, 140, 147, 150, 158, 162, 164, 165, 172, 173, 174, 182, 185, 188, 189, 190, 191, 192, 193, 210, 212, 213, 219, 233, 250, 253, 260, 305, 306, 331, 358
punishment, 3, 4, 8, 24, 27, 31, 37, 40, 42, 78, 98, 142, 159, 160, 163

queen, 42, 158, 165, 189

rape, xiv, 32, 33, 44, 95, 96, 97, 98, 99, 100, 101, 102, 106, 107, 108, 109, 110, 145, 230
reason, xii, 5, 9, 19, 20, 25, 66, 78, 80, 81, 82, 84, 87, 105, 119, 124, 153, 155, 156, 157, 160, 162, 164, 172, 173, 174, 183, 184, 185, 191, 192, 198, 212, 213, 214, 217, 222, 226, 230, 231, 232, 233, 252, 258, 271, 273, 284, 296, 300, 321, 322, 325, 335, 349, 353
reciprocal, 122, 124, 128, 151, 190, 280
reciprocity, 124, 128, 195
religion, 151
religious, xviii, 140, 189, 210, 212, 261, 269, 297, 304, 329, 333
republic, xii, 95, 96, 97, 98, 99, 100, 101, 102, 103, 104, 105, 106, 108, 110, 141, 142, 200, 215, 221, 222, 223
Republican, 95, 100, 103, 215, 221
republicanism, 101, 103, 109, 110, 115, 150, 153, 209, 211, 220, 221, 222, 223
respect, 5, 26, 65, 86, 102, 124, 125, 155, 156, 166, 168, 175, 183, 187, 195, 197, 212, 222, 223, 228, 235, 247, 250, 267, 268, 272, 276, 277, 279, 284, 302, 303, 304, 314, 322, 323, 324, 325, 331, 354, 359, 364
responsibility, 104, 172, 251, 297, 298, 307, 314, 315
reveal, xvi, 55, 60, 67
revelation, 8, 167, 296, 343, 357, 362
right, xii, xv, 4, 8, 11, 23, 39, 56, 78, 82, 99, 101, 102, 105, 116, 124, 148, 149-54, 159, 160, 162, 164-71, 183, 185, 190, 195, 197, 198, 209, 220, 228, 232, 235, 249, 254, 268, 271, 275, 277, 295, 298, 299, 300, 301-8, 315, 322, 337, 343, 344, 353, 355
romance, 332, 352, 353, 358
romantic love, 195, 302, 303, 304, 315
romanticize, 317
Rome, 23, 30, 36, 95, 97, 98, 100, 105, 107, 109, 128, 141, 142, 148, 215, 217, 218, 236
rule, 9, 10, 26, 29, 61, 62, 63, 69, 73, 76, 79-85, 89, 96, 97, 101, 127, 138, 139, 144, 145, 146, 149, 150, 152, 153, 156, 158, 159, 161, 162, 163, 164, 166, 167, 169, 172, 185, 189, 190, 193, 197, 198, 211, 213, 214, 219, 220, 227, 235, 295, 298, 301, 305, 306, 308, 321, 322, 323
ruler, 1, 10, 11, 13, 74, 75, 76, 81, 84, 86, 89, 97, 138, 139, 140, 145, 169, 219

rules, 21, 65, 143, 155, 163, 168, 189, 258, 265, 297, 320, 345

scriptural, 152, 156, 169
scripture, 153, 156, 164
self, 3, 4, 9, 13, 28, 35, 43, 153, 155, 159, 167, 169, 153, 209, 210, 220, 245, 257, 261, 266, 267, 301, 302, 316, 321, 323, 329, 332, 343, 344, 352, 354, 355, 358, 359, 363
self-control, 79, 87, 271, 279, 297
self-esteem, 246, 254
self-interest, 142, 171, 197, 245, 249
self-love, 183, 195, 196, 210, 217, 218, 219, 221, 233, 258, 259
self-preservation, 11, 154, 155, 162, 171
self-respect, 232
Seneca, 19, 22, 24, 28-33, 35, 36, 37, 39, 41-46
sensual, 9, 344
sentiment, 103, 190, 195, 197, 255, 308, 322
separate, 1, 23, 32, 65, 69, 86, 87, 125, 158, 166, 210, 223, 230, 257, 329, 338, 343
sex, xii, xv, xvi, 4, 12, 20, 59, 61, 68, 87, 115, 118, 119, 122, 173, 174, 182-88, 190, 191, 192, 198, 199, 210, 211, 220, 224, 226, 228, 229, 230, 231, 235, 285, 302, 305, 320, 324, 329, 330, 346, 360
sexual, xv, 59, 60, 61, 62, 64, 67
Shakespeare, 355, 356
Shanley, 151, 152, 200, 309
sin, 37, 353
slave, 34, 65, 73-90, 95, 96, 97, 105, 109, 141, 189, 213, 301, 305, 306, 323
slavery, xvi, 34, 75, 80, 194, 228
soul, 4, 5, 13, 29, 53, 57-68, 73, 74, 76-81, 83, 97, 115, 121, 124, 128, 173, 183, 189, 194, 197, 249, 268, 321, 324, 332
sovereign, xiv, 209, 216
sphere, 22, 25, 30, 33, 44, 80, 86, 87, 88, 96, 102, 106, 107, 121, 150, 158, 162, 164, 165, 166, 172, 174, 189, 191, 210, 211, 212, 216, 231, 233, 276, 286, 287, 300, 329, 330, 338
spirit, xii, 27, 38, 103, 119, 190, 193, 226, 231, 234, 273, 282, 283, 284, 285, 304, 321, 322, 343, 353, 359, 361
spiritual, xiv, xvii, 302, 356, 357, 362
standards, xiii, xiv
state of nature, 151, 161, 162, 163, 165, 184, 187, 194, 195, 219
statesman, 73
status, xiv, 1, 4, 10, 21, 22, 25, 26, 29, 30, 31, 32, 35, 36, 41, 42, 44, 45, 56, 82, 87, 88, 101, 105, 117, 149, 151, 157, 158, 159, 162, 163, 166, 168, 171, 173, 175, 183, 184, 186, 198, 210, 211, 247, 301, 305, 309, 332, 347
submissive, 273
suicide, 95, 99, 100, 101, 106, 107, 108, 110, 141, 142, 143, 346
superior, xv, 11, 27, 63, 81, 82, 86, 119, 185, 186, 223, 227, 228, 230, 268, 279, 285, 301, 359
superiority, xi, xvi, 25, 30, 34, 97, 109, 149, 150, 158, 173, 175, 186, 224, 226, 227, 228, 229, 234, 246, 247, 251, 278
sympathize, 39, 231, 255, 307
sympathy, 26, 28, 34, 224, 225, 231, 246, 247, 249, 251, 253, 255, 257, 258, 261, 280, 306, 307, 345

theorist, 45, 95, 96, 121, 296
title, xi,, 13, 120, 164, 167, 168, 169, 185, 274, 359, 361
Tocqueville, 223
Tower of Babel, 12
tragedy, 19, 20, 22, 26, 29, 31, 34, 35, 38, 44, 95, 105, 154, 155, 258, 305, 353, 360
tragic, 4, 19, 26, 27, 28, 29, 30, 31, 32, 34, 36, 38, 39, 41, 42, 43, 44, 45, 95, 335, 353, 355, 356, 358
trust, xvi, 108, 124, 125
tyrannical, 29, 38, 97, 99, 102, 105, 106, 129, 166
tyrannies, 105, 211
tyranny, xiv, xvii, 64, 96, 99, 101, 104, 105, 106, 196, 210, 211, 213, 214, 215, 216, 227, 272
tyrant, 42, 97, 99, 100, 101, 102, 125, 214, 220, 235

unequal, 173, 184
union, 1, 3, 6, 7, 11, 116, 117, 125, 152,

153, 154, 155, 166, 175, 183, 184, 186, 188, 195, 231, 249, 302, 333
unjust, 42, 77, 87, 168, 235, 248, 279, 280

vain, 219, 246, 247, 251, 269, 273, 277, 278, 279
value, 20, 21, 39, 40, 41, 95, 106, 107, 108, 123, 137, 143, 188, 192, 245, 266, 274, 281, 284, 304, 314, 331, 338, 361
vanity, 217, 233, 245-53, 255, 256, 257, 259, 260, 261, 276-80
vice, 38, 65, 124, 137, 138, 139, 187, 225, 226, 227, 228, 230, 232, 245, 248, 253, 254, 256, 258, 266, 271, 272, 275, 276, 277, 279, 280, 285, 306
virtue, xv, 5, 38, 41, 53, 57, 60, 66, 67, 68, 73, 79, 80, 81, 83, 84, 87, 88, 89, 105, 115, 118, 119, 121, 122, 137, 139-44, 158, 165, 174, 182, 189, 192, 194-98, 210, 211, 213, 214, 216, 219, 223, 226, 228, 231, 234, 245, 247, 248, 249, 250, 252-59, 261, 267, 268, 271, 272, 275-82, 287, 321
virtuous, 41, 45, 85, 87, 88, 89, 101, 139, 141, 189, 190, 192, 197, 230, 248, 259, 268, 269, 270, 271, 272, 274, 281, 282, 285, 359

war, 34, 39, 41, 57, 59, 60, 65, 88, 146, 162, 168, 34
weakness, 65, 102, 145, 173, 187, 230, 231, 284, 317, 324
whore, 123, 350

wife, 6, 7, 11, 12, 25, 26, 42, 75, 80, 81, 89, 97, 98, 99, 101, 105, 106, 116, 117, 118, 120, 121, 123-28, 139, 140, 141, 145, 146, 150, 156, 157, 158, 159, 161, 162, 163, 165, 166, 167, 168, 184, 185, 189, 191, 193, 195, 196, 211, 270, 274, 279, 287, 299, 303, 305, 308, 319, 320, 321, 322, 333
woman, xi, xv, xvi, xvii, xviii, 1-13, 19-23, 25-34, 37-45, 53-61, 63, 66, 67, 68, 73, 74, 75, 80-86, 88, 89, 95, 96, 98-102, 104-10, 115, 117, 118, 119, 121, 122, 123, 124, 126, 128, 139, 140-44, 146, 147, 149, 150-54, 156, 157, 158, 159, 161-76, 181-200, 210, 211, 213, 224, 227-31, 235, 245, 247, 256, 265, 266, 267, 272, 274, 276, 278, 282, 285, 286, 287, 295, 299, 300-308, 313-25, 329-38, 342, 343, 344, 346, 347, 348, 350, 352-57, 359, 360
womanhood, 25, 29, 34, 39, 329
womb, 31, 35, 45, 346, 347
work, 1, 4, 5, 11, 22, 29, 40, 41, 42, 45, 57, 58, 68, 78, 79, 85, 97, 106, 115, 120, 124, 126, 128, 143, 173, 174, 154, 181, 183, 184, 187, 214, 217, 223, 226, 229, 249, 265, 266, 300, 308, 318, 324, 330, 333, 341, 351, 357, 360, 362

Xenophon, 116, 124

Zeus, 2, 3, 4, 25

About the Authors

STEVEN BERG is an assistant professor at Loyola University of New Orleans. He has published articles on Aristophanes' *Clouds* and Nietzsche's *Thus Spoke Zarathustra*. At present he is working on a study of Plato's *Symposium*.

INGER SIGRUN BRODEY, an assistant professor at the University of Puget Sound, earned her Ph.D. as a Mellon fellow in the humanities at the committee on Social Thought at the University of Chicago. She has published numerous articles on the history of the eighteenth-century novel in England, France, and Germany, as well as on the twentieth-century Japanese novel, in journals such as *Philosophy and Literature, Comparative Literature, Mosaic,* and *Persuasions*. She serves on the board on directors of the Jane Austen Society of North America and the Association of Literary Scholars and Critics. She is coeditor and cotranslator of *Rediscovering Natsume Sôseki* (Weatherhill, 1999), and the author of *Authorizing Ruin*: *Constructions of Hypocrisy in the Novel of Sensibility*, which is currently under review. The latter volume continues her interest in the intersection of moral philosophy, landscape gardening, and the history of the novel.

RONNA BURGER is a professor of Philosophy at Tulane University, where she teaches courses on Plato and Aristotle, political philosophy, and philosophy of religion. She received her Ph.D. in philosophy from the New School for Social Research in 1975. She is the author of *Plato's Phaedrus: A Defense of a Philosophic Art of Writing*, University of Alabama Press, 1980, and *The Phaedro: A Platonic Labyrinth*, Yale University Press, 1984 (to be reprinted this spring by St. Augustine's Press). Her articles on Plato and Aristotle have appeared in *Review of Metaphysics, Interpretation,* and *Proceedings of the Boston Area Colloquium in Ancient Philosophy*, among other journals or collections. She is currently at work on a book on Aristotle's *Ethics*.

NICHOLAS CAPALDI is McFarin professor of philosophy at the University of Tulsa. He is a past editor of the *Public Affairs Quarterly* and current editor in chief of the Peter Lang series *Masterworks in the Western Tradition*. His interests in modern and contemporary philosophy as well as political theory are reflected in his latest published book *The Enlightenment Project in the Analytic Conversation*. His current research is focused on an intellectual biography of John Stuart Mill.

MARC CONNER is an assistant professor in the department of English at Washington and Lee University. He has published essays on the work of

Thomas Pynchon, Salman Rushdie, Toni Morrison, and Sherwood Anderson, and is the editor of *Speaking the Unspeakable: The Aesthetic Dimensions of Toni Morrison* (Mississippi, forthcoming). His teaching specialties include American and African-American literature, Modern Irish literature, the Bible as literature, and literature and religion.

MATTHEW B. CRAWFORD is a doctoral candidate in political science at the University of Chicago.

MELISSA MATTHES teaches political philosophy at the University of Maryland, College Park.

DOMNICA RADULESCU is an associate professor of romance languages and literatures at Washington and Lee University. She has also taught at the University of Chicago, where she received her Ph.D. in French and Italian. She is the author of a book on the French writer André Malraux (1994), of scholarly articles on Cervantes, Mihai Eminescu, André Malraux, and Albert Camus, and of encyclopedia articles (Malraux and Moldovans). She has also directed plays by Eugène Ionesco, Fernando Arrabal, and Samuel Beckett. She just finished a book entitled *Sisters of Medea: the Tragic Heroine Across Cultures*. She is also the editor of *Exile: Discourse and Experience*.

ARLENE W. SAXONHOUSE is a professor of political science and women's studies at the University of Michigan. She is the author of *Athenian Democracy: Modern Mythmakers and Ancient Theorists* (1996); *Fear of Diversity: The Birth of Political Science in Ancient Greek Thought* (1992); *Women in the History of Political Thought: Ancient Greece to Machiavelli* (1985); and editor with Noel B. Reynolds of *Three Discourses: A Critical Modern Edition of Newly Identified Work of the Young Hobbes* (1995). She has published numerous articles in such journals as *Political Theory* and the *American Political Science Review* on gender and ancient political thought and is currently working on free speech and democratic theory in ancient Greece.

DENISE SCHAEFFER is an assistant professor of political science at the College of the Holy Cross. Her teaching and research interests include classical and modern political philosophy, feminist theory, and political thought in literature. She is currently writing a book on Rousseau's *Emile*.

EVANTHIA SPELIOTIS received a Ph.D. in philosophy from Tulane University, an M.A. in philosophy from the Catholic University of America, and a B.A. in philosophy from the University of Michigan, Ann Arbor. She is currently an assistant professor of philosophy at Bellarmine College, Louisville, Kentucky.

EDUARDO A. VELÁSQUEZ received his B.A. from the University of California at Santa Barbara, and his M.A. and Ph.D. from the University of Chicago. He presently teaches political philosophy at Washington and Lee University where he is an assistant professor of politics. He is working on a second volume of essays entitled *Love and Friendship* and on a book entitled *From Manly Honor to Civic Androgyny: The Reconstitution of Self and Society in Early Modern Political Thought.*

GERMAINE PAULO WALSH is an assistant professor of political science at Texas Lutheran University. She currently is working on a book manuscript that examines the role of friendship in Aristotle's ethical thought, and an article that compares Jane Austen's views of happiness, friendship, and sexual difference with those of Willa Cather.

LEE WARD is a doctoral candidate in political science at Fordham University in New York. His research interests are in ancient and modern political philosophy. He is currently completing a dissertation entitled "The Liberal Critique of Patriarchy and the Origin of Modern Politics," which involves an examination of the works of Robert Filmer, James Tyrrell, Algernon Sidney, and John Locke.

LESLEY WHEELER is an assistant professor of literature at Washington and Lee University. She is currently completing a book-length manuscript, *The Poetics of Enclosure*, about American women poets.

DEBORAH L. WINKLE wrote her dissertation on "The Politics of Feminine Persuasion: Jean-Jacques Rousseau on the Moral Influence of Women" at the University of Chicago, where she was an Olin Fellow. She has also studied in Paris at the Institut d'Etudes Politiques and the Université de Paris VII. Her most recent teaching position was at Washington and Lee University; currently she writes and researches in northern California where she lives with her husband and young daughter.